I0749093

WASHINGTON

½ Mile Circles from the Capitol

References

A Capitol
B Presidents House
C State Dep. & Ltrs Office
D War Departments
E Navy "
F Treasury "
G General P. O. & City do.
H Patent Office
I Navy Magazine
J Observatory
K Marine Barracks
L Arsenal
M Penitentiary
NY. Navy Yard
O City Hall
P Jail
Q Poor House
R Colemans Hotel
S Browns "
T Gadsbys "
U Fullers "
V Verandah "
W Exchange "
X Metropolis Bank
a Patriotic "
b Washington "
c Eastern Cemetery
d E. Branch "
e St. Johns "
f Methodist "
g St. Peters "

Rail Road
Boundaries

GEORGETOWN
Rock Cr.
MASONS I.
POTOMAC RIVER
EAST BR. OF POTOMAC RIVER
Greenleafs Pt.
Sth. Part of Washington
E. BRANCH
Ches. & Ohio Canal
MALL
Washington Monument
Smithsonian Inst.
Lafayette Sq.

PLAN OF THE CAPITOL

Hall of Representatives 96 by 60
Depth of Wings 121 ft.
Central Rotunda 95 ft.
Senate Chamber 78 by 45
Library 92 by 34
West Loggia
East Portico
East Front
352 feet
Projection E. 65 ft.
Projection West 83 ft.

THE

WASHINGTON AND GEORGETOWN

DIRECTORY,

STRANGERS' GUIDE-BOOK FOR WASHINGTON,

AND

CONGRESSIONAL AND CLERKS' REGISTER.

COMPILED AND PUBLISHED BY ALFRED HUNTER.

He who steals my purse steals trash;
But he who borrows my Directory
Filches me most villanously.

Price Two Dollars.

WASHINGTON:
PRINTED BY KIRKWOOD & McGILL.

1853.

PREFACE.

I shall make no apology for any defects in this Book, as I am satisfied that under the circumstances it is as nearly perfect as possible. Few persons are aware of the labor in getting up a work of this kind; and as to profit, it is well known no person ever published a second book after trying the first: whether I shall follow the example of my predecessors remains to be seen. I look upon this as an experiment. Almost the whole of this work had to be modeled from original matter. I can say that every house in the city has been visited by faithful agents, and every reasonable person must be aware that wrong answers and misspelling are very liable to be met with, as has been the case. This volume will contain about 12,000 names, and every name has been canvassed separately, and scrutinized with care. Where there has been doubt, it has been the subject of special inquiry. It is with a great deal of pleasure I have to say, that my agents have been met with politeness, and a disposition always to forward the business in hand as much as could be expected.

From the officers of Government and the Departments generally, special thanks are due for the facilities they have tendered, and information that has been volunteered. I found that a book of this kind was universally needed, and to my immediate subscribers and advertisers, without whose encouragement this book could never have been published, I can say, it has been the subject of constant anxiety, night and day, from the first projection to the completion of the work; if, as I hope it will be found useful and profitable, I shall continue the work yearly, with the advantage of experience and a model to work by; and I also hope that the City Fathers will order the numbering of the city, after the plan I proposed to them before the commencement of the book, which will greatly facilitate the object of the work, and it will then be what it purports, a complete City Directory.

TABLE OF CONTENTS.

NOTE.—In examining the Table of Contents, notice that there are three different pagings, which was unavoidable.

ADDENDA.

Barclay, John, (spelled Barkley, clerk Department.)
Baldwin, George, (given up business to C. Cherry.)
Bohn, Casimer, bookseller, s side East Capitol, btw 1 and 2 e.
Buckingham, E. F., Periodical Depot, under National Hotel.
Baker, Potomac House, Pa. av., btw 3d and 4½ w.
French, Avenue House, cor. 7th and La. av.
Morrison, Wm. M., & Co., bookstore, 4½ st., near Pa avenue.
Gilbert, J. M., St. Charles Hotel, cor 3 w and Pa av.
Stewart, Charles H., n side N Y av, btw 13 and 14 w.
Platt & Stewart, attorneys, 15, btw F n and Pa. av.
Crawford, R. R., Georgetown, (see advertisement page, 105.)

ARRIVAL AND DEPARTURE OF THE CARS.

Leave Washington at 7 and 8½ o'clock A. M.
Leave Washington at 3½ and 5 o'clock P. M.
On Sundays at 7 o'clock, A. M. and 5 P. M.

Leave Baltimore at 4 and 9½ o'clock A. M.
Leave Baltimore at 4.45 and 6.35 o'clock P. M.
On Sundays at 4 o'clock A. M. and 4.45 o'clock P. M.

WASHINGTON AND GEORGETOWN

DIRECTORY.

A.

Abbreviations.—All points start from the Capitol; s south, n north, e east, w west, btw between, cor corner, av avenue, h house, (col) colored.

Abbot, G. J., clerk State Department, s side I n, btw 17 and 18 w.
Abbot, Charles, clerk, Gay, btw Congress and Washington, Georgetown.
Abbot, Mrs., s e cor West and Washington, Georgetown.
Abbot, George, clerk, Bridge, btw Jefferson and Washington, Georgetown.
Abbot, Mrs., Bridge, btw Jefferson and Washington, Georgetown.
Abbit, Rich., gardener, e side 22 w, btw Pa av and I n.
Abert, Charles, agent for claims, n side F n, btw 14 and 15 w.
Abert, J. J., chief engineer, n side I n, btw 17 and 18 w.
Academy of the Visitation, (Mother Julianna Matthews, Superior,) Convent Place.
Academy, (Catholic,) Fayette, btw 3 and 4, Georgetown.
ACKER, NICHOLAS, stone mason, e side 2 w, btw B and C n.
Acton, John, bricklayer, n side E s, btw 4½ and 6 w.
Acton, Wallace, s side I s, btw 12 and 13 e.
Acton, Theodore, plasterer, s side K s, btw 10 and 11 e.
Acton, Osborn, teamster, cor South Capitol and N n.
ADAM, WILLIAM, Bookstore, n side Pa av, btw 3 and 4½ w.
ADAMS & CO.'S Express Office, n side Pa av, btw 2 and 3 w.
Adams, Thomas, huckster, s side Md av, btw 6 and 7 w.
Adams, Edward, huckster, w side 7 w, btw G and H s.
Adams, West, laborer, w side 7 w, btw E and F s.
Adams, Samuel, captain steamboat Mount Vernon, w side 7 w, btw G and H s.
Adams, William W., huckster, w side 7 w, btw G and H south.
Adams, Calis, (col,) laborer, w side 3 w, btw M and N s.
Adams, Elijah, (col,) laborer, w side 3 w, btw M and N s.
Adams, Washington, grocer, w side 7 w, btw H and I n.
Adams, Samuel, huckster, s side Md av, btw 6 and 7 w.
Adams, J. G., grocer, cor 8 w and L n.
Adams, Robert, (col,) laborer, w side 8 w, btw L and M n.
Adams, C. B., clerk Post Office Department, w side 9 w, btw F and G n.
Adams, Mrs. Mary, boarding, s side Pa av, btw 6 and 7 w.
Adams, Mrs. Mary, n side F n, btw 13 and 14 w.
Adams, Mrs. M. A. tailoress, w side 10 w, btw N Y av, and K n.
Adams, Nelson, clerk Pension Office, n side L n, btw 8 and 9 w.
Adams, James, cashier Bank Wash'n, n side B s, btw N J av and 1 e.
Adams, A., (col,) laborer, s side A s, btw 1 and 2 e.
Adams, West, laborer, s side F s, btw 7 and 8 w.
Adams, A., grocer, n side F s, btw 9 and 10 w.
Adams, Samuel, grocer, n side C s, btw 3 and 4½ w.
Adams, John, gunner, U S N Y, w side 7 e, btw I and K s.
Adams, B., laborer, e side 11 e, btw M and N s.
Adams, Jonah, police office, s side L s, btw 4 and 5 e.
Adams, John, constable, s side 2, near High, Georgetown.

Abbreviations.—All points start from the Capitol; s south, n north, e east, w west, btw between, cor corner, av avenue, h house, (col) colored.

ADAMSON, ALEXANDER, Periodical Store, 7, opposite Gen. Post Office Dep't.
Addison, D. D., agent for claims against the Gov't, n side H n, btw 17 and 18 w.
Addison, A. & Co., lumber merchants, w side 11 e, btw N and O s.
Addison, Thomas B., clerk, e side Congress, btw West and Road, Georgetown.
Addison, Henry, (MAYOR,) Bridge, btw Congress and Washington, Georgetown.
Adjutant General's office, 1st story War Department.
Adler, Morris, clerk, out High, near Poor House, Georgetown.
Adrean, George, bricklayer, w side 8 w, btw P and Q n.
ADVOCATE PRINTING OFFICE, n e corner High and Gay, Georgetown.
African M. E. Church, Va av, btw 8 and 9 e.
AGER & McLEAN, Sash and Blind Factory, e side 6 w, btw Pa av and Md av.
Ager, James, carpenter, w side 13 w, btw N Y av and I n.
Ager, Uriah, carter, Frederick, btw 5 and 6, Georgetown.
AIGLER, J., Confectioner, s side L n, btw 11 and 12 w.
Aigler, A., confectioner, s side A, btw N J av and 1 e.
Aiken, Mrs. Prudence, bath house, n side C n, btw 4½ and 6 w.
Alden, Albert G., brickmaker, 6 w, btw H and I s.
ALEXANDER, J., Upholsterer, n side Pa av, btw 12 and 13 w.
House 12 w, btw C and D n.
Alexander, Mrs., widow, w side 12 w, btw D and C n.
Alexander, Columbus, printer, e side 14 w, btw N Y av and G n
Alexander, F., printer, s side F n, btw 17 and 18 w.
Alexander, Wm., collector, w side Mongomery, btw Dunbarton and Gay, Geo'town.
Allan, Edward, plasterer, s side Va av, btw 6 and 7 w.
Allan, James, (col,) n side D s, btw 4 and 5 e.
Allen, Mrs. H., n side Va av, btw 3 and 4 e.
ALLEN, G. F., Dry Goods, n side Pa av, btw 9 and 10 w.
House, s side Pa av, btw 14 and 15 w.
Allen, Mary, w side 3 w, btw Va av and Md av.
Allen, Mrs. Letitia, bonnet store, s side Pa av, btw 9 and 10 w.
Allen, A., carpenter, s side I n, btw 6 and 7 w.
Allen, James, carpenter, s side N Y av, btw 9 and 10 w.
Allen, Thomas, carpenter, n side F s, btw 7 and 8 w.
Allen, William, bricklayer, w side D s, btw 1 and 2 w.
Allen, Samuel E., laborer, e side 11 e, btw N and O s.
Allen, William, razor powder, s side 3, near High, Georgetown.
Allen, (col.) laundress, e s N J av, btw D and E s.
Allyn, Lucius B., clerk Navy Dep't, e side 9 w, btw I and N Y av.
Altemus, Thomas, engineer, w side 8 e, btw G and I s.
Alyet, ——, dressmaker, s side Md av, btw 4½ and 6 w.
Ambush, Augustus, (col,) laborer, e side 11 w, btw N Y av and K.
Ames, George C., s side G n, btw 14 and 15 w.
Amos, William, bricklayer, s side E s, btw 4½ and 6 w.
Anacostia Engine House, s side K s, btw 8 and 9 e.
Anderson, James, shoemaker, n side Pa av, bet 14 and 15 w
House, s side Pa av, btw 14 and 14 w.
ANDERSON, Mrs. G., Music Store, n side Pa av, btw 11 and 12 w.
Anderson, T. G., clerk Treasury Dep't, w side 6 w, btw D and E n.
Anderson, Dr. S. J., s side I n, btw 9 and 10 w.
Anderson, John L., messenger Pension Office, e side 13 w, btw N Y av and I n.
Anderson, Charles, printer, w side B w, btw E and F n.
Anderson, Mrs. Susan, widow, s side K n, btw 25 and 26 w.
Anderson, Robert P., n side F n, btw 10 and 11 w.
Anderson, M. L., widow, s side G n, btw 21 and 22 w.
Anderson, J. W., shoemaker, s side G n, btw 18 and 19 w.
Anderson, Hezekiah, laborer, e side 11 e, btw M and N s.
Anderson, S. B., e side n Capitol, btw B and C n.
Andrews, Mrs. Marie Hacker, Dunbarton, btw Wash. and Green, Georgetown.
Angel, John, sr., cabinet maker, n side D s, btw 4½ and 6 w.
Angel John, jr., painter, n side D s, btw 4½ and 6 w.

Abbreviations.—All points start from the Capitol; s south, n north, e east, w west, btw between, cor corner, av avenue, h house, (col) colored.

Angell, Henry, blacksmith, Bryantown, Georgetown.
Angermann, Johan, shoestore, e side 4½ w, btw Pa av and C n.
Angney, Isaac, s side F n, btw 10 and 11 w.
Angus, Job, carpenter, s side I n, btw 9 and 10 w.
Anthony, Joseph, hatter, n side C n, btw 11 and 12 w.
Applegate, John, blacksmith, n side E s, btw 6 and 7 e.
Archer, Daniel, clerk Post Office Department, boards at Mrs. Spaulding's.
Ardursur, John, carpenter, w side 7 w, btw N Y av and L n.
Armstead, Samuel, laborer, e side 7 e, btw Va av and L s.
Armstrong, J. W., ship carpenter, n side E s, btw 6 and 7 w.
Armstrong, Robert, editor of Union, n side G n btw 14 and 15 w.
Armstrong, George B., clerk Post Office Dep't, n side H n, btw 7 and 8 w.
Armstrong, C., (col,) candy shop, w side 21 w, btw E and F n.
Arney, A. L., confectioner, Bridge, btw Congress and Washington, Georgetown.
Arnold, Ann, seamstress, w side 4½ w, btw F and G s.
Arnold, S. & J., grocers, s side 8 e, btw I and K s.
Arnold, Joseph, (& Co.,) h n side G s, btw 7 and 8 e.
Arnold, J. W., n side C n, btw 2 and 3 w.
Arnold, Thomas, grocer, corner G and 7 e; house, e side 7 e, btw E and G s.
Arnold's Bookbindery, n side B n, btw 10 and 11 w.
Arnold, Charles W., baker, s side K s, btw 7 and 8 e.
A. ARNOLD, Patent Agent, 7, opposite Patent Office.
Arnold, Aquilla, Bridge, near the bridge, Georgetown.
Arnold, A. K., justice's office, e side High, near Bridge, Georgetown.
Arsenal, United States, s end 4½ w.
Arthur, Dr. R., dentist, n side Pa av, btw 12 and 13 w.
Asbury Church, Rev. Mr. Bull, (col,) s side K n, btw 11 and 12 w.
Ascension, Church of the, s side H n, btw 9 and 10 w.
Ash, Michael, collector, s side L s, btw 8 and 9 e.
Ash, Mrs., widow, n side H n, btw 9 and 10 w.
Ashdown, William, machinist, n side G s, btw 4½ and 6 w.
Ashford, Craven, magistrate, w side 7 w, btw D and E s.
Ashford, John, s side B s, btw 9 and 10 w.
Ashley, James, printer, n side L n, btw 6 and 7 w.
Ashton, C. H. T., carter, w side 4½ w, btw M and N s.
Ashton, Mrs. Pegg, corner G and 14 w.
Ashton, William, (col,) waterman, s side F s, btw 2 and 3 w.
Ashton, Mrs., confectionary, Water, near Foundry, Georgetown.
Athey, John, woodyard, s side I n, btw 10 and 11 w; house, 9, btw I and N Y av.
Atchison, Ignatius, grocery, s side e Capitol, btw 1 and 2 e.
Atchison, John, blacksmith, e side 7 e, btw Va av and L s.
Atkinson, Henry, brickmaker, n side N s, btw s Capitol and 1 e.
Atkinson, Rev. Mr., West, btw High and Congress, Georgetown.
Attorney General's Office, first story Treasury Department.
Atz, C., confectioner, n side G n, btw 11 and 12 w.
August, Samuel, blacksmith, s side K s, btw 13 and 14 e.
Aukward, H., pumpmaker, w side 3 e, btw M and N s.
Auld, James, clerk Globe office, n side G n, btw 12 and 13 w.
Aulick, Com. John H., U S N, n side I n, btw 18 and 19 w.
Austin, Dr. James M., n side F n, btw 10 and 11 w.
Austin, Sarah, w side 12 w, btw D and E n.
Austin, Dr., e side High, near Bridge, Georgetown.
Avery, Thomas, plasterer, w side 12 w, btw C and D s.
Aylmer, R. R., grocery, corner Pa av and 17 w.

B.

Baar, William, blacksmith, n side G n, btw 22 and 23 w.
Bache, Alexander, Superintendent Coast Survey, w side N J av, btw Pa av and B.

Abbreviations.—All points start from the Capitol; s south, n north, e east, w west, btw between, cor corner, av avenue, h house, (col) colored.

BACON, SAMUEL, & CO., Grocers, corner Pa av and 7 w.
Bacon, Samuel, (& Co.,) house, s side E, btw 6 and 7 w.
Bacon, Peter F., (& Co.,) house, Ia av, btw 3 and 4½, s side.
Bacon, Washington, carpenter, w side 6 w, btw N Y av and K n.
BADEN, J. W., Hardware, s side Pa av, btw 6 and 7 w.
House, n side F n, btw 6 and 7 w.
Baden, E, Hardware, e side 13 w, btw B and C s.
Baggott, James, printer, corner 13½ and D n.
Bagnan, William, hackman, e side 13 w, btw E and F n.
Bailey, John, shoemaker, corner 8 w and D n.
Bailey, William L., clerk War Department, e side 10 w, btw N Y av and I.
Bailey, William T., laborer, n side H s, btw 9 and 10 w.
Bailey, Robert, pattern maker, s side Va av, btw 3 and 4½ w.
Bailey, Gamaliel, editor National Era, w side 7 w, btw D and E n.
House, n side C n, btw 3 and 4½ w.
Bailey, James, (col,) laborer, w side 8 w, btw D and E s.
BAIN, JOHN, Confectioner, n side Pa av, btw 2 and 3 w.
Bair, John, wheelwright, e side 5 e, btw E and G s.
Bair, Thomas, blacksmith, e side 5 e, btw E and G s.
BAIRD, DAVID A., Upholsterer and Paper-hanger, w side 8 w, btw Pa av and D n.
Baird, James, stone-cutter, n side H n, btw 18 and 19 w.
Baird, Matthew, engineer, n side Va av, btw 3 and 4 e.
Baker, Mrs. H. D. P., widow, e side N J av, btw B and C. s.
Baker, Butler, carpenter, w side 7 w, btw D and E s.
Baker, John, carpenter, e side 4½ w, btw G and H s.
BAKER, C., Exchange Hotel, n side C, btw 4½ and 6 w.
Baker, William E., laborer, n side G n btw 18 and 13 w.
Baker, John E., s side B s, btw 9 and 10 w.
Baker, Thomas, Franklin Hotel, corner D and 8 w.
Baker, Elizabeth, w side Frederick, near Water, Georgetown.
Baker, Captain, coal merchant, yard on Water, Georgetown.
House, n side West, btw Congress and Washington, Georgetown.
Baker, Arthur, blacksmith, s side Beall, near High, Georgetown.
H, n side Dumbarton, btw Congress and Washington, Geo'town.
Balch, C. B., U S N, n side Pa av, btw 21 and 22 w.
BALDING, GEORGE, Currier, e side 6 w, btw Mo av and Pa av.
BALDWIN, A., Door and Sash Manufacturer, w side 3, btw D and Ia av n.
House, D, btw 2 and 3 w.
Baldwin, Benjamin H., clerk Land Office, e side 6 w, btw Mass av and K.
Baldwin, Henry, clerk Patent Office, s side H n, near corner 12 w.
Baldwin, Gabriel, bricklayer, n side e Capitol, btw 3 and 4 e.
Ball, William L., printer, w side 8 w, btw I and K n.
Ball, John, grocer, e side 9 w, btw Pa av and D n; h, 5 w, btw G and H n.
Ball, I. S., watchmaker, w side 8 e, btw G and H s.
Ball, Richard, painter, e side 10 w, btw N Y av and K n.
Ball, William N., printer, e side 13 w, btw G and H n.
Ball, George, chandler, w side Frederick, btw Prospect and First, Georgetown.
Ball, Alfred, butter merchant, Market, btw 2d and 3d, Georgetown.
Ballager, Francis, laborer, n side Md av, btw 6 and 7 w.
Ballantyne, William, (Gray &); house, e side 7 w, btw G and H n.
Ballard, Mrs. L., widow, boarding house, e side N J av, btw Pa av and B s.
Ballinger, George, bricklayer, n side Va av, btw 3 and 4½ w.
Ballinger, Richard, wheelwright, e side Congress, south of Bridge, Georgetown.
Ballinger, Rich., wheelwright, n side Water, btw High and Congress, Georgetown.
Balmain, A., clerk Surveyor Gen's Office, War Dep't, n side H n, btw 17 and 18 w.
Baltimore, Thomas, plasterer, e side 10 w, btw D and E s.
Baltimore, T., (col,) hackman, e side 22 w, btw K and L n.
Baltzer, Mrs. Susan, widow, corner H and 9 n.
Baltzers, Misses, n side Bridge, btw High and Potomac, Georgetown.
Bangs, James, carpenter, w side 8 w, btw L and M n.

Abbreviations.—All points start from the Capitol; s south, n north, e east, w west, btw between, cor corner, av avenue, h house, (col) colored.

Bangs, John T., shoemaker, s side Bridge, btw High and Congress, Georgetown.
Bangs, Thomas, shoemaker, e side High, btw Gay and Bridge, Georgetown.
House, s side Gay, btw Congress and High, Georgetown.
Bannerman, Mrs., Mary A., boarding, corner 8 w and E n.
Bannerman, Mrs., fancy store, n side La av, btw 8 and 9 w.
Bank of the Metropolis (J. W. Maury, president) 15, opposite Treas. Department.
Bank of Washington (W. Gunton, president) cor C n and La av.
Bank, Washington City Savings (Lewis Johnson, treasurer) cor 10 w and Pa av.
Bank, Patriotic (G. C. Grammer, president) 7, near D n.
Bank, Exchange (of Selden, Withers & Co.) 7, near Pa av.
BANK OF THE REPUBLIC (J. K. Bailey, President) corner 7 w and La av.
Bank, Freemen's, 7, near Odd-Fellows' Hall.
Bank, Farmers & Merchants' (C. W. Statham, pres.) n side Pa av, btw 4½ and 6 w.
Bank, Corcoran & Riggs', 15, opposite Treasury Department.
Bank, Chubb & Brothers, cor F n and 15 w.
Bank, Pairo & Nourse, 15, opposite Treasury Department.
BANK OF COLUMBIA (R. P. Stowe, president) n side Pa av, btw 4½ and 6 w.
Bank of Commerce, (C. E. Ritenhouse, pres.) Bridge, btw High & Congress, G'twn.
Bank, Farmers and Mechanics' (R. Read, pres't) cor Bridge and Congress, G'twn.
Bank, Mechanics' (G. Myers, president) Bridge, btw Green and Wash'n, Geo'town.
Commercial Bank (J. P. Wiggins, president) Bridge, btw High and Potomac, G'twn.
Banks, Joshua, feed-store, corner 5 and H n.
Banuclos, Chevalier, 1st Sec'ry to Spanish Legation, n side Mo av, btw 4½ and 6 w.
Barbarien, Dr., dentist, e side Congress, near Bridge, Georgetown.
Barbarien, Mr., clerk, Dumbarton, near Congress, Georgetown.
Barber, Albert (col) w side 14 w, btw H and I n.
Barber, Walter T., grocer, w side 7 w, btw Va av and D s.
Barber, J. C., stove-dealer, s side Pa av, btw 4½ and 6 w.
House 4½, btw Md av and C s.
Barber, George, butcher, w side 5 e, btw K and L s.
Barber, Andrew, mason, Dumbarton, btw Congress and Washington, Georgetown.
BARBOUR & SEMMES, Grocers, opposite Bank of Washington.
Barbour, J. L. (& Semmes); house opposite Bank of Washington.
Bardin, Wm., n side M s, btw 7 and 8 e.
Bargar, Jacob, bootmaker, w side 7 w, btw R and S n.
Bargy, Mrs. Hannah, e side High, btw Dumbarton and Beall, Georgetown.
Barker, James W., carpenter, s side H n, btw 11 and 12 w.
Barker, J. W., & Co., wood and coal yard, w side 12 w, btw C and D.
Barker, Mrs., milliner, e side 10 w, btw Pa av and C n.
Barker, John, grocer, n side L s, btw 4 and 5 e.
Barker, Murray, huckster, n side 4, btw Bridge and Market, Georgetown.
Barker, Rebecca, 4, btw Frederick and Fayette, Georgetown.
Barker, James, plasterer, 4, btw Frederick and Fayette, Georgetown.
Barker, Murrah (col) huckster, Market, btw 3 and 4, Georgetown.
Barker, Richard (col) plasterer, s side 1, near Lingan, Georgetown.
Barkley, John, clerk, w side 18 w, btw Pa av and G n.
Barnaclo, William H., police officer, n side G n, btw 12 and 13 w.
Barnard, C. C. P., s side H n, btw 17 and 18 w.
Barnard, Mr., clerk, s 1, btw Frederick and Market, Georgetown.
Barnard & Buckey, auctioneers, Bridge, near cor of Congress, Georgetown.
Barneclough, J. W., clerk, w side 9 w, btw I and N J av.
Barnes, M. A. (col) laundress, w side 10 w, btw E and F s.
Barnes, H., e side 6 w, btw D and E s.
Barnes, Henry, ship carpenter, s side L s, btw 4½ and 6 w.
Barnes, Vincent, clerk at Stratton's, auctioneer, s side H s, btw 8 and 9 w.
Barnes, John (col) laborer, s side F s, btw 2 and 3 w.
Barnes, Sarah A., confectioner, e side 11 e, btw M and N e.
Barnes, John (col) laborer, n side Va av, btw 1 and 2 w.
Barnes & Mitchell, drygoods, n side La av, btw 8 and 9 w.
Barney, S. C., lieutenant U S navy, n side E n, btw 6 and 7 w.

Abbreviations.—All points start from the Capitol; s south, n north, e east, w west, btw between, cor corner, av avenue, h house, (col) colored.

Barnhouse, Richard, carpenter, s side Md av, btw 4½ and 6.
Barnhouse, C., carpenter, n side E s, btw 4½ and 6 w.
Barnum, George, e side Market space, Georgetown.
Barret, Mrs., 3, extreme west, Georgetown.
Barron, Mrs., widow, e side N J av, btw B and C s.
Barry, Richard, clerk, Navy Yard, e side N J av, btw L and M s.
Barry, G. W., clerk Treasury Department, e side 11 w, btw N Y av and I.
Barry, Mrs. Margaret, grocery, e side 2 w, btw F and G n.
Barry, James, laborer, s side A s, btw 2 and 3 w.
Barry, Thomas, U S navy, n side L s, btw 8 and 9 e.
Barry, George, baker, s side Va av, btw 3 and 4 e.
BARTHAL, JOHN, Dyer, 4½ w, btw Pa av and Mo av.
Bartley, James, clerk City Post Office, n side I n, btw 8 and 9 w.
Bartlett, Walter, grocer, n side Va av, btw 2 and 3 w.
Bartlett, John H., clerk, s side H n, btw 11 and 12 w.
Bartlett, George, clerk State Department, w side 12 w, btw H and G n.
Bartlett, P., omnibus driver, w side 12 w, btw C and D s.
Bartlett, Thomas, clerk Post Office Department, e side 19 w, btw G and H n.
Barton, —— (col) w side 3 w, btw C and Va av.
Barton, Mrs., w side 13 w, btw E and F n.
Barton, Isaac, clerk, cor 2 and Lingan, Georgetown.
Bashlin, Frederick, blacksmith, s side M n, btw 6 and 7 w.
Bastianelli, T., & Co., fancy store, n side Pa av, under Brown's hotel.
Basset, Agur, sadler, n side D n, btw 6 and 7 w.
Basset, Mrs. E., widow, n side East Capitol s, btw 1 and 2 e.
Basset, Robert, clerk Coast Survey Office, n side East Capitol s, btw 3 and 4 e.
Bassett, John, laborer, s side A s, btw 2 and 3 e.
Bassett, D., laborer, s side A s, btw 2 and 3 e.
Bassett, Isaac, messenger in Senate, w side 2 e, btw E Cap and A n.
Bassett, Mr., clerk, n e cor Dumbarton and Washington, Georgetown.
Bateman, N., stonecutter, w side 2 e, btw C and D n.
Bateman, Mrs., tailoress, s side 3, west part, Georgetown.
Bateman, Joshua, grocer, cor 1 and Fayette, Georgetown.
Bates & Brother, soap and candle factory, n side G n, btw 6 and 7 w.
Bates, Frederick (& Bro.); house s side H n, btw 6 and 7 w.
Bates, ——, clerk Post Office, w side 10 w, btw K and I n.
Bates, R. W., clerk Treasury Department, n side Pa av, btw 17 and 18 w.
Bates, John E., druggist, cor 7 and L s.
Bathen, John, watchman Navy Yard, w side 7 e, btw I and K s.
Baum, William, carpenter, n side E s, btw 4½ and 6 w.
Bawmann, Charles, cabinetmaker, n side F n, btw N J av and 2 w.
Baxter, James, blacksmith, s side K s, btw 6 and 7 e.
Baxter, W., blacksmith, n side E s, btw 6 and 7 w.
Bayly, William, carter, e side 2 w, btw G and Mass av.
Bayly, Thos. H., s side F n, btw 6 and 7 w.
BAYLY, WM. F., Stationery, n side Pa av, btw 11 and 12 w.
House w side 10 w, btw H and N Y av.
Bayly, Benj. S., collector, w side 6 w, btw H and Mass av.
Bayliss, William P., carpenter, w side 4 w, btw I and K.
Bayliss, B., real estate ag't, n side Pa av, btw 6 and 7 w; h Mo av, btw 4½ and 6 w.
Bayne, John, ship carpenter, n side Va av, btw 4 and 5 e.
Bayne, Thomas J., shoestore, w side 8 e, btw I and J s.
Beach, Levi, plasterer, w side 5 e, btw L and M s.
Beach, John, foundryman, s side Bridge, extreme west, Georgetown.
Beall, Ellenor, w side 7 w, btw L and M n.
Beall, Benjamin (Middleton &); h opposite City Hall.
Beall, George, carpenter, n side L n, btw 6 and 7 w; h H, btw 4 and 5 w.
Beall, G. W., tailor, s side Bridge, btw High and Congress, Georgetown.
Beall, Robert (col) Beall, btw Congress and Washington, Georgetown.
Beams, Francis (col) carpenter, s side I n, btw 6 and 7 w.

Abbreviations.—All points start from the Capitol; s south, n north, e east, w west, btw between, cor corner, av avenue, h house, (col) colored.

Bean, John, hackman, n side D n, btw 13 and 13½ w.
Bean, Ann (col) cook, n side I n, btw 15 and 16 w.
Bean, William, cartman, n side East Capitol s, btw 1 and 2 e.
Bean, George, laborer, n side K s, btw 10 and 11 e.
Bean, H., gardener, n side D s, btw 3 and 4 e.
Bean, B. B., carpenter, w side 3 e, btw K and L s.
Bean, Mrs., widow, boarding, s side N s, btw N J av and 3 e.
Beard, Thomas, clerk Census Office, s side Pa av, btw 21 and 22 w.
Beasley, Joseph, livery stable, s side La av, btw 6 and 7 w.
Beatty, John A., clerk Treasury Department, s side L n, btw 6 and 7 w.
Beck, Mrs. O. M., widow, e side 4½ w, btw E and F s.
Beck, Zebulon, carpenter, e side 4½ w, btw E and F s.
Beck, Richard W., carpenter, e side 4½ w, btw E and F s.
Beck, Rezin, teacher, s side Pa av, btw 10 and 12 w.
Beck, Jos. W., magistrate, cor C and 6 w; h, cor 3 e and A s.
Beeker, George, carpenter, s side L n, btw 6 and 7 w.
Becker, William, tailor, w side 8 w, btw K and L n.
Becket, Chas., moulder, w side 18 w, btw H and I n.
Bede, George, hat and bonnet presser, cor 5 w and F n.
Bedle, Francis, messenger Treasury Department, s side D n, btw 13 and 13½ w.
Beers, Isaac, Temperance Hotel, w side 3 w, btw B and C n.
Belfils, Eugene, huckster, w side 7 w, btw Va av and D.
Bell, Thomas (col) laborer, e side 3 w, btw Md av and C.
Bell, William, dyer, s side Pa av, btw 4½ and 6 w.
Bell, Mrs. Susan, grocery, s side F n, btw 9 and 10 w.
Bell, Louisa (col) seamstress, s side Pa av, btw 3 and 4 e.
Bell, William, clerk Post Office, w side 12 w, btw N Y av and H n.
Bell, Mrs. Ann, widow, w side 12 w, btw D and E n.
Bell, P. B., county constable, e side 10 w, btw E and F n.
Bell, G. W., ship carpenter, n side I n, btw 6 and 7 w.
Bell, Mrs., Female Academy, n side L n, btw 9 and 10 w.
Bell, Charles, carpenter, n side H n, btw 4 and 5 w.
Bell, Benjamin N., carpenter, e side 12 w, btw C and Md av
House w side 10 w, btw C and Va av s.
Bell, James (col) e side 18 w, btw K and L n.
Bell, A. (col) waiter, w side 22 w, btw Pa av and I n.
Bell, E. F., cabinetmaker, s side F s, btw 7 and 8 w.
Bender, George, n side I n, btw 20 and 21 w.
Bender, Jacob A., bricklayer, n side L n, btw 6 and 7 w.
Benezett, H., grocer, cor 11 w and Md av; h w side 13 w, btw C and D s.
Benedict, William B., National Observatory, n side H n, btw 15 and 16 w.
Benjamin, Joseph D., carpenter, n side H n, btw 4 and 5 w.
BENNETT, ——, Daguerreotypist, n side Pa av, btw 6 and 7 w.
Bennett, Alexander, n side D n, btw 9 and 10 w.
Bennett, Richard, laborer, s side D n, btw Md av and North Capitol.
Bennett, C. W., agent for claims, e side 11 w, btw E and Pa av.
House cor H n and 11 w.
Bennett, Wm., merchant tailor, n side Mass av, btw 9 and 10 w.
Bennett, Andrew, w side 13½ w, btw Md av and D s.
Bennett, Jonah, laborer, w side 20 w, btw E and F n.
Benson, William B., carpenter, n side Mass av, btw 9 and 10 w.
Benter, Miss Ann, s side La av, btw 9 and 10 w.
Benter, W. F., restaurant, cor 6 and Pa av; h n side Md av, btw 4½ and 6 w.
Benter, Henry, carpenter, n side D s, btw 13 and 13½ w.
Bentley, Thomas, finisher, n side M s, btw 10 and 11 e.
Benton, Thomas H., s side C n, btw 3 and 4½ w.
Benton, T., laborer, e side 23 w, btw G and H n.
Bentz, Leonard, s side L s, btw 4½ and 6 w.
Berault, Mrs. Charles, s side K n, btw 25 and 26 w.
Bergershausen, J. W., tailor, w side 12 w, btw M and N n.

Abbreviations.—All points start from the Capitol; s south, n north, e east, w west, btw between, cor corner, av avenue, h house, (col) colored.

Bergling, George, tailor, n side Pa av, btw 11 and 12 w.
Bergman, Peter, overseer at Patent Office, e side 8 w, btw L and M n.
Bergman, L. M., shoe findings, s side Pa av, btw 9 and 10 w.
House e side 8 w, btw G and H.
Bergman, H. W., carpenter, n side N n, btw 5 and 6 w.
Bergman, W., music teacher, n side N n, btw 5 and 6 w.
BERKLEY, J. T., Dyer, s side Pa av, btw 9 and 10 w.
House n side C n, btw 9 and 10 w.
Berkley, ——, clerk, Capitol, s side I n, btw 17 and 18 w.
Berkley, Joseph, laborer, s side I s, btw 10 and 11 e.
Berkley, Enos, butcher, s side G s, btw 11 and 12 e.
Bernard, Mrs. Matilda, widow, w side 8 w, btw D and E n.
Berns, F., baker, e side 11 w, btw Md av and F s.
Berret, John, s side C n, btw 4½ and 6 w.
Berrian, Hobart, clerk Treasury Dep't, n side M n, btw 9 and 10 w.
Berry, Washington O., tin and sheet iron worker, e side 7 w, btw D and E.
Berry, Thomas, stonecutter, w side 8 w, btw G and H n.
Berry, Doctor W. H., n side Pa av, btw 9 and 10 w.
Berry, Michael R., e side 6 w, btw D and E s.
Berry, Washington O., tinner, w side 9 s, btw 4½ and 6 w.
Berry, William, machinist, n side E s, btw 3 and 4½ w.
Berry, Nelson (col) laborer, w side 4 e, btw K and L s.
Berry, J. H., laborer, e side 5 e, btw G and I s.
Berry, Horatio, drygoods, n side Bridge, btw Congress and Washington, Geo'town.
House, s side West, two doors from Washington, Georgetown.
Berry, Peter, grocery and commission merchant, Water, Georgetown.
House, Beall, near Christ church, Georgetown.
Berry, Philip T., wholesale grocer, Water, west of High, Georgetown.
House, s w cor Dumbarton and Congress, Georgetown.
Berryman, Leroy, clerk Indian Bureau, e side 12 w, btw C and D n.
Besley, George, trainer, w side 14 w, btw Pa av and E n.
Best, A., messenger State Department, e side 10 w, btw Pa av and C n.
Best, Mrs. R., dress-maker, e side 10 w, btw Pa av and C n.
Bester, W., cashier Exchange Bank, s side D n, btw 2 and 3 w.
Betout, Eugene, hairdresser, n side Pa av, btw 12 and 13 w.
Betsette, Hazel, grocer, s side D s, btw 10 and 11 w.
Biays, Jane, widow, s side I n, btw 19 and 20 w.
Bevan, Thomas, grocer, cor 13 w and L n.
Beveridge, Mrs., boarding h, s side Pa av. btw 3 and 4½ w.
Bicker, Henry (col) laborer, w side 6 e, btw D and E s.
Bidleman, Daniel, tinner, n side I n, btw 4 and 5 w
Bigelow, ——, e side 7 w, btw E and F n.
Bigler, Philip, musician, cor 12 e and E s.
Billing, Mrs., seamstress, n side H n, btw 6 and 7 w.
Billy, Andrew (col) laborer, e side 3 e, btw C and D s.
Bing, John, cooper, Water, cor Congress, Georgetown.
Binnax, Edward, boarding h, s side Md av, btw 6 and 7 w.
Birch, Richard, carpenter, e side N J av, btw M and N s,
BIRCH, W. H., Livery Stable, w side 14 w, btw Pa av and D n.
House n side D n, btw 14 and 15 w.
Birch, Thomas, carpenter, w side 11 w, btw F and G n.
Birch, Wesley, watchman, w side 13½ w, btw Md av and D s.
Birch, ——, clerk, 1, btw Market and Frederick, Georgetown.
Birch, Joseph, cabinetmaker, s e cor Jefferson and Bridge, Georgetown.
House n side Bridge, opposite, Georgetown.
Birch, Isaac, carpenter, s side Prospect, btw High and Potomac, Georgetown.
Bird, Aaron H., & Co., carpenters, w side 10 w, btw E and F n.
Bird, Ebon, carpenter, s side F s, btw 8 and 9 w.
Bird, W., woodyard, cor C and Canal.
Birdine, William, machinist, n side G s, btw 6 and 7 e.

Birth, William, grocer, w side B, Ia av and C n; h, 3, btw B and C, e side.
Birth, W. W. (Harkness &) h, e side 3 w, btw B and C n.
Biscoe, Ann, s side L s, btw 6 and 7 e.
Bitner, William G., gunsmith, n side H n, btw 18 and 19 w.
Birch, F., bricklayer, e side 14 w, btw Pa av and F.
Birkhead, Miss E., boardinghouse, e side 4½ w, btw Ia av and C n.
Bishop, D. J., bookstore, n side Pa av, btw 14 and 15 w.
Bishop, Henry, plasterer, s side I n, btw 4 and 5 w.
Bishop, Joseph, blacksmith, s side F s, btw 4½ and 6 w.
Bishop, John, shoemaker, n side Va av, btw 1 and 2 w.
Bittinger, ——, livery stable, cor Jefferson and Bridge, Georgetown.
Black, Moses (col) whitewasher, s side C s, btw 4½ and 6 w.
Blackford, Mrs. (col) laundress, n side B s, btw 1 and 2 w.
Blackford, J. S., watchmaker, s side Bridge, btw High and Congress, Georgetown.
Blackman, Mr., shoemaker at Bangs, n side 1, near High, Georgetown.
Blackson, Mary (col) laundress, w side 12 w, btw Pa av and C n.
Blagden, Thomas, wharf Eastern Branch, btw 3 and 4 e; h N J av, btw K and L s.
Blagrove, William, clerk, Water, btw Congress and Jefferson, Georgetown.
Blanchard, Mrs. Ann, widow, w side 8 w, btw E and F n.
Blanchard, Dr. S. B., w side 9 w, btw D and E n.
Blanchard, V., s side Pa av, btw 12 and 13 w.
Blanchard, Claude D., s side K n, btw 25 and 26 w.
Bland, William H., iron founder, n side Va av, btw 6 and 7 e.
Blake, Dr. John B., clerk Register's office, Treas. Dep't, boards cor Pa av and 4½.
Blake, Mrs. M. A., widow, e side 11 w, btw E and F n.
Blake, G. S., s side I n, btw 18 and 19 w.
Blank, John, baker, n side H n, btw 17 and 18 w.
Bleau, Joseph, carpenter, n side F n, btw 11 and 12 w.
Blenco, Mrs., widow, s side M n, btw 12 and 13 w.
Blois, John, carpenter, East Montgomery, Georgetown.
Bloise, Thomas, tinner, w side 8 e, btw I and J s.
Blunden, ——, porter at Cemetery, Road, near Washington, Georgetown.
Blunt, Lieutenant Simon F., U S N, w side 3 w, btw B and C n.
Blunt, H. W., grocer, s e cor High and Gay, Georgetown.
Boak, William L., boardinghouse, s e cor Pa av and 4½ w.
Boarman, S. B., clerk Bank Washington, n side L n, btw 9 and 10 w.
Boarman, Richard, gunner N Y, n side L s, btw 6 and 7 e.
Boch, M., shoemaker, s side Pa av, btw 21 and 22 w.
Bode, Taylor, shoemaker, n side K n, btw 6 and 7 w.
Bodisco, Alexandre de, Russian Minister, s side 2, btw Potomac and Frederick, Georgetown.
Boehler, Mr., carpenter, n side 2 and Fayette, near College, Georgetown.
Bogan, Dr., n side H n, btw 7 and 8 w.
Boggess, T. L., blacksmith, w side 10 w, btw D and E s.
Bogue, J. J., grocer, e side Market space, Georgetown.
Bohrer, George, grocer, store w side High, btw 1 and 2, Georgetown.
House e side High, btw West and Road, Georgetown.
Bohrer, Dr., n w cor Gay and Congress, Georgetown.
Bohrer, Benj., livery stable, n side Beall, near High, Georgetown.
Bolayer, D. C., butcher, s side I s, btw 8 and 9 e.
Bogle, Mrs., widow, s side La av, btw 9 and 10 w.
Bolden, T. (col) laborer, w side 20 w, btw E and F.
Bolder, M. (col) widow, n side C s, btw 3 and 4½ w.
Bolton, Mary, widow, n side F n, btw 19 and 20 w.
Bond, David (col) waiter, n side K n, btw 15 and 16 w.
Bond, Levi (col) laborer, n side K n, btw 17 and 18 w.
Bond, Samuel, carpenter, n side F s, btw 9 and 10 w.
Bond, J. L., flour store, s side La av, btw 9 and 10 w.
Bontz, Henry, second-hand furniture, s side Pa av, btw 12 and 13 w.
Bontz, Miss E., dress maker, e side 11 w, btw F and G n.

Booz, E., printer, s side D n, btw 13½ and 14 w.
Boone, Julia (col) laundress, w side 5 e, btw D and E s.
Boone, John B., wood yard, 9, near canal.
Bootes, Samuel, clerk, 1, btw Potomac and Market, Georgetown.
Booth, R. E., butter merchant, n side F n, btw 24 and 25 w.
House w side 10 w, btw D and E n.
Booth, James, blacksmith, n side Ga av., btw 10 and 11 e.
Boqusch, G., tobacconist, n side E n, btw 8 and 9 w.
Borrimans, C., grocer, n side Pa av, btw 21 and 22 w.
Borrows, Dr. Joseph, n side E n, btw 9 and 10 w.
Borland, A., carpenter, n side L n, btw 15 and 16 w.
Bosall, Mrs., widow, w side 4 e, btw K and L s.
Boscoe, Arthur, grocer, w side 7 w, btw R and S n.
BOSS, A. & J. S., Carpenters and Builders, 4, near City Hall.
House I, btw 6 and 7 w.
Boss, James H., carpenter, n side H n, btw 4 and 5 w.
Boss, William, police office, n side C n, btw 13 and 14 w.
Boss, John, printer, n side I n, btw 4 and 5 w.
Boss, A. B., carpenter, n side I n, btw 6 and 7 w.
Boswell, Henry T., laborer, n side L s, btw 3 and 4 e.
Boswell, Miss, dress-maker, s side I n, btw 6 and 7 w.
Boswell, John C., cor 7 w side and H s.
Boswell, William H., blacksmith, e side 9 w, btw Pa av and H.
Boswell, T., cabinetmaker, s side M n, btw 12 and 13 w.
Bosworth, Mrs., widow, s side M n, btw 12 and 13 w.
BOTELER, CHARLES W., sen., China Store, n side Pa av, btw 9 and 10 w.
House n side D n, btw 2 and 3 w.
Boteler, Charles W., jun., China store, n side Pa av, btw 9 and 10 w.
House e side 4½ w, btw Pa av and C n.
Boteler, J. D., shoe store, w side 8 e, btw I and K s.
Boteler, Philip, n side G n, btw 12 and 13 w.
Boteler, Richard, laborer, n side L n, btw 7 and 8 w.
Boucher, Offert, butter merchant, w side Potomac, btw Bridge and Prospect, Georgetown.
Boucher, Theodore, grocer, cor Bridge and Potomac, Georgetown.
Boudenot, ——, n side L n, btw 15 and 16 w.
Boulanger, J., restaurant, s side G n, btw 17 and 18 w.
Bourroughs, William, carpenter, n side C s, btw 12 and 13 w.
Bowen, Theodore, shoemaker, s side L s, btw 7 and 8 e.
Bowen, H., sweep master 7th ward, e side 4½ w, btw G and H s.
Bowen, John, printer, n side Mass av, btw 6 and 7 w.
Bowen, John, tailor, n side H n, btw 4 and 5 w.
Bowen, L., clerk, s side B s., btw 6 and 7 w.
Bowen, A. (col) laborer, s side E s, btw 9 and 10 w.
Bowen, S. J., agency, w side 12 w, btw I and K n.
Bowen, P. A., schoolhouse, s side Dumbarton, btw Congress and High, Geo'town.
Bowen, Philander A., teacher, n side West, near Washington, Georgetown.
Bowen, R. J., grocer, n e cor Washington and Dumbarton, Georgetown.
BOWERS, JOHN, Grocer and Baker, w side 4½ w, btw C and D s.
Bowie, William, bricklayer, e side 13 w, btw B and C s.
Bowie, Allen P., planter, cor D s and 2 e.
Bowie, Robert, clerk, Beall, near Christ church, Georgetown.
Bowlin, Thomas, laborer, s side Va av, btw 3 and 4½ w.
Bowlinger, Mrs. Rosina, widow, confectioner, e side 7 w, btw Md av and B.
Bowman, Charles, carpenter, Washington, btw Canal and Water, Georgetown.
Bowman, Dorothy, n side 2 and Fayette, near College, Georgetown.
Boyce, J., grocery, e side 3 w, btw Va av and E.
Boyce, Captain, n side Road, btw Congress and Washington, Georgetown.
Boyd, Robert B., doorkeeper General Post Office, e side 7 w, btw D and E n.
Boyd, George K. (Noell &); h C, btw 12 and 13 w.

Abbreviations.—All points start from the Capitol ; s south, n north, e east, w west, btw between, cor corner, av avenue, h house, (col) colored.

Boyd, Mrs. J. K., n side D n, btw 10 and 11 w,
Boyd, Robert, grocer, n side K n, btw 25 and 26 w.
Boyd, ——, iron finisher, w side 7 e, btw L and M s.
Boyer, Peter, gent., boards at Mrs. Lang's hotel, cor Bridge and High, Georgetown.
Boylau, Patrick, laborer, n side D n, btw 13½ and 14 w.
Boyle, Doctor C., w side 4½ w, btw C n and Pa av.
Boyle, C., grocer, s side Pa av, btw 3 and 4½ w.
Boyle, J. J., captain U S N, w side 21 w, btw F and H n.
Boyle, Thomas, cabinetmaker, w side Potomac, btw 3 and 4, Georgetown.
Brackenridge, Wm. D., superinten't of public gardens, w side 6 w, btw G and H n.
Bradbury, L., n side I n, btw 19 and 20 w.
Bradford, Wm. J., exchange office, e side 6 w, btw H and I n.
Bradford, E., bookkeeper, n side F n, btw 13 and 14 w.
Bradford, Wm. R., clerk Patent Office, n side I n, btw 9 and 10 w.
Bradley, Mrs. Maury, seamstress, w side 7 w, btw G and H n.
Bradley, Charles, sec. Franklin Ins. Co., n side C n, btw 2 and 3 w.
Bradley, Mrs., dressmaker, n side L n, btw 8 and 9 w.
Bradley, W. A., city postmaster, s side La av, btw 4½ and 6 w.
Bradley, Henry, carpenter, s side Va av, btw 5 and 6 e.
Brady, M., Railroad hotel, n side Pa av, btw 1 and 2 w.
Brady, Thomas, watchman, n side D n, btw 13 and 13½ w.
Brady, ——, s side N Y av, btw 11 and 12 w.
Brady, James S., blacksmith, n side I s, btw 9 and 10 e.
Brandt, John D., gunner U S N, n side M s, btw 10 and 11 e.
Brannan, Ann, widow, e side 8 w, btw L and M n.
Bransome, William (col) porter National Era office, w side 11 w, btw K and I n.
Brashears, Thomas, bootmaker, w side 6 w, btw Pa av and La av.
Braxter, John, cabinetmaker, e side 11 w, btw Md av and F s.
Brashears, Thomas N., butter merchant, e side 7 w, btw D and E s.
Brashears, W. B., grocer, n side Pa av, btw 2 and 3 w.
Brazill, William, laborer, n side N s, btw South Capitol and 1 e.
Bray, George W., grocer, n side East Capitol s, btw 2 and 3 e.
Bremer, George, shoemaker, w side 11 w, btw E and Pa av.
House e side 12 w, btw N Y av and H n.
Brenner, P., confectioner, n side Pa av, btw 3 and 4½ w.
Brenner, John, clerk, w side 6 w, btw M and N n.
Brent, John C., s side E n, btw 6 and 7 w.
Brent, John, laborer, w side 18 w, btw K and L n.
Brereton & Brothers, grocers, cor 7 w and F n.
Breslyn, Michael, blacksmith, e side 7 e, btw L and M s.
Brest, J. A., laborer, s side I n, btw 4 and 5 w.
Brewer, Dr. Wm., boardinghouse, e side Potomac, btw Prospect and 1, Georgetown.
Brewer, Henry, clerk, n side West, btw Green and Montgomery, Georgetown.
Brickert, George, plaster ornament maker, n side E s, btw 12 and 13 e.
Bricklay, Mary Ann, w side 3 e, btw N and Ga av s.
Bridget, Richard B., blacksmith, e side 11 w, btw L and M n.
Bridget, John, coachmaker, n side Mass av, btw 4 and 5 w.
Bridget, R. B., blacksmith, s side La av, btw 9 and 10 w.
Bridget, John, laborer, w side 3 e, btw L and M s.
Bridget, James A., cartman, w side 23 w, btw G and H n.
Brient, Mrs. E. (col) laundress, s side E n, btw 17 and 18 w.
Briggs, Samuel, finisher, n side K s, btw 8 and 9 e.
Bright, Rebecca, widow, n side I s, btw 4 amd 5 e.
Bright, James, clerk, s side E s, btw 13 and 14 e.
Bright, Edward, finisher, n side L s, btw 3 and 4 e.
Brightharp, John, carpenter, s side D s, btw 3 and 4 e.
Brintnall, S., clerk Capitol, s side E n, btw 9 and 10 w.
Briscoe, Ann, boardinghouse, w side 17 w, btw F and G n.
Briscoe, Richard G., merchant, n side Mo. av, btw 3 and 4½ w.
Briscoe, Mrs. (General,) s side Dumbarton, eastern part, Georgetown.

Abbreviations.—All points start from the Capitol; s south, n north, e east, w west, btw between, cor corner, av avenue, h house, (col) colored.

Brissy, William, currier, e side Frederick, btw 3 and 4, Georgetown.
British Minister (J. F. Crampton) s side K n, btw 24 and 25 w.
Broadhead, Dr., e side N J av, btw B and C s.
Brodbeck, Jacob, jun., confectioner, n side Pa av, btw 17 and 18 w.
Bronaugh, Mary, boardinghouse, e side 8 w, btw Pa av and D.
Bronaugh, J. W., clerk, cor Prospect and Frederick, Georgetown.
Bronough, William, clerk Post Office, w side 13 w, btw N Y av and I n.
Brook, Theodore, (col) laborer, n side Mass av, btw 12 and 13 w.
Brooke, Robert, e side 7 w, btw L and M n.
Brooke, Mrs., widow, w side 13 w, btw G and H n.
Brooke, E. (col) laborer, w side 24 w, btw I and K n.
Brooks, Howard, tailor, w side 3 w, btw G and H n.
Brooks, Charles, hackman, w side 3 w, btw C and Va av.
Brooks, Clem. (col) laborer, e side 3 w, btw E and F.
Brooks, J. W. (col) shoemaker, s side H n, btw 8 and 9 w.
Brooks, Frances (col) laundress, s side D s, btw 1 and 2 w.
Brooks, Peter (col) laborer, s side D s, btw 1 and 2 w.
Brooks, Richard (col) laborer, s side C s, btw 1 and 2 w.
Brooks, Richard, blacksmith, e side 11 e, btw M and N s.
Brooks, Lewis, grocer, w side High, btw 1st and 2d, Georgetown.
Brooks, Joseph, s e cor Prospect and Potomac, Georgetown.
Brosnen, C., grocer, cor 6 w and G n.
Brothers, Doc. J. L., German and Indian physician, s side B s, btw 9 and 10 w.
Brower, Mrs. Mary, n side Pa av, btw 1 and 2 w.
Brower, George, jeweller, cor K n and 8 e.
Brown, R. R., printer, w side 4 w, btw G and H n.
Brown, John, whitewasher, e side 3 w, btw L and N Y av.
Brown, Thomas B., dry goods, cor 7 w and I n; h, I, near cor 6 w.
Brown, Reuben, trader, w side 7 w, btw L and M n.
Brown, A., blacksmith, s side D n, btw 8 and 9 w.
House w side 7 w, btw S and T n.
Brown, Rachel (col) laundress, w side 8 w, btw I and K n.
Brown, Charles, huckster, w side 8 w, btw P and Q n.
Brown, William, blacksmith, e side 3 w, btw F and G n.
Brown, Mrs. Mary, widow, boardinghouse, w side 8 w, btw K and I n.
Brown, Eleazar, 2d Auditor's offico,
Brown, Sarah Ann, widow, seamstress, w side 8 w, btw D and E s.
Brown, John, laborer, w side 8 w, btw G and H s.
Brown, John D., furniture store, s side Pa av, btw 14 and 15 w.
Brown, Dr. Wm. V. H., s side E n, btw 8 and 9 w.
Brown, Jesse, Brown's hotel, n side Pa av, btw 6 and 7 w.
Brown, John, barber, n side Pa av, btw 14 and 15 w.
Brown, James, shoestore, w side 8 e, btw I and J s.
House n side K s, btw 5 and 6 e.
Brown, Henry (col) waiter, e side 6 w, btw N and O n.
Brown, Lewis (col) laborer, e side 6 w, btw N and O n.
Brown, J. W., clerk 2d Aud. office, Winder's Building, n side F n, btw 14 and 15 w.
Brown, William (col) brickmaker, e side 11 w, btw H and I n.
Brown, Nathan, porter, s side Mass av, btw 9 and 10 w.
Brown, Linny (col) s side Mass av, btw 12 and 13 w.
Brown, Robert, carpenter, cor 10 w and I n; h, cor 9 w and I n.
Brown, J. S., dairyman, n side I n, btw 4 and 5 w.
Brown, Emily (col) laundress, n side N n, btw 19 and 20 w.
Brown, Maria (col) laundress, n side N n, btw 19 and 20 w.
Brown, J. Ross, n side I n, btw 6 and 7 w.
Brown, John, barber, s side I n, btw 14 and 15 w.
Brown, C. B., s side I n, btw 6 and 7 w.
Brown, Mary, laundress, s side L n, btw 3 and 4 w.
Brown, Isaac (col) laborer, s side K n, btw 9 and 10 w.
Brown, Mrs. D. (col) laundress, s side L n, btw 6 and 7 w.

Abbreviations.—All points start from the Capitol; s south, n north, e east, w west, btw between, cor corner, av avenue, h house, (col) colored.

Brown, F. (col.) laborer, n side N n, btw 14 and 15 w.
Brown, Charles (col) laborer, n side N n, btw 14 and 15 w.
Brown, Mary (col) laundress, s side M n, btw 14 and 15 w.
Brown, Thomas, clerk Treasury Department, n side H n, btw 20 and 21 w.
Brown, John L., carpenter, n side N n, btw 5 and 6 w.
Brown, Robert (col) servant, n side N n, btw 4 and 5 w.
Brown, M. (col) servant, n side N n, btw 4 and 5 w.
Brown, Mrs. Elizabeth, w side 12 w, btw E s and Md av.
Brown. Robert, stonecutter, s side A s, btw N J av and 1 e.
Brown, William, plasterer, e side 20 w, btw G and H n.
Brown, Mrs., boardinghouse, e side 20 w, btw E and F n.
Brown, Mrs., widow, seamstress, e side 20 w, btw E and F n.
Brown, H. (col) laborer, e side 23 w, btw G and H n.
Brown, Daniel, tailor, e side 14 w, btw B and C s.
Brown, W. E., carpenter, s side La av, btw 6 and 7 w.
Brown, James A., grocer, n side La av, btw 6 and 7 w.
House B, btw Del av and 1 e.
Brown, Margaret (col) laundress, s side F s, btw 2 and 3 w.
Brown, John, carpenter, s side D s, btw 9 and 10 w.
Brown, William, stonecutter, n side E s, btw 3 and 4½ w.
Brown, William (col) laborer, w side 2 e, btw A s and East Capitol.
Brown, Richard, laborer, n side L s, btw 7 and 8 e.
Brown, Basil (col) porter, s side Va av, btw 3 and 4 e.
Brown, Mrs. Barbary, widow, n side La av. btw 9 and 10 w.
Brown, William (col) laborer, n side D s, btw 4 and 5 e.
Brown, William (col) laborer, n side I s, btw 3 and 4 e.
Brown, Henry (col) laborer, n side I s, btw 3 and 4 e.
Brown, George, cabinetmaker, n side I s, btw 7 and 8 e.
Brown, William, steward hospital, n side I s, btw 9 and 10 e.
Brown, Ebenezer, cracker baker, s w cor 3 and Market, Georgetown.
Brown's bakery, Water street, near aqueduct.
Brown, Washington, laborer, Water, near aqueduct, Georgetown.
Brown, Alexander, shoemaker, Water w, cor Scott's row, Georgetown.
Brown, Capt. T., bakehouse; h, s side West, btw Congress and High, Georgetown.
Browning, Mrs. widow, n side Md av, btw 4½ and 6 w.
Browning, P. W., merchant tailor, n side Pa av, btw 3 and 4½ w.
House Md av, btw 3 and 4½ w.
Browning, Mrs. George, and George, cor Jefferson and Bridge, Georgetown.
Bruff, E. C., draughtsman, w side 19 w, btw I and K n.
Brunner, W., messenger Paymaster's office, e side 20 w, btw G and H n.
Brunner, James, carpenter, n side C s, btw 12 and 13 w.
Brunett, Lewis, carpenter, n side Mass av, btw 4 and 5 w.
Brush, Z. B., grocer, w side 8 e, btw G and I s.
Bryan, J. agent, n side Pa av, btw 9 and 10 w.
Bryan, Joseph, carpenter, n side I, btw 9 and 10 w.
Bryan, Mrs., widow, n side G s, btw 7 and 8 w.
Bryan, Samuel, blacksmith, n side K s, btw 11 and 12 e.
Bryan, Mrs., w side Frederick, btw 1 and 2, Georgetown.
Bryan, William, shoestore, Fayette, btw 2 and 3, Georgetown.
Bryant, Mrs. Emma, widow, w side 9 w, btw H and I n.
Bryant, John Y., clerk Capitol, n side M n, btw 9 and 10 w.
Bryson, Rev. Mr., Beall, btw High and Congress, Georgetown.
Buckey, Mr. (Barnard &) auctioneer, Bridge, btw Congress and High, Georgetown.
Buckly, Timothy, laborer, w side 3 w, btw C and D s.
Buckly, Anthony, cabinetm'r, s side Pa av, btw 9 and 10 w; boards Mrs. Martin's.
Buckly, James S., bridge keeper, end 11 e.
Buckingham, C., blacksmith, C, btw 10 and 11 w; h, n side E n, btw 9 and 10 w.
Buckingham, E. F., clerk Dep't Interior, n side D n, btw 9 and 10 w.
Buckingham, J. T., blacksmith, e side 2 w, btw Mass av, and G n.
Buell & Blanchard, printing office, e side 6 w, btw Mo av, Pa av.

Abbreviations.—All points start from the Capitol; s south, n north, e east, w west, btw between, cor corner, av avenue, h house, (col) colored.

Budd, William, lumber yard, cor Md av, and 11 w.
Budd, William (col) laborer, w side 21 w, btw K and L n.
Bulger, Mrs. M., w side Capitol, btw B and C s.
Bull, Marcus, clerk Pension office, w side 9 w, btw F and G n.
Bull, Rev. Mr. (col) Ashbury church.
Bulley, A. F., refectory, n side Va av, btw 7 and 8 e.
Bulley, Mrs. E. C., fancy store, Va av, btw 7 and 8 e.
Bumbaugh, Mr., tailor, s side Prospect, btw High and Potomac, Georgetown.
Burch, Thomas W., n side H n, btw 4 and 5 w; h, cor 5 and H n.
Burch, Margaret, widow, e side 4½ w, btw C and Md av.
Burch, Charles J., tailor, w side 9 w, btw D and E w.
Burch, Richard, bricklayer, s tide F n, btw 9 and 10 w.
Burch, R., carpenter, e side 6 w, btw M and N n.
Burch, John, s side D n, btw 2 and 3 w.
Burch, E., widow, n side Mass av, btw 6 and 7 w.
Burch, Joseph, A., carpenter, n side N Y av, btw 3 and 4 w.
Burche, Mrs. Susan, e side 6 w, btw D and E n.
Burche, John C., clerk Dep't Interior, s side C n, btw 2 and 3 w.
Burdine, Reuben, n side H n, btw 6 and 7 w.
Burg, F., gardener, n side N Y av, btw 4 and 5 w.
Burgdoff, Louis, carpenter, s side C n, btw 9 and 10 w.
Burger, Frederick, tobacconist, n side F n, btw 9 and and 10 w.
Burgerin, Julia, widow, w side 12 w, btw C and D n.
Burgess, Charles, blacksmith, e side 14 e, btw K and L s.
Burgess, James, chimneysweep master, e side 14 e, btw K and L s.
Burgess, Andrew, engineer, n side M s, btw 10 and 11 e.
Burgess, Teresa, seamstress, w side 4½ w, btw C and D s.
Burgess, Bradley, boiler-maker, e side N J av, btw K and L n.
Burgess, Richard, agent, s side F n, btw 13 and 14 w.
Burgess, Washington G., barber, e side 8 w, btw D and E n.
BURGESS, CHARLES H., Bill-poster, n side B n, btw 10 and 11 w.
Burkardt, Lewis E., shoemaker, n side F n, btw 8 and 9 w.
Burke, H. (col) carpenter, e side 20 w. btw L and M n.
Burkley, Benjamin, butcher, n side Ga av, btw 13 and 14 e.
Burl, John (col) servant, s side D n, btw 5 and 6 w.
Burnett, E., pottery, cor 8 w, and H n; h, I n, btw 7 and 8 w.
Burnett, Miss C., and Miss, confectioners, e side 7 w, btw I and K n.
Burnett, Enoch, stoneware manufacturer, n side I n, btw 7 and 8 w.
Burnly, A. T., (Republic office,) s side F n, btw 17 and 18 w.
Burns, John W., confectioner, w side 7 w, btw I and N Y av.
Burns, George, shoestore, n side Pa av, btw 4½ and 6 w.
House e side 6 w, btw F and G n.
Burns, Patrick, blacksmith, n side C n, btw 4½ and 6 w.
Burns, Patrick, carpenter, s side Mass av, btw 2 and 3 w.
Burns, Patrick, carpenter, w side 15 w, btw L and M n.
Burns, Michael, gardener, n side Va av, btw 8 and 9 w.
Burns, George, shoestore, n side La av, btw 8 and 9 w; h 6 btw F and G n.
Burns, Ann, widow, s side B s, btw 10 and 11 w.
Burns, Alfred, teacher, s w cor Dumbarton and Green, Georgetown.
Burns, James, huckster, s side Bridge, near Market, Georgetown.
Burnside & Co., clothingstore, cor 7 e and L s.
Burr, T. S., n side Mass av, btw 2 and 3 w.
Burr, R. R., constable, cor F n and 3 w.
Burr, David, e side Del av, btw B and C n.
Burroughs, William, carpenter, n side C s, btw 12 and 13 w.
Burrows, Wm., farmer, w side Frederick, btw Prospect and 1, Georgetown.
Burrows, —— (at Edes' feed store) e side Washington, btw Bridge and Canal, Georgetown.
Burrows, John, laborer, e side Potomac, btw Bridge and Prospect, Georgetown.
Burruss, Mrs., boardinghouse, n side D n, btw 6 and 7 w.

Bury, Mrs. Eliza, milliner, w side 8 e, btw I and J s.
Busey, Doctor, w side 1 e, btw A and B s.
BUTHMANN, JOHN, Wine Merchant, s side Pa av, btw 4½ and 6 w; boards at Waverley House.
Buthmann, James (col) woodsawyer, e side 3, btw C and D s.
Butibaugh, George, tailor, n side D s, btw 4½ and 6 w.
Butt, Samuel, druggist, n side Pa av, btw 12 and 13 w.
House w side 12 w, btw C and Pa av.
Butt, Solomon, coachsmith, e side 14 w, btw C and D n.
Butt, L. W., tinner, s side F s, btw 7 and 8 w.
Butler, H. (col) laborer, n side F n, btw 21 and 22 w.
Butler, —— (col) e side N J av, btw B and C s.
Butler, Wm. (col) laborer, w side 9 w, btw G and H s.
Butler, Benjamin (col) laborer, w side 9 w, btw G and H s.
Butler, F., Monument House, cor Pa av and 14 w.
Butler, Matthew, baker, e side 6 w, btw G and H n.
Butler, Rev. C. M., pastor Trinity Church, n side C, btw 4½ and 6 w.
Butler, Andrew (col) carpenter, e side 10 w, btw L and M w.
Butler, Rev. J. G., pastor Eng. Luth'n church, e side 12 w, btw K and L n.
Butler, William, carpenter, n side L n, btw 9 and 10 w.
Butler, Mrs. (col) s side L n, btw Vt av and 15 w.
Butler, Eliza (col) landress, s side A s btw 1 and 2 e.
Butler, Walter, (col,) servant, w side 17 w, btw C and D.
Butler, H. (col) laborer, w side 20 w, btw L and M n.
Butler, L. (col) laundress, e side 22 w, btw K and L n.
Butler, Amelia (col) n side K n, btw Vt av and 15 w.
Butler, M. S. (col) servant, s side C s, btw 1 and 2 w.
Butler, Mrs. E., widow, e side 4 e, btw K and L s.
Butler, Joseph, carpenter, n side Dumbarton, eastern part, Georgetown.
Butler, Charles, tailor, Frederick, btw 3 and 4, Georgetown.
Byer, ——, carpenter, n side C s, btw 12 and 13 w.
Byers, Noah (col) laborer, w side 9 w, btw G and H s.
BYERS & McKNEW, Drygoods, n side La av, btw 8 and 9 w.
Byers, J. F. (& McKnew); h 7, btw G and H.
BYINGTON & CO., S., brick yard, South Capitol, btw M and N s.
Byington, S. (& Co.) Half street w, btw M and N s.
BYRNE, C. R., Grocer, cor Pa av and 10 w.
Byrne, Mrs. Mary Ann, grocery, s side F n, btw 13 and 14 w.
Byrne, P. A., blacksmith, w side 1 w, btw B s and Md av.

C.

Cadle, William, s side D s, btw 3 and 4 e.
Cady, D. H., barber, n side Pa av, btw 14 and 15 w.
House n side D n, btw 9 and 10 w.
Cahhall, James, laborer, e side 4½ w, btw C and Md av.
Caho, J. T., agent, n side H n, btw 6 and 7 w.
Calahan, Denis, blacksmith, n side D s, btw 3 and 4 e.
Calbert, G. (col) laundress, s side C s, btw 1 and 2 w.
Caldwell, J., clerk Post office, n side Md av, btw 12 and 13 w.
Caldwell, John, provision store, s side Pa av, btw 21 and 22 w.
Caldwell, Rev. —— (Episcopal) Gay, btw Congress and Washington, Georgetown.
Callahan, Jerome, bricklayer, w side 4½ w, btw I and J s.
Callahan, David, sergeant of the arsenal, s end 4½ w.
Callahan, Jeremiah, confectioner, n side Pa av, btw 1 and 2 w.
Callahan, Thomas, blacksmith, n side D n, btw 13½ and 14 w.
Callaher, James, hackman, n side Mo av, btw 4½ and 6 w.
Callan, John F., Pres. Poto. Sav. Bank, n side E n, btw 6 and 7 w.
CALLAN, NICHOLAS, Notary Public, s side F n btw 14 and 15 w.

Callan Michael, clerk City Po office, s side F n, btw 14 and 15 w.
Callan, Lawrence, laborer, s side B n, btw 5 and 6 e.
Callan, James, fireman U S N, s side B, btw 6 and 7 w.
Callan, Mrs., grocer, s side 2, btw Frederick and Fayette, Georgetown.
Callard, George, cor M and 4 s.
Calvert, Charles, clerk War Dep't, e side 19 w, btw I and K n.
Calvert, Charles, National Hotel, cor Pa av and 6 w.
Cameron, ——, artist, n side Pa av, btw 4½ and 6 w.
CAMERON, H., agent Mohawk Fire Insurance, n side Pa av, btw 6 and 7 w.
Cameron, Gilbert, stonecutter, s side B s, btw 10 and 11 w.
Cameron, —— (& Andrews) auctioneer, n side Bridge, btw Potomac and High, Georgetown; h cor Market and Bridge.
Cameron, Edward, s side Prospect, btw High and Potomac, Georgetown.
Cammack, Christopher, tailor, n side F n, btw 14 and 15 w.
Cammack, William, collector, s side Va av, btw 6 and 7 w.
Cammack, William, jr., engineer, s side Va av, btw 6 and 7 w.
Cammack, John, tailor, n side Prospect, cor Potomac, Georgetown.
Cammack, Edward, tailor, n side Bridge, btw Potomac and High, Georgetown.
Cammil, Thomas, stonecutter, w side, btw I and Mass av.
Camp, Mrs., n w cor Bridge and Washington, Georgetown.
Campbell, Q. A., Coast Survey, w side N J av, btw D and E s.
CAMPBELL, WILLIAM, Dealer in Plaster and Cement, w side 7 w.
House w side 9 w, btw D and E n.
Campbell, William H., grocer, cor 7 w and M n.
Campbell, Mrs. L., milliner, w side 9 w, btw D and E n.
Campbell, Daniel, saddler, n side Pa av, btw 4½ and 6 w.
House Mass av, btw 6 and 7 w.
Campbell & Coyle, hardware store, s side Pa av, btw 6 and 7 w.
Campbell, W. H. (& Coyle); h e, btw 6 and 7 w.
Campbell, R. Gray, s side Mass av, btw 4 and 5 n,
Campbell, Archibald, clerk War Dep't, n side H n, btw 17 and 18 w.
Campbell, Robert, n side N n, btw 4½ and 6 w.
Campbell, John, grocer, s w cor Beall and Montgomery, Ghorgetown.
Canal packet office, Congress, btw Bridge and Canal, Georgetown.
Canfield, Charles, clerk Census office, e side 10 w, btw N Y av and K n.
Cannon, Ann, s side K n, btw 24 and 25 w.
Cannon, John, blacksmith, e side 10 w, btw I and K s.
Canter, Mrs. L. (col) s side Pa av, btw 24 and 25 w.
Cantine Jos. C., clerk Treas. Dep't, 3d Aud. office, n side Mo av, btw 3 and 4½ w.
Canvau, James, laborer, n side F n, btw N J av and 2 w.
Caperton, Hugh, attorney, s side Bridge, btw High and Potomac, Georgetown.
House e side High, near Bridge, Georgetown.
Car, John, brass moulder, n side C n, btw 13 and 14 w.
Carberry, T. C., w side 17 w, btw C and D n.
Carberry, Lewis, surveyor, n side 2, on Lingan, near College, Georgetown.
Cardwell, David A., clerk Republic Office, s side D n, btw 2 and 3 w.
Cares, B., sailmaker, n side La av, btw 9 and 10 w.
Carico, Mrs. A., widow, tailoress, n side I n, btw 9 and 10 w.
Carico, Peter, grocer, s side H n, btw 21 and 22 w.
Carico, Wm. B., clerk N Y, e side 11 e, btw N and O s.
Carleton, Wm., printer, s side G w, btw 13 and 14 w.
Carlin, John E. F., carpenter, w side 12 w, btw D and E s.
Carlisle, J. M., attorney, cor Pa av and 4½ w.
Carmichael, Doctor E. H., e side 12 w, btw E n and Pa av.
Carmody, Jeremiah, laborer, w side 3, btw F and G n.
Carpenter, Sophy, laundress, w side 4½ w, btw Va av and F s.
Carpenter, John R., carpenter, n side N Y av, btw 21 and 22 w.
Carr, William, clerk, Maine av, btw 3 and 4½ w.
Carr, John, tailor, Frederick w, btw 1 and 2, Georgetown.
Carrico, James, carpenter, e side 20 w, btw E and F n.

Abbreviations.—All points start from the Capitol; s south, n north, e east, w west, btw between, cor corner, (col) colored, av avenue, h house.

Carothers, Rev. Andrew, n side F n, btw 11 and 12 w.
Carroll, Thomas, laborer, n side Ohio av, btw 13½ and 14 w.
Carroll, Daniel, laborer, s side G s, btw 12 and 13 e.
Carroll, John (col) shoemaker, n side K s, btw 6 and 7 e.
Carroll, William (col) laborer, s side Va av, btw 4½ and 6 w.
Carroll, Walter, laborer, n side E s, btw 12 and 13 e.
Carroll, Wm. T., clerk Supreme Court, n side F n, btw 18 and 19 w.
Carroll, Miss Ann, cor H and N J av, e side.
Carroll, John B., tailor, w side 7 w, btw L and M n.
Carroll, Michael, finisher, cor I n and 8 e.
Carroll, Peter, laborer, n side G n, btw 12 and 13 w.
Carroll, David (col) furniture car, s side G n, btw 13 and 14 w.
Carroll, J., shoemaker, s side Pa av, btw 19 and 20 w.
Carroll, James, shoemaker, n side H n, btw 18 and 19 w.
Carroll, Thomas, laborer, n side B s, btw 1 and 2 w.
Carrol, John, s side Bridge, btw Washington and Jefferson, Georgetown.
Carter, R. W., drygoods, La av, btw 7 and 8 w; h w side 19 w, btw D and E n.
Carter, James (col) huckster, e side 11 w, btw F and G n.
Carter, James, agent, s side L n, btw 9 and 10 w.
Carter, William, captain steamboat Columbia, w side 12 w, btw E s and Md av.
Carter, R., doorkeeper Treasury Dep't, e side 20 w, btw G and H n.
Carter, Mrs., boardinghouse, n side A n, btw 13 and Del av.
Carter, J. H., laborer, n side F s, btw 2 and 3 w.
Carter, J., laborer, n side I s, btw 10 and 11 e.
Carter, Mrs., s side Road, near Congress, Georgetown.
Carter, John G., dry goods, s side Bridge, btw High and Congress, Georgetown.
House Gay, cor Green, Georgetown.
Carter, Mr., barber and confectioner, n side Bridge, btw Potomac and High, G'twn.
Carttorill, George, carpenter, w side 3 w, btw C and D s.
Cartwright, Mr., carter, e side Montgomery, near Bridge, Georgetown.
Carusi, Samuel, music-store, n side Pa av, btw 12 and 13 w.
House n side K n, btw 12 and 13 w.
Carusi's Saloon, cor 11 w and C n.
Carusi, Nathaniel, music teacher, e side 13 w, btw E and F n.
Carvallo, Manuel, Chilian Minister, e side 7 w, btw E and F.
Cary, Isaac N. (col) barber, w side 6 w, btw La av and Pa av.
H n side C, btw 6 and 7 w.
CASPARIS, J., Refectory Congress Hall, s side A s, btw N J av, and 1 e.
Casper, John, carpenter, w side 7 w, btw N and O n.
Cassadavant, Dr., surgeon dentist, n side Pa av, btw 8 and 9 w.
Cassell, John T., painter, n side of Md av, btw 6 and 7 w.
House e side 7 w, btw B and Md av.
Cassell, J. A., bricklayer, n side Va av, btw 6 and 7 w.
Cassidy, A., Coast Survey, w side N J av, btw D and E s.
Cassidy, Mr., Catholic sexton, Fayette, Georgetown.
Cassin, Com., n w cor Beall and Washington, Georgetown.
Castel, John, grocer, w side 8 e, btw G and I s.
Catalano, Antonia, carpenter, n side I s, btw 7 and 8 e.
Cater, John, shoemaker, e side 7 e, btw Va av and L s.
Cathcart, Thomas, clerk Treas. Dep't, s side B n, btw Del av and 1 e.
Catherell, Captain Jonathan, s side West, btw Congress and Washington, Geo'town.
Caton, A., s side D n, btw 5 and 6 w.
Cattrell, William, B., butcher, w side 8 w, btw P and Q n.
Causten, James H., consul for Equador, and general agent, s side F n, btw 14 and 15 w.
Causten, James H., jr., w side 10 w, btw D and E n.
Cawood, Alexander, watchman President's House, s side K n, btw 18 and 19 w.
Caywood, Thomas, w side N J av, btw L and M s.
Cecil, Salrit S., laborer, e side 6 w, btw H and I n.
Cemetery, n side Road, gate facing Washington street, Georgetown.

Abbreviations.—All points start from the Capitol; s south, n north, e east, w west, btw between, cor corner, (col) colored, av avenue, h house.

Census Office, U. S., w side 8 w, btw E and F n.
Centre Market, s side Pa av, btw 7 and 9 w.
Central Academy, cor 10 and E n.
Centus, Eliza, widow, n side L n, btw 6 and 7 w.
Chamberlyn, George, shoemaker, s side 3d, btw High and Potomac, Georgetown.
Chamberlyn, David, blacksmith, e side Frederick, btw 3d and 4th, Georgetown.
Chamberlyn, James, (col) 4th, near Fayette, Georgetown.
Chamberlyn, William, blacksmith, High, btw 2d and 3d, Georgetown.
Chambers, J. C., engraver, n side Pa av, btw 2 and 3 w.
Chambers, Benjamin, engraver, e side 10 w, btw D and E n.
Chambers, William, cabinetmaker, n side L n, btw 9 and 10 w.
Chambers, Mrs., 2d, near College, Georgetown.
Champion, Samuel, blacksmith, w side 6 e, btw D and Pa.
Champion, Thomas, blacksmith, n side Va av, btw 7 and 8 e.
Chandler, Mrs., n w corner of West and Congress, Georgetown.
Chaney, Peter, feed store, w side Jefferson, near Bridge, Georgetown.
Chapin, E. M., cor 8 w and K n.
Chapman, James A., Dep't Interior, n side E n, btw 6 and 7 w.
Chapman, J., fancy store, s side Pa av, btw 19 and 20 w.
Chapman, William, clerk, cor Dumbarton and Congress, Georgetown.
Charles A., laborer, cor 19 w and Pa av.
Chase, Amelia (col) laundress, w side 3, btw M and N Y av.
Chase, Elizabeth (col) laundress, w side 10 w, btw M and N n.
Chase, Harriet (col) laundress, w side 10 w, btw M and N n.
Chase, William (col) blacksmith, n side I n, btw 11 and 12 w.
Chase, S. P., clerk Pension office, w side 1 e, btw A and B n.
Chattam, James, horse dealer, w side 14, btw D and E n.
Chedal, James D., printer, n side D n. btw 6 and 7 w.
Cheever, B. H., office opposite Treas. Department.
Cheny, Warren J., machinist, s side F s, btw 9 and 10 w.
Cherry, Mr., 2d, near College, Georgetown.
Chestney, James, attorney, s side B n, btw 2 and 3 w.
CHEVY, CLAYTON, currier, e side 6 w, btw Mo av and Pa av.
Chew, Robert F., carpenter, e side 8 w, btw L and M n.
Chew, Robert S., clerk State Dep't, n side Pa av, btw 15 w and Vt av.
Chew, Captain, superintendent Alexandria canal, s side Bridge, extreme west, Georgetown.
Chezum, Miss Catharine, grocery, n side C s, btw 12 and 13 w.
Chick, Richard, plasterer, s side Gay, extreme east, Georgetown.
Chilian Minister (Manuel Carvallo) e side 7, btw E and F n.
Chilton, Washington, blacksmith, n side I s, btw 2 and 3 e.
Chisel, George, carpenter, w side 22 w, btw Pa av and I n.
Chiseltine, L. (col) servant, w side 2 e, btw C and D n.
Chisholm, Miss, s side Md av, btw 4½ and 6 w.
CHOATE, WARREN, Cupper and Leecher, w side 4½ w., btw C n and Pa av.
CHOATE, Mrs., Fancy Milliner, w side 4½ w, btw C n and Pa av.
Choppin, William, carpenter, s side G n, btw 12 and 13; h cor G n and 13 w.
Chubb, Charles, banker, w side 14 w, btw F and G n.
Chubb, Brothers, bankers, e side 15 w, cor F n.
Chubb, Monroe (& Bro.) s side F n, btw 20 and 21 w.
Church, First Baptist (Stephen P. Hill, pastor) 10, btw E and F n.
Church, Second Baptist (Isaac Cole, pastor) cor Va av and 4 e.
Church, Third Baptist (G. W. Sampson, pastor) E n, btw 6 and 7 w.
Church, Fifth Baptist (T. C. Teasdale, pastor) 5th street, Island.
Church, First Baptist, (col,) (Mr. Brown, pastor) cor I n and 19 w.
Church, St. Patrick's (Wm. Mathews, pastor—Mr. O'Toole, assistant pastor) F n, btw 9 and 10 w.
Church, St. Matthew's (Jas. B. Donelan, pastor) cor 15 and H n.
Church, St. Peter's (E. A. Knight, pastor—B. McManes, ass't pastor) Capitol Hill.
Church, St. Mary's (Matthias Alig, pastor) 6 w, btw G and H n.

Abbreviations.—All points start from the Capitol; s soath, n north, e east, w west, btw between, cor corner, (col) colored, av avenue, h house.

Church, St. John's (Smith Pyne, D. D., rector) President square.
Church of the Epiphany (J. W. French, rector) G n, btw 14 and 15 w.
Church of the Ascension (L. J. Gillis, rector—Henry Stanley, assistant rector) H n, btw 11 and 12 w.
Church, Grace (Alfred Holmead, rector) cor D and 9 w, Island.
Church, Trinity (C. M. Butler, D. D., rector) cor 3 w and C n.
Church, Christ (Wm, Hodges, rector) G s, btw 6 and 7 e, Navy Yard.
Church, Methodist Episcopal—Wesley Chapel—(S. S. Rossell, pastor) cor of F n and 5 w.
Church, Methodist Episcopal—Foundry Chapel—(Jesse T. Peck, pastor) cor of 14 w and G n.
Church, Methodist Episcopal—M'Kendree Chapel—(W. T. Hamilton, pastor) Mass av, btw 9 and 10 w.
Church, Deutsche Evangelische Kirshe, s side G n, btw 19 and 20 w.
Church, Methodist Episcopal—Ryland Chapel—(Rev. Mr. Hodges, pastor) cor D s and 11 w.
Church, Methodist Episcopal—Union Chapel—(Rev. Mr. Dashiel, pastor) 19 w, btw H and Pa av.
Church, Methodist Episcopal—Ebenezer Chapel, Navy Yard—(Rev. Philip Lipscomb, pastor) 4 e, btw G and E s.
Church, Methodist Protestant—(Rev. Mr. ———, pastor) 9th, btw E and F.
Church, F street Presbyterian—(Rev. James Laurie, D. D., pastor—D. X. Junkin, D. D., associate pastor) on F street n, btw 14 and 15.
Church, First Presbyterian—(no pastor at present) on 4½ w, btw C and La av.
Church, Second Presbyterian—(Rev. J. R. Eckard, pastor) on N Y av and H n, near 13th.
Church, Fourth Presbyterian—(Rev. J. C. Smith, pastor) on 9th, btw G and H.
Church, Fifth Presbyterian—(Rev. A. G. Carothers, pastor) cor I n and 5 w.
Church, First Presbyterian, (col'd) 15th, btw I and K—(Rev. J. F. Cook, pastor.)
Church, Christ—(Rev. Mr. Caldwell) on cor of Beall and Congress, Georgetown.
Church, St. John's—(Rev. Mr. Tillenhast) cor of 2d and Potomac, Georgetown.
Church, Methodist Episcopal—Slicer's Chapel—(Rev. Samuel Bryson, pastor—Rev. John C. Dice, associate do.) on Dumbarton, btw High and Congress, Georgetown.
Church, Methodist Episcopal, (col'd)—Asbury—(Rev. John C. Dice, pastor) on Montgomery, near Lyon's Mill, Georgetown.
Church, Methodist Protestant—Rev. S. K. Cox, pastor) on Congress, btw Bridge and Gay, Georgetown.
Church, Presbyterian—(Rev. J. M. P. Atkinson, pastor) on Bridge, btw Green and Washington, Georgetown.
Church, Catholic—(Rev. Mr. ———,) on Lingan, btw 1st and 2d.
Church, Alfred (col) laborer, s side C s, btw 3 and 4½ w.
Churn, James, sawyer, w side 7 e, btw L and M s.
Cissel, G. W., laborer, e side 7 w, cor O n.
Cissel, Dr. R. S. T., drug store, cor Congress and Bridge, Georgetown.
Cissel's carpenter shop, e side Congress, btw Gay and Bridge, Georgetown.
City Hall contains rooms for the offices of the Circuit, Criminal, and Orphans' Courts; chamber of the Chief Justice, offices of the Attorney and Marshal of the District of Columbia, Clerk of the County of Washington, Register of Wills, City Council, Mayor of Washington, Register of the Corporation, City surveyor, Collector of City Taxes, Board of Health, office of the Chesapeake and Ohio Canal Company, and Commissioner of the Third Ward. See initial letter for each.
Clagett, Mrs., s side I n, btw 18 and 19 w.
Clagett, Wm. H., drygoods, w side 7 w, btw E and Pa av; boards at Mrs. Clare's.
Clagett, Newton, May & Co., drygoods, n side Pa av, btw 9 and 10 w.
Clagett, Darius, (Newton, May & Co.;) resides in the country.
CLAGETT & DODSON, Carpet Warerooms, La av, near cor of 9 w.
Clagett, J. B., (Clagett, Newton, May & Co.) C, btw 4½ and 6 w.
Claphan, John, pyrotechnist, n side 8 e, btw M and L s.
Clara, N., clerk, w side 19 w, btw F and G n.
Clark, J., w side btw G and H n.

Abbreviations.—All points start from the Capitol; s south, n north, e east, w west, btw between, cor corner, (col) colored, av avenue, h house.

Clark, John F., patent agent, cor 8 w and E n; h cor 3 w and D n.
Clark, R. B., grocer, w side 4½ w, btw M and N s.
Clark, Edward, architect office, e side 7 w, btw F and G n.
Clark, H. B., clerk foundry, w side 7 w, btw C and D s.
Clark, John W., dentist, w side 7 w, btw I and N Y av.
Clark, James B., clerk Bank of Metropolis, L, btw 9 and 10 w.
Clark, Edmund M., clerk, s side Md av, btw 12 and 13 w.
CLARK, L. F., Upholsterer, n side Pa av, btw 12 and 13 w.
House n side N Y av, btw 12 and 13 w.
Clark, Captain M. M., U S A, n side F n, btw 13 and 14 w.
CLARK, WM. H., Grocer, cor 12 and B n; h, n side C n, btw 12 and 13 w.
Clark, Thomas, hack driver, s side D n, btw 5 and 6 w.
Clark, J. T., clerk post office, w side 10 w, btw H and N Y av.
Clark, Richard, messenger Pension Office, w side 11 w, btw N Y av and H n.
Clark, J. D., magistrate, office w side 12 w, btw C and D n.
House s side H n, btw 12 and 13 w.
Clark, Charles (col) laborer, e side 12 w, btw M and N n.
Clark, John, milk and cream dealer, n side Mass av, btw 12 and 13 w.
Clark, C., n side K n, btw 17 and 18 w.
Clark, Mrs., widow, s side I n, btw 6 and 7 w.
Clark, James, tailor, s side I n, btw 9 and 10 w.
Clark, John G., n side H n, btw N Y av and 16 w.
Clark, Samuel, stone mason, w side 12 w, btw C and D s.
Clark, M. M., office asst. quartermaster, cor 17 w and Pa av.
Clark, R. H., attorney at law, cor 6 and La av; residence at Mrs. Scott's, Pa av.
Clark, Thomas D., painter, n side C s, btw 12 and 13 w.
Clark, Stephen (col) bricklayer, n side D s, btw 1 and 2 w.
Clark, Thomas, messenger Capitol, n side East Capitol, btw 3 and 4 e.
Clark, William, farmer, e side 14 e, btw I and K s.
Clark, Robert, undertaker, n side K s, btw 8 and 9 e.
Clark, Thomas, wood merchant, s side G s, btw 6 and 7 e.
Clark & Hamilton, grocers, cor 6 w and Va av, Island.
Clark, Ignatius, hay-weigher, n w cor Bridge and 2d, Georgetown.
Clarke, Daniel, drugstore, cor Md av and 11 w.
House w side 13 w, btw B and C s.
Clarke, Abraham, carpenter, e side 6 w, btw G and H n.
Clarke, James, n side L n, btw 9 and 10 w.
Clarke, Isaac, gent, n side H n, btw 7 and 8 w.
Clarke, R. C., barber, s side Pa av, btw 19 and 20 w.
Clarke, H. A., grocer, n side C s, btw 12 and 13 w.
Clarke, Dr. Samuel, dentist, s side Bridge, near Jefferson, Georgetown.
Clarke, Mrs. A. H., milliner, s side Bridge, near Jefferson, Georgetown.
Clarke, Rev. Wm. J., ladies' academy, (formerly Miss English's,) n e cor Gay and Congress, Georgetown.
Clayton, Philip, 2d Aud. office (Winder's Building) n side G n, btw 12 and 13 w.
Clayton, J. M., fancy store, s side Bridge, btw Potomac and Bridge, Georgetown.
Claxton, A. B., printer, 9th, btw H and I.
Claxton, Mrs. Susan, fancy store, s side Bridge, btw Potomac and Bridge, Georgetown.
Cleary, William, clerk Land office, Maine av, btw 4½ and 6 w.
Clements, Aloysius, chairmaker and painter, w side 4½ w, btw C and D s.
Clements, Rachel, seamtress, w side 4½ w, btw C and D s.
Clements, John S., Post Office Department, n side I n, btw 4 and 5 w.
Clements & Daly, wood and coal merchants, s side N Y av, btw 13 and 14 w.
Clements, Joseph, laborer, s side M n, btw 4 and 5 w.
Clements, B. H., painter, n side Pa av, btw 17 and 18 w; h M, btw 18 and 19 w.
Clements, J. F., attorney at law, s side La av, btw 4½ and 6 w.
Clements, Charles, huckster, w side 3 e, btw M and N s.
Clements, John T., shoemaker, s side 2d, btw Frederick and Fayette, Georgetown.
Clements, Bennet, s side 3d, cor Market, Georgetown.

Abbreviations.—All points start from the Capitol; s south, n north, e east, w west, btw between, cor corner, (col) colored, av avenue, h house.

Clements, Mrs. Wm., 4th, cor Potomac, in Twenty Buildings, Georgetown.
Clements, Mrs., confectioner, e side Fayette, btw 1st and 2d, Georgetown.
Clements, Samuel, hardware clerk, w side Lingan, btw 2d and 3d, Georgetown.
Clephane, James, printer, s side G n, btw 12 and 13 w.
Clerk House of Representatives, office Capitol, s wing, rotundo story.
Clerk Supreme Court, office Capitol, s wing, basement story.
Clerk of Washington County, City Hall, east wing, second story.
Click, John, clothier, n side Pa av, btw 4½ and 6 w.
Clinton, T. G., patent agent, e side 7 w, btw D and E n.
Clitch, Mrs. H., fancy store, n side Pa av, btw 9 and 10 w.
Clokey, Robert B., carpenter, n side G n, btw 12 and 13 w.
Clokey, John, carpenter, e side 15 w, btw D and Pa av; h 11, btw E and F s.
Clubb, John L., clerk Senate, n side I n, btw 6 and 7 w.
Cluskey, C. B., architect, n side Pa av, btw 12 and 13 w.
House, w side 10 w, btw G and H n.
Clumerford, ——, grocer, s side Ga av, btw 11 and 12 e.
Coakley, Mrs. Ann, (col) candy shop, n side G n, btw 18 and 19 w.
Coast Survey office, w side N J av, btw A and B s.
Coban, George, tanner, s side N Y av, btw 9 and 10 w.
Coburn, John, refectory, n side Pa av, btw 14 and 15 w.
Cochrane, Anna, widow, s side N Y av, btw 9 and 10 w.
Cochran, James, upholsterer, s side F n, btw 10 and 11 w.
GOCHRAN, GEORGE W., Tobacconist, e side 7 w, btw D and E n.
House, w side 6 w, btw G and H n.
Cochran, R., clerk Treasury Department, s side B s, btw 13 and 13½ w.
Cockrell, George H., wood yard, s side Md av, btw 2 and 3 w.
Cockerill, Mr., wheelwright, e side High, near Bridge, Georgetown.
Coddington, John, banker, n side G n, btw 12 and 13 w.
Codrick, Frederick, driver, n side C s, btw 13 and 13½ w.
Codrick, John, meal wagon, w side 9 w, btw G and H s.
Coffin, Isaac N., agent for claims and pensions, Green's row, opposite Capitol.
Coffin, John H. C., professor mathematics U S Navy, cor I n and 19 w.
Coggswell, Albert, shoemaker, n side Dumbarton, between Green and Montgomery, Georgetown.
Cohen, Robert, shoe store, s side Pa av, btw 6 and 7 w; h G, btw 5 and 6 w.
Coke, William, (col) porter, s side F n, btw 21 and 22 w.
Colbart, John, boarding, e side 3 w, btw G and Mass av.
Colbert, Michael, grocer, cor 10 w and F n.
Colbot, ——, blacksmith, (col) e side 15 w, btw H and I n.
Colbot, E., (col) laundress, w side 21 w, btw K and L n.
Colburt, Michael, laborer, e side 10 w, btw E and F n.
Colclager, Francis W., carpenter, n side La av, btw 6 and 7 w.
Cole, Samuel, clerk Pension Office, w side 9 w, btw E and F n.
Cole, S. L., clerk Census Office, s side Pa av, btw 10 and 12 w.
Cole, E., (col) laundress, s side I n, btw 9 and 10 w.
Cole, Doctor, n side I s, btw 4 and 5 e.
Coleman, Rev. T. K., e side 9 w, btw M and N n.
Coleman, Mrs., s side Dumbarton, btw Green and Montgomery, Georgetown.
Coleman, John, laborer, w side Lingan, btw Bridge and Prospect, Georgetown.
College, Catholic, 2d, extreme west, Georgetown.
Colley, James W., (Maxwell, Sears &) n side Pa av, btw 9 and 10 w.
Collier, Joseph, shoestore, cor 7 w and H n.
Collier, Joseph, shoemaker. w side 10 w, btw G and H n.
Collins, A. G., tailor, e side 4½ w, btw M and N s.
Collins, Levy, laborer, (col) w side 8 w, btw I and K n.
Collins, John, laborer, w side 8 w, btw L and M n.
Collins, William, cabinetmaker, n side G n, btw 11 and 12 w.
Collins, Mrs. William, boarding house, n side G n, btw 2 and 3 w.
Collins, Frederick, e side 2 w, btw G n and Mass av.
Collins, D, confectioner, e side 13 w, btw Pa av and E n.

Abbreviations.—**All points start from the Capitol; s south, n north, e east, w west, btw between, cor corner, (col) colored, av avenue, h house.**

Collins, Julia, widow, s side K n, btw 24 and 25 w.
Collins, George W., carpenter, n side M n, btw 6 and 7 w.
Collins, J. H., messenger War Department, n side G n, btw 17 and 18 w.
Collins, Joseph, n side Dumbarton, btw Green and Montgomery, Georgetown.
Collison, Mrs. E., milliner, w side 6 w, btw La av and Pa av.
Colman, Charles, stonecutter, s side Md av, btw 4½ and 6 w.
Colman, Samuel M., s side E n, btw 10 and 11 w.
Colnan, Mrs. M. M., widow, e side 10 w, btw E and F n.
Colston, Josiah, clerk Navy Department, n side I n, btw 18 and 19 w.
Colt, I., clerk Post Office, w side 12 w, btw K and L n.
Coltman, Charles L., brickmaker, n side M n, btw 13 and 14 w.
Colton, E., agent Wash'n and N. O. Tel. Comp., boards at Baker's Franklin House.
Colvin, Lawson, laborer, w side 7 w, btw G and H s.
Columbus, Francis W., plasterer, e side 8 w, btw L and M n.
Columbian engine house, w side N J av, btw A and B s.
Columbus, Charles, confectioner, opposite Odd Fellow's Hall.
House, 8, btw I and N Y av.
Columbus, C. J., plasterer, s side I n, btw 4 and 5 w.
Combs, M. R., Irving restaurant, cor 10 w and Pa av.
Combs, R. M., dry goods, s side 8 e, btw I and K s.
Combs, Samuel, messenger Treasury Department, e side 12 w, btw I and K n.
Commanding General United States Army, office 1st story War Department.
Commodore, O., (col) w side 7 w, btw C and D s.
Commissioner Public Buildings, office Capitol, centre basement.
Compton, Mrs., school, n side West, btw Congress and High, Georgetown.
Compton, W. T., flour merchant, s side Water, btw High and Jefferson; residence at Mr. French's, Bridge, Georgetown.
Comstock, Geo. F., Solicitor of the Treasury, Brown's Hotel.
Conaway, John, painter, n side E s, btw 4½ and 6 w.
Congressional Globe office, (John C. Rives,) n side Pa av, btw 4½ and 6 w.
Congressional Burying Ground, e end of E s.
Conlin, Peter, grocer, cor 3 w and G n.
Connell, Robert, bookbinder, w side 8 w, btw I and K n.
Connell, John W., printer, s side F s, btw 4½ and 6 w.
CONNOLLY, JOHN, Cabinetmaker and Undertaker, w side 7 w, btw G and H n.
House, 10, btw G and H n.
Conner, Thomas, stove dealer, w side 7 w, btw I and N Y av; h cor K and 7 w.
Conner, William, baker, e side 8 w, btw L and M n.
Conner, John, laborer, n side G n, btw North Capitol and 1 e.
Conner, John, messenger Smithsonian Institute, s side B s, btw 9 and 10 w.
Conner, Mrs. S. M., dressmaker, w side 5 e, btw E and G s.
Conner, Michael, moulder, n side G s, btw 9 and 10 s.
Conner, James, blacksmith, n side L s, btw 3 and 4 e.
Connerse, A., laborer, n side A n, btw 2 and 3 e.
Connolly, T. C., 9 w, near L n.
Conrad, Charles M., Secretary of War, n side F n, btw 13 and 14 w.
Conrad & Co., shoemakers, e side 10 w, btw Md av and F s.
Contee, James, (col) laborer, w side 15 w, btw L and M n.
CONTNER & CO., Furniture Store, n side E n, btw 8 and 9 w.
Conway, James, s side F s, btw 6 and 7 w; h F n, btw 4½ and 6 w.
Cook, J., tobacconist, w side 7 w, btw D and E n.
Cook, John C., painter, e side 4½ w, btw G and H s.
Cook, John C., n side Md av, btw 6 and 7 w.
Cook, Philip, tobacconist, n side Pa av, btw 3 and 4½ w.
Cook, C. J., cabinetmaker, n side E n, btw 8 and 9 w.
Cook, Henry, limeburner, w side 22 w, btw Pa av and I n.
Cook, ——, painter, n side G s, btw 4½ and 6 w.
Cook, L. O., cabinetmaker, s side D s, btw 6 and 7 w; h cor 7 w and D s.
Cook, John, blacksmith, w side 10 e, btw J and K s.
Cook, Samuel, cartman, w side 2 e, btw C and D n.

Cook, Wm., blacksmith, w side 7 e, btw G and I s.
Cook, Thomas, machinist, e side 7 e, btw I and Va av.
Cook, Wm. L., laborer, n side K s, btw 7 e and Va av.
Cook, James R., blacksmith, n side K s, btw 7 e and Va av.
Cook, Richard, carpenter, s side G s, btw 9 and 10 e.
Cook, William, (col) laborer, s side L n, btw 15 and 16 w.
Coolidge, James M., clerk, n side Gay, btw High and Congress, Georgetown.
Coombs, James W., clerk Census Office, n side I n, btw 19 and 20 w.
Coombs, Joseph, agent for claims, n side H n, btw 9 and 10 w.
Coombs, J. J., attorney, e side 15 w, btw F and N Y av.
Coombe, Dr. James G., w side 3 e, btw N and Ga av s.
Coombs, Mrs., seamstress, Bridge, btw Congress and Washington, Georgetown.
Coones, Mary, mantuamaker, s side Gay, btw Congress and Washington, Geo'town.
Cooper, John, w side 4½ w, btw Pa av and Mo av.
Cooper, L. N., carpenter, w side 12 w, btw G and H n.
Cooper, H. D., plumber, n side H n, btw 4 and 5 w.
Cooper, L., laborer, e side 14 w, btw L and M n.
Cooper, Wm., clerk Census Office, s side D s, btw 9 and 10 w.
Cooper, C. S., adjutant general U. S. A., cor F n and Pa av.
Cooper, Wm., (col) laborer, s side East Capitol, btw 3 and 4½ e.
Cooper, Mrs., s side 3d, btw High and Potomac, Georgetown.
COPP, MOSES, Pavilion, s side La av, btw 4½ and 6 w.
Corbin, Abel Rathbone, e side 4½ w, btw C n and Ia av.
Corbitt, Abraham, umbrella factory, s side Pa av, btw 4½ and 6 w.
Corcoran and Riggs, bankers, cor 15 w and Pa av.
Corcoran, Wm. W., (& Riggs) n side H n, btw 16 w and Conn av.
Corcoran, John, blacksmith, n side Pa av, btw 21 and 22 w.
Corcoran, Mrs., n side Gay, btw Congress and Washington, Georgetown.
Cornell, ——, (col) laborer, e side Congress, near Beall, Georgetown.
Corney, Thomas, grocer, cor 3 e and Mass av.
Cornivall, J., wheelwright, w side 10 w, btw E and F n.
Cornwall, John, sawyer, n side F s, btw 10 and 11 w.
Correy, William, (col) laborer, s side Mass av, btw 9 and 10 w.
Corrigan, B., grocer, cor Pa av and 24 w.
Corry, James L., carpenter, n side I s, btw 4 and 5 e.
Corwin, Thos., Secretary of Treasury, n side Pa av, btw Conn av and 17 w.
Costallo, Timothy, laborer, e side 3 w, btw G and Mass av.
Costen, Wm., (col) barkeeper, s side A s, btw 1 and 2 e.
Costen, Mrs. Ann and Charlotte, (col) mantuam'rs, s side A s, btw N J av and 1 e.
Coster, Mrs. C., w side N J av, btw L and M s.
Coster, Stephen, brick yard on 1, btw L and M s; h N J av, btw L and M s.
Costin, Wm. G., (col) laborer, s side C s, btw 1 and 2 w.
Costigan, John, grocer, cor 9 w and M n.
Cotton Factory, south of market-house, Georgetown.
Couch, J. W., cashier Mechanics' Bank, n side Bridge, near Washington, (at Union Hotel,) Georgetown.
Coumbe, John T., carpenter, e side 13½ w, btw D and E n.
Cowing, G., clerk Treasury Department, n side I, btw 6 and 7 w.
Cowling, E., livery stable, n side G n, btw 13 and 14 w.
Cox, Mrs. William, widow, s side C n, btw 3 and 4½ w.
Cox, Mrs. Ellen, n side Mass av, btw 2 and 3 w.
Cox, W. W., clerk s side I n, btw 9 and 10 w.
Cox, C, widow, s side I n, btw 9 and 10 w.
Cox, Wm., constable, n side E s, btw 3 and 4 e.
Cox, Rev. ——, Methodist Pr. minister, e side Congress, btw Gay and Bridge, Georgetown.
Cox, Walter S., attorney, s w corner Gay and Congress, Georgetown.
Cox, Richard J., clerk, s side Gay, btw High and Congress, Georgetown.
Cox, J. E., leather dealer, e side High, btw Gay and Bridge, Georgetown.
Coxe, Richard S., attorney, n side F n, btw 6 and 7 w.

Coxe, George G., clerk Post Office Department, boards at Mrs. Spaulding's.
Coyle, Fitzhugh, agricultural warehouse, w side, 7 w, btw D and Pa av.
House, s side C n, btw 3 and 4½.
Coyle, L., (Campbell &) H n, btw 6 and 7 w.
Coyle, Randolph, civil engineer, s side E n, btw 9 and 10 w.
Coyle, J. F., National Int. Office, n side Mo av, btw 4½ and 6 w.
Coyle, James, old iron dealer, n e cor Green and Bridge, Georgetown.
Craft, Philip, blacksmith, e side 7 w, btw N Y av and L n.
House, cor L n, and 8 w.
Craig, Col. H. K., n side Pa av, btw 19 and 20 w.
Craig, J. H., police officer, e side 19 w, btw G and H n.
Craig, Doctor, n side Pa av, btw 19 and 20 w.
Craig, Henry G., teacher, n side Beall, near Congress, Georgetown.
Craig, Mrs., boarding house, s side Bridge, btw Bridge and Potomac, Georgetown.
Craigin, Dr. C. H., office cor High and Prospect, Georgetown.
House n side Dumbarton, near High, Georgetown.
Crain, Thos., laborer, n side H n, btw 4 and 5 w.
Crampsey, John T., coachmaker and wheelwright, e side 8 w, btw M and N n.
Crampsey, Mrs. E., fancy corset store, s side F n, btw 10 and 11 w.
Crampter, Mrs., widow, w side 12 w, btw E and F n.
Crampton, John F., British Minister, s side K n, btw 24 and 25 w.
Cramsheir, Miss, dressmaker, s side H n, btw 17 and 18 w.
Crandell, George, w sido 9 w, btw I and N Y av.
Crandell, James, magistrate 6th ward, e side 7 e, btw G and I s.
Cranch, Wm., Chief Judge D. C., e side Del av, btw B and C n.
Cranch, W. G., clerk Patent Office, e side Del av, btw B and C n.
Crane, Thomas I, saddler, w side 8 w, btw P and Q n.
Crane, Michael, tavern, cor L s and 8 e.
Cranston, Robert, carver, w side 10 w, btw B and C n.
Cratty, Michael, laborer, n side A n, btw 2 and 3 w.
Craver, Philip, coppersmith, w side 5 e, btw K and L s..
Crawford, T. Hartley, Judge of Criminal Court, cor 7 w and F n.
Crawford, Adam, w side 8 e, btw G and F s.
Crawford, Rachel, (col) laundress, s side E s, btw 3 and 4½ w.
Crawford, W. R., attorney, Mrs. Lang's boarding h; office e side Montgomery, Georgetown.
Cray, Oliver, laborer, e side N J av, btw L and M s.
CREASER, T., Shoestore, s side F n, btw 8 and 9 w.
Creecy, James R., clerk Treasury Department, w side 13 w, btw B and C s.
Creighton, John, agricult'l implements, 7, near canal; h w side 10 w, btw B and C s.
Crews, John, shoemaker, w side 12 w, btw G and H n.
House, s side G n, btw 12 and 13 w.
Crier, Berg, (col) wagoner, n side K n, btw 17 and 18 w.
Crider, Michael, clerk Census Office, w side 9 w, btw F and G n.
CRIPPS, WM. McL., Chair Manufactory, e side 11 w, btw E and Pa av.
CRIPPS, W. M., grocer, n side La av, btw 6 and 7 w; h 11, btw Pa av and E n.
Criter, Wm., huckster, end of 6 w, w side.
Crittenden, T., n side H n, btw 17 and 18 w.
Crittenden, Josiah D., stonecutter, w side North Capitol, btw Md av and G n.
Croggin, Thomas, blacksmith, w side 3 w, btw G and H n.
Croggin, H. B., messenger Treas. Department, w side 12 w, btw Mass av and L n.
Croggin, John, grocer, e side 8 w, btw F and G n.
Crome, Mrs. H., milliner, e side 7 w, btw G and H n.
Cronin, Mrs. Margaret, widow, grocery, w side 6 w, btw G and H n.
Crook, George, gent., e side 4½ w, btw C and Md av.
Cropley, Samuel, grocer, s e corner market house; h corner Frederick and Bridge, Georgetown.
Cropley, Mrs., s side 3d, btw High and Potomac, Georgetown.
Cropley, Horatio, dyer, e side Potomac, btw Bridge and Prospect, Georgetown.
Cross, A. V., confectioner, cor of 7 w and G n.

Abbreviations.—All points start from the Capitol; s south, n north, e east, w west, btw between, cor corner, (col) colored, av avenue, h house,

Cross, Wm. B. B., attorney at law, office e side 7 w, btw D and E n. House s side F n, btw 13 and 14 w.
Cross, A. V., blacksmith, n side G n, btw 6 and 7 w.
Cross, Lloyd, grocer, n side K n, btw Vt av and 15 w.
Cross, Henry L., shoemaker, n side Pa av, btw 19 and 20 w.
Cross, Alexander, finisher, s side G s, btw 6 and 7 e.
Cross, James, woodsawyer, w side 3 e, btw L and M s.
Cross, Thomas B., blacksmith, n side K s, btw 14 and 15 e.
Cross, Jeremiah, Navy Yard laboratory, n side Ga av, btw 10 and 11 e.
Cross, W. B. B., attorney, e side 7 w, btw D and E n.
Cross, Thomas, blacksmith, n side Va av, btw 9 and 10 e.
Crossfield, James, printer, w side 9 w, btw I and N Y av.
Crossfield, A. E., widow, n side M n, btw 8 and 9 w.
Crossfield, Wm., clerk Bank Metropolis, n side G n, btw 21 and 22 w.
Crosson, Doctor H. J., n side H n, btw 10 and 11 w.
Crown, S., laborer, e side 10 w, btw M and N n.
Crown, Saml., messenger Post Office, n side L n, btw 6 and 7 w.
Crown, John, grocer, 4th, cor Potomac, in Twenty Buildings, Georgetown.
Crown, William, carpenter, e side Market, btw 2d and 3d, Georgetown.
Cruikshanks, Richard, clerk, n side Bridge, btw Potomac and High, Georgetown.
Cruikshanks, Mrs., e side Potomac, btw 1st and 2d, Georgetown.
Cruit, John, watchmaker, n side Pa av, btw 4½ and 6 w; h L n, btw 6 and 7 w.
Cruit, Robert, n side F n, btw 14 and 15 w.
Cruit, Richard, horseshoer, n side C n, btw 6 and 7 w; h cor 4½ and Mo av.
Cruit, John, silversmith, s side L n, btw 6 and 7 w.
Cruit, James, huckster, Bridge, btw Congress and Washington, Georgetown.
Crumbaugh, John, butcher, n side Bridge, extreme west, Georgetown.
Crump, Danl., constable, w side 7 w, btw Va av and D s.
Crump, D., carpenter, n side F n, btw 24 and 25 w.
Crump, James T., grocer, s side K s, btw 6 and 7 e.
Cruser, H., (col) feedman, s side G n, btw 18 and 19 w.
Crutchett, J., cor North Capitol and C.
Crutchett, J. P., French cook, w side 6 w, btw D and E n.
Cryer, James, clerk City Post Office, w side 12 w, btw C and Va av.
Cull, James, shoemaker, s side 8 e, btw K and L s.
Cullum, John, engraver, s side F n, btw 13 and 14 w.
Culverwell, Mrs. M. A., n side L n, btw 9 and 10 w.
Cumberland, Charles, n side C s, btw 13½ and 14 w.
Cummings, Charles, huckster, s side Beall, btw High and Washington, Georgetown.
Cunningham, George, laborer, n side L s, btw 7 and 8 e.
Cunningham, Jane J., boarding h, n side Pa av, btw 2 and 3 w.
Cunningham, A. F., clerk Treasury Department, n side H n, btw 9 and 10 w.
Cunningham, Mrs., dressmaker, n side Va av, btw 17 and 18 w.
Cunnington, Michael, laborer, e side 13½ w, btw C and D s.
Cunningham, Robert, huckster, e side Market, btw 3d and 4th, Georgetown.
Cunningham, Mrs., dressmaker, w side Congress, btw Gay and Bridge, Geo'town.
Curran, Wm. W., reporter, s side [illegible] av, btw 3 and 4½ w.
Curran, Barney B., architect, n side E s, btw 5 and 6 e.
Currigan, Patrick, laborer, e side 4½ w, btw F and G s.
Curry, James, (col) laborer, w side 12 w, btw C and D n.
Curry, John, grocer, n side C s, btw 3 and 4½ w.
Curson, Samuel, contractor, w side 7 w, btw R and S n.
Curtain, James J., laborer, w side 4½ w, btw G and H s.
Curtin, Daniel, laborer, n side G n, btw N Cap and 1 e.
Curtis, Henry B., carpenter, e side 8 w, btw L and M n.
Curtis, Thomas, (col) well-digger, e side 11 w, btw K and N Y av.
Curtis, Benjamin R., Associate Justice Supreme Court, cor 4½ and C n.
Cusack, P., stonemason, s side A s, btw 1 and 2 e.
Cushman, R. W., s side Ia av, btw 3 and 4½ w.
Custard, William, carpenter, e side Bridge, btw West and Road, Georgetown.

Abbreviations.—All points start from the Capitol; s south, n north, e east, w west, btw between, cor corner, (col) colored, av avenue, h house.

Cuthbert, James, refectory, e side 7 w, btw H and I n.
Cutts, R. D., engineer, n side I n, btw 16 and 17 w.
Cutts, J. Madison, chief clerk 2d Compt. Office, n side 15 w, btw N Y av and H n.
Cuviller, Joseph, gardener, n side E s, btw 11 and 12 e.

D.

Dacoursy, James, grocery, e side 6 w, btw H and I n.
Dacy, F., confectioner, e side 12 w, btw C and A n.
Dade, E. C., clerk Treasury Department, e side 19 w, btw F and G n.
Daggy, P., clerk General Land Office, 8 w, btw H and I n.
Dahlgren, Lieut. John A., U S N, w side 4½ w, btw La av and C n.
Dailey, Dr. O., dentist, n side Pa av, btw 10 and 11 w.
House n side D n, btw 6 and 7 w.
Daldare, Jordine, stonecutter, s side Md av, btw 4½ and 6 w.
Dallas, S. J., clerk Treasury Department, w side 12 w, btw M and Mass av.
Dallay, Hooper, grocer, n side L n, btw 12 and 13 w.
Daily, Richard, (col) carter, n side Bridge, btw Congress and Washington, Geo'tn.
Dalton, John, hack-driver, e side 4½ w, btw E and Va av.
Dalton, William, hackman, s side F n, btw 6 and 7 w.
Dalton, William, tailor, n side Va av, btw 1 and 2 w.
Dankworth, Frederick, artist, Coast Survey, n side C s, btw 11 and 12 w.
Daniel, Thomas C., clerk Treasury Department, boards Mrs. Spaulding's.
Dant, William, bricklayer, n side Md av, btw 6 and 7 w.
Dant, Thomas, tailor, s side Md av, btw 4½ and 6 w.
Dant, Wm. T., hackman, n side Md av, btw 4½ and 6 w.
Dant, F. X., & Co., clothiers, n side Pa av, btw 6 and 7 w.
Dant, William, messenger Capitol, n side D n, btw 2 and 3 w.
Dant, J., (col) laborer, s side I n, btw 12 and 13 w.
Dany, Peter, shoemaker, s side N Y av, btw 14 and 15 w.
Darley, Franklin, printer, n side G s, btw 8 and 9 w.
Darnell, F. H., painter, w side 18 w, btw H and I n.
Darnes' livery stable, Bridge, btw Potomac and Market, Georgetown.
Darnes, Mary, s side Bridge, near Mayor's office, Georgetown.
Darrel, W. S., clerk Post Office, n side L n, btw 9 and 10 w.
Dashiell, Rev. Mr., (Methodist Union Chapel.)
Dashiell, Mrs. E., milliner, s side Bridge, near Jefferson, Georgetown.
Dasy, J., laborer, s side Mass av, btw 2 and 3 w.
Datcher, Thomas, (col) laborer, e side 1 w, btw B and C s.
Datcher, C., shoemaker, (col) e side 15 w, btw Pa av and F n.
Davey, Mrs. Eliza, confectionary, n side F n, btw 14 and 15 w.
Davidge, W. D., attorney, s side La. av, btw 4½ and 6 w.
Davidson, John B., carpenter, w side 11 w, btw E and F s.
Davidson, S. G., attorney, s side La av, btw 4½ and 6 w.
Davidson, John H., carpenter, n side M s, btw 9 and 10 e.
Davidson, John, flour warehouse, s side Water, near Congress.
House, s e cor Gay and Montgomery, Georgetown.
Davis, James, shoe store, w side 7 w, btw D and E n.
House w side 4 w, btw G and H n.
Davis, Mrs. J. A., teacher, e side 4½ w, btw Pa av and C n.
Davis, Elias, laborer, w side 3 w, btw I and K n.
Davis, Miss Catherine, furnished rooms, w side 7 w, btw G and H n.
Davis, Edward, shoemaker, w side 7 w, btw L and M n.
Davis, William, e side 7 w, btw N and O n.
Davis, Henry, laborer, cor 7 w and O n.
Davis, Mary, widow, w side 8 w, btw M and N n.
Davis, George G., furniture store, e side 9 w, btw Pa av and D n.
Davis, Henry S,, carpenter, w side 9 w, btw E and F n.
Davis, Mrs. D. W., boarding, s side Pa av, btw 4½ and 6 w.

Abbreviations.—All points start from the Capitol; s south, n north, e east, w west, btw between, cor corner, (col) colored, av avenue, h house.

Davis, Addison, laborer, e side 11 e, btw M and N s.
Davis, Abel G., Navy Yard, e side 11 e, btw G and I s.
Davis, James B., grocer, n side L s, btw 3 and 4 e.
Davis, William, moulder, n side K s, btw 3 and 4 e.
Davis, John, n side I s, btw 10 and 11 e.
Davis, George, cooper, s side D s, btw 3 and 4 e.
Davis, William M., carpenter, s side G s, btw 9 and 10 e.
Davis, Richard, music store, n side Pa av, btw 9 and 10 w.
Davis, J., refectory, s side Pa av btw 6 and 7 w.
Davis, Joseph W., letter-carrier, s side F n, btw 7 and 8 w.
Davis, John, laborer, s side F n, btw 6 and 7 w.
Davis, Dr. Alexander M., s side E n, btw 6 and 7 w.
Davis, Thomas J., tailor, w side 8 e, btw I and J s.
House n side K s, btw 9 and 10 e.
Davis, Edward, shoemaker, w side 6 w, btw H and Mass av.
House 7 w, near L n.
Davis, Ari, machinist, w side 6 w, btw K and N Y av.
Davis, James Y., hatter, (Todd,) e side 6 w, btw F and G n.
Davis, George M., bank clerk, cor 11 w and G n.
Davis, John, paper-hanger, s side Mass av, btw 6 and 7 w.
Davis, Eli, shoemaker, 12 w, btw N Y av, and I n.
House w side 11 w, btw N Y av and H n.
Davis, Mrs., mantua-maker, w side 11 w, btw E and F n.
Davis, William, coal merchant, n side I n, btw 20 and 21 w.
Davis, G. T., carpenter, e side 8 w, btw E and F n.
Davis, Robert, laborer, cor 4 w and M n.
Davis, H. J., police officer, n side H n, btw 4 and 5 w.
Davis, E. Charles, clerk Land Office, s side H n, btw 20 and 21 w.
Davis, C. A., clerk War Department, n side H n, btw 19 and 20 w.
Davis, Mrs., corset-maker. n slde H n, btw 20 and 21 w.
Davis, Joseph, carpenter, e side 12 w, btw B and C s.
Davis, Mrs., dress-maker, n side C s, btw 13 and 13½ w.
Davis, David, n side D s, btw 13½ and 14 w.
Davis, J. S., w side 7 e, btw L and M s.
Davis, Mrs. B. A., widow, e side 11 e, btw M and N s.
Davis, R., clothing store, s side Bridge, few doors east of market house, Geo'town.
Davis, Saml., lottery office, n side Bridge, btw Congress and Washington, Geo'tn.
Davis, Mrs. James, near n w cor West and Washington, Georgetown.
Davis, John, tavern, e side High, btw Gay and Dumbarton, Georgetown.
Davis, Gustavus, huckster, w side Jefferson, Georgetown.
Davis, John, tailor, e side Market space, Georgetown.
Davis, Sarah, (col) s side Mass av, btw 4 and 5 w.
Davis, Mary, (col) laundress, w side 6 e, btw E and Pa av.
Davison, John, wood-merchant, n side G n, btw 7 and 8 w.
Davison, Samuel, constable, e side 10 w, btw B and C n.
DAVISON, JOSEPH, Brewery, n side K n, btw 26 and 27 w.
Daw, Reuben, gunsmith, n side Bridge, btw Congress and Washington; h s side Bridge, next Farmer's and Mechanics' Bank, Georgetown.
House s side K n, btw 26 and 27 w.
Dawes, Richard M., n side N Y av btw 2 and 3 w.
Dawson, Edward, barber, s side E n, btw 7 and 8 w.
Dawson, A., hatter, s side K n, btw 11 and 12 w.
Dawson, Sam., (col) waiter, s side N n, btw 9 and 10 w.
Dawson, Wm., constable, n e cor 1 and Fayette, Georgetown.
Daws, Misses, hat-trimmers, e side 6 w, btw G and H n.
Daws, William, sadler, w side 22 w, btw Pa av and I n.
Daws, Rufus, clerk Treasury Department, e side Del av, btw B and C n.
Day, R., (col) laborer, n side I s, btw 3 and 4 e.
Dayton, A. O., 4th Auditor Treas Dep't, w side 6 w, btw D and E n.
Dayton, Mr., n side West, btw Congress and Washington, Georgetown.

Abbreviations.—All points start from the Capitol; s south, n north, e east, w west, btw between, cor corner, (col) colored, av avenue, h house.

Deakins, Mrs. John, grocer, w side Lingan, btw 1 and 2, Georgetown.
Dean, Hiram, laborer, w side 7 e, btw L and M s.
Dean, George, rigger, s side E s, btw 6 and 7 e.
Dean, Mr., (ropewalk) s side West, extreme east, Georgetown.
Dearing, George, carpenter, w side 4½ w, btw Pa av and Mo av.
Decatur, Mrs., (Commodore) n side 2, near College, Georgetown.
De Chaner, John, hair-dresser, n side E n, btw 8 and 9 w.
Dechman, D., grocer, n side B s, btw 1 and 2 w.
Deeble, Edward, bookbinder, n side I n, btw 9 and 10 w.
Deeble, Joseph, bookbinder, s side I n, btw 9 and 10 w.
DEETH, S. G., Bookseller, at late residence of George Templeman, Georgetown.
Defalco, Pasquale, musician, s side E s, btw 9 and 10 e.
Degges, Edward, plasterer, cor 11 e and M s.
Degges, Robert H., carpenter, n side G n, btw 17 and 18 w.
Degges, William, carpenter, n side I n, btw 17 and 18 w.
Degges, Edwin, carpenter, n side I n, btw 19 and 20 w.
Degrofft, A., carpenter, n side G n, btw 18 and 19 w.
Deitz, Mrs. W. H., boarding house, s side F n, btw 12 and 13 w.
De Krafft, J. W., clerk Interior Department w side 11 w, btw G and H n.
Delany, H., (col) laundress, n side L n, btw 13 and 14 w.
Delany C., (col) hackman, s side F s, btw 9 and 10 w.
Delany, Michael, custom-house, (California,) n side Mo av, btw 4½ and 6 w.
Delany, Mrs., (col) n side D s, btw 5 and 6 e.
De la Roche, Captain, engineer, s w cor Washington and Beall, Georgetown.
Delarue, Mrs., fancy store, n side Pa av, btw 12 and 13 w.
Dellaway, J. W., segar store, s side Pa av, btw 19 and 20 w.
House, 19 w, btw I and K n.
Dellinger, Henry, carpenter, n side Mass av, btw 6 and 7 w.
Delphy, O. R., cabinetmaker, w side 12 w, btw M and N n.
Demenow, Charles, cigar store, w side 19 w, btw H n and Pa av.
Dement, Richard, clerk Post Office Department, boards at Mrs. Kesley's, Pa av.
Denham, Z. W., clerk architect's office, Adams's Express Building.
Denham, C., bookbinder, w side 10 w, btw H and N Y av.
Denham, A., clerk, e side 19 w, btw N Y av and F n.
Dening, Major St. Clair, U. S. A., n side Pa av, btw 18 and 19 w.
DENNIS, J., Jr., Patent Agent, w side 7 w, btw E and F n.
Dennis, Thomas, n side G s, btw 6 and 7 e.
Dennison, John T., printer, w side 6 w, btw G and H n.
Dennison, William, printer, w side 6 w, btw G and H n.
Dennison, John, carpenter, s side Bridge, near Mayor's office, Georgetown.
Dennison, Thos., boarding house, n side Bridge, btw Congress and Wash'n, Geo'tn.
Dennison, John, huckster, e side Congress, btw West and Beall, Georgetown.
Dennison, Sanford, fisherman, n side Water, east part, Georgetown.
Dent, Miss Emma, n side Gay, near High, Georgetown.
De Osma, J. Y., Peruvian Minister, n side H n, btw 17 and 18 w.
Department of Interior, s side F n, btw 14 and 15 w.
Department of State, s side Pa av, near 15 w.
Department of War, s side Pa av, near 17 w.
Department of Treasury, e side 15 w, near Pa av.
Department of Navy, w side 17 w, near Pa av.
Derrick, Mrs. W. S., widow, n side I n, btw 18 and 19 w.
Derrick, A. H., clerk State Department, n side Pa av, btw 21 and 22 w.
De Saules, P., Waverley House, s side Pa av, btw 4½ and 6 w.
DE SELDING & WYLIE, Law and Agency Office, Notaries Public and Commissioners of Deeds, w side 7 w. opposite Odd Fellow's Hall.
De Selding, Charles, e side 6 w, next cor F n.
Desmond, D., restaurant, n side F s, btw 9 and 10 w.
Devaughn, Harriet, w side 3 w, btw C and Va av.
Devaughn, Dr. Samuel, s side E n, btw 9 and 10 w.
Devaughn, Mrs., seamtress, n side H n, btw 19 and 20 w.

Abbreviations.—All points start from the Capitol; s south, n north, e east, w west, btw between, cor corner, (col) colored, av avenue, h house.

Deveny, C., dry goods, w side 8 e, btw I and J s.
Devereux, Robert, cartman, s side G s, btw 5 and 6 e.
Devlin, John S., s e cor Pa av and 2 e.
De Weall, George, s side B s, btw 9 and 10 w.
Dewdney, John, county constable, e side 22 w, btw Pa av and I n.
Dexter, Mrs. Emily, furnished rooms, s side E n, btw 9 and 10 w.
DEXTER & CALVERT, National Hotel, cor Pa av and 6 w.
Dice, John, laborer, w side 9 w, btw D and E n.
Dice, George, laborer, w side 10 w, btw L and M n.
Dick, Robert, farmer, n side Gay, btw Congress and Washington, Georgetown.
Dick, John W., tailor, e side 8 w, btw L and M n.
Dick, Moses, (col) carter, e side 11 w, btw Mass av and K n.
Dick, L., (col) servant, s side C s, btw 3 and 4½ w.
Dickins, Asbury, Secretary of Senate, n side F n, near 13 w.
Dickins, F. A., agent United States claims, office opposite Treasury Department.
Dickins, Thos. W., clerk Senate, n side A, btw 1 e and Del av.
Dickinson, J. P., clerk Pension Office, e side 12 w, btw M n and Mass av.
Dickson, John, (& Gordon,) wood and coal, &c., n side Water, near the bridge; lumber-yard s side Water; house s w cor Green and Stoddard, Georgetown.
Dickson, John, coach shop, w side Green, near Bridge, Georgetown.
Dickson, ——, watchman, e side 8 w, btw D and E n.
Dier, W. J., carpenter, s side Bridge, extreme west, Georgetown.
Diggs, Mrs. L., (col) laundress, e side 10 w, btw M and N n.
Diggs, R. H., carpenter, e side 20 w, btw G and H n.
Diggle, James, carpenter, cor N and 4½ w.
Digny, H., gas works, n side Md av, btw 3 and 4½ w.
Dille, H. W., clerk arsenal, s end 4½ w.
Dillow, William, grocer, n side G n, btw 22 and 23 w.
Dines, Maria, (col) laundress, s side C s, btw 4½ and 6 w.
Dingel, Valentine, tailor, w side 8 w, btw L and M n.
Dison, Robert, (col) brickmaker, s side C s, btw 2 and 3 w.
Divine, Lewis, printer, w side 10 w, btw G and H n.
Dixon, Mrs., (col) servant, w side 8 w, btw L and M n.
Dixon, Mrs. R., widow, w side 11 w, btw E and F n.
Dixon, James, laborer, e side 10 w, btw I and K s.
Dixon, William, clerk navy store, n side E s. btw 4 and 5 e.
Dobbins, W. B., bootmaker, cor L s and 8 e.
Dobson, J., tailor, w side 20 w, btw K and L n.
Dodd, Reuben, wagoner, e side 10 w, btw D and E s.
Dodge, Robert, s w cor Stoddard and Montgomery, Georgetown.
Dodge, Frank, s e cor Stoddard and Washington, Georgetown.
Dodge, Hamilton, merchant, n e cor West and Washington, Georgetown.
Dodge, Charles, cor West and Congress, Georgetown.
Dodge, F. & A. H., importers, &c., s side Water, btw High and Congress, Geo'town.
Dodge, Francis, sr., (deceased) family, n e cor Gay and Congress, Georgetown.
Dodson, James, (Clagett &,) house 6 w, btw E and F n.
Dodson, Samuel B., e side 6 w, btw E and F n.
Dodson, James, (col) woodsawyer, w side 3 w, btw E and Va av.
Dodson, Aivry, (col) laundress, w side 8 w, btw I and K n.
Donaldson, C., huckster, w side 4½, btw G and H n.
Donaldson, Dr. R. B., dentist, n side Pa av, btw 9 and 10 w.
Donaldson, James, omnibus driver, e side 20 w, btw Pa av and H n.
Donalson, William, carpenter, s side F s, btw 8 and 9 w.
Donelan, Rev. J. B., (St. Matthew's Catholic Church,) n side 15 w, btw H and I n.
Donelan, Edward, stonecutter, w side N Cap, btw Mass av and G n.
Donlin, Thomas, laborer, e side 6 e, btw A and B s.
Donn, A., painter, w side 4½, btw F and G s.
DONN, JOHN M., & G. W., furnishing store, n side D n, btw 9 and 10 w.
Donn, John M, (& G. W.,) house 12 w, btw G and H n.
Donn, G. W., (& John M.,) house w side H n, btw 4 and 5 w.

Abbreviations.—All points start from the Capitol; s south, n north, e east, w west, btw between, cor corner, (col) colored, av avenue, h house.

Donn, O. P., w side H n, btw 4 and 5 w.
Donn, Joseph W. H., furnishing store, s side H n, btw 4 and 5 w.
Donn, Thomas C., magistrate, s side La av, btw 6 and 7 w.
House s side H n, btw 4 and 5 w.
Donnell, J. O., n side H n, btw 17 and 18 w.
Donoho, Thomas S., attorney, n side N n, btw 13 and 14 w.
Donovan, Randall, laborer, e side 4½ w, btw C and Md av.
Dorothy, Washington, carpenter, w side 8 w, btw N. Y. av and L n.
Dorsett, F. R., carpenter, shop n side G n, btw 18 and 19 w.
House w side 18 w, btw I and K n.
Dorsett, James, clerk Post Office Department, s side K n, btw 17 and 18 w.
Doudin, Charles, stonecutter, e side 8 w, btw D and E n.
Dougal, W. H., engraver, e side 15 w, btw F and N Y av.
DORSEY, P. W., Hotel and Wagon Yard, corner 7 w and I n.
Dorsey, E. J., painter, s side Md av, btw 4½ and 6 w.
Dorsey, Mrs., (col) store, w side Potomac, btw 1 and Prospect, Georgetown.
Dorsey, J., (col) whitewasher, n side N Y av, btw 4 and 5 w.
Dorsey, Catherine, (col) laundress, e side Conn av, btw I and K n.
Dory, Captain, s side West, 2 doors from Congress, Georgetown.
Dotzbe, John, tailor, w side 6 w, btw H and Mass av.
Dougherty ——, Metropolis Livery Stable, s side D n, btw 13½ and 14 w.
Dougherty, John, laborer, e side 2 w, btw G n and Mass av.
Dougherty, Hugh, brickmaker, n side L s, btw 7 and 8 e.
Dougherty, William, superin't Washington Monument, e side 13 w, btw E and F n.
Dougherty, Henry, tailor, s side B n, btw 2 and 3 w.
Douglas, William, s side B s, btw 9 and 10 w.
Douglas, S. A., U S Senator, corner I and N J av.
Douglass, William, carpenter, s side H n, btw 4 and 5 w.
Douglass, Lewis, (col) drayman, e side 12 w, btw K and L n.
Douglass, James, carpenter, n side F n, btw N J av and 2 w.
Douglass, S. E., woodyard, n side Pa av, btw 17 and 18 w.
Douglass, John, (col) whitewasher, n side 15 w, btw L and M n.
DOUGLASS, H., Green-house, cor 15 w and G n.
Douglass, H., (col) laborer, e side 13½ w, btw D and E n.
Douglass, John, restaurant, s side La av, btw 4½ and 6 w.
Dove, John, carpenter, e side N J av, btw K and L s.
Dove, John, cartman, w side 8 w, btw L and M n.
Dove, W. T., coal-yard, s side Pa av, btw 17 and 18 w.
House e side 19 w, btw G and H n.
Dove, Dr. George M., n side I s, btw 6 and 7 e.
Dover, J., (col) porter, n side H n, btw 13 and 14 w.
Dovilliers, Dr. L., e side 13 w, btw E and F n.
Dow, Mrs. J. E., widow, n side F n, btw 13 and 14 w.
Dowden, Mrs. E., seamstress, e side 14 w, btw H and I n.
Dowling, John, clerk Indian Office, n side I n btw 6 and 7 w.
Dowling, P., stonecutter, n side N Y av, btw 2 and 3 w.
Dowling, James, tavern, Bridge, btw Montgomery and the Bridge, Georgetown.
DOWNER, R. M., Segar-store, n side Pa av, btw 11 and 12 w.
Down, John, bricklayer, w side 7 e, btw Va av and L s.
Downing, Joseph, carpenter, e side 8 w, btw L and N Y av.
House n side D n, btw 13 and 14 w.
Downing, William, n side M n, btw 8 and 9 w.
Downs, William, painter, n side N s, btw 2 and 3 w.
Downs, John, Navy Yard, n side I s, btw 9 and 10 e.
Doyle, Thomas, cabinetmaker, w side Potomac, btw 3 and 4, Georgetown.
Drake, Willard, w side 11 w, btw E and F n.
Drain, Charles, messenger Indian office, e side 10 w, btw N Y av and K n
Draper, Mrs. Susannah, widow, Me av, btw 3 and 4½ w.
Doyle, Robert, stonemason, w side 11 w, btw E and F n.
Doyle, George cabinetmaker, s side L n, btw 6 and 7 w.

Dree, ——, cartman, s side I n, btw 9 and 10 w.
Drew, Edward M., merchant tailor, e side 7 w, btw D and E n.
House w side 10 w, btw G and H n.
Drew, G. W., cloth-dresser, s side Pa av, btw 9 and 10 w.
Drew, William O., carpenter, w side 6 w, btw H and Mass av.
Drill, Mr., miller, e side High, btw Gay and Bridge, Georgetown.
Drover's Rest, a mile or two out, new cut road, Georgetown.
Drudge, James, blacksmith; shop n side K s, btw 6 and 7 e.
House cor Va av and 6 e.
Drummond, John, carpenter, e side 4½ w, btw F and G s.
Drury, William, brickmaker, w side 11 w, btw G and H n.
Drury, Samuel, magistrate, s side Pa av, btw 21 and 22 w.
Drury, John H , w side Vt av, btw K and L n.
Dubant, P. M., barber and restaurant, cor Pa av and 3 w.
Dubant M., barber, s side Pa av, btw 12 and 13 w; h e side 13½, btw C and D n.
Dudley, Henry, gun-carriage maker, arsenal, s end 4½ w.
Duffey, Mrs. Eliza, Frederick, btw 7 and 8, Georgetown.
Duffy, Thomas, house carpenter, e side 3 w, btw G and Mass av.
Duffy, Andrew, tinner, e side 7 w, btw G and H n.
Duffy, Michael, grocer, s side F n, btw 6 and 7 w.
Duffy, Mrs. E., widow, s side A s, btw 1 and 2 e.
Duhamel, Dr. W. J. C., w side 7 w, btw I and N Y av.
Duivan, Michael, coachman, s side F s, btw 4½ and 6 w.
Dulen, Mrs., widow, e side 4 e, btw L and M s.
Duley, Michael, clerk in Capitol, w side 4 w, btw B and C s.
Dully, Michael, laborer, e side 3 w, btw Md av and C s.
Dulim, J. V., & Co., blacksmiths, Me av, btw 3 and 4½ w.
Dulin, William, blacksmith, w side 4½ w, btw G and H s.
Dummer, Charles, clerk Treasury Department, w side 13 w, btw G and H n.
Dunaly, William, laborer, w side 2 w, btw C and D n.
Dunarvier, William, carpenter, cor Mass av and 15 w.
Dunavin, John, laborer, w side 16 w, btw M and N n.
Dunavin, D., laborer, w side 16 w, btw L and M n.
Dunbar, Mrs., seamstress, Frederick, btw 1 and 2, Georgetown.
Dunbar, Jerry, (col) laborer, w side 11 w, btw L and M n.
Duncan, Stephen, n side D n, btw 5 and 6 w.
Duncanson, J. A. M., clerk Post Office Dep't, n side H n, btw 9 and 10 w.
Dunham, L. J., feed store, n side B n, btw 10 and 11 w.
House s side Pa av, btw 9 and 10 w.
Dunkin, Henry, (col) waiter, n side F n, btw 18 and 19 w.
Dunlop, H., driver, e side 14 w, btw L and M n.
Dunlop, Judge James, s e cor Gay and Green, Georgetown.
Dunn, Ellen, n side Md av, btw 6 and 7 w.
Dunn, Mary, boarding h, e side 13 w, btw E and F n.
Dunn, Mrs., widow, laundress, n side A n, btw 2 and 3 w.
Dunn, Samuel, brickmaker, n side n s, btw 4½ and 6 w.
Dunn, Peter, head cook in garrison, n side K s, btw 9 and 10 e.
Dunnington, Charles W. C., principal police at Capitol, n side B s, btw N J av and 1 e.
Dunnington, J. T., huckster, e side 20 w, btw H and I n.
Dunniven, W., laborer, s side Md av, btw 4½ and 6 w.
Dunscombe, Mrs. Jane, e side 11 w, btw-F and G n.
Durham, Mrs. C. F., (col) widow, s side Pa av, btw 3 and 4 e.
Durham, James H., boarding house, Carroll Place, btw E Cap and A s.
Dusby, Lemuel, finisher in iron, n side I s, btw 11 and 13 e.
Dutton, Thomas, machinist, s side B s, btw 6 and 7 w.
Duvall, Mrs. L. dressmaker, w side 7 w, btw D and E n; boards cor 7 w and E n.
Duvall & Brother, merchant tailors, n side Pa av, btw 3 and 4½ w.
Duvall, W. T., (& Brother,) h Mo av, near 4½ w.
Duvall, John P., laborer, cor 6 w and H n.

Abbreviations.—All points start from the Capitol; s south, n north, e east, w west, btw between, cor corner, (col) colored, av avenue, h honse.

Duvall, Jackson, (& Brother,) n side C n, btw 3 and 4½ w.
Duvall, Samuel, grocer, n side Pa av, btw 19 and 20 w.
Dnvall, Eli, clerk Patent Office, n side A n, btw 1 e and Del av.
Duvall, Mrs. James, n side G s, btw 9 and 10 e.
Duvall, Washington, block-maker, Navy Yard, e side 11 e, btw M and N s.
Duvall, B., merchant tailor, n side Ind av, btw 1 and 2 w.
Duvall, Wm., machinist, s side 2, Petit's new house, Georgetown.
Duvan, William, grocer, n side E s, btw 3 and 4½ w.
Duvine, Hugh, tailor, at Welch's, n side Bridge, west of Congress, Georgetown.
Dyer, Benjamin F., feed store, w side N J av, btw D and E s.
Dyer, Dr. J. L., near cor 7 w and G n.
Dyer, George F., grocer, s side Pa av, btw 3 and 4½ w.
DYER, E. C., Importer Wines and Segars, n side Pa av, btw 12 and 13 w. House 11 w, btw G and H n.
Dyer, Margaret, seamstress, n side I n, btw 7 and 8 w.
Dyer & Skippen, merchant tailors, n side Pa av, btw 17 and 18 w.
Dyer, Joseph, shoemaker, e side Warren, Georgetown.
Dynes, Mary, (col) w side 10 w, btw L and M n.
Dyson, Owen, n side E Cap s, btw 2 and 3 e.

E.

Eames, Charles, ass't editor Wash'n Union, n side G n, btw 14 and 15 w.
Easler, A., huckster, s side East Cap, btw 5 and 6 e.
Eagen, Peter, grocer, cor 4½ w and F s.
Eagliston, John, butcher, e side N J av, btw K and L n.
Eagliston, S., butcher, n side N Y av, btw 6 and 7 w.
Earl, Richard, hackdriver, w side 20 w, btw F and H n.
Earl, Robert, livery stable, n side H n, btw 20 and 21 w.
Earp, J. W., painter and glazier, cor E and 9 w.
Easby, Wm., Commissioner of Public Buildings, office basement Capitol. House, cor 8 e and Pa av.
Easby, John W., shipbuilder, n side G n, btw 20 and 21 w.
Easby, H. N. & J. W., lumber yard, D, btw 25 and 26, near Observatory.
Easby, H. N., (& J. W.) h D, btw 26 and 27 w.
East Capitol street, running east from centre of Capitol.
Eastman, Captain Seth, U. S. A., n side E n, btw 10 and 11 w.
Easton, John, carpenter, at Pettit's, w side Potomac, btw 4th and 5th, Geo'town.
Eaton, Mrs. M. A., boarding house, s side Pa av, btw 6 and 7 w.
Eaton, John, attorney, n side I n, btw 20 and 21 w.
Eaton, Mary A., grocery, e side 8 w, btw D and E n.
Eaton, Mrs. Susan, widow, n side K s, btw 3 and 4 e.
Ebberly, William, shoemaker, w side High, two doors from Prospect, Georgetown.
Ebbert, Mr., currier, s side 2d, near High, Georgetown.
Ebeling, M., grocer, cor N n and 5 w.
Eberley, Danl., cabinetmaker, e side 7 w, btw N and O n.
EBERLY, ANTHONY, Stove Dealer, w side 7 w, btw G and H n.
Eberbach, J. H., restaurant, n side Pa av, btw 1 and 2 w.
Eckard, Rev. J. R., (2d Presbyterian church) s side N Y av, btw 9 and 10 w.
Eckardt, Thos., confectioner, n side F n, btw 9 and 10 w.
Eckloff, E. C., tailor, s side Pa av, btw 9 and 10 w.
Eckloff, J. W., clerk at Washington Monument, s side I n, btw 4 and 5 w.
Eckloff, G. F., tailor, n side La av, btw 6 and 7 w.
Ecton, E., blacksmith, n side G s, btw 7 and 8 e.
EDDY, STEPHEN, Jeweller, n side Pa av, btw 4½ and 6 w; boards at Mrs. Taylor's.
Edelin, Edward, w side N J av, btw K and L s.
Edelin, Mrs., widow, s side H n, btw 12 and 13 w.
Edgar, Joseph, Commissioner of Public Buildings, w side 3 w, btw B and C n.
EDGAR, JOHN, Professor of Music, n side Pa av, btw 1 and 2 w.

Abbreviations.—All points start from the Capitol; s south, n north, e east, w west, btw between, cor corner, (col) colored, av avenue, h house,

Edes, Mrs., s side Green, btw Beall and Dumbarton, Georgetown.
Edes, Wm. H., flour merchant, warehouse n side Water, btw High and Congress; h s side Gay, btw High and Congress, Georgetown.
Edgerter, Joseph, (col) laborer, n side I s, btw 3 and 4 e.
Edmondson, Mrs. Mary L., widow, w side 6 w, btw D and E n,
Edmondston, E., shoemaker, w side 7 w, btw D and E n.
House n side H n, btw 4 and 5 w.
Edmonson, Mr., clerk, n side West, btw Gay and High, Georgetown.
Edmonson, Mr., miller, w side Frederick, btw 3d and 4th, Georgetown.
Edmonston, E. A., grocer, cor Mass av and 6 w.
Edmonston, Franklin, printer, n side D n, btw 6 and 7 w.
Edmonston, Chas., carpenter, n side G n, btw 6 and 7 w.
House, I n, btw 9 and 10 w.
Edmonston, Jackson, carpenter, s side H n, btw 4 and 5 w.
Edmonston, Decies, baker, n side High, btw Beall and West, Georgetown.
Edwards, Mrs. Catharine, boarding, w side 7 w, btw D and E n.
Edwards, James L., s side Pa av, btw 14 and 15 w.
Edwards, John S., agent for claims, n side H n, btw 4 and 5 w.
Edwards, L., grocer, w side 12 w, btw M and Mass av.
Edwards, Saml., clerk General Post Office, w side 13 w, btw B and C s.
Edwards, Thos., grocer, cor I and 15 w.
Edwards, Jas., watchman navy yard, w side 7 e, btw G and I s.
Edwards, G., musician, marine barracks, n side G s, btw 7 and 8 e.
Edwards, James M., carpenter, w side 23 w, btw H and I n.
Edwards, Wm., plasterer, w side North Capitol, btw B and C n.
Edwards, J. L., s side F n, btw 19 and 20 w.
Egan, Peter, grocer, e side 4½ w, btw E and F s.
EGAN, WM., & SON, Dry Goods, s side Pa av, btw 6 and 7 w.
Eglen, Jas., Major U. S. A., n side B s, btw 2 and 3 e.
Eglin, Mrs. Sarah, n side Mass av, btw N J av and 4 w.
Eglin, J. H., laborer, s side I n, btw 12 and 13 w.
Eichen, Rodolph, baker, cor 3 w, and F n.
Eigentroth, G., shoemaker, s side Pa avenue, btw 19 and 20 w.
Eikens, Wm., gardener, w side 9 w, btw I and N Y av.
Eivai, John, stonecutter, s side Md av, btw 4½ and 6 w.
Ela, R., s side N Y av, btw 9 and 10 w.
Elbert, John, tailor, w side 10 w, btw N Y av and K.
Eldridge, Platt, & Stewart, attorneys, e side 15 w, btw Pa av and F n.
Eliason, E. A., tanner, n e cor High and Dumbarton; h out High, e side, G'town.
Eliot, Dr. Johnson, opposite Odd Fellow's Hall, 7 w.
Eliot, Wallace, druggist, cor F n and 12 w.
Eliot, Wm. G., clerk Post Office Department, s side Ia av, btw 3 and 4½ w.
Elkins, S., (col) blacksmith, btw 4½ and 6 w.
Ellicott, James P., engineer, n side I s, btw 7 and 8 e.
Elliot, Jefferson, omnibus driver, n side E s, btw 3 and 4½ w.
ELLIOT, WM. P., Patent Agent, office cor 8 w and F n.
House, North Capitol, btw B and C n.
Elliot, Seth A., clerk in Senate, B H, Capitol Hill, near N J av.
Elliot, G., clerk Land Office, s side N Y av, btw 12 and 13 w.
Elliot, Wm., clerk Navy Department, e side 20 w, btw G and H n.
Ellis, ——, cartdriver, w side 4½ w, btw Md av and C s.
Ellis, J. B., warden of penitentiary, foot of 4½ w.
Ellis, Edward, (& Bro.) carpenter, h w side 8 w, btw G and H n.
Ellis, V., attorney at law, s side Pa av, btw 12 and 13 w.
Ellis, Wm. M., chief engineer navy yard, w side 8 e, btw G and H s.
Ellis, John, watchman Patent Office, e side 6 w, btw F and G n.
Ellis & Bro., carpenters, s side H n, btw 7 and 8 w.
Ellis, Henry, grocer, n side Mass av, btw 6 and 7 w.
Ellis, James, carpenter, s side I n, btw 6 and 7 w.
Ellis, M., gunner, w side 11 e, btw I and K s.

Abbreviations.—All points start from the Capitol; s south, n north, e east, w west, btw between, cor corner, (col) colored, av avenue, h house.

Ellis, Mrs. Mary, widow, n side Ga av, btw 8 and 9 e.
Ellis, Mr., s side Market, near Water, Georgetown.
Ellis, Francis, carpenter, w side Potomac, btw Bridge and Prospect, Georgetown.
Ellis, George, grocery, e side Fayette, btw 1st and 2d, Georgetown.
Ellis, Richard, grocery, n side Water, btw Potomac and High, Georgetown.
Elmore & Topping, painters, cor 8 w and D n.
Elmore, Richard, (& Topping) h w side 8 w, btw G and H n.
Elmore, James, painter, s side H n, btw 8 and 9 w.
Elvin, Mary Ann, widow, n side Md av, btw 9 and 10 w.
Elwell, Francis, musician, w side 8 w, btw E and G s.
Emerson, George W., butcher, n side I n, btw 19 and 20 w.
Emerson, James, blacksmith, w side 7 e, btw L and M s.
Emmert, Henry, tinner, s side Pa av, btw 19 and 20 w.
Emory, M. G., stonecutter, e side 2 w, btw B and C n; h Mass av, btw 4 and 5 w.
Engelbreght, Charles, tavern, w side 1 w, btw B and C n.
Engle, D., baker, n side F n, btw 10 and 11 w.
English, David, jr., & Son, hardware, Bridge, btw Congress and High; house of David, s e cor 1st and Potomac, Georgetown.
English, Henry, hardware, n side Gay, west of Montgomery, Georgetown.
English, Miss Lydia, n e cor Gay and Washington, Georgetown.
Ennis, Gregory, n side F n, btw 12 and 13 w.
Ennis, Mrs., boarding house, n side A n, btw 1 e and Del av.
Ennis, J. F., attorney at law, s side La av, btw 4½ and 6 w.
Entwistle, T. B., carpenter, La av, btw 6 and 7 w; h w side 10 w, btw E and F n.
Ernolf, George, bootmaker, n side E n, btw 10 and 11 w.
Erwin, S. B., clerk Navy Department, 12 w, btw F and G n.
Eslin, Wm., brickmaker, w side 3 w, btw O and P n.
Espey, James, (Lee &) s side Md av, btw 4½ and 6 w.
Espey & Morrison, druggists, cor 7 w and E n.
Espey, S. C., (& Morrison) druggist, s side I n, btw 4 and 5 w.
Espey, John, bookbinder, s side F n, btw 17 and 18 w.
House, n side G n, btw 20 and 21 w.
Essex, Josiah, carpenter, s side I n, btw 6 and 7 w.
Essex, James F., flour merchant and cooper, warehouse s side Water, btw High and Aqueduct; h s side High, near Water, Georgetown.
Etchison, Lemuel, stonemason, e side 6 w, btw G and H n.
Etchison, James, work on canal, btw 3d and 4th, Georgetown.
European Hotel, (W. Levy) n side Pa av, btw 3 and 4½ w.
Eustace, Philip C., coachmaker, w side 12 w, btw E s and Md av.
Evans, J. D., grocer, cor 11 e and K s.
Evans, Walter, laborer, n side L s, btw 3 and 4 e.
Evans, Mrs., widow, n side I s, btw 11 and 13 e.
Evans, John, jr., hatter, n side Pa av, btw 12 and 13 w.
Evans, C., grocer, w side 9 w, btw B and C n; h cor 9 w and I n.
Evans, Isaac, stonecutter, s side F s, btw 2 and 3 w.
Evans, W. T., druggist, cor 7 w and H n.
Evans, Jane, boarding house, n side Md av, btw 13½ and 14 w.
Evans, E., grocer, w side 9 w, btw B and La av; h I n, first door below 9 w.
Evans, J. T., jr., n side Pa av, btw 12 and 13 w.
Evans, Edward, sr., blacksmith, w side 8 e, btw E and G s.
Evans, Edward, jr., clerk, w side 8 e, btw E and G s.
Evans, Traverse, shoemaker, w side 8 e, btw E and G s.
Evans, E., attorney, s side I n, btw 8 and 9 w.
Evans, F. S., Agent for Claims, opposite Treasury Department.
House, n side M n, btw 9 and 10 w.
Evans, B., clerk Treasury Department, e side 14 w, btw H and I n.
Evans, Mrs., milliner, s side La av, btw 6 and 7 w.
Evans, Burton, barber, n side Bridge, btw High and Potomac, Georgetown.
Evely, James, clerk Pension Office, w side 19 w, btw G and H n.
Everett, Dr. S. W., w side 7 w, btw G and H n.

Everett, Thomas T., Examiner Patent Office, n side M n, btw 9 and 10 w.
Everett, Charles, general agent, cor M n and Del av.
Everett, Edward, Secretary of State, cor 18 w and G n.
Everett, Dr. S. W., w side 6 w, btw G and H n.
Everly, ——, stove store, w side 7 w, btw G and H n.
Ewbank, Thomas, e side 6 w, btw D and E.
Exchange Bank, (Selden, Withers & Co.) w side 7 w, btw Pa av and D n.

F.

Fagan, Mary Ann, widow, s side Md av, btw 4½ and 6 w.
Fairfax, W. M. C., civil engineer, s side Pa av, btw 2 and 3 e.
Falconer, James H., carpenter, e side 7 w, btw L and M n.
Fales, G. W., messenger Treasury Department, n side M n, btw 8 and 9 w.
Fales, N. W., clerk Ordnance Department, n side H n, btw 9 and 10 w.
Farley, Edward W., messenger Sixth Auditor's Office, w side 8 w, btw G and H n.
Farmers and Mechanics' Bank, s e cor Bridge and Congress, Georgetown.
Farnham, R., bookstore, cor Pa av and 11 w; h M n, btw 11 and 12 w.
Farr, ——, Exchange Office, e side 13 w, btw Pa av and E n.
Farrar, ——, n side Mo av, btw 4½ and 6 w.
Farwell, George, Coast Survey, w side N J av, btw D and E s.
Faulkner, Joseph, baker, w side 7 w, btw Va av and D.
FAULKNER, WM. H., Shirtmaker, s side Pa av, btw 3 and 4½ w.
Faultner, Samuel, boatbuilder, Water, btw Scott's Row and High, Georgetown.
Faunce, Conrad, fishdealer, n side Md av, btw 13½ and 14 w.
Faunce, George, fishdealer, w side 13½ w, btw Md av and D s.
Fearson, Mr., grocer, w side High, btw 2d and 3d, Georgetown.
Fearson, Samuel, wood yard, s side Water, next the bridge; h, n e cor Water and Congresss, Georgetown.
Fearson, Jos. N., grocer and ship chandler, s side Water, btw High and Aqueduct; h, w side Congress, Georgetown.
Feeney, Wm., confectioner, n side Pa av, btw 2 and 3 w.
Felger, Francis, musician, w side 7 e, btw E and G s.
Fell, John, leatherstore, e side 9 w, btw I and N Y av.
Fendall, P. R., District Attorney, s side Ia av, btw 3 and 4½ w.
Fenley, Edward, Joseph, and John, plasterer, painter, and carpenter, s side West, extreme east, Georgetown.
Fennell, Walter H., farmer, s side Pa av, btw 14 and 15 w.
Fennell, Simon, shoemaker, n side L n, btw 9 and 10 w.
Fenton, Wm. R., printer, n side G s, btw 8 and 9 w.
Fenton, Charles W., clerk Treasury Department, n side G n, btw 8 and 9 w.
Fenwick, R. M. A., restaurant, basement cor Pa av and 1 w.
Fenwick, Mrs., e side Fayette, opposite Catholic Academy, Georgetown.
Fenwick, Frank, weaver, w side Lingan, Georgetown.
Fearson, Robert, grocer, w side Market space, Georgetown.
Ferguson, Alfred B., gunsmith, e side N J av, btw M and N s.
Ferguson, Rev. W. W., n side L n, btw 9 and 10 w.
Ferguson, John, clerk First Comptroller's Office, s side L n, btw 7 and 8 w.
Ferguson, James R., carpenter, n side E s, btw 2 and 3 e.
Ferman, Mrs., widow, w side 13 w, btw G and H n.
Ferril, Dennis, waterman, s side D s, btw 13½ and 14 w.
Fhrester, Mrs., widow, s side B s, btw N J av and 1 e.
Fickett, Mrs. Jane, widow, tailoress, n side G n, btw 18 and 19 w.
Fidny, Mrs. Martha, n side N s, btw 1 e and N J av.
Fiel, D., tinner, cor F n and 11 w.
Field, Wm. D., clerk, e side 14 w, btw F n and Pa av.
Fields, George, musician, n side I s, btw 9 and 10 e.
Fields, Mrs. Jane, widow, confectioner, n side Va av, btw 6 and 7 e.
Fields, George, (col) laborer, n side Va av, btw South Capitol and 1 w.

Abbreviations.—All points start from the Capitol; s south, n north, e east, w west, btw between, cor corner, (col) colored, av avenue, h house.

Fill, John, Prof. Penmanship and Mathematics, w side 10 w, btw D and E n.
Fillebrown, Thos., chief clerk Bureau Provisions and Clothing, Navy Department, n side H n, btw 19 and 20 w.
Fillius, Jacob, laborer, w side 3 w, btw Va av and D s.
Fillmore, Millard, Presd't U. S., President's house, s side Pa av, btw 15 and 17 w.
Fillmore, M. P., private secretary, same place.
Finch, D., painter, w side 13 w, btw N Y av and I n.
Finckman, Conrad, restaurant, s side Pa av, btw 12 and 13 w.
Finegan, P., e side 10 w, btw E and F n.
Finigan, Charles, hackman, n side G s, btw 5 and 6 e.
Fischer, Mrs. Wm., widow, music store, n side Pa av, btw 11 and 12 w.
House, s side C n, btw 3 and 4½ w.
Fischer, Charles, clerk Treasury Department, w side 11 w, btw K and L n.
Fisher, T. J., clerk, w side 12 w, btw N Y av and H.
Fisher, Morris, confectioner, e side 7 w, btw H and I n.
Fisher, Percival, machinist, s side G s, btw 6 and 7 e.
Fisher, David, (col) hackman, n side I n, btw 15 and 16 w.
Fitch, Patrick, grocer, w side 11 w, btw E and F n.
Fitman, T., clerk Pension Office, n side I n, btw 6 and 7 w.
Fitten, William H., finisher, e side 13 e, btw G and I s.
Fitz, Patrick, laborer, e side 2 w, btw G and Mass av.
Fitzgerald, John, laborer, w side 3 w, btw G and H n.
Fitzgerald, Patrick, laborer, w side 3 w, btw G and H n.
Fitzgerald, J., boarding house, n side Pa av, btw 3 and 4½ w.
Fitzgerald, Wm. A., printer, s side F n, btw 9 and 10 w.
Fitzgerald, Mrs. Susan, widow, grocery, n side E n, btw 12 and 13 w.
Fitzgerald, M., laborer, n side G n, btw 2 and 3 w.
Fitzgerald, Susan, (col) laundress, s side Mass av, btw 12 and 13 w.
Fitzgerald, Davis, grocer, n side F n, btw 2 and 3 w.
Fitzgerald, E., carpenter, w side 13 w, btw N Y av and I n.
Fitzgerald, W. P. N., attorney, n side M n, btw 9 and 10 w.
Fitzgerald, John, laborer, e side 2 w, btw F and G n.
Fitzpatrick, Wm. J., architect, office Adam's Express Building.
Fitzpatrick, John C., clerk Senate, B, btw 1 and N J av.
Fitzpatrick, John, shoemaker, s side East Capitol, btw 1 and 2 e.
Fitzhugh, Samuel, clerk General Post Office, w side 7 w, btw I and N Y av.
Fitzhugh, H. G., carpenter, n side I n, btw 12 and 13 w.
House, w side 11 w, btw I and K n.
Fitzhugh, John W., carpenter, e side 12 w, btw I and K n.
Fitzhugh, Michael, laborer, s side A n, btw N J av and 2 w.
Fitzhugh, Wm. M., Union Hotel, n e cor Bridge and Washington, Georgetown.
Flack, Jacob, baker, n side East Capitol, btw 3 and 4 e.
Flaherty, William, bootmaker, s side F n, btw 6 and 7 w.
Flannigan, Mrs., n side Second, near College, Georgetown.
Flaut, Julia, (col) Canal, near Va av and 3 w.
Flenner, William, clerk Land Office, s side I n, btw 8 and 9 w.
Fleischmann, C. L., draughtsman, s side F n, btw 7 and 8 w.
Flint, C. W., refectory, E, Union Square; h e side 14 w, btw F and Pa av.
Fletcher, Mrs. L., tailoress, n side N s, btw 3 and 4½ w.
Fletcher, Philip, brickmaker, n side N s, btw 3 and 4½ w.
Fletcher, W. A., carpenter, s side L s, btw 4 and 5 e.
Flaherty, John, plasterer, s side M n, btw 6 and 7 w.
Fleming, John, hackdriver, w side 4½ w, btw M and Md av.
Fletcher, John, grocer, cor I and 4 w.
Fletcher, B., (col) laborer, w side 3 w, btw E and F s.
Fletcher, Mrs. Sarah M., boarding house, s side Pa av, btw 3 and 4½ w.
Fletcher, Noah, bookkeeper Colonization Office, n side E n, btw 6 and 7 w.
Fletcher, Mrs. H., fancy store, n side D n, btw 7 and 8 w.
Fletcher, James, (col) servant, n side G n, btw 2 and 3 w.
Fletcher, Mr., paver, Market, btw 2d and 3d, Georgetown.

Flinn, Thomas, laborer, n side Mass av, btw N J av and 4 w.
Flinn, M., laborer, n side N Y av, btw 6 and 7 w.
Flood, Geo. W., messenger Topographical Engineers, w side 20 w, btw K and L n.
Flowers, Richard D., janitor Temperance Hall.
Foley, Martin, laborer, w side 18 w, btw H and I n.
Foley, Elix., s side Water, btw High and Aqueduct, Georgetown.
Folk, Harriet, widow, s side K n, btw 4 and 5 w.
Follansbee, J., grocer, s side B n, btw 2 and 3 w.
Forbes, Samuel, bricklayer, e side 8 w, btw L and M n.
Forbes, John M. D., carpenter, e side 6 w, btw E and F n.
Forbes, G. C., printer, e side 19 w, btw F and G n.
Foreman, Dr. Edward, cor Md av and 12 w.
Foote, A., hackdriver, s side I n, btw 9 and 10 w.
Force, Peter, historian, e side 10 w, btw D and E n.
Ford, Thomas, shoe-findings, e side 7 w, btw G and H n.
Ford, John B., wheelwright, e side 7 w, btw N Y av and L n.
House n side N Y av, btw 2 and 3 w.
Ford, William, (col) carter, n side G n, btw 2 and 3 w.
Ford, P., laborer, n side H n, btw 4 and 5 w.
Ford, Mrs., boarding h, n side F n, btw 19 and 20 w.
Ford, John A., clerk Land Office, s side Va av, btw 11 and 12 w.
Ford, Mrs., schoolmistress, Fayette, 2d and 3d, Georgetown.
FORREST, WILLIAM H., jeweller, w side 7 w, btw N Y av and L n.
House 18 w, btw H and I n.
Forrest, Henry, carpenter, e side 8 w, btw L and M n.
Forrest, Alexander, s side 8 e, btw I and K s.
Forrest, Charles, w side 18 w, btw F and G n.
Forrest, John, shoemaker, n side N s, btw S Cap and 1 e.
Forrest, Bladen, n e cor First and Frederick, Georgetown.
Forrester, James, laborer, e side 10 w, btw K and Mass av.
Forrester, Mrs. Ann, widow, n side I s, btw 6 and 7 e.
Forsyth, William, engineer, n side Pa av, btw 17 and 18 w.
Fortney, Edward, clerk Post Office Department, n side I n, btw 9 and 10 w.
Foskey, E., (col) driver, n side F n, btw 21 and 22 w.
Foster, Robert, bookbinder, w side 12 e, btw G and I s.
Fouk, Samuel, carpenter, s side D s, btw 6 and 7 w.
Foulkes, Elizabeth A., widow, n side E s, btw 11 and 12 w.
FOWLER, CHARLES S., China store, e side 7 w, btw D and E n.
Fowler, John, auxiliary guard, e side 7 w, btw D and E s.
FOWLER & SHILES, Lumber-yard, s side Md av, btw 3 and 4½ w; and s side Md av and 14 w.
Fowler, Samuel, (& Shiles,) n side Md av, btw 4½ and 6 w.
Fowler, Mrs. M. A., boarding h, n side Pa av, btw 3 and 4½ w.
Fowler, ——, w side 12 w, btw M and N n.
Fowler, Mrs. Julia A., n side H n, btw 20 and 21 w.
Fowler, Thomas, laborer, n side Pa av, btw 24 and 25 w.
Fowler, Mrs., widow, s side B s, btw N J av, and 1 e.
Fowler, Joseph, carpenter, s side E s, btw 6 and 7 w.
Fowler, John A., laborer, e side 11 e, btw Va av and M s.
Fowler, John L., jr., carpenter, n side Va av, btw 9 and 10 w.
Fowler, A. G., bookkeeper at Metropolis Bank: boards at Byington's.
Fowler, Mrs., n side Bridge, extreme west, Georgetown.
Fowler, Robert, clerk, s e cor Bridge and Congress, Georgetown.
Fowler, Wm. R., confectioner, s side Bridge, cor Montgomery, Georgetown.
Fowler, John, painter, e side High, near Bridge; h, cor of Frederick and 7th, Georgetown.
Foy, John, Mount Pleasant Hotel, cor 1 e and Delaware av.
Fox, L., (col) laborer, e side 11 w, btw K and N Y av.
Fox, Mrs., s side Second, btw Bridge and Potomac, Georgetown.

Abbreviations.—All points start from the Capitol; s south, n north, e east, w west, btw between, cor corner, (col) colored, av avenue, h house.

Foxwell, James, messenger War Department, e side 11 w, btw E and F n.
Frailer, Charles, grocer, n side Md av, btw 6 and 7 w.
Frailey, Doctor Charles S., s side N Y av, btw 13 and 14 w.
France, J. H., exchange broker, cor 7 w and D n.
House s side E n, btw 10 and 11 w.
France, Mrs. M., boarding, w side 7 w, btw D and E n.
France, Thomas E., exchange broker, n side Pa av, btw 4½ and 6 w.
House, n side C n, btw 11 and 12 w.
France, John, exchange broker, n side Pa av, btw 12 and 13 w.
France, James E., exchange broker, n side Pa av, btw 12 and 13 w.
Francis, Richard, stonecutter, s side Va av, btw 3 and 4½ w.
Frank, Jacob, butter merchant, n side K n, btw 17 and 18 w.
FRANKENBERGER & WITTENAUER, Refectory, cor 7 w and G n.
Franklin Engine House, e side 14, btw E and Pa av.
Franklin, Benjamin, M. D., e side 7 w, btw E and F n.
Franklin, William A., dentist, e side 7 w, btw E and F n.
Franklin, William, printer, s side E n, btw 9 and 10 w.
Franklin, Mrs., music teacher, s side E n, btw 9 and 10 w.
Franklin, S. P., upholsterer, n side Pa av, btw 9 and 10 w.
Franklin, A., laborer, n side F s, btw 2 and 3 w.
Franklin, Alexander, sailmaker, cor Jefferson and Water, Georgetown.
Franzoni, John C., printer, e side 6 w, btw H and I n.
Franzoni, Jane, widow, s side D s, btw 9 and 10 w.
Fraser, Hannah, w side 7 w, btw D and E s.
Frasher, Miss Lucy, laundress, w side 3, btw N Y av and L n.
Frasier, J. F., baker, s side F n, btw 13 and 14 w.
Frazer, James, gardener, Half, btw S and T s.
Frazier, William H., carpenter, e side 8 w, btw M and N n.
Frazier, Benjamin, messenger Census office, e side 11 w, btw E and F n.
Frazier, John, grocer, s side I n, btw 17 and 18 w.
Frazier, L., (col) laborer, w side 20 w, btw L and M n.
Frazier, James, blacksmith, s side F s, btw 7 and 8 w.
Freeman, Mrs., teacher, e side 7 e, btw Va av and L s.
Freeman, John, baker, e side 7 w, btw L and M n.
Freeman, Col. W. G., U. S. A., n side F n, btw 13 and 14 w.
Freeman, W., (col) carpenter, n side M n, btw 15 and 16 w.
Freeman, Henry, refectory, e side 7 w, btw L and M n.
House, n side N n, btw 5 and 6 w.
Freeman, Benjamin, (col) laborer, w side 18 w, btw K and L n.
Freeman, Peter, tailor, w side High, btw Prospect and First; h, s side Second, btw Fayette and College, Georgetown.
French, James B., tailor, side F s, btw 9 and 10 w.
French, Mrs. E., widow, laundress, n side N Y av, btw 6 and 7 w.
French, B. B., attorney and counsellor at law and general agent, n side Pa av, btw 4½ and 6 w; h n side East Capitol, btw 1 and 2 e.
French, Mrs. S. B., s side E n, btw 6 and 7 w.
French, Ephraim, stonecutter, e side 6 w, btw E and F n.
French, Rev. J. W., w side 13 w, btw G and H n.
French, M., shoemaker, n side L n, btw 9 and 10 w.
French, Mrs., s side Bridge, near the bridge, Georgetown.
Frere, E., widow, e side 20 w, btw I and K n.
Fresh, ——, woodyard, e side Washington, Georgetown.
Freund, L., bootmaker, n side L n, btw 9 and 10 w.
Fridenwald, Jos., clothing store, cor 4½ and Pa av; h e side 7 w, btw B and Md av.
Fridenwald & Co., n side Pa av, btw 9 and 10 w.
Frizzel, John, James, and William, gardeners, Fayette, btw 2d and 3d, Geo'town.
Frost, L., painter, e side 13 w, btw Pa av and E n.
Fry, Joseph, carpenter, w side N J av, btw D and E s.
Fry, William, laborer, s side East Capitol, btw 5 and 6 e.
Fry, James, shoemaker, Sixth, west of Frederick, Georgetown.

Abbreviations.—All points start from the Capitol; s south, n north, e east, w west, btw between, cor corner, (col) colored, av avenue, h house.

Fry, Thomas E., shoemaker, s side 1st, btw High and Potomac, Georgetown.
Fry, William, carpenter, w side Washington, btw Gay and Bridge, Georgetown.
Frye, N., chief clerk War Department, n side Pa av, btw 19 and 20 w.
Fugit, Joseph, lumber merchant, w side 9 w, btw La av and C n.
House, s side D n, btw 3 and 4½ w.
Fugitt, J., lumber yard, s side La av, btw 9 and 10 w.
Fugitt, G., laborer, e side 5 e, btw L and M s.
Fugitt, Thomas M., cor N J av and N s.
Fugitts, T. J., grocer, s side L s, btw 4 and 5 e.
Fullalove, James, tailor, n side Bridge, btw Washington and Green, Georgetown.
Fullalove, Richard, clothing store, s side Bridge, btw High and Congress, G'town.
Fulmer, George, clerk Barracks, n side I s, btw 4 and 5 e.
Furgerson, F., segar store, w side 13 w, btw N Y av and I n.
Furse, James, plumber, n side Pa av, btw 17 and 18 w.
Furtner, Richard, watchman Post office, s side Mass av, btw 6 and 7 w.
Furton, Susannah, grocery, w side 11 w, btw I and K n.

G.

Gaddis, Adam, foreman navy yard, s side Ga av, btw 9 and 10 e.
Gadsby, Wm., Hotel, n w cor Pa av and 3 w.
Gadsden, Thomas, clerk Patent office, w side 9 w, btw F and G n.
Gahan, Peter, barkeeper, n side D n, btw 7 and 8 w.
Gahmonn, F., tailor, n side F n, btw 10 and 11 w.
Gaine, George, grocer, e side 9 w, btw Pa av and D n.
Gainer, John, messenger Patent office, e side 6 w, btw H and I n.
Gaither, Mrs. Margaret, widow, w side 6 w, btw G and H n.
Gaither, Mrs. Sarah Ann, widow, e side 6 w, btw G and H n.
Gale, Leonard, D., M. D. s side E n, btw 5 and 6 w.
Gales & Seaton, printing office, (National Intelligencer) cor D n and 7 w.
Gallagher, Danl., laborer, e side 10 w, btw E and F n.
Gallaher, J. S., 3d auditor, w side 9 w, btw E and F n.
Gallant, Edward, carpenter, e side 6 w, btw O and P n.
Galligan, James, n side D n, btw 6 and 7 w.
Galt, Mrs. Eliza, widow, w side 9 w, btw D and E n.
Galt, M. W. & Broth, jewellers, n side Pa av, btw 9 and 10 w.
Gannen, Edwin, n side Va av, btw 6 and 7 e.
Ganter, Samuel, laborer, n side 1 s, btw 2 and 3 e.
Gapperal, Wm. H., carpenter, w side Washington, btw Stoddart and West, G'town.
Gardiner, Col., e side N J av, btw B and C s.
Gardiner, Nelly, (col) laundress, s side Mass av, btw 9 and 10 w.
GARDNER, MRS. MARY, Cigar Store, n side Pa av, btw 1 and 2 w.
Gardner, Richard, boarding house, s side Pa av, btw 3 and 4½ w.
Gardner, Charles T., n side G n, btw 13 and 14 w.
Gardner, Franklin, clerk Post Office Department, n sido I n, btw 9 and 10 w.
Gardner, D., s side N Y av, btw 14 and 15 w.
Gardner, Doctor J. B., druggist, s side A s, btw N J av and 1 e.
Garner, Mary, widow, w side 12 w, btw M and N n.
Garner, Wm., blacksmith, n side K s, btw 7 e and Va av.
Garner, Mrs., widow, n side D s, btw 3 and 4 e.
Garner, Charles, blacksmith, w side 11 e, btw I and K s.
Garnet, Frank, (col) w side N J av, btw L and M s.
Garnett, Dr. A. Y. P., w side 9 w, btw E and F n.
Garret, George W., carpenter, w side 7 w, btw D and E s.
Garret, John, saddler, s side Bridge, at Mrs. Lang's hotel, Georgetown.
Garrett, David, barber, e side 7 w, btw G and H n.
Garrett, Richard, clerk, s side Mass av, btw 4 and 5 w.
Garrett, S., carpenter, n side K n, btw 10 and 11 w.
Garrett, Mr., blacksmith, Bridge, nearly opposite Market, Georgetown.

Garrett, Mortimer, Frederick, btw Prospect and First, Georgetown.
Garrettson, Nimrod, merchant, w side 8 e, btw I and K s; h n side I s, btw 6 and 7 e.
Garrison, George, (col) whitewasher, e side 8 w, btw L and N Y av.
Garrison, James, engineer, e side Dumbarton, near High, Georgetown.
Gasworks, s side Me av, btw B and 4½ w.
Gassaway, Mrs. Kitty E. A., widow, s side D n, btw 7 and 8 w.
Gasaway, R., laborer, n side L n, btw Vt av and 14 w.
Gates, S., carpenter, n side I s, btw 9 and 10 e.
Gates, George, bleacher, e side 6 w, btw G and H n.
Gates, W. H., laborer, w side 10 e, btw G and I s.
Gates, James, laborer, w side 11 e, btw I and K s.
Gates, S. F., carpenter, w side 11 e, btw M and N s; h I, btw 9 and 10.
Gates, Charles, moulder, w side Lingan, btw 1st and Water, Georgetown.
Gatewood, Wm., shoemaker, w side 7 w, btw M and N n.
Gatewood, John S., n side D n, btw 6 and 7 w.
Gatton, Henry, clerk Navy Department, e side 20 w, btw E and F n.
Gaubert, John A., confectioner, w side 7 w, btw L and M n.
Gauner, John, paver, w side 8 w, btw M and N n.
Gaut, James, (col) servant, s side B s, btw 4 and 5 e.
Gaut, Jerry, (col) laborer, e side Conn av, btw I and K n.
Gaut, Benjamin, (col) laborer, n side Va av, btw 3 and 4½ w.
Gautier, C., confectioner, cor Pa av and 11 w; h w side 11 w, btw E and F n.
GAWLERS, JOSEPH, Cabinetmaker, n side Pa av, btw 17 and 18 w.
Gayman, Mrs., seamstress, w side 11 w, btw G and H n.
Gee, Henry P., turner, s side Va av, btw 8 and 9 e.
Gedney, Thos. R., Commodore, U. S. N., s side F n, btw 19 and 20 w.
Geiger, Frederick, carpenter, e side 7 w, btw I and K n.
Genan, D., bootmaker, s side A s, btw N J av and 1 e.
Gentry, Meredith P., M. C., N. C., s side B n, btw Del av and 1 e.
GERECKE, F. C. & W., Wine Dealer, s side Pa av, btw 4½ and 6 w.
House, 7, btw G and H n.
GERECKE, CHARLES, Liquor Store, e side 7 w, btw G and H n.
German, Francis, currier, n side H n, btw 9 and 10 w.
German, W. C., laborer, w side 10 w, btw E and F n.
German, Stephen, engineer, w side 13½ w, btw B and C s.
Germellir, F., harnessmaker, w side 7 w, btw I and N Y av.
Gerolt, Mons., Prussian Minister, s w cor Green and Gay, Georgetown.
Getier, Frank, cabinetmaker, e side 7 w, btw L and M n.
Getril, Andrew, butcher, n side Mass av, btw 9 and 10 w.
House, s side D n, btw 5 and 6 w.
Getty, George, stonecutter, n side Mass av, btw N J av and 4 w.
Getzaendanner, Henry, blacksmith, e side 7 e, btw L and M s.
Giberson, G. L., attorney, n side La av, btw 6 and 7 w.
Gibbins, Patrick, blacksmith, n side D n, btw 13½ and 14 w.
Gibbins, S. Matthew, marine, navy yard, n side G s, btw 9 and 10 e.
Gibbons, John W., clerk Treasury Department, e side 6 w, btw D and E n.
Gibbs, Mrs., fancy store, n side Pa av, btw 9 and 10 w.
Gibbs, J., (col) laborer, n side H n, btw 21 and 22 w.
Gibbs, S. H., w side 15 w, btw L and M n.
Gibson, R., drawing and painting academy, w side 12 w, btw C and D n.
GIBSON & WERNER, Refectory, cor 7 w and E n.
Gibson, John, hotel, n side Md av and 14 w.
Gibson, Louisa, widow, w side 8 w, btw D and E s.
Gibson, George, Commissary General, U. S. A., s side F n, btw 14 and 15 w.
Gibson, Lieut. A. A., U. S. A., n side H n, btw 5 and 6 w.
Gibson, F., (col) laborer, s side L n, btw 13 and 14 w.
Gibson, S., (& Werner,) n side C s, btw 12 and 13 w.
Gideon, Jacob, printer, opposite City Post office, 7 w.
Gideon & Co. G. S., printers and bookbinders, w side 9 w, btw Pa av and D n.
Gideon, G. S., (& Co.) cor F, near 7 w.

Abbreviations.—All points start from the Capitol; s south, n north, e east, w west, btw between, cor corner, (col) colored, av avenue, h house,

Gideon, Jacob, rag warehouse, s side D n, btw 8 and 9 w.
Gieskins, ——, baker, n w cor Green and Bridge, Georgetown.
Gilbert, H., St. Charles Hotel, cor 3 w and Pa av.
GILBERT, H. N., Boarding House, n side Pa av, btw 1 and 2 w.
Gill, Robert, plasterer, s side Va av, btw 3 and 4½ w.
Gillespie, A., major in marines, n side H n, btw 18 and 19 w.
Gillis, Rev. L., (Church of the Ascension) s side N Y av, btw 9 and 10 w.
Gillis, J. M., Lieut. U. S. N., n side F n, btw 18 and 19 w.
Gilman, Vincent, currier, n side M n, btw 7 and 8 w.
Gilman, W. H., druggist, n side cor Pa av and 4½ w; h 2 w, near C n.
GILMAN, Z. D. & W. H., Druggists, n side Pa av, btw 6 and 7 w; h 2, near C.
Gingenback, Mrs. D., w side 7w, btw S and T n.
Ginnaty, Thomas, porter at Willard's, s side D n, btw 13½ and 14 w.
Gipson, Samuel, boatswain, n slde Md av, btw 13½ and 14 w.
Gipson, Susan, confectionary, e side 12 w, btw A and C n.
Given, John T., wood and coal merchant, yard near 14 st bridge.
House, n side C s, btw 12 and 13 w.
Gladdon, Mrs., Sarah, widow, s side Va av, btw 1 and 2 w.
Gladman, Addison B., carpenter, cor 8 w and M n.
Gladman, Asa, carpenter, w side 9 w, btw H and I n; h cor 9 w and M n.
Glauding, David, carpenter, n side Mass av, btw N J av and 2 w.
Globe, (see Congressional.)
Glorius, G., bootmaker, s side D n, btw 11 and 12 w.
Glover, Jane, w side 10 w, btw D and E n.
Glover, Mary, widow, n side I n, btw 9 and 10 w.
Glover, John, bookbinder, e side 11 w, btw E and Pa av.
Gobright, L. A., reporter, s side E n, btw 9 and 10 w.
Goddard, John H., magistrate, e side 7 w, btw F and G n.
Goddard, D. C., attorney at law, s side F n, btw 14 and 15 w.
Goddard, Solomon, messenger Treasury Department, e side 11 w, btw L and M n.
Goddard, W. C., watchman Treasury Department, w side 10 w, btw N Y av and K n.
Goddard, Isaac, grocer, w side 12 w, btw F and G n.
Goddard, Thomas, messenger Treasury Department, w side 11w, btw E and F n.
Goddard, D. C., attorney at law, n side H n, btw 9 and 10 w.
Goddard, James, painter, n side Gay, east of Montgomery, Georgetown.
Goddard, Mr., grocer, Dumbarton, btw Green and Montgomery, Georgetown.
Goddard, James, painter and grocer, Dumbarton, btw Green and Montg'y, Geo'tn.
Goddard, J. A., painter, w side Montgomery, btw Beall and Dumbarton, G'town.
Godey, Edward, tailor, n side I n, btw 4 and 5 w.
Godey, W., carpenter and grocer, n side Dumb'tn, btw Cong. and Wash., G'town.
Godey, Wm., painter and grocer, s w cor High and Prospect, Georgetown.
Godey, George, lottery office, Bridge, Georgetown.
Godfrey, Lewis, painter, w side 12 w, btw M and Mass av.
Goens, P., (col) laborer, n side F n, btw, 21 and 22w.
Goggin & Saunders, job printers, n side Pa av, btw 3 and 4½ w.
Goggin, Mrs. Julia, boarding n side Pa av, btw 6 and 7 w.
Gohens, John T., plasterer, e side [illegible] w, btw L and M n.
Golden, Edward' mason, w side 4½ w, btw C and D s.
Golden, John A., Our House, n side 8 e, btw I and K s.
Golden, S., hack driver, n side C n, btw 12 and 13 w,
Golden, John, boot maker, n side D n, btw 7 and 8 w.
Golden, Wm., laborer, e side Washington, btw Bridge and Canal, Georgetown.
Golden, George, omnibus driver, Water, west Scott's row, Georgetown.
Goldsmith, Mrs. Samuel, widow, w side 2 e, btw East Capitol and A n.
Goldsmith, Mrs., tailoress, s side Second, btw Frederick and Fayette, Georgetown.
Goldsmith, Mrs., grocery, s e cor Fourth and Market, Georgetown.
Goo, Anne Maria, widow, e side 9 e, btw F and G s.
Gooch, John, bookstore, n side Pa av, btw 2 and 3 w; h e side 8 w, btw I and K n.
Gooch, Mrs., Sarah, widow, trimming store, e side 6 w, btw F and G n.
Good, C. K. L., shoestore, s side Bridge, near Market-house, Georgetown.

Abbreviations.—**All points start from the Capitol; s south, n north, e east, w west, btw between, cor corner, (col) colored, av avenue, h house.**

Good, S., lottery office, Bridge, Georgetown.
Good, Mrs., school, s side First, near High, Georgetown.
Goodall, J., Professor of Music, boards at Mrs. Banneman.
Goodall, George, gasfitter, n side Va av, btw 6 and 7 e.
Goodloe, Dan. R., clerk Navy Department, n side D n, btw 14 and 15 w.
Goodman, William, s side Second, btw Frederick and Fayette, Georgetown.
Goodrich, James, blacksmith, Frederick, btw 3d and 4th; lottery office, Bridge, Georgetown.
Goodrich, J., lottery office, n side Bridge, btw Congress and Washington, G'town.
Goodriche, John, laborer, e side 13, btw G and I s.
GOODS, WM. H., Saddler, cor 7 w and I n; h 10, btw N Y av and K.
Goodwin, Thomas, watchman, e side 6 w, btw M and N n.
Gordon, Charles, clerk Navy Yard, s side K s, btw 7 and 8 e.
Gordon, E., laborer, n side G s, btw 6 and 7 e.
Gordon, Manuel, carpenter, n side K s, btw 10 and 11 e.
Gordon, James A., blacksmith, n side M s, btw 10 and 11 e.
Gordon, John, clerk Post Office Department, s side G n, btw 13 and 14 w.
Gordon, Wm., (col) n side I n, btw 11 and 12 w.
Gordon, George, printer, n side Mass av, btw 6 and 7 w.
Gordon, C., s side I n, btw 17 and 18 w.
Gordon, Wm., clerk Pension office, e side 13 w, btw E and F n.
Gordon, John, shoemaker, n side M s, btw 10 and 11 e.
Gordon, Charles A., clerk, n side West, btw Green and Montgomery, Georgetown.
Gordon, Daniel S., wood and lumber, w side Washington, btw Bridge and Canal, Georgetown.
Gormly, John, inspector of gas works, w side 1 w, btw B and Md av.
Goslin, James, laborer, w side 8 w, btw G and H n.
Gott, Richard, chief clerk Commissary General's office, e side 13 w, btw E and F n.
Gotzler, Mrs., confectionary, s side Bridge, west of Scott's row, Georgetown.
Gotzler, James, clerk, Prospect, btw Fayette and Frederick, Georgetown.
Gould, John, clerk Land Office, s side E n, btw 20 and 21 w.
Gould, Mrs. Stephen, n side G s, btw 9 and 10 e.
Grace, James, laborer, e side N J av, btw B and C s.
Graeme, Robert, clerk Treasury Department, e side 13 w, btw N Y av and I n.
Graham, C. B., lithographer, s side D n, near cor 12 w.
Graham, Col. James D., U S A, n side I n, btw 20 and 21 w.
Graham, J. M., bricklayer, w side 13 w, btw G and H n.
Graham, William, cartman, s side K n, btw 24 and 25 w.
Gramebaum, Moses, clothing, s side Bridge, btw Congress and Jefferson, G'town.
Granger, William, carpenter, w side 4½ w, btw L and M s.
Grant, George, bricklayer, n side I n, btw 4 and 5 w.
Grant, William, blacksmith, w side 7 w, btw G and H s.
Grant, E. (col) laborer, n side I n, btw 4 and 5 w.
Grant, Alexander, grocer, n side La av, btw 9 and 10 w.
Graham, G. W., farmer, n side 15 w, btw N Y av and H n.
Grasen, Sarah, laundress, e side 8 w, btw D and E n.
Grason, Butler, n side H n, btw 9 and 10 w.
Gratiot, Gen. C., Six Buildings, Pa av.
Graves, Wm., driver, Dumbarton, btw Green and Montgomery, Georgetown.
Graveyard, Presbyterian, on Frederick, btw 4th and 5th, Georgetown.
GRAY & BALLANTYNE, Bookstore, e side 7 w, btw D and E n.
Gray, Austin (& Ballantyne) e side 7 w, btw G and H n.
Gray, Thomas K., tailor, e side 8 w, btw Pa av and D.
House n side Md av, btw 4½ and 6 w.
Gray, John W. D., carpenter, e side 12 w, btw G and H n.
Gray, Daniel (col) laborer, n side K n, btw 4 and 5 w.
Gray, J., laborer, s side B s, btw 1 and 2 e.
Gray, Thomas, (col) porter, s side C s, 4½ and 6 w.
Gray, Anthony, s side B n, btw 5 and 6 e.

Abbreviations.—All points start from the Capitol; s south, n north, e east, w west, btw between, cor corner, (col) colored, av avenue, h house.

Gray, George, shoemaker, n side Bridge, two doors from Congress, Georgetown.
House s side Bridge, btw Montgomery and Green, Georgetown.
Gray, Hiram, (col) blacksmith, w side Montgomery, btw Gay and Bridge, G'town.
Greason, Mrs., boardinghouse, w side 13 w, btw E and F n.
Green, Jonas, M. D., homœopathic physician, n side C, btw 4½ and 6 w.
Green, B. E., attorney at law, n side Pa av, btw 4½ and 6 w.
Green, Edwin, cabinetmaker, cor Pa av and 11 w.
House w side 11, btw Pa av and C.
Green, William (col) laborer, e side 6 w, btw N and O n.
GREEN & SCOTT, Auctioneers, cor 6 w and Pa av.
Green, A. (& Scott,) n side C, btw 4½ and 6 w.
Green, E. (col) laborer, e side 11 w, btw K and N Y av.
Green, G. W. (col) waterman, n side N, btw 9 and 10 w.
Green, Patrick, cartman, w side 13 w, btw C and D s.
Green, Michael, grocer, w side 11 w, btw H and I n.
Green, M. (col) cartman, e side 1 w, btw B and C s.
Green, Duff, attorney, office over Lane & Tucker's, Pa av.
House Carroll Place, btw East Capital and A s.
Green, John F., dairy, cor 7 and Md av.
Greenfield, Henry, grocer, cor 11 e and M s.
Greenleaf, W. C., Republic office, cor 9 and L n.
Greenleaf, C., machinist, w side 3 e, btw I and Va av.
Greenough, James, office for patents, s side F n, btw 7 and 8 w.
House cor H n and 11 w.
Greenwell, J. B., pump maker, e side 4½ w, btw F and G s.
Greer, Mrs., dressmaker, w side 10 w, btw I and K n.
Greer, A. A., carpenter, e side 8 w, btw L and M n.
Greer, William, printer, office at Temperance Hall, E, btw 9 and 10 w.
House w side 11 w, btw G and H n.
Gregg, Mrs. Letty (col) laundress, s side D n, btw 5 and 6 w.
Gregg, Samuel, contractor, n side G s, btw 8 and 9 w.
Gregory, John, bricklayer, s side Mass av, btw 6 and 7 w.
Gregory, George, printer, n side H n, btw 4 and 5 w.
GREHAM, J. THOMPSON, General Agent, 18, btw H and I n.
Greham, Mrs. George, n side G n, btw 17 and 18 w.
Greham, James, laborer, s side B n, btw 5 and 6 e.
Grentrup, F., paper box maker, n side I n, btw 4 and 5 w.
Gretsenr, M., clerk Post Office Department, e side 9 w, btw I and N Y av.
Griffin, Clarissa R., Union Ben. Employ. Society, e side 7 w, btw D and E n.
Griffin, James C,, carpenter, w side 8 w, btw L and M n.
Griffin, T. B., shoestore, Pa av, btw 9 and 10 w; h, n side D, btw 9 and 10 w.
Griffin, E. W. W., printer, s side Bridge, btw High and Gongress, Georgetown.
Griffith, William T., merchant tailor, e side 9 w, btw Pa av and D n.
House on K, opposite Northern Liberties Market.
Griffith and McKnew, grocers, n side H n, btw 7 and 8 w.
Griffith, N., gardener, n side L n, btw 4 and 5 w.
Griffith, J., tailor, w side 11 w, btw Md av and E s.
Griffith, Philip, secretary of legation, (England,) w side 21 w, btw H and I n.
Griffith, Thomas, moulder, w side 7 e, btw I and K s.
Griffith, John H., gunsmith, w side 3 e, btw I and K s.
Griffith, William A., stonecutter, cor C n and 12 e.
Grigsby, Mrs. Ann, widow, confectionary, n side F n, btw 13 and 14 w.
Grimes, Henry, shoemaker, n side K s, btw 7 e and Va av.
Grimes, Michael H., shoemaker, n side 8 e, btw I and K s.
Grimes, William, carpenter, n side I n, btw 4 and 5 w.
Grimes, J. F., shoemaker, w side 18 w, btw K and L n.
Grimes, William, (col) laborer, w side 21 w, btw K and L n.
Grimes, John A., flour and com. merchant, agent Boston packets, warehouse s side Water, btw High and Aqueduct; h, s side West, btw Congress and Washington, Georgetown.

Abbreviations.—All points start from the Capitol; s south, n north, e east, w west, btw between, cor corner, (col) colored, av avenue, h house.

Grimes, George, shoemaker, e side High, btw Gay and Bridge, Georgetown.
Grindall, Edward, coppersmith and tinner, e side 7 w, btw E and F s.
Grindle, ——, gardener, Navy Yard, s side F s, btw South Capitol and 1 w.
Griner, Mrs. E,, widow, n side C s, btw 3 and 4½ w.
Griner, Anthony W., grocer, n side C s, btw 3 and 4½ w.
Grinnell, ——, cartman, s side Va av, btw South Capitol and 1 w.
Grisset, William W., laborer, w side 21 w, btw E and F n.
GRITZNER, M. C., Draughtsman, s side F n, btw 7 and 8 w.
Grives, John, lumber merchant, cor 9 w and Mass av.
Gross, Thomas, blacksmith, n side Va av, btw 9 and 10 e.
Gross, James, grocer, n side Water, cor Scott's row, Georgetown.
Gross, John, omnibus driver, s side Bridge, near Mayor's office, Georgetown.
Gross, Frank, butcher, n side First, cor Warren, Georgetown.
Grouard, George M., printer, e side 6, btw F and G n.
GROUX, D. E., Professor of Languages, s side Pa av, btw 6 and 7 w.
Grove, Philip, blacksmith, e side 8 w, btw L and M n.
Grubb, Samuel, magistrate, e side 9 w, btw Pa av and D n.
House s side M n, btw 6 and 7 w.
Grupe, William, confectioner, s side Pa av, btw 3 and 4½ w.
Gulager, Mrs. Bella, boardinghouse, s side Pa av, btw 6 and 7 w.
Guitard, Repetti, musician Navy Yard, w side 7 e, btw I and K s.
Gunnell, James S., dentist, n side Pa av, btw 9 and 10 w.
Gunnell, Henry D., commissioner 7th ward, cor Half and 7 s.
Gunton, William, president Bank of Washiugton, n side Pa av, btw 9 and 10 w.
Gurley, Rev. R. R., e side 12 w, btw E and Pa av.
Gutridge, Wm., (col) carpenter, w side 19 w, btw K and L n.
Guttenshon, John, confectioner, n side Pa av, btw 21 and 22 w.
Guyton, Mrs. Ophelia, widow, grocery store, w side 7 w, btw E and F s.
Gwinn, William, U. S. Senator, w side cor 3 and C n,

H.

Hackney, R. H. B., United States Hotel, n side Pa av, btw 3 and 4½ w.
Haden. A. D., dentist, e eide 6 w, btw G and H n.
Hader, Frederick, carpenter, e side 7 w, btw L and M n.
Hagan, John, gunner Navy Yard, w side 7 e, btw D and E s.
Hager, C., baker, e side 18 w, btw I and K n.
Hager, Frederick A., butcher, n side F n, btw 24 and 25 w.
Hagermann, Henry, grocer, e side cor 4½ w and E s.
Hagerty, Wm., grocer, e side 22 w, btw Pa av and I n.
Hagner, Mrs., s side H n, btw 18 and 19 w.
Haines, Joseph, (col) laborer, n side D s, btw 4 and 5 e.
Halder, Michael, clerk Post Office, s side Mass av, btw 6 and 7 w.
Haliday, James F., printer, w side 11 w, btw Pa av and C n.
Hall, David A., attorney at law, cor 3 w and C n.
Hall & Brother, dry goods, w side 7 w, btw D and Pa av.
Hall, R. B., dry goods, w side 7 w, btw I and N Y av.
Hall, .G J., tobacconist, n side Md av, btw 9 and 10 w.
Hall, Mary, cor 4½ w, and Md av.
Hall, Catharine, e side 8 w, btw L and M n.
Hall, P. W., tobacconist, n side Pa av, btw 2 and 3 w.
Hall, Dr. James C., n side Pa av, btw 9 and 10 w.
Hall, Dan. W., s side C n, btw 3 and 4½ w.
Hall, W. F., clerk Post Office Department, n side D n, btw 2 and 3 w.
Hall, J. H., clerk, dry goods, w side 11 w, btw G and H n.
Hall, Margaret, (col) laundress, n side L n, btw 5 and 6 w.
Hall, Levi, carpenter, w side 13 w, btw N Y av and I n.
Hall, Edward, grocer, n side La av, btw 7 and 8 w; h H, btw 9 and 10 w.
Hall, Thomas, laborer, s side B s, btw 6 and 7 w.

Abbreviations.—All points start from the Capitol; s south, n north, e east, w west, btw between, cor corner, (col) colored, av avenue, h house.

Hall, Francis, (col) whitewasher, n side D s, btw 4½ and 6 w.
Hall, Wm. R., finisher, w side 10 e, btw I and K s.
Hall, ——, blacksmith, n side G s, btw 6 and 7 e.
Hall, George, clerk Treasury Department, e side Del av, btw B and C n.
Halleck, John, printer, w side 9 w, btw I and N Y av.
Haman, A., tinner, w side N J av, btw D and E s.
Hamback, C., watchman, w side 4½ w, btw P and Q s.
Hambury, George, painter, w side 6 w, btw D and E s.
Hamil, Mrs. Sarah, widow, s side Va av, btw 3 and 4½ w.
Hamilton, Miss E., widow, s side Pa av, btw 2 and 3 e.
Hamilton, Dorcas, (col) laundress, w side 3 w, btw E and F s.
Hamilton, Rev. M. G., s side Pa av, btw 4½ and 6 w.
Hamilton, Mrs., milliner, s side Pa av, btw 9 and 10 w.
Hamilton, C. Captain U. S. A., n side G n, btw 13 and 14 w.
Hamilton, Samuel & Co., grocers, s side Pa av, btw 3 and 4½ w.
Hamilton, Mrs. General, n side H n, btw 13 and 14 w.
Hamilton, Wm., barber, s side Pa av, btw 17 and 18 w.
Hamilton, ——, clerk Patent office, e side 10 w, btw Va av and B s.
Hamilton, R., Secretary to General Scott, e side 18 w, btw I and K n.
Hamilton, Maria, (col) laundress, n side L s, btw 4 and 5 e.
Hamilton, Mrs., fancy store, w side Green, btw Green and Dumbarton, Geor'tn.
Hammack, D., grocer, cor 13½ and D n.
Hampton, Emily, (col) n side L n, btw 15 and 16 w.
Hammell, Wm., grocer, e side 7 w, btw L and M n.
Hammersley, Edward, confectioner, e side 10 w, btw Md av and F s.
Hammond, Edward, laborer, w side 3, btw N Y av and L n.
Hammond, Nelson, wood merchant, w side 7 w, btw G and H n.
Hammond, N, printer, s side I n, btw 6 and 7 w.
Hancock, A., Bald Eagle House, s side Pa av, btw 12 and 13 w
Hand, Edward, police officer, w side 8 w, btw G and H n.
Hand, John, tobacconist, n side Pa av, btw 14 and 15 w.
Hand, John, exchange broker, w side 6 w, btw Pa av and La av.
House, s side I n, btw 8 and 9 w.
Handley, James, fancy store, e side 7 w, btw G and H n.
Handley, Mrs. Jane, widow, n side G n, btw 20 and 21 w.
Handsome, Amelia, (col) washwoman, near I and Mass av.
Handsome, Samuel, e side N J av, btw B and C s.
HANDY, SAML., Paper Hanger, n side C n, btw 12 and 13 w.
Handy, S. W. K. & Co, grocers, s side Pa av, btw 14 and 15 w.
Hane, David, wheelwright, n side Prospect, btw High and Potomac.
House, n side West, btw Congress and Washington, Georgetown.
Hane, Frank, n side West, btw Congress and Washington, Georgetown.
Hanes, W., huckster, e side 18 w, btw I and K n.
Hanly, Hugh, fancy store, s side Pa av, btw 17 and 18 w.
Hanly, Henry, clerk, w side 17 w, btw H and I n.
Hanley, Edmund, clerk, n side G n, btw 20 and 21 w.
Hannavan, Mrs. Catharine, widow, e side 11 w, btw F and G n.
Hansell, Edward, carpenter, w side 8 w, btw I and K n.
Hanson, ——, clerk Post Office Department, e side 4½ w, btw C n and Ia av.
Hanson, Henry, (col) brickmaker, w side 3 w, btw C and Va av.
Hanson, G., clerk Post Office, s side B s, btw N J av and 1 e.
Harbaugh, Joseph, measurer of builders work, w side 7 w, btw D and E n.
Harbaugh, V., druggist, cor 7 w and G n.
Harbaugh, J. R., carpenter, w side 10 w, btw C s and Va av.
Harbin, Philip, shoemaker, s side G, btw 6 and 7 e.
Harbin, Jas., machinist, n side G s, btw 6 and 7 e.
Hardin, L. B., clerk Navy Department, n side H n, btw 14 and 15 w.
Hardy, Walter, blacksmith, s side G, btw 10 and 11 e.
Hardy, Mr., n side Bridge, btw Montgomery and the Bridge, Georgetown.
Hare, D. O., engraver, n side Pa av, btw 12 and 13 w.

Abbreviations.—All points start from the Capitol; s south, n north, e east, w west, btw between, cor corner, (col) colored, av avenue, h house.

Haren, Henry, (col) carpenter, n side F s btw 2 and 3 w.
Harkins, Charles, clerk Treasury Dep't., e side 12 w btw C and B s.
Harkness, J. C., architect, s side N Y av, btw 9 and 10 w.
Harkness & Birth, architects, n side E n, btw 8 and 9 w.
Harkness, John C., (& Birth,) N Y av. btw 9 and 10 w.
Harkness, Daniel, carpenter, s side H, n btw 11 and 12 w.
Harley, Smith, (col) well digger, e side 11 w, btw M and L n.
Harman, James, coach maker, s side H, n btw 6 and 7 w.
Harman, John L., coach painter, w side, 10 w, btw N Y av. and K.
Harman, John, laborer, Frederick, btw 5 and 6, Georgetown.
HARPER, WM. C., & CO., Grocers, s side Pa av, btw 4½ and 6 w.
Harper, Dr. James, s side F n, btw 13 and 14 w.
Harper, C., grocer, High st., Georgetown.
Harper, Grafton, watchman, n side Water, btw Aqueduct and Scott's Row, Geo'tn.
Harper, Walter & Co., dry goods, n side Pa av, btw 9 and 10 w.
Harren, Chas., paver, s side F s, btw 9 and 10 w.
Harrington, George, chief clerk, Treasury Department, n side, E n, btw 6 and 7 w.
Harrington, Mrs. Mary A., widow, n side, 8 E, btw M and L s.
Harrington, James, watchman, e side 10 w, btw 12 and Mass. av.
Harrington, J., carpenter, w side 1st w. btw B and Md. av.
Harrington, Mrs., n side E Capitol s, btw 2 and 3 e.
Harris, Elizabeth, cake shop, n side Md av. btw 13½ and 14 w,
Harris, ———, w side 8 w, btw I and K n.
Harris, H. C., (col) shoe maker, n side E n.
Harris, Margaret, (col) laundress, s side Mass av. btw 9 and 10 w.
Harris, Wm. J. painter, e side 12 w, btw M n and Mass av.
Harris, Rev. W. A., clerk Land Office, n side L n, btw 9 and 10 w.
Harris, Samuel L., house s side N Y av. btw 9 and 10 w.
Office n side Pa av. btw 4½ and 6 w.
Harris, Wm. A., carpenter, w side 10 W, btw E and F s.
Harris, Mrs., widow, e side 11 E, btw Pa av and M s.
Harris, H. C., (col) shoemaker, n side E n, btw 12 and 13 w.
HARRIS & GRIFFIN, shoe store, n side Pa av. btw 9 and 10 w.
Harrison, Joseph, billiard saloon, n side Pa av. btw 4½ and 6 w.
Harrison, Mrs. E., boarding h, s side Pa av. btw 4½ and 6 w.
Harrison, James, blacksmith, n side C n btw 11 and 10 w.
Harrison, Richard, Mess. State Department w side 20 W btw H and F n.
Harrison, Wm., carpenter, w side 22 w, btw H and G n.
Harrison, Mrs., dress maker, s side E Capitol btw 5 and 6 E.
Harrison, Robert M., carpenter, e side Va av. btw H and I.
HARRISON'S GREEN HOUSE, s side Pa av, btw 4½ and 6 w.
Harrison, Wm. Henry, laborer, Fayette, btw 2 and 3, Georgetown.
HARROVER, W. H., Stove Warehouse, e side 7 w, btw D and La av.
Harry, John, clerk, cor Stoddard and Congress, Georgetown.
Hartley, Nimrod, wholesale grocer, s side Water, btw High and Aqueduct, Geo'tn.
Hart John, laborer, s side D n, btw Mass av., and n Capitol.
Hartley John, s side N Y av, btw 9 and 10 w.
Hartman, Mrs., A., widow, w side 6 E, btw G and E s.
Hartnell, Patrick, stonecutter, n side M n, btw 7 and 8 w.
Harven, ———, carpenter, w side 8 w, btw L and M n.
Harvey, James F., cabinet maker, e side 7 w, btw G and H n.
Harvey & Co., Jasper S., grocer, cor Md av. and 13½ w.
Harvey, T. M., carpenter, s side F n, btw 9 and 10 w.
House, cor 10 w, and N Y av.
Harvey, Mr,. Mary Ann, widow, s side G n, btw 13 and 12.
Harvey, George, painter, s side H, n btw 7 and 8 w.
House, n side M n, btw 8 and 9 w.
Harvey, J. S., wood merchant, e side 10 w, btw D and E n.
Harvey, Wm., printer, e side 10 w, btw H and 1 n.
Harvey, Arenius, grocer, n side C s, btw 12 and 13 w.

Abbreviations.—All points start from the Capitol; s south, n north, e east, w west, btw between, cor corner, (col) colored, av avenue, h house.

Harvey, H. L., clerk Navy Department, w side, 17 w, near I n.
Harvey, A. F., clerk Navy Department, w side 17 w, near I n.
Harvey, F. A., exchange broker, n side Pa av. btw 14 and 15 w.
Harvey, T. M., grocer, cor 10 w and N Y av.
Haslup, Thomas M., furniture dealer, w. side 7 w btw Va av. and D.
Haslup, Mary C, widow, w side 9 w, btw I and N Y av.
Haslup, Lewis, coach maker, cor 9 and Market Place.
House s side 10 w, btw B and C.
Haslup & Wieden, coachmakers, cor C n and 9 w.
HASSLER, F. E., General Agent for Claims, 4½ near Pa av.
Residence at Fitzgerald's, Pa av.
Hastings, Mrs., e side Potomac, btw Bridge and Prospect, Georgetown.
Hatch, A. Jr., camphine and lamp store, w side 9 w, btw Md av and F n.
Hatton, Mrs., widow, boards at Mrs. Fletcher's, Pa av.
Haveland, James C., clerk Treasury Department, s side K n, btw 11 and 12 w.
Havvener, John F., baker, w side 11 w, btw Md av and E s.
Havvener, Thomas H., baker, s side C n, btw 4½ and 6 w.
House, n side C n, btw 4½ and 6 w.
Havenner, P., bricklayer, n side D n, btw 6 and 7 w.
Hawes, Charles W., machinist, e side 4½ w, btw M and n s.
Hawes, Wm., (col) laborer, e side 3 e, btw F and G s.
Hawke, Thomas, w side 3 e, btw Va av and I s.
Hawke, Rob., A., messenger Post Office Department, n side M n, btw 7 and 8 w.
Hawkins, Susannah, w side 10 w, btw M and N n.
Hawkins, Mrs. A. A., boarding house, n side H, btw 8 and 9 w.
Hawkins, Mrs. P., (col) laundress, n side H, btw 12 and 13 w.
Hawkins, John, tinner, w side High, 2 doors from 1, Georgetown.
Hawkins, Charles, huckster, w side High, btw 3 and 4, Georgetown.
Hawkins, Matilda, (col) laundress, w side Vt av, btw K and L n.
Hawks, John, clerk Treasury Department, e side 8 w, btw L and M n.
Hawley, Mrs. Wm., s side Pa av, 6 doors from War Department.
Hauptman, D & Sons, tinners, e side 11 w, btw E and Pa av.
Hay, Edward, waiter, e side 13 w, btw G and H n.
Hay, Henry, painter, e side 6 w, btw Mass av and K n.
Hayden, Mrs., dressmaker, n side F n, btw 13 and 14 w.
Hayer, Thos., watchman at Observatory, w side 22 w, btw G and H n.
Hayer, Jas., (col) carpenter, s side D s, btw 1 and 2 w.
Hayer, John, laborer, e side 6 e, btw A and B n.
Hayman, E., carpenter, (col) s side Pa av, btw 21 and 22 w.
Haymes, Col. James, (col) laborer, e side 3 w, btw F and G n.
Hays, Bertrand, E, tobacconist, w side 7 w, btw Va av and D s.
Hays, Mrs. Sarah, nurse, s side F n, btw 11 and 12 w.
Hays, J. L., attorney, e side 15 w, btw F and N Y av.
House, e side 11 w, btw E and F n.
Hazard, O. E. P., exchange broker, n side Pa av, btw 14 and 15 w.
Hazard, R. R., constable, e side 14 w, btw B and C s.
Hazel, Wm., shoestore, e side Market Space, Georgetown.
Headley, John P., shoemaker, w side 11 w, btw Md av and E s.
Heap, Dr. D. P, cor 9 w and D n.
Heard, Joseph, (Medhurst &) cor 6 w and H n.
Hecker, Father, s side 1, btw Fayette and College, Georgetown.
Hecter, Uriah, confectionery, w side High, 2 doors from Bridge, Georgetown.
Hedges, Rev. J. W., n side Md av, btw 4½ and 6 w.
Hedlen, C., carpenter, w side 7 e, btw G and I s.
Heffermann, Mrs. B., grocery, w side N J av, btw K and L s.
Hefferman, Patrick, printer, s side D n, btw 13 and 13½ w.
Heger, Jahan F., grocer, w side N J av, btw K and L s.
Hegerty, Danl., laborer, e side 10 w, btw M and N n.
Heile, Joseph, shoemaker, s side Mass av, btw 2 and 3 w.
Hein, George, laborer, s side East Capitol, btw 5 and 6 e.

Abbreviations.—All points start from the Capitol; s south, n north, e east, w west, btw between, cor corner, (col) colored, av avenue, h house,

Heinlaim, V., rag merchant, n side Va av, btw 1 and 2 w.
Heisler, Mary, w side 3 w, btw C and Va av.
Heisler, John, confectioner, w side 8 w, btw P and Q n.
Hellen, Johnson, attorney, cor 5 and D n.
Hemlay, L., (col) porter, w side 8 w, btw D and E s.
Hempler, J. G., tailor, n side C n, btw 6 and 7 w.
Henderson, General, (Marine barracks,) n side 8 e, btw G and I s.
House, s side G s, btw 8 and 9 e.
Henderson, Mr., carpenter, w side 13 w, btw C and D n.
Henderson, Mr., s e cor Green and Beall, Georgetown.
Henderson, Wm., bricklayer, s e cor, Green and Dumbarton, Georgetown.
Henderson, Anna, (col) laundress, w side 14 w, btw H and I n.
Hendley, George, tinner, w side 7 w, btw D and E n.
Hendley, Richard, tinner, e side 4 w, btw I and K n.
Hendley, James, Metropolis refectory, n side Pa av, btw 4½ and 6 w.
Heney, Patrick, laborer, w s N J av, btw L and M s.
Henley, Mrs. Com., n side H n, btw 14 and I5 w.
Hennessy, Jeremiah, laborer, n side Pa av, btw 1 and 2 w.
Henning, Nelson, bricklayer, w side 6 w, btw G and H n.
Henning, Bennett, carpenter, n side I n, btw 6 and 7 w.
Henning, James, grocer, cor L n and 18 w.
Henning, S., dry goods, w side 11 e, btw I and K s.
Henry, Jos., Prof. and Sect'ry Smiths'n Institute, w side 10 w, btw Md av and C s.
Henry, Mrs., grocery, e side 18 w, near I n.
Henry, P. M., clerk War Department, n side N Y av, btw 17 and 18 w.
Henry, C. H., laborer, e side 6 w, btw M and N n.
Henry, Dr. Charles, clerk Treasury Department, w side 13 w, btw N Y av and I.
Hens, William, plasterer, w side cor K and 4 w.
Hensley, Mrs. M., n side H n, btw 20 and 21 w.
Henson, Charles, cartman, s side D s, btw 13 and 13½ w.
Henson, Thomas (col) laborer, s side E, btw 3 and 4½ w.
Henson, Ellen, (col) servant, n side D s, btw 1 and 2 w.
Henson, Wm., (col) hackman, s side East Capitol, btw 3 and 4½ w.
Henshaw, Foster, machinist, e side 4½ w, btw C and Md av.
Henshaw, Joshua, clerk Marshal's Office, s side Mass av, btw 6 and 7 w.
Hepburn, Jerry, grocer, s side East Capitol, btw 1 and 2 e.
Hepburn, D., bricklayer, w side 12 w, btw C and Va av.
Hepburn, Peter, grocer, s side F s, btw 8 and 9 w.
Hepburn, George, carpenter, s side F s, btw 8 and 9 w.
Hepburn, H. C., carpenter, s side F s, btw 9 and 10 w; h 10, btw Va av and C.
Hereford, T. P., M. D., w side 7 w, btw D and E s.
Herbert, Wm., carpenter, n side H n, btw 6 and 7 w.
Hercus, George, grocer, n side Md av, btw 9 and 10 w.
Herd, John, miller, s side 2, near College, Georgetown.
Herrell, John, bricklayer, s side L n, btw Vt av and 15 w.
Herrick, George R., clerk Capitol, w side 12 w, btw I and N Y av.
Herring, ——, cor 1 and Frederick, Georgetown.
Herold, Adam G., clerk Navy Yard, n side 8 e, btw L and M s.
Hess, E., laborer, e side 13½ w, btw C and D n.
Hess, Jacob, clerk Coast Survey Office, s side East Capitol, btw 5 and 6 e.
Hess, John, tanner, cor new cut road and Fayette, Georgetown.
Hess, John, laborer, n side 7, btw Frederick and Fayette, Georgetown.
Heyzel, John, carpenter, e side 6 e, btw A and B n.
Hiberger, F. J., (Loudon &,) boards at Exchange Hotel.
Hickerson, Wm., watchman, e side 14 w, btw C and D n.
Hickerman, Joseph, (col) Boatman, w side 14 w, btw J and H n.
Hickey, Miss E., dressmaker, e side 10 w, btw C and Pa av.
Hickey, Daniel, bricklayer, n side F s, btw 1 and two w.
Hickman, Anthony, (col) whitewasher, w side 3, btw D and K n.

Abbreviations.—All points start from the Capitol; s south, n north, e east, w west, btw between, cor corner, (col) colored, av avenue, h house.

Hickman, Lewis, laborer, (col) n. side L n, btw 3 and 4 w.
Hicks, Charles, (col) cartman, n side B s, btw 3 and 4 e.
Hicks, L., (col) laborer, s side C s, btw 1 and 2 w.
Hicks, James, cabinetmaker, w side High, btw 1 and Prospect, Georgetown.
Higby, James, shoemaker, w side 10 w, btw F and G n.
Higgins, Martin, laborer, e side 2 w, btw F and G n.
Higgins, Judge, w side 17 w, btw H and I n.
Higgins, ——, (col) sexton at colored church, w side Green, near Bridge, Geo'tn.
Highfield, Mary, seamstress, n side G n, btw 22 and 23 w.
HILBUS, GEORGE, Music Store, s side Pa av. btw 10 and 11 w.
House, s side E n, btw 11 and 12 w.
Hilbus, Francis, n side D n, btw 13½ and 14 w.
Hill, Joseph, shoe store, w side 7 w, btw D and E n.
Hill, John W., barber, w side 7 w, btw I and N Y av.
Hill, Alice, widow, cor Md av. and 3 w, n side.
Hill, Isaac, wood merchant, cor Canal and 8th; h w side 9 w, btw G and H n.
Hill, Mrs. M., fancy store, s side Pa av. btw 9 and 10 w.
Hill, S. H., Treasury Dept., Prest. Board Aldermen, n side E n, btw 6 and 7 w.
Hill, Mrs. A., dressmaker, s side Pa av. btw 10 and 12 w.
Hill, Rev. S. P., s side H n, btw 15 and 16 w.
Hill, Richard A., tinner, n side F n, btw 14 and 15 w.
Hill, Mrs., tailoress, w side 10 w, btw G and H n.
Hill, George, & Co., rag warehouse, n side B n, btw 10 and 11 w.
Hill, Ann S., widow, n side H n, btw 14 and 15 w.
Hill, Clement, planter, n side H n, btw Conn av and 17 w.
Hill, Dr. F. H., e side 1 e, btw A n and East Capitol.
Hill, Mrs. M. A., e side 1 e, btw A n and East Capitol.
Hill, John, laborer, (col) e side 5 e, btw C and D s.
Hill, Caroline, (col) laundress, n side L n, btw 13 and 14 w.
Hill, Geo., paper merch't, n side Bridge s, btw Congress and Washington, Geo'tn.
Hillary, John, tavern, e side Market Space, Georgetown.
Hilgard, J. E., United States Coast Survey, w side 4½ w, btw Pa av and C.
Hillery, L., n side I s, btw 10 and 11 e.
Hillyard, Mrs. C., grocery, w side 7 w, cor L n.
Hilton, A. R., cabinetmaker, e side 13 w, btw E and F n.
Hilton, Joseph H., police officer, n side Pa av. btw 23 and 24 w.
Hilton, John P., carpenter, e side 14 w, btw I and H n.
Hilton, Joshua, bricklayer, lockkeeper, w side Washington, btw Bridge and Canal, Georgetown.
Hines, Philip, mess. Treasury Department, n side H n, btw 12 and 13 w.
Hines, Henry, n side H n, btw 18 and 19 w.
Hines, David, grocer, cor 20 and Pa av.
Hines, C., w side 20 w, btw Pa av. and H n.
Hines, A., packer Land Office, w side 20 w, btw Pa av. and H n.
Hines, Ann, (col) huckster, n side E s, btw 3 and 4 e.
Hines, Saml., clerk, n e cor 1 and Potomac, Georgetown.
Hinson, ———, clerk, n side H n, btw 18 and 19 w.
Hinton, G. W., grocer, s side Md av. btw 4½ and 6 w.
Hinton, G. W., merchant tailor, n side Pa av. btw 4½ and 6 w.
House, Md av. 1st door w of 4½ w.
Hinton, Mary A., teacher, n side D s, btw 6 and 7 w.
Hipkins, John, tinner, n side H n, btw 4 and 5 w.
Hipkins, L., cabinetmaker, n side H n, btw 4 and 5 w.
Hisker, Dr., n side L n, btw 13 and 14 w.
Hitchcock, R. J., mattress maker, s side K s, btw 10 and 11 e.
Hitz, F. & J., grocers, s side A s, btw N J av. and 1 e.
Hoban, Mrs. M., widow, w side 9 w, btw F and G n.
Hobbs, John, carpenter, n side D n, btw 14 and 15 w.
Hobbs, Wm., laborer, n side D s, btw 4½ and 6 w.
Hobbs, Lucretia, cor 3 and Warren, Georgetown.

Hobbie, S. R., w side 14 w, btw G and F n.
Hocke, Mrs. A., widow, n side 8 e, btw G and E s.
Hodge, Wm. L., Ass't Sec. Treasury, n side H n, btw 15 and 16 w.
Hodges, Silas H., Commissioner of Patents.
Hodgkin, John, laborer, w side 13½ w, btw Md av. and D s.
Hodgkins, George W., stove store, s side Pa av. btw 14 and 15 w.
House, 14, 3 doors south Pa av.
Hodgson, John W., gun and locksmith, w side 6 w, btw G and H n.
Hodgson, J. T., tinner, n side H n, btw 6 and 7 w.
Hoe, Catharine, (col) laundress, n side B n, btw 1 and 2 w.
Hoerrick, Augustus, tinner, s side A s, btw N J av. and 1 e.
Hoffman, Henry, refectory, e side 7 w, btw Pa av. and B.
Hoffman, John, hackman, s side D n, btw 1 and 2 w.
Hoffman, J., bricklayer, s side N Y av. btw 12 and 13 w.
Hogan, Philip, laborer, w side 8 w, btw G and H n.
Hogan, Miss Sarah, teacher, s side F n, btw 13 and 14 w.
Hogan, Henry, (col) messenger at Institute, s side I n, btw 12 and 13 w.
Hoking, Lewis, grocer, cor 6 w and N n.
Holcomb, Albert, lieutenant U. S. Navy, s side Pa av. btw 2 and 3 e.
Holdon, Thomas, stonecutter, n side F s, btw 2 and 3 w.
Holland, Wm., refectory, n side Pa av. btw 4½ and 6 w.
House, w side 8 w, btw G and H n.
Holland, James S., clerk Union office, w side 6 w, btw H and Mass av.
Holland, George, laborer, (col) n side L n, btw 7 and 8 w.
Holland, Isaac, ass't doorkeeper Sen., w side 17 w, btw Pa av. and H n.
Holleter, Morris, laborer, w side 10 w, btw L and M n.
Hollingshead, John S., clerk Census office, n side I n, btw 9 and 10 w.
Hollohan, John, stonecutter, w side N J av. btw D and E s.
Hollohan, John, carver, e side North Capitol, btw B and C n.
Hollran, John, laborer, n side F n, btw 2 and 3 w.
Holmead, Elizabeth, boarding, e side 4½ w, btw Pa av. and C n.
Holmead, J. B., furniture store, s side Pa av. btw 3 and 4½ w.
Holmead, Mrs., boarding h, s side Pa av, btw 3 and 4½ w.
Holmead, Anthony, grocer, s side F n, btw 9 and 10 w.
Holmead, Rev. Alfred (Grace Church,) s side B s, btw 9 and 10 w.
Holmead, L. R., grocer, cor 7 w and Md av.
Holmes, Sophia, (col) laundress, n side L n, btw 13 and 14 w.
Holt, Walter, painter, s side B s, btw 10 and 11 w.
Holtzman, G. H., clerk Indian office, s side B s, btw 13 and 13½ w.
Holtzman, James, restaurant, High, btw 1 and Prospect, at Forrest Hall.
House, e of Cotton Factory, Georgetown.
Home, Edward, steamboat hotel, e side 7 w, btw Pa av. and B n.
Hood, George, wheelwright, e side 4½ w, btw C and Md av.
Hooe, Broth. & Co., dry goods, n side La av. btw 7 and 8 w.
Hooe, P. H., merchant, n side La av. btw 7 and 8 w; h cor 8 w and La av.
Hooe, R. A., merchant, boards at Browns Hotel.
Hook & Co., coach factory, n side D n, btw 9 and 10 w.
Hook, William, (& Co.,) n side D n, btw 9 and 10 w.
HOOVER, A., & SONS, Shoe Store, s side Pa av. btw 6 and 7 w.
Hoover, C. P., (Hoover & Sons,) s side Pa av. btw 19 and 20 w.
Hoover, A. P., (Hoover & Sons,) E, btw 6 and 7 w.
Hoover, L. P., s side Pa av. btw 19 and 20 w.
Hoover, Wm., messenger Gen. Post Office, w side 6 w, btw M and N n.
Hoover, John, butcher, s side N Y av. btw 9 and 10 w.
Hoover, J. D., shoe merchant, n side La av. btw 7 and 8 w.
Hoover, Michael, drover, w side 7 w, btw O and P n.
Hopkins, Philip, tailor, n side H n, btw 4 and 5 w.
Hopkins, Margaret, (col) laundress, w side 11 w, btw L and M n.
Hopkins, John, stonecutter, n side Fourth, btw High and Market, Georgetown.
Hopkins, Mr., grocer and flour store, s side Water btw Congress and High, Geo'tn.

Abbreviations.—All points start from the Capitol; s south, n north, e east, w west, btw between, cor corner, (col) colored, av avenue, h house,

Hopkins, Captain John, brickyard, w side Congress, near West, Georgetown.
Hornberger, John, tavern, n side Bridge s, btw Congress and Washington, Geo'tn.
Horning, David, confectionery, n side F n, btw N J av. and 2 w.
Horning, J., confectionery, s side K s, btw 6 and 7 e.
Horseman, James W., waterman, s side F s, btw 7 and 8 w
Horstkamp, H., grocer, n side N Y av. btw 1 and 2 w.
Hoskins, George, stove manufacturer, w side 14 w, btw Pa av. and E n.
Hotel, Brown's, (T. P. & M. Brown,) n side Pa av, btw 6 and 7 w.
Hotel, National, (Dexter and Calvert,) n side Pa av, cor 6 w.
Hotel, United States, (Hackney,) n side Pa av, btw 3 and 4½ w.
Hotel, Gadsby's, (Gadsby,) n side Pa av, cor 3 w.
Hotel, Beers' Temperance, (Isaac Beers,) w side 3 w, btw B and C n.
Hotel, St. Charles, (H. N. Gilbert,) e side 3 w, cor Pa av.
Hotel, Baker's Franklin, (Baker,) cor D n and 8 w.
Hotel, Baker's Exchange, (Baker,) C n, btw 4½ and 6 w.
Hotel, Irving, (Thomas,) cor Pa av and 12 w.
Hotel, Steamboat, (Edward Home,) e side 7 w, btw Pa av and B n.
Hotel, Potomac, n side Pa av, btw 3 and 4½ w.
Hotel, Columbian, (J. Wingenroth,) cor 8 w and E n.
Hotel, City, (Willard,) cor Pa av and 14 w.
Hough, Lucinda, boarding house, w side 8 w, btw I and K n.
Houghton, Cylon, finisher, n side L s, btw 7 and 8 e.
Hounschild, W., upholsterer, n side Pa av. btw 17 and 18 w.
Housam, Frederick, tailor, s side F n, btw 8 and 9 w.
Houston, John H., Treasury Department, Carroll Place, btw E Capitol and A s.
Houston, Samuel A, & Co., n side Mo av. btw 4½ and 6 w.
Howard, Dr. H. P., cor 10 and F n.
Howard, Wm. E., tax clerk Corporation of Washington, s side D n, btw 2 and 3 w.
Howard, Lewis, (col) e side 11 w, btw Mass av. and K n.
Howard, Dr. F., cor 10 and F n.
Howard, Joseph, attorney, n side H n, btw 9 and 10 w.
Howard, George T., hotel, e side 11 w, cor G n.
Howard, Thomas, huckster, s side Va av, btw 1 and 2 w.
Howard, Mrs., s side 1, btw High and Potomac, Georgetown.
Howe, Richard, blacksmith, w side 8 e, btw E and G s.
Howe, Mrs. John, n side L s, btw 8 and 9 e.
Howell, Wm. P., grocer, cor 9 w and L n.
Howell & Shoemaker, flour and wholesale grocer, cor High and Water.
Howell's dwelling, e side Market, at Dr. Brewer's, Georgetown.
Howes, John, carpenter, s side D s, btw 9 and 10 w.
Howes, Horace, millwright, s side 4, btw Frederick and Fayette, Georgetown.
Howlett, John, florist, cor of 5 and N Y av.
Houye, Robert, shoemaker, s side Pa av. btw 4½ and 6 w.
Hubbard, Solomon, boarding house, s side I n, btw 6 and 7 w.
Hubbard, S. D., Postmaster Gen'l., n side Pa av. cor 16.
Hubbert, Sarah, widow, w side 12 w, btw I and K n.
Hubert, James, laborer, n side H n, btw 4 and 5 w.
Hubert, L., jeweller, n side Ohio av. btw 13½ and 14 w.
Huggins, Joseph, jeweller, n side Pa av. btw 12 and 13 w.
House, s side Pa av., btw 13 and 13½ w.
Hugh, Miss Polly, e side Congress, btw Gay and Bridge, Georgetown.
Hughes, J. O., nursery, cor 7 and Va av. Island.
Hughes, Charles, clerk Treasury Department, w side 12 w, btw N Y av. and H n.
Hughes, Wm., grocer, n side G n, btw 1 and 2 e.
Hughes, George W., baker, e side 7 w, btw M and N n.
Hughes, Eden, merchant tailor, n side Pa av. cor 13 w; h cor 13 w and N Y av.
Hughes, Mrs. Ann, boarding house, s side D n, btw 12 and 13 w.
Hughes, Mrs., widow, s side I n, btw 10 and 11 w.
Hughes, Ezekiel, Editor "Advocate," n e cor Gay and High.
House, e side West, btw Congress and Washington, Georgetown.

Abbreviations.—All points start from the Capitol; s south, n north, e east, w west, btw between, cor corner, (col) colored, av avenue, h honse.

Hughes, John E., baker, s side Bridge, btw Congress and Washington, Georgetown.
Hughes, Mrs., huckster, n side Bridge s, btw Green and Montgomery, Georgetown.
Hughes, Robert, baker, w side Montgomery, btw Beall and Dumbarton, Geo'tn.
Hull, Wm. H., clerk Pension office, e side 7 w, btw I and K n.
Hume, Francis, clerk Post Office, w side 11 w, btw G and H n.
Humphreys, ——, dentist, n side E n, btw 13 and 14 w.
Humphreys, Mrs. Gertrude, widow, w side 9 w, btw G and H n.
Humphreys, Hezekiah, laborer, n side Mass av. btw 2 and 3 w.
Hungerford, Henry, clerk Interior Department, s side N Y av. btw 12 and 13 w.
HUNT, WM., (attorney at law, and ag't for claims,) opposite Odd Fellow's Hall 7 w.
Hunt, Taylor, tailor, w side 7 w, btw L and M n.
Hunt, Dr. R. F., dentist, n side Pa av. btw 9 and 10 w.
Hunt, Wm. E., air furnace dealer, n side D n, btw 14 and 15 w.
Hunt, Mrs. Wm., widow, n side La av. btw 6 and 7 w.
Hunt, Wm. B., tailor, w side 8 w, btw P and Q n.
Hunt, A., printer, e side 12 w, btw A and C n.
Hunt, Thomas, sergeant garrison, n side L s, btw 3 and 4 e.
HUNTER, ALFRED, Book store, n side Pa av. btw 3 and 4½ w.
Hunter, Mrs. L., widow, s side C n, btw 4½ and 6 w.
Hunter, Wm., clerk General Post Office Dep't, e side 12 w, btw N Y av. and H n.
Hunter, Wm., chief clerk State Department, Cox's Row, Georgetown.
Hunter, Gen. Thomas, n side 1, btw Market and Frederick, Georgetown.
Hunter, Thos., cooper shop, Water, btw Congress and Jefferson, Georgetown.
Hunter, Charles S., paper merchant, w side High, btw 1 and 2, Georgetown.
Hunter, Mrs., w side Jefferson, near Water, Georgetown.
Hunter, Thomas, shoemaker, e side Market Space, Georgetown.
HURDLE, THOMAS, Carpenter, cor 4½ and Md av; h, e side 4½, btw I and K n.
Hurdle, Alfred, clerk, w side 7 w, btw Va av. and D s.
Hurdle, Samuel, bricklayer, e side 20 w, btw I and H n.
Hurdle, Richard, bricklayer, w side 18 w, btw K and I n.
Hurdle, Jas., bricklayer, n side Dumbarton, btw Green and Montgomery, Geo'tn.
Hurdle, Henry, grocer, e side High, btw Dumbarton and Beall, Georgetown.
Hurdle, Noble, bricklayer, e side High, btw West and Road, Georgetown.
Hurley, Wm., laborer, s side N n, btw 11 and 12 w.
Hurley, James, omnibus driver, s side N n, btw 11 and 12 w.
Hutchins, Wm., (col) laborer, s side B s, btw 1 and 2 e.
Hutchins, Wm. H., bricklayer, w side Washington, btw Stoddard and West, Geo'tn.
Hutchinson, John, wood & coal merchant, w side 1 e, btw A and B s.
House, O s, btw 2 and 3 e.
Hutchinson, Thomas, grocer., w side 7 e, btw G and I s.
House, n side I s, btw 11 and 13 e.
Hutchison, Jerry, (col) laborer, n side Mass av. btw 12 and 13 w.
Hutchison, S., n side I n, btw 19 and 20 w.
Hutchison, Susan, widow, w side 1 w, btw Pa av. and B n.
Hutton, Mrs. S. R., n side H n, btw 17 and 18 w.
Hutton, Mrs. C. S., milliner, n side E s, btw 6 and 7 w.
Hutton, George, blacksmith, n side M s, btw 9 and 10 e.
HYATT, R. G., Dry Goods, w side 7 w, btw I and N Y av.
House, s side I n, btw 6 and 7 w.
Hyatt, Seth, s side Pa av, btw 6 and 7 w.
Hyde, Richard, laborer, cor 8 w and M n.
Hyde, Mrs. E. D., widow, s side E n, btw 7 and 8 w.
Hyde, Anthony, clerk, e side Washington, btw Dumbarton and Gay, Georgetown.
Hyder, Mrs. Eliz., n side High, btw West and Road, Georgetown.

I.

IARDELLA, FRANCIS C., Hardware Store, w side 7 w, near cor I n.
Iardella, (& Thaw) Dorsey's Hotel, cor 7 w and I n.

Abbreviations.—All points start from the Capitol; s south, n north, e east, w west, btw between, cor corner, (col) colored, av avenue, h house.

Iardella, John, professor of music, boards at Mrs. Bannerman's.
Iardella, Nicholas, clerk Treasury Department, s side Pa av, btw 1 and 2 e.
Iardella, Charles, clerk Coast Survey, s side Pa av, btw 1 and 2 e.
Iddins, J. V., shoemaker, n side Pa av, btw 17 and 18 w.
Indermauer, Margaret, boarding and confectionery, e side 7 w, btw B and Md av.
Ingersoll, Mrs. A., boarding and dressmaker, w side 9 w, btw H and I n.
Ingham, Washington, (col) boarding, w side 4½ w, btw La av and C n.
Ingman, John, shoemaker, e side North Capitol, btw G and H n.
Ingle, Joseph, clerk, e side N J av, btw B and C s.
Ingle, Henry, clerk City Post Office, n side D n, btw 9 and 10 w.
Ingle, John, clerk, e side N J av, btw B and C s.
Ingle, C., attorney at law, s side La av, btw 4½ and 6 w.
Ingraham, Mrs. Margaret A., mantua maker, e side 7 w, btw F and G n.
Ingraham, Benj. T., clerk Land office, s side N Y av, btw 9 and 10 w.
Ingram, Wm., (col) laborer, e side 18 w, btw K and L n.
Insurance Company, Franklin, cor 7 w and D n.
Insurance Company, Firemen's, cor 7 w and La av.
Insurance Company, Potomac, n side Bridge street, btw Congress and Washington, Georgetown.
Iron works, Water, east of Aqueduct, Georgetown.
Irving, William, clerk Census office, boards cor 4½ and Pa av.
Irving House, (John Thomas,) cor Pa av and 12 w.
Irving, David, tobacconist, s side D s, btw 9 and 10 w.
Irving, Thomas, U. S. M., w side 11 e, btw G and I s.
Isamann, H., musician, n side G s, btw 6 and 7 e.
Israel & Green, auctioneers, e side 7 w, btw La av and D.
Ivey, Mrs. Catharine, teacher, n side G s btw 7 and 8 e.

J.

Jack, James, w side 4½, btw Pa av and Mo av.
Jack, Mary, dressmaker, w side 4½, btw Pa av and Mo av.
Jackson, Andrew, plasterer, n side Ohio av, btw 13½ and 14 w.
Jackson, W. R., s side S C av. btw 11 and 12 e.
Jackson, V. R., grocer, cor N Y av and 12.
Jackson, Mary Jane, tailoress, w side 11 w, btw F and G n.
Jackson, James, wheelwright, e side 7 w, btw G and H n.
Jackson Hall, n side Pa av, btw 3 and 4½ w.
Jackson, B. L., Brothers & Co., grocers, s side Pa av, btw 6 and 7 w.
Jackson, W. B., (Brothers & Co.,) same place.
Jackson, Mrs., dressmaker, n side West, btw Congress and Washington, G'town.
Jackson, Frederick, wheelwright, n side Beall, btw High and Congress, G'town.
Jackson, R. P., attorney, s side Bridge, btw High and Potomac, Georgetown.
Jackson, Thomas, currier, n side High, btw Bridge and Canal, Georgetown.
Jackson, Eliza, (col) laundress, w side 11 w, btw L and M n.
Jackson, Pompey, (col) cart driver, w side 4½, btw Va av and F s.
Jackson, Jane, (col) laundress, w side 10 w, btw M and N n.
Jackson, S., (col) laborer, w side 4 e, btw K and L s.
Jackson, James F., (col) wheelwright, s side H n, btw 6 and 7 w.
Jackson, N., (col) brickmaker, e side 18 w, btw K and L n.
Jacobi, A., tailor, n side Pa av, btw 14 and 15 w; h F, btw 11 and 12 w.
Jacobi, Wm., confectioner, n side H n, btw 18 and 19 w.
Jacobs, C., tailor, w side 7 w, btw E and F s.
Jacobs, Mrs., laundress, w side 7 w, btw G and H n.
Jacobs, George K., machinist, w side 12 w, btw C and D s.
Jocobs, Mrs., widow, n side B n, btw 2 and 3 w.
Jacobs, C., laborer, w side 12 e, near bridge.
Jairdain, Harriet, widow, s side D s, btw 3 and 4½ w.
James, Mrs. M. W., boarding house, s side F n, btw 12 and 13 w.

Abbreviations.—All points start from the Capitol; s south, n north, e east, w west, btw between, cor corner, (col) colored, av avenue, h house.

James, Charles H., clerk at Corcoran & Riggs, e side 14 w, btw F and G n.
James, R., butcher, n side G n, btw 18 and 19 w.
James, Saml., e side Vt av, btw H and I n.
Jameson, E., (col) hackman, n side I n, btw 13 and 14 w.
Jameson, J. M., w side 2 e, btw B and C s.
Janney, Ann, boarding house, w side 8 w, btw Pa av and D.
Janney, Henry, shoe store, w side 8 w, btw D and E n.
Janvier, Benj. A., clerk Treasury Department, w side 9 w, btw F and G n.
Jarboe, Thomas, carpenter, e side 6 w, btw Mass av and K.
Jarvis, S., laborer, s side L n, btw 6 and 7 w.
Jarvis, John, marine, e side 11 e, btw G and I s.
Jasper, Wm., hack driver, (col) n side K n, btw 21 and 22 w.
Jeet, John, mate "Thomas Collyer," w side 7 w, btw G and H s.
Jeffers, Mrs., widow, n side Mo av, btw 3 and 4½ w.
Jefferson, Ferdinand, assistant editor Republican office, w side 10 w, btw L and M n.
Jenkens, Wm. T., blacksmith, w side 7 w, btw L and M s.
Jenkins, Wm., stonecutter, w side 7 w, btw P and Q n.
Jenkins, D. B., grocer, n side Md av, btw 13½ and 14 w.
Jenkins, Miss Elizabeth, confectionary, w side 6 w, btw D and E n.
Jenkins, Thornton A., Lieut. U. S. N., s side G n, btw 20 and 21 w.
Jenkins, Francis, blacksmith, e side 10 w, btw K and L s.
Jessup, Gen. Thos., U. S. A., s side F n, btw 12 and 13 w.
Jett, Mrs., cake shop, n side Water, btw High and Congress, Georgetown.
Jeubert, John, confectioner, w side 7 w, btw L and M n.
Jewell, Thomas, clerk, n side High, btw Beall and West, Georgetown.
Jewell, William, clerk to Corporation, n e cor Gay and High, Georgetown.
Jewell, Miss Ann, school, cor Gay and High, Georgetown.
Jewell, George, notary, cor Gay and High, Georgetown.
Jewett, J. C., & Co., druggists, s side F s, btw 7 and 8 w.
Jillard, George, paint and oil store, n side Pa av, btw 12 and 13 w.
House, n side H n, btw 11 and 12 w.
Johns, Thomas, clerk, n side I n, btw 9 and 10 w.
Johnson, James, shoemaker, cor 7 w and H n.
Johnson, James, butcher, e side 4½ w, btw M and N s.
Johnson, Derbin, laborer, n side Md av, btw 13½ and 14 w.
Johnson, Wm., messenger Senate, cor 8 w and L n.
Johnson, P. C., chief clerk Bureau of Construction, Navy Dep't, s side E n, btw 9 and 10 w.
Johnson, Martin, clerk Post Office Department, n side E n, btw 9 and 10 w.
Johnson, John M., w side 6 w, btw H and Mass av.
Johnson, L., n side G n, btw 10 and 11 w.
Johnson, W. R., w side 12 w, btw E and F n.
Johnson, Wm., cabinetmaker, n side Mass av, btw 9 and 10 w.
Johnson, Peter, chief clerk Pension office, n side Mass av, btw 13 and 14 w.
Johnson, George, s side K n, btw 25 and 26 w.
Johnson, Ann, widow, n side M n, btw 7 and 8 w.
Johnson, T. W., dry goods, s side Pa av, btw 19 and 20 w.
Johnson, Dr. R., n side Pa av, btw 24 and 25 w.
Johnson, D., laborer, s side E s, btw 7 and 8 e.
Johnson, John H., grocer, cor 7 w and E n; h n side I n, btw 4 and 5 w.
Johnson, Dr. Wm. P., opposite City Post Office, 7 w.
Johnson, George, messenger Treasury Department, s side Md av, btw 6 and 7 w.
Johnson, Samuel, messenger House of Representatives, e side 8 w, btw L and M n.
Johnson, Lorenzo Dow, clerk Census office, boards at Mrs. Kesley's.
Johnson, H. D., office opposite Treasury Department.
Johnson, Richard, assistant Examiner Patent Office, w side 17 w, btw H and I n.
Johnson, Moses, music teacher, e side 20 w, btw E and F n.
Johnson, James H., coach painter, n side F s, btw 3 and 4½ w.
Johnson, Robert W., painter, n side C s, btw 13 and 13½ w.
Johnson, John, clerk City Post Office, w side 2 e, btw B and C s.

Johnson, Thomas, laborer, e side 7 e, btw Va av and L s.
Johnson, G. W., cabinetmaker, n side L s, btw 7 and 8 e.
Johnson, James, blacksmith, cor Half and 7 w.
Johnson, French, boardinghouse, s side Bridge, east of market-house, Georgetown.
Johnson, Robert, shoemaker, w side Frederick, btw 1st and 2d, Georgetown.
Johnson, William, carpenter, w side Washington, btw Bridge and Canal, G'town.
Johnson, Robert, (col) hackdriver, e side Montgomery, near Bridge, Georgetown.
Johnson, H., (col) laborer, n side F n, btw 21 and 22 w.
Johnson, R., (col) waiter, s side B s, btw 4 and 5 e.
Johnson, W., (col) w side 14 w, btw H and I n.
Johnson, Benj. (col) laborer, e side 18 w, btw K and L n.
Johnson, Thomas, (col) butcher, s side L n, btw 3 and 4 w.
Johnson, Rachel, (col) laundress, s side F n, btw 6 and 7 w.
Johnson, Richard, (col) barber, s side Pa av, btw 3 and 4½ w.
Johnson, C., (col) hackman, w side 3 w, btw C and Va av.
Johnson, John, (col) laborer, w side 7 w, btw E and F s.
Johnson, T., (col) cartman, n side Va av, btw 3 and 4½ w.
Johnston, C. V., dressmaker, e side 10 w, btw C n and Pa av.
Joiner, James H., blacksmith, cor Market and 2d, Georgetown.
Jolly, John, e side 4 e, btw M and N s.
Jones, Charles Lee, w side 3 w, btw B and C n.
Jones, William, blacksmish, w side 4½ w, btw P and Q s.
Jones, Wm. H., grocer, cor K and 7 w.
Jones, Mrs. S., widow, w side 8 w, btw F and G s.
Jones, Mrs. Emma, boarding, cor 9 w and F n.
Jones, J. W., Police Capitol, boards at Mrs. Williams', Pa av.
Jones, R., Lieut. U. S. A., cor 10 and F n.
Jones, Dr. William, s side C n, btw 2 and 3 w.
Jones, Wm. O., carpenter, n side I n, btw 7 and 8 w.
Jones, Charles S., n side H n, btw 9 and 10 w.
Jones, Noah, huckster, e side 10 w, btw E and F s.
Jones, Thomas, shoemaker, n side F n, btw 24 and 25 w.
Jones, Wm., watchman, s side East Capitol, btw 5 and 6 e.
Jones, Thomas, woodmerchant, w side 3 e, btw M and N s.
House, n side M s, btw N J av and 3 e.
Jones, Raphael, grocer, e side 8 w, btw Pa av and D n.
Jones, Rhyre, finisher, n side I s, btw 9 and 10 e.
Jones, James, painter, n side G s, btw 6 and 7 e.
Jones, William, grocer, n side High, near Potomac; h, s side Prospect, btw High and Potomac, Georgetown.
Jones, Washington, (col) laborer, e side 8 w, btw L and M n.
Jones, P., (col) waiter, n side D n, btw 13 and 14 w.
Jones, Mrs. Mary, (col) laundress, n side G n, btw 13 and 14 w.
Jones, Mrs. Mary, (col) w side 10 w, btw E and F n.
Jones, Wm., (col) laborer, e side 20 w, btw K and L n.
Jones, N. (col) laundress, w side 21 w, btw K and L n.
Jones, A., (col) feed store, s side La av, btw 9 and 10 w.
Jones, Joseph, (col) laborer, w side 3 w, btw C and Va av.
Jones, J., (col) laborer, s side Va av, btw 4½ and 6 w.
Jordon, J. W., carpenter, s side 6 w, btw D and La av.
House, s side E n, btw 9 and 10 w.
Jordon, John A., sashmaker, n side C n, btw 13 and 14 w.
Joseph, Peter, watchman, n side I s, btw 3 and 4 e.
JOST, B., Liquor Store, s side Pa av, btw 17 and 18 w,
Jourdon, T., n side L n, btw 8 and 9 w.
Joy, Wm., cabinetmaker, e side 8 w, btw L and M n.
Joy, Joseph, w side 13½ w, btw B and C s.
Joy, Morris, laborer, s side A n, btw N J av and 2 w.
Joyce, Edward, (col) e side N J av, btw B and Pa av.
Joyce, John J., grocer, cor F n and 13 w.

Abbreviations.—All points start from the Capitol; s south, n north, e east, w west, btw between, cor corner, (col) colored, av avenue, h house.

Joyce, Michael, stonemason, s side N n, btw 11 and 12 w.
Joyce, Andrew J., blacksmith, e side 14 w, btw C and D n.
Joyce, A. J., wheelwright, cor E and 14 w.
Joyce, Mrs. Ann, widow, w side 18 w, btw H and I n.
Joyce, Mrs. Susan, s side B s, btw 1 and 2 e.
Judge, John M., 12, btw H and N Y av.
Juenimann, George, refectory, s side Pa av, btw 4½ and 6 w.
Julien, Miss, school, e side 13 w, btw G and H n.
Junkin, Rev. D. X., (F st. Presbyterian Church) s side K n, btw 11 and 12 w.

K.

Kable, John B., carpenter, n side F n, btw 11 and 12 w.
Kahl, J. F., piano forte manufactory, n side N Y av, btw 17 and 18 w.
Kain, Patrick, grocer, w side 15 w, btw L and M n.
Kain, Adam, carpenter, 5 w, btw N and O n.
Kaiser, Henry, cabinetmaker, e side 8 w, btw L and M n.
Kaiser, John C., locks, e side High, btw Gay and Bridge, Georgetown.
Kaisser, H., baker, s side F n, btw 13 and 14 w.
Kaller, Michael, laborer, n side G n, btw 2 and 3 w.
Kane, T., s side G n, btw 18 and 19 w.
Kapper, John, bootmaker, s side Pa av, btw 4½ and 6 w.
Karll, Henry, laborer, w side 8 w, btw Pa av and D n.
Kavanagh, Thomas, fruit dealer, e side 8 w, btw L and M n.
Kay, J. W., grocer, n side Mass av, btw 4 and 5 w.
Kazanberger, John, refectory, e side 7 w, btw Pa av and B n.
Kealey, D. E., letter carrier, n side 8 e, btw K and L s.
Keath, John P., painter, e side N J av, btw M and N s.
Keefe, Arthur, carpenter, w side 3 w, btw M and N s.
Keefe, William, grocer, n side Pa av, btw 21 and 22 w,
Keefer, Joseph A., tailor, w side 9 w, btw D andE n.
Keese, A. E. L., police officer and collector, office at Squire Donn's. House N n, near 5 w.
Kearn, Robert, mess. Library Capitol, e side 8 w, btw L and M n.
Kearney, Col. Robert, Top'l Engineers, n side First, btw Matket and Frederick, Georgetown.
Kearny, Mrs. Kate, widow, e side 11 w, btw G and H n.
Keenan, James, laborer, e side 4½ w, btw E and F s.
Keener, Patrick, laborer, n side D n, btw 12 and 13 w.
Keifer, John A. H., tailor, at Freeman's, w side High, btw Prospect and First, Georgetown.
Keiger, Alfred, (col) hackdriver, n side H n, btw 5 and 6 w.
Kernan, Mr., "Sun" carrier, e side Dumbarton, east part, Georgetown.
Keithly, Francis, blacksmith, n side M s, btw 9 and 10 e.
Keithly, John, carpenter, w side 3 e, btw M and N s.
Keller, J. P., clerk in War Department, e side Pres. Square, btw Pa av and H n.
Keller, Mrs. S. A., boardinghouse, e side President Square, btw Pa av and H n.
Kelley, N., ornamental painter, w side 8 w, btw L and M n.
Kelley, William, watchman Department Interior, n side M n, btw 14 and 15 w.
Kelley, Henry, machinist, w side 2 e, btw B and C s.
Kelligan, James, hackdriver, s side F n, btw 6 and 7 w.
Kelligan, Richard, clerk Census office, s side G n, btw 13 and 14 w.
Kelly, John, grocer, e side 4½ w, btw C and Md av.
Kelly, Thomas, stonemason, e side 4½ w, btw Md av and Mo av.
Kelly, Michael, laborer, w side 6 w, btw D and E n.
KELLY, JOHN, Farmer's Hotel, cor 8 w and D n.
Kelly, John, laborer, s side F n, btw 6 and 7 w.
Kelly, Thomas, blacksmith, e side 10 w, btw E and F n.
KELLY, JAMES, Stove Manufactory, n side Pa av, btw 17 and 18 w.

Abbreviations.—All points start from the Capitol; s soath, n north, e east, w west, btw between, cor corner, (col) colored, av avenue, h house.

Kelly, J. M., boardinghouse, n side La av, btw 6 and 7 w.
Kelsey, John, bricklayer, n side L s, btw 3 and 4 e.
Kenan, James, hackman, n side B s, btw 1 and 2 w.
Kendall, W., blacksmith, n side B n, btw 2 and 3 w.
House C, btw 4½ and 6 w.
Kendrick, Mrs. Ann, widow, w side 11 w, btw Md av and E s.
Keney, Mrs., grocery, s side East Capitol, btw 1 and 2 e.
Kengla, Mrs. Jacob, boardinghouse, High, btw Canal and Water, Georgetown.
Kengla, Henry, butcher, out High, w side, extreme north, Georgetown.
Kennedy, Mrs., s side Ia av, btw 3 and 4½ w.
Kennedy, William A., clerk General Post Office, w side 8 w, btw G and H n.
Kennedy, Thomas, stonecutter, e side 3 w, btw F and G n.
Kennedy, John, stonecutter, e side 3 w, btw F and G n.
Kennedy, John P., Secretary of the Navy, n side I n, btw 17 and 18 w.
Kennedy, Joseph C. G., Superintendent Census, n side H n, btw 9 and 10 w.
Kennedy, C., stonecutter, s side F s, btw 2 and 3 w.
Kennedy, William, blacksmith, w side 10 e, btw G and I s.
Kennedy, James, (col) barber, w side 11 w, btw E and F n.
Kennon, P. S., printer, n side G n, btw 22 and 23 w.
Keppler, S., clerk Post Office Department, n side B n, btw 2 and 3 w.
Kerbey, James P., n side D n, btw 14 and 15 w.
Kernan, Charles, grocer, e side 4½ w, btw Va av and D.
Keron, John, carpenter, s side E n, btw 20 and 21 w.
Kerr, James D., clerk War Department, e side 13 w, btw F and G n.
Kerr, W. W. S., hatter, s side Va av, btw 10 and 11 w.
Kesley, Mrs. Julia A., boarding house, s side Pa av, btw 3 and 4½ w.
Kesley, Mrs., teacher, s side East Capitol, btw 1 and 2 e.
Key, J. W., grocer, cor 4 w and Mass av.
Key, P. B., attorney, n side C n, btw 3 and 4½ w.
Key, Mrs. John, widow, n side H n, btw 15 and 16 w.
Key, G., (col) hackman, n side N n, btw 14 and 15 w.
Keyworth, Mrs. E., dressmaker, s side Pa av, btw 4½ and 6 w.
Keyworth, R., jeweller, n side Pa av, btw 9 and 10 w.
Kibbey, W. B., leather store, s side Pa av, btw 6 and 7 w ; h C, btw 3 and 4½ w.
Kibbey, John B., & Co., grocers, n side La av, btw 7 and 8 w.
KIDWELL & LAURENCE, Druggists, cor 14 w and Pa av.
Kidwell, John, laborer, e side 7 e, btw E and G s.
Kidwell, ——, paver, w side 8 w, btw L and M n.
Kidwell, George F., clerk lumber yard, w side 18 w, btw H and I n.
Kidwell, A., moulder, e side 6 e, btw G and I s.
Kidwell, James H., grocer, w side High, btw 2d and 3d, Georgetown.
Kidwell, John L., druggist, n w cor High and Prospect, Georgetown.
Kieckhoffer, Adolphus, Corcoran & Riggs' Bank, e side 13 w, btw E and F n.
Killmon, J. T., grocer, cor Pa av and 1 w.
Kimball, John S., machinist, s side L s, btw 4½ and 6 w.
Kimmell, A. F., livery stable, C n, btw 4½ and 6 w.
King, John S., carpenter, w side 8 w, btw G and H n.
King, William, clerk in Navy Department, boards at Mrs. Fletcher's.
King, E. H., cabinet maker, s side E n, btw 10 and 11 w.
House w side 10 w, btw E and F n.
King, James, agency office, n side Pa av, btw 14 and 15 w.
King, James, printer, s side E n, btw 6 and 7 w.
King, Mrs. Charles, boardinghouse, cor 11 w and F n.
King, William W., clerk Land Office, n side F n, btw 13 and 14 w.
King, William R., Vice President U S, s side C n, btw 3 and 4½ w.
King, Mrs. Rosanna, s side D n, btw 2 and 3 w.
King, C. B., portrait painter, e side 12 w, btw E and F n.
King, J. W., fancy store, s side I n, btw 19 and 20 w.
King, H., principal clerk post office, n side H n, btw 7 and 8 w.
King, Joseph W., auxiliary guard, w side 13 w, btw C and D s.

King, Charles, clerk Navy Department, w side 17 w, btw Pa av and H n.
King, Miss Mary Anna, n side G n, btw 17 and 18 w.
King, John, messenger in Penitentiary, n side N s, btw 4½ and 6 w.
King, Benjamin, laborer, n side N s, btw 4½ and 6 w.
King, Thomas A., weighmaster at market-house, n side C s, btw 3 and 4½ w.
King, William, laborer, e side 4 e, btw L and M s.
King, Martin, grocer, w side 7 e, btw I and K s.
King, Z. M. P., grocer, w side Vt av, btw H and I n.
King, William, cabinetmaker, e side Congress, btw Canal and Water, Georgetown.
King, John, cabinetmaker, e side Congress, btw Canal and Water, Georgetown.
King, John H., agent and farmer, e side Market space, near Canal, Georgetown.
King, Wm. Albert, Market space, near Canal, Georgetown.
King, Mr., e side High, btw Gay and Dumbarton, Georgetown.
King, Benjamin, tanner, e side Frederick, btw 4th and 5th, Georgetown.
King, John A., grocer, e side Fayette, cor Second, Georgetown.
King, Nace, tavern, n side Water, btw Potomac and High, Georgetown.
King Henry, Insurance office, n side Bridge, btw Congress and Washington, G'tn.
King, Alexander, grocer, s w cor Second and Lingan, Georgetown.
King, Mr., laborer at Libbey's, e side Dumbarton, east part, Georgetown.
King, E., (col) gardener, s side E n, btw 17 and 18 w.
King, Isaiah, (col) brickmaker, n side B s, btw 4 and 5 e.
King, Thomas, (col) w side South Capitol, btw C and D s.
King, Julia, (col) laundress, n side L n, btw 13 and 14 w.
Kinsday, Benjamin, cor Md av and 6 w.
KIRBY, SAMUEL, Cabinetmaker, w side 8 w, btw Pa av and D n.
House e side 8 w, btw D and E n.
Kirby, F. T., clerk Pension Office, e side 10 w, btw E and F n.
Kirby, Charles T., printer, s side I n, btw 4 and 5 w.
Kirby, Mary, widow, w side 20 w, btw Pa av and H n.
Kirk, George, sash and blind factory, w side 7 w, btw F and G s.
Kirk, G. E., painter, s side La av, btw 6 and 7 w.
House F, btw 7 and 8.
KIRKPATRICK, JOHN, Marble-yard, n side E n, btw 13 and 14 w.
House s side D n, btw 13 and 13½ w.
Kirkwood, Mrs., boarding house, e side 12 w, btw F and G n.
KIRKWOOD & McGILL, Printers, cor 8 w and D n.
Kirkwood, J., (& McGill,) e side 12 w, btw F and G n.
Kitchen, Jesse, watchman, w side Market, btw 3 and 4, Georgetown.
Kleiber, Mrs. Elizabeth, s side E n, btw 9 and 10 w.
Kley, F., professor of music, s side La av, btw 4½ and 6 w.
Klomann, Charles K., refectory, w side 7 w, btw D and E n.
Klopfer, Christian, printer, e side 7 w, btw F and G n.
Klopfer, C. G., shoe store, s side Pa av, btw 6 and 7 w; h F, btw 10 and 11 w.
Klopfer, Edward, printer, s side D n, btw 5 and 6 w.
Klopfer, Henry A., grocer, n side 8 e, btw I and K s.
Klotz, George, laborer, e side 3 w, btw G and Mass av.
Klotz, Frederick, tailor, n side G n, btw 2 and 3 e.
Knippel, Daniel bootmaker, e side 11 w, btw G and H n.
Knight, John, engraver, s side Md av, btw 11 and 12 w.
Knight, George, paver, e side 6 w, btw N and O n.
Knight, Samuel M., agent for claims, e side 11 w, btw E and Pa av.
Knight, Frederick, w side 13½, btw Md av and D s.
Knight, C., stonecutter, s side B s, btw 1 and 2 e.
Knight, Perry, bricklayer, s side E s, btw 4½ and 6 w.
Knight, Rev. Edward A., (St. Peter's Ch., Capitol Hill,) w side 2 e, btw D and C s.
Knight, Mrs. Jane, boardinghouse, n side Second, btw High and Potomac, G'town.
Knot, grocer, n e cor Green and Dumbarton, Georgetown.
Knott, George A., confectioner, s side Pa av, btw 2 and 3 w.
Knott, J., bookbinder, w side 6 w, btw D and E n.

Knott, J. H., wood and coal merchant, s side I n, btw 15 and 16 w.
House n side G n, btw 14 and 15 w.
Knott, William, miller, e side Warren, Georgetown.
Knowles, Edwin, (Thompson & Co.,) merchant tailor, n side Pa av, btw 3 and 4½ w.
Knowles, John, carpenter, e side 10 w, btw L and M n.
Knowles, Mr. Thomas, grocer, s e cor Bridge and Market space; h, First, btw High and Potomac, Georgetown.
Knowles, E., carpenter, s side M n, btw 12 and 13 w.
Knox, James, cartman, w side 1 w, btw Pa av and B n.
Koch, A., turner, s side Pa av, btw 12 and 13 w.
Koestner, J., shoemaker, n side Mass av, btw N J av and 4 w.
Koff, Mr., clerk, e side Frederick, btw 2d and 3d, Georgetown.
Kolb, George, tailor, e side 3 w, btw G n and Mass av.
Kolb, Jacob, confectioner, n side F n, btw 11 and 12 w.
Koones, E., clerk Census office, s side D n, btw 2 and 3 w.
Koons & Eurich, blacksmiths, s side Pa av, btw 1 and 2 e.
Korph, H. G., tinner, Bridge street, btw Congress and High, Georgetown.
Krafft, G. S., baker, s side Pa av, btw 17 and 18 w.
Krafft, J. M., baker, cor 12 w and F n.
Kraft, Christ., messenger Coast Survey, w side N J av, btw D and E s.
Krober, ——, n side K n, btw 19 and 20 w.
Kroff, C., confectioner, cor 11 w and Pa av; h e side 11 w, btw E and F n.
Krophizer, J. E., shoemaker, e side High, btw Gay and Congress, Goorgetown.
Krouse, Nancy and Edward, s side Fourth, btw Market and First, Georgetown.
Krouse, Ebbert, tavern, n side Water, btw Potomac and High, Georgetown.
Kuhl, H., refectory, n side Pa av, btw 12 and 13 w.
Kuhland, N., blacksmith, w side 20 w, btw L and M n.
Kummer, Charles, cabinetmaker, w side 8 w, btw D and E n.
Kurton, Richard, laborer, s side Va av, btw 8 and 9 e.
Kurtz, David, watchman War Dep't, s side F n, btw 9 and 10 w.
Kurtz, John D., U S Engineers, s side Gay, btw Congress and High, Georgetown.

L.

Lakenam, Charles, tailor, e side 6 w, btw H and I n.
Lallaouette, E., tailor, s side Pa av, btw 19 and 20 w.
Lacy, William H., moulder, n side E s, btw 4½ and 6 w.
Lacey, Emanuel, drayman, w side 3 w, btw I and K n.
Ladd, Mrs. H. G., n side B n, btw Del av and 1 e.
Ladde, Mrs. V. C., w side 10 w, btw Md av and C s.
Ladies' Union Benev. Employm't Soc'y, (branch) s side A s, btw N J av and 1 e.
Lafayette Square, north of President's House.
Lafontaine, Mrs., huckstress, s side Md av, btw 4½ and 6 w.
Laird, William, sen., at Mrs. Lang's hotel, Georgetown.
Laird, William, jun., cashier Farmers and Mechanics' Bank, cor Bridge and Congress, Georgetown.
Lairdick, J., (col) laborer, n side N, btw 9 and 10 w.
Lamb, Mrs. E., boarding, s side Pa av, btw 14 and 15 w.
Lamb, F., razormaker, s side Pa av, btw 12 and 13 w.
Lamb, George, saddler, n side Pa av, btw 12 and 13 w.
House, s side Pa av, btw 14 and 15 w.
Lambelin, Charles, coachmaker, e side 8 w, btw L and M n.
Lancaster, B., (col) laborer, w side 15 w, btw L and M n.
Lane, Charles H., furnishing store, n side Pa av, btw 4½ and 6 w.
House n side Ia av, btw 1 and 2 w.
Lane, George A., feed store, s side Bridge, 3 doors east Jefferson, Georgetown.
Lane, Mrs. M. L., milliner, s side Bridge, btw High and Congress, Georgetown.
Landly, Francis, carpenter, w side N J av, btw L and M s.

Abbreviations.—All points start from the Capitol; s south, n north, e east, w west, btw between, cor corner, (col) colored, av avenue, h house.

Lang, Mrs. Eleanor, and John Lang, hotel, s side Bridge, two doors from High' Georgetown.
Lange, John, watchmaker, e side 7 w, btw F and G n.
Lammond, Peter, clerk Treasury Department, s side L n, btw 15 and 16 w.
LAMMOND, A., Fancy Store, e side 7 w, btw D and E n.
House Me av, btw 3 and 4½ w.
Langfelt, Mary A., trimming store, e side 2 w, btw F and G n.
Landers, L., (col) barber, s side E n, btw 10 and 11 w.
Landrick, Sarah, (col) laundress, e side 2 w, btw F and G n.
Landvoight, D., widow, e side 11 w, btw E and Pa av.
Langley, Thos. H., huckster, w side 7 w, btw L and M n.
Langley, George T., bricklayer, n side L n, btw 9 and 10 w.
Langley, W., baker, n side East Capitol, btw 1 and 2 e.
Langley, Samuel, blacksmith, e side 11 e, btw M and N s.
Langley, Joseph, laborer, n side M s, btw 9 and 10 e.
Langley, John, shoemaker, n side M s, btw 7 and 8 e.
Langley, James, confectioner, n side L s, btw 4 and 5 e.
Langton, Mrs. C. A. T., s side A s, btw N J av and 1 e.
Lanham, M. A., widow, n side K n, btw 15 and 16 w.
Lanphier, Mrs. Eliza, millinery store, s side Pa av, btw 9 and 10 w.
Lansdale, Henry N., carpenter, n side I n, btw 4 and 5 w.
Lanum, Margaret, seamstress, e side 3 e, btw I s and Va av.
Laporte, Eugene, carpenter, w side 11 w, btw E and F n.
Larcomb, John, carpenter, s side B s, btw 6 and 7 w.
Larkey, Robert, wheelwright, w side 11 e, btw C and D s; h 9, btw D and E n.
Larkey, R. H., attorney, s side La av, btw 4½ and 6 w.
Larned, B. F., w side 13 w, btw E and F n.
Larner, Michael, messenger Capitol, s side F n, btw 6 and 7 w.
Larrainzar, Manuel, Minister from Mexico, n side F n, btw 20 and 21 w.
Lasselle, H., clerk Land Office, n side B n, btw 2 and 3 w.
Latham, John, & Co., dry goods, cor Pa av and 19 w.
Latham, Moses, butcher, s side G s, btw 11 and 12 e.
Latham, Woodville, clerk Post Office, cor Md av and 11 w.
Latham, Robert W., (Selden, Withers & Co.) banker, n side G n, btw 8 and 9 w.
Lathrop, John G., navy agent, cor F n and 15 w.
La Truitte, Mrs., boarding house, n side Mo av, btw 3 and 4½ w.
Lauck, Henry C., clerk Department of the Interior, n side G n, btw 12 and 13 w.
Lauck, Dr. Isaac S., n side Bridge, btw High and Potomac, Georgetown.
Laurie, Rev. Dr., s side Pa av, btw 14 and 15 w.
Laurie, S., clerk Post Office Department, s side E n, btw 5 and 6 w.
Law, ——, clerk War Department, w side 12 w, btw F and G n.
Lawerson, Andrew, brickmaker, s side Va av, btw 1 and 2 w.
Lawrence, A. H., attorney at law, n side E n, btw 6 and 7 w.
Lawrence, De Witt C., solicitor for Patents, e side F n, btw 6 and 7 w.
Lawrence, D. C., agent for Patents, s side H n, btw 11 and 12 w.
Lawrence, Mary Ann, widow, n side D s, btw 4½ and 6 w.
Lawrenson, J., clerk General Post Office, w side 6 w, btw H and Mass av.
Lawrie, John, stonemason, s side L n, btw 6 and 7 w.
Laws, Dr. C. H., e side 7 w, btw G and H n.
Lawson, Thos., surgeon general U. S. A., e side 20 w, btw E and F n.
Layer, John P., laborer, s side K s, btw 6 and 7 e.
Lazenby, E., carpenter, e side 8 w, btw L and M n.
Lazenby, Mary, widow, w side 12 w, btw M and Mass av.
Lazenby, T., china, n side Bridge, btw High and Congress, Georgetown.
Lea, Luke, Commissioner Indian Affairs, n side E n, btw 6 and 7 w.
Leach, Captain Wm., e side 10 w, btw Md av and F s.
Leach, Miss J. A. C., milliner, s side Bridge, 2d door east from Congress, G'town.
Leake, N., pension agent, e side 12 w, btw M n and Mass av.
Lear, Mrs., widow, s side Pa av, btw 21 and 22 w.
Leatherbarer, Littleton, (col) laborer, w side 8 w, btw D and E s.

Abbreviations.—All points start from the Capitol; s south, n north, e east, w west, btw between, cor corner, (col) colored, av avenue, h house.

Leclair, John B., barber, w side 7 w, btw D and E n.
Leckie, Mrs. Martha, widow, e side 6 w, btw G and H n.
Le Conte, Mrs. Harriet, s side C n, btw 4½ and 6 w.
Leddy, Owen, grocer, e side 7 w, btw G and H n.
Lederer, C., baker, n side K s, btw 6 and 7 e; h cor Va av and 6 e.
Leddon, Catharine, widow, grocery, cor Md av and 12 w.
Leddon, Benj., cor Md av and 12 w.
Leddy, Q., grocery, w side 11 w, btw I and K n.
Lee, Richard H., stonecutter, w side 7 w, btw Va av and D.
Lee, Henry, cabinetmaker, s side Md av, btw 4½ and 6 w.
Lee, Captain Sidney S., U. S. N., s side N Y av, btw 13 and 14 w.
LEE & ESPEY, Undertakers, s side Pa av, btw 3 and 4½ w.
Lee, Henry, (& Espey) Md av, btw 4½ and 6 w.
Lee, A., exchange broker, n side Pa av, btw 4½ and 6 w.
House, w side 6 w, btw D and E n.
Lee, Dr. A. H., cor I n and 12 w.
Lee, Captain T. S., Topographical Corps U. S. A., n side F n, btw 18 and 19 w.
Lee, John, clerk Census office, s side Va av, btw 10 and 11 w.
Lee, Alfred, (col) feedstore, e side 12 w, btw A and C n.
Lee, K., (col) laundress, n side K n, btw 17 and 18 w.
Lee, A., (col) feedman, n side K n, btw 21 and 22 w.
Lee, Henry, (col) laborer, s side L n, btw 3 and 4 w.
Lee, R., (col) servant, n side M n, btw 15 and 16 w.
Lee, R., (col) n side Pa av, btw 21 and 22 w.
Lee, Wm., (col) hackdriver, n side B s, btw 4 and 5 w.
Lee, Catherine, (col) laundress, e side 2 w, btw F and G n.
Lee, A., (col) laborer, w side 21 w, btw K and L n.
Lee, M., (col) laundress, n side I s, btw 3 and 4 e.
Lee, Josiah, (col) laborer, n side E s, btw 4 and 5 e.
Lee, F., (col) laborer, s side F s, btw 2 and 3 w.
Lee, Joseph, (col) laborer, s side Va av, btw 3 and 4 e.
Lee, Philip, (col) dining room servant, w side 3 w, btw E and Va av.
Lee, Aloisius, (col) feedman, s side Bridge, 1 door east Washington; also at n w cor Montgomery and Bridge, Georgetown.
Leenitzer, ——, tinner, s side F s, btw 4½ and 6 w.
Lehmann, Charles, bootmaker, n side F n, btw 13 and 14 w.
Lehmann, A., hotel, n side East Capitol, btw 1 and 2 e.
Leinhart, John, laborer, w side 6 e, btw D and Pa av.
Leitch, Mrs., widow, n side B n, btw 2 and 3 w.
Lemerle, A., messenger Land office, s side G n, btw 12 and 13 w.
Lemmon, Rev. Mr., (Methodist) n side Gay, east of Montgomery, Georgetown.
Lemon, Charles, bookbinder, n side G n, btw 11 and 12 w; h L, btw 9 and 10 w.
Lemon, Charles, (col) laborer, w side 24 w, btw I and K n.
Lender, Michael, bootmaker, w side 8 w, btw Pa av and D.
Lenman, J. T., lumber yard, 12, near Canal; h w side 12 w, btw G and H n.
Lenor, Wm., machinist, n side N s, btw 3 and 4½ w.
Lennox, Margaret, widow, n side E n, btw 9 and 10 w.
Lenox, Walter, attorney, n side La av, btw 6 and 7 w.
Lenthall, Miss Mary, n side Pa av, btw 12 and 13 w.
Lenthall, John, chief Naval Constructor, s side F n, btw 18 and 19 w.
Lepreux, Lewis, saddler, s side Pa av, btw 4½ and 6 w; h, 13½, btw C and D n.
Lepreux, L & A., grocers, s side Pa av, btw 11 and 12 w.
Letmate, C., watchmaker, w side 7 w, btw D and E n.
Levy, Mr., teacher, cor Warren and 2d, Georgetown.
Lewis, James, carpenter, w side 3, btw F and G n.
Lewis, James, hackman, w side 7 w, btw D and E s.
Lewis, J. C., agent Hudson Life Insurance Co., e side 7 w, btw E and F n.
Lewis, Wm., waterman, w side 9 w, btw G and H s.
Lewis, Samuel, silversmith, n side Pa av, btw 12 and 13 w.
House w side 9 w, btw G and H n.

Abbreviations.—All points start from the Capitol; s south, n north, e east, w west, btw between, cor corner, (col) colored, av avenue, h house.

Lewis, Wm. B., auctioneer, n side Pa av, btw 4½ and 6 w.
Lewis, Samuel, boardinghouse, s side Pa av, btw 3 and 4½ w.
Lewis, Washington, n side I n, btw 4 and 5 w.
Lewis, Wm, S., carpenter, n side I n, btw 4 and 5 w.
Lewis, Thos., bricklayer, s side I n, btw 8 and 9 w.
Lewis, John W., superintendent of chimney sweeps, n side I n, btw 18 and 19 w.
LEWIS, S. C., Attorney and General Agent and Commissioner of Deeds of the State of Virginia, s side K n, btw 24 and 25 w.
Lewis, R., fancy store, s side B s, btw N J av and 1 e.
Lewis, Mrs. Jane, furnished rooms, w side 17 w, btw Pa av and H n.
Lewis, John, carpenter, w side 17 w, btw D and E n.
Lewis, Mrs. Samuel, widow, w side 17 w, btw D and E n.
Lewis, John, (col) hackman, e side 1 w, btw B and C s.
Lewis, Wm., (col) waiter, n side C n, btw 12 and 13 w.
Leonard, Mrs. Honoria, n side Mass av, btw 2 and 3 w.
Leonberger, John L., baker, w side 6 w, btw F and G n.
Levy, W. W., European Hotel, n side Pa av, btw 3 and 4½ w.
Libbey, Joseph, & Son, lumber yard, s side Water, btw the bridge and Congress; h, n e cor 1st and Potomac; and "Plough Factory," s e cor High and Dumbarton, Georgetown.
Liebermann, Dr. Charles H., s side F n, btw 13 and 14 w.
Lindsay, Alfred, primary school, 1st District, e side 18 w, btw I and K n.
Lindsley, H., hardware store, n side Pa av, btw 9 and 10 w.
Lindsley, Dr. H., n side C n, btw 4½ and 6 w.
Lingam, Mr., wagoner, s side West, east of Montgomery, Georgetown.
Linkins, D., cartman, s side F n, btw 23 and 24 w.
Linn, Philip, laborer, s side F n, btw 11 and 12 w.
Linthicum, E. M., hardware, n side Road, fronting Congress; store n w cor Bridgo and High, Georgetown.
Linthicum, O. M., drugstore, s w cor Bridge and High; h, n side Third, 1st door from Frederick, Georgetown.
Linton, John A., attorney at law, w side 7 w, btw Pa av and D n.
Lippitts, Rev. E. R., seminary for young ladies, cor 9 w and E n; boards at Mrs. Bannerman's.
Lipscomb, Rev. Robert M., (Ebenezer Episcopal Church) e side 7 e, btw G and I s.
Lipscomb, Jesse, grocer, s w cor Bridge and Jefferson, Georgetown.
Lipscomb, George, grocer, n e cor Third and Market, Georgetown.
Lisberger, H., stove warehouse, s side Pa av, btw 19 and 20 w.
House, I, btw 20 and 21 w.
Lisher, Mrs., mantuamaker, e side High, btw Beall and West, Georgetown.
Lisher, Samuel, huckster, s side Bridge, near Market-house, Georgetown.
Litchfield, C. W., tailor, s side Me av, btw 3 and 4½ w.
Litchfield, C. W., tailor, w side 6, btw Pa av and La av.
House, B n, btw 3 and 4½ w.
Little, Mrs. B., widow, w side 6 w, btw Mass av and K n.
Little, Mrs. Anna, boarding house, s side C n, btw 4½ and 6 w.
Little, Mrs. Joseph, boarding house, s side D n, btw 9 and 10 w.
Little, Joseph, tailor, s side D n, btw 9 and 10 w.
Little, Franklin, clerk, w side 10 w, btw B and C n.
Little, Joseph F., carpenter, e side 5 e, btw I and K s.
Little, Samuel, butcher, n side L s, btw 6 and 7 e.
Little, James, carpenter, s side Va av, btw 6 and 7 e.
Little, Peter, clerk lumber yard, s side Va av, btw 5 and 6 e.
Little, Miss Susan, Beall, opposite Christ Church, Georgetown.
Littlejohn, Charles, clerk, e side Fayette, extreme north, Georgetown.
Liverpool, J., (col) ship caulker, n side F n, btw 21 and 22 w.
Lloyd, L., general agent, e side 15 w, btw F and N Y av.
Lloyd, Mrs. M., w side 13 w, btw C and D s.
Lloyd, John M., bricklayer, 6 w, btw H and I s.
Locay, J. B., carter, s side Md av, btw 4½ and 6 w.

Abbreviations.—All points start from the Capitol; s south, n north, e east, w west, btw between, cor corner, (col) colored, av avenue, h house.

Lochrey, Edward, coachmaker, e side 12 w, btw G and H n.
Lock, Loa, carpenter, e side 4½ w, btw C and Md av.
Logan, H., (col) n side H n, btw 21 and 22 w.
Lomax, Thomas, laborer, w side 7 w, btw G and H s.
Lomax, Wm., laborer, e side 4½ w, btw E and F s.
Lomux, Alfred, (col) huckster, e side 7 w, btw Va av and D.
Lombey, Jas., (col) laborer, w side 21 w, btw K and L n.
Long, David, carpenter, w side 24 w, btw H and I n.
Longster, S., (col) laundress, s side I n, btw 9 and 10 w.
Lorch, Herman C., refectory, e side 7 w, btw B and Md av.
Lord, William, grocer, cor 5 w and G n.
Lord, Francis, jr., shoestore, s side D n, btw 5 and 6 w.
Louden, W. H., (col) carpenter, s side I n, btw 12 and 13 w.
LOUDON, H. F., & CO., Merchant Tailors, under Brown's Hotel.
Loudon, H. F., (& Co.) n side C n, btw 4½ and 6 w.
Loudner, George, baker, n side G n, btw 1 and 2 w.
Lounge, Isaac, (col) laborer, e side 3 w, btw F and G n.
Loupsher, Peter, stonecutter, w side 3, btw F and G n.
Lovejoy, Dr. J. W. H., s side F n, btw 11 and 12 w; h, cor 12 w and I n.
Lovejoy, Mr., tailor, e side Market, btw 3d and 4th, Georgetown.
Loveless, G. H., carpenter, n side G s, btw 9 and 10 e.
Lovely, John, cartman, e side 23 w, btw G and H n.
Low, Joseph, carpenter, e side 4 e, btw I and K s.
Lowber, J., clerk Land Office, s side M n, btw 8 and 9 w.
Lowe, Mrs., fancy store, s side Pa av, btw 9 and 10 w.
Lowe, Bennett, blacksmith, n side Va av, btw 5 and 6 e.
Lowery, George, wholesale grocer, n e cor Water and Jefferson, Georgetown.
Lowmac, Wm., (col) waiter, n side B s, btw 4 and 5 e.
Lowndes, Henry, hackdriver, w side 4½ w, btw C and D s.
Lowndes, Wm., painter, n side F n, btw 13 and 14 w.
Lowndes, Frank, clerk, n side Bridge, cor Fayette, Georgetown.
Lowndes, Ann, (col) laundress, s side D s, btw 1 and 2 w.
Lowry, Wm. H., clerk Land office, s side F n, btw 8 and 9 w.
Lowry, James H., clerk War Department, n side G n, btw 12 and 13 w.
Lowry, George, s side K n, btw 24 and 25 w.
Loxman, M., laborer, cor North Capitol and G n.
Loxman, Martin, laborer, cor North Capitol and H n.
Lucas, David, corker, D n, btw 26 and 27 w.
Lucas, J. M., clerk Land office, n side I n, btw 9 and 10 w.
Lucas, Ann, (col) nurse, n side I n, btw 15 and 16 w.
Lucas, P. A., (col) laundress, n side L n, btw Vt av and 15 w.
Luce, Vinal, s side H n, btw 14 and 15 w.
Luckett, A., tinner, n side D s, btw 3 and 4 w.
Luckett, Legrand I., printer, w side 7 w, btw N Y av and L n.
Luff, Frederick, agent Baltimore Clipper, n side Md av, btw 4½ and 6 w.
Lullay, Meno, cigarstore, s side Pa av, btw 3 and 4½ w.
Lumsden, Mr., e side Montgomery, btw Dumbarton and Gay, Georgetown.
Lundy, E. K., bookstore, n side Bridge, btw High and Congress, Georgetown.
Lunsford, William, cigar vender, s side Bridge, btw High and Congress, G'town.
Lusby, Jasper, shoemaker, s side Md av, btw 4½ and 6 w.
Lusby, Wm., grocery, n side D s, btw 3 and 4 e.
Lusby, Samuel, carpenter, n side Ga av, btw 13 and 14 e.
Lusby, James A., blacksmith, n side Ga av, btw 13 and 14 e.
Luther, Mrs. Sarah, widow, e side 11 w, btw L and M n.
Lutheran Church, St. Paul's, English, (Rev. J. G. Butler) cor H n and 11 w.
Lutheran Church, German, cor G n and 20 w.
Lutz, Francis A., saddler, n side Pa av, btw 4½ and 6 w; h 6, btw G and H.
Lutz, Mrs. John, e side High, btw Gay and Bridge, Georgetown.
Lyles, Henry, carpenter, w side 6 w, btw G and H n.
Lynch, Robert, stonecutter, s side D n, btw Mass av and North Capitol.

Abbreviations.—All points start from the Capitol; s south, n north, e east, w west, btw between, cor corner, (col) colored, av avenue, h house.

Lynch, James L., plasterer, s side Mass av, btw 2 w and N J av.
Lynch, John T., paver, e side 8 w, btw E and F n.
Lynch, James, grocery, s side East Capitol, btw 1 and 2 e.
Lyon, Charles, brickmaker, w side 10 w, btw C and Pa av.
Lyons, Evan, flour merchant, s side Water, cor Congress: h, First, btw Potomac and Market, Georgetown.
Lysrught, John, laborer, n side G n, btw North Capitol and 1 e.

M.

Macbee, Wm., laborer on railroad, cor N J av and 2 w.
Mace, Dan., M. C. from Indiana, e side 10 w, btw Pa av and C n.
Mack, John, laborer, w side North Capitol, btw Mass av and G n.
Mackall, Brooke, n side F n, btw 14 and 15 w.
Mackall, Richard, cor 7th and Frederick, Georgetown.
Mackall, Brook, s side Dumbarton, btw Congress and Washington, Georgetown.
Mackall, Dr. Lewis, sen., w side Green, btw Road and Stoddart, Georgetown.
Mackall, Dr. Lewis, jr., s e cor Dumbarton and Montgomery, Georgetown.
Mackay, George, agent for claims, n side F n, btw 12 and 13 w.
Mackey, Thomas, blacksmith, w side 2 e, btw B and C s.
Mackey, Wm., fisherman, w side 6 w, btw E and G s.
Mackie, James S., State Department, n side H n, btw 7 and 8 w.
Mackmarrel, Dan., stonecutter, s side Md av, btw 3 and 4½ w.
Maclin, A. H., w side 19 w, btw I and K n.
Macomb, Mrs. Gen., n side I n, btw 17 and 18 w.
Macubbin, Mrs. Mary, widow, s side La av, btw 4½ and 6 w.
Maddox, Mrs., widow, n side N s, btw 3 and 4 e.
Madigan, Michael, shoemaker, n side F n, btw 2 and 3 w.
Madison, Francis, (col) waiter, w side 14 w, btw H and I n,
Madison Alfred, watchman, w side 3 e, btw M and N s.
Magar, John, constable, w side 4½ w, btw L and M s.
Magee, Samuel, baker, w side 7 w, btw G and H n.
Magee, James P., tailor, s side F s, btw 9 and 10 w.
Magill, Dr., n side Pa av, btw 3 and 4½ w.
Magill, J. B., painter, s side Pa av, btw 1 and 2 e.
Magill, ——, laborer, s side Mass av, btw 2 and 3 w.
Magill, Wm. W., tinner, n side L s, btw 7 and 8 e.
Magruder & Calvert, dry goods, n side La av, btw 8 and 9 w.
Magruder, Thomas C., (& Calvert,) E, btw 3 and 4 w.
Magruder, Jane, (col) washwoman, n side E s, btw 4 and 5 e.
Magruder, M. E., (col) laundress, w side 5 e, btw D and E s.
Magruder, Henry, (col) laborer, n side D s, btw 4½ and 6 w.
Magruder, Fielder, wood merchant, w side 3 w, btw F and G n.
Magruder, Richard, wood merchant, w side 3 w, btw F and G n.
Magruder, Thomas J., shoestore, n side Pa av, btw 8 and 9 w.
House n side G n, btw 4 and 5 w.
Magruder, R., (col) servant, s side K n, btw 17 and 18 w.
Magruder, B., tailor, n side N Y av, btw 6 and 7 w.
Magruder, Dr. W., s side Pa av, btw 21 and 22 w.
Magruder, Mrs., s side West, btw Washington and Congress, Georgetown.
Magruder, Dr. Hezekiah, n w cor 3d and Market, Georgetown.
Magruder, Nathan, currier, w side Fayette, btw 1st and 2d, Georgetown.
Magruder, James, commission merchant, s side 1st, btw Market and Frederick, Georgetown.
MAGUIRE, JAMES, Hat Store, n side Pa av, btw 3 and 4½ w.
Maguire, F., huckster, s side E n, btw 20 and 21 w.
Maguire, Rev. B., at Georgetown College, president.
Maher, James, public gardener and hotel, cor 13½ w and E n.
Mahagan, J., grocery, s side H n, btw 20 and 21 w.

Abbreviations.—All points start from the Capitol; s south, n north, e east, w west, btw between, cor corner, (col) colored, av avenue, h house.

Mahorney, George, grocer, s side 2d, btw Fayette and College, Georgetown.
Mallow, Robert, blacksmith, s side I s, btw 12 and 13 e.
Maloney, Michael, stonemason, s side D n, btw Mass av and North Capitol.
Maloney, Daniel, laborer, n side E n, btw N J av and 2 w.
Malster, William, dentist, n side Pa av, btw 9 and 10 w.
Maniette, Joseph, moulder, w side 7 e, btw I and K s.
Mankin, J., e side 9 w, btw H and I n.
Mankins, William, tailor, cor Pa av and 4½ w.
Mankins, Edmund, fisherman, e side Fayette, btw 2d and 3d, Georgetown,
Mankins, William, do do do.
Mankins, Washington, huckster, w side Market square, Georgetown.
Mann, Charles, bootmaker, e side 7 w, btw F and G n.
Mann, J., shoemaker, n side F n, btw 22 and 23 w.
Mansfield, Rev. Z. H., s w cor West and Washington, Georgetown.
Marbry, Dr. William, n side H n, btw 5 and 6 w.
Marbury, John, jr., hardware, n w cor High and Bridge; h, s side 1st, btw Market and Frederick, Georgetown.
Marbury, John, attorney, s e cor Frederick and Bridge, extreme west; office opposite Jefferson, on Bridge st.
Marceron, P. T., grocer, cor N J av and B s.
Marceron, John L., grocer, cor 10 w and Md av.
Marceron, Mrs. E., widow, cor B and N J av.
Marine Barracks (Gen. Henderson commandant,) n side 8 e, btw G and I s.
MARKLAND, A. H., office opposite Treas. Dep't; h n side L n, btw 10 and 11 w.
Markland M., w side 16 w, btw K and L n.
Markoe, Francis, clerk State Department, n side I n, btw 20 and 21 w.
Marks, Samuel, clerk Quartermaster's office, n side G s, btw 6 and 7 e.
Marks, Andrew, blacksmith, s side E s, btw 6 and 7 e.
Markwell, George, coach trimmer, w side 8 w, btw L and M n.
Marl, Joseph W., tinner, w side High, btw Prospect and Bridge; h, s side West, btw Congress and High, Georgetown.
Marll, John S., tinner, w side 7 w, btw E and F s.
Marquis, William, n side D n, btw 14 and 15 w.
Marrow Samuel, (col) laborer, s side G n, btw 21 and 22 w.
Marr, Thomas F., printer, n side Va av, btw 6 and 7 w.
Marr, James H., clerk Post Office Department, w side 8 w, btw K and L n.
Marr, J. T., painter, s side N Y av, btw 14 and 15 w; h cor 6 and N Y av.
Marron, J., Third Ass't Postmaster Gen., s side N Y av, btw 9 and 10 w.
Marselas, Henry E., bootmaker, w side 7 w, btw N Y av and L n.
Marsh, O. W., clerk Pension office, s side N Y av, btw 12 and 13 w.
Marshall, William, clothing store and auctioneer, n side Pa av, btw 6 and 7 w. House e side N J av, btw B and C s.
Marshall, William, ship carpenter, n side 8 e, btw L and M s.
Marshall, Jacob, blacksmith, n side 8 e, btw I and K s.
Marshall, Henry (col) servant, n side K n, btw 17 and 18 w.
Marten, William H., barber, s side Pa av, btw 19 and 20 w.
Martin, James, bookbinder, n side E n, btw 6 and 7 w.
Martin, William, police officer, n side D n, btw 6 and 7 w.
Martin, J., painter, w side 10 w, btw B and C n; h D, btw 6 and 7 w.
Martin, Z., shoemaker, s side I n, btw 10 and 11 w.
Martin, Josephine, (col) laundress, s side I n, btw 10 and 11 w.
Martin, Hamilton, hackdriver, n side L n, btw 3 and 4 w.
Martin, Mrs., (col) laundress, e side 8 w, btw F and G n.
Martin, Miss, dressmaker, n side Pa av, btw 21 and 22 w.
Martin, John W., blacksmith, w side 11 w, btw Md av and E s.
Martin, William S., carpenter, n side E s, btw 6 and 7 w.
Martin, John, gent., e side 1 e, btw C and D n.
Martin, Mrs., cor 1 e and C n.
Martini, Joseph, cabinetmaker, e side 7 w, btw F and G n.
Martin, Samuel, laborer, w side 5 e, btw L and M s.

Abbreviations.—All points start from the Capitol; s south, n north, e east, w west, btw between, cor corner, (col) colored, av avenue, h house.

Martin, Joseph S., carpenter, e side 7 e, btw E and G s.
Martin, James H., laborer, n side L s, btw 6 and 7 e.
Martin, George, laborer, n side I s, btw 6 and 7 w.
Martin, Mrs. C. D., teacher, (District school No. 3,) cor K and 11.
Martin, Henry, n side N s, btw N J av and 3 e.
Martin, Mrs. Mary, widow, s side F s, btw 9 and 10 w.
MASI, S., Jeweller, n side Pa av, btw 4½ and 6 w; h E n, btw 9 and 10 w.
Masi, F., n side E n, btw 9 and 10 w.
Mason, P., watchman, s side Md av, btw 4½ and 6 w.
Mason, Emeline, (col) cook, e side 8 w, btw M and N n.
Mason, John, agent for claims, cor G n and 12 w.
Mason, Henry, (col) hackdriver, n side K n, btw 17 and 18 w.
Mason, Mary, (col) widow, n side K n, btw Vt av and 15 w.
Mason, J. H., (col) waiter, e side 13 w, btw G and H n.
Mason, E., (col) huckster, w side 21 w, btw K and L n.
Masonic Hall, cor 10 w and E n.
Massey, George T., clerk, e side 9 w, btw H and I n.
Massie, J. E., (col) barber, s side N Y av, btw 12 and 13 w.
Masters, Mrs., milliner, s side F s, btw 9 and 10 w.
Masterson, Wm., bootmaker, e side 7 w, btw F and G n.
Mastin, Wm. E., constable, n side Pa av, btw 23 and 24 w.
Matlock, Simeon, merchant tailor, e side 9 w, btw Pa av and D n.
House, 8 w, btw G and H n.
Matthews, Mrs. S., s side F n, btw 6 and 7 w.
Matthews, Mary Jane, (col) laundress, e side 12 w, btw K and L n.
Matthews, Henry C., s e cor West and Washington, Georgetown.
Matthews, Dr. W., s e cor West and Washington, Georgetown.
Mattics, W., (col) laborer, e side 11 e, btw Ga av and L s.
Mattingly, George St Bt., agent, n side F s, btw 4½ and 6 w.
MATTINGLY, FRANCIS, Hatter, e side 7 w, btw D and E n.
House, e side 7 w, btw N Y av and L n.
Mattingly, John, blacksmith, s side D n, btw 13 and 13½ w.
Mattingly, Edward, e side 3 e, btw Ga av and N s.
Mattingly, ———, grocer, w side High, btw 3d and 4th, Georgetown.
Mattingly, ——, laborer, w side Washington, btw Bridge and Canal, Georgetown.
Mattox, George, paver, w side 11 e, btw M and N s.
Maud, Robert, carpenter, w side 15 w, btw L and M n.
Maury, Charles B., (Taylor &) cor E n and 10 w.
Maury, John W., mayor, s side C n, btw 2 and 3 w.
MAXWELL, SEARS & COLLEY, Dry Goods, n side Pa av, btw 9 and 10 w.
MAXWELL & SEARS, Fancy Store, n side Pa av, btw 9 and 10 w.
Maxwell, John S., (& Sears) fancy store, n side Pa av, btw 9 and 10 w.
Maxwell, C. D., clerk navy, s side I n, btw 17 and 18 w.
Maxwell, James, stonecutter, n side G n, btw 1 and 2 e.
Maxwell, Robert, printer, n side Mass av, btw 6 and 7 w.
Maxwell, George P., plasterer, s side D s, btw 9 and 10 w.
May, Joseph J., (Clagett, Newton, & Co.) boards at National Hotel.
May, F. R., exchange broker, cor 14 and F n.
May, F. R., watchman Treasury Department, e side 13 w, btw F and G n.
May, Dr., s side La av, btw 4½ and 6 w.
May, Mrs., n e cor Warren and Second, Georgetown.
May, Philip, baker, w side High, btw 1st and Prospect, Georgetown.
May, J. M., cabinetmaker, w side High, btw 1st and Prospect, Georgetown.
May, Thomas, grocer, n side Water, btw Cherry alley and Congress, Georgetown.
May, Mrs, and John, and Thomas, n w cor Second and Frederick, Georgetown.
Mayfield, ———, gunsmith, n side Bridge, btw Congress and Washington, G'town.
Mayfield & Brown, drygoods, s side Bridge, btw High and Congress, Georgetown.
Mayfield, Mrs., e side Congress, btw West and Beall, Georgetown.
MAYNARD, EDWARD, Dentist, n side Pa av, btw 11 and 12 w.
House, n side Pa av, btw 24 and 25 w.
Mayor's office, s side Bridge, btw High and Potomac, Georgetown.

Abbreviations.—All points start from the Capitol; s south, n north, e east, w west, btw between, cor corner, (col) colored, av avenue, h house,

McAllister, James, clerk Post Office Department, e side 4½ w, btw C n and Ia av.
McAndle, Eugene, stonecutter, w side 12 w, btw C and D s.
McBee, Joseph, carpenter, e side 6 w, btw G and H n.
McBlair, J. H., grocer, n side Pa av, btw 17 and 18 w.
House, w side Vt av, btw H and Pa av.
McBride, Thomas, laborer, n side E n, btw 9 and 10 w.
McCabe, Andrew, liquorstore, w side 7 w, btw G and H n.
McCafferty, Wm., dry goods, n side E n, btw 5 and 6 w.
McCaffrey, H., grocer, s side Pa av, btw 3 and 4½ w.
McCalla, John M., attorney, s side La av, btw 6 and 7 w.
McCalla, Jackson, blacksmith, n side I s, btw 11 and 13 e.
McCarter, Garrett, laborer, s side F s, btw 4½ and 6 w.
McCARTY, AUGUSTUS, Daguerreotypist, e side 4½ w, btw Pa av and C n.
McCarty, William, daguerreotypist, e side 4½ w, btw Pa av and C n.
McCarty, Thomas, watchman, w side 3 w, btw G and H n.
McCarty, Michael, merchant tailor, s side Pa av, btw 4½ and 6 w.
McCarty, James, clerk, n side E n, btw 5 and 6 w.
McCarty, James, laborer, w side 6 w, btw F and G n.
McCarty, Eugene, carpenter, s side G n, btw 12 and 13 w.
McCawly, Wm., eating house, n side Pa av, btw 1 and 2 w.
McCarty, Charles F., carpenter, n side 15 w, btw I and K n.
McCaskie, P., upholsterer, s side H n, btw 17 and 18 w.
McCauley, Joseph, blacksmith, w side 3 w, btw M and N s.
McCauley, Com. Charles, U. S. N., n side Pa av, btw 15 and Vt av.
McCauley, Wm., tinner, w side South Capitol, btw B and C s.
McCausland, Captain A., mailboat, e side 12 w, btw B and C s.
McCauley, John, laborer, n side L s, btw 4 and 5 e.
McClain, Wm., bookbinder, n side I n, btw 8 and 9 w.
McClain, J. P., Professor of Drawing, e side 7 w, btw D and E n.
McClelland, D., engraver, n side E n, btw 9 and 10 w.
McClelland, John, foundry, cor 10 w and E; h cor N Y av and 14 w.
McClenagan, James, carpenter, n side I n, btw 4 and 5 w.
McClery, Morven, J., U. S. Coast Survey, s side N Y av, btw 14 and 15 w.
McClerry, James, clerk Treasury Department, n side F n, btw 13 and 14 w.
McCloskey, Wm., coachman, e side 8 w, btw L and M n.
McCloud, John, clerk. Fayette, Georgetown.
McColgan, James, furnished rooms, s side Pa av, btw 12 and 13 w.
McConnell, W. P., dentist, s side Pa av, btw 6 and 7 w.
McConnell, Morris, messenger Capitol, s side East Capitol, btw 1 and 2 e.
McCormick, Sophia, teacher, w side 4½, near Pa av.
McCormick, Harriet, teacher, w side 4½, near Pa av.
McCormick, Hugh, e side N J av, btw L and M s.
McCormick, John, laborer, s side Md av, near canal.
McCormick, A. T., boardinghouse, s side Pa av, btw 4½ w, and 6 w.
McCormick, W. J., register of City, Carroll Place, btw East Capitol and A s.
McCoy, B., (col) teacher, s side L s, btw 3 and 4 w.
McCoy, Wm., watchman, w side 3 e, btw L and M s.
McCUBBIN, E., Barber, e side 8 w, btw Pa av and D.
McCubbin, Nicholas, laborer, e side 7 e, btw East Capitol and A s.
McCulloch, Mrs., widow, e side 15 w, btw Pa av and H.
McCune, John, grocer, w side 7 w, btw N Y av and L n.
McCutcheon, John, clerk Treasury Department, s side L n, btw 7 and 8 w.
McCutchen, James, wood merchant, e side 19 w, btw G and H n; h Georgetown.
McCutchen, J. H. G., attorney at law, office, 3, adjoining Gadsby's Hotel.
McCutchen, John and J., wood yard, w side Jefferson, btw Canal and Water, G'tn.
McDaniel, George, shoestore, w side 4 w, btw G and H n.
McDaniel, E. L., laborer, e side 11 e, btw L s and Va av.
McDaniel, Miss, milliner, n side Gay, btw Congress and Washington, Georgetown.
McDERMOTT, M., Coach Factory, s side Pa av, btw 3 and 4½ w.
House, Mo av, btw 3 and 4½ w.

Abbreviations.—All points start from the Capitol; s south, n north, e east, w west, btw between, cor corner, (col) colored, av avenue, h honse.

McDermott, Wm., clerk Ordnance office, s side I n, btw 18 and 19 w.
McDevitt, John, auction store, Pa av, btw 9 and 10 w.
House, n side La av, btw 6 and 7 w.
McDew, ——, n side L n, btw 9 and 10 w.
McDonald, John, paver, w side 7 w, btw D and E s.
McDonald, James, stonecutter, s side M n, btw 12 and 13 w.
McDonnell, C., refectory, s side A s, btw N J av and 1 e.
McDonnel, T., n side East Capitol s, btw 1 and 2 e.
McDuell, John, clerk Census office, e side 14 w, btw I and H n.
McDuffie, Mrs., boardinghouse, n side Pa av, btw 1 and 2 w.
McElfresh, G. S., tobacconist, s side Pa av, btw 9 and 10 w.
McElfresh, J. W., painter, e side 6 w, btw C and La av.
McElfresh, C. S., exchange broker, e side 6 w, btw F and G n.
McElwee, Saml., printer, e side 6 w, btw E and F n.
McEmory, Thomas, Coast Survey, w side N J av, btw D and E s.
McEmmy, Charles, messenger City Hall, n side East Capitol, btw 1 and 2 e.
McFarlan, Danl., w side 10 w, btw G and H n.
McFarland, George, w side 9 e, btw L and Va av.
McFarley, Wm., drummer in garrison, e side 9 e, btw I and K s.
McCarty, Dan., laborer, s side A n, btw N J av and 2 w.
McGarr, Owen, printer, e side 10 w, btw L and M n.
McGarbey, Mrs., s side Dumbarton, east of Montgomery, Georgetown.
McGarvey, John, porter and ale dealer, n side K n, btw 27 and 28 w.
McGaw, Mrs., milliner, s side Bridge, btw Congress and Jefferson, Georgetown.
McGee, Charles, laborer, n side G s, btw 5 and 6 e.
McGee, William, tailor, s side Bridge, east of market-house, Georgetown.
McGill, P. M., clerk Pension office, n side L n, btw 10 and 11 w.
McGill, John, painter, cor N J av and D s.
McGill, Emily, widow, w side 8 w, btw G and H n.
McGill, John H., s side G n, btw 13 and 14 w.
McGill, Henry M., clerk Census office, s side G n, btw 13 and 14 w.
MoGill, Thos., printer, (Kirkwood &) cor 12 w and F n.
McGinness, Peter, carpenter, w side 4½ w, btw L and M s.
McGlue, ——, wood yard, s side I n, btw 18 and 19 w.
McGoldrick, Wm. C., refectory, n side Pa av, btw 2 and 3 w.
McGonigle, A., carpenter, e side 11 w, btw E and F n.
McGrann, James, Green Tree House, n side Pa, btw 2 and 3 w.
McGrath, Mrs. T., boardinghouse, s side La av, btw 6 and 7 w.
McGregor, N. M., furnishing store, e side 7 w, btw La av and D n.
House, s side Pa av, btw 1 and 2 e
McGuire, Thomas, blacksmith, w side 8 w, btw D and E n.
McGUIRE, J. C., Auctioneer, n side D n, btw 10 and 11 w.
House, s side E n, btw 6 and 7 w.
McGuire, ——, w side 1 w, btw B and Md av.
McHenry, Hamilton, Superintendent Roads, n side D n, btw 9 and 10 w.
McIntire, J. C., druggist, cor 7 w and I n, boards at Dorsey's Hotel.
McIntosh, Job P., marble cutter, e side 4½ w, btw C and Md av.
McIntosh, James T., tailor, w side 9 w, btw I and N Y av.
McIntyre, A. L., clerk Patent office, s side M n, btw 11 and 12 w.
McJilton, Mrs., widow, e side 7 e, btw Va av and L s.
McKahan, S. Perry, clerk, Pa av, near United States Hotel.
McKEAN, JAMES P., Bookbinder, n side D n, btw 6 and 7 e.
McKEAN, P., Mineral Water Manufactory, s side B n, btw 2 and 3 w.
McKean, S. M., Treasury Department, w side 17 w, btw N Y av and F n.
McKelden, John C., e side 7 w, btw D and E n.
McKelden, Wm., baker, n side L n, btw 9 and 10 w.
McKenna, V., machinist, w side 11 e, btw N and O s.
McKenna, Patrick, grocer, s side Pa av, btw 3 and 4 e.
McKenney, Edward, finisher, e side 11 e, btw M and N s.
McKenny, Samuel, n side Dumbarton, btw High and Congress, Georgetown.

McKim, Dr. Sam. A. H., w side 8 e, btw G and I s.
McKIM, JOHN W., Attorney, opposite City Hall, Ia av.
Boards at Mrs. Tilley's, Mo av.
McKinney, James H., laborer, w side 8 w, btw G and H s.
McKinstry, Wm., Eagle Iron Works, Ohio av, btw 13 and 13½.
House, Ohio av, btw 14 and 15 w.
McKnew, Z., doorkeeper House Representatives, s side D n, btw 2 and 3 w.
McKnew, C., (Byers &) C, btw 2 and 3 w.
McKnight, Dr. G. B., w side 3 w, btw B and C n.
McKnight, James M., clerk, n side C n, btw 12 and 13 w.
McKnight, Francis, clerk, w side Green, btw Dumbarson and Gay, Georgetown.
McLain, Mrs. Catharine, widow, w side 8 e, btw E and G s.
McLain, Thomas, laborer, e side 6 w, btw D and E s.
McLain, Rev. W., Sec'y American Colonization Society, s side C n, btw 3 and 4½ w.
McLain, R. L., 6 w, btw G and H n.
McLean, R., (Ager &,) n side E n, btw 12 and 13 w.
McLean, William, carpenter, w side 13 w, btw N Y av and I n.
McLehesney, John H., grocer, cor 7 w and N n.
McLochly, Thomas, laborer, s side East Capitol, btw 3 and 4 e.
McMahan, James, laborer, w side 3 w, btw C and D s.
McMahon, John, carpenter, w side 8 w, btw G and H n.
McManners, Edward, doorkeeper at President's House, n side 15 w, btw I and K n.
McManaron, Michael, laborer, n side G n, btw North Capitol and 1 e.
McMihn, Mrs. M. A., e side 10 w, btw E and F n.
McNamee, John, machinist, s side A n, btw 1 and 2 e.
McNamee, Charles, clerk City Hall, East Capitol, btw 1 and 2 e.
McNantz, P. H., carpenter, s side B s, btw 1 and 2 e.
McNeay, B., engineer, n side D n, btw 12 and 13 w.
McNeil, A., marble finisher, s side K n, btw 11 and 12 w.
McNeir, George, general agent, cor F n and 6 w.
McNerhany, Francis, clerk in Capitol, e side 6 w, btw G and H n.
McNoughton, George, grocer, e side 6 w, btw G and H n.
McOllem, John, bricklayer, e side 7 w, btw G and H n.
McPeak, William, gent., n side Md av, btw 4½ and 6 w.
McPherson, William S., grocer, w side 7 w, btw G and H n.
McPherson, H. H., 9 w, btw H and I n.
McPherson, Mrs. H n., btw 4 and 5 w.
McPherson, John, clerk War Department, s side F n, btw 9 and 10 w.
McPherson, jr., H. H., druggist, cor Pa av and 1 e.
McPherson, John, w side 13 w, btw C and D s.
McPherson, Samuel, plasterer, e side 22 w, btw G and H n.
McQuay, Benjamin, feedstore, n side Md av, btw 9 and 10 w.
McQueen, Thomas, laborer, e side 2 w, btw G n and Mass av.
McQuillan, Mrs. Ann, widow, furnished rooms, w side 4½ w, btw Pa av and Mo av.
McQuillan, Mrs., s side F n, btw 14 and 15 w.
McRea, James W., e side 11 w, btw G and H n.
Mead, ——, w side 6 e, btw G and E s.
Mead, S. merchant tailor, s side Pa av, btw 4½ aud 6 w.
Mead, B,, grocer, n side M n, btw 8 and 9 w.
Meade, Edward, foreman at Capitol, n side H n, btw 4 and 5 w.
Mead, John, blacksmith, s side D s, btw 3 and 4 e.
Mead, James, blacksmith, cor 6 e and D s.
Meager, John, fancy store, e side 13 w, btw F and G n.
Meagle, Jacob, grocer, s side East Capitol, btw 5 and 6 e.
Means' Tavern, Georgetown—on new cut road, out of town.
Mechanics' Union Association, n side Pa av, btw 6 and 7 w.
Mechlin, W., chief clerk 2d Aud. office, I n, btw 18 and 19 w.
Medhurst & Heard, barbers, 6 w, under National Hotel.
Meehan, John S., librarian Congress, s side B n, btw Del av and 1 e.
Meekins, Charles H. clerk, boards Mrs. Speeding's, I, btw 7 and 8 w.

Abbreviations.—**All points start from the Capitol; s south, n north, e east, w west, btw between, cor corner, (col) colored, av avenue, h house.**

Megee, Robert, hackdriver, e side 8 w, btw E and F n.
Melcher, Andrew D., carpenter, e side 6 w, btw H and I n.
House n side I n, btw 4 and 5 w.
Mellfesh, Zachariah, carpenter, w side 4 w, btw G and H.
Mellington, Jane E., dressmaker, n side Mo av, btw 4½ and 6 w.
Melson, John, laborer Treasury Department, w side 6 w, btw K and N Y av.
Melvin, Dr. M. R., s side F s, btw 9 and 10 w.
Melvin, Josiah, printer, w side 10 w, btw G and H n.
Menadier, Capt. William, U S A, n side Pa av, btw 21 and 22 w.
Meredith, John H., tinner, w side 7 w, btw L and M n.
Meredith, Moses, grocer, w side 3 e, btw Ga av and N s.
Mercer, James, (col) cartman, n side B s, btw 4 and 5 e.
Meryman, Joseph, stonecutter, n side F s, btw 9 and 10 w.
Messer, Andrew, stonecutter, w side 7 w, btw F and G s.
Messer, Handry, stonecutter, w side 7 w, btw F and G s.
Mevillat, Mary, widow, cor H and 4 w.
Michlin, William, s side I n, btw 17 and 18 w.
Mickum, Samuel, messenger Navy Department, e side 22 w, btw K and L n.
Middleton, D. W., clerk Supreme Court, e side N J av btw B and C s.
Middleton, Richard, (col) laborer, w side 3 w, btw E and F s.
Middleton & Beall, grocers, s side Pa av, btw 4½ and 6 w.
Middleton, B. F., (& Beall,) opposite City Hall.
Middleton, Mrs. Eliza, widow, eatinghouse, n side 8 e, btw I and K s.
Middleton, E. J., clerk office Circuit Court, City Hall.
Middleton, L. J., clerk Post Office Department, n side M n, btw 12 and 13 w.
Middleton, ———, grocer, n side Prospect, near Market, Georgetown.
Milburn, Mrs. Margaret, widow, e side 7 w, btw C and Va av.
Milburn, Thomas, carpenter, n side D s, btw 6 and 7 w.
Milburn, Mrs., widow, s side Va av, btw 7 and 8 w.
Miles, Charles, (col) laborer, w side 8 w, btw D and E s.
Miles, Nicholas, laborer, w side 3 w, btw G and H n.
Miles, L. M., artist, n side Pa av, btw 3 and 4½ w.
Miles, George, brickmaker, n side G n, btw 2 and 3 w.
Miller, John, gardener, e side 3 w, btw P and Q n.
Miller, Royal E., confectioner, e side 7 w, btw D and E n.
Miller, James, painter, w side 7, btw E and F s.
Miller, James, baker, e side 9 w, btw Pa av and D n.
Miller, Mrs. M. S., mantua maker, s side Pa av, btw 9 and 10 w.
Miller, M. H., chief clerk 1st Auditor's office, n side H n, btw 9 and 10 w.
Miller, C., & G. M., barbers, s side Pa av, btw 4½ and 6 w.
Miller, Mary D., boarding, s side Pa av, btw 14 and 15 w.
Miller, James, Indian Department, s side E n, btw 7 and 8 w.
Miller, J., confectioner, s side Pa av, btw 10 and 11 w.
Miller, Edward, stonemason, n side C n, btw 13 and 14 w.
Miller, Frank, confectioner, n side G n, btw 1 and 2 e.
Miller, E. P., dry goods, n side G n, btw 12 and 13 w.
Miller, Charles, confectioner, w side 6 w, btw D and E s.
Miller, Michael, n side Mass av, btw 11 and 12 w.
Milller, James, grocer, cor 15 w and L n.
Miller, William, clerk Treasury Department, w side 13 w, btw G and H n.
Miller, Mary, s side M n, btw 14 and 15 w.
Miller, J. J., clerk Indian office, opposite city post office.
Miller, F., carpenter, s side East Capitol, btw 5 and 6 e,
Miller, R., stonecutter, w side 2 e, btw C and D n.
Miller, Doctor A. W., w side 6 e, btw G and I s.
Miller, George, butcher, s side K s, btw 13 and 14 e.
Miller, George, carpenter, n side Va av, btw 6 and 7 w.
Miller, Dr. Thomas, n side Pa av, btw 13 and 14 w.
Miller, John, stonemason, w side Washington, btw Stoddart and West, Geo'town.
Miller, Michael, ice, s w cor Beall and Green, Georgetown.

Abbreviations.—All points start from the Capitol; s south, n north, e east, w west, btw between, cor corner, (col) colored, av avenue, h house.

Millett, Mrs., s side G n, btw 13 and 14 w.
Milliken, N., messenger War Department, s side G n, btw 13 and 14 w.
Mills, Robert, architect, w side N J av, btw A and B s.
Mills, William, wheelwright, w side 11 e, btw M and N s.
Mills, William, pilot Chesapeake Bay, w side 4½ w, btw G and H s.
Mills, Charles C., wood merchant, e side 7 w, btw E and F s.
House F s, btw 9 and 10, Island.
Mills, J., shoestore, under Brown's Hotel; h w side 6 w, btw D and E n.
Mills, Clark, cor 15 w and Pa av; boards at Willard's.
Millstead, Thomas, grocer, cor 4½ w and F s.
Milstead, Ignatius, grocer, n side Va av, btw 1 and 2 w.
Milstard, Robert, grocer, e side N J av, btw M and N s.
Mimm, George, carpenter, s w cor Second and Frederick, Georgetown.
Mina, Nancy, (col) laundress, w side 10 w, btw M and N n.
Minitree, A., carpenter, n side Md av, btw 4½ and 6 w.
Minor, John, (col) laborer, n side D n, btw 12 and 13 w.
Minor, Benjamin, (col) brickmaker, s side H n, btw 12 and 13 w.
Minor, John, (col) laborer, e side 13½ w, btw D and E n.
Minnekheim, John, baker, w side 8 e, btw E and G s.
Missel, John, baker, w side 7 w, btw L and M n.
Mister, J., cartman, s side D s, btw 13 and 13½ w.
Mitchell, John T., hatter, n side D n, btw 6 and 7 w.
Mitchell, John, dry goods, La av, btw 6 and 7 w.
House n side G n, btw 9 and 10 w.
Mitchell, Caroline, (col) laundress, w side 11 w, btw I and K n.
Mitchell, Harvey, clerk Pension Office, n side Mass av, btw 13 and 14 w.
Mitchell, George, clerk Post Office Department, e side 12 w, btw K and L n.
Mitchell, James, captain steamboat, e side 11 w, btw Md av and F s.
Mitchell, Henry C., sand and wood merchant, n side La av, btw 6 and 7 w.
Mitchell, U. B., police officer, s side D s, btw 9 and 10 w.
Mitchell, Joseph, blacksmith, w side 6 e, btw D and Pa av.
Mitchell, Charles, captain steamboat "Osceola," n side I s, btw 7 and 8 e.
Mitchell, Thomas, foreman at penitentiary, w side 4½ w, btw N and O s.
Mitchell & Terrett, dry goods merchants, n side La av, btw 9 and 10 w.
Mitchell, Judson, broker, s side First, btw High and Potomac, Georgetown.
Mix, Charles E., clerk, e side High, btw West and Road, Georgetown.
Moaney, Michael, stonemason, n side C s, btw 13½ and 14 w.
Moe, Samuel, carpenter, n side L n, btw 8 and 9 w.
Mockbee, G. W., bootmaker, s side A s, btw N J av and 1 e.
Mockbee, J. B., gardener, n side East Capitol, btw 1 and 2 e.
Moffett, Joseph, fancy store, w side 7 w, btw D and E n.
Moffett, Hugh, cooper, w side 7 w, btw L and M n.
Moffett, Alexander, inspector telegraph lines, s side F n, btw 13 and 14 w.
Mohan, W. P., carpenter, w side 6 w, btw Pa av and La av.
House, 3d, btw F and G n.
Mohen, Francis, carpenter, w side 8 w, btw G and H n.
Mohun, William, carpenter, w side 3, btw F and G n.
Mohun, Philip, contractor, w side 3, btw F and G n.
Mohun, M. P., drygoods and grocery, e side 11 e, btw M and N s.
Moise, Mrs. E., widow, n side G n, btw 22 and 23 w.
Molden, G., laborer, s side K s, btw 13 and 14 e.
Monroe, Thomas, clerk, s side Md av, btw 6 and 7 w.
Monroe, George, (col) car driver, n side K n, btw 2 and 3 w.
Montgomery, J. B., U S N, e side 4½ w, btw C n and Ia av.
Moody, T. L., clerk, w side 11 w, btw G and H n.
Moone, Robert, drayman, w side 7 w, btw H and I s.
Moore, H. W., huckster, e side 7 w, btw N and O n.
Moore, Thomas, carpenter, e side 8 w, btw L and M n.
Moore, William, merchant tailor, n side Pa av, btw 4½ and 6 w.
Moore, John, baker, s side F n, btw 9 and 10 w.

Abbreviations.—All points start from the Capitol; s south, n north, e east, w west, btw between, cor corner, (col) colored, av avenue, h house.

Moore, William W., printer, s side F n, btw 6 and 7 w.
Moore, James, printer, cor 6 and Mass av.
Moore, Henry W., (col) bootmaker, s side D n, btw 6 and 7 w.
MOORE, DOUGLASS, Upholsterer, cor La av and 7 w.
House, D n, btw 9 and 10 w.
Moore, Wm., printer, w side 10 w, btw D and E n.
Moore, Robert B., wheelwright, w side 11 w, btw Pa and C.
Moore, J. M., clerk Department of Interior, s side I n, btw 17 and 18 w.
Moore, J. J., clerk Census office, s side M n, btw 6 and 7 w.
Moore, J. B., druggist, n side Pa av, btw 19 and 20 w.
Moore, J. P., clerk Quartermaster's Department, cor 17 w and Pa av.
Moore, Mrs., widow, w side 18 w, btw H and I n.
Moore, David, carpenter, n side Mo av, btw 4½ and 6 w.
Moore, Wm., (col) laborer, s side D s, btw 3 and 4 e.
Moore, Rev. J. P., clerk, s side West, btw Congress and High, Georgetown.
Moorhead, James W., clerk Post Office Department, s side K n, btw 11 and 12 w.
Moran, William, carter, w side 8 w, btw G and H s.
Moran, E., carpenter, s side Pa av, btw 21 and 22 w.
Moratte, Danl., laborer, s side A n, btw N J av and 2 w.
Morcoe, Wm. E., printer, w side 8 w, btw G and H n.
Mordecai, Major A., Superintendent of Arsenal, south end 4½ w.
Morehouse, A., w side 12 w, btw K and L n.
Morgan, Com. Charles W., commandant navy yard.
Morgan, Wm. S., e side 9 e, btw L and M s.
Morgan, Wm., blacksmith, n side G s, btw 8 and 9 e.
Morgan, J. B., grocer, w side 4½, btw Md av and C s.
Morgan, Henry, exchange broker, w side 8 w, btw G and H n.
Morgan, Dr. J. E., s side Md av, btw 11 and 12 w.
Morgan, John R., shoestore, s side Pa av, btw 9 and 10 w.
House, e side 8 w, btw L and M n.
Morgan, Wm., s side Pa av, btw 6 and 7 w; h 6, btw G and H n.
Morgan, A. C., grocery, w side 11 w, btw G and H n.
MORGAN, THOS. P. Commission Merchant, bone dust manufactory; office, foot of G, near river; h n side I n, btw 20 and 21 w.
Morgan, George, boatman, w side Jefferson, btw Canal and Water, Georgetown.
Morisey, Patrick, stonecutter, n side Mass av, btw 2 and N J av.
MORISON, G. F., Teacher, (Rugby Academy) cor 14 w and K n.
Morison, A., gardener, n side N, btw 12 and 13 w.
Morley, Mrs. H. L., fancy store, n side Pa av, btw 9 and 10 w.
Morley, Miss H. L., milliner, s side D n, btw 9 and 10 w.
Morris, John H., s side I n, btw 6 and 7 w.
Morris, Com. Charles, n side I n, btw 16 and 17 w.
Morris, Mary A., widow, n side Mass av, btw 6 and 7 w.
Morris, Wm., blacksmith, s side E s, btw 13 and 14 e.
Morrison, ——, (Espy &) druggist, cor 7 w and E n.
Morrison, A., dry goods, w side 7 w, btw I and N Y av.
MORRISON, WM., & CO., Bookstore, n side Pa av, btw 3 and 4½ w.
MORROW, ROBERT, exchange broker, n side Pa av, btw 6 and 7 w.
Morrow, Wm., n side D n, btw 2 and 3 w.
Morse, Mrs., seamstress, w side 8 w, btw L and M n.
Morse, J. E., gent., Me av, btw 3 and 4½ w.
Morsell, B. K., magistrate, 4th Dis., n side La av, btw 6 and 7 w.
House, n side Pa av, btw 6 and 7 w.
Morsell, R. J., clerk Land office, L n, btw Vt av and 15 w.
Morsell, Judge James, s w cor West and Congress, Georgetown.
Morsel, Samuel, carpenter, n side of G n, btw 4 and 5 w.
Morsel, B. F., grocer, n side La av, btw 6 and 7 w; boards at Mrs. Gallagher's.
Mortimer, James, carpenter, e side N J av, btw K and L n.
Mortimer, John T., grocer, cor E n and 9 w; n side Md av, btw 9 and 10 w.
Morton, Jackson, U. S. Senate, w side 4½ w, btw C n and Pa av.

Morton, J., clerk Capitol, n side Va av, btw 3 and 4 e.
Morton & Wilson, wholesale grocers, s side Water, opposite fish wharf, Geo'town.
Mosely, William, messenger War Department, n side G n, btw 22 and 23 w.
Mosher, Mrs., e side High, btw Gay and Bridge, Georgetown.
Moss, John J., blacksmith, n side G s, btw 7 and 8 e.
Moss, C. B., engineer, w side 10 w, btw D and E n.
Moss, Elizabeth, seamstress, w side 11 w, btw E and Pa av.
Moss, Philip D., teacher, e side 7 e, btw I and Va av.
Moton, Mary A., (col) laundress, e side 13½ w, btw D and C s.
Moulton, F., attorney, e side 12 w, btw E and F n.
Moulden, John A., carpenter, n side Va av, btw 9 and 10 w.
Moulder, John U., printer, s side I n, btw 8 and 9 w.
Mount, Sarah A., grocery, w side 10 w, btw N J av and K n.
Mountz, Mrs., & Son, w side Montgomery, cor Dumbarton, Georgetown.
Mountz, John, clerk, s side Bridge, btw Jefferson and Washington, Georgetown.
Moxley, Benjamin F., tobacconist, n w cor Bridge and Washington, Georgetown.
Moxley, William, blacksmith, s side Bridge, extreme west, Georgetown.
Mudd, Mary, widow, s side Md av, btw 12 and 13 w.
Mudd, J. F., tailor, n side D n, btw 7 and 8 w.
Mudd, Edward, n side G s, btw 11 and 12 e.
Mudd, Mrs., cake shop, n side Water, btw Cherry alley and Congress, Georgetown.
Mullen, William S., hackman, e side 7 w, btw E and F s.
Mullen, Pat., stonecutter, w side North Capitol, btw Mass av and G n.
Mulligan, Mary, grocery, n side C s, btw 3 and 4½ w.
Mullikin, James H., carpenter, e side 12 w, btw I and K n.
Mulliken, Miss, dressmaker, n side Bridge, one door east Green, Georgetown.
Mulloy, Thomas, bookbinder, s side D s, btw 6 and 7 w.
Mully, Betsey, (col) washerwoman, e side 5 e, btw C and D s.
Muncaster, Z. O., hardware, s side Bridge, btw Congress and High; house, s side Beall, cor Washington, Georgetown.
Munck, C. E., carpenter, n side D n, btw 6 and 7 w.
Munking, William, tailor, w side 4½ w, btw C and D s.
Munroe, Columbus, clerk Bureau Subsistence, n side E n, btw 6 and 7 w.
Munroe, Elizabeth, widow, n side La av, btw 6 and 7 w.
Murdoch, Wm. A., s side West, btw Washington and Congress, Georgetown.
Mure, L., (col) messenger Navy Department, e side 18 w, btw I and K n.
Murphy, Joseph, laborer, n side I s, btw 9 and 10 e.
Murphy, Cornelius, laborer, w side 3 w, btw C and D s.
Murphy, John, laborer, w side 7 w, btw N Y av and L n.
Murphy, Cornelius, laborer, w side 7 w, btw C and D s.
Murphy, Dennis, laborer, cor N J av and F n.
Murphy, Lawrence, saddler, n side F n, btw 13 and 14 w.
Murphy, Mrs. Mary, widow, seamstress, n side G n, btw 8 and 9 w.
Murphy, James, gardener, s side F s, btw 4½ and 6 w.
Murphy, John P., plasterer, s side B s, btw 13 and 13½ w.
Murphy, John, butcher, s side K s, btw 11 and 13 e.
Murray, Mrs, Sarah, w side 9 w, btw D and E n.
Murray & Semmes, grocers, s side Pa av, btw 4½ and 6 w.
Murray, J. R., (& Semmes,) C, btw 4½ and 6 w.
Murray, P. J., s side Pa av, btw 12 and 13 w.
Murray, H. G., grocer, cor K s and 8 e.
Murray, Mr., grocer, e side 20 w, btw E n and N Y av.
Murray, Owen, grocer, s side I n.
Murray, James, painter, s side Bridge, btw High and Potomac, Georgetown.
Murray, William A., huckster, w side High, btw 1st and 2d, Georgetown.
Murray, James, painter, e side High, btw West and Road, Georgetown.
Mustin, Thomas, clerk 5th Auditor's office, n side H n, btw 9 and 10 w.
MYERS & CO., Dry Goods, n side Pa av, btw 9 and 10 w.
Myers, Edward, (& Co.,) e side 9 w, btw L and M n.
Myers, Mrs. Ann, widow, boardinghouse, s side C n, btw 2 and 3 w.

Abbreviations.—All points start from the Capitol; s south, n north, e east, w west, btw between, cor corner, (col) colored, av avenue, h house,

Myers, Samuel, saddler, n side Mass av, btw 2 and 3 w.
Myers, Mary, (col) laundress, s side Mass av, btw 12 and 13 w.
Myers, F. S., magistrate, e side 15 w, btw Pa av and F n.
House w side 12 w, btw N Y av and H n.
Myers, Daniel, blacksmith, s side Pa av, btw 23 and 24 w.
Myers, A., laborer, n side N n, btw 4 and 5 w.
Myers, William, waiter, e side 14 w, btw L and M n.
Myers, George, grocer, w side 9 e, btw L s and Va av.
Myers, Joseph, machinist, e side 4 e, btw M and N s.
Myers, Charles, wood measurer, n side Dumbarton, btw High and Congress, G'tn.
Myers, Edward S., drygoods, n side Bridge, btw High and Congress; house, s side 2d, btw Market and Frederick, Georgetown.
Myers, Charles, carpenter, e side High, btw West and Road, Georgetown.

N.

Nailor, D., grocer, cor N n and 10 w.
Nairn, Joseph W., (Paterson &) druggist, n side Pa av, btw 9 and 10 w.
Nairn, John W., druggist, cor 15 w and N Y av.
Nally, James T., watchman, n side 8 e, btw K and L s.
Nally, Mrs., boardinghouse, e side 12 w, btw E and F n.
Nally, Joseph, laborer, s side L s, btw 8 and 9 e.
Nalley, Mrs. Mary Ann, n side G n, btw 8 and 9 w.
Nalley, Dennis, laborer, s side B n, btw 5 and 6 e.
Narle, Henry, laborer, n side B n, btw 1 and 2 e.
National Intelligencer, (Gales and Seaton,) office w side 8 w, cor D n.
National Hotel, (Dexter and Calvert,) cor Pa av and 6 w.
National Observatory, (Lieut. M. F. Maury, superin't,) s side E n, btw 24 and 25 w.
National Institute, Patent Office building, n side F n, btw 7 and 9 w.
National Era Office, w side 7 w, btw D and E n.
Navy Yard, United States, e end 8 e.
Navy Yard Market-house, s side K s, btw 6 and 7 e,
NAYLOR, F. G., Tin and Coppersmith, s side Pa av, btw 3 and 4½ w.
House s side C n, btw 2 and 3 w.
Naylor, William, coach trimmer, n side D n, btw 13½ and 14 w.
Naylor, James G., carpenter, n side Mass av, btw 6 and 7 w.
Naylor, A., w side 13 w, btw F and G n.
Naylor. Joshua, carpenter, e side 6 w, btw D and E s.
Neal, Raymond, (col) waiter, w side 3 w, btw N Y av and L n.
Neal, John T., laborer, n side D s, btw 3 and 4 e.
Neeckiver, Mrs., dressmaker, w side 16 w, btw M and N n.
NEELY, J. T., Attorney at Law and General Agent, cor 4½ w and Pa av.
Neil, John, clerk wood yard, n side H n, btw 4 and 5 w,
Neil, Ellen, (col) laundress, n side B s, btw 1 and 2 w.
Nelson, Samuel, n side G s, btw 6 and 7 e.
Nelson, Henry, wagon stand, n side Bridge, btw High and Potomac, Georgetown.
Nesbet, Mrs. Harriet, n side C n, btw 3 and 4½ w.
Netter, Dan., (col) laborer, s side E s, btw 3 and 4½ w.
Nevings, Mary, widow, s side I n, btw 6 and 7 w.
Newton, A. L., (Clagett, May & Co,) I n, btw 6 and 7 w.
Newton, Mrs. Elizabeth, widow, n side Mass av, btw 6 and 7 w.
Newton, William C., county constable, e side 18 w, btw K and L n.
Newland, John H. B., clerk Land Office, n side D n, btw 6 and 7 w.
Newman, Mrs., widow, dry goods, s side K s, btw 6 and 7 e.
Newman, Peter, shoemaker, e side 8 w, btw L and N Y av.
Newman, Dr. W. G. H., n side K n, btw 24 and 25 w.
House s side Pa av, btw 24 and 25 w.
Newman, T. A., shoemaker, s side Bridge, btw Congress and High, Georgetown.
Newmeger, Leopold, huckster, w side 7 w, btw L n and N Y av.

Nichols, Mrs. Ann, (col) laundress, n side E s, btw 4 and 5 e,
Nicholls, William, broker, n side West, btw Congress and High, Georgetown.
Nicholson, William, s side H n, btw 17 and 18 w.
Nicholson, Walter H., blacksmith, w side 3 e, btw L and M s.
Niedfeldt, J. F., tailor, n side E n, btw 8 and 9 w.
Niles, Samuel V., clerk General Land Office, e side 13 w, btw E and F n.
Nixon, Mr., watchmaker, s side Bridge, btw Washington and Jefferson, G'town.
Noakes, James, painter, w side 8 e, btw G and I s.
Noble, Rev. Mason, Principal Young Ladies' Sem., n side E n, btw 6 and 7 w.
Noble, Rezin, painter, e side Market, btw Bridge and Water, Georgetown.
Noell & Boyd, upholsterers, s side Pa av, btw 9 and 10 w.
Noell, William, (& Boyd,) blindmaker, s side Pa av, btw 9 and 10 w.
Noerr, Andrew, baker, cor 11 w and E n.
Nokes, Thomas, painter, e side 11 e, btw M and N s.
Noland, Jane, s side Mass av, btw 4 and 5 w.
Noland, Samuel, grocer, w side 15 w, btw L and M n.
Noonan, John, laborer, e side 4½ w, btw Miss av and Pa av.
Norbeck, George, confectioner, n side Pa av, btw 9 and 10 w.
Norflet, Thomas, saddler, n side G n, btw 1 and 2 e.
Norman, Richard, painter, w side 10 w, btw M and N n.
Norment, S., n side Mo av, btw 4½ and 6 w.
Norris, William G., painter, w side 11 w, btw Va av and C s.
Norris, Charles, engineer, w side 11 w, btw Md av and E s.
Norris, Mrs., widow, s side Va av, btw 3 and 4 e.
North, B., clerk, e side N J av, btw B and C s.
Northern Liberties Engine-house, N Y av, fronting 8 w.
Nott, William, printer, e side 9 w, btw Pa av and D n.
Nottingham, William, carpenter, w side 3 e, btw I and K s.
Nourse, Rev. James, Principal Central Academy, s side F n, btw 12 and 13 w.
Nourse, John, clerk Treasury Department, n side L n, btw 9 and 10 w.
Nourse, Michael, chief clerk Treasury Department, w side 13 w, btw E and F n.
Nourse, William, (Pairo &,) banker, n side N n, btw 10 and 11 w.
Nourse, H. M., attorney and agent, e side 15 w, btw F n and N Y av.
Noyes, George E., & Co., finishing shop, Me av, btw 3 and 4½ w.
Noyes, George, n side G n, btw 4 and 5 w.
Nicholson, Joseph, machinist, w side High, btw 1st and 2d, Georgetown.
Noyes, C. S. & H., agents for Baltimore Sun, n side C n, btw 6 and 7 w.
Noyes, T. L., clerk, n side H n, btw 4 and 5 w.
Noyes, Wm., wholesale boot merchant, n side La av, btw 6 and 7 w; h Georgetown.
Noyes, William, wholesale shoedealer, s w cor West and Green, Georgetown.
Noyes, Alb., s w cor West and Green, Georgetown.
Newton, Charles, cabinetmaker, n side Bridge, btw Green and Montgomery, G'tn.
Newton, John B., lottery, e side Market space, Georgetown.
Nugent, Eli, (col) porter, w side 8 w, btw L and M n.
Nugent, T. M., Falcon House, s side F n, btw 13 and 14 w.
Nunnery, w side Fayette, btw 3d and 4th, Georgetown.
Nutsill, Sally Ann, e side 18 w, btw I and K n.
Nye, J. W., carpenter, s side L n, btw 6 and 7 w.

O.

Oakes, John, laborer, w side 3 w, btw M and N s.
Oakes, Michael, omnibus driver, s side Prospect, btw High and Potomac, G'town.
Ober, Franklin, machinist, w side 10 e, btw K s and Va av.
O'BRIEN, CAPT. WM., Broker, w side 4½, 2 doors south Pa av.
O'Brien, Terence, laborer, s side D n, btw 2 and 3 w.
O'Brien, E. E., agent, s side Mass av, btw 6 and 7 w.
O'Brien, Wm., shoemaker, n side F n, btw N J av and 2 w.
O'Brien, Michael, laborer, e side 2 w, btw F and G n.

Abbreviations.—All points start from the Capitol; s south, n north, e east, w west, btw between, cor corner, (col) colored, av avenue, h house.

O'Brien, Patrick, laborer, n side C s, btw 10 and 11 e.
O'Brien, Rodey, stonecutter, s side C s, btw 6 and 7 w.
O'Brien, C., laborer, n side F n, btw 2 and 3 w.
O'Brien, Frank, shoestore, e side Market space; h, n side 2d, west of Frederick, Georgetown.
O'Brien, William, shoe store, s side Bridge, a few doors east of market-house, G'tn.
O'Bryon, James, painter, s side Pa av, btw 12 and 13 w.
House, s side D n, btw 12 and 13 w.
O'Conner, James, laborer, w side North Capitol, btw Mass av and G n.
O'Conner, Danl., machinist, n side G s, btw 7 and 8 e.
O'Conner, John, laborer, cor N J av and F n.
O'Conner, D., laborer, e side 3 w, btw Md av and C.
O'Conner, James A., city Express driver, w side 9 w, btw D and E n.
O'Conner, Thomas, laborer, e side 2 w, btw G and Mass av.
O'Conner, M., laborer, n side East Capitol, btw 1 and 2 e.
O'Donnell, John, carpenter, w side 8 e, btw G and I s.
O'Donnell, Mrs. Ellenor, widow, w side 8 e, btw G and I s.
Odd-Fellows' Hall, e side Congress, btw High and the Canal, Georgetown.
O'Donnoghue, P. & T., candle and soap factory, n side G n, btw 4 and 5 w.
O'Donoghue, Timothy, candle factory, s side 1st, near College, Georgetown.
O'Donoghue, Peter, clothing store, n e cor High and Bridge; also store and dwelling e side Market space, Georgetown.
O'Donohue, Miss, china store, e side market space, Georgetown.
Ofenstein, Caspar, blacksmith, s side B n, btw 2 and 3 e.
Offert, Artaxeres, grocer, s e corner Bridge and Market space, Georgetown.
Offert, Hilleary L., grocer, w side High, two doors from Bridge, Georgetown.
House, s side 1st, btw Market and Frederick, Georgetown.
Offut, Zachariah M., painter, n side 2d, btw Potomac and Frederick, Georgetown.
Offutt, John, carpenter, s side Mass av, btw 4 and 5 w.
Offutt, T. K., painter, s side I n, btw 6 and 7 w.
Offutt, Marion, painter, e side 4½ w, btw C and D s.
Offutt, Henry, clerk 6th Auditor's office, s side Pa av, btw 3 and 4½ w.
Ogle, Mrs., seamstress, Market, btw 4th and 5th, Georgetown.
Ogle, Benjamin, painter, w side Frederick, btw 3d and 4th, Georgetown.
Oh, George, pedlar, e side 4½ w, btw Md av and Me av.
O'Hare, Michael, stonemason, s side C s, btw 6 and 7 w.
O'Hare, C. S., grocer, cor 7 w and M n.
O'Hare, D., engraver, n side Pa av, btw 12 and 13 w.
O'Leary, Jerry, stonecutter, w side 4½ w, btw C and D s.
O'Leary, Mrs., Catharine, confectioner, s side Pa av, btw 4½ and 6 w.
Oliver, J. B., clerk Treasury Department, w side 11 w, btw F and G n.
Oliver, Thomas, tailor, w side 14 w, btw C and D n.
Olmstead, Rev. Mr., school, e side Montgomery, btw Beall and Dumbarton, G'twn.
O'Meara, John, confectioner, n side Pa av, btw 1 and 2 w.
O'Meara, William, confectioner, n side Pa av, btw 1 and 2 n.
O'Neal, Patrick, laborer, w side 3 w, btw G and H.
O'Neal, H. G., clerk Navy Department, n side M n, btw 9 and 10 w.
O'Neal, Mrs., and William, w side High, btw Prospect and First, Georgetown.
O'Neale, Timothy, new building 4th st., opposite Academy, on Fayette; h, w side Fayette, north of Academy, Georgetown.
O'Neall, John, laborer, n side F n, btw 22 and 23 w.
O'Neall, Mrs. Mary, widow, grocer, w side 8 e, btw G and I s.
Onor, M., fancy store, e side 10 w, btw Md av, and F s.
Oppenheim, L., pedlar, w side 4½ w, btw Md av and C s.
Orem, James B., (Young &) C, btw 6 and 7 w.
ORME, WM., Grocer, n side D n, btw 10 and 11 w.
House, e side 11 w, btw E and F n.
Orme, ——, clerk, n e cor Stoddart and Congress, Georgetown.
Orme, Jeremiah, store, s w cor Bridge and Congress; h, n side West, btw Congress and Washington, Georgetown.

Abbreviations.—All points start from the Capitol; s south, n north, e east, w west, btw between, cor corner, (col) colored, av avenue, h house.

Orphan Asylum, (male) St. Matthew's Church, w side Vt av, btw L and M n.
Orphans' school, Catholic, w side Fayette, n of Academy. Georgetown.
Orrison, Arthur, cartman, n side D s, btw 13½ and 14 w.
Ortool, Luke, stonecutter, n side F s, btw 2 and 3 w.
Osborn, James, carpenter, n side L n, btw 9 and 10 w.
Osborne, McK., drygoods, n side Bridge, btw Congress and High; h, s side Beall, btw Congress and High, Georgetown.
Osborne, Mrs., s w corner Bridge and Market, Georgetown.
Osgodby & Williamson, carpenters, 13, btw D and Pa av.
Ostermayer, B., bootmaker, s side F n, btw 12 and 13 w.
Ott, John, clerk Capitol, e side Va av, btw H and I n.
Otter, James, coachman, w side 10 w, btw D and E n.
Otterback, Philip, butcher, s side 8 e, btw L and M s.
Otterback, Philip, jr., grocer, e side 11 e, btw N and O s.
House, e side 8 e, btw L and M s.
Ould, Mrs., s side Dumbarton, near Green, Georgetown.
Ould, Robert, attorney, n side 1st, btw Potomac and Market; office, at Mayor's office, Georgetown.
Ourand, Elijah, messenger Treasury Department, e side 12 w, btw K and L n.
Over, Frances, (col) laundress, s side D s, btw 5 and 6 e.
Owen, Edward, & Son (Samuel) merchant tailors, n side Pa av, btw 14 and 15 w.
Owen, B. F., clerk Pension office, w side 12 w, btw M and N n.
Owens, Charles, shoemaker, s side B n, btw 2 and 3 w.
Owens, B., w side North Capitol, btw B and C s.
Owens, James, laborer, n side D s, btw 3 and 4 e.
Owens, James L., clerk, s side Prospect, btw High and Potomac, Georgetown.
Oyster, David, grocer, s w cor High and First, Georgetown.
Oxley, Thomas, grocer, s side Pa av, btw 19 and 20 w.
Oxley, Everett J., carpenter, n side C s, btw 13 and 13½ w.

P.

Padget, Joseph, navy yard, s side L s, btw 8 and 9 e.
Padgett, John, butcher, w side 3 e, btw Va av and I s.
Page, Y. P., clerk Capitol, n side Va av, btw 4 and 5 e.
Page, L. S., s side F s, btw 6 and 7 w.
Page & Paynter, flour mill, s side F s, btw 6 and 7 w.
Page, Wm., clerk Land Office, boards cor 4½ and Pa av.
Page, Quincy, miller, w side 7 w, btw E and F n.
Page, George A., shipbuilder, e side 7 w, btw F and G s.
Page, Charles G., agent for Patents, s side F n, btw 7 and 8 w.
Page, J., U. S. N., n side H n, btw 15 and Vt av.
Page, George, A., brickyard, 6 w, btw I and L s.
Page, ———, clerk at W. H. Bryan's, s side Bridge, extreme west, Georgetown.
Paget, John, huckster, w side 4½ w, btw M and N s.
PAIGE, BLANCHARD, Daguerreotypist, over Todd's hat store.
House, w side 6 w, btw H and I n.
Paine, Samuel, (col) laborer, s side D s, btw 4 and 5 e.
Painter, Vantine, w side 7 w, btw N Y av and L n.
Pairo, O. S., clerk Pension office, s side I n, btw 17 and 18 w.
Pairo & Nourse, bankers, e side 15 w, btw F n and Pa av.
Pairo, Charles W., banker, s side Prospect, near Frederick, Georgetown.
Pakinson, Wm., tinner, w side 6 w, btw G and H n.
Palmer, William, waiter, e side 3 w, btw G and Mass av.
Palmer, A., agency, cor 15 and Pa av.
Palmer, Dr. W. G., n side H n, btw 9 and 10 w.
Palmer, Mrs., confectioner, High, btw 2d and 3d, Georgetown.
Parhan, Wm. J., stonecutter, w side 10 w, btw E and F n.
Parish, Levi, w side 14 w, btw F n and Pa av.

Abbreviations.—All points start from the Capitol; s south, n north, e east, w west, btw between, cor corner, (col) colored, av avenue, h house.

Parker, Wm. P., barber, w side 4 w, btw I and Mass av.
Parker, Francis E., bricklayer, n side Md av, btw 6 and 7 w.
Parker, Henry T., tailor, e side 8 w, btw L and M n.
Parker, S., fancy store, n side Pa av, btw 4½ and 6 w.
Barker & Co., G. & Thomas, grocers, s side Pa av, btw 6 and 7 w.
Parker, George, (& Thomas) cor 4½ and C n.
Parker, Thos., (George &) w side 6 w, btw D and E n.
Parker, James, slate yard, s side F n, btw 12 and 13 w.
Parker, M. T., painter, n side C n, btw 6 and 7 w.
Parker, Henry, carpenter, s side Mass av, btw 6 and 7 w.
Parker & Spaulding, painters, n side Pa av, btw 17 and 18 w.
Parker, S. S., (& Spaulding) H, btw 21 and 22 w.
Parker, Wm., (col) laborer, e side 20 w, btw K and L n.
Parker, Mrs., widow, n side G n, btw 18 and 19 w.
Parker, M. T., painter, s side La av, btw 6 and 7 w; h C, btw 6 and 7 w.
Parker, James, (col) laborer, s side C s, btw 1 and 2 w.
Parker, William, painter, w side High, btw 1st and 2d, Georgetown.
Parkhill, Robert, blacksmith, w side 4½ w, btw C and D s.
Parkhurst, W. G., reporter, s side F n, btw 9 and 10 w.
Parkhurst, H. L., reporter, w side 14 w, btw Pa av and E n.
Parkins, Joseph, stonecutter, n side N Y av, btw 21 and 22 w.
Parmer, John, n side Md av, btw 13½ and 14 w.
Parris, Julia, widow, w side 19 w, btw Pa av and I n.
Parry, H., marble yard, s side H n, btw 18 and 19 w.
Pascoe, ——, baker, w side Jefferson, btw Water and the bridge, Georgetown.
Parsons, T. H., railroad agent, cor Del av and C.
Parsons, Mrs. Elizabeth, widow, e side 7 w, btw E and F s.
Parsons, Thomas, refectory, s side Pa av, btw 12 and 13 w.
Parsons, Mrs. Mary L., widow, e side 11 e, btw M and N s.
Parsons, William, shoemaker, w side High, btw 1st and 2d, Georgetown.
Patch, Mrs., widow, confectioner, n side G n, btw 12 and 13 w.
Patterson & Nairn, druggists, n side Pa av, btw 9 and 10 w.
Patterson, Lieut. T. H., U. S. N., n side I n, btw 20 and 21 w.
Patterson, James, refectory, cor H n and 19 w.
Patterson, B., (col) laborer, w side 15 w, btw L and M n.
Patterson, Wm., P. watchman Coast Survey office, e side 5 e, btw L and M s.
Patterson, Robert, clerk, n side West, 2d door east of Congress, Georgetown.
Patrick, Wm., (col) cooper, w side 21 w, btw K and L n.
Patton, L., (col) barber, s side C s, btw 2 and 3 w.
Paul, Isaac, clerk Law office, w side 17 w, btw H and I n.
Paul & Brown, flour and commission, s side Water, west of High, Georgetown.
Paul, John, carpenter, n side 2d, Georgetown.
Payne, William, carpenter, w side 4½ w, btw C and D s.
Payne, Henry, feed store, s side 1st, btw Frederick and Fayette, Georgetown.
Payne, ——, shoemaker, e side Washington, btw West and Beall, Georgetown.
Payne, Henry, coach factory, w side Washington, btw Gay and Congress, G'town.
Payne, John, coachmaker, e side Washington, btw Bridge and Canal; h, on Bridge street, Georgetown.
Payne, L., shoemaker, s side Bridge, btw Congress and High, Georgetown.
Payne, James, shoemaker, s side Fourth, btw Market and Frederick, Georgetown.
Peaco, Wm. H., fancy store, n side La av, btw 8 and 9 w.
Peak, Wm., laborer Treasury Department, e side 14 w, btw H and I n.
Peak, Mrs. Charlotte, widow, s side L s, btw 4 and 5 e.
Peake, John, blacksmith, w side 4½ w, btw I and J s.
Peake, John H., painter, s side 8 e, btw K and L s.
Peale, T. R., Examiner Patent office, n side G n, btw 14 and 15 w.
Pearce, T., exchange broker, n side Pa av, btw 3 and 4½ w.
Pearce, A., clerk Land office, w side 14 w, btw L and M n.
Pearce, Peter, plasterer, s side Va av, btw 3 and 4½ w.
Pearce, Gideon, clerk, s side Prospect, extreme west, Georgetown.

Pearson, Peter M., lumber and coal merchant, w side 7 w, btw Pa av and Canal.
Peck, Joseph, butcher, s side Pa av, btw 6 and 7 w.
Peck, Rev. Jesse T., pastor Foundry Methodist Church, n side G n, btw 13 and 14 w.
Peckham, Mrs. Sophia, widow, teacher, s side F n, btw 8 and 9 w.
Peddicord, Mrs. C. E., milliner, n side E n, btw 6 and 7 w.
Pegg, Wm., grocer, e side 11 w, btw M and N s.
Pelitsi, Mrs., widow, n side I s, btw 6 and 7 e.
Pendleton, A. G., Professor Mathematics U. S. N., w side 2 e, btw B and C s.
Penitentiary, south end 4½ w.
Penniman, B. J., M. C. from Michigan, s side B s, btw N J av and 1 e.
Penny, Charles, (col) laborer, w side 18 w, btw N Y av and F n.
Pension office, Winder's Building, cor 17 w and F n.
Pepper, J. P., office, rear Adam's Express office.
Percell, Vincent, laborer, e side 3 e, btw Ga av and N s.
Peregoy, Joseph, bricklayer, w side 9 w, btw D and E n.
Perkins, Mrs., dressmaker, e side 19 w, btw G and H n.
Perley, Sarah A., widow, n side I n, btw 10 and 11 w.
Perry, Augustus, (& Bro.,) opposite City Post office.
Perry, Wm., merchant, n side La av, btw 6 and 7 w.
Perry & Brothers, drygoods, n side La av, btw 7 and 8 w.
Perry, A. E., (& Bro.) 7, btw E and F n.
Perry, T. J. S., (& Bro.) La av.
Perry, ———, gunsmith, n side Bridge, btw Potomac and High, Georgetown.
Perrie, George, clerk, n side H n, btw 9 and 10 w.
Perseverance Engine House, s side Pa av, btw 7 and 8 w.
Peters, J. H., attorney, w side 2 e, btw B and C s.
Peters, Julius A., fancy store, n side Pa av, btw 9 and 10 w.
Peters, James, laborer, w side 11 w, btw I and K n.
Peters, John, driver, e side 22 w, btw K and L n.
Peters, Thomas, clerk Capitol, n side East Capitol, btw 1 and 2 e.
Peters, Mrs., s side Road, near Congress, Georgetown,
Peterson, Henry, (col) confectioner, w side 3 w, btw C n and Ia av.
Petersen, W. P., merchant tailor, w side 8 w, btw Pa av and D n.
House 10 w, btw E and F n.
Petit, Richard, carpenter, w side Frederick, btw 1st and 2d, Georgetown.
Petit, ——, cooper, w side High, btw 1st and 2d, Georgetown.
Pettibone, J., lumber merchant, Lennox wharf, s end 13½ w.
Pettit, Charles, messenger Treasury, n side E n, btw 5 and 6 w.
Pettit, Charles W., clerk Third Auditor's, e side 6 w, btw G and H n.
Pettit, Smith, blacksmith, n side C n, btw 13 and 14 w.
Peugh, S. A., e side 7 w, btw E and F n.
Peugh, Hugh, tailor, n side N Y av, btw 17 and 18 w.
Peyton, Eliza, boarding, cor 4½ w and Pa av.
Perper, Mrs., grocer, s w cor Green and Dumbarton, Georgetown.
PHELPS, OLIVER, Law Office, n side Pa av, btw 4½ and 6 w; boards Nat. Hotel.
Phelps, John, finisher, e side 5 e, btw G and I s.
PHILIP, WILLIAM H., Attorney at Law, Lane & Tucker's building, Pa av, btw 4½ and 6 w; boards National Hotel.
Philips, George, messenger, cor 4 and G w.
Philips, Samuel, document room Capitol, w side 3 w, btw B and C n.
Philips, G. W., exchange broker, n side Pa av, btw 6 and 7 w.
House s side D n, btw 2 and 3 w.
Philips, Thomas, blacksmith, s side D n, btw 8 and 9 w.
Philips, William, engraver, w side 11 w, btw E and F n.
Philips, William, printer, n side I n, btw 6 and 7 w.
Philips, John W., carpenter, w side 12 w, btw M and N n.
Philips, James, plasterer, n side H n, btw 6 and 7 w.
Philips, James, carpenter, w side 3 e, btw L and M s.
Phipps, John, gunsmith, e side 4½ w, btw M and N s.
Phisk, Richard, (col) s side A s, btw N J av and 1 e.

Abbreviations.—All points start from the Capitol; s south, n north, e east, w west, btw between, cor corner, (col) colored, av avenue, h house.

Pickerell, J. D., oyster house, e side 13½ w, btw D and E n.
Pickett, John B., n side Ky av, btw 14 and 15 e.
Pickrell, Mrs., and William, n side First, btw High and Prospect, Georgetown.
Pickrell, Esau, merchant, s side Water, near Congress; h, n side 2d, cor Market, Georgetown.
Pickrell, Adolphus, merchant, s side Water, near Congress; h, n side 3d, btw Market and Frederick, Georgetown.
Pierce, Daniel, umbrella maker, s side Pa av, btw 12 and 13 w.
Pierce, Mrs. Mary A., boardinghouse, w side 1 e, btw B and C s.
Pigott, Jennings, clerk 3d Auditor's office, n side D n, btw 14 and 15 w.
Pilling, James, grocer, cor 4½ w and Md av.
Pilling, James, carpenter, s side N Y av, btw 14 and 15 w.
Pilling, A., fancy store, e side 15 w, btw Pa av and F n.
Pimonds, Johnson, shoemaker, e side N J av, btw B and C s
Pipher, Joseph, shoemaker, e side 4 w, btw I and K n.
Plant, P., w side 7 w, btw E and F s.
Plant, James K., paperhanger, n side D n, btw 9 and 10 w.
Plant, John, bricklayer, w side 11 w, btw G and H n.
Platt, L., attorney at law, n side G n, btw 10 and 11 w.
Plant, Joseph T. K., paper hanger, n side D n, btw 9 and 10 w.
Plant, J. Wm., cabinetmaker, same place.
Pleasants, G. W., attorney at law, w side 4½ w, btw La av and C n.
Pleasants, B. F., chief clerk office Solicitor Treas., n side E n, btw 6 and 7 w.
Pleasanton, Stephen, 5th Aud. Treas. Dep't, w side 21 w, btw E and F n.
Plowman, William R., bricklayer, w side 4 w, btw I and K n.
Plummer, P., carpenter, s side G n, btw 12 and 13 w.
Plummer, M. A., (col) laundress, e side 15 w, btw H and I n.
Plumbe, ——, daguerreotypist, Brown's Hotel building.
Poe, Jacob, n side Bridge, btw Frederick and Fayete, Georgetown.
Polk, J. F., clerk Treasury Department, s side K n, btw 26 and 27 w.
Polkinhorn, Richard, saddler, s side Md av, btw 6 and 7 w.
House n side D n, btw 6 and 7 w.
Polkinhorn, Charles, carpenter, e side 6 w, btw G and H n.
Polkinhorn, Henry, printer, cor Pa av and 10 w; h s side B n, btw 9 and 10 w.
Pollard, R. J., ornithologist National Museum, s side B s, btw 6 and 7 w.
Pollard, ——, (col) porter at Gadsby's Hotel, s side I n, btw 12 and 13 w.
Pollard, A., carpenter, e side 20 w, btw G and H n.
Polly, ———, butcher, Market, btw 4th and 5th, Georgetown.
Pomeroy, George, cabinetmaker, e side Conn av, btw I and K n.
Pomeroy, Walter, barber, e side High, btw Gay and Dumbarton, Georgetown.
Pons, Antonio, musician marine band, n side 8 e, btw F and G s.
Pool, Wilson E., huckster, e side 7 w, btw N and O n.
Poor, John, blacksmith, w side 18 w, btw Pa av and G n.
Poor, Frederick, painter, n side West, east of Montgomery, Georgetown.
Pope, Charles T., 6th Auditor's office, s side Pa av, btw 3 and 4½ w.
Pope, William, clerk, n side Mass av, btw 11 and 12 w.
Pope, F., carpenter, s side [illegible] s, btw 8 and 9 e.
Porter, D., blacksmith, e side 10 w, btw K and L s.
Porter, J. E., painter, n side I n, btw 9 and 10 w.
Porter, David, brickmaker, w side 3 w, btw M and N s.
Porter, Mrs. W. T., boarding, s side Pa av, btw 4½ and 6 w.
Porter, William T., painter, over Green's auction store.
Porter, Denton S., billiard saloon, cor Pa av and 6 w; h Pa av btw 4½ and 6 w.
Porter, ——, clerk at Farmers and Mechanics' Bank, s e cor Bridge and Congress, Georgetown.
Porterfield, George A., clerk, Prospect, btw Market and Frederick, Georgetown.
Potter, Mrs. H., widow, n side G n, btw 14 and 15 w.
Potter, Thomas, furniture store, s side Mass av, btw 4 and 5 w.
Poulton, Wm., woodenware manufacturer, w side 8 w, btw Pa av and D n.
Pourtales, L. F., clerk Coast Survey, n side B s, btw N J av and 1 e.

Abbreviations.—All points start from the Capitol; s south, n north, e east, w west, btw between, cor corner, (col) colored, av avenue, h house.

Powell, H. C., grocer, cor 13 w and E n; h cor 14 w and Ohio av.
Powell, William C., clerk Treasury Department, w side 10 w, btw L and M n.
Powell, G., clerk Treasury Department, e side 14 w, btw C and D n.
Power, J. E., tobacconist, n side C n, btw 6 and 7 w.
Power, Mrs., widow, n side G n, btw 22 and 23 w.
Power, Mrs., widow, n side E s, btw 6 and 7 w.
Posey, J., (col) laundress, s side I n, btw 12 and 13 w.
Posey, R., (col) plasterer, n side N n, btw 14 and 15 w.
Posey, Thomas, laborer, e side 14 w, btw B and C s.
Post Office, General, n side E n, btw 7 and 8 w.
Post Office, City, w side 7 w, btw E and F n.
Poston, John, constable, n side K n, btw 27 and 28 w.
Potts, Samuel J., clerk War Department, w side 17 w, btw H and I n.
Potts, John, chief clerk War Department, w side 17 w, btw H and I n.
Prander, John W., messenger State Department, w side 6 w, btw F and G n
Prather, Leonard, cartman, n side I n, btw 4 and 5 w.
Prather, O. J., contractor, n side M n, btw 6 and 7 w.
Pringle, Miss Mary A., n side Mass av, btw 12 and 13 w.
Preinkert, Conrad, baker, cor 7 w and M n.
President's House, s side Pa av, btw 15 and 17 w.
Prettyman, Mary, widow, n side H n, btw 17 and 18 w.
Prater, William, (col) carpenter, alley e side 4½ w, btw Mo av and Pa av.
Prather, Joseph, butcher, e side 3 w, btw N and O n.
Prenot, Henry, machinist, w side 4 w, btw G and H n.
Prentice, Rufus, clerk post office, s side Mass av, btw 6 and 7 w.
Prentice, W. H., messenger State Department, n side L n, btw Vt av and 15 w.
Preston, John T., slater, w side 12 w, btw E and F n.
Preuss, Charles, surveyor, w side 4½ w, btw N and O s.
Preuss, Thaddeus, clerk Treasury Department, n side I n, btw 18 and 19 w.
Pribram, Solomon, fancy store, cor 7 w and H n.
Price, W. F., clerk Capitol, n side A n, btw 1 e and Del av.
Pritchard, H. F., e side N J av, btw M and N s.
Pritchard, Mrs. Lettia, widow, e side 10 w, btw H and I n.
Proctor, Abner B., carpenter, e side 11 w, btw E and F n.
Proctor, Samuel, (col) laborer, s side I n, btw 12 and 13 w.
Prosperi, Francis, musician, n side G s, btw 7 and 8 e.
Prout, Jonathan, gent., n side Va av btw 3 and 4 e.
Protestant Orphan Asylum, s side H n, btw 9 and 10 w.
Prott, B. F., bootmaker, s side Mass av, btw 2 and 3 w.
Pulin, Hanson, driver, n side G s, btw 8 and 9 e.
Pumphrey & Vermillion, grocers, cor 4½ w and N s.
Pumphrey, Jackson, carpenter, n side G n, btw 4½ and 6 w.
House w side 4½ w, btw F and G s.
Pumphrey, John W., laborer, cor 7 w and L n.
Pumphrey, Dennis, livery stable, cor C n and 6 w.
Pumphrey, Levy, livery stable, n side C, btw 4½ and 6 w.
Pumphrey, J. H., carpenter, n side I n, btw 4 and 5 w.
Purdy, Richard G., shoemaker, w side 3 w, btw F and G n.
PURDY, JOHN P., Coal and Lumber Merchant, 1 w, btw Pa av and B n.
House n side Pa av, btw 1 and 2 w.
Purdon, Mrs., grocery, w side 14 w, near Pa av.
Purrington, Dr. T., s side G n, btw 14 and 15 w.
Pursell, William F., Judge, s side Md av, btw 6 and 7 w.
PURSELL, T., & SON, China Store, s side Pa av, btw 6 and 7 w.
Pyne, Rev. Dr., (St. John's Episcopal Church,) n side H n, near cor 16 w.
Pywell, Robert, porter National Hotel, n side D n, btw 6 and 7 w.

6

Abbreviations.—All points start from the Capitol; s south, n north, e east, w west, btw between, cor corner, (col) colored, av avenue, h house.

Q.

Quaid, Francis, waterman, w side 7 w, btw G and H s.
Quantrill, Archibald R., claim agent, e side Vt av, btw H and I n.
Quaralles, Benj. (col) cook, w side 18 w, btw K and L n.
Queen, E. F. & Co., grocers, w side 7 w, btw I and N Y av.
Queen, Charles J., grocer, w side 7 w, btw L and M n.
Queen, John R., clerk in Capitol, n side 8 e, btw I and K s.
Queen, Richard T., clerk Treasury Department, n side I n, btw 4 and 5 w.
Queen, Richard, clerk, w slde 12 w, btw C and D s.
Queen, Theodore, cabinetmaker, w side 12 w, btw C and D s.
Queen, Thomas H., (col) clothdresser, w side 6 w, btw D and E n.
Queen, Wm., (col) waiter, n side C n, btw 12 and 13 w.
Quigley, William, grocery, w side 11 e, btw M and N s.
Quigley, Francis, grocer, w side 3, btw B and C n.
Quigley, Michael, grocer, w side 7 w, btw N and O n.
Quigley, Wm., grocer, w side 7 w, btw N and O n.
Quigley, Mary, grocer, s side C s, btw 12 and 13 e.
Quincy, Thos. H., clerk Land office, n side K n, btw 12 and 13 w.
Quinn, Dan., grocer, cor G n and 13 w.
Quinn, Alfred, (col) laborer, w side Vt av, btw K and L n.
Quynn, Mr., watchman at Factory, Georgetown.

R.

Raab, Adam, tailor, s side E n, btw 6 and 7 w.
Rabbitt, Saml. A., carpenter, e side 4½ w, btw C and D s.
Rabbitt, Thos., shoemaker, w side 10 w, btw N Y av and K.
Rabbitt, John, clerk, s side B s, btw 13 and 13½ w.
Radcliff, John W., carpenter, e side 4½ w, btw E and F s.
RADCLIFF, JOSEPH T., Grocer, e side 7 w, btw D and E n.
House, w side 6 w, btw E and F n.
Radcliff, Matilda, widow, w side 7 w, btw E and F s.
Radcliff, S. J., agricultural implements, w side 9 w, btw B and La av.
House, cor 6 w and F n.
Radcliff, Joseph, clerk City Hall, w side 6 w, btw F and G n.
Radcliffe, D., attorney at law, cor E n, and 8 w.
Radcliffe, Joseph, n side Gay, btw Congress and High, Georgetown.
Ragan, Thomas, cartman, n side D s, btw 13½ and 14 w.
Ragan, James, grocery, n side F n, btw 2 and 3 w.
Ragan, Dennis, laborer, e side 2 w, btw F and G n.
Ragan, Mrs. widow, n side H n, btw 4 and 5 w.
Ragan, Danl., cartman, w side 13½ w, btw Md av and D s.
Ragan, Richard R., grocer, s side Bridge, btw Green and Montgomery, Geo'town.
Raidey, John laborer, cor N J av and F n.
Raidy, John, grocer, cor 6 w and G n.
Railey, ——, n side Va av, btw 1 and 2 w.
Railroad Depot, e side N J av, btw C and D n.
Rainey, Robert, livery stable, w side 8 w, btw D and E n.
House, 8 w, btw G and H n.
Rainey, Charles, livery stable, s side E, btw 9 and 10 w.
Raley, Thomas, cartman, s side D n, btw 1 and 2 w.
Ramsey, Com. Wm., U S N, n side I n, btw 20 and 21 w.
Ran, J. W., professor of music, n side Pa av, btw 14 and 15 w.
Ran, G., bootmaker, n side Ga av, btw 10 and 11 e.
Rand, James R., Adams' Express office, w side 6 w, btw D and E n.
Randall, G. A. W., feedstore, cor D n and 12 w.

Abbreviations.—All points start from the Capitol; s south, n north, e east, w west, btw between, cor corner, (col) colored, av avenue, h house.

Reid, Robert, cashier Farmers and Mechanics' Bank, n side Gay, east of Montgomery, Georgetown.
Reid, Davis, flour merchant, s side Water, west of High.
House, n side Gay, east of Montgomery, Georgetown.
Reidy, John, laborer, n side D n, btw 12 and 13 w.
Reinhartt, Charles, shoemaker, e side 4½ w, btw Mo av and Pa av.
Reintzell, Samuel, carpenter, angle of Market and High, Georgetown.
Reiley, John, hackman, s side D s, btw 3 and 4½ w.
Reilley, Francis, messenger Capitol, n side 8 e, btw I and K s.
Reilly, B. T., clerk Treasury Department, w side 17 w, btw H and I n.
Reilly, Mrs., w side Lingan, btw 2d and 3d, Georgetown.
Reilly & Brother, (James and John) saddlers, e side High, btw Gay and Bridge, Georgetown.
Reily, Thomas B., clerk General Post Office, w side N J av, btw B s and Pa av.
Reily, James, machinist, w side 3 e, btw I and K s.
Reiss, B., professor of music, n side G n, btw 14 and 15 w.
Reiss, J. H., messenger Treasury Department, s side I n, btw 9 and 10 w.
Remick, Timothy, hats and caps, n side Bridge, btw Congress and High, G'town.
Remmington, Mr., e side Market, btw 2d and 3d, Georgetown.
Renn, Thomas, laborer, n side F n, btw 2 and 3 w.
Renwick, Edward S., (Watson &) boards at Mrs. Janney's.
Republic office, w side 9 w, btw Pa av and D n.
Reuss, Dr. P. T., e side 7 w, btw D and E n.
Reynolds, H. W., Coast Survey, w side N J av, btw D and E s.
Reynolds, E. K., painter, n side D n, btw 6 and 7 w.
Reynolds, Joseph, clerk Post Office Department, n side H n, btw 9 and 10 w.
Reynolds, Enos, foundryman, n side Water, near Aqueduct, Georgetown.
Reynolds, John, cooper, n side Bridge, btw Green and Montgomery, Georgetown.
Reynolds, Joseph, Cherry Alley, Georgetown.
Rhees, William Jones, clerk Census office, s side F n, btw 12 and 13 w.
Rhees, Henry Holcombe, clerk Census office, s side F n, btw 12 and 13 w.
Rhodes, Elizabeth, (col) laundress, n side K n, btw 17 and 18 w.
Rhodes, Harriet, laundress, s side K n, btw 9 and 10 w.
Rhodes, George, s side Bridge, near Market, Georgetown.
Rhodier, Jas. R., clothing, s side Bridge, btw Congress and High, Georgetown.
Rhodier, H., upholsterer, n side Bridge, btw Congress and Washington, Geo'town.
Rice, John, baker, s side F n, btw 6 and 7 w.
Rice, N., clerk War Department, n side F n, btw 6 and 7 w.
Rice, E. V., grocer, cor B s and 1 e.
Riceby, Alfred, commission merchant, s side F n, btw 6 and 7 w.
Richards, Dr. John, office over Hunter's bookstore; boards at Mrs. Spaulding's.
Richards, Geo. T., trader, s side B s, btw 6 and 7 w.
Bichards, Wm., brickmaker, n side G s, btw 6 and 7 e.
Richards, A & T. A., brickyard, South Capitol, btw N and O s.
House, cor ½ w and N s.
Richards, Z., teacher Union Academy, cor 14 w and N Y av.
Richardson, Wm., A., teacher of Penmanship, n side Pa av, btw 4½ and 6 w.
Richardson, Luke, n side M n, btw 13 and 14 w.
Richardson, James, gardener, s side M n, btw 4 and 5 w.
Richardson, A., driver, s side Va av, btw 8 and 9 e.
Richey, Hiram, tinner and stove dealer, cor 7 w and H n.
Richter, Peter, grocer, n side L n, btw 6 and 7 w.
Ricketts, R., clerk Land office, s side I n, btw 9 and 10 w.
Riddick, Richard H., clerk Department of Interior, n side D n, btw 14 and 15 w.
Riddle, W. C., clerk State Department, w side 13 w, btw G and H n.
Rider & White, Washington Foundry, s side Me av, btw 3 and 4½ w.
Rider, Geo. F., (& White) 6 w, btw D and E s.
Rider, Geo. F., sash and blind factory, Md av, btw 3 and 4½ w.
Ridgate, B. C., s side F n, btw 17 and 18 w.
Ridgeley, Fanny, widow, laundress, w side 3 w, btw N Y av and L n.

Ridgely, Wm., clerk, n side First, btw Market and Frederick, Georgetown.
RIDGLY & CO., Druggists, n side I n, btw 20 and 21 w.
Ridgway, Enoch, boardinghouse, w side 12 w, btw C and D n.
Ridgway, H., e side 14 w, btw H and I n.
Riggles, John, merchant tailor, e side 7 w, btw La av and D n.
Riggles, Charles, moulder, w side 18 w, btw H and I n.
Rigglis, Thos., grocer, e side 16 w, btw I and K n.
Riggs, Elisha, (Corcoran &) n side 1 n, btw 16 and 17 w.
Rigley, Miss, seamstress, s side Va av, btw 3 and 4 e.
Rigtstine, John W., confectioner, n side Mass av, btw 9 and 10 w.
Riley, Terence, coffee roaster, cor Union alley and N s.
Riley, John, confectioner, e side 7 w, btw La av and D n.
Riley, Dr. Richard J., n side F n, btw 14 and 15 w.
Riley, Major, clerk navy yard, w side 12 w, btw D and E n.
Riley, Wm. R., drygoods, n side La av, btw 7 and 8 w.
House, s side H s, btw 9 and 10 w.
Riley, Thomas S., boat agent, s side H s, btw 9 and 10 w.
Riley, ——, laborer, n side Ohio av, btw 13½ and 14 w.
Riley, Dr. Joshua, s side Gay, btw Congress and Washington, Georgetown.
Riley, James & J., saddlers, e side High, btw Gay and Bridge, Georgetown.
Ringgold, Frederick, clerk War Department, n side I n, btw 16 and 17 w.
Ringgold, Thos. L., Ordnance Department, U. S. A., n side F n, btw 18 and 19 w.
Riordan, James, n side 15 w, btw N Y av and H n.
Risen, Charles, carter, s side Mass av, btw 12 and 13 w.
Ritchie, Thomas, sr., n side H n, btw 16 and Conn av.
Ritchie, Mrs., widow, n side Ohio av, btw 13½ and 14 w.
Ritchie, Dr. Joshua, M. D., n w cor High and 3d, Georgetown.
Rittenhouse, Charles, Bank of Commerce, n side Bridge, btw Congress and High.
House, Stoddart street, east, Georgetown.
Ritter, Adam, engineer, s side D n, btw 13 and 13½ w.
Ritter, Dr. Henry, s side F s, btw 7 and 8 w.
Ritter, Obadiah, collector, Dumbarton, btw Green and Montgomery, Georgetown.
Ritter, Mrs., Cherry Alley, Georgetown.
Ritter, Wm,, woodyard, cor Scott's row and Canal, Georgetown.
Rives, John C., cor C n and 3 w.
Rixter, Miss, mantuamaker, w side 20 w, btw F and H n.
Roach, Edmond, laborer, w side 6 w, btw F and G n.
Roach, James, laborer, s side D n, btw 5 and 6 w.
Roach, Edward, Register of Wills, City Hall, w side 10 w, btw F and G n.
Roach, Robt. J., collector, w side 12 w, btw I and N Y av.
Roach, J. H., watchman navy yard, w side 10 e, btw I and K s.
Roane, Robt. J. P., messenger Capitol, w side 13 w, btw C and D s.
Robb, John, clerk Capitol, n side Mass av, btw 11 and 12 w.
Robb, A., tailor, n side I n, btw 4 and 5 w.
Robb, Michael, blacksmith, n side Va av, btw 7 and 8 e.
Robbins, Z. C., office for Patents, s side F n, btw 7 and 8 w.
Roberts, Lieut. B. L., U. S. A., w side 21 w, btw H and I n.
Roberts, Dr. John M., s side G s, btw 7 and 8 e.
Roberts, Mrs. E., widow, n side B n, btw 1 and 2 e.
Robertson, Samuel P., tobacconist, cor 8 w and L n.
Robertson, Daniel, grocer, s side L n, btw 13 and 14 w.
Robertson, James, butcher, n w cor Prospect and Potomac, Georgetown.
Robey, John C., blacksmith, n side 8 e, btw F and G s.
Robey, Thos., lawyer, w side 13½ w, btw Md av and D s.
Robey, Wm., carpenter, e side 4 e, btw I and K s.
Robey, John E., carpenter, e side 7 e, btw L and M s.
Robey, James, laborer, s side Ga av, btw 11 and 12 e.
Robins, Thomas, grocery, w side 12 w, btw Mass av and L n.
Robinson, J., jeweller, n side F s, btw 7 and 8 w.
Robinson, John, segar store, s side Pa av, btw 17 and 18 w.

Abbreviations.—All points start from the Capitol; s south, n north, e east, w west, btw between, cor corner, (col) colored, av avenue, h house.

Robinson, T. W., clerk Treasury, w side 10 w, btw H and N Y av.
Robinson, Edward B., printer, n side D n, btw 9 and 10 w.
Robinson, J. G., carpenter, n side G n, btw 6 and 7 w; h w side 7 w, btw G and H n.
Robinson, James H., tailor, n side Md av, btw 9 and 10 w.
ROBINSON, Mrs., Boarding house, n side Pa av, btw 1 and 2 w.
Robinson, John, auctioneer, s side Pa av, btw 6 and 7 w ; h F n, near 7 w.
Robinson, John, marine, w side 8 e, btw E and G s.
Robinson's Mill, n side Water, near Aqueduct, Georgetown.
Robinson, Col. James, s w cor High and Road, Georgetown.
Robison, Mary, (col) e side 10 w, btw M and N n.
Robison, George W., tailor, n side Mass av, btw 6 and 7 w.
Robison, James, (col) plasterer, n side H n, btw 21 and 22 w.
Robison, Wm., grocer, n side F n, btw 22 and 23 w.
Robison, Wm. B., e side 6 e, btw G and I s.
Roby, Henry, shoemaker, w side 7 w, btw Va av and D s.
Roby, Bazil, grocer, n side H n, btw 4 and 5 w.
Roby, John, sawyer, s side D s, btw 13½ and 14 w.
Roby, ——, w side Jefferson, btw Bridge and Canal, Georgetown.
Roby, D., laborer, n side K s, btw 10 and 11 e.
Roby, Mary A., widow, n side N s, btw 1 e and N J av.
Rockwell, James, s side F n, btw 14 and 15 w.
Rockwell, Charles W., cor F n and 20 w.
Roe, Samuel C., farmer, n side M n, btw 12 and 13 w.
Roemmele, John C., grocer, cor K n and 18 w.
Rodgers, Mrs., boarding, n side Pa av, btw 2 and 3 w.
Rodgers, Mrs. Comm., n side H n, btw 9 and 10 w.
Rodry, Robert, (col) laborer, e side 3 e, btw C and D s.
Rogers, Joseph, printer, s side F n, btw 6 and 7 w.
Rogers, John K., agent for claims, n side G n, btw 12 and 13 w.
Rogers, C. L., (col) blacksmith, s side I n, btw 14 and 15 w.
Rogers, Coyle, blacksmith, s side N Y av, btw 12 and 13 w.
Rogers, William, machinist, n side E s, btw 3 and 4½ w.
Rollé, Albert, eng. Coast Survey office, w side South Capitol, btw B and C s.
Rollins, Joshua, refectory, e side 7 w, btw Pa av and B n.
Rollins, William, potter, e side 8 w, btw L and M n.
Rollins, Washington, boatman, n side G n, btw 1 and 2 e.
Rollins, William, shoemaker, n side F n, btw 22 and 23 w.
Rollins, Isaac, finisher, n side I s, btw 3 and 4 e.
Rollins, Robert, watchman, n side Second, btw High and Potomac, Georgetown.
Rollow, William, ricker, e side 7 w, btw L and M n.
Rooker, Misses, boarding school, cor 6 w, and F n.
Rool, Michael, laborer, e side N J av, btw K and L s.
Rose, ——, clerk Post Office Department, boards at Mrs. Bannerman's.
Rose, Mary, mantuamaker, s side C s, btw 1 and 2 w.
Roseway, Godfrey, bookbinder, w side 4½ w, btw G and H s.
Rosier, John W., barber, n side Pa av, btw 3 and 4½ w.
Rosier, J., (col) laborer, n side C n, btw 10 and 11 w.
Ross, J., (col) whitewasher, e side 13½ w, btw C and D s.
ROSS, AUGUSTUS, Porter, cor 13½ w and D n.
Ross, Richard M., clerk Post Office Department, s side E n, btw 2 and 3 w.
Ross, William, (col) laborer, n side Mass av, btw 12 and 13 w.
Ross, William, plasterer, s side [illegible] n, btw 6 and 7 w.
Ross, R., (col) porter, n side 15 w, btw I and K n.
Rosser, Rev. Leslie, (Methodist Episcopal Church,) s side Mass av, btw 4 and 5 w.
Rosser, C. P., clerk post office, n side East Capitol, btw 2 and 3 e.
Rossiter, Basil, boatman, s side I n, btw 12 and 13 w.
Roszell, Rev. S. S., (Methodist Episcopal Church,) s side F n, btw 6 and 7 w.
Rotherdale, John, printer, w side 1 w, btw Pa av and B n.
Rother's Vinegar Depot, w side Green, near Bridge, Georgetown.
Rothwell, Daniel, stonecutter, w side N J av, btw D and E s.

Rothwell, Andrew, attorney at law, D, btw 6 and 7 w; h e side 7, near cor I.
Rothwell Richard, stonecutter, n side Mass av, btw N J av and 2 w.
Rowe, Mrs., confectionary, n side Bridge, btw Congress and Washington, G'town.
Rowland, David, exchange broker, n side Pa av cor 3 w.
Rowles, James, grocer, e side 4 e, btw D and E s.
Rowles, ——, wheelwright, e side High, btw Gay and Dumbarton, Georgetown.
Rowzer, John, (& Littleton) grocers, w side Market space, Georgetown.
Roy, Samuel, painter, w side 7 w, btw F and G s.
Royal, Mrs. Ann, editress of "Huntress," s side B n, btw 3 and 4 e.
Ruff, J. A., shoestore, n side Pa av, btw 3 and 4½ w.
House s side E n, btw 5 and 6 w.
Ruff, George, cabinetmaker, e side 7 e, btw G and I s.
Runnels, J. T., tailor, w side 6 w, btw H and Mass av.
Runnels C., segar store, w side 7 w, btw I and Mass av.
Rupert, Ignatius, steward President's House, w side 10 w, btw L and M n.
RUPP, WILLIAM, Refectory, n side Pa av, next to Adams' Express.
Ruppel, Gottleib, hotel, w side 6 w, btw Pa av and La av.
Ruppert, Caspar, tailor, w side 7 w, btw N Y av and I n.
Ruppert, Anthony, Northern Liberties Hotel, w side 8 w, btw L and M n.
Russell, Alfred, agent Hudson Ins. Co., w side 7 w, btw I and N Y av.
Russell, John T., plasterer, w side 7 w, btw L and M n.
Russell, John H., carpenter, w side 8 e, btw E and G s.
Russell, David, (col) laborer, n side Mass av, btw 12 and 13 w.
Rudd, Mrs. Elizabeth, confectioner, n side 8 e, btw K and L s.
RUTHERFORD, W., marbleyard, n side E n, btw 13 and 13½ w; wareroom e side 13 w, btw Pa av and E n; h cor 10 w and I n.
Rutherford, Alexander, stonecutter, n side D n, near cor 14 w.
Rutter, Miss Amelia, w side 3 w, btw I and K n.
Ryan, William, clerk Treasury Department, e side 13 w, btw N Y av and I n.
Rye, John, wheelwright, w side 22 w, btw Pa av and I n.
Ryne, Thomas, grocer, s side A s, btw 1 and 2 e.
Ryon, Richard J., grocer, n side La av, btw 7 and 8 w.
House w side 6 w, btw G and H n.
Ryon, Michael, stonemason, s side C s, btw 10 and 11 w.
Ryther, E. A., & Co., Navy Yard omnibus line, w side 8 e, btw I and G s.

S.

Sadler, T., shoemaker, e side 14 w, btw B and C s.
Saffell, Miss, dressmaker, w side 12 w, btw G and H n.
Sage, J. A., printer, e side 1 e, btw B and C n.
Salisbury, Mrs., milliner, s side L s, btw 4 and 5 e.
Sampson, James, blacksmith, n side G s, btw 8 and 9 w.
Sampson, H., cartman, s side F n, btw 25 and 26 w.
Sanders, Major, n side K, btw 12 and 13 w.
Sanderson, N., blacksmith, w side 11 e, btw G and I s.
Sandilands, Andrew, blacksmith, e side 4½ w, btw C and D s.
House, Md av, btw 4½ and 6 w.
Sands, Capt. B. F., s side F n, btw 9 and 10 w.
Sandy, Mrs. C. D., widow, w side 9 w, btw F and G n.
Sanford, Bushrod, waiter, s side I s, btw 4½ and 6 w.
Sanford, Linas, laborer, s side B n, btw 5 and 6 e.
Sanger, W. P. S., civil engineer, U. S. N., w side 17 w, btw Pa av and H n.
Sanner, Jerome, carpenter, w side 23 w, btw G and H n.
Sargeant, James, (col) stonecutter, s side B s, btw 1 and 2 e.
Sargent, J. O., Editor Republic, e side 14 w, btw F n and Pa av.
Sasscer, J., grocer, n side 8 e, btw I and K s.
Sasser, Wm., clerk, s side H n, btw 4 and 5 w.
Sautier, Wm., confectioner, e side 7 w, btw L and M n.

Sauerwein, G., bricklayer, s side N Y av, btw 12 and 13 w.
Saul, John, nurseryman, n side C s, btw 13 and 13½ w.
Saul, Lewis, barber, opposite Odd Fellows' Hall, 7 w.
Saunders, Lewis, (col) waiter, e side 14 w, btw B and C s.
Saunders, Harriet, (col) laundress, s side C s, btw 1 and 2 w.
Savage, G., variety store, n side Pa av, btw 9 and 10 w.
House, w side 9 w, btw D and Pa av.
Savage, J. L., hardware store, s side Pa av, btw 19 and 20 w.
Savoy, H., (col) laundress, s side I n, btw 9 and 10 w.
Sawkins, Wm., watchmaker, s side F n, btw 13 and 14 w.
Saxton, Joseph, Coast Survey, n side B s, btw N J av and 1 e.
Scala, Francis, musician, s side E s, btw 9 and 10 e.
Scammell, Wm., furnished rooms, e side 14 w, btw F n and Pa av.
Schad, H. L., grocery and liquor store, s side Pa av, btw 3 and 4½ w.
Schad, Charles, brewer, e side 7 w, btw G and H n.
Schad, B., refectory, s side Pa av, btw 3 and 4½ w.
Schadd, ——, music teacher, n side Bridge, btw Congress and Washington, G'town.
Schaefer, Wm. A., boardinghouse, s side D n, btw 2 and 3 w.
Schafer, G. F., merchant tailor, s side Pa av, btw 10 and 11 w.
Schaff, Mrs. Mary E., n side First, btw High and Potomac, Georgetown.
Scheel, John E., Prof. of Music, e side 14 w, btw F and G n.
Scheide, Henry, refectory, n side E n, btw 11 and 12 w.
Schiefley, J., gasfitter, s side La av, btw 9 and 10 w.
Schiefner, Edward, hatter, s side La av, btw 6 and 7 w.
Schlegel, F., clothier, e side 7 w, btw D and E n.
Schlegel, C, bellhanger, n side Pa av, btw 17 and 18 w.
Schloss, Nicholas, drygoods, w side High, btw 2d and 3d, Georgetown.
Schlossor, Henry, stonecutter, n side Mass av, btw N J av and 4 w.
Schmidt, Frederick, e side 18 w, btw I and K n.
Schneider, L. H. & G., brass foundry, s side Pa av, btw 10 and 11 w.
Schneider, F. & A., foundry, n side Pa av, btw 17 and 18 w.
Schneider, Miss, dressmaker, n side Pa av, btw 17 and 18 w.
Schneider, F., (& A) e side 18 w, btw H and I n.
Schneider, Gottlob, (L. H. &) C s, btw 12 and 13 w.
Schofield, Thomas, tailor, e side 8 w, btw L and M n.
Schools, Public, viz:

First District School, (Male Department.) Samuel Kelly, principal. School-room at the corner of 14th and G streets.

Female Department. Mrs. S. G. Henshaw, teacher. School-room on 11th street, in the German Hall.

Male Primary. A. Lindsay, teacher. School-room on 18th, btw H and I.

Primary No. I. Mrs. A. O. Johnson, teacher. School-room on New York avenue, btw 17th and 18th.

Primary No. 2. Mrs. M. E. Rodier, principal—Miss A. K. Lowe, assistant. School-room in basement of Union Chapel, 20th street.

Primary No. 3. Miss Alice English, principal—Miss M. G. Wells, assistant. School-room in the Washington Library building, 11th street.

Primary No 4. Miss M. F. Nevins, principal—Miss M. A. S. Davis, assistant. School-room in Friends' Meeting-house, I street,

Second District School, (Male Department.) T. M. Wilson, principal—George H. Ray, assistant.

Female Department. Mrs. S. P. Randolph, teacher. School-rooms, 5th street, Judiciary Square.

Male Primary. Rezin Beck, teacher. School-room F st., btw 5 and 6.

Primary No. 1. Miss M. A. Joyce, teacher. School-room, 5th street, Judiciary square.

Primary No. 2. Miss L. H. Randolph, principal—Miss E. H. Parsons, assistant. School-room, basement of Methodist Church south, on 8th street.

Schools, Public, viz:

Primary No. 3. Miss C. L. Nevitt, teacher. School-room, in Ninth Street Presbyterian Church.

Primary No. 4. Mrs. R. M. Ogden, principal—Miss E. V. Billing, assistant. School-room in Methodist Church south, on 8th street.

Third District School, (Male Department.) John Fill, principal—Joseph T. Goldsmith, assistant.

Female Department. Mrs. C. D. Martin, assistant. School-room, cor E and 13 e, Navy Yard.

Male Primary. W. M. McCathran, teacher. School-room at Navy Yard.

Primary No. 1. Miss F. Elvans, principal. Miss J. F. Acton, assistant. School-room, cor A and Pa av.

Primary No. 2. Mrs. M. Freeman, principal—Mrs. M. A. Skidmore, assistant. School-room in Methodist Protestant Church, cor Virginia avenue and 4th e, Navy Yard.

Primary No. 3. Mrs. Eliza Clarke, teacher. School-room on 11th e, Navy Yard.

Primary No. 4. Miss Jane Moss, teacher. School-room, Odd-Fellows' Hall, 7th e, Navy Yard.

Fourth District School, (Male Department.) J. E. Thompson, principal.

Female Department. Mrs. M. A. Hinton, teacher. School-rooms on south 6th, near Va av.

Male Primary. A. M. Smith, teacher. School-room on G s, btw 6 and 7.

Primary No. 1, Miss M. R. Anderson, teacher. School-room on C s, near 12th.

Primary No. 2. Miss M. P. Middleton, teacher. School-room on K s, btw 4½ and 6.

Primary No. 3. Miss M. A. Milburn, teacher. School-room on 4½ s, btw L and M.

School, (col) Miss E. Smith and Lucinda Jackson, teachers, s side B s, btw 1 w and South Capitol.

Schoolcraft, H. R., n side E n, btw 10 and 11 w.

Schott, John G., folder in Capitol, n side B n, btw Del av and 1 e.

Schroeder, ——, musician, n side G s, btw 6 and 7 e.

Schuermann, C. W., Prof. of Music, n side L n, btw 9 and 10 w.

Schureman, Rev. Peter, (col) s side A n, btw 1 and 2 e.

Schussler, Charles, refectory, cor 7 w and N Y av.

Schutz, S., bootmaker, e side 7 w, btw F and G n.

SCHWARTZE, J., Druggist, n side Pa av, btw 2 and 3 w.

Schwartze, R., refectory, basement, cor 11 w and E n.

Schwartze, S. R., printer, w side 10 w, btw N Y av and K n.

Schwartze, Andrew, hackman, e side 14 w, btw F and G n.

Schwartze, Joseph, messenger War Department, e side 18 w, btw H and I n.

Schweitzer, P., shoemaker, w side 15 w, btw L and M n.

Schwenghamer, E., root beer manufactory, n side D n, btw 12 and 13 w.

Schwetzer, Hiram, gardener, e side 3 w, btw Q and R n.

Sciller, Francis, btw ½ and 1, Point.

Scott, John, blacksmith, n side I s, btw 11 and 13 e.

Scott, Mrs. James, widow, e side 9 w, btw I and N Y av.

Scott, Mrs. H A., s side Pa av, btw 3 and 4½ w.

Scott, Fdward M., clerk Third Auditor's, n side D n, btw 13 and 14 w.

Scott, Wm. A., plasterer, n side N Y av, btw 3 and 4 w.

Scott, Winfield, Major General U. S. A., n side H n, btw 13 and 14 w.

Scott, W. B., s side H n, btw 19 and 20 w.

Scott, Samuel, boardinghouse, e side 1 e, btw B and C n.

Scott, T. A., (Green &) auctioneers, e side Del av, btw B and C n.

Scott, Mary, (col) laundress, e side Conn av, btw I and K n.

Scott, H., (col) servant, s side C s, btw 4½ and 6 w.

Scrivener, Elizabeth, w side 12 w, btw Mass av and L n.

Scrivener, Rev. John, n side I n, btw 8 and 9 w.

Abbreviations.—All points start from the Capitol; s south, n north, e east, w west, btw between, cor corner, (col) colored, av avenue, h house,

Scrivener, Thomas, grocer, cor Del av and B n; h n side A n, btw 1 e and Del av.
Scrivener, Mrs. R. widow, n side R s, btw 6 and 7 e.
Scrivener, ——, baker, e side Fayette, btw 1st and 2d, Georgetown.
Scroggins, George, carpenter, n side C s, btw 13 and 13½ w.
Scufferle, J. Jacob, baker, e side 6 w, btw F and G n.
Seaman, E. C., chief clerk First Comptroller's office, cor F n and 13 w.
Seanon, A. J., clerk Solic. office, w side 12 w, btw F and G n.
Sears, James W., (Maxwell &) boards at Mrs. King's, opposite General Post Office.
Seaton, W. W., (Gales &) s side E n, btw 7 and 8 w.
Sebastian, Caleb, butter merchant, w side Jefferson, near Bridge, Georgetown.
Sedgwick, Richard H., watch Patent office, e side 7 w, btw N Y av and L n.
Seibart, Selmar, engraver, cor Md av and 13 w.
Seibell, George C., tailor, w side 7 w, btw H and I.
Seiss, John, huckster, e side Frederick, btw 3d and 4th, Georgetown.
Seitz, M., tobacconist, s side Pa av, btw 4½ and 6 w.
Seitz, George, baker, cor 10 and N Y av.
Selby, Thos. W., cartman, w side 11 w, btw Md av and E s.
Selby, Henry, finisher in iron, n side I s, btw 9 and 10 e.
Selden, Withers & Co., bankers, 7th street, btw D and La av.
Selden, William, banker, s side N Y av, btw 13 and 14 w.
Selden, Francis, restaurant, n side Pa av, btw 14 and 15 w.
Selden, Mary, widow, s side N Y av, btw 9 and 10 w.
Seldner, A., clothier, n side Pa av, btw 6 and 7 w, and n side D n, btw 10 and 11 w.
Self, B., e side 4 e, btw L and M s.
Sellhausen, Frederick, tobacconist, e side 7 w, btw F and G n.
Selwyn, John W., laborer, e side 4½ w, btw E and F s.
Semmes, Dr. A. J., cor 17 and I n.
Semmes, J. H., grocer, w side 9 w, btw B and La av.
House, Md av, btw 6 and 7 w.
Semmes, T. F., wine merchant, n side Pa av, btw 3 and 4½ w.
House, 6, btw E and F n.
Semmes, B. J. & Brother, wholesale grocers, s side Pa av, btw 4½ and 6 w.
Semmes, B. J., (& Brother) wholesale grocers, Georgetown.
Semmes, Thos. J., (& Brother) wholesale grocers, New Orleans, La.
Semmes, J. H., (Murray &) D s, btw 7 and 8 w.
Semmes, J. B., (Barbour &) La av, btw 7 and 8 w.
Semmes, J. B., (Barbour &) opposite Bank of Washington.
House, Md av, btw 7 and 8 w.
Semmes, Mrs. Ralph, one door east of cor of First and Potomac, Georgetown.
Semmes, Dr. Alexander, do. do. do.
Semmes, Joseph, do. do. do.
Sengstack, Chas. P., printer, s side D n, btw 12 and 13 w.
Sengstack, C. A., painter, s side Mass av, btw 12 and 13 w.
Seoussa, John, porter, s side N Y av, btw 12 and 13 w.
Sergeant, John, bookbinder, n side E n, btw 9 and 10 w.
Serin, William, plasterer, w side 22 w, btw G and H n.
SESSFORD, JOHN Jr., Tobacconists, n side Pa av, btw 4½ and 6 w.
House cor L and 4 e.
Sessford, Joseph, carpenter, n side C n, btw 11 and 12 w.
Sessford, John H., printer, s side D n, btw 13½ and 14 w.
Sessford, John, clerk, s side D n, btw 11 and 12 w.
Sessford, Andrew, clerk Treas. Dep't, n side L n, btw 9 and 10 w.
Sessford, Margaret, widow, e side 14 w, btw B and C s.
Settle, Alexander, printer, n side Second, near the College, Georgetown.
Seymour, Richard, (col) laborer, cor 8 w and H n.
Seymour, W. F., hats and caps, n side Bridge, btw High and Congress, Geo'town.
Sewall, Rev. Thomas, clerk, n side West, btw Green and Montgomery, Georgetown.
Sewall, Wm., grocery store, e side Market space, Georgetown.
Seward, Wm. H., United States Senator, n side F n, btw 6 and 7 w.
Sewell, Walter, carpenter, e side N J av, btw K and L n.

Abbreviations.—All points start from the Capitol; s south, n north, e east, w west, btw between, cor corner, (col) colored, av avenue, h house,

Sewell, Mrs. Maria, (col) laundress, w side 3, btw F and G n.
Sewell, Walter, carpenter, e side N J av, btw K and L u.
Sewell, R. (col) laundress, w side 21 w, btw K and L n.
Shackelford, James, saddler, s side Pa av, btw 14 and 15 w.
Shaffer, Jacob F.. bricklayer, s side H n, btw 6 and 7 w.
Shaffner, Mrs. Peter R., mantua maker, w side 9 w, btw Pa av and D n.
Shafer, C., hotel, w side 9 w, btw B and La av.
Shafer, Jonathan, leather store, w side 6 w, btw G and H n.
Shafer, Peter, cabinetmaker, w side 6 w, btw G and Mass av.
Shanks, Michael, gent., cor 18 w and N Y av.
Shanllan, D., laborer, n side B n, btw 2 and 3 w.
Sharpless, William, printer, w side 10, btw N Y av and K n.
Shaw, Mrs. D., w side 8, btw I and Mass av.
Shaw, Mrs. Eliza, (col) laundress, w side 6 w, btw N Y av and L n.
Shaw, A., printer, s side N Y av, btw 12 and 13 w.
Shaw, Sandy, (col) shoemaker, e side 10 w, btw M and M n.
Shaw, Mrs. and Miss Jane, school, s side Bridge, btw High and Congress, G'town.
Sheahan, John, laborer, w side 3 w, btw G and H n.
Sheckells, B., trader, n side D n, btw 9 and 10 w.
Sheckels, Theodore, grocer, w side 7 w, btw I and N Y av.
Sheckels, Merit, rigger, n side L s, btw 3 and 4 e.
Sheckells, Richard, sen,, mason, n side 7th, cor of Market, Georgetown.
Sheckells, ——, & Bro., drygoods, s side Market, east of Market-house, Geo'town.
Shedd, Wm. P., clerk Post Office Department, e side 11 w, btw E and Pa av.
Shehan, James, confectioner, w side 1 w, btw Pa av and B n.
Sheid, T., turner, n side E n, btw 9 and 10 w; h, n side L n, btw 9 and 10 w.
Shenfelder, George E., printer, s side I n, btw 4 and 5 w.
Shepard, William, scavenger 6th ward, s side Ga av, btw 11 and 12 e.
Sherf, E., bootmaker, s side D n, near 9 w.
Sherman, Charles E., w side 3 w, btw B and C n.
Sherman, George, blacksmith, s side K s, btw 10 and 11 e.
Shermy, D., grocer, e side 11 e, btw M and N s.
Sherwood, Mrs. Sarah Ann, seamstress, s side F n, btw 10 and 11 w.
Sherwood, Samuel, e side 10 w, btw N Y av and K n.
Sherwood, Mr., blacksmith, n side Prospect, btw High and Prospect, Georgetown.
Sheton, Mrs. Elizabeth, n side M s, btw 10 and 11 e.
Shick, John, carpenter, w side 10 w, btw C s and Va av.
Shiel, T., stonecutter, n side M n, btw 7 and 8 w,
Shields, Miss, grocery, s side I n, btw 13 and 14 w.
Shields, J. W., mess. Interior Dep't, e side 14 w, btw I and H n.
Shiepler, Andrew, lacemaker, s side D n, btw 13 and 13½ w.
Shiles, J. W., (Fowler &) w side 10 w, btw C and Va av.
Shillington, Joseph, bookstore, cor Pa av and 4½ w.
Shinar, Michael, (col) painter, w side 8 e, btw E and G s.
Shine, Mr., stonemason, e side Congress, btw Canal and Water, Georgetown.
Shipley, John W., tailor, e side 4½ w, btw C and Md av.
Shiras, Capt. E. A., U S A, s side F n, btw 14 and 15 w.
Shoats, John, laborer, s side East Capitol, btw 5 and 6 e.
Shoemaker, Edward, grocer, cor 11 w and F n.
Shoemaker, George, flour inspector, s side West, btw Congress and High, G'town.
Shoemaker, Dr. W. L., s side West, btw Congress and High, Georgetown.
Shoemaker, ——, (of Howell &,) warehouse cor High and Water, Georgetown.
Shortel, Edward, laborer, e side N J av, btw B and C s.
Shorter, Charles, (col) whitewasher, w side 8 w, cor K n.
Shorter, Maria, (col) s side Mass av, btw 4 and 5 w.
Shorter, Charles, (col) oyster shop, n side H n, btw 20 and 21 w.
Shorter, Charles, (col) laborer, w side 20 w, btw I and K n.
Shreve, Samuel, huckster, w side 7 w, btw L and M n.
Shreve, James H., livery stable, e side 7 w, btw H and I n.
House, s side I n, btw 6 and 7 w.

Abbreviations.—All points start from the Capitol; s south, n north, e east, w west, btw between, cor corner, (col) colored, av avenue, h house.

Shreve, John, grocer, e side 7 w, btw M and N n.
Shubrick, Com. W. B., U. S. N., n side H n, btw Conn. av and 17 w.
Shulton, Samuel, laborer, n side Ga av, btw 13 and 14 e.
Shultz, Joseph, printer, e side 9 e, btw G and H s.
Shuster, William M., drygoods, w side 7 w, btw D n and Pa av; h 6, near cor F n.
Sibley, Solomon, folder Capitol, w side 8 w, btw L and M n.
Sibley, W. L., & Co., lumber yard, w side 14 w, btw C and D n.
Siebel, J. C., tailor, e side 7 w, btw H and I n; h L, btw 6 and 7 w.
Silence, Caroline, e side 20 w, btw M and N n.
Silence, Walter, painter, n side Dumbarton, btw Green and Montgomery, G'town.
Simmes, John H., printer,, s side B n, btw 3 and 4 e.
Simmes, Q., (col) laborer, n side E s, btw 3 and 4 e.
Simonds, John, blacksmith, s side Va av btw 6 and 7 e.
Simmons, P., plasterer, s side L n, btw 6 and 7 w.
Simmons, George, s side F s, btw 4½ and 6 w.
Simmons, A., cartman, s side D s, btw 9 and 10 w.
Simmons, Cephas, clerk Census office, boards cor 4½ and Pa av.
Simms, John T., barber, w side 7 w, btw G and H n; h Va av, btw M and N.
Simms, Elexius, grocer, s side F n, btw 12 and 13 w.
Simms, Edward, n side C n, btw 3 and 4½ w.
Simms, Richard, (col) laborer, e side 11 w, btw K and N Y av.
Simms, Milly, (col) laundress, n side L n, btw 7 and 8 w.
Simms, Sampson, carpenter, n side L n, btw 10 and 11 w.
Simms, Mrs., grocery, e side 10 w, btw Md av and F s.
Simms, Delilah, (col) laundress, s side E s, btw 3 and 4½ w.
Simms, ——, carpenter, n side Gay, near High; steam saw-mill, south of Water and Washington, Georgetown.
Simms, James, shoemaker, n side Fourth, btw Market and Frederick, Georgetown.
Simms, William, carpenter, w side Frederick, btw 1st and 2d, Georgetown.
Simpson, Presley, clerk Post Office Department, e side 12 w, btw G and H n.
Simpson, Mrs., n side B s, btw 3 and 4 e.
Simpson, M., (col) nurse, n side A n, btw 2 and 3 e.
Simpson, J., laborer, n side I s, btw 11 and 13 e.
Simpson, Rev. T. W., school, s side West, btw Congress and Washington, G'town.
Simpson, J. A., portrait painter, Georgetown.
SIMS, PALIN H., Plumber, e side 7 w, btw Pa av and D n.
House, n side D s, btw 6 and 7 w.
Sims, John M., clerk Treasury Department, s side E n, btw 9 and 10 w.
Sims, William (col) laborer, n side F s, btw 3 and 4½ w.
Sims, Jerry, (col) laborer, w side 5 e, btw D and E s.
Sinclair, John, laborer, e side 20 w, btw N and M n.
Sinsheimer, Luis, tailor, n side Pa av, btw 3 and 4½ w.
Sioussa, John, messenger Bank Metropolis, s side N Y av, btw 14 and 15 w.
Sioussa, F., plasterer, n side L n, btw 12 and 13 w.
Sioussa, Charles, plasterer, w side 18 w, btw H and I n.
Sipe, H., watchman, s side L n, btw 13 and 14 w.
Sisson, Jesse, tobacconist, e side 7 w, btw B and Md av; h D, btw 10 and 11 w.
Sisson, John A., clerk, s side F s, btw 4½ and 6 w.
Skelley, William, tailor, e side North Capitol, btw B and C n.
Skidmore, Miss M. E., n side G n, btw 13 and 14 w.
Skidmore, Samuel, wheelwright, n side K s, btw 10 and 11 e.
Skinner, Capt. William, w side 7 w, btw G and H s.
Skinner, Com. Charles W., U. S. N., cor 11 w and H n.
Skinner, F. G., clerk Treasury Department, n side 15 w, btw N Y av and H n.
SKIRVING, JAMES, Stove Dealer, cor Pa av and 11 w.
House 10 w, btw Pa av and C n.
Skirving, John, clerk, n side A n, btw 1 e and Del av.
Slade, William O., clerk Pension office, n side Pa av, btw 24 and 25 w.
Slater, William, w side N J av, btw D and E s.
Slatford, G. W., bricklayer, e side 3 w, btw G and Mass av.

Abbreviations.—All points start from the Capitol; s south, n north, e east, w west, btw between, cor corner, (col) colored, av avenue, h house,

Slavln, John, fancy store, n side Pa av, btw 21 and 22 w.
Slight, P., carpenter, w side South Capitol, btw A and B s; h Va av, near bridge.
Sly, John A., laborer, e side 11 e, btw Va av and M s.
Smallwest, Wm. (col) barber, e side 13 w, btw G and H n.
Smallwest, J., (col) waiter, w side South Capitol, btw C and D s.
Smallwest, Miss, (col) laundress, n side C s, btw 2 and 3 w.
Smallwood, John, ship carpenter, e side 7 e, btw Va av and L s.
Smallwood, Moses, (col) laborer, n side Mass av, btw 12 and 13 w.
Smallwood, George, carpenter, n side East Capitol, btw 1 and 2 e.
Smith, John W., watchman Capitol, 4½ w, btw Pa av and Mo av.
Smith, James, stonecutter, w side N J av, btw D and E s.
Smith, John G., lumber merchant, 6th, near the canal.
House, e side 7 w, btw D and E s.
Smith, John L., magistrate, e side 7 w, btw Pa av and D n.
Smith, James, barber, w side 7 w, btw I and N Y av.
Smith, Philip, laborer, e side 4½ w, btw F and G s.
Smith, Daniel, printer, e side 8 w, btw L and M n.
Smith, Mary, e side 3 w, btw Md av and C.
Smith, Simeon, claim agent, s side Pa av, btw 3 and 4½ w.
Smith, Chauncey, clerk Post Office Department, boards at Mrs. Fletcher's, Pa av.
Smith, jr., Ezra, Adelphi Saloon, s side Pa av, btw 4½ and 6 w.
Smith, Frederick, sculptor, s side Pa av, btw 12 and 13 w.
Smith, L., agent, s side Pa av, btw 14 and 15 w.
Smith, William, model maker, s side F n, btw 8 and 9 w; h Georgetown.
Smith, Thomas L., 1st Auditor, w side 6 w, btw D and E n.
Smith, Patrick, waiter, w side 6 w, btw F and G n.
Smith, James, hatter, e side 6 w, btw G and H n.
Smith, J. B. H., attorney, n side F n, btw 14 and 15 w.
Smith, E. G., clerk Land Office, n side C n, btw 3 and 4½ w.
Smlth, Wm. Joseph, bricklayer, s side D n, btw 1 and 2 w.
Smith, John A., laborer, s side D n, btw Mass av and North Capitol.
Smith, John H., clerk Treasury Department, n side G n, btw 12 and 13 w
Smith, John C., carpenter, s side D n, btw 3 and 4 w.
Smith, James, clerk Treasury Department, w side 12 w, btw G and H n.
Smith, Henry, shoemaker, e side 10 w, btw M and N n.
Smith, Dr. Philip, e side 12 w, btw E and F n.
Smith; J. M., cooper, n side I n, btw 6 and 7 w.
Smith, Mrs. E., widow, n side K n, btw 17 and 18 w.
Smith, Rev. J. C., (Third Presbyterian Church) s side N Y av, btw 9 and 10 w.
Smith, William J., clerk War Department, w side 13 w, btw G and H n.
Smith, James H., guard at jail, n side M n, btw 6 and 7 w.
Smith, B., attorney, n side H n, cor 15 w.
Smith, Norman B., clerk War Department, n side N n, btw 13 and 14 w.
Smith, H. T., cabinetmaker, n side H n, btw 9 and 10 w.
Smith, Thomas, harnessmaker, n side H n, btw 18 and 19 w.
Smith, Richard, cashier Bank Metropolis, n side Pa av, btw 15 and Vt av.
Smith, John L., magistrate and attorney at law, e side 8 w, btw Pa av and D.
House, w side 12 w, btw C and Va av.
Smith, Thomas, woodyard, 10, near Canal; h w side 15 w, btw K and L n.
Smith, Thomas, livery stable, e side 19 w, btw Pa av and I n.
Smith, A. Austin, attorney, s side La av, btw 4½ and 6 w.
House, cor 12 and G n.
Smith, ———, waterman, s side F s, btw 8 and 9 w.
Smith, Wm., engraver, n side C s, btw 10 and 11 w.
Smith, Stuart, grocer, cor 2 and B s.
Smith, Wm., shipcarpenter, e side 11 e, btw Va av and M s.
Smith, G. H., boilermaker, e side 11 e, btw Va av and M s.
Smith, John, shipcarpenter, n side M s, btw 10 and 11 e.
Smith, James S., watchman, n side K s, btw 9 and 10 e.
Smith, J., tinner, n side I s, btw 2 and 3 e.

Abbreviations.—All points start from the Capitol; s south, n north, e east, w west, btw between, cor corner, (col) colored, av avenue, h house.

Smith, James, n side I s, btw 2 and 3 e.
Smith, George B., brickmaker, e side 3 e, btw Ga av and N s.
Smith, Wm., (col) barber, cor 3 and Pa av, under Gadsby's Hotel.
Smith, Mrs. (col) w side 17 w, btw F and G n.
Smith, R., (col) laborer, n side F n, btw 21 and 22 w.
Smith, Wm., (col) laborer, n side N, btw 5 and 6 w.
Smith, Jos., (col) barber, e side 14 w, btw H and I n.
Smith, W. B., (col) laborer, n side K n, btw 17 and 18 w.
Smith, M., (col) blacksmith, n side N Y av, btw 4 and 5 w.
Smith, Mary, (col) laundress, s side Mass av, btw 4 and 5 w.
Smith, Thomas, (col) coachman, w side 3 w, btw E and F s.
Smith, Randall, (col) w side 3, btw K and L n.
Smith, Hamilton, jr., n side Stoddart, btw Congress and Washington, Georgetown.
Smith, Mrs. Clem., n e cor First and Potomac, Georgetown.
Smith, Alexander, carpenter, s side Water, near the bridge, Georgetown.
Smith, Lewis, pumpmaker, near n e cor High and West, Georgetown.
Smith, Alex., cooper, n w cor Water and Washington, Georgetown.
Smith, Anthony, carpenter, w side Montgomery, btw Gay and Dumbarton, G'town.
Smithson, John H., hackdriver, w side 4½ w, btw Me av and Md av.
Smithson, Wm. S., cashier Farmers and Merchants' Bank, boards at Mrs. Adams'.
Smithson, Thomas, engineer, n side N s, btw 4½ and 6 w.
Smithson, A., shoemaker, n side N s, btw 3 and 4½ w.
Smoot, A., lime merchant, n side H n, btw 11 and 12 w.
Smoot, L. R., n side K n, btw 26 and 27 w.
Smoot, Dr. Samuel, s side Pa av, btw 19 and 20 w.
Smoot, J. H., w side 7 e, btw I and K s.
Smoot, John H., drygoods, s side Bridge, btw High and Congress; h, First, btw Market and Frederick, Georgetown.
Smoot, Robert W., dry goods, n side Bridge, btw High and Congress, Georgetown.
Smoot, Walter, wood merchant, Canal, near Market-house; h, n e cor Prospect and Market, Georgetown.
Sneathen, Worthington G., attorney at law, 5 Carroll Place, Capitol Hill.
Snider, M., exchange office, n side Pa av, under National Hotel.
Sniffin, Theodore, laborer navy yard, w side 8 e, btw G and I s.
Snowden, G., (col) assistant messenger Post office, n side K n, btw 15 and 16 w.
Snyder, M., broker, s side Pa av, btw 4½ and 6 w; h cor 3 w and B n.
Snyder, Wm. & Co., refectory, n side D n, btw 9 and 10 w.
Snyder, John, baker, n side Mass av, btw 12 and 13 w.
Snyder, M., agent, n side B n, btw 2 and 3 w.
Snyder, N., wheelwright and blacksmith shop, n side B n, btw 10 and 11 w.
Snyder, Dr., w side Congress, btw Gay and Bridge, Georgetown.
Sollers, Wm., upholsterer, w side 7 w, btw D and E s.
Solomon, George, (col) laborer, w side Vt av, btw K and L n.
Somerville, Mrs. Mary, (col) laundress, w side 6 w, btw N Y av and L n.
Somerville, Arnold, (col) soapmaker, e side 6 w, btw Mass av and K.
Sommer, Edward, stonecutter, w side 8 w, btw G and H n.
Sommerville, Robt. A., clerk Pension office, n side L n, btw 8 and 9 w.
Sorrell, R., carpenter, w side 11 w, btw Md av and E s.
Sorris, ———, (col) w side 22 w, btw G and H n.
Sothoron, John messenger War Department, n side G n, btw 13 and 14 w.
Sothoron, W. B., drygoods and grocery, cor L s and 3 e.
Sothoron, Dr. John, and George, drug store, n e cor Bridge and Potomac; h, a few doors east, Georgetown.
Sower, John A., shoemaker, e side 4½ w, btw C and D s.
Spalding, H. C., attorney, boards at Irving House.
Sparrow, K., laborer, n side G n, btw 22 and 23 w.
Spaulding, Mrs., boardinghouse, s side C n, btw 3 and 4½ w.
Speak, Edward, tailor, n side Va av, btw 6 and 7 w.
Speake, Dr. R. H., n side F n, btw 10 and 11 w.
Speaks, Everitt, & Bro., coach factory, s side D n, btw 12 and 13 w.

Spedden, Edward M., printer, n side I n, btw 8 and 9 w.
Speer, Dr. A., w side 3, btw D and E n.
Speiden, Wm., purser U. S. N., n side F n, btw 17 and 18 w.
Speir, Mrs., milliner, n side D n, btw 9 and 10 w.
Spence, Christopher, shoemaker, e side 9 w, btw Pa av and D n.
Spencer, R. B., Freeman's Bank, e side 7 w, btw D and E n.
Spencer, R. D., e side 8 w, btw M and N n.
Spencer, John, stonecutter, w side 2 e, btw C and D n.
Sperin, ———, gilder, w side 13 w, btw N Y av and I n.
Spuring, James, clerk, e side 4 e, btw B and C s.
Spicer, F., butcher, w side 11 e, btw K s and Ga av.
Spicer, F., shoemaker, n side I s, btw 9 and 10 e.
Spooner, Mary, widow, w side 7 e, btw I and K s.
Spratt, ———, patent lightning rod, n side Pa av, btw 4½ and 6 w.
Sprigg, Mrs. B., boardinghouse, s side C n, btw 3 and 4½ w.
Sprigg, Horace, (col) laborer, n side L n, btw 5 and 6 w.
Sprignul & McKnew, grocers, cor 7 w and K n.
Springman, George, laborer, w side 4½ w, btw C and D s.
Springman, John M., n side Md av, btw 4½ and 6 w.
Stack, John, carpenter, s side Mass av, btw 2 and N J av.
Stallings, Wm., coachtrimmer, s side West, cor Montgomery, Georgetown.
Stanford, W. H., merchant tailor, n side Pa av, btw 3 and 4½ w.
House, e side North Capitol, btw B and C n.
Stanley, Thomas, painter, w side 9 w, btw E and F n.
Stanley, J. N., artist, s side Pa av, btw 10 and 12 w.
Stanley, John, painter, w side 20 w, btw F and H n.
Starbuck, N. H., e side C n, btw E and F n.
Stark, Benj. T., shoemaker, n side I n, btw 4 and 5 w.
Statham, Charles W., pres't Farmers and Mechanics' Bank.
Staunton, Mrs., w side Congress, btw Gay and Bridge, Georgetown.
Staunton, Mrs., w side Congress, btw Gay and Bridge, Georgetown,
St. Clair, George, refectory and eating house, e side 7 w, btw Pa av and B.
Stansbury, Charles F., clerk Patent office, s side B s, btw 9 and 10 w.
Stanton, John, laborer, e side 8 w, btw D and E n.
Steamboat wharf, extreme south end 11 w.
Steedman, Lieut. Charles, U. S. N., n side F n, btw 19 and 20 w.
Steel, Robert, carpenter, w side B, btw I and Mass av.
Steele, Rev. A., n side F n, btw 10 and 11 w.
Steele, Dr. Thos., w side 12 w, btw M and N n.
Steele, H. N., chief of Police, e side 10 w, btw N Y av and K n.
Steele, Major, n side H n, btw 9 and 10 w.
STEER, P. J., Merchant Tailor, e side 7, near Odd Fellows' Hall.
House, s side I n, btw 9 and 10 w.
Stell, Thomas, s side C n, btw 4½ and 6 w.
Stephens, Thomas, (Wall &) clothier, n side Pa av, btw 9 and 10 w.
Stephens, J. T., (col) laborer, s side Va av, btw 3 and 4 e.
Stephenson, J. T., n side I s, btw 7 and 8 e.
Stettinius, Saml., s side La av, btw 4½ and 6 w.
Stevens, ——, fancy store, n side La av, btw 8 and 9 w.
Stevens, Major Isaac, w side 3 w, btw B and C n.
Stevens, M. H. hat store, under Brown's Hotel; boards at Mrs. Boak's.
Stevens, Mrs. Lydia P., widow, e side 6 w, btw D and E n.
Stevens, Robt., lace store, e side 6 w, btw Mass av and K.
Stevens, Mrs., boardinghouse, e side 10 w, btw D and E n.
Stevens, John, clerk Treasury Department, s side I n, btw 10 and 11 w.
Stevens, Leonard, blacksmith, w side 7 e, btw I and K s.
Stevens, ——, justice, w side High, btw Bridge and Prospect, Georgetown.
Stevens, Rezin, tavern, s e cor High and Beall, Georgetown.
Stevenson, Thomas, baker, w side 7 w, btw F and G n.
Stevenson, Robt., (col) cook, s side F s, btw 2 and 3 w.

Abbreviations.—All points start from the Capitol; s south, n north, e east, w west, btw between, cor corner, (col) colored, av avenue, h house.

Steward, C., stonemason, n side N n, btw 5 and 6 w.
Stewart, Wm. T., messenger Capitol, w side 8 w, btw G and H n.
Stewart, Richard, carpenter, s side Md av, btw 4½ and 6 w.
Stewart, Charles, paver, e side 8 w, btw L and M n.
Stewart, Walter, billiard saloon, s side Pa av, btw 14 and 15 w.
Stewart, John, land merchant, n side C n, btw 12 and 13 w.
Stewart, ——, s side D n, btw 12 and 13 w.
Stewart, D., stonemason, s side H n, btw 10 and 11 w.
Stewart, Walter, clerk, w side 11 w, btw G and H n.
Stewart, G. W., grocery, w side 12 w, btw N Y av and H n.
Stewart, Walter, billiard room, w side 12 w, btw G and H n.
Stewart, Wm., carter, w side 12 w, btw F and G n.
Stewart, Captain, clerk Pension office, w side 12 w, btw N and O n.
Stewart, James W., bricklayer, e side 10 w, btw L and M n.
Stewart, Sarah J., widow, e side 10 w, btw B and C n.
Stewart, James H., clerk Pension office, n side I n, btw 19 and 20 w.
Stewart, Miss L., seamstress, s side L n, btw 13 and 14 w.
Stewart, Mrs., widow, seamstress, s side N n, btw 10 and 11 w.
Stewart, C. W., assistant doorkeeper Capitol, s side B s, btw N J av and 1 e.
Stewart, Charles, (col) plasterer, w side 15 w, btw L and M n.
Stewart, John C., huckster, s side D s, btw 13½ and 14 w.
Stewart, Wm., grocer, n side F s, btw 2 and 3 w.
Stewart, Henry, finisher, n side G s, btw 7 and 8 e.
Stewart, Mrs., widow, grocery, s side L s, btw 6 and 7 e.
Stewart, F. D., (Sessford &) H n, btw 7 and 8 w.
Stewart, William, agent, 1st st., btw Market and Frederick, Georgetown.
Stillins, John, cabinetmaker, n side L s, btw 7 and 8 e.
St. John, Mrs., widow, e side 4 e, btw I and K s.
Stocke, George, wheelwright, n side Va av, btw 6 and 7 w.
Stocket, Wesley, carpenter, s side K s, btw 13 and 14 e.
Stocks, Charles, (col) laborer, e side 1 w, btw B and C s.
Stockton, Francis B., purser U. S. N., w side Presid't Square, btw H n and Pa av.
Stoddard, Isaac, constable 7th ward, e side 4½ w, btw E and F s.
Stokes, Richard, (col) barber, s side Pa av, btw 4½ and 6 w.
Stone, John H., druggist, cor 7 w and L n.
Stone, Dr., cor F and 14 w.
Stone, Michael, gardener, e side 3 w, btw G and Mass av.
Stone, W. J., jr., attorney, n side F n, btw 13 and 14 w.
Stone, James, gardener, s side I n, btw 4 and 5 w.
Stone, Mrs., w side Del av.
Stone, Mrs., Rachel, grocery, n side K s, btw 7 and Va av.
Stone, W., woodyard on 7, at Canal Bridge.
Stone, Dr. John, druggist, w side High, btw 2d and 3d, Georgetown.
Stoops, Mrs. Margaret E., widow, grocery, e side 8 w, btw L and M n.
Stoops, Richard, grocer, cor 9 w and I n; h w side 9 w, btw I and N Y av.
Storm, Leonard, grocer, w side 7 w, btw I and N Y av; h cor N Y av and L n.
Stothard, Francis, grocery, w side 12 w, btw M and N n.
Stott, Charles, druggist, n side Pa av, cor 7 w.
Stott, Samuel, w side 19 w, btw G and H n.
Stotson, Ann, (col) laundress, s side C s, btw 1 and 2 w.
Stoughton, A. B., patent agent, n side F n, btw 6 and 7 w.
House n side H n, btw 6 and 7 w.
Strasburger, H. L., furniture store, w side 7 w, btw H and I n.
Stratton, E. N., auctioneer, cor Pa and 9 w; h w side 10 w, btw E and F n.
Straub, Joseph, potter, s side L n, btw 6 and 7 w.
Streekes, R., tailor, n side Pa av, btw 23 and 24 w.
Stroble, George, blacksmith, n side Va av, btw 6 and 7 w.
Strong, Samuel, superintendent Capitol, w side 1 e, btw B and C n.
Stroud, Geo. W., butter merchant, s side Bridge, two doors east of Jefferson, G'tn.
Stuart, A. H. H., Secretary of the Interior, s side C n, btw 3 and 4½ w.

Abbreviations.—All points start from the Capitol; s south, n north, e east, w west, btw between, cor corner, (col) colored, av avenue, h house,

Sotne, John, druggist, cor 7 w and L n.
Stutz, George F., refectory, e side 9 w, btw Pa av and D n.
St. Vincent Orphan Asylum, cor 10 w and G n.
Sufferle, George, (Jackson & Co.) e side 6 w, btw F and G n.
Sugrow, John, tailor, w side 7 w, btw L and M n.
Suit, James, plasterer, n side K n, btw 3 and 4 w.
Suit, John, laborer,, n side I s, btw 3 and 4 e.
Sullivan, John, opposite city post office, 7 w.
Sullivan, D. O., feedstore, s side Md av, btw 4½ and 6 w.
Sullivan, John, grocer, cor Md av and 7 w.
Sullivan, E. Marshall, undertaker and cabinetmaker, s side F n, btw 13 and 14 w.
Sullivan, William, clerk 6th Auditor's office, w side 12 w, btw F and G n.
Sullivan, C., laborer, n side K n, btw 3 and 4 w.
Sullivan, William, carpenter, w side 24 w, btw H and I n.
Sullivan, Wm., blacksmith, n side Water, btw High and Congress; h, Washington, btw Bridge and Canal, Georgetown.
Sullivan, Samuel, wheelwright, e side Frederick, btw 3d and 4th, Georgetown.
Sullivan, Samuel, plough factory, s side Prospect, btw High and Potomac, G'town.
Sulphey, Alfred, clerk Navy Department, s side H n, btw 18 and 19 w.
Summers, William, carpenter, n side I n, btw 7 and 8 w.
Summers, A., shoemaker, n side L s, btw 4 and 5 e.
Summons, John, laborer, n side K s, btw 10 and 11 e.
Suter, John, carpenter, n side G n, btw 5 and 6 w.
Suter, ——, s side G n, btw 21 and 22 w.
Sutherland, Isabella, grocery, East Capitol, btw 1 and 2 e.
Sutton, Robert, livery stable, n side D n, btw 8 and 9 w.
House w side 9 w, btw D and E n.
Sutton, Miss E., milliner, cor 15 w and Pa av.
Sutton, R. M., drygoods, s side Pa av, btw 19 and 20 w.
Sutton, ——, shoemaker, Washington, btw Bridge and Canal, Georgetown.
Swain, Washington G., tailor, e side 11 w, btw E and F n.
Swain, Mrs., widow, w side 13 w, btw N Y av and I n.
Swann, E., attorney, s side La av, btw 4½ and 6 w.
Schwarzmann, clerk Post Office, n side 10 w, btw E and F n.
Sweeny, Mary, widow, grocery, w side N J av, btw L and M s.
Sweeny, John, tailor, w side 6 w, btw F and G n.
Sweeny, H. B., banker, Georgetown; h s side H n, btw 6 and 7 w.
Sweeny, Patrick, clerk city post office, n side Mass av, btw 9 and 10 w.
Sweeny, H. B., cashier Bank of Commerce, n side Bridge, btw High and Congress, Georgetown.
Sweeney, Patrick, laborer, n side N s, btw South Capitol and 1 e.
Sweeny, H. M., grocery and flour, s side Water, btw High and Congress, G'town.
SYLVESTER, S. R., Druggist, cor 6 w and H n.
Sylvester, T. H., druggist, cor 6 w and H n; h n side H n, btw 4 and 5 w.
Sword, James, stonecutter, n side Pa av, btw 3 and 4½ w.

T.

Tableman, William, tobacconist, w side 7 w, btw H and I n.
Tschiffely, Charles K., s side G n, btw 12 and 13 w.
Taggerts, Mrs., widow, w side 22 w, btw F and G n.
Taif, Mrs., boardinghouse, w side 7 e, btw Va av and L s.
Tait, James A., canal commissioner, cor 7 w and B n; h Capitol Hill, cor A and 3 e.
Tait, William, blacksmith, n side G n, btw 12 and 13 w.
Talbert, James, clerk Treasury Department, s side Ia av, btw 3 and 4½ w.
Talbert, William, grocer, cor I s and 12 e.
Talbert, Tobias, refectory, cor 7 w and N n.
Talbert, James, carpenter, s side I s, btw 11 and 12 e.
Talbert, William, grocer, w side 11 e, btw M and N s.

Abbreviations.—All points start from the Capitol; s south, n north, e east, w west, btw between, cor corner, (col) colored, av avenue, h house.

Talbot, Alexander, carpenter, e side 7 w, btw G and H n.
Talbot, Adeline, widow, w side 13 w, btw E and F n.
Talbot, James, cor C n and 11 w.
Taliaferro, Samuel, barber, w side 6 w, btw D and E s.
Taltaval, Peter, cabinetmaker, w side 8 e, btw G and I s.
Tanner, Mrs. Mary, widow, n side C n, btw 12 and 13 w.
Tanner, L., (col) grocer, e side 14 w, btw H and I n.
Tarlton, Louis A., baker, n side F n, btw 14 and 15 w.
Tasker, Thos., (col) shoemaker, w side 21 w, btw K and L n.
Tastet, J. M., clerk Fifth Auditor's office, n side H n, btw 9 and 10 w.
Tate, Robt., hackdriver, n side F s, btw 9 and 10 w.
Tate, A., fancy store, n side D n, btw 10 and 11 w.
Tate, Joseph B., Editor Evening Star, cor 11 w and G n.
Tate, Robert, laborer, e side 13½ w, btw C and D s.
Taurill, Miss Frances, w side 7 w, btw D and E s.
Tayloe, Ann, widow, cor N Y av and 18 w.
Tayloe, Ben. Ogle, gent, e side President Square, btw Pa av and H n.
Taylor, John, e side 3 w, btw K and L n.
Taylor, S. T., messenger arsenal, s end 4½ w.
Taylor, Samuel, cabinetmaker, s side Md av, btw 4½ and 6 w.
Taylor, John H., grocer, n side cor Md av and 13½ w.
Taylor, Franck, bookstore, n side Pa av, btw 4½ and 6 w.
Taylor, Mrs., boardinghouse, s side Pa av, btw 4½ and 6 w.
Taylor & Maury, bookstore, n side Pa av, btw 9 and 10 w.
Taylor, Hudson (& Maury) cor 9 w and D n.
Taylor, Wm. M., (col) laborer, w side 6 w, btw H and Mass av.
Taylor, S., widow, e side 12 w, btw F and G n.
Taylor, Saml. H., messenger Treasury Department, n side L n, btw 8 and 9 w.
Taylor, John, stonecutter, s side L n, btw Vt av and 15 w.
Taylor, Lewis, clerk Treasury Department, n side H n, btw 6 and 7 w.
Taylor, Thos. H., grocery, w side 7 e, btw L and M s.
Taylor, Wm. H., butcher, n side Ga av, btw 10 and 11 e.
Taylor, D., (col) laborer, s side D s, btw 4 and 5 e.
Taylor, E., (col) woodsawyer, e side 3 e, btw F and G s.
Taylor, Mrs., n side Prospect, btw Potomac and Market, Georgetown.
Taylor, Vincent, miller, n w cor Potomac and First, Georgetown.
Taylor's Mill, n side Water, near aqueduct, Georgetown.
Taylor, ——, clerk, e side Washington, btw Stoddard and Gay, Georgetown.
Teacher, Robt., carpenter, w side 4 e, btw L and M s.
TEBBS, D. H., & Co., Drygoods, s side Pa av, btw 6 and 7 w.
Telegragh Companies, viz:
House's Printing Telegraph, office e side 6 w, near Pa av. A. B. Talcott, operator—W. B. Walworth, cashier.
Washington and New Orleans Telegraph, office cor D and 7 w. E. Colton, operator.
Morse's Western and Southwestern Telegraph, office n side Pa av, btw 6 and 7 w. John R. Mingle, operator.
Morse's Northern and Eastern Telegraph, office cor 6 and Pa av. J. R. Bailey, operator.
Morse's Telegrah, office cor High and Prospect, (at J. L. Kidwell's drug store,) Georgetown.
Temperance Hall, s side E n, btw 9 and 10 w.
Templeman, Mrs., s side Prospect, extreme west, Georgetown.
Temps, William, confectioner, e side 7 w, btw F and G n.
Tennant, Mrs., seamstress, Market, btw Fourth and Fifth, Georgetown.
Tenney, W. H., grocer, s e cor Bridge and High; h few doors east, Georgetown.
Tennison, Lieut. Wm. A., U. S. Revenue service, s side B s, btw 10 and 11 w.
Terry, E. S., Recorder General Land office, e side 7 w, btw I and N Y av.
Terrell, Edmond, (col) laborer, n side D s, btw 2 and 3 w.
THAW & IARDELLA, Wood merchants, cor 7 w and N Y av.

Abbreviations.—All points start from the Capitol; s south, n north, e east, w west, btw between, cor corner, (col) colored, av avenue, h house,

Thaw, Joseph, (& Iardella) I, btw 9 and 10 w.
Thecker, James, e side Cherry alley, Georgetown.
Thecker, Henry, e side Scott's Row, Georgetown.
Thecker, Henry, at Fresh's, Geogretown.
Thoma, L., German Hotel, s side D n, btw 11 and 12 w.
Thoma, Wm., butcher, n side F n, btw 24 and 25 w.
Thoma, Charles, butcher, w side North Capitol, btw L and M n.
Thomas, G., baker, n side F s, btw 9 and 10 w.
Thomas, Henry, carpenter, n side C s, btw 13 and 13½ w.
Thomas, Charles, (col) waiter, e side 5 e, btw D and E s.
Thomas, Henry, baker, w side 11 e, btw M and N s.
Thomas, Charles E., bookkeeper, (Selden, Withers & Co.,) w side 12, btw I and K.
Thomas, A. W., blacksmith, w side 11 w, btw G and H n.
Thomas, Saml., (col) waiter, e side 10 w, btw M and N n.
Thomas, Geo. C., attor'y, office opposite Treas. Dep't; h n side I n, btw 8 and 9 w.
Thomas, Charles, s side N Y av, btw 9 and 10 w.
Thomas, James, (col) waiter, n side K n, btw 4 and 5 w.
Thomas, Henry, auxiliary guard, s side L n, btw 6 and 7 w.
Thomas, Josephine, (col) s side Pa av, btw 24 and 25 w.
Thomas, Dr. John M., n side 15 w, btw N Y av and H n.
Thomas, Wm. H., barber, w side 11 w, btw Md av and E s.
Thomas, W., carpenter, s side B n, btw 2 and 3 w; h C, btw 4½ and 6 w.
Thomas, Edward A., carpenter, w side 4½ w, btw L and M s.
Thomas, Moses., laborer, w side 3 w, btw M and N s.
Thomas, John H., book agent, w side 7 w, btw H and I n.
Thomas, Gustus, (col) woodsawyer, w side 3 w, btw C and Va av.
Thomas, Noble, e side 4½ w, btw E and G s.
Thomas, Edward, stonecutter, w side 8 w, btw P and Q n.
Thomas, William, carpenter, w side 8 w, btw D and E s.
Thomas, George, w side 9 w, btw D and E n.
Thomas, John, Irving House, cor Pa av and 12 w.
Thomas, Miss Mary, and Sisters, bookstore, w side High, three doors n of 1st, G'n.
Thomas, Wm., binder, w side High, three doors n of First, Georgetown.
Thomas, Mrs., s side West, btw High and Congress, Georgetown.
Thomas, Jenkin, saddler, e side High, btw Gay and Bridge; h s side Gay, btw Congress and Washington, Georgetown.
Thompson, Mrs., w side 11 w, btw E and F n.
Thompson, Mrs., w side 11 w, btw E and Pa av.
Thompson, John, shoestore, w side 10 w, btw D and E n.
Thompson, Wm., 5th District police office, Editor Washington News and Notary Public; office and house, e side 2 w, btw B and C n.
Thompson, James, carpenter, s side L n, btw Vt av and 15 w.
Thompson, R. H., police officer, s side M n, btw 14 and 15 w.
Thompson, Wm., saddler, s side N n, btw 6 and 7 w.
Thompson, C,, carpenter, s side Pa av, btw 21 and 22 w.
Thompson, B., shoemaker, s side H n, btw 19 and 20 w.
Thompson, John, cartman, w side 11 w, btw Md av and E s.
Thompson, Wm. Henry, bricklayer, w side 20 w, btw E n and N Y av.
Thompson, John, teacher, s side E n, btw 2 w and N J av.
Thompson, Wm., laborer, n side F n, btw 22 and 23 w.
Thompson, Ann, (col) laundress, n side D s, btw 2 and 3 w.
Thompson, Mrs., widow, e side 14 e, btw K and L s.
Thompson, Elizabeth, (col) laundress, s side Va av, btw 4½ and 6 w.
Thompson, George W., carpenter, w side 3 e, btw L and M s.
Thompson, Mrs. Mary, grocery, n side N s, btw South Capitol and 1 e.
Thompson, John H., bricklayer, cor 4½ and G s.
Thompson, M., attorney and counsellor at law, w side 4½ w, btw La av and C n.
Thompson, C. T., Coast Survey, w side N J av, btw D and E s.
Thompson, John, laborer, w side 4½ w, btw G and H s.
Thompson, Josias, laborer, w side 4½ w, btw G and H s.

Thompson, James, tobacconist, w side 7 w, btw L and M n.
Thompson, Mrs. Henrietta, e side 7 w, btw M and N n.
Thompson, George C., tobacconist, s side Md av, btw 4½ and 6 w.
Thompson, Wm., carpenter, s side Md av, btw 4½ and 6 w.
Thompson, Mrs., fortuneteller, s side Md av, btw 6 and 7 w.
Thompson, John H., saddler, n side Pa av, btw 4½ and 6 w.
Thompson & Co., J. R., (& Knowles) merchant tailor, n side Pa av, btw 4½ and 3 w.
THOMPSON, ———, Daguerreotypist, n side Pa av, btw 4½ and 6 w.
House, n side G n, btw 4 and 5.
THOMPSON, J. W., Plumber and Gasfitter, s side Pa av, near cor 11 w.
House, e side 11 w, btw G and H n.
Thompson, George W., boards at Mrs. Gallagher, btw 6 and 7 w.
Thompson, Mrs. L., (col) cook, s side F n, btw 13 and 14 w.
Thompson & Davis, paperhangers, n side Pa av, btw 12 and 13 w.
Thompson, Mrs. Harriet E., fancy store, n side E n, btw 12 and 13 w.
Thompson, Wm. H., pyrotechnist, w side 8 e, btw E and G s.
Thompson, George, (col) servant, n side G n, btw 6 and 7 w.
Thompson, ——, clerk, n side First, four doors w Potomac, Georgetown.
Thomson, Mrs. E., cor 9 w and H n.
Thorn, Henry, wood merchant, e side 7 w, btw D and E n.
House, e side 8 w, btw D and E n.
Thorn, Benj. E., barkeeper, e side 8 w, btw L and N Y av.
Thornley, Thomas, grocer, cor I s and 8 e.
Threbaud, F. L., refectory, n side G n, btw 17 and 18 w.
Throop, J. V. N., engraver, n side Pa av, btw 3 and 4½ w.
Thumbert, W. T., shoestore, s side Pa av, btw 4½ and 6 w.
House, s side C n, btw 3 and 4½ w.
THYSON, P., Grocer, w side 7 w, btw H and I.
Tilghman, H., (col) waiter, s side M n, btw 8 and 9 w.
Tilley, Mrs., boardinghouse, n side Mo av, btw 3 and 4½ w.
Tilley, H. W., postm., s side Bridge, btw Congress and Jefferson, Georgetown.
Tillinghast, Rev. Mr., boards cor Potomac and First, Georgetown.
Timms, James F., watchman and city constable, e side 4½ w, btw E and F s.
Tingle, G. E., clerk Light house Board, s side E n, btw 10 and 11 w.
Tinley, A., laborer, n side D s, btw 3 and 4 e.
Tinney, J., laborer, n side K n, btw 21 and 22 w.
Tippett, Thomas, carpenter, n side Mass av, btw 9 and 10 w.
Tippett, ——, carpenter, n side Dumbarton, btw Washington and Green, Geo'town.
Titus, James, (col) laborer, w side 18 w, btw K and L n.
TODD, WM. B., hatstore, under Brown's Hotel; h n side F n, btw 10 and 11 w.
Todd, Wm. B., painter, boards at Mrs. Burns.
Todtschinder, John A., refectory, s side B n, btw 2 and 3 e.
Tomlingson Elizabeth, milliner, w side 8 w, btw M and N n.
Tolson, John F., baker, w side 12 w, btw C and Va av.
Tolty, ——, laborer, s side A n, btw N J av and 2 w.
Toomey, Jeremiah, laborer, Md av, btw B and C.
Toomey, Michael, carpenter, n side D s, btw 1 and 2 w.
Tooney, Wm., (col) n side K n, btw 2 and 3 w.
Topham, George W., w side 7 w, btw Va av and D.
Topping, Nathaniel H., (Elmore &) 12 n, btw M and N n.
Topping, E., (col) brickmaker, e side 1 e, btw Pa av and B s.
Totten, J. G., engineer, n side I n, btw 20 and 21 w.
Tourny, Patrick, laborer, n side C s, btw 12 and 13 w.
Touy, Hugh, teacher, e side 11 e, btw G and I s.
Towers, Wm., clerk Penitentiary, south end 4½ w.
Towers, Lemuel, printer, e side 6 w, btw C and La av.
House, e side 6, btw G and H n.
Towers, James M., clerk Telegraph office, e side 6 w, btw G and H n.
Towers, J. T., Superintendent Public Printing, n side H n, btw 9 and 10 w.
Towle, N. C., clerk Senate, B s, Capitol Hill.

Abbreviations.—All points start from the Capitol; s south, n north, e east, w west, btw between, cor corner, (col) colored, av avenue, h house,

Towles, James, agent, n side H n, btw 8 and 9 w.
Townly, J. D., tinner, s side Pa av, btw 4½ and 6 w.
House, D, btw 6 and 7 w.
Townly, Mrs., w side 12 w, btw G and H n.
Towson, Gen. Nathan, Paymaster Gen., U. S. A., w side 17 w, btw N Y av and F n.
Toy, Reuben, tinner, s side D s, btw 1 and 2 w.
Tracy, Mrs., seamstress, e side Fayette, btw Second and Third, Georgetown.
Tracy, Wm., carpenter, do. do. do.
Travers, E., grocer, n side Pa av, btw 12 and 13 w.
Travers, Mrs. E. H., dressmaker, w side 18 w, btw H and I n.
Travers, J., woodyard, Canal, near Market, Georgetown.
Tredway, L. D., carpenter, e side 10 w, btw H and I n.
House M n, btw 8 and 9 w.
Tree, L., clerk City Post office, w side 12 w, near N Y av.
Tretler, John, bookbinder, e side 7 w, btw D and E n.
Trenholm, John H., printer, n side E n, btw 9 and 10 w.
Trimble, Matthew, grocer, w side 7 e, btw Va av and L s.
Triplett & O'Neale, bookbinders, n side Pa av, btw 14 and 15 w.
Triplett, Thomas M., (& O'Neale,) 13, near Franklin Row.
Triplett, A., (col) baker, n side D s, btw 4½ and 6 w.
Triplett, Gasper, carpenter, e side 14 w, btw B and C s.
Triplett, F. F. C., attorney at law, office cor 15 w and Pa av.
Trocton, George, plasterer, e side 4½ w, btw G and H s.
Trook, John, clerk post office, s side Va av, btw 7 and 8 w.
Trott, T. P., chief clerk post office, e side N J av, btw B and C s.
True, L. B., agency, s side Pa av, btw 14 and 15 w.
House, e side 18 w, btw I and K n.
Tuay, J., laborer, n side D s, btw 2 and 3 w.
Tuell, Lawrence, carpenter, w side 7 e, btw I and K s.
TRUE, EDWARD E., Carpenter, w side Va av and F s; h G s, btw 7 and 8.
TRUE, WALTER A., Machinist, w side Va av and F s.
True, William, carter, e side 4½ w, btw G and H s.
Trueman, Campbell, (col) sexton Christ Ch., n side Dumbarton, btw Congress and Washington, Georgetown.
Truman, Richard, carpenter, w side 4 w, btw I and K n.
Truman, William, carpenter, n side I n, btw 4 and 5 w.
Trundle, Isaac, tailor, w side 7 w, btw L and M n.
Trundle, J. H., carpenter, n side N Y av, btw 2 and 3 w.
Trundle, John, grocer, n w cor Third and Frederick, Georgetown.
Trundle, Richard, coachpainter, s side Fourth, btw Frederick and Fayette, G'town.
Trundle, David, collector, w side Frederick, btw Third and Fourth, Georgetown.
Trundle, Henry, landlord, do. do. do.
Trunnell, Elizabeth, n side Md av, btw 4½ and 6 w.
Tucker, Henry, laborer, n side G s, btw 5 and 6 e.
Tucker, James, blacksmith, n side Va av, btw 7 and 8 e.
Tucker, William, pumpmaker, n side F n, btw 9 and 10 w.
Tucker, Charles G., agent, w side 12 w, near Pa av.
Tucker, James H., tailor, e side 8 w, btw L and M n.
Tucker, William, merchant tailor, n side Pa av, btw 4½ and 6 w.
House C, btw 4½ and 6 w.
TUCKER, F. A., Merchant Tailor, n side Pa av, btw 4½ and 6 w.
House 6 w, btw H and I n.
Tucker, Margaret, w side 10 w, btw B and C n.
Tucker, B., sawyer, w side 18 w, btw I and K n.
Tucker, John H., letter carrier, s side B s, btw 10 and 11 w.
Tucker, Andrew, wheelwright and blacksmith, s side Bridge, near bridge, Geo'twn.
Tuckson, Stewart, (col) carter, w side 8 w, btw D and E s.
Tuel, Lawrence, carpenter, w side 7 e, btw G and K s.
Tune, S. T., messenger city post office, next door n to post office.
Tuomy, Timothy, carpenter, s side D n, btw 18 and 13½ w.

Abbreviations.—All points start from the Capitol; s south, n north, e east, w west, btw between, cor corner, (col) colored, av avenue, h house.

Turner, Thomas, hackdriver, e side 4½ w, btw C and Md av.
Turner, John L., tailor, s side Md av, btw 1 and 2 w.
Turner, Henry, livery stable, s side F n, btw 11 and 12 w.
House w side 11 w, btw F and G n.
Turner, Henry L., s side D n, btw 13 and 13½ w.
Turner, Rev. M. A., s side K n, btw 11 and 12 w.
Turner, Mrs. Robert, (col) laundress, n side N n, btw 6 and 7 w.
Turner, G., painter, s side La av, btw 6 and 7 w.
Turney, Mrs., n side West, btw High and Congress, Georgetown.
Turney, Misses, school, s e cor Bridge and Washington, at Presb. Ch.; h e side Washington, cor Stoddard, Georgetown.
Turner, John, shoemaker, s side West, e of Montgomery, Georgetown.
Turpin, Thomas, tailor, w side 4½ w, btw F and G s.
Turpin, Rev. Nelson, (col) pastor Wesley Zion Church, s side E s, btw 3 and 4½ w.
Tumbelty, H., grocer, n side H n, btw 20 and 21 w.
Turnbull, Col. William, U. S. A., n side F n, btw 20 and 21 w.
Turnbull, George, painter, s side La av, btw 6 and 7 w.
Turton, John B., carpenter, e side 18 w, btw Pa av and G n.
Turvey, Capt. Thomas, huckster, w side Potomac, btw Bridge and Prospect, G'twn.
Tustin, Rev. Dr., n side I n, btw 18 and 19 w.
Tustin, J. P., attorney, n side I n, btw 18 and 19 w.
Tweedy, Robert D., clerk Census Office, n side G n, btw 12 and 13 w.
Tyler, H. B., captain Marine Corps, w side 6 w, btw D and E n.
Tyler, Samuel, (col) welldigger, s side K n, btw 11 and 12 w.
Tyler, William, clerk, s side H n, btw 20 and 21 w.
Tyler, Dr. Grafton, n w cor Gay and Washington, Georgetown.
Tyson, M. A., and Sisters, seminary, n side F n, btw 12 and 13 w.
Tyson, Dr. Samuel E., druggist, cor 10 w and I n.
House s side N Y av, btw 13 and 14 w.
Tyssouski, J., clerk Treasury Department, e side 12 w, btw I and K n.

U.

Uhrlands, H. E., Coast Survey, w side N J av, btw D and E s.
Ulrich, Mrs., boardinghouse, cor 15 w and G n.
Umberfield & Co., dyers, e side 20 w, btw H and I n.
Unack, John, contractor public works, s side Mass av, btw 12 and 13 w.
Underwood, John, claim agent, e side N J av, btw B and C s.
Unger, Henry, carpenter, s side D s, btw 6 and 7 w.
Unger, Mrs., e side High, btw Gay and Dumbarton, Georgetown.
Union Engine House, cor H n and 19 w.
Union Hotel, n e cor Washington and Bridge, Georgetown.
Upperman, Wm. H., grocer, n side Pa av, btw 3 and 4½ w.
Upperman, Charles R., grocer, cor 3d and Bridge, Georgetown.
Upperman, ——, clerk, n side High, btw Beall and West, Georgetown.
Upperman, George, restaurant, e side Congress, one door n Bridge, Georgetown.
Upshaw, John, (col) cook, w side 8 w, btw H and I n.
Urgewood, Jesse, blacksmith, s side G s, btw 6 and 7 e.
Usher, John, grocer, cor F and 8 w.
Uternivhbe, G. W., w side 7 w, btw M and N n.
Uttermuhle & Huntsbergeres, wood merchants, cor N Y av and 7 w.
Uttermuhle, G. W., wood merchant, w side 7 w, btw I and N Y av.
Utermahle, M., tailor, e side 9 w, btw Pa av and D n.

V.

Valentine, William, (col) hackman, n side K n, btw 17 and 18 w.
Valentine, Matthias, wood carver, w side 10 w, btw D and E n.
Vallane, Christian, baker, s side East Capitol, btw 1 and 2 e.

Abbreviations.—All points start from the Capitol; s south, n north, e east, w west, btw between, cor corner, (col) colored, av avenue, h house.

Van Allen, Mrs. D. D., boardinghouse, w side 12 w, btw F and G n.
Vanderventer, clerk Post Office Department, boards w side 9 w, btw D and E n.
Vanderwerken, George, omnibus prop'r, s side West, btw Cong. and Wash'n, G'tn.
Van Horn, Jeremiah, carpenter, s side L s, btw 4 and 5 e.
Van Kleeck, Elbert H., clerk Department, e side 15 w, btw F n and N Y av.
Van Ness, C. P., attorney, w side 6 w, btw D and E n.
Van Ness, Mrs. John P., widow, n side Mo av, btw 4½ and 6 w.
VAN PATTEN, Dr., Dentist, n side Pa av, btw 6 and 7 w.
Van Patten, Milford, office at penitentiary, n side N s, btw N J av and 3 e.
Van Reswick, Joseph, finisher, n side L s, btw 3 and 4 e.
Van Reswick, T., commissioner 5th and 6th wards, s side L s, btw 3 and 4 e.
Van Tyne, Mrs. Mary, widow, fancy store, s side F n, btw 13 and 14 w.
Van Zandt, Nicholas B., clerk Treasury Dep't, n side Mass av, btw 11 and 12 w.
Varnell, George H., painter and glazier, w side 8 w, btw I and K n; boards B. L. Bogan's, N Y av, btw 7 and 8 w.
Varnell, John, clerk Patent Office, w side 10 w, btw H and N Y av.
Vauscriber, Wm., fisherman, n w cor Montgomery and Bridge, Georgetown.
Vedder, N., clerk, n side L n, btw 9 and 10 w.
Veihmyer, Jacob, stonecutter, w side 13 w, btw C and D s.
VENABLE, CHARLES, Daguerreotypist, over Stott's drug store.
House Va av, btw 7 and 8 e.
Venable, William, Grocery, n side L s, btw 4 and 5 e.
Venable, Thomas, gunner U. S. Navy Yard, w side 7 e, btw G and I s.
Venable, Jonah, grocer, cor Va av and 7 e.
Venable, William S., stove dealer, cor Va av and 7 e.
Venson, Joseph, grocer, w side 12 w, btw E and F n.
Vermillion, G. R., & Pumphrey, grocer, cor 4½ w and N s.
Vermillion, Otho T., tailor, e side 7 e, btw Va av and L s.
Vernon, F. F., carpenter, n side G s, btw 4½ and 6 w.
Vernon, Henry Y., tailor, s side Pa av, btw 4½ and 6 w; h w side 4½, btw F and G s,
Vernon, John C., coachmaker, n side H n, btw 21 and 22 w.
Vickers, Thomas, arsenal, s end 4½ w.
Viedt, Julius, cabinetmaker, n side E n, btw 10 and 11 w.
Vigan, R., (col) laborer, s side K n, btw 4 and 5 w.
Villard, T. J., watchmaker and dentist, n side Bridge, btw Cong. and High, G'tn.
Vimson, Mary, (col) laundress, s side I n, btw 10 and 11 w.
Vincent, ——, shoemaker, s side First, btw Frederick and Fayette, Georgetown.
Vincon, Charles, Clerk Treasury Department, s side Pa av, btw 21 and 22 w.
Visser, J., fancy store, n side Pa av, btw 9 and 10 w.
Visser, J. & J., bakers, w side 10 w, btw E and F n.
Von Essen, Peter, n e cor Canal and Congress, Georgetown.
Voss, William, jeweller, n side Pa av, btw 12 and 13 w.

W.

Wade, John W., tailor, n side H n, btw 4 and 5 w.
Wade, J. R., carpenter, s side Mass av, btw 4 and 5 w.
Wade, Mrs., Jane, widow, e side 6 w, btw G and H n.
Wade, Hiram, (col) laborer, e side 12 w, btw K and L n.
Waddie, B. F., hatter, s side Prospect, btw High and Congress, Georgetown.
Wadsworth, H. N., dentist, Brown's Hotel Building.
Wadsworth, Mrs., widow, n side K n, btw 12 and 13 w.
Waggaman, Mrs., s side First, few doors east High, Georgetown.
Wagler, Mrs., widow, s side I n, btw 16 and 17 w.
Wagner, John, gilder, s side Pa av, btw 12 and 13 w; h K, btw 13 and 14 w.
Wagner, John, confectioner, s side Pa av, btw 1 and 2 e.
Wagner. F., musician navy yard, w side 7 e, btw G and I s.
Wagoner, Anthony, carpenter, w side 8 w, btw I and K n.
Wailes, J. H., police at Capitol, side B n, btw Del av and 1 e.

Abbreviations.—All points start from the Capitol; s south, n north, e east, w west, btw between, cor corner, (col) colored, av avenue, h house.

Wainwright, Mrs., widow, s side G n, btw 19 and 21 w.
Waite, Nathan, slater, w side 4½ w, btw C n and Pa av.
House, s side G n, btw 6 and 7 w.
Waite, Edward, printer, n w cor G s and 8 w.
Waite, Samuel Brett, druggist, s side G n, btw 6 and 7 w.
Wakeman, N. T., w s 12 w, btw M and N n.
Walbridge, ——, e side 15 w, btw D n and Pa av.
Walker, John, butcher, e side N J av, btw M and N n.
Walker, Thos. J., lumber yard, B, near canal, btw 10 and 11 w.
House, cor N Y av and 8 w.
Walker & Shadd, National eating house, basement, cor Pa av and 6 w.
Walker, Noah & Co., merchant tailors, under Browns Hotel.
Walker, Mrs. C. H., widow, w side 6 w, btw D and E n.
Walker, C. E., carpenter, s side La av, btw 9 and 10 w.
House, n side D n, btw 6 and 7 w.
Walker, Wm, messenger War Department, e side 12 w, btw F and G n.
Walker, Ocenal, widow, e side 12 w, btw F and G n.
Walker, Wm. H., shoemaker, e side 12 w, btw I and K n.
Walker, Henry, printer, e side 16 w, btw I and K n.
Walker, Wm., messenger War Department, e side 19 w, btw I and K n.
Walker, Lewis, butcher, n side G n, btw 18 and 19 w.
Walker, W. T., painter, n side C s, btw 12 and 13 w.
Walker, Maria, widow, n side C s, btw 12 and 13 w.
Walker, Henry, painter, e side 4 e, btw K and L s.
Walker, Mrs. Isabella, widow, n side Mo av, btw 3 and 4½ w.
Walker, Mrs., boardinghouse, n side Mo av, btw 4½ and 6 w.
Walker, Joseph T., Notary Public, w side 3 w, btw Pa av and C n.
Walker & Kemmel, National livery stable, s side C n, btw 4½ and 6 w.
Walker, David, bookkeeper, (Selden, Withers & Co.,) w side Mo av, btw 3 and 4½ w.
Walker, Richard, stonemason and tavern, Potomac, btw Bridge and Prospect, G'n.
Walker, David, stonemason, w side Fayette, north new cut road, Georgetown.
Walker, Henry, carpenter, w side Montgomery, btw Beall and Dumbarton, G'town.
Wall, Michael, laborer, w side 3, btw I and K n.
Wall, C. O., cabinetmaker and undertaker, e side 7 w, btw D and E n.
Wall, Robert, tailor, s side Md av, btw 12 and 13 w.
Wall, Wm., merchant tailor, n side Pa av, btw 4½ and 6 w.
WALL & STEPHENS, Clothing Store, n side Pa av, btw 9 and 10 w.
Wall, William (& Stephens) clothier, n side Pa av, btw 9 and 10 w.
Wall, Thomas, gardener, w side 12 w, btw M and Mass av.
Wall, S. T., shoestore, n side La av, btw 7 and 8 w.
House, e side 11 w, btw N Y av and I n.
Wall, William, shoemaker, e side Frederick, btw 5th and 6th, Georgetown.
Wallace, Dr. William F., n side Pa av, btw 1 and 2 w.
Wallace, William, clerk Post Office Department, n side E n, btw 5 and 6 w.
Wallace, L., (col) servant, n side C s, btw 3 and 4½ w.
Wallace, ——, cooper shop, n side Water, near Ray's Mill, Georgetown.
Wallace, ——, huckster, w side High, btw 3d and 4th, Georgetown.
Wallace, James, tobacconist, w side High, btw Prospect and Bridge; h e side High, btw Gay and Bridge, Georgetown.
Wallack, Samuel, fancy store, e side 7 w, btw G and H n.
Wallack, Charles S., attorney at law, s side La av, btw 4½ and 6 w.
House, s side Ia av, btw 3 and 4½ w.
Wallack, Richard, United States marshal, City Hall, n side La av, btw 5 and 6 w.
Wallack, Cuthbert P., deputy marshal, City Hall, s side C, near 4½ w.
Waller, William, clerk Fourth Auditor's office, s side N Y av, btw 9 and 10 w.
Waller, A. B., clerk Post office, s side N Y av, btw 9 and 10 w.
Wallingsford, Ellinor, boarding, e side 4½ w, btw Pa av and C n.
Wallingsford, W., butter dealer, market, e side 19 w, btw I and K n.
Wallis, William, teacher, s side H n, btw 6 and 7 w.
Walmsley, Robert, cabinetmaker, e side 13 w, btw Pa av and E n.

Walsh, Francis S., n side 8 e, btw I and K s.
Walsh, John, grocer, n side I n, btw 13 and 14 w.
Walsh, R. M., s side Pa av, btw 17 and 18 w.
Walter, Theodore, grocer, e side 20 w, btw L and M n.
Walter, Charles, music teacher in German Hall, 11 st.; h w side 3, btw F and G n.
Walter, John, bootmaker, w side 7 w, btw L and M n.
Walter, Thos., architect Public Buildings, Adams' Express Building.
House 13, btw F n and Pa av.
Walter, J., cabinetmaker, cor 13 and Pa av.
Walter, Mrs. M. L., widow, n side C n, btw 12 and 13 w.
Walter, W. E., coal merchant, cor 12 and C.
Walter, John, w side 24 w, btw I and K n.
Walter, Robert, mariner, s side F s, btw 8 and 9 w.
Walter, Samuel, carpenter, e side 7 e, btw L and M s.
Wanderlich, J., baker, w side 7 e, btw Va av and L s.
Wannall, Charles P., grocer, cor 9 w and N Y av.
Waple, Robert, carpenter, w side 8 e, btw E and G s.
Waple, Obed., laborer, n side E s, btw 4½ and 6 w.
Ward, Mrs. C., boardinghouse, w side 4½ w, btw Pa and Mo avs.
Ward, John, book pedlar, w side 4½ w, btw Pa and Mo avs.
Ward, George, bricklayer, w side 4½ w, btw Pa and Mo avs.
Ward, Helen, (col) laundress, e side N J av, btw D and E s.
Ward, James, carpenter, cor 7 w and M n.
WARD, WM. H., Attorney at Law, office Brown's Hotel Building.
House, w side 10 w, btw C s and Va av.
Ward, Milton M., guard at jail, w side 6 w, btw M and N.
WARD, J. B., Lumber Merchant, 12, near canal; h Mo av, 1 door w 4½.
Ward, Enoch, cartman, w side 11 w, btw Md av and E s.
Ward, J. D., assistant doorkeeper Capitol, w side 6 w, btw D and E s.
Ward, Ulysses, n side Mo av, btw 4½ and 6 w.
Wardell, Mrs., seamstress, w side 11 w, btw G and H n.
Wardell, Mrs. James, shop n side Bridge, btw Washington and Green, Geo'town.
Wardell, Samuel, grocer, n side Bridge, btw Green and Montgomery, Georgetown.
Warder, William, wood and coal yard, w side 12 w, btw C and D n.
House, C, btw 11 and 12.
Warder, Walter, clerk Census office, e side 9 w, btw I and N Y av.
Warder, Wm., woolcarder, e side 2 w, btw F and G n.
Ware, Catharine, (col) laundress, s side F s, btw 2 and 3 e.
Warivole, Columbus, cabinetmaker, w side 6 w, btw E and F n.
Warnall, Joseph, saddler, s side F n, btw 10 and 11 w.
Warner, Henry, shoemaker, e side Lingan, north, Georgetown.
Warren, John, shoemaker, s side West, west of Montgomery, Georgetown.
Warrington, Lewis, purser navy yard, n side H n, btw 19 and 20 w.
WARRINER, C., & CO., Jewellers, n side Pa av, btw 9 and 10 w.
Warner, N., (col) servant, w side 3 w, btw C and Va av.
Warner, N., (col) porter, e side 11 w, btw Mass av and K n.
Warner, T., (col) laundress, e side 23 w, btw G and H n.
Warner, Charles, blacksmith, n side K s, btw 10 and 11 e.
Warren, Thomas, tailor, e side 7 w, btw N Y av and L n.
Warren, Henry, (col) tinner, s side Pa av, btw 12 and 13 w.
House, C, btw 12 and 13 w.
Warren, Louise, (col) n side K n, btw Vt av and 15 w.
Warwick, John, shoemaker, e side 7 w, btw L and M n.
Washburn, Ann, widow, w side 12 w, btw G and H n.
Washington, Mrs. P., (col) laundress, s side Va av, btw 3 and 4 e.
Washington, B., (col) laborer, s side C s, btw 3 and 4½ w.
Washington, W., (col) barber, e side N J av, btw Pa av and B.
Washington, Perrin, clerk Post office Department, s side F n, btw 6 and 7 w.
Washington Ladies' Depository, n side Pa av, btw 14 and 15 w.
Washington, Dr. B., w side 6 w, btw D and E n.

Abbreviations.—All points start from the Capitol; s south, n north, e east, w west, btw between, cor corner, (col) colored, av avenue, h house.

Washington, Richard C., clerk Post office Depart't, n side F n, btw 11 and 12 w.
Washington, Mary, widow, n side K n, btw 17 and 18 w.
Washington, Henry, (col) carpenter, e side 16 w, btw K and L n.
Washington Infirmary, s side F n, btw 4 and 5 w.
Washington City Club, (Geo. Washington, President) n side G n, btw 17 and 18 w.
Washington, G., (col) laborer, n side F s, btw 9 and 10 w.
Washington, Col. George C., cor Washington and Road, Georgetown.
Wason, Israel, carpenter, n side K s, btw 9 and 10 e.
House, 10 e, btw I and K s.
Waters, Robert, printer, w side 19 w, btw F and G n.
Waters, Robert, shoestore, w side 4 w, btw G and H n.
Waters, Samuel, (col) waiter, w side 3, btw N Y av and L n.
Waters, Gustavus, woodmerchant, cor 8 w and F n.
House, w side 8 w, btw E and F n.
Waters, J., drygoods, s side Pa av, btw 6 and 7 w.
Waters, John, market master, (centre) n side E n, btw 10 and 11 w.
Waters, David J., s side Mass av, btw 6 and 7 w.
Waters, Susannah, (col) laundress, e side 10 w, btw M and N n.
Waters, Thos., hackman, w side 1 w, btw Pa av and B n.
Waters, George, flour and corn, s e cor Water and High; h w side Market, btw Prospect and 1st, Georgetown.
Waters, John, wholesale grocer, s side Water, west of High, Georgetown.
Waters, Thomas, grocer, s side High, btw 2d and 3d, Georgetown.
Waters, John, do. do. do.
House e side High, btw West and Road, Georgetown.
Watkins, Robt., (col) huckster, s side E s, btw 3 and 4½ w.
Watson, Mrs. Sarah, n side E s, btw 4 and 5 e.
Watson, G. W., office, n side of Pa av, btw 4½ and 6 w.
Watson, W. H., clerk Pension office, w side 19 w, btw G and H n.
Watson, Lewis, shoemaker, e side 13½ w, btw C and D.
Watson & Renwick, patent agents, s side F n, btw 7 and 8 w.
Watson, P. H., (& Renwick) boards at Mrs. Janney's.
Watson, Edward, shoemaker, n side K n, btw 17 and 18 w.
Watson, James, messenger Post office Department, n side H n, btw 4 and 5 w.
Watson, Mrs., widow, e side 13½ w, btw C and D s.
Watt, John, grocer, s side D n, btw 14 and 15 w.
Watts, Saml., (col) w side N J av and E s.
Watts, Mrs. Eliza, boardinghouse, s side D n, btw 12 and 13 w.
Watts, G., (col) laborer, w side 22 w, btw G and H n..
Watupouski, H., Land office, n side L n, btw 9 and 10 w.
Waugh, Wm. A., grocer, s w cor Bridge and Washington; h Bridge, few doors w, Georgetown.
Waugh, A. P., woodyard, Washington, btw Canal and Water; h s side Bridge, west of Washington, Georgetown.
Wayne, James, Coast Survey, w side N J av, btw D and E s.
Wayne, James, judge Supreme Court, s side H n, btw 17 and 18 w.
Wayne, Major H. C., U. S. A., n side G n, btw 17 and 18 w.
Wayson, Israel, carpenter, w side 10 e, btw I and K s.
Weaver, Mrs. Helen, fancy store, w side 7 w, btw G and H n.
Weaver, J. G., confectioner, s side G n, btw 13 and 14 w.
Weaver, William, clerk Post Office, w side 15 w, btw L and M n.
Weaver, Michael, butcher, out High, Georgetown.
Webb, Pollard, agent National L. and F. Assurance Society, and Actual Life Insurance Company, n side Pa av, btw 4½ and 6 w.
Webb, W. B., attorney, e side 6 w, btw D and E n.
Webb, Miss Frances, n side G n, btw 11 and 12 w.
Webb, Wm. P. S., turning establishment, n side D n, btw 5 and 6 w.
Webb, Richard J., miller, s side Frederick, btw 3d and 4th, Georgetown.
Webber, C., saddler, e side 18 w, btw K and L n.
Webster, Charles, plasterer, n side G n, btw 4 and 5 w.

Abbreviations.—All points start from the Capitol; s south, n north, e east, w west, btw between, cor corner, (col) colored, av avenue, h house.

Webster, Samuel, carpenter, w side 11 e, btw M and O s.
Webster, Mrs. A., laundress, w side 7 w, btw H and I n.
Webster, T. W., cabinetmaker, w side 11 w, btw I and K n.
Webster, John, stonemason, n side Va av, btw South Capitol and 1 w.
Webster, William, cabinetmaker, n side West, btw Cong. and Washington, G'town.
Weeden & Ryther, stables, n side K s, btw 8 and 9 e.
Weeden, W., livery stable, w side 1 w, btw B and Md av.
Weeden, H. A., coachmaker, cor 9 w and Market space.
Weeks, Miss Rachel, e side 8 w, btw L and M n.
Weesbecker, A., shoemaker, cor 11 w and I n.
Weggerman, Bernard, shoemaker, e side 7 w, btw M and N n.
Weightman, Henry T., clerk city post office, w side 6 w, btw E and F n.
Weightman, R. H., Delegate New Mexico, e side 6 w, btw D and F n.
Weightman, Roger C., chief clerk Patent Office, n side La av, btw 6 and 7 w.
WEIRMAN, C., Ladies' Shoestore, e side 15 w, btw N Y av and H n.
Weisenfield & Co., clothiers, n side Pa av, btw 3 and 4½ w.
Welch, Thomas, hackdriver, s side Mass av, btw 4 and 5 w.
Welch, ——, n side La av, btw 9 and 10 w.
Welch, Robert, clerk, n side Bridge, btw High and Potomac, Georgetown.
Welch, C. D., tailor, n side Bridge, e Cong.; h s side West, btw High and Congress, Georgetown.
Wells, William Henry, baker, e side 6 w, btw G and H n.
Wells, Samuel, carpenter, w side 10 w, btw L and M n; h F n, btw 13 and 14 w.
Wells, Mrs., boardinghouse, Carroll Place, btw East Capitol and A s.
Wells, Philip, (col) hackman, w side 5 e, btw G and I s.
Werner, J. H. T., gunsmith, n side La av, btw 6 and 7 w.
Wescott, Mrs. Susan, grocery, cor 8 e and G s.
Wessen, ——, laborer Navy Yard, w side 8 e, btw E and G s.
West, James, barkeeper, e side 10 w, btw Va av and B s.
West, John, laborer, e side 3 e, btw Ga av and N s.
West, John, & Son, Columbia Central Hotel, C, btw 4½ and 6 w.
West Market, w side 20 w, btw I n and Pa av.
West, John, brickmaker, s side Md av, btw 6 and 7 w.
West, Clement L., draughtsman, architect's off., Cap'l, n side Pa av, btw 2 and 3 w.
West, G. R., patent agent, s side F n, btw 7 and 8 w.
West, John, (col) plasterer, w side 6 w, btw Mass av and K n.
West, John D., n side C n, btw 13 and 14 w.
West, Mrs., s side Mass av, btw 6 and 7 w.
West, Henry, stonecutter, w side 10 w, btw C and Va av.
Westerfield, David, cabinetmaker, e side 3 w, btw Va av and F.
Westerfield, James, grocer, s side G n, btw 18 and 19 w.
Weyrich, Joseph, blacksmith, w side 7 w, btw N and O n.
Whalen, Pat., mason, w side 8 w, btw L and M n.
Whalen, Wm., laborer, n side B s, btw 1 and 2 w.
Whalen, Morton, painter, e side Potomac, btw Bridge and Prospect, Georgetown.
Whalen, John, workman canal, n side Market, btw 4th and 5th, Georgetown.
Whalen, ——, tanner, w side Fayette, north new cut road, Georgetown.
Whaley, H. H., drygoods and furniture store, s side Pa av, btw 12 and 13 w.
Whaley, John, omnibus driver, cor 13½ w and C n.
Wheat, Mrs. Mary, w side 4½ w, btw N and O s.
Wheat, William, county constable, e side 5 e, btw E and G s.
Wheatley & Walker, lumberyard, s side Water, near bridge, Georgetown.
Wheatley, ——, (& Walker,) w side Jefferson, near bridge, Georgetown.
Wheatley, Franklin J., feed merchant, s side Water, west of High, Georgetown.
Wheatly, William, drygoods, e side N J av, btw B and C s.
Wheatly, J., shoestore, s side A s, btw N J av and 1 e.
Wheatly, George, huckster, s side C s, btw 4½ and 6 w.
Wheatly, Francis, s side Water; h s side Bridge, btw High and Congress, G'town.
Wheeler, Ephraim, agricultural warehouse, e side 7 w, btw Pa av and B n.
Wheeler, T., s side Md av and 13 w.

Abbreviations.—All points start from the Capitol; s south, n north, e east, w west, btw between, cor corner, (col) colored, av avenue, h house.

Wheeler, E., hardware store, s side Pa av, btw 6 and 7 w.
House n side Md av btw 10 and 11 w.
Wheeler, William, carpenter, w side 8 w, btw G and H n.
Wheeler, J., clerk, w side 6 w, btw G and H n.
Wheeler, G. W., cabinetmaker, n side Pa av, btw 17 and 18 w.
Wheeler, Henry, (col) laborer, s side N Y av, btw 9 and 10 w.
Wheeler, William A., & Co., stationers, n side B n, btw 10 and 11 w.
Wheeler, Mrs. Gen., school, n side Prospect, cor Fayette, Georgetown.
Whelan, Dr. William, U. S. N., n side G n, btw 14 and 15 w.
Whitaker, John, printer, s side Pa av, btw 17 and 18 w.
White, Charles, (Rider &) Me av, btw 4½ and 6 w.
White, ———, 4½, btw C and Ia av.
White & Sons, drygoods, cor La av and 8 w.
White, Mrs., dressmaker, e side 7 w, btw L and M n.
White, John, laborer, w side 3 w, btw C and D s.
White, M. M., coffin warehouse, s side Pa av, btw 3 and 4½ w.
White, W. G. W. & Bro., drygoods, s side Pa av, btw 6 and 7 w.
White, W. G. W., (& Bro.) 4½ w, btw Ia av and C n.
White, James L., (& Bro.) E n, btw 5 and 6 w.
White, Margaret, (col) laundress, n side L n, btw 5 and 6 w.
White, Richard, clerk Post office, s side M n, btw 6 and 7 w.
White, Thos., pilot, w side 13½ w, btw Md av and D s.
White, T., (col) carter, s side B s, btw 1 w and South Capitol.
White, E. E., & Co., grocers, n side La av, btw 6 and 7 w.
White, James, s side D s, btw 9 and 10 w.
White, Patrick, laborer, n side East Capitol s, btw 1 and 2 e.
White, Basil, printer, w side 7 e, btw L and M s.
White, Joseph, tinner, e side 5 e, btw G and I s.
White, Mrs. Ann, widow, n side M s, btw 9 and 10 e.
White, Mrs., widow, n side L s, btw 8 and 9 e.
White, Frederick, clerk Coast Survey office, n side D s, btw 3 and 4 e.
White, Robert, moulder, n side Va av, btw 9 and 10 w.
White, Robert, grocer, s w cor Bridge and market space; h n side Prospect, western part, Georgetown.
WHITEHURST, J. H., Daguerreotypist, n side Pa av, btw 3 and 4½ w.
Whitemore, H. O., shoemaker, w side 4½ w, btw Md av and C s.
Whitemore, Samuel, shoemaker, n side G s, btw 8 and 9 w.
Whitemore, U., shoemaker, n side E n, btw 10 and 11 w.
Whiting, W. B., shoemaker, s side F s, btw 8 and 9 w.
Whiting, G. W., clerk Selden, Withers & Co., Franklin Row, Pa av.
Whitlock, William, n side F n, btw 19 and 20 w.
Whitney, Joseph, shoestore, cor 9 and D n; h e side 6 w, btw F and G n.
Whitney, F., clerk Pension office, s side G n, btw 17 and 18 w.
Whittlesey, Oliver, lamp and oil store, s side C n, btw 6 and 7 w.
House, s side Ia av, btw 3 and 4½ w.
Whittlesey, C. S., s side Ia av, btw 3 and 4½ w.
Whitwell, Mrs., widow, s side B n, btw 2 and 3 w.
Whitwell, John C., (Kibbey & Co.) boards at Adams', opposite Brown's Hotel.
Widdicombe, Robert, s side F n, btw 13 and 14 w.
Widle, John, baker, e side 11 w, btw Md av and F s.
Wiechmann, J. C., tailor, s side Pa av, btw 6 and 7 w; h C n, btw 6 and 7 w.
Wight, O. C., Principal Rittenhouse Academy, cor Ia av and 3 w, boards at United States Hotel.
Wilburn, Mrs., widow, s side M n, btw 12 and 13 w.
Wilcox, Mrs. A. F., widow, s side E n, btw 9 and 10 w.
Wilcox, Charles, clerk War Department, cor 12 and N n.
Wiles, Lemuel M., artist, Lane & Tucker's Building, Pa av.
Wild, ——, blacksmith arsenal, south end 4½ w.
Wilkes, Com. Charles, U. S. N., office North Capitol, btw B and C n.
s side H n, btw 15 and Vt av.

Abbreviations.—All points start from the Capitol; s south, n north, e east, w west, btw between, cor corner, (col) colored, av avenue, h house.

Wilkins, John L., grocery, w side 12 w, btw M and Mass av.
Wilkinson, Wm., (col) waiter, n side Mass av, btw 12 and 13 w.
Wilkinson, John, carpenter, n side M n, btw 6 and 7 w.
Wilkison, Wm., n side K n, btw 15 and 16 w.
Wilkison, Wm., moulder, e side 7 e, btw Va av and L s.
Wilkison, ——, carpenter, s side L s, btw 8 and 9 e.
Willard, Henry A., hotel, n side Pa av, btw 14 and 15 w.
Willburn, R., laborer, n side L s, btw 3 and 4 e.
Willet, John, Post office, w side 7 e, btw L and M s.
Willet, Col., e side High, btw West and Road, Georgetown.
Willett, V., dealer in live stock, n side Ia av, btw 1 and 2 w.
Williams, Joseph O., moulder, w side 4½ w, btw Md av and C s.
Williams, James, cabinetmaker, e side 7 w, btw D and E n.
House, e side 4½ w, btw Pa av and C n.
Williams, George, carpenter, e side N J av, btw B and C s.
Williams, Martha, widow, baker, e side 8 w, btw L and M n.
Williams, John, shoemaker, e side 8 w, btw K and L n.
Williams, Mrs. C. E., boarding house, s side Pa av, btw 4½ and 6 w.
Williams, Giles, laborer, s side F n, btw 6 and 7 w.
Williams, Wm., clerk, s side G n, btw 12 and 13 w.
Williams, T. J., w side 12 w, btw I and K n.
Williams, Wm., w side 12 w, btw D and E n.
Williams, Thomas, navy yard, w side 12 w, btw D and E n.
Williams, Mrs., ladies' dressmaker, e side 11 w, btw E and Pa av.
Williams, J. W., n side K n, btw 17 and 18 w.
Williams, Mrs., widow, s side M n, btw 6 and 7 w.
Williams, J. S., clerk Navy Department, n side H n, btw 9 and 10 w.
Williams, J. O., drygoods, n side Pa av, btw 19 and 20 w.
Williams, L., cabinet warerooms, n side Pa av, btw 17 and 18 w.
Williams, B. B., banker, e side 15 w, btw F n and Pa av.
Williams, Mrs., widow, s side B s, btw N J av and 1 e.
Williams, Mrs. Ann D., widow, w side 20 w, btw G and H n.
Williams, Jesse, n side F s, btw 1 and 2 w.
Williams, Lemuel, draughtsman, w side 7 e, btw G and I s.
Williams, Wm. F., laborer, e side 7 e, btw L and M s.
Williams, Zadock, grocer, e side 3 e, btw Ga av and N s.
Williams, Mary S., widow, shoestore, e side 3 e, btw Ga av and N s.
Williams, Saml., (col) laborer, e side 6 w, btw N and O n.
Williams, Danl., (col) waiter, e side 11 w, btw Mass av and K n.
Williams, Mrs., (col) laundress, s side K n, btw 4 and 5 w.
Williams, Charles, (col) servant, n side 15 w, btw L and M n.
Williams, Lucy, (col) laundress, n side B s, btw 2 and 3 e.
Williams, Betsy, laundress, (col) n side E n, btw N J av and 2 e.
Williams, Mrs., (col) laundress, e side 20 w, btw K and L n.
Williams, J., (col) laborer, e side 20 w, btw L and M n.
Williams, Wm., (col) driver, n side C s, btw 3 and 4½ w.
Williams, Brooke B., s side Road, btw Congress and Washington, Georgetown.
Williams, Henry, shoemaker, s side West, btw Congress and Washington, Geo'twn.
Williams, Mrs., mantuamaker, do. do. do.
Williams, Jeremiah, s side Dumbarton, btw Congress and Washington, Geo'town.
Williams, Mr., shoemaker, n side Bridge, btw Green and Montgomery, Georgetown.
Williams, Mrs., confectionery, s side Bridge, btw Congress and Jefferson, Geo'town.
Williams, Wm., shoemaker, s side Bridge, two doors west Washington, Geo'town.
Williams, Mort. L., drygoods, n side Bridge, few doors east Congress; h e side Washington, cor Dumbarton, Georgetown.
Williams, Barbara, n side Prospect, west of Fayette, Georgetown.
Williams, John, farmer and boardinghouse, e side High, btw Gay and Bridge, G'n.
Williams, Henry, shoemaker, at Grimes', do. do. do.
Williams, Wm., shoemaker, w side Washington, btw Bridge and Canal, Geo'town.
Williamson, James, messenger State Department, w side 2 e, btw B and C s.

Abbreviations.—All points start from the Capitol; s soath, n north, e east, w west, btw between, cor corner, (col) colored, av avenue, h house.

Williamson & Osgodby, carpenters, w side 12 w, btw E and F n.
Williamson, Benj., carpenter, s side H n, btw 10 and 11 w.
House 10 w, btw G and H n.
Williamson, John B., (& Osgodby,) carpenter, w side 10 w, btw G and H n.
Williamson, R. H., w side 10 w, btw D and E n.
Williamson, Josh. A., editor, cor Washington and Bridge; h s side West, few doors east Congress, Georgetown.
Willis, Mrs., boardinghouse, cor F n and 13 w.
WILLNER, GEORGE, Upholsterer, e side 9 w, btw Pa av and D n.
Wills, R., w side N J av, btw B and Pa av.
Willson, Wm. P., wheelwright, cor 4½ w and Md av; h n side Md av, btw 4½ and 6 w.
Willson, John Q., clerk, n side G n, btw 4 and 5 w.
Willson, ——, teacher, n side Beall, btw High and Congress, Georgetown.
Wilson, George, bricklayer, w side B, btw I and Mass av.
WILSON, WILLIAM P., Blacksmith and wheelwright, w side 4½ w, btw Me and Md avs; h n side Md av, btw 4½ and 6 w.
Wilson, John M., coachmaker, w side 4½ w, btw N and O s.
Wilson, William, hatter, e side 7 w, btw D and E n.
Wilson, Miss Harriet, seamstress, w side 7 w, btw G and H n.
Wilson, J. P., restaurant, cor N J av and Pa av.
Wilson, David M., w side 9 w, btw I and N Y av.
Wilson, Ephraim K., clerk Republic office, w side 9 w, btw I and N Y av.
Wilson, Henry, dyer and clothes cleaner, s side Pa av, btw 3 and 4½ w.
Wilson, J. B., grocer, s side Pa av, btw 6 and 7 w; h 9 w, btw N Y av and I n.
Wilson, Mrs. N., boarding, s side Pa av, btw 9 and 10 w.
Wilson, Mrs., boarding, n side F n, btw 11 and 12 w.
Wilson & Hayward, Union Hall, n side C, btw 6 and 7 w.
Wilson, Mrs., cigar store, w side 10 w, btw C and Pa av.
Wilson, Patrick, grocer, e side 10 w, btw E and F n.
Wilson, Thomas, carpenter, e side 10 w, btw B and C n.
Wilson, John D., clerk Pension office, n side Mass av, btw 11 and 12 w.
Wilson, William B., contractor, n side M n, btw 6 and 7 w.
Wilson, Mrs., widow, n side B n, btw 2 and 3 w.
Wilson, J., woodyard, s side Pa av, btw 17 and 18 w.
House, w side 17 w, btw H and I n.
Wilson, E., w side 11 w, btw Md av and E s.
Wilson, J. P., refectory, s side A s, btw N J av and 1 e.
Wilson, John, Commissioner Land Office, N Y av, near 14 w.
Wilson, William, w side 20 w, btw F and H n.
Wilson, Mrs. H., widow, e side 22 w, btw G and H n.
Wilson, C. H., attorney, s side La av, btw 4½ and 6 w.
Wilson, John, carpenter, s side D s, btw 6 and 7 w.
Wilson, George R., finisher, e side 7 e, btw L and M s.
Wilson, Mrs., widow, n side L s, btw 6 and 7 e.
Wilson, George, grocer, s side I s, btw 12 and 13 e.
Wilson, John L., huckster, n side La av, btw 9 and 10 w.
Wilson, H. T. L., constable, 1, btw Capitol and Ind av.
Wilson, Joseph S., clerk Department Interior, 13 w, btw E and F n.
Wilson, Henry, (col) cake shop, e side N J av, btw Pa av and B.
Wilson, William, (col) servant, n side N n, btw 9 and 10 w.
Wilson, John, barber, w side High, btw Prospect and Bridge; h e side High, btw Gay and Bridge, Georgetown.
Wilson, Mrs., dressmaker, w side Washington, btw Stoddard and West, Geo'town.
Wilson, Lewis, feedstore, cor Montgomery and Bridge, Georgetown.
Wilson, Henry, tailor, s side Gay, one door e High, Georgetown.
Wilson, Henry G., watchm., e side High, btw Beall and West, Georgetown.
Wilson, James, clerk, s side Bridge, near the bridge, Georgetown.
Wilson, ——, marbleyard, s side Prospect, btw High and Congress, Georgetown.
Wilson, Charles, miller, n side Water, near aqueduct; h n side 1st, btw Market and Frederick, Georgetown.

Abbreviations.—All points start from the Capitol; s south, n north, e east, w west, btw between, cor corner, (col) colored, av avenue, h house.

WIMER, JAMES, Stationery and Fancy Store, w side 6 w, btw C and La av.
Wimsatt, J., grocer, cor Pa av and 13 w; h 12, btw E and F n.
Winder, Mrs. John H., confectionary, e side 9 w, btw I and N Y av.
Winder, Charles H., w side 17 w, btw F and G n; h F n, btw 18 and 19 w.
Winder's Building, (public offices,) 17 w, btw G and H n.
Windsor, John A., drygoods, w side 7 w, btw H and I n.
Windule, Catharine, furnished rooms, e side 12 w, btw E and F n.
WINGENROTH, FREDERICK, Columbian Refectory, w side 8 w, cor E n.
Wingerd, Abraham, farmer, s side Beall, btw High and Congress, Georgetown.
Winkfield, Elizabeth, (col) w side 12 w, btw E and F n.
Winner & Gibson, restaurant, cor 7 w and E n.
Winner, Charles, (& Gibson,) cor 7 w and E n.
Winship, Mrs., grocery, n side West, e Montgomery, Georgetown.
Winter, W. H., contractor Capitol, n side La av, btw 6 and 7 w.
Winwright, Mrs. Maria, boarding, s side E n, btw 10 and 11 w.
Wirt, John L., watchman Capitol, e side North Capitol, btw B and C n.
Wise, John, bricklayer, w side 4½ w, btw Md av and C s.
Wise, James A., blacksmith, w side 7 w, btw G and H n.
Wise, Samuel, carpenter, n side E n, btw 9 and 10 w.
House n side I n, btw 6 and 7 w.
Wise, Mrs. M. D. P., boardinghouse, e side 13 w, btw Pa av and E n.
Wise, Charles J., carter, n side Fourth, btw Market and Frederick, Georgetown.
Witherow, Lawrence, hatter, e side 8 w, btw L and M n.
Withers, J. O., saddler, s side F n, btw 17 and 18 w.
Witherspoon, A. S., ass't surgeon U. S. A., Winder's building.
House w side 17 w, btw Pa av and H n.
Wittenauer, ——, (Frankenberger &,) cor 7 w and G n,
Witthaft, ——, wheelwright, s side Pa av, btw 1 and 2 e.
Wollard, J. F., constable, s side D n, btw 7 and 8 w.
Woltz, T., chairmaker, n side H n, btw 4 and 5 w.
Wood, George, at Dr. J. C. Hall's, Pa av, btw 10 and 11 w.
Wood, Wm., cabinetmaker, e side 10 w, btw E and F n.
Wood, Thomas, (col) waiter, s side A s, btw N J av and 1 e.
Wood, D., laborer, w side South Capitol, btw C and D s.
Wood, Isaac C., agent Empire State Ins. Co., s side A n, btw 1 and 2 e.
Wood, Henry S., w side 4 w, btw B and C s.
Woods, John, blacksmith, w side 11 e, btw M and N s.
Wood, Thomas, tailor, e side 7 w, btw N Y av and L n.
Woodbury Academy, s side H n, btw 12 and 13 w.
Woodfield, Benj., shoemaker, e side 4 e, btw K and L s.
Woodhull, M., U. S. N., s side F n, btw 6 and 7 w.
Woodland, Thomas, (col) laborer, w side 3 w, btw M and N s.
Woodruff, J. B., n side H n, btw 8 and 9 w.
Woodward, Clement, clerk, w side 11 w, btw G and H n.
Woodward, Wm. R., carpenter, e side 6 w, btw M and N n; h cor 5 w and O n.
Woodward, C., hardware, n side D n, btw 9 and 10 w.
Woodward, Daniel T., grocer, s side K n, btw 26 and 27 w.
Woodward, A., blockmaker, w side 3 e, btw M and N s.
Woodward, Thomas, deputy marshal, n side West, extreme west, Georgetown.
Woodward, William R., attorney, do. do. do.
Woolard, Mrs., confectionery, n side Bridge, btw Congress and Washington, Geo'tn.
Worden, shoemaker, s side 1 n, btw 6 and 7 w.
Wormly, Winney, (col) w side 3 w, near Ia av.
Wormly, Wm., (col) n side I n, btw 15 and 16 w.
Worrell, William, carpenter, s side S, btw 9 and 10 w.
Worthington, Thomas, wood and coal merchant, e side 14 w, btw C and D n.
Worthington's Temperance Hotel, n side D n, btw 9 and 10 w.
Wren, George W., refectory, n side Pa av, btw 14 and 15 w.
Wrench, U. S., musician, G s, btw 8 and 9 e.
Wright, W. S., stove manufacturer, cor 4½ w and E s.
Wright, Lewis, grocer, w side 4½, btw F and G s.

Abbreviations.—All points start from the Capitol; s south, n north, e east, w west, btw between, cor corner, (col) colored, av avenue, h house.

Wright, George, machinist arsenal, s end 4½ w.
Wright, Benj. C., printer, w side 7 w, btw F and G n.
Wright, George H., cooper, n side Md av, btw 6 and 7 w.
WRIGHT, MRS. ROBERT, Corsetstore, n side Pa av, btw 12 and 13 w.
Wright, Charles J., carpenter, w side 6 w, btw G and H n.
Wright, C. M., hatter, n side C n, btw 9 and 10 w.
Wright, James, hackdriver, w side 20 w, btw I and K n.
Wright, Ed. S., s side First, btw Market and Frederick, Georgetown.
Wright, Mrs., (col) laundress, s side F n, btw 13 and 14 w.
Wroe, Wm., bricklayer, w side 13 w, btw N Y av and I n.
Wroe, Richard, bricklayer, n side G n, btw 12 and 13 w.
Wroe, J. R., bricklayer, e side 12 w, btw N Y av and H n.
WURDEMANN, WM., Mathematical instrument maker, cor Del av and B n.
Wylie, Andrew, jr., (De Selding &) Alexandria.

Y.

Yager, Mrs. M. A., confectionery, s side Bridge, few doors east High, Georgetown.
Yateman, Thomas, butter merchant, e side 7 w, btw D and E s.
Yates, John L., w side 12 w, btw C and Va av.
Yates, ——, grocer, s side West, extreme east, Georgetown.
Yawk, John, (col) laborer, w side 8, btw K and L n
Yeatman, Arthur, H., cabinetmaker, w side 7 w, btw E and F s.
Yeatman, J. H., butter store, s side E n, btw 6 and 7 w.
Yerby, Wm. G., merchant, cor La av and 7 w.
Yerkes, Harman, carpenter, e side 10 w, btw H and I n.
Young, William, saddler, w side 4 w, btw G and H n.
Young, Dr. Alex., w side 4½ w, btw La av and C n.
Young, R. M., attorney at law, w side 7 w, btw Pa av and D n.
Young, A. H., clerk city Post office, w side 9 w, btw E and F n.
Young, Dr. Noble, s side Pa av, btw 3 and 4½ w.
Young, Thomas, coachmaker, s side Pa av, btw 4½ and 6 w.
House, Mo av, btw 3 and 4½ w.
Young & Orem, merchant tailors, under Brown's Hotel.
Young, Abner, (& Orem) I, btw 9 and 10 w.
Young, John M., coachmaker, Me av, btw 3 and 4½ w.
Young, Henry N., e side 8 w, btw G and H n.
Young, McClintock, attorney at law, s side F n, btw 12 and 13 w.
Young, G. W., farmer, w side 6 w, btw D and E n.
Young, Mrs. A. E., dressmaker, w side 6 w, btw H and Mass av.
Young, Wm., clerk, w side 6 w, btw H and Mass av.
Youug, Mrs., schoolteacher, s side I n, btw 18 and 19 w.
Young, Abner, tailor, s side I n, btw 9 and 10 w.
Young, James, clerk Navy Department, s side Pa av, btw 21 and 22 w.
Young, Dr. R. W., agent for Claims, e side 16 w, btw I and K n.
Young, Coleby, e side 12 w, btw B and C s.
Young, Wm., painter, s side Va av, btw South Capitol and 1 w.
Young, Wm., laborer, n side I s, btw 11 and 13 e.
Young, John Y., contractor, Mrs. Lang's, s side Bridge, near High, Georgetown.
Young, Anthony, carter, s side Fourth, btw Market and Frederick, Georgetown.
Young, Jacob, clerk at H. L. Offert's, e side High, btw West and Road, Geo'town.
Yulee, R., clerk Treasury Department, s side Pa av, btw 2 and 3 e.
Yunghans, J. M., shoemaker, n side D s, btw 3 and 4 e.

Z.

Zantzinger, Wm. C., clerk State Department, cor E n and 9 w.
ZAPPONE, A., Teacher, n side Pa av, btw 4½ and 6 w.
Zimmerman, H. F., furniture store, s side Pa av, btw 12 and 13 w.
House, w side 6, btw G and H n.

CONGRESSIONAL DIRECTORY

FOR THE

SECOND SESSION

OF THE

THIRTY-SECOND CONGRESS

OF THE

UNITED STATES OF AMERICA,

AND

GUIDE BOOK THROUGH THE PUBLIC OFFICES.

WASHINGTON:
PUBLISHED BY ALFRED HUNTER.

1853.

TABLE OF CONTENTS.

CONGRESSIONAL DIRECTORY.

[*In the alphabetical list, the Boarding Houses of Members will be found, see page* 20.]

Maine—New Hampshire.

Name.	Post Office.	Congressional District.
MAINE.		
SENATORS.		
James W. Bradbury....	Augusta.	
Hannibal Hamlin........	Hampden.	
REPRESENTATIVES.		
Moses McDonald.........	Biddeford	1. The county of York, together with the towns of Hiram, Potter, Brownfield, Denmark, Freyburg, Lovell, Stow, Stoneham, Sweden, Waterford, Albany, Mason, Gilead, Bethel, Newry, Batchelder's Grant, Riley Plantation, Greenwood, Norway, Oxford, and Hebron, from Oxford county.
John Appleton...........	Portland	2. Cumberland county.
Robert Goodenow.......	Farmington.........	3. Kennebec and Franklin, except the town of Greene.
Isaac Reed...............	Waldoboro'..........	4. Lincoln, together with that part of Oxford not annexed to the first district, with the town of Greene from Kennebec county.
Ephraim K. Smart......	Camden.	5. Waldo and Somerset, except North Haven and Vinalhaven.
Israel Washburn, jr.....	Orono	6. Penobscot and Piscataquis.
Thomas J. D. Fuller....	Calais	7. Hancock, Washington, and Aroostook, together with the towns of North Haven and Vinalhaven, in Waldo county.
NEW HAMPSHIRE.		
SENATORS.		
John P. Hale............	Dover.	
Moses Norris............	Manchester.	
REPRESENTATIVES.		
Amos Tuck...............	Exeter	1. Rockingham, Strafford, and part of Carroll.

Maine—Vermont—Rhode Island.

Name.	Post Office.	Congressional District.
Charles H. Peaslee......	Concord.............	2. Belknap, Carroll, and parts of Grafton and Merrimack.
Jared Perkins............	Winchester..........	3. Cheshire, Hillsborough, and the towns of Henniker, Hopkinton, Dunbarton, and Bow, in the county of Merrimack.
Harry Hibbard...........	Bath..................	4. Sullivan, Coos, and part of Grafton.
VERMONT.		
SENATORS.		
William Upham..........	Montpelier.	
Solomon Foot............	Rutland.	
REPRESENTATIVES.		
Ahiman L. Miner........	Manchester.........	1. Windham, Bennington, Rutland.
William Hebard..........	Chelsea.............	2. Windsor and Orange.
James Meacham.........	Middlebury........	3. Addison, Chittenden, Franklin, and Grand Isle.
Thomas Bartlett, jr.....	Lyndon.............	4. Washington, Caledonia, Essex, Orleans, and Lamoille.
MASSACHUSETTS.		
SENATORS.		
John Davis...............	Worcester.	
Charles Sumner..........	Boston.	
REPRESENTATIVES.		
William Appleton.......	Boston	1. Suffolk.
[Deceased.]		2. Parts of Essex, Middlesex, and Suffolk.
James H. Duncan.......	Haverhill...........	3. Parts of Essex and Middlesex.
[Deceased.]		4. Parts of Middlesex and Worcester.
Charles Allen............	Worcester...........	5. Part of Worcester.
George T. Davis.........	Greenfield..........	6. Parts of Hampshire, Franklin, Hampden, and Worcester.
John Z. Goodrich........	Glen Dale...........	7. Berkshire, parts of Franklin, Hampshire, and Hampden.
Horace Mann.............	West Newton.......	8. Norfolk, and parts of Middlesex and Plymouth.
[Deceased.]		9. Parts of Bristol and Plymouth.
Zeno Scudder............	Barnstable..........	10. Nantucket, Dukes, Barnstable, and part of Bristol.
RHODE ISLAND.		
SENATORS.		
John H. Clarke..........	Providence.	
Charles T. James.......	Do.	

Rhode Island—Connecticut—New York.

Name.	Post Office.	Congressional District.
REPRESENTATIVES.		
George G. King	Newport	1. The Eastern District contains the following towns: Newport, Middletown, Portsmouth, Little Compton, Tiverton, Bristol, Warren, Barrington, North Providence, Smithfield, and Cumberland, and the city of Providence.
Benjamin B. Thurston	Hopkinton	2. The Western District contains the following: New Shoreham, Westerly, South Kingston, North Kingston, Charlestown, Exeter, Richmond, Hopkinton, Jamestown, East Greenwich, West Greenwich, Warwick, Coventon, Cranston, Johnston, Scituate, Foster, Gloucester, and Burrilville.
CONNECTICUT.		
SENATORS.		
Truman Smith	Litchfield.	
Isaac Toucey	Hartford.	
REPRESENTATIVES.		
Charles Chapman	Hartford	1. Hartford and Tolland.
Colin M. Ingersoll	New Haven	2. New Haven and Middlesex.
Chauncey F. Cleveland	Hampton	3. New London and Windham.
Origen S. Seymour	Litchfield	4. Fairfield and Litchfield.
NEW YORK.		
SENATORS.		
Hamilton Fish	New York.	
William H. Seward	Auburn, Cayuga county.	
REPRESENTATIVES.		
John G. Floyd	Moriches	1. Suffolk and Queens.
Obadiah Bowne	Richmond	2. Kings and Richmond.
Emanuel B. Hart	New York	3. New York city and county, 1st, 2d, 3d, 4th and 5th wards.
J. H. Hobart Haws	New York	4. 6th, 7th, 10th and 13th wards.
George Briggs	New York	5. 8th, 9th and 14th wards.
James Brooks	New York	6. 11th, 12th, 15th, 16th, 17th, 18th, 19th and 20th wards.
Abraham P. Stephens	Nyack	7. West Chester and Rockland.
Gilbert Dean	Poughkeepsie	8. Dutchess and Putnam.
William Murray	Goshen	9. Orange and Sullivan.
Marius Schoonmaker	Kingston	10. Ulster and Delaware.
Josiah Sutherland	Hudson	11. Columbia and Greene.

New York—New Jersey—Pennsylvania.

Name.	Post Office.	Congressional District.
David L. Seymour......	Troy..................	12. Rensselaer.
John L. Schoolcraft....	Albany................	13. City and county of Albany.
John H. Boyd...........	Whitehall.............	14. Washington and Essex.
Joseph Russell.........	Warrensburgh	15. Clinton, Franklin Warren, and north half of Hamilton.
John Wells..............	Johnston	16. Saratoga, Schenectady, Fulton, and balance of Hamilton.
Alexander H. Buell....	Fairfield	17. Herkimer and Montgomery.
Preston King............	Ogdensburg.........	18. St. Lawrence and Lewis.
Willard Ives............	Watertown	19. Jefferson.
Timothy Jenkins........	Oneida Castle......	20. Oneida.
William W. Snow.......	Oneonto..............	21. Otsego and Schoharie.
Henry Bennett..........	New Berlin.........	22. Chenango, Broome, and Tioga.
Leander Babcock.......	Oswego	23. Madison and Oswego.
Daniel T. Jones.........	Baldwinsville.......	24. Onondaga.
Thomas Y. Howe, jr....	Auburn...............	25. Cayuga and Courtland.
Henry S. Walbridge...	Ithaca	26. Tompkins, Chemung and Yates.
William A. Sackett.....	Seneca Falls........	27. Seneca and Wayne.
A. M. Schermerhorn..	Rochester	28. Monroe.
Jerediah Horsford......	Moscow	29. Ontario and Livingston.
Reuben Robie...........	Bath	30. Steuben and Allegany.
Frederick S. Martin...	Olean.	31. Cattaraugus and Chautauque.
Solomon G. Haven.....	Buffalo	32. Erie.
Augustus P. Hascall...	Le Roy..............	33. Genesee and Wyoming.
Lorenzo Burrows.......	Albion...............	34. Orleans and Niagara.
NEW JERSEY.		
SENATORS.		
Jacob W. Miller.........	Morristown.	
Robert F. Stockton....	Princeton.	
REPRESENTATIVES.		
Nathan T. Stratton.....	Mullica Hill	1. Atlantic, Cape May, Cumberland, Salem, Gloucester, and Camden.
Charles Skelton.........	Trenton.	2. Burlington, Monmouth, Mercer.
Isaac Wildrick..........	Blairstown	3. Hunterdon, Warren, and Sussex.
George H. Brown.......	Somerville	4. Middlesex, Somerset, and Morris.
Rodman M. Price.......	Hoboken.............	5. Essex, Hudson, Passaic, and Bergen.
PENNSYLVANIA.		
SENATORS.		
James Cooper............	Pottsville.	
Richard Brodhead.......	Easton.	
REPRESENTATIVES.		
Thomas B. Florence....	Philadelphia.........	1. Southwark, Moyamensing, Passyunk, (county of Philadelphia,) and Cedar & Newmarket wards, in city.

Pennsylvania—Delaware—Maryland.

Name.	Post Office.	Congressional District.
Joseph R. Chandler....	Philadelphia.........	2. City of Philadelphia, except Cedar and Newmarket wards.
Henry D. Moore.........	..........do............	3. Northern Liberties and Spring Garden, county of Philadelphia.
John Robbins, jr.........	Kensington, Phila.	4. Kensington, Richmond, Penn district, North Penn, Roxborough, Germantown, Bristol, unincorporated Northern Liberties, Oxford, Lower Dublin, Byberry, Morland, Blockley, West Philadelphia, and Kingsessing, county of Philadelphia.
John McNair...............	Norristown	5. Delaware and Montgomery.
Thomas Ross..............	Doylestown..........	6. Bucks and Lehigh.
John A. Morrison.......	Cochranville	7. Chester.
Thaddeus Stevens.......	Lancaster	8. Lancaster.
J. Glancy Jones	Reading	9. Berks.
Milo M. Dimmick.......	Stroudsburg	10. Northampton, Monroe, Pike, Wayne, and Carbon.
Henry M. Fuller.........	Wilkesbarre	11. Columbia, Luzerne, Wyoming, and Montour.
Galusha A. Grow........	Glenwood.	12. Bradford, Susquehanna, and Tioga.
James Gamble............	Jersey Shore	13. Lycoming, Northumberland, Union, Clinton, and Sullivan.
Thomas M. Bibighaus..	Lebanon	14. Dauphin, Lebanon, and Schuylkill.
William H. Kurtz.......	York.....................	15. Adams and York.
James X. McLanahan..	Chambersburg.......	16. Cumberland, Perry, and Franklin.
Andrew Parker...........	Mifflintown	17. Huntington, Centre, Juniata, Mifflin, and Blair.
John L. Dawson.........	Brownsville..........	18. Greene, Somerset, and Fayette.
Joseph H. Kuhns........	Greensburgh	19. Westmoreland, Bedford, Cambria, and Fulton.
John Allison..............	Beaver..................	20. Beaver and Washington.
Thomas M. Howe.......	Alleghany city.......	21. Alleghany.
John W. Howe...........	Franklin...............	22. Venango, Crawford, and Mercer.
Carlton B. Curtis........	Warren	23. Erie, Warren, McKean, Clarion, Potter, and Jefferson.
Alfred Gilmore...........	Butler..................	24. Armstrong, Butler, Indiana, and Clearfield.
DELAWARE.		
SENATORS.		
Presley Spruance	Smyrna.	
James A. Bayard........	Wilmington.	
REPRESENTATIVE.		
George Read Riddle....	Wilmington.	
MARYLAND.		
SENATORS.		
James A. Pearce	Chestertown, Kent co.	
Thomas G. Pratt.	Annapolis.	

Maryland—Virginia.

Name.	Post Office.	Congressional District.
REPRESENTATIVES.		
Richard I. Bowie.......	Rockville............	1. St. Mary's, Calvert, Charles, Prince George's, Montgomery, and part of Anne Arundel.
William T. Hamilton...	Hagerstown........	2. Frederick, Washington, and Alleghany.
Edward Hammond......	Ellicott's Mills.....	3. Baltimore and Carroll counties, Howard District, 12th, 13th, and 14th wards in Baltimore city.
Thomas Y. Walsh.......	Baltimore...........	4. 1st, 2d, 3d, 4th, 5th, 6th, 7th, 8th, 9th, 10th, and 11th, in Baltimore.
Alexander Evans........	Elkton...............	5. Hartford, Cecil, Queen Anne, Kent, and Caroline.
Joseph S. Cottman......	Upper Trappe, Somerset co...	6. Worcester, Somerset, Dorchester, and Talbot.
VIRGINIA.		
SENATORS.		
James M. Mason........	Winchester.	
Robert M. T. Hunter..	Lloyds, Essex co.	
REPRESENTATIVES.		
John S. Millson..........	Norfolk..............	1. Isle of Wight, Nansemond, Princess Ann, Norfolk county, Norfolk borough, Sussex, Surrey, and Southampton.
Richard K. Meade......	Petersburg..........	2. Nottoway, Greensville, Mecklenburg, Brunswick, Prince George, Amelia, Dinwiddie, and Petersburg.
Thomas H. Averett.....	Halifax C. H.......	3 Halifax, Henry, Patrick, Franklin, and Pittsylvania.
Thomas S. Bocock......	Appomattox C. H.	4. Campbell, Buckingham, Charlotte, Prince Edward, Cumberland, Fluvanna, and Lunenburg.
Paulus Powell............	Amherst C. H......	5. Albemarle, Nelson, Bedford, Greene, Orange, Amherst, and Madison.
John S. Caskie...........	Richmond..........	6. Henrico, city of Richmond, Chesterfield, Powhatan, Hanover, Louisa, and Goochland.
Thomas H. Bayly.......	Accomac C. H......	7. York, Accomac, Northampton, Elizabeth City, Warwick, James City, Williamsburg, New Kent, Charles City, Matthews, Gloucester, Lancaster, and Northumberland.
Alexander R. Holladay.	Mansfield, Louisa co.	8. Essex, Middlesex, King and Queen, Richmond county, Westmoreland, Caroline, Spottsylvania, King Geo., and King William.
James F. Strother,......	Rappahannock C. H.	9. Alexandria, Fauquier, Stafford, Rappahannock, Prince William, Fairfax, Loudon, and Culpepper.

Virginia—North Carolina.

Name.	Post Office.	Congressional District.
Charles J. Faulkner....	Martinsburg........	10. Frederick, Hampshire, Morgan, Berkeley, Jefferson, Clarke, Warren, and Page.
John Letcher............	Lexington.	11. Rockingham, Rockbridge, Augusta, Pendleton, Hardy, and Shenandoah.
Henry A. Edmundson..	Salem, Roanoke co.	12. Boone, Monroe, Botetourt, Roanoke, Montgomery, Pulaski, Floyd, Giles, Mercer, Greenbrier, Pocahontas, Logan, Bath, Alleghany, Highland, and Wyoming.
Fayette McMullen......	Rye Cove...........	13. Washington, Lee, Scott, Russell, Smythe, Wythe, Grayson, Carroll, and Tazewell.
James M. H. Beale.....	Point Pleasant.....	14. Kanawha, Jackson, Mason, Cabell, Wayne, Lewis, Braxton, Harrison, Wood, Fayette, Nicholas, Ritchie, Gilmer, Putnam, Raleigh, Pleasants, Upshur, and parts of Barbour, Taylor, and Doddridge.
Sherrod Clemmens......	Wheeling, Va......	15. Monongalia, Brooke, Hancock, Ohio, Marshall, Tyler, Marion, Randolph, Preston, Wetzel, and parts of Barbour, Taylor, and Doddridge.
NORTH CAROLINA.		
SENATORS.		
George E. Badger.......	Raleigh.	
Willie P. Mangum......	Red Mountain.	
REPRESENTATIVES.		
Thomas L. Clingman...	Asheville...........	1. Cherokee, Macon, Haywood, Buncombe, Henderson, Rutherford, Burke, Yancey, Cleveland, and Caldwell.
Joseph P. Caldwell.....	Statesville..........	2. Rowan, Davie, Surrey, Ashe, Wilkes, Catawba, and Iredell.
Alfred Dockery..........	Dockery's Store....	3. Lincoln, Gaston, Mecklenburgh, Cabarrus, Stanly, Union, Anson, Montgomery, Moore, and Richmond.
James T. Morehead....	Greensboro'.........	4. Stokes, Guilford, Davidson, Randolph, and Rockingham.
Abraham W. Venable...	Brownsville.........	5. Granville, Orange, Person, Caswell, and Chatham.
John R. J. Daniel.......	Halifax..............	6. Halifax, Warren, Franklin, Wake, Johnson, Edgecombe, and Nash.
William S. Ashe.........	Wilmington.........	7. Bladen, Brunswick, Columbus, Duplin, New Hanover, Onslow, Sampson, Robeson, and Cumberland.
Edward Stanly..........	Washington.........	8. Wayne, Cartaret, Greene, Pitt, Lenoir, Beaufort, Jones, Hyde, Craven, Tyrrell and Washington.

North Carolina—South Carolina—Georgia.

Name.	Post Office.	Congressional District.
David Outlaw	Windsor	9. Martin, Bertie, Hertford, Northampton, Gates, Chowan, Perquimans, Pasquotank, Camden, and Currituck.
SOUTH CAROLINA.		
SENATORS.		
Andrew P. Butler	Edgefield C. H.	
W. F. De Saussure	Columbia.	
REPRESENTATIVES.		
Daniel Wallace	Jonesville	1. Spartansburg, Union, York, and Chester.
James L. Orr	Anderson C. H.	2. Pickens, Anderson, Greenville, and Laurens.
Joseph A. Woodward	Winnsborough	3. Lancaster, Kershaw, Fairfield, Richland, and Sumpter.
John McQueen	Bennettsville	4. Chesterfield, Marlborough, Darlington, Marion, Horry, Georgetown, and Williamsburg.
Armistead Burt	Willington	5. Abbeville, Newberry, Edgefield, and Lexington.
William Aiken	Charleston	6. Charleston District, except the parish of St. John Colleton.
William F. Colcock	Grahamsville	7. Orangeburg, Barnwell, Beaufort, and Colleton Districts, and the Parish of St. John Colleton.
GEORGIA.		
SENATORS.		
Robert M. Charlton	Savannah.	
William C. Dawson	Greensboro'.	
REPRESENTATIVES.		
Joseph W. Jackson	Savannah	1. Chatham, Effingham, Bryan, Liberty, McIntosh, Glynn, Camden, Ware, Lowndes, Thomas, Telfair, Apling, Montgomery, Tatnall, Emanuel. Bullock, Wayne, Clinch and Scriven,
James Johnson	Columbus	2. Muscogee, Stewart, Randolph, Early, Decatur, Baker, Lee, Sumpter, Marion, Macon, Houston, Pulaski, Dooley, and Irwin,
David J. Bailey	Jackson	3. Twiggs, Monroe, Pike, Talbot, Bibb, Crawford, Upton, Jasper, Jones, Butts, and Wilkinson.
Charles Murphy	Decatur	4. Troop, Meriwether, Coweta, Heard, Carroll, Campbell, Fayette, Henry, Harris, and De Kalb.

Georgia—Alabama—Mississippi.

Name.	Post Office.	Congressional District.
Elijah W. Chastain	Tacoah	5. Cobb, Cherokee, Forsyth, Gwinnett, Lumpkin, Union, Gilmer, Cass, Paulding, Floyd, Chatooga, Gordon, Murray, Walker, and Dade.
Junius Hillyer	Monroe	6. Walton, Clarke, Jackson, Hall, Habersham, Franklin, Rabun, Madison, and Newton.
Alexander H. Stephens	Crawfordsville	7. Oglethorpe, Greene, Morgan, Putnam, Baldwin, Laurens, Hancock, Washington, and Taliaferro.
Robert Toombs	Washington	8. Elbert, Wilkes, Lincoln, Warren, Richmond, Burke, Jefferson, and Columbia.
ALABAMA.		
SENATORS.		
William R. King, *Vice President elect.*	Selma.	
Jeremiah Clemens	Huntsville.	
REPRESENTATIVES.		
John Bragg	Mobile	1. Mobile, Washington, Baldwin, Clark, Monroe, Conechu, Butler, Wilcox, and Marengo.
James Abercrombie	Girard	2. Covington, Dale, Henry, Coffee, Pike, Barbour, Macon, Montgomery, and Russell.
Sampson W. Harris	Wetumpka	3. Dallas, Lowndes, Autauga, Perry, Bibb, Jefferson, Shelby, and Coosa.
William R. Smith	Fayette C. H.	4. Greene, Sumpter, Pickens, Tuscaloosa, and Fayette.
George S. Houston	Athens	5. Limestone, Lauderdale, Franklin, Lawrence, Morgan, Marion, and Walker.
W. R. W. Cobb	Bellefonte	6. Madison, Jackson, Marshall, De Kalb, Blount, and St. Clair.
Alexander White	Talladega	7. Cherokee, Butler, Talladega, Randolph, Chambers, and Tallapoosa.
MISSISSIPPI.		
SENATORS.		
Walker Brooke	Lexington.	
Stephen Adams	Aberdeen.	
REPRESENTATIVES.		
Benjamin D. Nabers	Hickory Flat	1. Tishamingo, Tippah, Marshall, De Soto, Tunica, Panola, Lafayette, Pontotoc, and Itawamba.
John A. Wilcox	Aberdeen	2. Chickasaw, Monroe, Lowndes, Noxubee, Oktibbeha, Carroll, Choctaw, Yalabusha, Tallahatchie, Coahoma, Bolivar, and Sunflower.

Mississippi—Louisiana—Ohio.

Name.	Post Office.	Congressional District.
John D. Freeman......	Jackson....	3. Warren, Isaguina, Washington, Hinds, Madison, Yazoo, Holmes, Attala, Winston, Kemper, Lauderdale, Newton, Neshoba, Leake, Scott, and Rankin.
Albert G. Brown.......	Gallatin.............	4. Claiborne, Copia, Covington, Smith, Jasper, Clark, Greene, Perry, Jones, Wayne, Pike, Amité, Franklin, Jefferson, Adams, Wilkinson, Jackson, Harrison, Hancock, Marion, Simpson, and Lawrence.
LOUISIANA.		
SENATORS.		
Solomon W. Downs.....	Monroe.	
Pierre Soulé.......,......	New Orleans.	
REPRESENTATIVES.		
Louis St. Martin.......	New Orleans.	1. First and Third Municipalities, Parishes of Plaquemine and St. Barnard.
J. Aristide Landry.....	Donaldsonville.....	2. That part of the parish of Orleans, situated on the right bank of the river, Second Municipality, Parishes of Jefferson, St. Charles, St. John, St. James, Ascension, Assumption, Terrebonne, and Lafourche Interior.
Alezander G. Penn......	Covington...........	3. St. Tammany, St. Helena, Livingston, Washington, East and West Baton Rouge, East and West Feliciana, Point Coupee, Iberville, Catahoula, Avoyelles, Concordia, Madison, and Carroll,
John Moore...............	New Iberia..........	4. St. Martin's, St. Mary, Lafayette, St. Landry, Rapides, Natchitoches, Caddo, Union, Caldwell, Ouachita, Claiborne, Bossier, Sabine, Jackson, Vermillion, De Soto, Morehouse, and Calcasieu.
OHIO.		
SENATORS.		
Salmon P. Chase........	Cincinnati.	
Benjamin Wade..........	Jefferson.	
REPRESENTATIVES.		
David T. Disney.........	Cincinnati	1. Hamilton.
Lewis D. Campbell.....	Hamilton	2. Butler, Warren, and Clinton.
Hiram Bell................	Greenville	3. Montgomery, Greene, Preble, and Darke.
Benjamin Stanton	Bellefontaine	4. Logan, Champagne, Union, Clarke, and Miami.

Ohio—Kentucky.

Name.	Post Office.	Congressional District.
Alfred P. Edgerton	Hicksville	5. Mercer, Vanwert, Paulding, Williams, Lucas, Henry, Putnam, Allen, Shelby, and Hardin.
Frederick W. Green	Tiffin	6. Wood, Hancock, Crawford, Wyandot, Seneca, Sandusky, and Ottowa.
Nelson Barrere	Hillsborough	7. Clermont, Brown, and Highland.
John L. Taylor	Chillicothe	8. Ross, Pike, Jackson, Scioto, and Adams.
Edson B. Olds	Circleville	9. Fairfield, Pickaway, Fayette, and Madison.
Charles Sweetser	Delaware	10. Franklin, Delaware, and Licking.
George H. Busby	Marion	11. Knox, Richland, Marion, and part of Ashland.
John Welch	Athens	12. Lawrence, Gallia, Meigs, and Athens.
James M. Gaylord	McConnellsville	13. Perry, Morgan, and Washington.
Alexander Harper	Zanesville	14. Muskingum and Guernsey.
William F. Hunter	Woodsfield	15. Monroe, Belmont, and Harrison.
John Johnson	Coshocton	16. Holmes, Coshocton, and Tuscarawas.
Joseph Cable	Carrollton	17. Jefferson, Carroll, Columbiana, and five townships of Mahoning.
David K. Cartter	Massillon	18. Stark, Wayne, and part of Ashland.
Eben Newton	Canfield	19. Trumbull, Portage, Summit, and ten townships of Mahoning.
Joshua R. Giddings	Jefferson	20. Ashtabula, Geauga, Lake, and Cuyahoga.
Norton S. Townshend	Avon	21. Medina, Lorain, Huron, and Erie.
KENTUCKY.		
SENATORS.		
Jos. R. Underwood [Deceased.]	Bowling Green.	
REPRESENTATIVES.		
Linn Boyd, (*Speaker House.*)	Paducah	1. Ballard, Caldwell, Calloway, Crittenden, Graves, Hickman, Hopkins, Livingston, Marshall, McCracken, Trigg, and Union.
Benj. Edwards Gray	Hopkinsville	2. Breckenridge, Butler, Christian, Daviess, Edmonson, Grayson, Hancock, Henderson, Meade, Muhlenberg, and Ohio.
Presley Ewing	Russellville	3. Allen, Barren, Hart, Hogan, Monroe, Simpson, Todd, and Warren.
William T. Ward	Greensburg	4. Adair, Boyle, Casey, Clinton, Cumberland, Greene, Sinclair, Pulaski, and Wayne.
James W. Stone	Elizabethtown	5. Anderson, Bullit, Hardin, La Rue, Marion, Mercer, Nelson, Spencer, and Washington.
Addison White	Richmond	6. Clay, Estill, Floyd, Harlan, Garrard, Johnson, Knox, Laurel, Letcher, Madison, Owsley, Perry, Pike, Rockcastle, and Whitley.

Kentucky—Tennessee—Indiana.

Name.	Post Office.	Congressional District.
William Preston	Louisville	7. Carroll, Henry, Jefferson, Louisville city, Oldham, Shelby, and Trimble.
John C. Breckenridge	Lexington	8. Bourbon, Fayette, Franklin, Jessamin, Owen, Scott, and Woodford.
John C. Mason	Owensville	9. Bath, Breathett, Carter, Clarke, Fleming, Greenup, Lawrence, Lewis, Montgomery, and Morgan.
Richard H. Stanton	Maysville	10. Braken, Boone, Campbell, Gallatin, Grant, Harrison, Kenton, Mason, Nicholas, and Pendleton.
TENNESSEE.		
SENATORS.		
John Bell	Nashville.	
J. C. Jones	Memphis.	
REPRESENTATIVES.		
Andrew Johnson	Greenville	1. Johnson, Carter, Sullivan, Washington, Hawkins, Greene, and Cocke.
Albert G. Watkins	Panther Springs	2. Jefferson, Granger, Claiborne, Campbell, Anderson, Morgan, Sevier, Blount, and Monroe.
Wm. M. Churchwell	Knoxville	3. Knox, Roane, Bledsoe, Rhea, Meigs, McMinn, Polk, Bradley, Hamilton, and Marion.
John H. Savage	Smithville	4. Fentress, Overton, Jackson, White, De Kalb, Van Buren, Warren, and Coffee.
George W. Jones	Fayetteville	5. Franklin, Lincoln, Bedford, and Marshall.
William H. Polk	Columbia	6. Hickman, Maury, Giles, Lawrence, Wayne, and Hardin.
Meredith P. Gentry	Richmond	7. Wilson, Rutherford, Cannon, and Williamson.
William Cullom	Carthage	8. Smith, Summer, and Davidson.
Isham G. Harris	Paris	9. Robertson, Montgomery, Stewart, Dickson, Humphreys, Benton, and Henry.
Frederick P. Stanton	Memphis	10. McNairy, Hardeman, Fayette, Shelby, Tipton, Haywood, Lauderdale, and Dyer.
Chris. H. Williams	Lexington	11. Perry, Henderson, Madison, Carroll, Gibson, Weakley, and Obion.
INDIANA.		
SENATORS.		
Jesse D. Bright	Madison.	
Charles W. Cathcart	Laporte.	
REPRESENTATIVES.		
James Lockhart	Evansville	1. Posey, Vanderburg, Gibson, Pike, Dubois, Warwick, Spencer, Perry, Crawford, Orange, and Harrison.

Indiana—Illinois.

Name.	Post Office.	Congressional District.
Gyrus L. Dunham.......	Payntersville.......	2. Clark, Washington, Scott, Jackson, Jefferson, Jennings, and Floyd.
John L. Robinson.......	Rushville............	3. Dearborn, Ripley, Rush, Switzerland, Decatur, and Franklin.
Samuel W. Parker......	Connersville........	4. Fayette, Union, Wayne, and Henry.
Thomas A. Hendricks..	Shelbyville..........	5. Hamilton, Marion, Hancock, Shelby, Johnson, Bartholomew, Brown, Madison, and Tipton.
Willis A. Gorman.......	Bloomington........	6. Monroe, Lawrence, Martin, Daviess, Knox, Owen, Green, Sullivan, and Morgan.
John G. Davis............	Rockville............	7. Vigo, Clay, Putnam, Park, Vermillion, and Hendricks.
Daniel Mace..............	Lafayette............	8. Montgomery, Fountain, Warren, Tippecanoe, Clinton, Boone, Carroll, and Richardsville.
Graham N. Fitch.........	Logansport.........	9. Jasper, White, Cass, Miami, Fulton, Pulaski, Kosciusco, Marshall, Starke, Elkhart, St. Joseph, Laporte, Porter, Lake, Wabash, and Benton.
Samuel Brenton.........	Fort Wayne.........	10. Randolph, Delaware, Grant, Blackford, Jay, Adams, Wells, Huntington, Allen, Whitley, Noble, De Kalb, Steuben, and Lagrange.
ILLINOIS.		
SENATORS.		
Stephen A. Douglas....	Chicago.	
James Shields............	Belleville.	
REPRESENTATIVES.		
William H. Bissell......	Belleville............	1. Alexander, Union, Jackson, Perry, Randolph, Monroe, Washington, St. Clair, Clinton, Bond, Madison, and Pulaski.
Willis Allen...............	Marion...............	2. Johnson, Pope, Hardin, Williamson, Gallatin, Franklin, Hamilton, White, Wabash, Edwards, Wayne, Jefferson, Marion, and Massac.
Orlando B. Ficklin......	Charleston..........	3. Lawrence, Richland, Crawford, Cumberland, Jasper, Effingham, Fayette, Montgomery, Christian, Shelby, Moultrie, Coles, Clarke, Clay, Edgar, Macon, Piatt, and De Witt.
Richard S. Molony......	Belvidere............	4. Lake, McHenry, Boone, Cook, Kane, De Kalb, Du Page, Kendall, Grundy, La Salle, Will, Iroquois, Livingston, McLean, Champaign, Vermillion, and Bureau.
William A. Richardson.	Quincy...............	5. Green, Jersey, Calhoun, Pike, Adams, Marquette, Brown, Schuyler, Fulton, Peoria, and Macoupin.

Illinois—Missouri—Arkansas.

Name.	Post Office.	Congressional District.
Thompson Campbell	Galena	6. Jo Daviess, Stephenson, Winnebago, Carroll, Ogle, Lee, Whiteside, Rock Island, Henry, Stark, Mercer, Henderson, Warren, Knox, McDonough, and Hancock.
Richard Yates	Jacksonville	7. Putnam, Marshall, Woodford, Tazewell, Mason, Menard, Cass, Morgan, Scott, Logan, and Sangamon.
MISSOURI.		
SENATORS.		
David R. Atchison	Platte City.	
H. S. Geyer	St. Louis.	
REPRESENTATIVES.		
John F. Darby	St. Louis	1. St. Louis, Jefferson, St. Genevieve, St. François, Perry, Madison, Reynolds, Shannon, Cape Girardeau, Scott, Stoddard, Wayne, Ripley, Dunklin, New Madrid, Mississippi, and Oregon.
Gilchrist Porter	Bowling Green	2. Marion, Ralls, Pike, Lincoln, St. Charles, Warren, Montgomery, Audrian, Callaway, Osage, Gasconade, Franklin, Washington, Crawford, Pulaski, and Texas.
John G. Miller	Boonville	3. Camden, Miller, Morgan, Cole, Moniteau, Cooper, Chariton, Howard, Boone, Randolph, Macon, Monroe, Shelby, Lewis, Knox, Scotland, Schuyler, and Clark.
Willard P. Hall	St. Joseph's	4. Adair, Andrew, Atchison, Buchanan, Caldwell, Carroll, Clinton, Clay, Daviess, De Kalb, Gentry, Grundy, Harrison, Holt, Lind, Livingston, Mercer, Platte, Putnam, Ray, Sullivan, and Nodoway.
John S. Phelps	Springfield	5. Barry, Bates, Benton, Cass, (lately Van Buren,) Cedar, Dade, Dallas, Green, Henry, Hickory, Jackson, Jasper, Johnson, part of Laclide, Lafayette, Lawrence, McDonald, Newton, Ozark, Pettis, Polk, St. Clair, Saline, Stone, Taney, Vernon, and Wright.
ARKANSAS.		
SENATORS.		
Solon Borland	Hot Springs.	
William K. Sebastian	Helena.	

Arkansas—Michigan—Florida—Texas.

Name.	Post Office.	Congressional District.
REPRESENTATIVE.		
Robert W. Johnson	Little Rock.	
MICHIGAN.		
SENATORS.		
Alpheus Felch	Ann Arbor.	
Lewis Cass	Detroit.	
REPRESENTATIVES.		
Ebenezer J. Penniman	Plymouth	1. Monroe, Lenawee, Washtenaw, Wayne, and Hillsdale.
Charles E. Stuart	Kalamazoo	2. Branch, St. Joseph, Cass, Berrien, Van Buren, Kalamazoo, Calhoun, Jackson, Allegan, Barry, Ionia, Eaton, Kent, Ottawa, Oceana, Newaygo, Mecosta, Notipecago, Aishcum, Manistic, and Kautawabet, and all other counties in this State not included in the first and third Districts.
James L. Conger	Mount Clemens	3. Macomb, Oakland, Livingston, Ingham, Clinton, Shiawassee, Genesee, Lapeer, St. Clair, Mackinack, Chippewa, Saginaw, Tuscola, Midland, Gladwin, Arenac, Ogemaw, Canotin, Sanilac, and Huron.
FLORIDA.		
SENATORS.		
Jackson Morton	Pensacola.	
S. R. Mallory	Jacksonville.	
REPRESENTATIVE.		
E. Carrington Cabell	Monticello, M. F.	
TEXAS.		
SENATORS.		
Sam Houston	Huntsville.	
Thomas J. Rusk	Nacogdoches.	
REPRESENTATIVES.		
Richardson Scurry	Clarksville	1. *Eastern Texas.*—Anderson, Angelina, Bowie, Cass, Cherokee, Collin, Cooke, Dallas, Denton, Fanning, Grayson, Harrison, Henderson, Hopkins, Houston, Hunt, Jasper, Jefferson,

Texas—Iowa.

Name.	Post Office.	Congressional District.
		Kaufman, Lamar, Liberty, Nacogdoches, Newton, Panola, Polk, Red River, Rusk, Sabine, San Augustine, Shelby, Smith, Titus, Tyler, Trinity, Wood, Upshur, and Van Zandt.
Volney E. Howard......	San Antonio.........	2. *Western Texas.*—Austin, Brazoria, Bexar, Bastrop, Brazos, Burleson, Caldwell, Calhoun, Comal, Colorado, Cameron, De Witt, Fayette, Fort Bend, Galveston, Gonzales, Guadaloupe, Goliad, Grimes, Gillespie, Harris, Hays, Jackson, Lavaca, Leon, Limestone, Matagorda, Montgomery, Milam, Medina, Neverro, Nueces, Robertson, Refugio, Santa Fé, San Patricio, Starr, Travis, Victoria, Washington, Walker, Wharton, Williamson, and Webb.
IOWA.		
SENATORS.		
Augustus C. Dodge......	Burlington.	
George W. Jones........	Dubuque.	
REPRESENTATIVES.		
Bernhart Henn...........	Fairfield.............	1. Lee, Van Buren, Davis, Appanoose, Henry, Jefferson, Wapello, Monroe, Keokuk, Mahaska, Marion, Jasper, Polk, Dallas, Poweshiek, Guthrie, Audubon, Shelby, Harrison, Pottawatomie, Cass, Adair, Madison, Warren, Lucas, Clarke, Union, Adams, Montgomery, Mills, Frémont, Page, Taylor, Ringgold, Decatur, and Wayne.
Lincoln Clark............	Dubuque	2. Desmoines, Louisa, Washington, Johnson, Iowa, Muscatine, Scott, Cedar, Jones, Linn, Clinton, Jackson, Delaware, Buchanan, Benton, Clayton, Dubuque, Blackhawk, Fayette, Alamakee, Winnesheik, Howard, Mitchell, Worth, Winnebago, Bancroft, Emmett, Dickinson, Osceola, Buncombe, Sioux, O'Brien, Clay, Palo Alto, Kossuth, Hancock, Cerro Gordo, Floyd, Chickasaw, Bremer, Butler, Franklin, Wright, Humboldt, Pocahontas, Buena Vista, Cherokee, Plymouth, Wahkaw, Ida, Sac, Fox, Yell, Risley, Hardin, Grundy, Tama, Marshall, Story, Boone, Greene, Carroll, Crawford, and Monona.

Wisconsin—California—Minnesota—Oregon—New Mexico—Utah.

Name.	Post Office.	Congressional District.
WISCONSIN.		
SENATORS.		
Henry Dodge............	Dodgeville.	
Isaac P. Walker.........	Milwaukie.	
REPRESENTATIVES.		
Charles Durkee.........	Kenosha	1. Racine, Walworth, Wausheka, Milwaukie, and Kenosha.
Ben. C. Eastman.........	Platteville..........	2. Rock, Green, Dane, Sauk, Iowa, Lafayette, Grant, Richland, Crawford, St. Croix, La Point, Adams, Portage, Chippewa, and Marathon.
James Duane Doty......	Menasha............	3. Washington, Jefferson, Dodge, Columbia, Marquette, Fond du Lac, Winnebago, Sheboygan, Manitoowoc, Calumet, Brown, Outaugamee, Oconto, and Door.
CALIFORNIA.		
SENATORS.		
William M. Gwin........	San Francisco.	
John B. Weller...........	Do.	
REPRESENTATIVES.		
Joseph W. McCorkle...	Marysville.	
Edward C. Marshall....	Sonora.	
MINNESOTA.		
DELEGATE.		
Henry H. Sibley.........	Mendota.	
OREGON.		
DELEGATE.		
Joseph Lane.............	Oregon City.	
NEW MEXICO.		
DELEGATE.		
Richard H, Weightman	Santa Fé.	
UTAH.		
DELEGATE.		
John M. Bernhisel......	Salt Lake City.	

United States Ministers, &c.

DEPARTMENT OF STATE.

List of Ministers, Consuls, and other Diplomatic and Commercial Agents of the United States in foreign countries, and of the places of their residence.

BRITISH DOMINIONS.

Joseph R. Ingersoll, Envoy Extraordinary and Minister Plenipotentiary, London.
John C. B. Davis, Secretary of Legation, London.

England.

Thomas Aspinwall, consul, London.
Albert Davy, consul, Leeds.
Thomas L. Crittenden, consul, Liverpool and Manchester.
Francis B. Ogden, consul, Bristol.
Robert W. Fox, consul, Falmouth.
Thomas Were Fox, consul, Plymouth.
James R. Croskey, consul, Southampton and Cowes.

Scotland.

John Broadfoot, consul, Leith, Port of Edinburgh.
James McDowell, consul, Dundee.
Day O. Kellogg, consul, Glasgow.

Ireland.

James Foy, consul, Dublin.
Valentine Holmes, consul, Belfast.
Robert L. Loughead, consul, Londonderry.
Alfred Mitchell, consul, Cork.
Thomas M. Persse, consul, Galway.

China.

Frederick T. Bush, consul, Hong Kong.

East Indies.

Edward Ely, consul, Bombay.
James H. Adams, consul, Singapore.
Charles Huffnagle, consul, Calcutta.

In and near Europe and Africa.

Horatio J. Sprague, consul, Gibraltar.
William Winthrop, consul, Island of Malta.
Gideon S. Holmes, consul, Cape Town, Cape of Good Hope.
George M. Farnum, consul, Port Louis, Isle of France.

North America.

Israel D. Andrews, consul, St. John's, N. B., and Canada.
T. B. Livingston, consul, Halifax, Nova Scotia.
Benjamin H. Norton, consul, Pictou, Nova Scotia.
Wm. S. H. Newman, St. John's, Newfoundland.

South America.

Charles Benjamin, consul, Demerara, British Guiana.

United States Ministers, &c.

Australia.

Frederick W. Clarke, consul, Sidney, N. S. Wales.
E. Hathaway, jr., consul, Hobart Town.
Joseph Augustus Henriques, consul, Melbourne.

West Indies.

Wm. Tudor Tucker, consul, Bermuda.
Timothy Darling, consul, Nassau, Bahama Islands.
Benjamin E. Smith, consul, Turk's Island.
Robert Monroe Harrison, consul, Kingston, Jamaica.
Winston J. Towbridge, consul, Barbadoes.
E. B. Marache, consul, Island of Trinidad.

Central America.

——— ———, consul, Belize, Honduras.

George W. Kimball, commercial agent, Island of St. Helena.
Wm. T. Thurston, commercial agent, St. Christopher.
Richard S. Higinbothom, commercial agent, Antigua.
John Black, commercial agent, Ceylon.

RUSSIA.

Neill S. Brown, Envoy Extraordinary and Minister Plenipotentiary, St. Petersburg.
Edward H. Wright, Secretary of Legation, Saint Petersburg.

On the Baltic Sea.

Wm. H. Ropes, consul, Saint Petersburg.
Alexander Schwartz, consul, Riga.
Edmund Brandt, consul, Archangel.
Reynold Trenckill, consul, Helsingfors.

On the Black Sea.

John Ralli, consul, Odessa.

FRENCH DOMINIONS.

Wm. C. Rives, Envoy Extraordinary and Minister Plenipotentiary, Paris.
Henry Shelton Sanford, Secretary of Legation, Paris.
Samuel G. Goodrich, consul, Paris.
Chas. S. J. Goodrich, consul, Lyons.
J. B. C. Antoine, consul, Sedan.
August Furtado, consul, Bayonne.

Ports on the Atlantic.

Lorenzo Draper, consul, Havre.
Hypolite Roques, consul, Nantes.
Francis M. Auboyneau, consul, La Rochelle.
Frederick Kahl, consul, Bordeaux.
Charles Audouy, consul, Napoleon Vendée.

Ports on the Mediterranean.

John L. Hodge, consul, Marseilles.

United States Ministers, &c.

West Indies.

John W. Fisher, consul, Point-a-Pitre, Guadaloupe.
Alexander Campbell, consul, St. Pierre, Martinique.
George Hughes, commercial agent, St. Pierre, Miquelon.

French Guiana.

J. W. Fabens, consul, Cayenne.

Africa.

Henri Stuekle, consul, Algiers.

SPANISH DOMINIONS.

Daniel M. Barringer, Envoy Extraordinary and Minister Plenipotentiary, Madrid.
Horatio J. Perry, Secretary of Legation, Madrid.
Maximo de Aguirre, consul, Bilbao.
Alexander Burton, consul, Cadiz.
John Summers Smith, consul, Malaga.
Paul Anguera, consul, Barcelona.
Manuel Barcena, consul, Vigo.
Spiridion Ladico, consul, Port Mahon, Island of Minorca.
John Morand, consul, Denia.

Cuba.

W. S. Sharkey, consul, Havana.
Thomas M. Rodney, consul, Matanzas.
Samuel McLean, consul, Trinidad-de-Cuba.
William Newton Adams, consul, Saint-Iago-de-Cuba.

Puerto Rico.

James C. Gallaher, consul, Ponce.
George Latimer, consul, San Juan or St. John's.

Other Spanish Islands.

Edward F. Weld, consul, Teneriffe, Canary.
Alfred H. P. Edwards, consul, Manilla, Phillippine.

PORTUGUESE DOMINIONS.

Charles B. Hadduck, Chargé d'Affaires, Lisbon.

Portugal.

Nicholas Pike, consul, Lisbon.
Robert P. De Silver, consul, Macao.

Portuguese Islands.

Charles W. Dabney, consul, Fayal, Azores.
John H. March, consul, Funchal, Madeira.
John Z. Forney, consul, Saint Jago, Cape Verd.
William E. Hines, consul, Mozambique.

BELGIUM.

Richard H. Bayard, Chargé d'Affaires, Brussels.
William H. Vesey, consul, Antwerp.

United States Ministers, &c.

DOMINIONS OF THE NETHERLANDS.

George Folsum, Chargé d'Affaires, Hague.

Holland.

C. Goethe Bayl r consul, Amsterdam.
William S. Campbell, consul, Rotterdam.

Colonies of the Netherlands.

Frederick V. B. Morris, consul, Batavia, Java, East India Island.
Francis W. Cragin, consul, Paramaribo, Surinam.
Hierome O. Claughton, commercial agent, St. Martin.
——— ———, commercial agent, Curaçoa, West India Island.

DANISH DOMINIONS.

Miller Grieve, Chargé d'Affaires, Copenhagen.

Denmark.

Charles F. Ryan, consul, Copenhagen.
H. T. A. Rainals, oonsul, Elsineur.

West Indies.

David Rogers, consul, Sainte Croix, or Santa Cruz.
Hardy M. Burton, commercial agent, St. Thomas.

SWEEDEN AND NORWAY.

Francis Schroeder, Chargé d'Affaires, Stockholm.
Charles D. Arfwedson, consul, Stockholm, Sweeden.
Alexander Barclay, acting consul, Gothenburg, Sweeden.
Helmich Janson, consul, Bergen, Norway.
——— ———, consul, Porsgrund.

PRUSSIA.

Daniel D. Barnard, Envoy Extraordinary and Minister Plenipotentiary, Berlin.
Theodore S. Fay, Secretary of Legation, Berlin.
Isaac C. Bates, consul, Aix La Chapelle.
Frederick Schillow, consul, Stettin.

AUSTRIA.

Thomas M. Foote, Chargé d'Affaires, Vienna.
——— ———, consul, Vienna.
L. W. Jerome, consul, Trieste.
Edmund Flagg, consul, Venice.

SAXONY.

John M. Fessenden, consul, Dresden.
John G. Flugel, consul, Leipsick.

DUTCHY OF SAXE MEINENGEN HILBURGHAUSEN.

Louis Linder, consul, Sonneberg.

United States Ministers, &c.

BAVARIA.

Charles Obermayer, consul, Augsburg.
Phillip Geisse, consul, Nuremburg.

WURTEMBURG.

Charles L. Fleischmann, consul, Stuttgard.

HANOVER.

Charles Graebe, consul.

GRAND DUCHY OF HESSE CASSEL, AND GRAND DUCHY OF HESSE DARMSTADT.

Gharles Graebe, consul, Darmstadt.

BAADEN.

John Reichard, consul, Mannheim.

HANSEATIC OR FREE CITIES.

Samuel Bromberg, consnl, Hamburg.
Ralph King, consul, Bremen.
Ernest Schwendler, consul, Frankfort on the Mayn.

SWITZERLAND.

Nathan Burchard, consul, Basil, or Basle.
Wm. L. J. Kiderlin, consul, Zurich.

SARDINIAN STATES.

Wm. B. Kinney, Chargé d'Affaires, Turin.
George G. Baker, consul, Genoa.
J. B. Wilber, sen., consul, Nice.

TUSCANY.

J. A. Binda, consul, Leghorn.
Francis Lance, consul, Florence.

PONTIFICAL STATES.

Lewis Cass, jr., Chargé d'Affaires, Rome.
——— ———, consul, Rome.
Joseph Mozier, consul, Ancona.
James W. Irwin, consul, Ravenna.
William Walton, consul, Carrara in Modena.

KINGDOM OF THE TWO SICILIES.

E. Joy Morris, Chargé d'Affaires, Naples.
Alexander Hammett, consul, Naples.
Julius C. Kretschmar, consul, Palermo, Sicily.
Alexander H. Clements, consul, Messina, Sicily.

United States Ministers, &c.

TURKISH DOMINIONS.

George P. Marsh, Minister Resident, Constantinople.
John P. Brown, Drogaman, Constantinople.
Henry A. Homes, Assistant Drogaman, Constantinople.
George A. Porter, consul, Constantinople.
E. S. Offley, consul, Smyrna.
George Mountfort, consul, Candia.
J. Hosford Smith, consul, Beirout, Damascus, and Said, in Syria.
Merino de Mattey, consul, Cyprus.

Under the Government of the Pasha of Egypt.

Daniel S. McCauley, consul general, Alexandria, Egypt.

GREECE.

John D. Diernatari, consul, Athens.

BARBARY STATES.

George V. Brown, consul, Tangiers, Morocco.
Joseph H. Nicholson, consul, Tunis, Tunis.
Marcus Junius Gaines, consul, Tripoli, Tripoli.

AFRICA.

James W. Lugenbeel, commercial agent, Monrovia.
Alexander J. Cotheal, commercial agent, River Djeb.

DOMINIONS OF THE IMAUM OF MUSCAT.

——— ———, consul, Muscat.
William McMullen, consul, Island of Zanzibar, near the east coast of Africa.

CHINA.

Humphrey Marshall, Commissioner.
Peter Parker, Chargé d'Affaires *ad interim*, secretary and interpreter.
Paul S. Forbes, consul, Canton.
Dwight Webb, consul, Fouchow.
Charles William Bradley, consul, Amoy.
J. N. A. Griswold, consul, Shang Hai.

SANDWICH OR HAWAIIAN ISLANDS.

Luther Severance, commissioner, Honolulu.
Elisha H. Allen, consul, Honolulu.
Charles Bunker, consnl, Lahaina.
Thomas Miller, consul, Hilo.

NAVIGATOR'S ISLANDS.

——— ———, commercial agent, Apia.

SOCIETY ISLANDS.

William H. Kelley, consul, Tahiti.

NEW ZEALAND.

John B. Williams, consul, Bay of Islands.

FEEJEE ISLANDS.

John B. Williams, commercial agent, Lanthala.

United States Ministers, &c.

HAYTI OR SAN DOMINGO.

George F. Usher, commercial agent, Port Au Prince.
Sidney Oaksmith, commercial agent, Aux-Cayes.
John L. Wilson, commercial agent, Cape Haytien.
Jonathan Elliot, commercial agent, City of St. Domingo and Porto Plata.

MEXICAN REPUBLIC.

Alfred Conkling, Envoy Extraordinary and Minister Plenipotentiary, Mexico.
William Rich, Secretary of Legation, Mexico.
John Black, consul, Mexico.
——— ———, consul, City of Monterey, State of New Leon.
David R. Diffenderffer, consul, Paso del Norte.

On the Atlantic side.

Franklin Chase, consul, Tampico, or Santa Anna de Tamaulipas.
James F. Waddell, consul, Matamoros.
Wm. R. Glover, consul, Vera Cruz and Alvarado.
Edward Porter, consul, Tabasco.
——— ———, Laguna, Carmen Island.
Lewis Morris, Campeché.
Wills de Hass, Merida and Sisal.

On the Pacific side.

Robert R. Gatton, consul, Mazatlan.
Hector C. Ames, consul, San Blas.
John A. Robinson, consul, Guaymas.
Charles R. Webster, consul, Tehuantepec and Huatulco.
Bennett Riddells, consul, Chihuahua.

CENTRAL AMERICA.

John B. Kerr, Chargé d'Affaires, Nicaragua.
B. M. Edney, Chargé d'Affaires, Guatemala.
——— ———, consul, Guatemala.
A. Follin, consul, Omoa and Truxillo.
Wm. F. Boone, commercial agent, San Juan de Nicaragua.

Costa Rica.

Marquis L. Hine, consul, San José.

NEW GRANADA.

Yelverton P. King, Chargé d'Affaires, Bogota.

On the Atlantic side.

Ramon Leon Sanchez, consul, Cartagena.
——— ———, consul, Santa Martha.
Harvey Gleason, consul, Chagres.

On the Pacific side.

Amos B. Corwine, consul, Panama.
John A. Bennet, consul, Bogota.
Henry Munro, consul, Aspinwall.

United States Ministers, &c.

VENEZUELA.

J. Nevett Steele, Chargé d'Affaires, Caracas.
Roland Dubs, consul, Maracaibo.
Southy Grinalds, consul, Puerto Cabello.
Nicholas J. Keefe, consul, Laguayra.
Adolphus H. Wappaus, consul, Angostura, now Cuidad Bolivar.

EQUADOR.

Courtland Cushing, Chargé d'Affaires, Quito.
M. P. Game, consul, Guayaquil.

BRAZIL.

Robert C. Schenck, Envoy Extraordinary and Minister Plenipotentiary, Rio de Janeiro.
Ferdinand Coxe, Secretary of Legation, Rio de Janeiro.
John U. Pettit, consul, Maranham Island.
Henry L. Norris, consul, Para.
James Wright Gordon, consul, Pernambuco.
Edward Kent, consul, Rio de Janeiro.
——— ———, consul, Santos.
Robert S. Cathcart, consul, St. Catharine's Island.
George F. Upton, consul, Rio Grande.
John S. Gillmer, consul, Bahia de San Salvador.

URUGUAY OR CISPLATINE REPUBLIC.

Robert M. Hamilton, consul, Montevideo.
Wm. H. Smiley, commercial agent, Faulkland Islands.

ARGENTINE REPUBLIC OR BUENOS AYRES.

John S. Pendleton, Chargé d'Affaires.
Joseph Graham, consul, Buenos Ayres.
Wm. H. Smiley, consul, Rio Negro.

PARAGUAY.

Edward A. Hopkins, consul.

CHILE.

Balie Peyton, Envoy Extraordinary and Minister Plenipotentiary, Sant-Iago.
Jesse B. Holmer, Secretary of Legation, Sant-Iago.
Wm. Duer, consul, Valparaiso.
Samuel Eckel, consul, Talcahuano.
Samuel F. Haviland, consul, Coquimbo.

PERU.

John R. Clay, Chargé d'Affaires, Lima.
Edward McCall, consul, Lima.
——— ———, consul, Arica.
Alexander Ruden, jr., consul, Paita.
Samuel J. Oakford, consul, Tumbez.

BOLIVIA.

Horace H. Miller, Chargé d'Affaires, Chuquisaca.

DEPARTMENT OF STATE.

DIPLOMATIC CORPS.

List of Foreign Ministers, their Secretaries and Attachés, accredited to the Government of the United States.

[Corrected to January, 1853.]

ENVOYS EXTRAORDINARY AND MINISTERS PLENIPOTENTIARY.

ENGLAND.

John F. Crampton, esq., Envoy Extraordinary and Minister Plenipotentiary, corner K and 23d sts.
Philip Griffith, esq., Secretary of Legation.

FRANCE.

M. le Compte de Sartiges, Envoy Extraordinary and Minister Plenipotentiary, G street, between 17th and 18th streets.
M. Boilleau, Secretary of Legation.

RUSSIA.

Mr. Alexandre de Bodisco, Envoy Extraordinary and Minister Plenipotentiary, Georgetown, D. C.
——— ———, Secretary of Legation.

NETHERLANDS.

Baron Testa, Chargé d'Affaires, Mrs. Ulrich's, opposite Department of State.

SPAIN.

Señor Don A. Calderon de la Barca, Envoy Extraordinary and Minister Plenipotentiary, Capitol Hill, B street.
Chevalier Don M. de los Santos Bañuelos, Secretary of Legation.

PORTUGAL.

The Commander J. C. de Figaniere è Morâo, Minister Resident.
——— ———, Attaché.

PRUSSIA.

Baron Von Gerolt, Minister Resident, corner of Gay and Green streets, Georgetown, D. C.
——— ———, Attaché.

DENMARK.

Steen de Billé, Chargé d'Affaires.

TWO SICILIES AND PARMA.

Chevalier Martuscelli, Chargé d'Affaires.

SARDINIA.

Chevalier L. Mossi, Chargé d'Affaires.

BELGIUM.

M. Henri Bosch Spencer, Chargé d'Affaires.

Foreign Ministers, &c.

MEXICO.

Señor Don Manuel Larrainzar, Envoy Extraordinary and Minister Plenipotentiary, cor. F n and 21 w.
Don. J. M. Gonzales de la Vega, Secretary of Legation.
Don Antonio Sierra, Clerk.
Don Angel Huici, Attaché.

GUATEMALA.

Señor Don Felipe Molina, Chargé d'Affaires.

NICARAGUA.

Señor Don José de Marcoleta, Envoy Extraordinary and Minister Plenipotentiary, at Kieckofer's, east side 13th street, between E and F streets.

COSTA RICA.

Señor Don Felipe Molina, Envoy Extraordinary and Minister Plenipotentiary.

VENEZUELA.

Señor Don Lucio Palido, Minister Plenipotentiary.

BRAZIL.

The Chevalier F. J. de Carvalho Moreira, Envoy Extraordinary and Minister Plenipotentiary.
F. V. da Costa Aguiar de Andrada, Attaché, and Secretary *ad interim.*

CHILE.

Señor Don Manuel Carvallo, Envoy Extraordinary and Minister Plenipotentiary, 7th street, opposite City Post Office.
——— ———, Secretary of Legation.

PERU.

Señor Don J. J. Osma, Envoy Extraordinary and Minister Plenipotentiary.
——— ———, Secretary of Legation.

STANDING COMMITTEES—HOUSE OF REPRESENTATIVES.

Committee of Elections.

Mr. William S. Ashe, of N. C.
Christopher H. Williams, of Tenn.
William T. Hamilton, of Md.
Abr'm M. Schermerhorn, of N. Y.
John S. Caskie, of Va.
Presley Ewing, of Ky.
George T. Davis, of Mass.
James Gamble, of Pa.
Nathan T. Stratton, of N. J.
Room No. 32, *attic story.*

Committee of Ways and Means.

Mr. George S. Houston, of Ala.
George W. Jones, of Tenn.
Edward Stanly, of N. C.
Harry Hibbard, of N. H.
James Brooks, of N. Y.
J. Glancy Jones, of Pa.
William Appleton, of Mass.
Cyrus L. Dunham, of Ind.
John S. Phelps, of Mo.
Room No. 44, *2d story, west.*

Committee of Claims.

Mr. John R. J. Daniel, of N. C.
Alfred P. Edgerton, of Ohio.
Richard I. Bowie, of Md.
Origen S. Seymour, of Conn.
Chauncey F. Cleveland, of Conn.
William A. Sackett, of N. Y.
Carlton B. Curtis, of Pa.
Gilchrist Porter, of Mo.
Daniel Mace, of Ind.
Room No. 50, *first story, east.*

Committee on Commerce.

Mr. David L. Seymour, of N. Y.
Andrew Johnson, of Tenn.
Alexander H. Stephens, of Ga.
Thomas J. D. Fuller, of Me.
James H. Duncan, of Mass.
John Robbins, jr., of Pa.
Louis St. Martin, of La.
William Aiken, of S. C.
Thomas Y. Walsh, of Md.
Room No. 40, *2d story, west.*

Committee on Public Lands.

Mr. Willard P. Hall, of Mo.
W. R. W. Cobb, of Ala.
Henry Bennet, of N. Y.
James L. Orr, of S. C.
Albert G. Watkins, of Tenn.
John D. Freeman, of Miss.
Henry D. Moore, of Pa.
Bernhart Henn, of Iowa.
Joseph W. McCorkle, of Cal.
Room No. 30, *attic story.*

Com. on the Post Office and Post Roads.

Mr. Edson B. Olds, of Ohio.
Alexander G. Penn, of La.
William Cullom, of Tenn.
Paulus Powell, of Va.
John L. Schoolcraft, of N. Y.
Richardson Scurry, of Texas.
Ben. Edwards Grey, of Ky.
Edward C. Marshall, of Cal.
Lincoln Clark, of Iowa.
Room No. 42, *2d story, west.*

Committee for the District of Columbia.

Mr. Orlando B. Ficklin, of Ill.
Thomas H. Averett, of Va.
Wm. Preston, of Ky.
Edward Hammond, of Md.
Charles Allen, of Mass.
Junius Hillyer, of Ga.
Hiram Bell, of Ohio.
Alexander H. Buell, of N. Y.
Daniel Mace, of Indiana.
Room No. 49, *basement.*

Committee on the Judiciary.

Mr. James X. McLanahan, of Pa.
Richard K. Meade, of Va.
David Outlaw, of N. C.
Abraham W. Venable, of N. C.
Isham G. Harris, of Tenn.
James Meacham, of Vermont.
John Bragg, of Ala.
Samuel W. Parker, of Ind.
Preston King, of New York.
Room No. 77, *2d story, south.*

Committee on Revolutionary Claims.

Mr. Moses McDonald, of Maine.
James F. Strother, of Va.
James M. Gaylord, of Ohio.
Henry M. Fuller, of Pa.
John Letcher, of Va.
Charles Murphy, of Ga.
Richard Yates, of Ill.
Gilbert Dean, of New York.
John McQueen, of S. C.
Room No. 41, *2d story, west.*

Committee on Public Expenditures.

Mr. Charles Sweetser, of Ohio.
Marius Schoonmaker, of N. Y.
Nathan T. Stratton, of N. J.
John Letcher, of Va.
Thomas M. Howe, of Pa.
James T. Morehead, of N. C.
Leander Babcock, of N. Y.
Thomas Campbell, of Ill.
John G. Davis, of Indiana.
Room No. 80, *basement.*

Committees—House of Representatives.

Committee on Private Land Claims.

Mr. Timothy Jenkins, of N. Y.
Sherrard Clemens, of Va.
James Abercombie, of Ala.
John L. Dawson, of Pa.
Lewis D. Campbell, of Ohio.
Benjamin D. Nabers, of Miss.
J. Aristide Landry, of La.
William W. Snow, of N. Y.
John G. Miller, of Mo.
Room No. 39, 2d story, west.

Committee on Manufactures.

Mr. James M. H. Beale, of Va.
Thomas B. Florence, of Pa.
Isaac Reed, of Me.
Chauncey F. Cleveland, of Conn.
Addison White, of Ky.
William Murray, of N. Y.
Jared Perkins, of N. H.
Frederick W. Green, of Ohio.
Emanuel B. Hart, of N. Y.
Room No. 28, attic story.

Committee on Agriculture.

Mr. John G. Floyd, of N. Y.
Fayette McMullen, of Va.
Alfred Dockery, of N. C.
Joseph Cable, of Ohio.
Charles Skelton, of N. J.
Samuel Brenton, of Ind.
Eben Newton, of Ohio.
James Duane Doty, of Wis.
John McNair, of Pa.
Room No. 31, attic story.

Committee on Indian Affairs.

Mr. Robert W. Johnson, of Ark.
Volney E. Howard, of Texas.
George Briggs, of N. Y.
Joseph W. Jackson, of Ga.
James L. Conger, of Mich.
Graham N. Fitch, of Ind.
Joseph P. Caldwell, of N. C.
Edward C. Marshall, of Cal.
Charles Durkee, of Wis.
Room No. 62, 2d story, south.

Committee on Military Affairs.

Mr. Wm. H. Bissell, of Ill.
Meredith P. Gentry, of Tenn.
Willis A. Gorman, of Ind.
Alexander Evans, of Md.
Ephraim K. Smart, of Me.
Thaddeus Stevens, of Pa.
John A. Wilcox, of Miss.
Solomon G. Haven, of N. Y.
Chas. J. Faulkner, of Va.
Room No. 27, attic story.

Committee on the Militia.

Mr. Chas. H. Peaslee, of N. H.
John H. Savage, of Tenn.
Geo. G. King, of R. I.
John G. Davis, of Ind.
William F. Hunter, of Ohio.
William Hebard, of Vt.
Elijah W. Chastain, of Ga.
William T. Ward, of Ky.
Alfred Gilmore, of Pa.
Room No. 69, 2d story, south.

Committee on Naval Affairs.

Mr. Frederick P. Staunton, of Tenn.
Thomas S. Bocock, of Va.
Lorenzo Burrows, of N. Y.
Sampson W. Harris, of Ala.
E. Carrington Cabell, of Fla.
Ebenezer J. Penniman, of Mich.
Isaac Wildrick, of N. J.
Robert Goodenow, of Me.
Thomas B. Florence, of Pa.
Room No. 34, attic story.

Committee on Foreign Affairs.

Mr. Thomas H. Bayly, of Va.
Joseph A. Woodward, of S. C.
Robert Toombs, of Ga.
William H. Polk, of Tenn.
John L. Taylor, of Ohio.
John Appleton, of Me.
Colin M. Ingersoll, of Conn.
Joseph R. Chandler, of Pa.
John C. Breckenridge, of Ky.
Room No. 29, attic story.

Committee on the Territories.

Mr. William A. Richardson, of Ill.
Alexander R. Holladay, of Va.
Thomas L. Clingman, of N. C.
James W. Stone, of Ky.
Joshua R. Giddings, of Ohio.
David J. Bailey, of Ga.
Zeno Scudder, of Mass.
Charles E. Stuart, of Mich.
James Lockhart, of Ind.
Room No. 28, attic story.

Committee on Revolutionary Pensions.

Mr. John S. Millson, of Va.
Joseph Russell, of N. Y.
Amos Tuck, of N. H.
Norton S. Townshend, of Ohio.
George H. Brown, of N. J.
William M. Churchwell, of Tenn.
Joseph S. Cottman, of Md.
John Z. Goodrich, of Mass.
Willis Allen, of Ill.
Room No. 43, 2d story, west.

Committees—House of Representatives.

Committee on Invalid Pensions.

Mr. Isham G. Harris, of Tenn.
Rodman M. Price, of N. J.
Frederick S. Martin, N. Y.
Richard S. Molony, of Ill.
Ben. C. Eastman, of Wis.
John Moore, of La.
Joseph H. Kuhns, of Pa.
Daniel T. Jones, of N. Y.
Charles Chapman, of Conn.

Room No. 63, *2d story, west.*

Committee on Roads and Canals.

Mr. John L. Robinson, of Ind.
Wm. F. Colcock, of S. C.
John W. Howe, of Pa.
John C. Mason, of Ky.
Benjamin Stanton, of Ohio.
Emanuel B. Hart, of N. Y.
Charles J. Faulkner, of Va.
Josiah Sutherland, of N. Y.
James Johnson, of Ga.

Room No. 31, *attic story.*

Committee on Patents.

Mr. David K. Cartter, of Ohio.
Milo M. Dimmick, of Pa.
William T. Ward, of Ky.
Benjamin B. Thurston, of R. I.
Alexander White, of Ala.

Room No 70, *2d story, south.*

Committee on Public Buildings and Grounds.

Mr. Richard H. Stanton, of Ky.
Henry A Edmundson, of Va.
Richard I. Bowie, of Md.
James Duane Doty, of Wis.
John H. Boyd, of N. Y.

Room No. 49, *basement.*

Committee on Revisal and Unfinished Business.

Mr. W. R. W. Cobb, of Ala.
Thomas Y. Howe, Jr., of N. Y.
Thomas M. Bibighaus, of Pa.
Georgo H. Busby, of Ohio.
Israel Washburn, jr., of Me.

Room No 70, *2d story, south.*

Committee on Accounts.

Mr. John C. Mason, of Ky.
John A. Morrison, of Pa.
John Welch, of Ohio.
Reuben Robie, of N. Y.
James H. Duncan, of Mass.

Room No 64, *2d story, south.*

Committee on Mileage.

Mr. Thomas A. Hendricks, of Ind.
John D. Freeman, of Miss.
J. H. Hobert Haws, of N. Y.
A. P. Stephens, of N. Y.
John Allison, of Pa.

Committee on Engravings.

Mr. George Reed Riddle, of Del.
Ahimar L. Miner, of Vt.
Timothy Jenkins, of N Y.

Joint Committee on the Library of Congress.

On the part of the House—
Mr. Joseph R. Chandler, of Pa.
Joseph A. Woodward, of S. C.
Horace Mann, of Mass.

Committee on Enrolled Bills.

Mr. Isaac Wildrick, of N. J.
Nelson Barrere, of Ohio.

Joint Committee on Printing.

On the part of the House—
Mr. Willis A. Gorman, of Ind.
Solomon G. Haven, of N. Y.
Richard H. Stanton, of Ky.

Committee of Expenditures in the State Department.

Mr. Charles E. Stuart, of Mich.
William S. Ashe, of N. C.
John Wells, of N. Y.
Thompson Campbell, of Ill.
Alexander Harper of Ohio.

Room No. 80, *basement.*

Committee on Expenditures in the Treasury Departmenl.

Mr. Benjamin B. Thurston, of R. I.
Thomas A. Hendricks, of Ind.
Henry S. Walbridge, of N. Y.
Galusha A. Grow, of Pa.
John Allison, of Pa.

Committees—Senate.

Committee on Expenditures in the War Department.

Mr. Milo M. Dimmick, of Pa.
Willard Ives, of N. Y.
Obadiah Bowne, of N. Y.
Andrew Parker, of Pa.
Elijah W. Chastain, of Ga.
Room No. 45, basement.

Committee on Expenditures in the Navy Department.

Mr. Fayette McMullen, of Va.
Sampson W. Harris, of Ala.
Jerediah Horsford, of N. Y.
Thomas B. Florence, of Pa.
E. Carrington Cabell, of Fla.

Committee on Expenditures in the Post Office Department.

Mr. Alexander G. Penn, of La.
William H. Kurtz, of Pa.
George T. Davis, of Mass.
Augustus P. Hascall, of N. Y.
John H. Savage, of Tenn.

Committee on Expenditures on the Public Buildings.

Mr. Thomas Bartlett, jr., of Vt.
J. H. Hobart Haws, of N. Y.
David Outlaw, of N. C.
Wm. M. Churchwell, of Tenn.
John L. Taylor, of Ohio.

LIST OF COMMITTEES IN THE SENATE.

On Foreign Relations.

Mr. Mason, Chairman,
Douglas,
Norris,
Mangum,
Underwood.

On Finance.

Mr. Hunter, Chairman,
Bright,
Gwin,
Pearce,
Miller.

On Commerce.

Mr. Hamlin, Chairman,
Soulé,
Dodge, of Wisconsin.
Davis,
Seward,

On Manufactures.

Mr. Sebastian, Chairman,
Bayard,
James,
Upham,
Fish.

On Agriculture.

Mr. Soulé, Chairman,
Atchison,
Spruance,
Wade.

On Military Affairs.

Mr. Shields, Chairman,
Clemens,
Borland,
Dawson,
Jones, of Tennessee.

On the Militia.

Mr. Houston, Chairman,
Dodge, of Wisconsin.
Cathcart,
Morton,
Spruance.

On Naval Affairs.

Mr. Gwin, Chairman,
Stockton,
Mallory,
Badger,
Fish.

On Public Lands.

Mr. Felch, Chairman,
Borland,
Dodge, of Iowa,
Underwood,
Pratt.

On Private Land Claims.

Mr. Downs, Chairman,
Cathcart,
Clemens,
Davis.

Committees—Senate.

On Indian Affairs.

Mr. Atchison, Chairman,
Sebastian,
Rusk,
Bell,
Cooper.

Of Claims.

Mr. Brodhead, Chairman,
Bayard,
Adams,
Pratt,
Wade.

On Revolutionary Claims.

Mr. Brodhead, Chairman,
Foot,
Brooke.

On the Judiciary.

Mr. Butler, Chairman,
Downs,
Bradbury,
Geyer,
Badger.

On the Post Office and Post Roads.

Mr. Rusk, Chairman,
Soulé,
Hamlin,
Upham,
Morton.

On Roads and Canals.

Mr. Bright, Chairman,
Douglas,
Adams,
Spruance,

On Territories.

Mr. Douglas, Chairman,
Houston,
Weller,
Cooper,
Jones, of Tennessee.

On Pensions.

Mr. Jones, of Iowa, Chairman,
Weller,
Stockton,
Foot,
Geyer.

For the District of Columbia.

Mr. Shields, Chairman.
Bradbury,
Norris,
Clarke,
Brooke,

On Patents and Patent Office.

Mr. James, Chairman,
De Saussure,
Charlton,
Dawson,
Smith.

On Retrenchment.

Mr. Bradbury, Chairman,
Bright,
Felch,
Mangum,
Fish.

On Public Buildings.

Mr. James, Chairman,
Hunter,
Clarke.

On Printing.

Mr. Borland, Chairman,
Hamlin,
Smith,

On Engrossed Bills.

Mr. Bayard, Chairman,
Mallory,

On the Library.

Mr. Pearce, Chairman,
Clemens,
Dodge, of Iowa.

On Enrolled Bills.

Mr. Jones, of Iowa, Chairman,
Badger.

To audit and control the Contingent Expenses of the Senate.

Mr. Dodge, of Iowa, Chairman,
Underwood.

SUPREME COURT OF THE UNITED STATES.

Roger B. Taney, Chief Justice, Brenner's, n side Pa. av., between 3d and 4½ sts.
John McLean, Associate Justice, Mrs. Carter's, Capitol Hill.
James M. Wayne, Associate Justice, H street, between 18th and 19th streets.
John Catron, Associate Justice, Brown's Hotel.
Peter V. Daniel, Associate Justice, Brenner's, n side Pa. av., btw. 3d and 4½ sts.
Samuel Nelson, Associate Justice, Gadsby's Hotel.
Robert C. Grier, Associate Justice, Brenner's, n side Pa. av., btw. 3d and 4½ sts.
Benjamin R. Curtis, Associate Justice, corner of 4½ and C streets.
Benjamin C. Howard, Reporter, Brenners, n side Pa. av., between 3d and 4½ sts.
William Thomas Carroll, Clerk, corner 20th and F streets.
J. W. Middleton, Deputy Clerk, New Jersey avenue, south of Capitol.
Richard Wallach, Marshal, corner Louisiana avenue, btw 5th and 6th w.

OFFICERS OF THE SMITHSONIAN INSTITUTE.

MEMBERS.—*Ex officio.*

Hon. Millard Fillmore,
" Edward Everett,
" Thomas Corwin,
" Charles M. Conrad,
" J. P. Kennedy,
Hon. S. D. Hubbard,
" J. J. Crittenden,
" Roger B. Taney,
" Silas H. Hodges,
" John W. Maury.

Board of Regents.

Hon. William R. King, Vice President of the United States.
" Roger B. Taney, Chief Justice of the United States.
" John W. Maury, Mayor of Washington City.
" James A. Pearce, United States Senate.
" James M. Mason, United States Senate.
" Robert M. Charlton, United States Senate.
" James Meacham, House of Representatives U. S.
" Graham N. Fitch, House of Representatives U. S.
" William F. Colcock, House of Representatives U. S.
Rufus Choate, citizen of Massachusetts.
Gideon Hawley, citizen of New York.
William C. Preston, citizen of South Carolina.
Richard Rush, citizen of Pennsylvania.
Alexander D. Bache, member of the National Institute.
Joseph G. Totten, member of the National Institute.

Officers.

The President of the United States, *ex officio* presiding officer of the Institution.
The Vice President of the United States, *ex officio* second presiding officer of the Institution.
Roger B. Taney, Chancellor of the Institution.
Joseph Henry, Secretary of the Institution.
Charles C. Jewett, Assistant Secretary, in charge of the Library.
Spencer F. Baird, Assistant Secretary, in charge of the Museum.
Edward Foreman, General Assistant.
W. W. Seaton, Treasurer.

Joseph G. Totten,
Alex. Dallas Bache,
James A. Pearce, } Executive Committee.

——— ———,
John W. Maury,
——— ———, } Building Committee.

Officers Smithsonian Institute—Residences of Public Officers in Washington.

Honorary Members.

Robert Hare,
Albert Gallatin,*
Benjamin Silliman,
Washington Irving.

LIBRARY OF CONGRESS.

John S. Meehan, Librarian to Congress, north B street, Capitol Hill.
E. B. Stelle, Assistant Librarian to Congress, D, btw 9th and 10th streets.
C. H. W. Meehan, Assistant Librarian to Congress, north B street, Capitol Hill.
Robert Keoran, messenger, 8th, btween L and M.

RESIDENCES OF PUBLIC OFFICERS.

FILLMORE, MILLARD, of New York, President of the United States, Executive Mansion.
Fillmore, M. P., Private Secretary, Executive Mansion.
KING, WM. R., of Alabama,, President of the Senate of the United States, south side C n, between 3 and 4½ w.
Boyd, Linn, of Ky., Speaker House of Representatives; boards at U. S. Hotel.

STATE DEPARTMENT.

Everett, Edward, Secretary of State, Mrs. Smith's, 17th street, opposite Navy Department.
Hunter, William, Chief Clerk, Cox's Row, Georgetown.

ATTORNEY GENERAL.

Crittenden, J. J., Attorney General, Mr. Burnley's, s side F n, btw. 17 and 18 w.
Reid, J. T., Clerk, e side 12 w, btw E and Pa. av.

TREASURY DEPARTMENT.

Corwin, Thomas, Secretary of the Treasury, Pa. av., opposite President's.
Hodge, Wm. L., Assistant Secretary, n side H n, btw 15 and 16 w.
Harrington, George, Chief Clerk, n side E n, btw 6 and 7 w.
Rockwell, Charles W., Commissioner of Customs, cor F n and 20 w.
Barclay, John D., Chief Clerk, w side 18 w, btw G and Pa. av.
Bache, A. D., Superintendent Coast Survey, N. J. av., btw Pa. av. and B.
Whittlesey, Elisha, First Comptroller, Mrs. Seth Hyatt's, opposite Brown's Hotel.
Seaman, E. C., Chief Clerk, corner F and 13 w.
Phelps, Edward J., Second Comptroller, Mrs. Spaulding's, s side C, btw 3 and 4½.
Cutts, J. Madison, Chief Clerk, e side 15, btw Pa. av. and H s.
Sargent, Nathan, Register of the Treasury, Mrs. Willis's, corner F and 13.
Nourse, Michael, Chief Clerk, w side 13 w, btw E and F n.
Smith, T. L., First Auditor. w side 6 w, btw D and C n.
Miller, M. H., Chief Clerk, n side H n, btw 9 and 10 w.
Clayton, P., Second Auditor, (Winder's Building,) n side G n, btw 12 and 13 w.
Mechlin, William, Chief Clerk, (Winder's building,) I, btw 17 and 18.
Gallagher, J. S., Third Auditor, 9, btw E and F n side.
Thompson, James, Chief Clerk, corner 24 and M n.
Dayton, Aaron O., Fourth Auditor, w side 6 w, btw D and E n.
Mackall, R. L., Chief Clerk, Georgetown.
Pleasanton, Stephen, Fifth Auditor, w side 21 w, btw E and F n.
Mustin, Thomas, Chief Clerk, n side H n, btw 9 and 10 w.
Sloan, John, Treasurer, Brown's Hotel.
Randolph, W. B., Chief Clerk, s side Md. av., btw 12 and 13 w.
Comstock, George F., Solicitor of the Treasury, Brown's Hotel.
Pleasants, B. F., Chief Clerk, n side E n, btw 6 and 7 w.

*Deceased.

Residences of Public Officers in Washington.

DEPARTMENT OF THE INTERIOR.

Stuart, Alexander H. H., Secretary of the Interior, s side C, btw 3 and 4½.
Whiting, Georgе C., Chief Clerk, Mrs. Reed's, F street.
Kennedy, Jos. C. G., Superintendent Census, office 8 w btw E and F; house n side H n, btw 9 and 10 w.
Lea, Luke, Commissioner of Indian Affairs, (Winder's Building;) house n side E n, btw 6 and 7 w.
Mix, C. E., Chief Clerk, Georgetown.
Heath, James E., Commissioner of Pensions, (Winder's Building,) Mrs. Wise's boarding house, 13 w, near Pa. av.
Metcalf, George T., Chief Clerk, (Winder's Building,) Dr. Jones's, corner 9 and F.
Wilson, John, Commissioner General Land Office, (Treasury Building,) corner 11 and I streets.
Terry, E. S., Recorder General Land Office, (Treasury Department,) e side 7, btw I and N. Y. av.
Wilson, Joseph S., Principal Clerk Private Land Claims, (Treasury Department,) 13, btw E and F n.
Moore, John M., Principal Clerk of Surveys, (Navy Department,) s side I n, btw 17 and 18 w.

Hodges, Silas H., Commissioner of the Patent Office.
Weightman, R. C., Chief Clerk, n side La. av., btw 6 and 7 w.
Easby, Wm., Commissioner Public Buildings, (office, Capitol,) cor Pa. av. and 8 e.

WAR DEPAREMENT.

Conrad, Charles M., Secretary of War, n side F n, btw 13 and 14 w.
Potts, John, Chief Clerk, 17, btw H and I.
Scott, Major General Winfield, Commander-in-Chief, n side H n, btw 13 and 14.
Thomas, Lieutenant Colonel S., near Georgetown.
Totten, Colonel J. G., Chief Engineer, n side I n, btw 20 and 21.
Jessup, Thomas S., Quartermaster General, s side F n, btw 12 and 13 w.
Gordon, William A., Chief Clerk, Georgetown.
Gibson, George, Commissary General, s side F n, btw 14 and 15 w.
Gott, Richard, Chief Clerk, e side 13 w, btw E and F n.
Cooper, C. S., Adjutant General of the Army, corner F and 20 w.
Towson, Nathan, Paymaster General, w side 17 w, btw N. Y. av. and F n.
Frye, Nathaniel, Chief Clerk, n side Pa. avenue, btw 19 and 20 w.
Craig, Colonel H. K., Chief of the Ordnance Department, n side Pa. av., btw 19 and 20 w.
Maynadier, Captain William, Assistant, Six Buildings, Pa. avenue, btw 20 and 21.
Bender, George, Chief Clerk, n side I, btw 20 and 21 w.
Lawson, Thos., Surgeon General, (Winder's Building,) e side 20 w, btw E and F n.
Abert, Col. John J., Chief of Topographical Engineers, n side I n, btw 17 and 18 w.
Thomas, George, Chief Clerk, Georgetown.

NAVY DEPARTMENT.

Kennedy, John P., Secretary of the Navy, H, btw 17 and 18 w.
Etheridge, John, Chief Clerk, n side 12, btw E and F n.
Morris, Commodore Charles, Chief of Bureau of Ordnance and Hydrography, corner I and 16 n.
McCorkle, Joseph P., Chief Clerk, Georgetown.
Shubrick, Commodore W. B., Chief of Bureau of Construction, Equipment, and Repair, n w corner of H and Conn. avenue.
Johnson, Philip C., Chief Clerk, s side E n, btw 9 and 10 w.
Smith, Commodore Joseph, Chief of Bureau of Yards and Docks; house, 9 near L.
Ridgely, William G., Chief Clerk, Cox's Row, Georgetown.
Sinclair, William, Chief of Bureau of Provisions and Clothing, Mrs. Keller's, President's Square.

Residences of Public Officers in Washington.

Fillebrown, Thomas, Chief Clerk, corner 20 and H n.
Harris, Dr. Thos., Chief of Bureau of Medicine and Surgery, (Winder's Building,) Mrs. Keller's, near Lafayette Square.
Addison, Dr. S. R., U. S. N., Assistant to the Chief, corner I and 16 w.
Skinner, Commodore Charles W., Inspector of Ordnance, corner 11 w and H n.
Morgan, Commodore Charles W., Commandant U. S. Navy-Yard.
Lenthal, John, Constructor, Navy Department, (Winder's Building,) house, F n, btw 18 and 19 w.
Stuart, Gen. Charles B., Engineer-in-Chief, U. S. Navy, (office, Winder's Building.)
Isherwood, B. F., Chief Engineer U. S. N., office Winder's Building; boards at Coburn's, Pa. avenue.
Geddes, C. W., First Assistant Engineer, Lamb's, opposite Willard's.
Long, R. H., Second Assistant Engineer, Lamb's, opposite Willard's.
Houston, Samuel, Third Assistant Engineer, Dr. Houston's, Mo. avenue.

POST OFFICE DEPARTMENT.

Hubbard, S. D., Postmaster General, corner of 16 w and Pa. av., three doors west of Corcoran and Riggs's Banking House.
Jacobs, S. D., First Assistant Postmaster General, Mrs. Janney's, cor. 8 and Pa. av.
Dundas, William H., Second Assistant Postmaster General, residence in the country.
Marron, John, Third Assistant Postmaster General, s side N. Y. av, btw 9 and 10 w.
Trott, Thomas P., Chief Clerk, e side N. J. av., btw B and C s.
Farrelly, J. W., Auditor Post Office Department, Widdecombe's, F, btw 13 and 14.
Ball, Gideon J., Chief Clerk Auditor's office, Widdecombe's, F, btw 13 and 14.
King, Horatio, Principal Clerk for Foreign Mails, H, btw 7 and 8 w.
Bradley, William A., City Postmaster, s side La. av., btw 4½ and 6 w.

Officers of the Senate.

Dickens, Asbury, Secretary, F street, btw 12th and 13th.
Machen, Lewis H., Chief Clerk, at Mr. H. N. Gilbert's, Pa av, btw 1st and 2d.
Hickey, William, Clerk, county of Washington.
Dickens, Thomas W., Clerk, n side A, btw 1 e and Del av.
McDonald, W. J., Clerk, cor Del. avenue and C, Capitol Hill.
Fitzpatrick, J. C., Clerk, B st. s, Capitol Hill.
Patton, William, Clerk, Mrs. Morton's, e side 4½, near Pa av.
Elliot, S. A., Clerk, South Capitol, near N. J. av.
Price, William F., Clerk, near the Capitol, Capitol Hill.
Beale, Robert, Sergeant-at-Arms and Doorkeeper, Pa. avenue, Capitol Hill.
Holland, Isaac, Assistant Doorkeeper, w side 17 w, btw Pa av and H n.

Officers of the House of Representatioes, &c.

Forney, John W., Clerk of the House of Representatives, 10th st, btw D and E sts.
Hayes, P. Barry, Chief Clerk, Mrs. Esterly's, Penna. av., between 2d and 3d sts.
Buck, Daniel, Clerk, Mrs. Wise's, corner 13th and E sts.
Barclay, John M., Clerk, 13th, between F and G streets.
Galpin, John, Clerk, Mrs. Esterly's, Penna. av., between 2d and 3d sts.
Bailey, John, Clerk, Mrs. Chase's, Capitol Hill.
Lee, William, Clerk, Mrs. Kley's, Louisiana avenue.
Coll, Cornelius, Clerk, Mrs. Esterly's, Penna. avenue, between 2d and 3d sts.
Sproule, R. S., Clerk, Mr. Wirt's, Capitol Hill.
Harris, Thomas De Kalb, National Hotel.
Minnix, W. H., Clerk, corner F and 21st streets.
Martin, Matthias, Reading Clerk, do.
Parker, John A., Librarian, United States Hotel.
Messengers in Clerk's office.—Queen, John R., Garrison street, Navy Yard.
Hunnicutt, J. A., Congress Hall, Pennsylvania avenue.
Glossbrenner, A. J., Sergeant-at-Arms, Gadsby's Hotel.
Flood, William G., Clerk, 11th, near Pennsylvania avenue.
Messenger to the Sergeant-at-Arms.—Cole, Christopher, Van Patten's, Penna. av.

Officers of the House—Arrangement of the Mails.

McKnew, Z. W., Doorkeeper, D, between 2d and 3d sts.
Stewart, Charles W., Assistant Doorkeeper, south B street, Capitol Hill.
Galt, Thomas J., Superintendent Folding Room.
Lamborn, Samuel H., Assistant Superintendent Folding Room.
Messengers to Doorkeeper.—Joseph Wright, Samuel J. Johnson, Wm. McKnew, Wm. Sanborn, James J. Randolph, Samuel Phillips, Wm. T. Stewart, Joseph D. Ward, H. W. Moore, J. P. Raub, M. McConnell, H. B. Taylor, G. M. Kendall.
A. H. Allen and W. A. Hacker, in charge of Document Room.
Johnson, J. M., Postmaster, Exchange Hotel.
Messengers in the Post Office.—P. Laphen, Jas. Henry, J. Owner, and Alex. Gillespie.

Agricultural Index of Claims.

Ezra Williams, superintendent, at Mr. Lee's, P st. s.
Albert Greenleaf.
David H. Wood, U. S. Hotel.
Joseph J. Anderson, Baker's Franklin House.
Harmon H. Heath.
Abraham M. Farquhar.
Thomas E. S. Russwurm.
Sewall Brintnall, E street, near 10th.
Hilliard F. Webb, United States Hotel.
Benjamin H. Dorsey.
Leonidas McIntosh, U. S. Hotel.
Benjamin Morrison.
Benjamin C. Cook.
Horace S. Knapp.
William P. Reyburn.
C. C. Rockwell.
Charles J. Wilbur.
John E. Helms.
A. H. Allen.
William Schall, Mrs. McDuffie's, Pa av.
Edw. S. Mosely, Mrs. Esterly's, Pa av.

Superintendent of the Public Printing.

Towers, J. T., (office in the Capitol,) H, btw 9 and 10.

Arrangement of the Mails at the Washington Post Office, December, 1852.

The *Great Eastern Mail*, from Baltimore, Philadelphia, New York, Boston, &c., and Buffalo, &c., arrives at 6 a. m., and 9 p. m., daily; and the mail to be sent from this office, to and by those places, will be closed, as heretofore, at 3 and 9 p. m., daily.

The *Southern Mail* will be closed hereafter daily at 7 and 9 o'clock, p. m., and will be received, as heretofore, daily, by 6 o'clock, a. m., and 4 p. m.

The *second Eastern* and *Great Western Mails* are received by 6 p. m; the latter closes at 2 p. m., the former at 9 p. m., daily. The mail trains north of Philadelphia, are to arrive there in time to connect with the train for Baltimore, which brings the Great Mail, to arrive here by 6 a. m. No eastern mail is received at this office on Sunday night, and no eastern mail, to be sent beyond Baltimore, is made up on Saturday night.

The mail for *Annapolis, Md.*, and *Norfolk,** and *adjacent places in Virginia*, is closed every night, *except Saturday*, at 9 p. m., and is received six times a week, with a mail from *Baltimore, Md.*, by 12 m.

The mail from *Georgetown, D. C.*, is received twice daily, by 8 a. m. and 5 p. m., and it is closed for that place at the same hours.

The mail from *Rockville, &c., Md.*, is received Monday, Wednesday, and Friday, of each week, by 6 p. m., and it is closed for those places at 9 p. m., of same days.

The mail from *Brookville, &c., Md.*, is received by 5 p. m., of Monday, Wednesday, and Friday, each week, and closes same days at 9 p. m.

Papers and pamphlets can be sent, without being prepaid, to any part of the United States; but double postage is charged on delivery. The postage on foreign printed matter must be prepaid.

The office is open from 8½ o'clock a. m. to 8 o'clock p. m. daily, *except Sunday*, and on that day it is open from 8 to 10 a. m., and from 7 to 8 o'clock p. m.

* Norfolk, &c., three times by Baltimore; four times by Richmond.

GUIDE TO THE PATENT OFFICE,

On F street north, opposite 8th street.

Prepared by J. DENNIS, Jr., Agent for procuring Patents, west side of 7th street, next to corner of F street.

East Wing.

1st room. Chief clerk, R. C. Weightman; clerk, S. T. Shuger.
2d room. Draughtsman, Arthur L. McIntire; assistant, William G. Cranch.
3d room. Commissioner, Hon. Silas H. Hodges.
4th room. Examiner, Henry B. Renwick; assistant, Dr. Thomas T. Everet.
5th room. Recorder's office. Hugh McCormick, Amos B. Little, Wm. H. Ball.
6th room. Library. W. W. Turner, Librarian; Thomas Gadsden, and Philander Wilson, clerks.
7th room. Examiner, Henry Baldwin; assistant, Capt. R. W. Johnson.
8th room. Examiner, F. S. Smith; assistant, Lieut. James L. Henry.
9th room. Examiner, Jonathan H. Lane; assistant, Prof. Wm. O. Langdon.
10th room. Examiner, Prof. George C. Schaeffer; assistant, Dr. Daniel Breed.

West Wing.

11th room. Examiner, Dr. Leonard D. Gale; assistant, Titian R. Peale.
12th room. Machinist, Samuel P. Bell; assistants, James S. Ewbank, ——— McCauly.
Charles F. Stansbury, clerk, basement, east wing.

GUIDE TO THE ROOMS CONTAINING THE MODELS OF PATENTED INVENTIONS.

Vestibule, or first room as you enter the building.

1st case right hand. 1st, 2d and 3d shelves. Machinery for making, cutting, folding, ruling, sizing, marking, and printing paper for books, walls, &c., including telegraphs.

4th shelf. Machines for the manufacture of paper, electro-magnetic telegraphic machines. Top of the case: Machines for printing floor cloths, wall paper, copper-plate engraving.

Entrance to the East Wing.

2d case on the right. Lower shelf. Lamps and lanterns, pens, inkstands, and photographic printing.

2d shelf. Lamps and lanterns, daguerreotype apparatus, artificial limbs and joints.

3d shelf. Mathematical, nautical, surveying, surgical, dental and optical instruments.

4th. shelf. Time pieces, astronomical instruments, instruments for gymnasiums. Top of the case: Designs for furnace registers.

Left hand side.—1st case. 1st shelf. Boilers for generating steam.

2d and 3d shelves. Reciprocating, vibrating and rotary steam engines.

4th shelf. Steam, air, and gas engines. Top of the case: Ditto.

2d case on left hand. 1st shelf. Electro-magnetic machines and apparatus, fire alarms, and machines for taking yeas and nays.

2d shelf. Locks, fastenings for doors and shutters.

3d. shelf. Glass and mineral knobs for door fastenings, bolts, hinges, fire alarms, telegraphs, annunciators for hotels, and mail locks.

4th shelf, and top of the case. Hinges, fastenings for doors, shutters, &c.

West Wing.

Case next to the door. 1st, 2d and 3d shelves, right hand side. Seed planters.

4th shelf. Threshing machines.

Guide to the Patent Office.

Entrance to Machinist's Office.

First case against the wall. 1st and 2d shelves. Washing machines.

3d, 4th, 5th and 6th shelves. Churns, &c.

2d case against the wall. 1st and 2d shelves. Straw-cutters.

3d shelf. Straw-cutters, machines for working butter, turning cheese, and milking cows.

4th, 5th and 6th shelves. Bee-hives.

1st case. Lower shelf. Horse-rakes, cultivators, rotary harrows, grassburners, &c.

2d shelf. Ploughs, harrows, cultivators, apparatus for feeding chickens, destroying insects on trees, &c.

3d shelf. Smut machines, machines for rubbing, separating, and cleaning grain, hulling cloverseed, hulling and pearling rice, &c.

4th shelf. Smut machines, fanning mills, machines for cleaning grain, &c. Top of the case: Bridges, ships, &c.

2d case. Lower shelf. Mowing, reaping, and flax-pulling machines.

2d shelf. Mowing and reaping machines, grain cradles, scythes, pitchforks, hoes, clover harvesters, &c.

3d shelf. Machines for harvesting grass, grain, hemp, shelling corn, &c.

4th shelf. Harvesting machines, machine for crushing sugar cane, &c. Top of the case: Machine for harvesting, improvements in rigging vessels, &c.

3d case. Lower shelf. Horse-powers, gearing for varying the speed of machinery, apparatus for changing a reciprocating into a rotary motion, &c.

2d shelf. Mills for grinding grain, paints, ores, bark, &c.; mill stones, and machines for packing flour, horse-powers, &c.

3d shelf. Apparatus for cooling flour; cider mills, coffee mills, machines for cutting corn-fodder; also mills for grinding, crushing, &c., flour bolts, bran dusters, scrubbing brushes, brooms; also gearing for changing, regulating, and governing the motion of machinery.

4th shelf. Straw-cutters, churns, beehives, and machines for washing and pressing clothes. Top of case: Straw-cutters, grain driers, and machines for cutting hemp, &c.

Small case against the post. Bedsteads, chairs, sofas, tailors' geese, speaking trumpets, smoothing irons, swifts, &c.

2d case against the post. Bedsteads.

4th case. 1st shelf. Bedsteads, matresses, fly-traps, shower-baths, braiding machines, machine for crushing ice, traps for catching animals, &c.

2d shelf. Extension and billiard tables, rocking chairs, sofas, invalid chairs, bread and cheese cutters, gongs, elevating desks, &c.

3d shelf. Machines for kneading dough, cutting crackers, drying cloths, embossing candy, mincing blubber, cutting sausage-meat, fly-brush, crushing, cutting and grinding vegetables, paring apples, ice-cream freezers, refrigerators, &c.

4th shelf. Machines for turning irregular forms, head and tail blocks for self-setting saw-mills, self-waiting tables, bed-clothes clasps, machines for cutting tallow, bruising beefsteaks, carving meat. Top of the case: Bridges, carding machines, &c.

5th case. 1st and 2d shelves. Saw-mills.

3d and 4th shelves. Machines for planing, tongueing, and grooving; machinery for working lumber into irregular forms, planing slats for blinds, &c. Top of the case: Machine for cutting mouldings and figures.

6th case. 1st shelf. Machinery for cutting, sawing, and jointing staves; turning shoe-lasts and irregular forms; for turning spokes, oars, spools, and hoe and broom handles.

2d shelf. Machines for jointing and dressing staves, making barrels, cutting and splitting hoops, sawing staves, &c.

3d shelf. Machines for cutting screws for bedsteads, chucks for lathes; machines for sawing, riving, dressing, and jointing shingles.

4th shelf. Machines for boring and mortising wood, boring bobbins, making tenons, plugs, &c. Top of the case: Machines for turning bobbins and irregular forms.

7th case. 1st shelf. Machines for smoothing and cleaning tobacco leaves, tobacco

Guide to the Patent Office.

presses; machines for making cigars, cheese presses, oil presses, oil filters, stump extractors, hoisting machines, weighing machines, jacks, &c.

2d shelf. Dove-tailing machines, machines for making boxes for goods and pills, blinds, cutting veneers, weighing and platform balances.

3d shelf. Machines for cutting lathes, making window sashes, matches, match-splints, carving, working ivory, cutting corks, cutting bungs, splints for baskets, cutting shreds of wood and crimping it for matresses, cutting pegs for boots and shoes, cutting dye woods, splitting and dressing rattan, manufacturing woods for stuffing beds, matresses, &c., sawing rabbets, manufacturing brooms, cutting splints for brooms, mitre boxes, hewing irregular forms, cutting felloes, making carriage wheels, &c.

4th shelf. Machine for filling rockets, charging percussion caps, making safety-fuse for blasting rocks, casting ordnance, casting balls, drop shot, manufacturing bullets, making and charging percussion caps, points and insulators for lightning rods, improvement in construction of roofs, arranging stair-cases, &c. Top of the case: Weighing apparatus, and machinery for dressing tobacco.

8th case. 1st shelf. Machines for making faucets, graduating carpenters' measures, for making flasks, and fixtures for making car wheels, for boring and turning circular grooves, beveling washers, forming rotary cutters, punching and boring metal, drilling machines, boring and cutting screws, punching nuts and washers, tools for working sheet metal, lamp tops, button backs, forming the joints of elliptical springs, riveting pipes, engraving, crimping metals, riveting boiler plates, for making shovels, spades, &c.

2d shelf. Machines for making wire grating, wire rope, cleaning wire, moulds for casting butts, making sand cores, flasks for moulds for cast-iron dies for sheet lead, lead pipe machinery, improvements in apparatus for chilling cast iron.

3d shelf. Screw lever, and hydraulic presses for cotton, hay, and other articles operated by steam and other power, &c. Top of the case: Machines for straightening iron rods, and manufacturing wrought-iron tubes, &c.

9th case. 1st shelf. Machinery for making screws, spikes, bolts, rivets, nails, &c.

2d shelf. Machinery for making jack chains, railroad chains, rolling wrought iron, tires, irregular figures, axes, cutting brads, feeding plates to nail machinery, nail machines, horse-shoe nails, rolling and twisting iron, &c.

3d shelf. Machinery for cutting teeth in circular saws, for hardening, sharpening, and setting saws, cutting files, grinding and polishing spiral and conical knives and other instruments, grinding cards, &c.

4th shelf. Rotary shears, machines for making button moulds and buttons, making pins, buckles, horse-shoes, blacksmiths' strikers, machines for hammering and planishing metals, steam hammers, &c., making anvils, &c. Top of the case: Machines for making wrought iron nails, chains, buckles, &c.

Case next to the wall, in the corner. 1st shelf. Augers, machines for making wrought-iron butt hinges.

2d shelf. Designs for spoons, &c., machines for making hinges.

3d shelf. Apparatus for making spoons and car wheels.

4th shelf. Patent vices, securing tools in handles, planes and bench hooks.

5th shelf. Twisted and other spikes, hammers, screw-wrenchers, box-openers.

6th shelf. Safes and planes.

Room in the corner. Stoves, furnaces, stills, saddles, bridles, harness, &c.

Entrance to the West Wing.

Left hand side.—Case next the door. 1st, 2d, 3d, 4th and 5th shelves. Seed drills and planters.

Entrance to Examiner's Room.

Small case. Specimens for forming compositions.

Case next the wall. Straw-cutters, washing machines, churns, beehives, and machine for wringing clothes.

Guide to the Patent Office.

2d case against the wall. Skates, machines for making boots, shoes, harness, working and splitting leather, &c.

1st case. 1st shelf. Machines for carding and cleaning cotton, wool, and other fibrous substances, cotton gins, &c.

2d shelf. Machines for carding wool, cotton, &c.; grinding, and preparing flax, combing worsted, &c.

3d shelf. Machines for manufacturing carpets, rugs, &c., fulling mills, sizing and dyeing cotton batting, yarn, &c., spreading and stretching cloth, warping machines, improvements in cocooneries, fixtures for silk worms, cotton whippers, apparatus for wetting flannels, &c.

4th shelf. Machines for making felt cloth, hat-bodies, &c., making paper, napping, shearing, and pressing cloth, making wadding, batting, &c. Top of the case: looms, &c.

2d case. 1st shelf. Self-operating mule, looms, shuttles, temples, &c.

2d, 3d and 4th shelves. Looms, and rotary knitting machine, &c. Top of the case: Windmill, &c.

3d case. 1st and 2d shelves. Looms.

3d shelf. Machines for sewing, making weavers' harness, looms, machinery for knitting, twisting fringes for shawls, for making mats, India-rubber and gutta-percha goods.

4th shelf. Machinery for treeing boots and cutting welts and heels, making hat bodies; pressing, polishing, and blocking hats; pressing bonnets, making pegs for boots. Top of the case: Machines for pressing bonnets, &c.

4th case. 1st shelf. Knitting machinery, machinery for brushing, dressing, stretching, drying, folding, and measuring cloth.

2d shelf. Self-operating mules, ring and flyer spinning, drawing frames, winding and reeling yarn; machinery for spinning hemp, wool, flax, &c.

3d shelf. Cap and cup spinning, winding wool for carding machines, roving cotton, making card, preparing and spinning hemp.

4th shelf. Cordage, twine and rope-making machines; reeling, spinning. and twisting silk. Top of the case: Bridges, boats, &c.

5th case. 1st shelf. Machinery for breaking, hackling, and dressing flax, hemp, &c., pumps.

2d shelf. Sewing machines, fire-engines, pumps, hydraulic apparatus, &c.

3d shelf. Water filters, rams, faucets, rotary pumps, and other hydraulic fixtures.

4th shelf. Fire-engines and apparatus, escape ladders, cordage, manufacturing and picking oakum, steamboat signals, buoys, sailing vessels, sounding instruments, attaching yards to trusses, ventilating ships, tarring rope yarns, &c. Top of the case: Boats, vessels, water-wheels, windmills, etc.

6th case. 1st shelf. Construction of boats and vessels,

2d shelf. Propellers for boats and vessels, fishing apparatus, nets, harpoons, hooks, spears, grains, capstans, windlasses, steering apparatus, blocks, sails, anchors, grapnels, &c.

3d shelf. Propellers.

4th shelf. Machinery for accumulating, cutting, raising, and depositing ice; propellers, &c. Top of the case: Boats, and bridges, &c.

7th case. 1st shelf. Windmills, organs, pianos, twisting wires, canal locks, adjustable flood-gates, dams, wiers, &c.

2d shelf. Apparatus for regulating and governing the speed of water-wheels; melodeons, pianos, sounding boards, violins, seraphims, reed instruments, &c.

3d shelf. Water-wheels.

4th shelf. Floating and other dry docks, bridges. Top of the case: Bridges and telegraphs, &c.

8th case. 1st shelf. Apparatus for opening and closing gates, improvements in fence and fencing; axles, hubs, and wheels.

2d and 3d shelves. Wagons, carriages, and other vehicles, and parts of the same.

4th shelf. Apparatus for driving piles, floating docks; hoisting apparatus, and telegraphs. Top of the case: Ditching machines.

Guide to the Patent Office.

9th case. 1st shelf. Car seats, turn tables, trucks and running gear for cars, &c.
2d shelf. Car couplings, springs, brakes, improvements in locomotive engines.
3d shelf. Cow catchers, snow-ploughs, canal boats for railroads, ventilating and excluding dust from cars, and protecting cars from sparks and locomotive engines, &c.
4th shelf. Apparatus for draining marshes, excavating and removing earths, dredging machines, trenching and laying pipes, road scrapers, net shears, floating excavators, box-cutting machines, apparatus for forming embankments, augurs for boring earth, ditching ploughs, &c. Top of the case: Spark arresters, apparatus for smelting ores, distilling, &c.

Case against the wall. 1st shelf. Comb machines, machines for dressing tortoise shell, umbrellas, band-boxes, canes, guns, &c.

3d shelf. Tailors' shears, eyelets, buttons, hooks and eyes; cannons, machinery for making bullets.

4th shelf. Suspenders, stocks, apparatus for suspending garments; cannon locks, tent frames, &c.

5th shelf. Pantaloon straps, cannon for chain shot, cartridge box, machine for making fuses.

Case in the corner. Car-wheels and tires.

Room in the corner. Lime, brick, and other kilns and machines, switches for railroads, stone-dressing machines, harnesses, whips, and machinery for making whips, fire-arms.

Case in the machinist's room.

The foregoing guide to the Patent Office was prepared by J. Dennis, Esq., attorney for inventors, and agent for procuring American and Foreign patents; office, west side of 7th street, next to the corner of F street north, between the City Post Office and Patent Office, where maps, with guides, to the City of Washington, Patent Office, and National gallery, are furnished gratis to strangers, or sent to any person forwarding his address and enclosing a stamp. For further particulars, see advertisement in the Washington City Directory.

GUIDE TO THE NATIONAL MUSEUM IN THE U. S. PATENT OFFICE,

Commencing with the numbering of Cases on your right, entering the door.

PREPARED BY R. J. POLLARD, ESQ.

1. War implements, &c., from the Feejee Islands.

Cast your eyes up to the wall, and you will see the full-length portrait of of Mons. Guizot, the celebrated Prime Minister of Louis Philippe, presented to the National Institute Society by the citizens of Paris, and painted by Healey, the celebrated artist, who executed the great painting of Webster, replying to Hayne, in the Senate of the United States.

2. Fishing implements, mats, &c., from the Feejee Islands.

3. Pottery used by the Feejee islanders for carrying water, cooking, &c.; mats, Tapa, &c., used as clothing.

4. Personal ornaments, clothing (consisting merely of a girdle fastened round the loins.)

5. Implements of manufactures from the Samoa or Navigator Islands, some of which are equal to civilized work.

6. Implements of war, and specimens of manufacture from the Sandwich Islands; some such as were used at the time of the murder of Captain Cook, and also a fragment of the rock on which the lamented Cook was murdered. Also specimens of spinning and weaving from the same group of islands, which have been taught them by the missionaries.

7. Implements of war, and fishing spears, &c., from Kingsmill, Paumotu, Marquesas Islands.

8. Implements, &c., from New Holland, (the region in which the gold is found in great abundance,) among which may be found the boomering and shield, the implement which the natives throw with great force, and cause it to rebound so as to be caught in the hand ready for another throw. A small collection from Siam. Specimens of Japanese swords and other warlike implements; also several models of Japanese piratical vessels, called the Proa, which are said to sail very fast, some as high as twenty miles the hour. Chinese mask, umbrella, book, lady's slipper, &c.

10. A similar collection from the East Indies and Terra del Fuego.

11. Articles from Oregon and California; among which is a very remarkable dress made of feathers; also two others made of the interior coating of the intestines of the sea lion; many masks, pipes, &c.

13. American manufactures belonging to the Patent Office. Also a number of curiously trained roots, representing men and animals from Siam, belonging to the National Institute.

14. Minerals, geological specimens, lavas, &c.; one specimen of lava, which was dipped up in a frying-pan by one of the missionaries at the great crater on the island of Hawii. Immediately after he had dipped it up, he was called to by the natives who were with him, to run, which he did, and immediately after the place where he was standing was all in commotion.

15. Rocks and earth from icebergs near the antarctic land, &c.

16. Mineralogical and geological specimens from New Holland, (the land of gold.)

17. Mineral and geological specimens from Brazil, Patagonia, Terra del Fuego, Chili, and Peru.

18. Mineral and geological specimens from Oregon and California, &c.

19, 20, 21. Corals and sponges from the vicinity of the Feejee Islands.

22. Geological specimens of our own county, belonging to the National Institute Society.

23. Personal effects of the late James Smithson, Esq., of England, the founder of the Smithsonian Institution in the city of Washington, consisting of silver plate

much corroded, which looks like old copper, but is solid silver. A fine collection of minerals and geological specimens, though small in size.

24. The original copy of the Declaration of Independence; the dress worn by Gen. George Washington when he resigned his commission in 1783, (see the picture in the Capitol;) the sword worn by him in all of the revolutionary war; the staff of Franklin, presented by him to Gen. Washington; part of the camp equipage used by Washington, and his camp chest, (of pewter plates and indifferent knives and forks, in comparison with now-a-days,) and many other things which belonged to that illustrious person; the great Persian carpet which was presented by the Imaum of Muscat to President Van Buren, valued at near five thousand dollars; the treaties with the different Powers, with the signatures of the then reigning monarchs, among which are those of Napoleon and George III. acknowledging the independence of the United States. This is the case from which the jewels were stolen, and which are now a shapeless mass, locked up in the State Department.

25, 26. Insects belonging to M. Castelnau, a French nobleman, and deposited with the National Institute.

27. Collection made by Captain H. Stansbury, on his expedition to the Great Salt Lake near the Rocky Mountains, consisting in part of a Rocky Mountain sheep, (a fine specimen,) a very rare animal called the wolverine, cross fox, badgers, whooping cranes, ducks, geese, the skeleton of a pelican, and many other things, which are deposited by Col. J. J. Abert; all of which has been prepared and arranged by R. J. Pollard, Esq. In the same case are some specimens of Ophir fruit from the Dead Sea, brought home and deposited by Lieutenant Lynch.

28, 29. Collection of the National Institute Society, in boxes.

30. Here you will find the Guanaca, adult and young, (the finest wool-growing animal known)—is from South America; the next is the Patagonia deer from the land of hurricanes and giants; for the sake of comparison, the Virginia deer is set along side of him, a young elk, one year old.

31. In this case you will find the sea leopards or seals and a porpoise, and also a small whale's jawbone.

32. In this case you will find a number of small mammalia, a moose head and horns, under which are a number of little musk deer from the East Indies; also a small antelope, elk horns, &c.

33 and 34. A number of specimens of mammalia.

35. Mammalia from New Holland, &c.; and also a fine specimen of the black ourang-outang, from the coast of Africa, and a young red ourang-outang from the island of Borneo.

36. Fishes, &c., in alcohol.

37. Egyptian mummies belonging to John Varden, esq.; Peruvian mummies, crania, &c., and one very fine skull of the African elephant. Amongst the human crania is the head of the Feejee chief Vendovi.

38. Quadrupeds, reptiles, and fishes in alcohol.

39. Crustacea in alcohol.

40. You will find a collection of parrots, Trogons, Cuckoos, and Bucchos.

41. American birds, consisting of hawks, owls, &c., also a few from Mazatlan by Colonel Abert; and several of the most beautiful birds in the collection, of the Trogon family, deposited by Mr. Pollard, the native name of which is Quesal.

42. Kingfishers, woodpeckers, humming-birds, and quails.

43. Sylvicolæ, finches, nectarinæ, &c.

44. Waders, pigeons, doves, &c.

45. Rails, plovers, petrels, oyster-catchers, cape pigeons, &c.

46. Penguins, geese, ducks, &c.

47. Albatrosses, geese, ducks, &c.

48. Here you behold one of the largest frames of the feathered tribe—the skeleton of the ostrich; the pelican, the harp-tailed pheasant of New Holland, the Argus pheasant of the East Indies; and above you see the enormous rhinoceros hornbill, with several others of the same class.

Guide to the National Museum.

49. A large number of small specimens of birds from various parts of the world; the most beautiful are the Pittas, at the north end of the case.

50. Eagles, hawks, owls, &c.; one specimen of the skeleton of the eagle, prepared by Mr. Pollard.

51 to 54. Herbarium of the Exploring Expedition, 10,000 specimens of plants.

55 and 56. Crustacea; below, reptiles.

57. Echini and star-fish; below, fishes.

58 Shells from the East Indies; land shells of Luzon.

59 to 63. Shells of the Exploring Expedition. In the lower part of 62 you will find the collection made by Lieutenant Herndon on the Amazon river, in Central America, in the years 1850-'51.

59. Lower shelf: Shawls presented to various officers of our government by different monarchs, valued at from $500 to $1,500 each.

58. Lower shelf: The fossil remains of the Mastodon and other animals, from the State of Missouri.

At the east end of the room you will find a case containing the old printing press which Dr. Benjamin Franklin worked on when a journeyman printer, in London—the particulars you will find attached thereto.

In the alcove, immediately in the rear of case 49, you will find a full length portrait of General Washington, taken by Charles Wilson Peale, esq., for Lafayette.

Immediately to the left as you enter the door, you will find a case of fine rich specimens of California gold.

Immediately over the entrance door you will see a fine old painting of Constantinople, as it was upwards of a hundred years ago, purchased in that city, and presented to the National Institute. Now, walk down stairs in the basement, and you will find the old sarcophagus which was brought from Greece by Commodore Elliott, and tendered to General Andrew Jackson, but which was declined by him.

REPORTERS IN CONGRESS.

SENATE.

Union.

H. M. Parkhurst, 14th, btw E & Pa av.
W. H. Burr, Mrs. Willis's, cor F and 13.
W. B. Lord, Mrs. Willis's, cor F and 13.
W. G. Parkhurst, F, btw 9th and 10th.
Philo M. Slocum, E, btw 9th and 10th.

Globe.

R. Sutton, Brown's Hotel.
D. F. Murphy, Mrs. Holmead's, 4½ st.
Robert M. Patterson, Mrs. Kesley's, Pa av, btw 3d and 4½.
H. E. Rockwell, Mrs. Ward's, cor 4½ st and Mo av.
J. A. Rowland, Mrs. Browning's, 9th, btw D and E.
H. Pardon, at Mrs. Gassaway's, D street.

Intelligencer.

W. A. Rind, at Copp's Saloon, La av.

N. Y. Ass. Press and Republic.

James W. Sheahan, 21st, betw H and I.

HOUSE OF REPRESENTATIVES.

Globe.

W. W. Curran, Ia av, opposite City Hall.
T. F. Andrews, Mr. Robinson's, D street, btw 9th and 10th.
Charles B. Collar, Mrs. Kesley's, Pa av, btw 3d and 4½ sts.
William Hincks, Mrs. Griffin's, D, btw 9th and 10th.
J. J. McElhone, Mrs. Esterley's, Pa av, btw 2d and 3d.
F. H. Smith, Mrs. Stettinius', s side La av, btw 4½ and 6th.

Intelligencer.

William G. Moore, cor 6th and F.

Union.

D. Wallach.

N. Y. Associated Press.

L. A. Gobright, E st, btw 9th and 10th.

Baltimore Sun.

Edmund Ward, Mrs. Ward's, 4½ street.

Baltimore Argus.

Douglas Howard, Capitol Hill.

ALPHABETICAL LIST OF SENATORS.

Names.		Residences in Washington.
Adams, Stephen	Miss.	Brown's Hotel.
Atchison, D. R.	Mo.	Brown's Hotel
Badger, G. E.	N. C.	Brown's Hotel.
Bayard, J. A.	Del.	Irving Hotel.
Bell, John	Tenn.	
Borland, Solon	Ark.	Mrs. Hill's, Capitol Hill.
Bradbury, J. W.	Me.	National Hotel.
Bright, J. D.	Ind.	Private, Georgetown Heights.
Brodhead, R.	Penn.	National Hotel.
Brooke, Walker	Miss.	Mrs. Walingsford's, e side 4½, btw Pa av and C sts.
Butler, A. P.	S. C.	Brown's Hotel.
Cass, L.	Mich.	St. Charles Hotel.
Cathcart, Chas. W.	Ind.	Mr. Peabody's, s side B, North Capitol Hill.
Charlton, Robert M.	Ga.	Brown's Hotel.
Chase, S. P.	Ohio.	Private, s side C, btw 3 and 4½ sts.
Clarke, J. H.	R. I.	Willard's Hotel.
Clemens, Jeremiah	Ala.	Mr. Campbell's, n side Pa av, btw 4½ and 6 sts.
Cooper, James	Pa.	National Hotel.
Davis, John	Mass.	Willard's Hotel.
Dawson, W. C.	Ga.	National Hotel.
De Saussure, W. F.	S. C.	Brown's Hotel.
Dodge, A. C.	Wis.	Mrs. Ennis's, Capitol Hill.
Dodge, Henry	Iowa.	Mrs. Ennis's, Capitol Hill.
Douglass, S. A.	Ill.	Private, cor J and N J av.
Downs, S. W.	La.	Private, n side of F, btw 13 and 14 sts.
Felch, A.	Mich.	St. Charles Hotel.
Fish, H.	N. Y.	Private, s side of H, btw 17 and 18 sts.
Foot, S.	Vt.	Mrs. Carter's, Capitol Hill.
Geyer, H. S.	Mo.	Mrs. Harrison's, Pa av, btw 4½ and 6 sts.
Gwin, W. M.	Cal.	Private, cor 3 and C st,
Hale, J. P.	N. H.	National Hotel.
Hamlin, H.	Me.	Mrs. Scott's, Pa av, btw 3 and 4½ sts.
Houston, S.	Texas.	
Hunter, R. M. T.	Va.	Brown's Hotel.
James, C. T.	R. I.	National Hotel.
Jones, G. W	Iowa.	
Jones, J. C.	Tenn.	National Hotel.
King, W. R.	Ala.	Private, s side C, btw 3 and 4½ sts.
Mallory, S. R.	Fla.	Gadsby's Hotel.
Mangum, W. P.	N. C.	Mrs. Stettinius', s side La av.
Mason, J. M.	Va.	Brown's Hotel.
D. Meriwether	Ky.	United States Hotel.
Miller, J. W.	N. J.	Willard's Hotel.
Morton, Jackson	Fla.	Private, w side 4½, btw Pa av and C sts.
Norris, M.	N. H.	United States Hotel.
Pearce, J. A.	Md.	Mrs. Duncan's, s side La av.
Pratt, T. G.	Md.	National Hotel.
Rusk, T. J.	Texas.	Brown's Hotel.
Sebastian, W. K.	Ark.	
Seward, W. H.	N. Y.	Private, n side F, btw 6 and 7 st.
Shields, J.	Ill.	Mrs. Burr's, n side Del av, Capitol Hill.
Smith, T.	Conn.	Private, e side 12, btw F and G sts.
Soulé, P.	La.	
Spruance, P.	Del.	Mrs. Harrison's, Pa av, btw 4½ and 6 sts.
Stockton, R. F.	N. J.	National Hotel.

Alphabetical list of Representatives.

Names.	Residence in Washington.
Sumner, C.................Mass.	Mrs. Ulrick's, opposite State Department.
Toucey, Isaac..............Conn.	Brown's Hotel.
Underwood, J. R............Ky.	Brown's Hotel.
Upham, W....................Vt.	Irving Hotel.
Wade, B. F.................Ohio.	Mr. Hyatt's, s side Pa av, btw 6th and 7th.
Walker, Isaac P...... ......Wis.	Mrs. Hill's, Old Capitol.
Weller, John B..............Cal.	Brown's Hotel.

REPRESENTATIVES.

Names.	Residence in Washington.
Abercrombie, James.......Ala.	Brown's Hotel.
Aiken, William.............S. C.	Willard's Hotel.
Allen, Charles.............Mass.	Mr. Reily's, w side N J av, near Capitol.
Allen, Willis....................Ill.	Mrs. Beveridge's n side Pa av, btw 3d and 4½ sts.
Allison, John....................Pa.	Mrs. Carter's, Capitol Hill, A, btw 1 and Del av.
Appleton, John...............Me.	Georgetown.
Appleton William.........Mass.	
Ashe, William S............N. C.	Private, n side H, btw 9 and 10 w.
Averett, Thomas H......... Va.	United States Hotel.
Babcock, Leander.........N. Y.	National Hotel.
Bailey, David J............. Geo.	Private, s side B, btw 1st and N. J. av
Bayly, Thomas H.............Va.	Private, s side F, near 7th.
Barrere, Nelson............Ohio.	Mrs. Stettinius', La av, btw 4½ and 6.
Bartlett, Thomas, jr.........Vt.	John Foy's, cor Del av and A.
Beale, James M. H.........Va.	United States Hotel.
Bell, Hiram....................Ohio.	Mrs. Gulager's, s side Pa av, btw 6th and 7th.
Bennett, Henry............N. Y.	Mrs. Randall's, Capitol Hill.
Bernhisel, J. M............Utah.	Mr. Upperman's, Pa av, btw 3d and 4½ sts.
Bibighaus, Thomas M......Pa.	Mr. Grouxe's, Pa av, btw 4½ and 6.
Bissell, William H........... Ill.	National Hotel.
Bocock, Thomas S..........Va.	
Bowie, Richard I............Md.	Mrs. Stettinius', La av, btw 4½ and 6.
Bowne, Obadiah............N. Y.	National Hotel.
Boyd, John H...............N. Y.	National Hotel.
Boyd, Linn (Speaker)......Ky.	United States Hotel.
Bragg, John...................Ala.	National Hotel.
Breckenridge, John C......Ky.	Mrs. Peterson's, 10th, btw E and F n.
Brenton, Samuel.............Ia.	Mrs. Harrison's, s side Pa av, btw 4½ and 6th sts.
Briggs, George ....N. Y.	Gilman's Building, cor 4½ and C.
Brooks, James .... N. Y.	Willard's Hotel.
Brown, Albert G...........Miss.	Fitzgerald's, n side Pa av, btw 3d and 4½ sts.
Brown, George H..........N. J.	Willard's Hotel.
Buell, Alexander H.......N. Y.	Mrs. Scott's, s side Pa av, btw 3d and 4½ sts.
Burrows, Lorenzo.........N. Y.	National Hotel.
Burt, Armstead ....S. C.	
Busby, George H..........Ohio.	Mr. Grouxe's, Pa av, btw 4½ and 6.
Cabell, E. Carrington......Fla.	National Hotel.
Cable, Joseph...............Ohio.	Mr. Reily's, w side N J av, near Capitol.
Caldwell, Joseph P....... N. C.	Brown's Hotel.
Campbell, Lewis D........Ohio.	National Hotel.
Camphell, Thompson........Ill.	Mr. Gibbon's, 6 w, btw La av and E.
Cartter, David K.......... Ohio.	Mrs. Harrison's, s side Pa av, btw 4½ and 6th sts.
Caskie, John S.............. Va.	Brown's Hotel.

Alphabetical list of Representatives.

Names.	Residence in Washington.
Chandler, Joseph R.........Pa.	Mrs. Harrison's, s side Pa av, btw 4½ and 6th sts.
Chapman, Charles........Conn.	National Hotel.
Chastain, Elijah W.........Geo.	Mrs. Ennis's, Capitol Hill, A, btw 1 and Del av.
Churchwell, Wm. M......Tenn.	Brown's Hotel.
Clark, Lincoln............. Iowa.	Baker's Exchange Hotel, C street, btw 4½ and 6.
Clemens, Sherrard..........Va.	Brown's Hotel.
Cleveland, C. F............Conn.	Mrs. Esterly's, Pa avenue, between 2d and 3d sts.
Clingman, Thomas L.....N. C.	Mrs. Heydon's, Pa av, btw 4½ and 6th sts.
Cobb, W. R. W...............Ala.	Mrs. Rawlin's, E, btw 5 and 6.
Colcock, Wm. F............ S. C.	Gadsby's Hotel.
Conger, James L..........Mich.	Mrs. McCormick's, Pa av, btw 6 and 7.
Cottman, Joseph S..........Md.	Gadsby's Hotel.
Cullom, William.......... Tenn.	National Hotel.
Curtis, Carlton B............ Pa.	Fitzgerald's, n side Pa av, btw 3d and 4½ sts.
Daniel, John R. J........ N. C.	Dr. Brewer's, Georgetown.
Darby, John F...............Mo.	Mrs. Ennis's, Capitol Hill, A, btw 1 and Del av.
Davis, George T...........Mass.	National Hotel.
Davis, John G.............. Ind.	United States Hotel.
Dawson, John L............ Pa.	National Hotel.
Dean, Gilbert............. N. Y.	National Hotel.
Dimmick, Milo M.............Pa.	Mrs. Bronaugh's, 8th, btw La av and D st.
Disney, David T............Ohio.	Willard's Hotel.
Dockery, Alfred............N. C.	Mrs. Shields', 5th, btw La av and E n.
Doty, James Duane........Wis.	United States Hotel.
Duncan, James H.........Mass.	National Hotel.
Dunham, Cyrus L.......... Ind.	United States Hotel.
Durkee, Charles............ Wis.	Mrs. Gullager's, Pa av, btw 6 and 7 w.
Eastman, Ben. C........... Wis.	Mrs. Esterly's, Pa avenue, between 2d and 3d sts.
Edgerton, Alfred P....... Ohio.	National Hotel.
Edmundson, Henry A...... Va.	Mrs. Murray's, Pa av, btw 12th and 13th sts.
Evans, Alexander........... Md.	Mrs. Gautier's, 11th, btw D and E.
Ewing Persley................Ky.	National Hotel.
Faulkner, Charles J.........Va.	Brown's Hotel.
Ficklin, Orlando B.......... Ill.	Mrs. Hill's, Old Capitol.
Fitch, Graham N............Ind.	Fitzgerald's, n side Pa av, btw 3d and 4½ sts.
Florence, Thomas B.........Pa.	Dr. Holmead's, 4½, btw Pa av and C.
Floyd, John G............. N. Y.	
Freeman, John D..........Miss.	Mrs. Wallingsford's, e side 4½, btw Pa av and C.
Fuller, Henry M............. Pa.	National Hotel.
Fuller, Thomas J. D....... Me.	Irving Hotel.
Gamble, James...............Pa.	Mr. Crutchett's, cor D and 6 w.
Gaylord, James M.........Ohio.	Mrs. Adams's, s side Pa av, btw 6 and 7 w.
Gentry, Meredith P......Tenn.	Private, B n, btw Del av and 1 e, Capitol Hill.
Giddings, Joshua R...... Ohio.	Mr. Reily's, w side N. J. avenue, near Capitol.
Gilmore, Alfred...............Pa.	National Hotel.
Goodenow, Robert.......... Me.	Mrs. Harrison's, s side Pa av, btw 4½ and 6th sts.
Goodrich, John Z......... Mass.	National Hotel.
Gorman, Willis, A.........Ind.	St. Charles Hotel.
Green, Frederick W...... Ohio.	Brown's Hotel.
Gray, Ben. Edwards....... Ky.	Gilman's Building, cor 4½ and C.
Grow, Galusha A............ Pa.	Room at Crutchett's, 6th, btw La av and E; boards at Baker's Exchange Hotel, C st.
Hall, Willard P............. Mo.	Mrs. Wallingsford's, e side 4½, btw Pa av and C.
Hamilton, William T...... Md.	St. Charles Hotel.
Hammond, Edward.........Md.	Brown's Hotel.
Harper, Alexander........Ohio.	Mr. Hyatt's, s side Pa av, btw 6th and 7th.

Alphabetical list of Representatives.

Names.	Residence in Washington.
Harris, Isham G.......... Tenn.	Mrs. Cunningham's, Pa av, btw 2 and 3 w.
Harris, Sampson W.........Ala.	Mrs. Hill's, Old Capitol.
Hart, Emanuel B..........N. Y.	National Hotel.
Haws, John H. H.........N. Y.	Mrs. Gautier's, 11th, D and E n.
Hascall, Augustus P......N. Y.	Mrs. Esterly's, Pa avenue, between 2d and 3d sts.
Haven, Solomon G....... N. Y.	Willard's Hotel.
Hebard, William............ Vt.	Irving Hotel.
Hendricks, Thomas A......Ind.	Fitzgerald's, n side Pa av, btw 3d and 4½ sts.
Henn, Bernhart........... Iowa.	Mrs. Ennis's, Capitol Hill, A, btw 1 and Del av.
Hibbard, Henry........... N. H.	Gadsby's Hotel.
Hillyer, Junius...............Ga.	Mrs. Scrivener's, A n, btw E and Del av.
Holladay, Alexander R.... Va.	Irving Hotel.
Horsford, Jerediah....... N. Y.	
Houston, George S......... Ala.	Brown's Hotel.
Howard, Volney E...... Texas.	Brown's Hotel.
Howe, John W................Pa.	Mrs. Carter's, Capitol Hill, A, btw 1 and Del av.
Howe, Thomas M............Pa.	Mrs. Carter's, Capitol Hill, A, btw 1 and Del av.
Howe, Thomas Y., jr.....N. Y.	National Hotel.
Hunter, William F.........Ohio.	Mrs. Gullager's, Pa av, btw 6 and 7 w.
Ingersoll, Colin M.........Conn.	Campbell's, Pa av, btw 4½ and 6 w.
Ives, Willard............... N. Y.	Mrs. Scott's, s side Pa av, btw 2d and 4½ sts.
Jackson, Joseph W......... Ga.	Gadsby's Hotel.
Jenkins, Timothy.........N. Y.	Mrs. Scott's, s side Pa av, btw 3d and 4½ sts.
Johnson, Andrew.........Tenn.	United States Hotel.
Johnson, James................Ga.	Brown's Hotel.
Johnson, John............. Ohio.	St. Charles Hotel.
Johnson, Robert W..........Ark.	Mrs. Wallingsford's, e side 4½, btw Pa av and C.
Jones, Daniel T............N. Y.	Mrs. Scott's, s side Pa av, btw 3d and 4½ sts.
Jones, George W..........Tenn.	Campbell's, Pa av, between 4½ and 6th streets.
Jones, J. Glancy............. Pa.	United States Hotel.
King, George G.............R. I.	Mrs. Carter's, Capitol Hill, A, btw 1st and Del av.
King, Preston.............. N. Y.	Mrs. Scott's, s side Pa av, btw 3d and 4½ sts.
Kuhns, Joseph H.............Pa.	Gadsby's Hotel.
Kurtz, William H............Pa.	Gadsby's Hotel.
Landry, J. Aristide..........La.	Reily's, New Jersey avenue, Capitol Hill.
Lane, Joseph............Oregon.	Mr. Wirt's, North Capitol, btw Del. avenue and C.
Letcher, John................ Va.	Brown's Hotel.
Lockhart, James............ Ind.	St. Charles Hotel.
Mace, Daniel................ Ind.	Private, 10th, btw Pa av and C st.
Mann, Horace............. Mass.	National Hotel.
Marshall, Edward C........Cal.	National Hotel.
Martin, Frederick S......N. Y.	National Hotel.
Mason, John C...............Ky.	United States Hotel.
McCorkle, Joseph W.......Cal.	Brown's Hotel.
McDonald, Moses........... Me.	Irving Hotel.
McLanahan, James X...... Pa.	National Hotel.
McMullen, Fayette.........Va.	Dr. Daily's, D st, btw 6th and 7th sts.
McNair, John................ Pa.	Fitzgerald's, n side Pa av, btw 3d and 4½ sts.
McQueen, John.............S. C.	Gadsby's Hotel.
Meacham, James.............Vt.	Mrs. Carter's, Capitol Hill, A, btw 1st and Del av.
Meade, Richard K.......... Va.	Brown's Hotel.
Miller, John G...............Mo.	Mrs. Harrison's, s side Pa av, btw 4½ and 6th sts.
Millson, John S...............Va.	United States Hotel.
Miner, Ahiman L............ Vt.	Irving Hotel.
Molony, Richard S.......... Ill.	St. Charles Hotel.
Moore, Henry D............ Pa.	Mrs. Davis's, Pa. avenue, btw 6th and 7th sts.

Alphabetical list of Representatives.

Names.	Residence in Washington.
Moore, John..................La.	National Hotel.
Morehead, James T.......N. C.	Mrs. Shields', 5th, btw La av and E n.
Morrison, John A............Pa.	Fitzgerald's, n side Pa av, btw 3d and 4½ sts.
Murphy, Charles............Ga.	Mr. Duvall's, A, btw 1st and Del av.
Murray, William.......... N. Y.	Willard's Hotel.
Nabers, Benj. D........... Miss.	Mrs. Wallingsford's, e side 4½, btw Pa av and C.
Newton, Eben.............. Ohio.	St. Charles Hotel.
Olds, Edson B............. Ohio.	United States Hotel.
Orr, James L............... S. C.	Mrs. Cly's, La av, btw 4½ and 6.
Outlaw, David............. N. C.	Gadsby's Hotel.
Parker, Andrew............. Pa.	Mrs. Esterly's, Pa avenue, between 2d and 3d sts.
Parker, Samuel W..........Ind.	Mr. Hyatt's, s side Pa av, btw 6th and 7th.
Peaslee, Charles H.......N. H.	Willard's Hotel.
Penn, Alexander G......... La.	Private, n side F, btw 13 and 14 w.
Penniman, E. J........... Mich.	Private, B street s, Capitol Hill.
Perkins, Jared.............N. H.	Mrs. Tubbs', L street.
Phelps, John S.............. Mo.	Campbell's, Pa av, btw 4½ and 6th sts.
Polk, William H.......... Tenn.	National Hotel.
Porter, Gilchrist............Mo.	Mrs. Harrison's, s side Pa av, btw 4½ and 6th sts.
Powell, Paulus............... Va.	Irving Hotel.
Preston, William............ Ky.	Brown's Hotel.
Price, Rodman M..........N. J.	Willard's Hotel.
Reed, Isaac...................Me.	
Richardson, William A..... Ill.	Mr. Gibbon's, 6th, btw La av and E.
Riddle, George Read.......Del.	Dr. Boyle's, 4½ street, near Pa av.
Robbins, John, jr...........Pa.	National Hotel.
Robie, Reuben............ N. Y.	Willard's Hotel.
Robinson, John L.......... Ind.	Fitzgerald's, n side Pa av, btw 3d and 4½ sts.
Ross, Thomas.................Pa.	Gadsby's Hotel.
Russell, Joseph............N. Y.	Mrs. Esterly's, Pa avenue, between 2d and 3d sts.
Sackett, William A.......N. Y.	Willard's Hotel.
Savage, John H............Tenn.	Brown's Hotel.
Schermerhorn, A. M..... N. Y.	Rev. Mr. Gurley's, e side 12, btw Pa. av and E st.
Schoolcraft, John L...... N. Y.	Senator Seward's, F, btw 6 and 7 sts.
Schoonmaker, Marius....N. Y.	Mrs. Davis's, Pa. avenue, btw 6th and 7th sts.
Scudder, Zeno............ Mass.	Mrs. Carter's, Caaitol Hill, A, btw 1st and Del av.
Scurry, Richardson..... Texas.	Dr. Boyle's, 4½ street, near Pa av.
Seymour, David L.........N. Y.	Dr. J. Green's, n side C, btw 4½ and 6.
Seymour, Origen S.......Conn.	Rooms at Dr. J. Green's, n side C, btw 4½ and 6; boards at Baker's Exchange Hotel.
Skelton, Charles........... N. J.	Mr. Fowler's, Pa. avenue, btw 3 and 4½ sts.
Sibley, H. H.................Min.	
Smart, Ephraim K..........Me.	Mrs. Esterly's, Pa avenue, between 2d and 3d sts.
Smith, William R.......... Ala.	Fitzgerald's, n side Pa av, btw 3d and 4½ sts.
Snow, William W..........N. Y.	Mrs. Cunningham's, n side Pa av, btw 2d and 3d.
Stanly, Edward............N. C.	Willard's Hotel.
Stanton, Benjamin........Ohio.	Mr. Hyatt's, s side Pa av, btw 6th and 7th.
Stanton, Frederick P.....Tenn.	Mrs. Wells's, Duff Green's Row, Capitol Hill.
Stanton, Richard H.........Ky.	United States Hotel.
Stevens, Abraham P......N. Y.	Mrs. Beveridge's, n side Pa av, btw 3d and 4½ sts.
Stephens, Alexander H.... Ga.	Mrs. Duncan's, La av, btw 4½ and 6th.
Stevens, Thaddeus...........Pa.	National Hotel.
Stone, James W.............Ky.	United States Hotel.
St. Martin, Louis............La.	National Hotel.
Stratton, Nathan T....... N. J.	St. Charles Hotel.
Strother, James F......... Va.	Irving Hotel.

Alphabetical list of Representatives—Boarding-Houses, and Members in Messes.

Names.	Residence in Washington.
Stuart, Charles E.........Mich.	St. Charles Hotel.
Sutherland, Josiah........N. Y.	National Hotel.
Sweetser, Charles......... Ohio.	Mr. Gibbon's, 6th, btw La av and E.
Taylor, John L............ Ohio.	Mrs. Stettinius', La av, btw 4½ and 6.
Thompson, Benj..........Mass.	
Thompson, George W...... Va.	
Thurston, Benjamin B....R. I.	St. Charles Hotel.
Toombs, Robert............. Ga.	Mrs. Duncan's, La av, btw 4½ and 6th.
Townshend, Norton S....Ohio.	Senator Chase's, C street, btw 3d and 4½ sts.
Tuck, Amos................N. H.	Mrs. Harrison's, s side Pa av, btw 4½ and 6th sts.
Venable, Abraham W.... N. C.	Mrs. Chase's, Capitol Hill, 1st, btw A and B sts.
Walbridge, Henry S......N. Y.	Mrs. Esterly's. Pa avenue, between 2d and 3d sts.
Wallace, Daniel............ S. C.	Dr. Holmead's, 4½, btw Pa av and 6th st.
Walsh, Thomas Y.......... Md.	Brown's Hotel.
Ward, William T............ Ky.	Mrs. Fletcher's, s side Pa av, btw 3d and 4½ sts.
Washburn, Israel, jr....... Me.	Willard's Hotel.
Watkins, Albert G....... Tenn.	Brown's Hotel.
Weightman, R. H.....N. Mex.	Private, e side 6 n, btw E and F sts. n.
Welch, John............... Ohio.	Hyatt's, opposite Brown's Hotel.
Wells, John................ N. Y,	
White, Addison...............Ky.	National Hotel.
White, Alexander..........Ala.	Brown's Hotel.
Wilcox, John A...........Miss.	Brown's Hotel.
Wildrick, Isaac..............N J.	Mrs. Scott's, s side Pa av, btw 3d and 4½ sts.
Williams, Chris. H....... Tenn.	Mr. Scrivener's, Capitol Hill, A, btw E and Del av.
Woodward, Joseph A..... S. C.	Gadsby's Hotel.
Yates, Richard......... ...... Ill.	Mrs. Harrison's, s side Pa av, btw 4½ and 6th sts.

ALPHABETICAL LIST OF BOARDING HOUSES,

And Members in Messes.

BAKER'S EXCHANGE HOTEL, n side C st., between 4½ and 6 sts.

Lincoln Clark,
Origen S. Seymour.

Mrs. BEVERIDGE'S, south side Penna. avenue, between 3d and 4½ streets.

Willis Allen,
Abraham P. Stephens,

Dr. BOYLE'S, near corner 4½ street.

James Duane Doty,
George Read Riddle,
Israel Washburn, jr.

BROWN'S HOTEL, Penna. avenue.

James Abercrombie,

BROWN'S HOTEL—Continued.
Joseph P. Caldwell,
John S. Caskie,
William M. Churchwell,
Sherrard Clemens,
Charles J. Faulkner,
Frederick W. Green,
Edward Hammond,
George S. Houston,
Volney E. Howard,
James Johnson,
John Letcher,
Joseph W. McCorkle,
Richard K. Meade,
William Preston,
John H. Savage,
Thomas Y. Walsh,
Albert G. Watkins,
Alexander White,
John A. Wilcox.

Alphabetical list of Boarding Houses, and Members in Messes.

CAMPBELL'S, Pa. av., btw 4½ *and* 6.

Jeremiah Clemens, S.
George T. Davis,
George W. Jones,
John S. Phelps.

Mrs. CARTER'S, Capitol Hill.

John Allison,
John W. Howe,
Thomas M. Howe,
George G. King,
James Meacham,
Zeno Scudder.

Mrs. CLY'S, La. av., between 4½ *and* 6.

Pierre Soulé, S.
James L. Orr.

Mr. CRUTCHETT'S, corner 6th and D.

James Gamble,
Galusha A. Grow.

Mr. GROUXE'S, Pa av, btw 4½ *and* 6.

Thomas M. Bibighaus.
George H. Busby.

Mrs. CUNNINGHAM'S, north side Pa. avenue, between 2d and 3d streets.

Isham C. Harris,
William W. Snow.

Mrs. DAVIS', Pa. av., bet. 6th and 7th.

Henry D. Moore,
Marius Schoonmaker,

Mrs. DUNCAN'S, La. av., btw 4½ *and* 6.

James Cooper, S.
James A. Pearce, S.
Alexander H. Stephens,
Robert Toombs.

Mrs. ENNIS'S, Dowson's Row, Capitol Hill.

Elijah W. Chastain,
Bernhart Henn.

Mrs. ESTERLY'S, Pa. av., btw 2 *and* 3.

Chauncey, F. Cleveland,
Ben. C. Eastman,
Augustus P. Hascall,
Andrew Parker,
Joseph Russell,
Ephraim K. Smart.
Henry S. Walbridge.

FITZGERALD'S, north side Penna. av., between 3d and 4½ *streets.*

Albert G. Brown,
Carlton B. Curtis,
Graham N. Fitch,
Thomas A. Hendricks,
John McNair,
John A. Morrison,
John L. Robinson,
William R. Smith.

GADSBY'S HOTEL, Penna. avenue.

William F. Colcock,
Joseph S. Cottman,
Harry Hibbard,
Colin M. Ingersoll,
Joseph W. Jackson,
Joseph H. Kuhns,
William H. Kurtz,
John McQueen,
David Outlaw,
Thomas Ross,
Daniel Wallace,
Joseph A. Woodward.

GAUTIER'S, 11th st., btw D and E.

Alexander Evans,
John H. H. Haws.

Mr. GIBBON'S, 6th, btw La. av. and E.

Thompson Campbell,
William A. Richardson,
Charles Sweetser.

Mrs. GULAGER'S, south side Pa. av., between 6th and 7th streets.

Hiram Bell,
Charles Durkee,
William F. Hunter.

Mrs. HARRISON'S, south side Pa. av., between 4½ *and 6th streets.*

H. S. Geyer, S.
P. Spruance, S.
Samuel Brenton,
David K. Cartter,
Joseph R. Chandler,
Robert Goodenow,
John G. Miller,
Gilchrist Porter,
Amos Tuck,
Richard Yates.

Mrs. HILL'S, Capitol Hill.

Isaac P. Walker, S.
Orlando B. Ficklin,
Sampson W. Harris.

Alphabetical list of Boarding Houses, and Members in Messes.

HYATT'S, south side Pa. avenue, between 6th and 7th streets.

Alexander Harper,
Samuel W. Parker,
Benjamin Stanton,
John Welch.

Mr. INGRAHAM'S corner C and 4½ w.

George Briggs,
Ben. Edwards Grey.

IRVING HOTEL, Penna. avenue.

James A. Bayard, S.
William Upham, S.
John C. Breckenridge,
Thomas J. D. Fuller,
Alexander R. Holladay,
Moses McDonald,
Ahiman L. Miner,
Paulus Powell,
James F. Strother.

NATIONAL HOTEL, Penna. avenne.

J. W. Bradbury, S.
W. C. Dawson, S.
A. Dixon, S.
John P. Hale, S.
C. F. James, S.
J. C. Jones, S.
Thomas G. Pratt, S.
R. F. Stockton, S.
E. Allen,
Leander Babcock,
John H. Boyd,
Obadiah Bowne,
William H. Bissell,
John Bragg,
Lorenzo Burrows,
E. Carrington Cabell,
Lewis D. Campbell,
Charles Chapman,
William Cullom,
George T. Davis,
John L. Dawson,
Gilbert Dean,
James H. Duncan,
Alfred P. Edgerton,
Presley Ewing,
H. M. Fuller,
Alfred Gilmore,
John Z. Goodrich,
Emanuel B. Hart,
Thomas Y. Howe, jr.
Horace Mann,
Edward C. Marshall,
Frederick S. Martin,

NATIONAL HOTEL—Continued.

John Moore,
James X. McLanahan,
William H. Polk,
John Robbins, jr.
Thaddeus Stevens,
Louis St. Martin,
Josiah Sutherland,
Addison White,

Mr. REILY'S, N. J. av, near Capitol.

Charles Allen,
Joseph Cable.
J. R. Giddings,
J. Aristide Landry.

ST. CHARLES HOTEL, Penna. avenue.

Willis A. Gorman,
William T. Hamilton,
John Johnson,
James Lockhart,
Richard S. Molony,
Eben Newton,
Charles E. Stuart,
Nathan T. Stratton,
Benjamin B. Thurston.

Mrs. SCOTT'S, south side Penna. avenue, between 3d and 4½ streets.

Alexander H. Buell,
Willard Ives,
Timothy, Jenkins,
Daniel T. Jones,
Preston King,
Isaac Wildrick.

Mrs. SCRIVENER, Capitol Hill.

Junius Hillyer,
Christopher H. Williams.

STETTINIUS', La. av., btw 4½ and 6.

Willie P. Mangum, S.
Nelson Barrere,
Richard I. Bowie,
John L. Taylor.

UNITED STATES HOTEL, Pa. av.

Thomas H. Averett,
James M. H. Beale,
John H. Boyd,
John G. Davis,
James Duane Doty,
Cyrus L. Dunham,

List of Boarding Houses, &c.—Rates of charges for Hackney Carriages, &c.

UNITED STATES HOTEL—Contin'd.

Sampson W. Harris,
Andrew Johnson,
J. Glancy Jones,
John C. Mason,
John S. Millson,
Edson B. Olds,
Richard H. Stanton,
James W. Stone.

Mrs. WALLINGSFORD'S, east side 4½, between Pa. avenue and C st.

Walter Brooke, S.
John D. Freeman,
Willard P. Hall,
Robert W. Johnson,
Benjamin D. Nabers.

WILLARD'S HOTEL, Penn. avenue.

Richard Brodhead, S.
J. H. Clarke, S.
John Davis, S.
J. W. Miller, S.
William Aiken,
James Brooks,
George H. Brown,
David T. Disney,
Solomon G. Haven,
William Murray.
Charles H. Peaslee,
Rodman M. Price,
Reuben Robie,
William A. Sackett,
Edward Stanly,
Israel Washburn, jr.,

The *Railroad Cars* leave the depot, Washington, daily, at 6 and 8¾ a. m., and 12½ m., and 4 p. m., and arrive at the depot, Baltimore, in about two hours and a quarter; they leave the depot, Baltimore, at 4 and 8¾ a. m., and 4 and 6¾ p. m., and arrive at the depot, Washington, in about two hours and a quarter.

On *Sundays*, leave Washington at 6 a. m. and 4 p. m.; and leave Baltimore at 4 a. m. and 4 p. m.

MOUNT VERNON.

The steamer George Washington or Thomas Collyer leaves the wharf every Tuesday, Thursday, and Saturday, at 10½ o'clock a. m., for Mount Vernon and Fort Washington. A line of omnibusses which connects with the boat, leaves the capitol at a quarter to 10 o'clock each day.

RATES OF CHARGES FOR HACKNEY CARRIAGES, CABS, &c.

[Extract from an act of the Corporation, approved March 20, 1842.]

Sec. 12. *And be it enacted*, That, from and after the passage of this act, the following rates of fare or charges for the conveyance of persons from one place to another in the city of Washington, in hackney carriages, cabs, or other vehicles, carrying passengers for pay or hire, between daybreak and eight o'clock, p. m., shall not be exceeded, that is to say: for each and every passenger, for any distance not over one and a half mile, twenty-five cents; for any distance over one and a half mile, and not exceeding three miles, fifty cents: *Provided*, In case any hackney carriage, cab, or other vehicle, shall be detained for a longer period than five minutes, the driver thereof shall be allowed for the whole hack, cab, or other vehicle, the sum of twelve and a half cents for every fifteen minutes so detained; and for all conveyances or other detentions later than eight o'clock, p. m., the owner or driver of hackney carriages, cabs, or other vehicles, may demand and receive at the rate of fifty per centum on the foregoing charges in addition thereto.

Changes—Arrivals.

CHANGES.

Since my work went to press, the following changes have been made:

The Hon. William R. King has resigned the office of President *pro tem.* of the Senate; the Hon. David R. Atchison, of Missouri, has been elected in his place.

The Senate has decided in favor of the Hon. Archibald Dixon, Senator from Kentucky, in place of Mr. Meriwether.

Major James M. Baker appointed Commissioner of Customs, in place of Charles W. Rockwell, resigned.

Abraham J. Jerusun has been appointed commercial agent at Curaçoa, W. I.

P. C. Johnston, chief clerk to Commissioner of Pensions, residence on Missouri avenue, btw 3 and 4½.

For "Mrs. Cly," read "Mrs. Kley," page 54.

For "Agricultural Index of Claims," read "Alphabetical Index of Private Claims," page 39.

Hon. Edward Everett, Secretary of State, cor 18 w and G n.
Hector C. Ames, consul to Acapulco, Mexico.
Richard B. Jones, consul at Alexandria, Egypt.
Hon. H. Hamlin, in mess at Mrs. Scott's, Pa av, btw 3 and 4½.
Hon. Arch. Dixon, at National Hotel.
Hon. P. Soulé—residence at Mrs. Kley's, La. av, between 4½ and 6th sts.
Hon. W. K. Sebastian, at Mrs. Wallingsford's.
Hon. D. R. Atchison, at Birth's, e side 3 w, btw Pa av and C n.
Hon. A. P. Butler, same place.
Hon. W. F. De Saussure, same place.
Hon. R. M. T. Hunter, same place.
Hon. J. M. Mason, same place.
Hon. G. E. Badger, Gadsby's Hotel.
Hon. John Bell, Mrs. Smith's, opposite War Department.
Hon. James Cooper, Mrs. Duncan's, La. avenue.
Hon. Sam Houston, Mrs. Crutchett's, cor D and 6th.
Hon. G. W. Jones, Mrs. Ennis's, Capitol Hill.
Hon. Thomas S. Bocock, at Mrs. Murray's, Pa. av, btw 12 and 13.
Hon. R. Brodhead, Willard's Hotel.
Hon. James Abercombie, Mrs. Stone's, w side 8 w, btw D and E n.
Hon. William Aiken, Mrs. Smith's, opposite War Department.
Hon. Wm. Appleton, private, cor 16½ and H.
Hon. A. Burt, Mrs. Smith's, opposite War Department.
Hon. L. D. Campbell, Stettinius', La av, btw 4½ and 6.
Hon. J. D. Doty, at Boyle's, w side 4½ w, btw Pa av and C.
Hon. J. Reed, at Hall's, e side Del av, btw B and C n.
Hon. John L. Dawson, at Heydon's, btw 4½ and 6 w.
Hon. J. G. Floyd, at Casparis', Capitol Hill.
Hon. E. Hammond, at Dixon's, cor F n and 11 w.
Hon. E. B. Hart, at Col. Forney's, w side 10, btw D and E.
Hon. J. Horsford, Mrs. Harrison's, s side Pa av, btw 4½ and 6.
Hon. James Johnson, Mrs. Stone's, w side 8 w, btw D and E n.
Hon. W. H. Kurtz, Mr. Edgar's, n side Pa av, btw 1 and 2 w.
Hon. H. Mann, at Ladd's, cor B n and 1 e, Capitol Hill.
Hon. Paulus Powell, at McColgin's, s side Pa av, btw 12 and 13 w.
Hon. Thaddeus Stevens, Mrs. Taylor's, s side Pa av, btw 4½ and 6 w.
Hon. Louis St. Martin, at Murray's, w side 10 w, btw D and E n.
Hon. John Wells, National Hotel.
Hon. G. H. Brown, Shackelford's, opposite Willard's.
Hon. J. R. J. Daniel, Brown's Hotel.
Hon. J. G. Davis, Campbell's, Pa. avenue, btw 4½ and 6 w.
Hon. D. T. Disney, Shackelford's, opposite Willard's.

Changes.

Hon. C. L. Dunham, Campbell's, Pa. avenue, btw 4½ and 6 w.
Hon. F. B. Fay, Irving Hotel.
Hon. A Gilmore, Mrs. Kley's, La avenue, btw 4½ and 6 w.
Hon. E. V. Howard, Walker's, Mo. avenue, btw 3 and 4½ w.
Hon. J. A. Landry, Mill's, Capitol Hill.
Hon. E. P. Little, National.
Hon. H. D., Moore, Harrison's, Pa. avenue, btw 4½ and 6 w.
Hon. L. Sabine, Willard's.
Hon. M. Schoonmaker, Mrs. Harrison's, Pa. avenue, btw 4½ and 6 w.
Hon. Richard Scurry, Brown's.
Hon. D. L. Seymour, National.
Hon. H. H. Sibley, National.

Hon. W. Upham, Senator from Vermont, died at two o'clock on Friday, January 14, 1853.

THE STRANGER'S GUIDE

IN

WASHINGTON AND ITS VICINITY,

AND THROUGH

The Public Buildings;

WITH A

HISTORY OF THE FOUNDATION OF WASHINGTON CITY.

In consequence of the immense numbers who annually visit Washington on business or pleasure, to whom, in addition to a Directory, a guide book through the city will be useful and convenient, the following is added for their benefit.

In visiting this metropolis, there are many objects which strangers would like to view, but are deterred from various considerations, the chief of which is the want of a good guide book. To make it interesting, I shall give the history connected with the establishment, upon this site, of the city of Washington. The first knowledge we have of the situation was derived from Gen. Washington, to whose influence the act of Congress, which created the territory of the District, was passed in 1790, now 63 years since, on the 16th July. The vote in the House of Representatives was 32 to 29, and in the upper branch 12 to 14. In passing the law provision was made that the seat of government should not be removed from Philadelphia until the year 1800, and that commissioners should be appointed for the purpose of preparing suitable buildings for the Departments, a house for the President, and a suitable place for the deliberations of Congress. One hundred square miles were set apart, making exactly a square of ten miles. This included Alexandria, then a flourishing city, and having an extensive commerce with the West Indies; and Georgetown, also a place of considerable importance, then belonging to Maryland, as well as Alexandria to Virginia.* The Potomac at this spot is at the head of ship navigation, and some of the largest ships of the United States Navy have anchored off the navy yard.

The following extracts from a letter of the President to the Secretary of State, will show when and on what terms the site was ceded to the Government:

MOUNT VERNON, *March* 31, 1791.

DEAR SIR: Having been so fortunate as to reconcile the contending interests of Georgetown and Carrollsburgh, and to unite them in such an agreement as permits he public purposes to be carried into effect on an extensive and proper scale, I have the pleasure to transmit to you the enclosed proclamation, which, after annexing the seal of the United States, and your counter-signature, you will cause to be published.

The terms entered into by me, on the part of the United States, with the landholders of Georgetown and Carrollsburgh, are, that all the land from Rock creek, along the river, to the Eastern Branch, and so upwards to or above the ferry, including a breadth of about a mile and a half, the whole containing from three to five thousand acres, is ceded to the public, on condition that when the whole shall be surveyed and laid off as a city, (which Major L'Enfant is now directed to do,) the present proprietors shall retain every other lot; and for such part of the land as may be taken for public use, for squares, walks, &c., they shall be allowed at the rate of £25 per acre, the public having the right to reserve such parts of the wood on the land as may be thought necessary to be preserved for ornament—the landholders to have the use and profits of the grounds until the city is laid off into lots, and sale is made of those lots which, by this agreement, become public property. Nothing is to be allowed for the ground which may be occupied for streets and alleys. * * * * * * * *

It was found, on running the lines, that the comprehension of Bladensburgh within them must have occasioned the exclusion of more important objects; and of this I am convinced, as well by my own observation, as Mr. Elliot's opinion.

With great regard and esteem, I am, dear sir, your most obedient servant,

GEORGE WASHINGTON.

Extract from Mr. Jefferson's reply.

PHILADELPHIA, *April* 10, 1791.

The acquisition of ground at Georgetown is really noble, considering that only £25 an acre is to be paid for any grounds taken for the public, and the streets not to be counted, which will, in fact reduce it to about £19 an acre. I think very liberal reserves should be made for the public.

A more beautiful site for a city could hardly be obtained. From a point where the Potomac, at a distance of 295 miles from the ocean, and flowing from northwest to southeast, expands to the width of a mile, extended back is an almost level plain, hemmed in by a series of gradually sloping hills, terminating with the heights of Georgetown; the plain being nearly three miles in length, from east to west, and varying from a quarter of a mile to two miles in breadth; bounded on the east by the eastern branch of the Potomac, where are now the navy-yard and Congressional cemetery, and on the west by Rock creek, which separates it from Georgetown.

The corner-stone of the District was laid at Jones' Point with all the Masonic ceremonies appropriate to the occasion; and we have the following account of the ceremony of laying the corner-stone of the Capitol. The orator of the day was Joseph Clarke, Esq., architect of the State-house at Annapolis, instead of Gen. Washington, as has been supposed:

GEORGETOWN, *September* 21, 1793.

On Wednesday one of the grandest Masonic processions took place, for the purpose of laying the corner-stone of the Capitol of the United States, which perhaps ever was exhibited on the like important occasion. About 10 o'clock, Lodge No. 9 was visited by that congregation so graceful to the craft, Lodge No. 22 of Virginia, with all their officers and regalia; and directly afterwards appeared, on the southern banks of the Grand River Potowmack, one of the finest companies of Volunteer Artillery that hath been lately seen, parading to receive the President of the United States, who shortly came in sight with his suite, to whom the Artillery paid their military honors; and his Excellency and suite crossed the Potowmack, and was received in Maryland by the officers and brethren of No 22, of Virginia, and No. 9, of Maryland, whom the President headed, and, preceded by a band of music, the rear brought up by the Alexandria Volunteer Artillery, with grand solemnity of march, proceeded to the President's square, in the city of Washington, where they were met and saluted by No. 15, of the city of Washington, in all their elegant badges and clothing, headed by brother Joseph Clarke, Rt. W. G. M., P. T., and conducted to a large lodge prepared for the purpose of the reception. After a short space of time, by the vigilance of brother Clotworthy Stephenson, Grand Marshal P. T., the brotherhood and other bodies were disposed in a second order of procession, which took place amidst a brilliant crowd of spectators of both sexes, according to the following arrangement, viz:

The Surveying Department of the city of Washington.
Mayor and Corporation of Georgetown.
Virginia Artillery.
Commissioners of the city of Washington, and their attendants.
Stone Cutters. Mechanics.

(Here follow all the various officers of Free Masonry, among whom appears Grand Master P. T. George Washington; Worshipful Master of No. 22, Virginia.)

The procession marched two abreast, in the greatest solemn dignity, with music playing, drums beating, colours flying, and spectators rejoicing from the President's square to the Capitol in the city of Washington, where the Grand Marshal ordered a halt, and directed each file in the procession to incline two steps, one to the right, and one to the left, and faced each other, which formed a hollow oblong square, through which the Grand Sword Bearer led the van, followed by the Grand Master P. T. on the left, the President of the United States in the centre, and the Worshipful Master of No. 22 Virginia on the right; all the other orders that composed the procession advanced in the reverse of their order of march from the President's square, to the southeast corner of the Capitol, and the artillery filed off to a destined ground to display their manœuvres and discharge their cannon; the President of the United States, the Grand Master P. T., and Worshipful Master of No. 22, taking their stand to the east of a huge stone, and all the craft forming a circle westward, stood a short time in awful order.

The artillery discharged a volley.

The Grand Marshal delivered to the Commissioners a large silver plate with an inscription thereon, which the Commissioners ordered to be read, and was as follows:

This south-east corner-stone of the Capitol of the United States of America, in the city of Washington, was laid on the 18th day of September, 1793, in the thirteenth year of American Independence, in the first year of the second term of the Presidency of George Washington, whose virtues in the civil administration of his country have been so conspicuous and beneficial, as his military valour and prudence have been useful in establishing her liberties, and in the year of Masonry 1793, by the President of the United States, in concert with the Grand Lodge of Maryland, several Lodges under its jurisdiction, and Lodge No. 22 from Alexandria, Virginia.

THOMAS JOHNSON,
DAVID STUART,
DANIEL CARROLL, } *Commissioners.*
JOSEPH CLARKE, *R. W. G. M., P. T.*
JAMES HOBAN,
STEPHEN HALLATE, } *Architects.*
COLLIN WILLIAMSON, *M. Mason.*

The artillery discharged a volley.

The plate was then delivered to the President, who, attended by the Grand Master P. T. and three Most Worshipful Masters, descended to the cavazion trench and deposited the plate, and laid it on the corner stone of the Capitol of the United States of America, on which was deposited corn, wine, and oil, when the whole congregation joined in reverential prayer, which was succeeded by Masonic chanting honors, and a volley from the artillery.

The President of the United States, and his attendant brethren, ascended from the cavazion to the east of the corner-stone, and there the Grand Master P. T., elevated on a triple rostrum, delivered an oration fitting the occasion, which was received with brotherly love and commendation. At intervals, during the delivery of the oration, several volleys were discharged by the artillery. The ceremony ended in prayer, Masonic chanting honors, and a 15 volley from the artillery.

The whole company retired to an extensive booth, where an ox of 500 lbs. weight was barbacued, of which the company generally partook, with every abundance of other recreation. The festival concluded with fifteen successive volleys from the artillery, whose military discipline and manœuvres merit every commendation.

Before dark the whole company departed, with joyful hopes of the production of their labor.

General Washington directed the design of the city himself, which was carried out by Major L'Enfant, a private gentleman, who evidently had reference to the city of Paris, as there are many points decidedly alike in the two cities. The city extends from southwest to east about two miles and a half, and from northwest to southeast about four miles and a half. There are fifteen avenues, named after the fifteen States, which at the time belonged to the Union, now numbering thirty-one. Although the streets cross each other at right angles, as in other cities, strangers find it difficult to learn localities—unless they have a good guide-book, which I trust I have supplied. The proprietors of the original Ground reserved one-half for their own use, the other half was assigned to the United States. Property remained at a low valuation for many years, for the reason that the question had been agitated as to removing the seat of government to the West, but which fear has been effectually removed by Government expending large sums in improving the city, and, in particular, the extension of the Capitol, which is now in progress, and when completed will compare with any building of the kind in Europe.

Speaking of a removal of the seat of government, Mr. Calhoun said:

"Our capital had been placed here, very wisely in his judgment, and he believed it would always continue here as long as there was a necessity for a seat of government. If it were ever removed, the change would proceed from some other cause than the necessity for placing it in a more central position. The attendance of members might be found inconvenient and oppressive; but he would here remark that there was a wise provision in the statute-book—a provision for the allowance of mileage to members for the expenses of travel. As long as that law prevailed, the Representatives of the most distant quarters would stand in as eligible a position as those of the nearest. They ought to be paid in a proportion equal to the square of the distance traveled. It was an error to suppose that the mere extent of the intervening distance should be paid. Greater distances should be paid a higher rate. Because distance disturbed all the social relations, broke in upon the comfort of families, and robbed them of the enjoyment of home, it should therefore be liberally compensated. He was convinced that no one here, as far as he was individually concerned, desired a removal of the seat of government."

Our city could hardly have been placed upon a more eligible spot. With the modern improvements of railroads and telegraphic wires, a few hours place us within reach of every point in the Union; and I venture to say, when my next Directory in 1854 is published, we shall have news from California, in as short a time as from the city of Baltimore.

Our city is nearly three hundred miles from the ocean, and, in point of salubrity, cannot be excelled. The climate has been gradually ameliorating, and variations must be expected. Our last winter was excessively cold, more snow fell than had been known by that respectable gentleman, the oldest inhabitant, for many years; while, on the contrary, the present season has been remarkably mild and open.

When the site of Washington was first chosen for the seat of government, Baltimore was two days' journey from us, now one hour and a quarter; Philadelphia, four days, now six hours; New York, two weeks, and sometimes three, now twelve hours; New Orleans, two months or six weeks, now five days; and it must be recollected, that this time was the quickest, not allowing for delays or accidents. It will thus be seen, in the time I give now, a person may safely calculate upon reaching his destination, it being the ordinary mail time. The soil is light sand or clay; and notwithstanding the time which has elapsed since the first foundation of the city, articles of country produce remains much dearer than in any other city in the United States: the uncertainty as to real estate, the long and short sessions of Congress, the vast influx of strangers, (of which the calculation this year, from January to April, is 150,000,) prevents, in a great measure, all regularity in the price of country produce. The Eastern Branch of the Potomac, upon which is situated the navy-yard and Congressional Burying Ground, debouches from the arsenal at Greenleaf's Point, and forms the eastern part of the city. There are many improvements going on in this part of the city; new buildings rising up at every point; streets newly opened; and what was formerly dreary commons now present the appearance of a busy city—property in this quarter of the city assuming a value never before known.

The small stream from the North, over which the railroad bridge now passes, on entering the city, emptied into a bay or inlet of the Potomac, about 400 feet wide, which jutted in from the West to within a quarter of a mile of the Capitol Hill, and nearly divided the plain. Not far from the head of this, and south of the Capitol Hill, a small stream took its rise in a large number of springs, and emptied into the river, at a place now called Greenleaf's Point, formed by the intersection of the Eastern Branch with the Potomac, and was known as James' Creek. There is a stream above Georgetown which has always been called Goose Creek; but, from a certificate of a survey now preserved in the mayor's office, at Washington, dated 1663, it appears that the inlet from the Potomac was then known by the name of *Tiber*, and probably the stream from the North emptying into it bore the same name; so that Moore did injustice to the history of the place and confounded streams when he wrote the well-known line:

"And what was Goose Creek once, is Tiber now."

By the same survey, it appears that the land, comprising the Capitol Hill, was called Rome or *Room*, two names which seem to have foreshadowed the destiny of the place. Mr. Force, of Washington, suggests that they probably originated in the fact that the name of the owner of the estate was *Pope*, and, in selecting a name for his plantation, he fancied the title of "Pope of Rome."

In his observations on the river Potomac, published in 1793, Mr. Andrew

Ellicott, who afterwards assisted in laying out the city, remarks as follows:

"No place has greater advantages of water, either for the supply of the city, or for cleaning the streets, than this ground. The most obvious source is from the head-waters of Rock creek, which takes its rise in ground higher than the city, and can readily be conveyed to every part of it. But the grand object for this purpose, which has been contemplated by those best acquainted with the country hereabouts, and the circumstances attending it, and which has been examined with an eye to this purpose, by good judges, is the Potomac. The water of this river, above the great falls, fourteen miles from the city, is 108 feet higher than the tide-water. A small branch, called 'Watts' Branch,' just above the falls, goes in a direction towards the city. From this branch to the city, a canal may be made, (and the ground admits of it very well,) into which the river, or any part of it, may be turned, and carried through the city. By this means, the water may not only be carried over the highest ground in the city, but, if necessary, over the tops of the houses."

The advantages which would thus be presented for mill-seats, are also dwelt upon by Mr. Ellicott, and the whole plan subsequently attracted much attention, having been proposed to Congress by President Jefferson. It is greatly to be regretted that it was not adopted instead of the plan for bringing water from the spring near the Capitol.

It is said that Washington's attention had been called to the advantages which this place presents for a city, as long previous as when he had been a youthful surveyor of the country round. His judgment was confirmed by the fact that two towns were afterwards planned on the spot, and the first maps of the city represent it as laid out over the plans of Hamburgh and Carrollsville.

In the original plan of the city, as submitted to Congress by the President, in January, 1790, mention is made of the subjoined magnificent intentions:

"An equestrian figure of George Washington, a monument voted in 1783, by the late Continental Congress.

"An historic column, also intended for a mile or itinerary column, from whose station (at a mile from the Federal House) all distances and places through the continent are to be calculated.

"A naval itinerary column, proposed to be erected to celebrate the first rise of a navy, and to stand a ready monument to perpetuate its progress and achievements.

"A church intended for national purposes, such as public prayer, thanksgivings, funeral orations, &c., and assigned to the special use of no particular sect or denomination, but equally open to all. It will likewise be a proper shelter for such monuments as were voted by the late Continental Congress, for those heroes who fell in the cause of liberty, and for such others as may hereafter be decreed by the voice of a grateful nation.

"Five grand fountains, intended with a constant spout of water.

"A grand cascade, formed of the water of the sources of the Tiber.

"A grand avenue, four hundred feet in breadth, and about a mile in length, bordered with gardens, ending in a slope from the houses on each side. This avenue leads to the monument of Washington, and connects the Congress garden with the President's park.

"Fifteen squares were to be divided among the several States in the Union for each of them to improve; the centres of these squares designed for statues, columns, obelisks, &c., such as the different States may choose to erect.

"The water of Tiber creek to be conveyed to the high ground, where the Congress House stands, and, after watering that part of the city, its overplus will fall from under the base of the edifice, and, in a cascade of twenty feet in height, and fifty in breadth, into the reservoir below, thence to run, in three falls, through the gardens in the grand canal."

The Executive was informed early in the summer of 1800 that the buildings were ready for the public use, accordingly preparations were made in June for Congress to meet, which they did on the third day of November. Adams, who was then President, in his address to Congress, said:

"I congratulate the people of the United States on the assembling of Congress at the permanent seat of their government; and I congratulate you, gentlemen, on the prospect of a residence not to be exchanged. It would be unbecoming the representatives of this nation to assemble for the first time in this solemn temple, without looking up to the Supreme Ruler of the universe, and imploring his blessing. It is with you, gentlemen, to consider whether the local powers over the District of Columbia, vested by the constitution in the Congress of the United States, shall be immediately exercised. If, in your opinion, this important trust ought now to be executed, you cannot fail, while performing it, to take into view the future probable situation of the territory, for the happiness of which you are about to provide. You will consider it as the capital of a great nation, advancing with unexampled rapidity in arts, in commerce, in wealth, and in population, and possessing within itself those resources, which, if not thrown away, or lamentably misdirected, will secure to it a long course of prosperity and self-government.

The Senate, in their reply, said:

"We meet you, sir, and the other branch of the national legislature, in the city which is honored by the name of our late hero and sage, the illustrious Washington, with sensations and emotions which exceed our power of description."

The House of Representatives, in reply, said:

"The final establishment of the seat of national government, which has now taken place in the District of Columbia, is an event of no small importance in the political transactions of our country. Nor can we on this occasion omit to express a hope that the spirit which animated the great founder of this city, may descend to future generations; and that the wisdom, magnanimity, and steadiness, which marked the events of his public life, may be imitated in all succeeding ages. A consideration of those powers which have been vested in Congress over the District of Columbia, will not escape our attention; nor shall we forget, that, in exercising those powers, a regard must be had to those events which will necessarily attend the capital of America."

THE PRESIDENT'S HOUSE,

Commonly known throughout the Union as the White House, was commenced in 1792. Partially burnt by the Vandals who took Washington during the last war, and rebuilt in 1815, it was one of the points representing the Tuilleries, on the plan of Major L'Enfant. It occupies a plat of ground forty-four feet above the waters of the Potomac. The house itself is plain and simple, having the appearance of some of the club houses in the English Metropolis. About 170 feet front and 86 feet deep, is built of white freestone with Ionic columns, making two stories high.

The north front has a beautiful portico composed of four Ionic columns and a projecting screen of three columns. The outer range forms a landing for visitors and a convenient pass for their carriages; a space is also reserved for visitors who arrive on foot.

There has been much said of the interior of the Executive mansion. To our foreign visistors it may appear very plain, but it is well adapted to the wants of the republic and purposes for which it was designed.

There are usually two evenings in the week during the Congressional season, when the stranger is privileged to pay his respects to the President, and promenade the east room of such celebrity. While Congress is in session the President usually gives official dinners about twice a week.

In front of the house stands a bronze statue of Jefferson, procured in Europe by Capt. Levy, United States Navy, and by him offered to the United States Senate, who refused to receive it; it being uniformly the practice of the Senate never to accept any gifts in their official capacity. He then gave it to John Tyler, President of the United States, and it was deposited in the vaults of the Executive mansion, from which it was rescued by some of our citizens, who contributed to building the pedestal upon which it at present stands, so that it does not belong to the United States Government, and it would be difficult to say who was the proper owner.

There have been many improvements in the public grounds under the superintendence of the late Mr. Downing. Mr. Breckenridge has been appointed to succeed him, and the grounds are gradually assuming an elegance which visitors will be highly pleased with. Lafayette Square, directly in front of the President's, shows the hand of a skilful artist, and will be one of the principal ornaments of the city when finished. In the middle of the square stands Mr. Mill's equestrian statue of Gen. Jackson.

NATIONAL OBSERVATORY.

The National Observatory, about a mile west from the President's, occupies a commanding site, and commands a beautiful view of the Potomac, Washington, and Georgetown. Under the direction of Lieut. Maury it has attained a reputation equal if not superior to any of the older observatories of long established reputation, and whose merits are acknowledged throughout the scientific world. At 12 m. a ball is dropped from a flag-staff, similar to the one at Greenwich, which enables navigators leaving the Potomac to regulate their time to a second, and also regulates the city time.

The chronometer room is one of great importance, and the most severe rules regulate it—upon the faithfulness with which they are observed depends the safety of our national vessels.

The visitor will be highly gratified in observing the splendid machinery attached to the large telescope: it is mounted in the revolving dome, which moves by this machinery.

There are many other things worthy of note. The visitor is recommended to go between the hours of 9 a. m. and 3 p. m., when they will find a person appointed to show them the building, who points out the various curiosities very politely, and, not like the usual Continental guides expects nothing in the way of a fee. You may now continue on to

GEORGETOWN.

It was formerly a place of considerable trade, and had a large commerce with the West Indies. The Heights of Georgetown form an important part of that city to be visited by the stranger to Washington; and while in Georgetown, recollect that the Georgetown College is well worthy of a visit, and where the stranger will meet with every attention. For description of the college, see another page.

Lately there has been many improvements going on. The new hotel is gradually earning a reputation due to the exertions of its proprietor, (Mr. Fitzhugh,) where you can stop and refresh, or continue on to

THE AQUEDUCT,

To which I will next call your attention. It has attracted the notice of every scientific architect in Europe and America; even Prince Albert's attention was called to it, though unfortunately he placed its locality upon the Delaware. It has stood the pressure of floods probably as severe as any that it will ever be called upon to endure. It rises forty-two and a half feet above the water, and is fourteen hundred and fifty feet long.

You may now take the stage and return to Washington, at a cost six cents, or five tickets for twenty-five cents. They will land you at any point up to the Capitol—to which I will then call your attention.

THE CAPITOL.

The cost of building the Capitol was nearly $2,000,000. Extensions on each side are now in course of progress, under the superintendence of the able architect, Thomas U. Walter, esq. The corner-stone was laid by his Excellency the President, July 4th, 1851, with Masonic honors; on which occasion, the late Secretary of State delivered an oration with his usual ability. The visitor will be able to observe the strength of the walls, and the construction of the basement, now nearly completed.

In the Capitol, the first point which calls the attention of the visitor is the Rotundo. The room is divided into eight panels, in which there are seven paintings, all national subjects, and the eighth panel will be filled with a painting representing De Soto discovering the Mississippi, now nearly finished, painting by the celebrated young painter, Mr. Powell, who has resided several years in Paris, from which city he may be expected shortly with his picture. The price paid for these paintings was $10,000 each. You will find hanging beneath each one an accurate drawing and explanation. There is a police attached to the Capitol, whom the visitor will always find very attentive and polite, always ready to give the visitors any information they may desire.

The Senate Chamber is in the north wing, and is very badly constructed for the purpose for which it was intended. Ionic columns, called a screen in architecture, supports the gallery. Ladies are sometimes admitted into the body of the house, when a speech is expected from some member of great fame. Peale's likeness of Washington, and a copy of the Declaration of Independence, are all the objects hanging on its walls in the way of fine arts.

The House of Representatives naturally comes next, and is in the south wing, directly opposite as you come from the Senate Chamber. It contains twenty-four columns of Potomac marble, which are well worthy of notice. There is a fine, full-length portrait of Washington and Lafayette on each side of the Speaker's platform. On the outside of the right hand window back of the Speaker's chair, is the sun-dial referred to in the following lines, which are placed in a small mahogany frame, in the hand-writing of the late Ex-president John Quincy Adams.

To the Sun-dial under the window of the Hall of the House of Representatives.

BY HON. JOHN QUINCY ADAMS.

Thou silent herald of Time's ceaseless flight,
Say, couldst thou speak, what warning voice were thine—
Shade who can only show how others shine—
Dark, sullen witness of resplendent light.

In day's broad glare, and when the noontide bright
Of laughing Fortune sheds the ray divine,
Thy ready favors cheer us—but decline
The clouds of morning and the gloom of night.

Yet are thy counsels faithful, just, and wise,
They bid us seize the moments as they pass,
Snatch the retrieveless sunbeam as it flies,
Nor lose one sand of L fe's revolving glass,
Aspiring still, with energy sublime,
By virtuous deeds to give eternity to time.

The galleries are extensive, and usually not so crowded as the Senate Chamber, being larger and not thought so attractive. Strangers may visit all parts of the House during the hours when Congress is not in session, ; but when sitting, only a few persons are privileged, though a member may introduce a friend into the lobby.

The officers and clerks are very efficient. In each House there are a number of well-dressed and active boys, called pages, who are ready to execute any message that the members may desire. The business of Congress is immense; but with the aid of its army of clerks, its business is despatched with great celerity. Next in order comes

THE LIBRARY,

So unfortunately destroyed by fire the last winter. It was lamentable to see the destruction, caused in a few hours, of works of art, and valuable and costly books impossible to be replaced. The fire, it is supposed, was caused by a defective flue, and the anxiety of the nation was intense in the cities reached by telegraph during the progress of the flames. President Fillmore and the officers of the Departments were on the ground, and every exertion was made to overcome the raging element, but water could not be had, owing to the intense cold. The visitor will now see an iron room, which has been in progress night and day during the recess of Congress, and there have been many books purchased, ready to place on the shelves when this extraordinary and beautiful work is completed.

If you look from the balcony leading from the library you will have a beautiful view of the city, extending in every direction, with a fine view of the Potomac, extending west until lost among the hills of Georgetown. Immediately below you is the monument erected to the memory of the brave men who fell at Tripoli, by their brother officers: it is of marble, and when first erected was put up at the Navy Yard, but was removed to its present position a few years since. It is situated in the centre of a pool of water filled with gold-fish, and is about forty feet in height. There are emblematic figures surrounding the base—Mercury, Fame, History, and America—and words to the memory of the heroes who fell before Tripoli. The naval heroes of England, perhaps somewhat jealous of the fame acquired by their American brethren, partially destroyed it when they were in possession of the Capitol, in 1814.

There is one point, however, which has been neglected. Of every engraving that is copyrighted, a copy is obliged to be deposited in this library and in the Smithsonian Institute. There should be a cheap frame furnished by Government, and the picture hung upon walls designed for the purpose. At present they are deposited in portfolios, and not one out of a thousand ever sees them.

The library is in charge of a librarian (John S. Meehan) and two assistants, who will furnish the visitor with any information that may be required. There is a committee of the two Houses appointed to regulate its affairs. It is open every day, while Congress is in session, and three times a week during the recess; and it is supposed, when the room is finished, and the books in their proper places, it will present an appearance superior and more beautiful than any other library in Europe or America.

SUPREME COURT ROOM.

In the basement you will find the highest judicial court in the United States—badly lighted, and badly ventilated: along dark passages and in an out of the way corner, you will find this room. It is to be hoped when the new extension is completed, a more suitable room will be appropriated for this august body. The Judges occupy chairs, and wear, in their official capacity, black robes, omitting the wigs usually worn by the English judges. In another place you will find the names of the Judges and officers of the court.

The statue of Columbus and the Indian girl, by Persico, is well worthy the attention of the visitor. It stands upon the eastern portico, which you will notice as the place where the Presidents have stood during their inauguration, and have addressed their fellow-citizens.

You now leave the Capitol, and directly in front you will see the celebrated statue of Washington, by Greenough, nearly in the centre of the lawn—a work of art worthy of the fame of its distinguished sculptor, but not likely to find much favor with the casual visitor. This statue formerly stood in the Rotundo of the Capitol, but was removed a few years since to its present site. The distinguished sculptor, lately deceased, received

$25,000 from Government for this beautiful work of art. It was brought to this country from Italy in the national ship Ohio, as it was found difficult to find an ordinary merchant ship able to carry it.

THE NAVY YARD

Will next call your attention. You will find an omnibus leaving Sixth street, on Pennsylvania avenue, and passing the Capitol grounds to the east of the Capitol, every few minutes, which lands you directly at the gate. The ground was selected by the Government in the year 1800, and occupies about twenty acres. The Commodore in command has a comfortable house appropriated to his use; the several officers attached to the yard also live in it.

Two large ship-houses will attract the attention of visitors, from one of which has been recently launched the steamer "Water Witch," to take the place of the old iron steamer of the same name. There is usually employed here from four to five hundred mechanics of the first class, who are generally intelligent, educated men, quiet and regular in their habits, and are gradually building up a town around the Yard, which makes a respectable appearance. The work done at this yard will compare favorably with any navy-yard in the Union.

In the blacksmith shop there is a *small* hammer weighing nearly two tons, and another about a ton. These are used in the manufacture of anchors for our largest ships of war, which are preferred to any made at any other yard. Chain cables of enormous size are made and tested by a machine made for the purpose. The machinery used in the different shops are of the most perfect and massive description. Ingenious experiments are being constantly made by the officers of the various branches in the service, and the intelligent and scientific visitor will receive instruction and profit in his journey through the yard. Admittance can at all times be had at proper hours. We will now take you to the

CONGRESSIONAL BURYING-GROUND

It is in the northeastern quarter, about a mile and a half from the Capitol, affording a pleasant ride on a good road, and contains ten acres of land on the Eastern Branch of the Potomac. A number of our distinguished men are buried here; and some fine monuments will pay the curiosity of the visitor for his excursion. Many of the inscriptions are interesting: A Minister from the Court of Prussia, who died in Washington in 1823; Judge Barbour, a Judge of the Supreme Court of the U. States; Gen. Jacob Brown; a Choctaw Chief, who died in 1824, in this city, and to whom a monument was erected by his brother chiefs; with several monuments erected to the memory of some who fell in the late Mexican war. A simple yet handsome style of monument has been designed for those members of Congress who have died in Washington, of which, at present, there are about one hundred and ten. Also the tomb of Elbridge Gerry, Vice President of the United States, who died at the age of 70.

We now return; and you can vary your ride by returning on Virginia avenue, a broad and well laid out street. You may now drive to the

Arsenal, passing by the United States Penitentiary, to visit which you will have to obtain an order from one of the inspectors, of whom there are three. For a full description see another place.

THE ARSENAL

Is situated at the foot of Four-and-a-half street. The water in front is deep, and a few years since the two steamers Mississippi and Missouri, (the latter unfortunately has been destroyed by fire in the Bay of Gibraltar,) anchored off the arsenal for the purpose of being visited by the members of Congress, the officers of government and citizens. In coming up from Alexandria, (the fare to and back varying from five to twelve and a half cents) there is a beautiful view of the arsenal, the river, the city, and the dome of the Capitol, which can be seen for miles around.

All kinds of ordnance are prepared at this arsenal, by the best and latest improvements in machinery adapted for the purpose. The machinery for making percussion caps is a wonder for those who have never seen these articles made. The turning machine invented by Blanchard, and bought by the United States government for $10,000, is here to be seen, turning out all kinds of irregular shapes; that which formerly occupied days in the construction, now takes but a few minutes; but for turning musket stocks is the chief use to which it is applied here.

The storehouses of the arsenal are spacious, and filled with warlike implements of all kinds, enough to supply any army the United States should see fit to bring into the field; many of them have also seen service in Mexico. The celebrated Bragg and Duncan battery is now peacefully laid aside here, which had so large a share in contributing to the result of the celebrated battle of Buena Vista. In the square you will see many old pieces that were used during the Revolution of '76, which are here preserved, and curious foreign cannon, (unknown how they came into the possession of the United States,) and some presented by the French Government after the battle of Yorktown. Inquire for the model office, and you will be much pleased if you are curious, in arms of old and new inventions. Two curiously-looking buildings, having the appearance of a pair of pyramids, contain machinery for testing the strength and quality of gunpowder. A heavy gun is put in a sling, and by the force with which it rebounds, its quality is tested. You can then call at the

SMITHSONIAN INSTITUTION.

The Smithsonian Institution derives its name and endowment from James Smithson, esq., of England.

Mr. Smithson was a son of the first Duke of Northumberland. He was educated at Oxford, where he distinguished himself by his scientific attainments. In 1787, the year after taking his Master's degree, he was elected a Fellow of the Royal Society. To the "Philosophical Transactions" he contributed, at different times, eight valuable papers. He was an associate of most of the eminent men of science of the last generation in England, and was much respected for his proficiency in the department of chemistry, as well as for his amiable and unassuming manners. He had no fixed residence, and formed no family ties. The last years of his life were spent mostly on the continent, and he died at Genoa, June 27th, 1829.

From the property which he received by his mother, and the ample annuity allowed him by his father, his frugality enabled him to accumulate a fortune, which, at the time of his death, amounted to 120,000 pounds sterling.

By his will, he directed that the income of this property, (after deducting some small annuities) should be paid to his nephew, Henry James Hungerford, during his life, and that the property itself should descend to his children, if he had any, absolutely and forever.

"In case of the death of my said nephew without leaving a child, or children, or of the death of the child or children he may have had, under the age of 21 years, or intestate, I then bequeath the whole of my property (subject to an annuity of 100 pounds to John Fitall, and for the security and payment of which, I mean stock to remain in this country,) *to the United States of America, to found at Washington, under the name of the Smithsonian Institution, an establishment for the increase and diffusion of knowledge among men.*"

Such are the words of the will, and the only words of Smithson which have come to us relating to this remarkable bequest.

Of the reasons which led him to make this disposal of his fortune, we know nothing except by inference. He was never in America, had no friends or acquaintances here, and is supposed to have had no particular fondness for republican institutions. No sentence among his papers, no book in his library, no recollection of his associates, shows that he had made our country an object of special thought and study. It was, we may suppose, to perpetuate his name as the friend and patron of science and learning that he made this bequest; and it is the highest compliment that he could pay our country, to select it as the trustee of his noble purposes, and to abstain from tramelling the legacy by any condition, restriction, reservation, or direction.

Young Hungerford died at Pisa, on the 5th of June, 1835, without issue. The event thus occurred in in which the claim of the United States attached. The particulars of the bequest were communicated to our government, and both Houses of Congress passed a bill, which was approved the first of July, 1836, authorizing the President to appoint an agent to prosecute, in the Court of Chancery of England, the right of the United States to the bequest; and pledging the faith of the United States to the application of the fund to the purposes designated by the donor.

Hon. Richard Rush, of Philadelphia, was by the President appointed the agent of the United States. He proceeded to England, instituted a suit in the Court of Chancery, recovered the fund and paid it into the Treasury of the United States, in sovereigns, during the month of September, 1838.

The amount of the fund at this time was $515,169. It was not till eight years after this period, 10th August, 1846, that the act establishing the Smithsonian was finally passed.

This act creates an establishment, to be called the Smithsonian Institution, composed of the President and Vice President of the United States, the Secretaries of State, of the Treasury, of War, and the Navy, the Postmaster General, Attorney General, and Mayor of Washington, with such others as they may elect Honorary Members. It devolves the immediate government of the Institution upon a Board of Regents, of fifteen members, namely, the Vice President of the United States, the Chief Justice of the Supreme Court, and the Mayor of the city of Washington, *ex officio*, three members of the Senate, to be appointed by the President thereof, three members of the House, to be appointed by the Speaker, and six persons to be chosen from the citizens at large, by joint resolution of the Senate and House, two of whom shall be members of the National Institute, and the other four inhabitants of States, and no two from the same State.

The act establishes a permanent loan of the original fund ($515,169) to the United States at six per cent. interest; appropriated the accumulated interest, then amounting to $242,129, or so much as might be needed, together with so much of the accruing income as might be unexpended in any year, for the erection of a building; provided for the establishment of a Library, Museum, Chemical Laboratory, &c., and left most of the details of the organization to the Board of Regents.

As the result of the conscientious labors of the Board of Regents, a plan of organization has been adopted, which seems to give universal satisfaction, and promises the widest usefulness.

The cost of the building was limited (with furniture, grading the grounds, &c.) to $250,000, to be taken mostly from the income of the original and building funds, so as to save $150,000 of the building fund, which will be added to the original fund, making a permanent fund of $675,000, yielding nearly $40,000 per annum. The building will, however, cost nearly $300,000; though by delaying the time of finishing, the original plan will be carried out.

The income is to be divided between two methods of increasing and diffusing knowledge—the first by publications, researches and lectures—the second by collections of literature, science and art.

Four volumes of a series entitled "Smithsonian Contributions to Knowledge," in 4to., have been issued; also, several works in a series of a more popular character, and in 8vo form, entitled "Smithsonian Reports." It is proposed, also, to publish, for still wider circulation, a monthly "Bulletin." Researches in various departments of science have been instituted or aided by the Institution, and several courses of free lectures have been delivered.

The various publications of the Institution have been very liberally distributed among the literary and scientific Institutions of this country and of foreign countries.

The Library has been commenced, and though the funds have not been available for its rapid growth, it has continued to increase by means of purchases, donations, and exchanges for the publications of the Institution, and is destined to be a valuable collection for reference and research. The cabinets of Natural History and of Art, have been commenced.

The following rules are those adopted for the distribution of the quarto volumes:

1. They are to be presented to all learned societies which publish transactions, and give copies of these, in exchange, to the Institution.

2. Also, to all foreign libraries of the first class, provided they give in exchange their catalogues or other publications, or an equivalent for their duplicate volumes.

3. To all the colleges in actual operation in this country, provided they furnish in return meteorological observations, catalogues of their libraries and their students, and all other publications issued by them relative to their organization and history.

4. To all States and Territories, provided there be given, in return, copies of all documents published under their authority.

5. To all incorporated public libraries in this country, not included in any of the foregoing classes, now containing more than 7000 volumes; and to smaller libraries, where a whole State or a large district would be otherwise unsupplied.

The building is in the later Norman or Lombard style. It consists of a centre and two wings, united by connecting ranges. Its extreme length is 447 feet, and its greatest breadth 132 feet. It is adorned by nine towers, the highest of which is 135 feet. The central portion of the building contains, on the first floor, a Library, and a large Lecture Room. The second story contains the Museum, 200 feet by 50. This is divided into three aisles, the centre aisle being 40 feet in height.

The east wing contains a small Lecture-Room. The eastern range contains laboratories, workshops, rooms for apparatus, offices, &c.

The western wing and range contains two large rooms, one of which will be used as a Reading-Room. Beneath are rooms for unpacking books, and other purposes of the Library.

WASHINGTON MONUMENT.

A feature which is likely every year to more and more beautify the place, and endear it in the hearts of the American people, is the erection here, from time to time, of monuments to the illustrious dead. In 1783, Congress voted an equestrian statue to General Washington at the future seat of Government; and in the plan of the city, the commissioners, selected a site at the west end of the Mall, near the Potomac, but, for the want of appropriations, it was never carried into execution. A monument was also voted to General Greene, to be erected at the seat of government, which for a like reason, only exists on the statute book. The subject of one to Washington has several times of late years been revived in Congress, but nothing more was done than to order a statue, which Greenough has executed. The National Monument Association collected, some years since, about $30,000, in subscriptions of one dollar, all over the country; this sum was well invested, and amounted, with the interest, to about $70,000. A new subscription was opened, under the direction of the Hon. Elisha Whittlesey, as general agent, and every encouragement has been received for believing that the building will be rapidly completed. The plan adopted is on a most extensive scale, comprising a grand pantheon, which may be commemorative of all the heroes of the Revolution. The site has been recently granted by Congress, and the erection has been commenced, which is visible from every point of the city, and is now about 120 feet high. The height to which it is intended to be raised is near 600 feet; higher than any building in the known world. As every stranger will visit this spot, he will see the plan upon which it is intended to be finished, and the various blocks contributed by individuals, States and societies—beautiful specimens of art from all parts of our common country. A piece of deception was practised in the quartz specimen from California. It cost $6,000; but on opening the case which contained it, it proved to be worthless. The name of the individual who perpetrated the fraud should be handed down to posterity along with that of *Erostratus*, who burnt the temple of Diana. The block from Michigan is a splendid piece of native copper, which you will not fail to inquire for. Visitors are presented with a book, in which they can register their names, and contribute any sum their means and inclination permits. We believe this is the only national monument we are to have; for, besides the obvious propriety of erecting one at the city founded by Washington, in the vicinity of his birth-place, and on ground expressly set apart for the purpose, when the place was established as the seat of government, and in Washington's lifetime, this is the only one of all the projects for which any considerable sum has been given from the people at large. A State may with propriety erect one, which, while it does honor to the Father of his Country, shall at the same time bear testimony more particularly to the part her own sons have taken in the contest for freedom; but there should be only one, peculiarly *national*, in order that it may be on a scale worthy of the nation, and that the subscriptions may not be divided amongst one at Washington, another at New York, and still another at some other place, which may present equal claims to the honor with the commercial emporium. Washington, too, is the only *neutral* spot, as being the only place without the precincts of any State, and common to the whole Union.

We now walk among the grounds, now being laid out from the designs of the late Mr. Downing and carried into execution by Mr. Breckenridge, who succeeded him in his office, crossing the canal to the Patent office, containing in the lower rooms, all the articles patented, which for a full description, see page 40, Congressional Directory. Also, in the second story is the rooms of the National Institute, a short catalogue, see page 44, Congressional Directory, which is extracted from a full one I am now engaged in preparing. To the right you will see the elegant hall, into which it is intended to remove the curiosities to give them more space, and which has been granted by Government for the use of the Mechanics' Institute of this city, who intend holding a fair here, which promises to be well supported by our citizens and inhabitants of the surrounding country.

We are now near the General Post Office, one of the finest buildings in Washington. It is built of white marble, designed and executed by Mr. Mills, the architect. It is three stories high, and contains about ninety rooms in all, but nothing more particular to attract the attention of the visitor. If you have business with the Department, a list of the clerks is appended, and directly in front, after you enter, you will find a room for inquiry, where you will be directed to any bureau you may desire. We next call your attention to the Treasury Department, which stands on Fifteenth street, in a prominent situation near Pennsylvania avenue, and cannot fail to please you with its general appearance; when finished it wil be near 500 feet long. In front is an immense colonnade, forming a screen of columns stretching the whole length of the building. In this building there is more business done than in any of the other Departments, and literally swarms with clerks. Washington, like the Bank of England, could furnish about two regiments of clerks to act as soldiers in case of necessity; and probably no country in the world could furnish a similar number of men, equal in talents, industry, and business capacity, as can be found in the different Departments of Washington City. You now turn north a few steps and you come to the State Department, the home of the Adamses, Clays and Websters of the country, an old fashioned building, not worthy of the wealth and power of the country. It has a handsome library, which is well kept, and if the visitor has an hour of leisure, he cannot better dispose of it than looking through the books of this Department. There are about 18,000 volumes, and a large quantity of copyright works, which are here carefully preserved. For a list of all the clerks in the Department, you will see the appropiate heads. We next direct your attention to the War Department, which you come to by crossing to the northwest corner of President Square. There is nothing particularly interesting to the casual visitor here; and if you have business with the Department, you will find the officers obliging and gentlemanly.

South from this is the Navy Department.

Much of the business of the Navy Department is carried on here; but there is a building called Winder's building, where many of the offices of Government are located.

Between the War and Navy Departments is an extraordinary piece of copper, brought from the banks of the river Ontonagon, near Lake Superior, to which the natives attached an extraordinary history. This piece of copper was known over two hundred years ago. The Jesuits, who first visited this part of the country, first heard of it from the Indian priests, and were anxious to be conducted to the spot where it lay; but an ancient superstition concerning it prevented the Indians from conducting them to the spot; they believed that when the white man had seen it, the Indians would be destroyed, and the control of the country pass away from their hands. It was the general belief that the evil Manitou resided therein, and it was used as a place of sacrifice. We have the following account by Father Charlevoix, in a letter to his Superior:

HEAD OF LAKE SUPERIOR.

REV. AND DEAR SIR: As you are aware, I was sent the last spring, by the Right Rev. Bishop of Quebec, on an exploring expedition, in order to ascertain the disposition of the Indians, and the prospect of success we might have if we were to establish a mission in the country. In my first voyage to the country I had heard of the Manitou of the savages, which was of pure copper, and used as a place of sacrifice. The natives, though addicted to the practice of lying and stealing, yet (what must appear wonderful) are in some respects believers with regard to a future life, and display a Pharisaical punctuality in the observance of their religious rites. The Indians believe that they will die if they should communicate the locality of their Manitou to strangers. The most common worship among them is a sacrifice of birds, which are filled with herbs and roots, and living animals. They suppose that this Manitou had been sent to their ancestors by the Morning Star, to be their mediator when they should stand in need of some particular favor. In order to render the spirit more propitious to them, they smoke the calumet, and cover the rock with the first smoke that issues from it. They imagine it often speaks to them and demands a human sacrifice in a voice of thunder; and, on solemn occasions, a human sacrifice was added to the oblation of the calumet; and the priests, according to what they pretend to have learned from the Great Spirit, that an enemy be immolated, which is done in the most cruel manner. I listened with horror to the circumstances that attended the sacrifice of a young female who had been taken prisoner during an excursion of a war party of the natives. An expedition had been resolved upon, and they thus thought to insure success and the favor of their powerful Manitou. The young maiden was only fifteen years old. After having a lodge appointed for her use, attendants to meet every wish, her neck, arms, and ancles covered with bracelets of silver and copper, and she was led to believe she was to be the bride of the son of the head chief. The time appointed was the end of winter; and she felt rejoiced as the time rolled on, waiting for the season of her happiness. The day fixed upon for the sacrifice having dawned, she passed through all the preparatory ceremonies, and was dressed in her best attire, covered with all the ornaments the settlement could command, after which she was placed in the midst of a circle of warriors dressed in their war suits, who seemed to escort her for the purpose of showing her deference. Besides their usual arms, each one carried several pieces of wood which he had received from the girl She had carried wood to the rock on the preceding day, which she had helped gather in the forest. Believing she was to be elevated to a high rank, her ideas being of the most pleasing character, the poor girl advanced to the altar with rapturous feelings of joy and timidity, which would naturally be raised in the bosom of a young female of her age.

As the procession proceeded, which occupied some time, savage music accompanied them, and chants, invoking the intervention of their Manitou, that the Great Spirit would prosper their enterprise; so that, being excited by the music and dancing, the deceitful delusion under which she had been kept remained till the last moment. But as soon as they had reached the place of sacrifice, where nothing was to be seen but fires, torches, and instruments of torture, her eyes were opened—her fate was revealed to her, and she became aware of her horrible destiny, as she had often heard of the mysterious sacrifices of the Copper Rock. What must have been her feelings! how great her surprise! how terrible the change, when she no longer had any doubt of their intentions! Who could describe the terrible horror of the moment! She shed tears of blood; her cries resounded through the forest; but neither tears nor entreaties prevailed. She conjured the stern warriors who surrounded her to have pity on her youth, her innocence, but all in vain; the Indian priests coolly proceeded with the horrid ceremonies. Nothing could prevail against their superstition, and the horrid demands of the copper monster, who called for a human sacrifice. She was tied with withs to the top of the rock. The fire was gradually applied to her body with torches made of the wood which she had with her own hands distributed to the warriors. When exhausted with her cries, and about expiring, her tormentors opened the circle that had surrounded her, and the great chief shot an arrow into her heart, which was followed by the spears and arrows of his followers, which, after being turned and twisted in the wounds, were torn from her body in such a manner that it presented but one shapeless mass of human flesh, and the blood poured down the glistening sides of the rock in streams. When the blood had ceased to flow, the high priest approached the body of the victim, and, to crown the horrible deed, tore out her heart, and after invoking the blessing of the bloody Manitou, devoured the bleeding flesh, amid the acclamations of the whole tribe. The mangled remains were then left to be destroyed by wild beasts. Their weapons were sprinkled with her blood, to render them invincible, and all retired to their cabins cheered and encouraged with the hope of a glorious victory. At the sight of so much cruelty, who could mistake the agency of the enemy of mankind? and who would refuse to exert himself for these benighted nations? * * * * *

Reverend and dear Father, yours,

PETERFRANCIS XAVIER DE CHARLEVOIX.

The good father did not get a sight of the rock; he was conducted to a spot where he was told it was situated, but nothing was to be seen; and the savages attempted to persuade him that the Spirit was displeased with their intrusion, and had disappeared. One of the Jesuits at Montreal, who had been at the place, was told by the Indians that it was about seven feet long and five feet thick, and was bright and yellow as gold. They seemed to regard it with great veneration. Henry, a trader, who, soon after the conquest of Canada by the English, set out on a trading voyage to Fort Mackinaw, and was preseut at the dreadful massacre of the whole garrison, and was saved by being adopted as a brother by one of the Indians. Referring to his interesting and truthful narrative for an account of his voyage and perils, he says: "On my way back to Michilimackinac, I encamped at the mouth of the Ontanagon river, and now took the opportunity of going ten miles up the river with the Indian guides. The object for which I had expressly went, and to which I had the satisfaction of being led, was the great sacrificial rock, which I found to be a mass of copper, of the weight, according to my estimate, of no less than five tons. (This is the copper rock now on the ground near the War Department, in Washington.—Charles T. Jackson, U. S. Geologist.) Such was its pure and malleable state, that with an axe I was able to cut off a portion weighing near a hundred pounds. On viewing the surface, I conjectured that the mass at some period or other had rolled from the side of a lofty hill which rises at its back; but how it came there I am at a loss to conceive, unless the Indian account be correct, that it was brought there by supernatural means." In more modern times we have the observations of Henry R. Schoolcraft, who accompanied Gen. Cass in his travels on the lake, and who visited the great block of native copper at Ontonagon. And soon after the last war with England, Dr. Francis Le Baron of Plymouth visited Lake Superior, and brought home a piece of the great copper rock of the Ontonagon.

In the year 1841 J. Eldred procured from an Indian agent a license to trade with the Indians on Lake Superior, and purchased from Okondokon, the head chief of the Ontonagon tribe, the large mass of copper usually called the copper rock, then lying in the bed of the Ontonagon river, for the sum of one hundred and fifty dollars. Eldred employed a large force of men, and with boats ascended the Ontonagon river to the rapids, then crossed over the mountain to the rock, which they raised on skids, but were unable to remove it to the boats. In 1842 he made another effort to remove the rock, but did not succeed. He then prepared at Detroit a portable iron railway and car, and with a capstan, tackle and blocks, in the year 1844, succeeded, with the assistance of 20 men, in removing it to the shore of the lake, where it was claimed by Gen. Cunningham as the property of the United States. Cunningham agreed that if Eldred would give up the rock, he should be paid for his time and expenses in removing it to Detroit; and that when government should remove it to Washington, Eldred should act as the agent of Government, and be compensated for his services. It appears in 1843 the Secretary of War wrote to Cunningham to take possession of the copper rock, and to have it shipped to the Sault, thence to be taken on board the revenue cutter, on Lake Erie.

Eldred, according to agreement, removed it to Detroit, when the officers of Government took charge of it, and were at the expense of bringing it to Washington, and deposited it where it now lies. The object of Eldred in procuring this mass of copper was to exhibit it as a great natural curiosity in this country and in Europe. He had thought of it a long time previous to his first attempt, and persuaded his sons to assist him in his design. The committee of Congress came to the conclusion that as he acted under the direction of the Secretary of War in delivering up the rock, and was promised to be reimbursed for his time and expenses, he should be paid, and was paid, by order of Congress, the sum of $5,654 98, for one of the most remarkable mineral specimens in the known world.

The Department of the Interior is a new branch of the Government, and the building intended for it is not yet completed. It has a very valuable library, but not so extensive as the other Departments. The Patent, Census, Land, Indian, and Pension offices, National Institute, &c., are all connected with this Department.

As you pass on Pennsylvania avenue to 4½ street, you will see the City Hall, a large building, well adapted for the use of the city. The members of council, mayor's office, as well as the circuit and criminal courts hold their sessions here.

I now call your attention to Mount Vernon, that hallowed spot to which every American approaches with so much veneration, and is undoubtedly the Mecca of America, which every visitor to the city will wish to see. It is about fourteen miles from Washington, and the usual mode of getting there is by steamboat which leaves, (see Congressional Directory, page 56.)

The mansion, which is of wood, the appearance of which every American is familiar with, is situated on the bank of the Potomac, from which a view can be had of the river some twenty-five miles. It was named after Admiral Vernon, under whom the brother of Washington served, who built the main building; the wings were added by Washington himself. Many of the plants in the green-house, and tropical fruits, were planted by Washington's own hands. Unfortunately, a few years since, the green-house was destroyed by fire, which injured a great many of them. The noble sarcophagus, in which the remains of Washington and his consort Martha are deposited, were presented by a public-spirited citizen of Pennsylvania, by the name of Strothers. When the British captured Washington city, in descending the river, upon passing Mount Vernon, the yards were manned, and Mount Vernon saluted in memory of Washington. There are some pictures of the Washington family, to be seen in the house, and a key of the Bastile, presented to Washington by Lafayette—that building which caused so many tears, and witnessed so much tyranny, now surmounted by the column of July, and the burial place of its victims. It has been often agitated that Government should buy this estate, and it should do so. We see lately a foreign government expending $500,000 te bury its great general in St. Paul's. Ours could well appropriate a less sum for Washington. The contributions at the polls of the late election show that the people will sanction every measure of the general government in showing regard to his memory.

"It was, many years ago, proposed that the United States should become the proprietors of the estate of Mount Vernon, and maintain it in memory of the Father of his Country, in the precise condition in which he left it. It was urged that the family, after being multiplied, could not afford to keep up the place, which had always been an expense to General Washington and his nephew, the Justice; that even the remains of Washington were not safe there, without greater care of them, as had been once proved by the abstraction from the old vault of a coffin supposed by the robber to contain those of the General; that the family ought not to be burdened with the necessary attention to visitors, who in vast numbers flock to the place from all parts of the Union, and, indeed, of the world; and, in fine, that it was the duty of the Government to take care of the spot where the remains of the hero repose, and render it accessible also to all those of his countrymen, who in time to come might make a pilgrimage to his tomb.

"It is understood that there is a large sum in the Treasury, which has escheated to it in consequence of the decease, without heirs, of sailors and marines in the navy. The whole amount is estimated at three millions. There is a large sum due on account of prize money alone.

"The government does not claim this fund, but merely the right of its safe-keeping. There is no chance that it will ever be called for. It would be very proper, therefore, to appropriate the sum, or a portion of it, to the purchase of Mount Vernon, and the establishment there of an institution for the benefit of invalid and superannuated seamen and mariners. If the fund does not belong to them, it belongs to nobody. It would seem that they have, as a body, a right to all its benefits, at least to the benefit of the interest of the fund."

The steamboat bell rings, and you will reach the city in time to take an early supper and visit the theatre, which you will find on Pennsylvania avenue near 13th street.

THE UNITED STATES PENITENTIARY FOR THE DIST. OF COLUMBIA,

Situated at the south end of Four-and-a-half street, is a building built of brick, surrounded by a high wall, and well adapted to the purposes for which it is built. In order to visit it, it is necessary to have an order from one of the inspectors, which having obtained, will enable you to visit the interior, and where you will be received with much politeness by the officers in attendance, and who will show you over the building, explaining the parts, and the various branches of manufacture carried on in the Penitentiary.

There are 80 prisoners confined here, who are received mostly from the District of Columbia, and a few from the western part of Virginia.

There are various mechanical arts carried on here, such as coaches, wagons, furniture of various kinds, meat safes, brooms; and more particularly the shoe business is carried on pretty extensively. The articles are made and finished in the best manner, and sold, both at wholesale and retail, at very reasonable prices. The prison labors under the disadvantage of having no shop where they can expose the articles for sale, and perhaps few persons are aware of the variety and goodness of the articles made. A very handsome coach is sold for about $250; carryalls, strong and neatly made, varying in price from $100 to $125; and a strong grocer's wagon from $75 to $100; handsome boots and shoes of every kind and every price, and to suit every taste. There is a very neat chapel, suitably provided with seats, where divine service is performed every Sunday by a regularly-appointed chaplain, service commencing at

10 o'clock in the morning. Before and after the service, the convicts are marched through the yards for exercise, and afterwards attend afternoon service. The wards are well arranged, and capable of accommodating many more prisoners than are ever likely to be confined here. The cells are clean, and appear to be well adapted for the safe-keeping of the prisoners, and to make them as comfortable as circumstances will permit. The comfort, cleanliness, and order displayed, show that the warden and officers are attentive to their duties, and feel the responsibility of their respective situations.

The prisoners are well fed, being allowed coffee and tea morning and evening, fresh meat every day, excepting Friday, when they are served with fish and rice, and on Sundays an alteration is made, and they have a change of diet.

It will be a pleasure to the observant visitor to visit the bake-house. Everything is remarkably clean and neat. Bread is baked three times a week, in loaves of a size sufficient for a day's consumption of each convict, of good, wholesome bread, made of wheat flour. There is a blacksmith shop, where the iron work used in the construction of the wagon and coach department is made; but the principal portion of the convicts are employed in the shoe department, in which there are 45 engaged; carpenters, 8; blacksmiths, 2: tailoring, shoemaking, &c., 8; baking and cooking, 2; barber, 1; picking oakum, 9; laborers and servants, 3. Of the infirm, unable to work, there is 1; and at present only 1 on the sick list.

In the infirmary, which is well supplied with every variety of medicine, a small library is placed, to which the prisoners have access, presented by that eminent philanthropist, Miss Dix, consisting of religious works calculated to benefit and instruct the readers.

Congress makes an annual appropriation for the support of the prison. The last one, for the year ending June, 1853, which is the end of the fiscal year, was $9,212. The amount sold in the year 1850 was $5,676; in 1851, $11,635; in 1852, $11,353; and the amount of cash received in the same years was, 1850, $5,362; 1851, $7,677; 1852, $10,839; from the sales of articles manufactured by the convicts: showing a state of financial affairs very flattering to the officers of the institution, and one that has never been equalled at the prison heretofore.

The number of convicts at the end of the year, Dec. 31, 1851, was		66
Received during the year - - - - - - -		40
Making a total of - - - - - - -		106
The number discharged by expiration of sentence during the year was - - - - - - - -	22	
Pardoned by the President of the United States - -	2	
Deaths - - - - - - - - -	2	
		26
Remaining for the commencement of the new year - -		80
Of which there were white males, - - - -	43	
white females - - - -	3	

colored males - - -	29
colored females - - -	5
	80

The inspectors of the Prison, Messrs. Thomas Donaho, Wm. H. Edes, and Dr. Harvey Lindsey, receive a salary of $100 per annum, visit the prison once a week, and have the general supervision of the affairs of the prison. The regular officers are—

Mr. Jonas B. Ellis, warden, salary $1,500.
James H. Shekell, clerk, $1,000.
Francis Miller, Thomas Mitchell, } assistant keepers, $750.

There are four guards, who take turns alternately on the walls and in the interior of the prison, and who are required to superintend the mechanical operations of the prisoners.

Edward Short, $650.
Dennis Calaghan, George W. Johnson, Wilfred Van Reswick, } $550 each.
John King, messenger, $350.
Noble Young, physician, $500.
Austin Gray, chaplain, $250.

INAUGURATIONS

OF

THE PRESIDENTS OF THE UNITED STATES.

In view of the approaching inauguration of General Pierce, it will be interesting to have a description of the ceremonies that have formerly taken place in the inauguration of the Chief Magistrate of the United States—commencing with General Washington, the first President, who was inducted into office, in the city of New York, in 1789, to President Fillmore, in 1850, who succeeded to office by the death of the lamented Taylor

On the 1st of May, 1789, Washington was inaugurated President of the United States. The ceremony which took place was truly grand and pleasing. His Excellency was escorted from his house by a troop of light dragoons, and the legion under the command of the well-known Col. Morgan Lewis, attended by a committee of the House and Senate, to Federal Hall, where he was received by both Houses of Congress, assembled in the Senate Chamber, at 12 o'clock, m., conducted to the gallery in front of the City Hall, accompanied by all the members, when the oath prescribed by the constitution was administered to him by Chancellor Livingston, who then said "Long live Gen. Washington, President of the United States," which was received with great applause by the citizens assembled. Washington then addressed the two Houses of Congress, and afterwards attended divine service in St. Paul's church, after which his Excellency proceeded in form to his own house. In the evening there were fireworks, and the houses of the French and Spanish ministers were brilliantly illuminated, and many beautiful transparencies exhibited to the public. The building in which the ceremony took place was then the City Hall of New York, where the splendid New York Custom House now stands.

In 1793, Washington was again re-elected, upon which occasion the following ceremonies took place: On Monday, March 4, a number of the members of the Senate, the Speaker and members of the late House of Representatives, together with the Heads of Departments, Judges of the Supreme Court, &c., with foreign ministers, together with a great many ladies and gentlemen of distinction, assembled in the Senate Chamber at 12 m. The President entered the Hall. The President *pro tem.* then arose and said: "Sir, one of the Judges of the Supreme Court is now present and ready to administer to you the oath required by the constitution to be taken by the President of the United States." The President then made a short address, when Judge Cushing read the oath, which the President repeated after him, sentence by sentence, as follows:

"I. George Washington, do solemnly swear that I will faithfully execute the office of President of the United States, and will, to the best of my ability, preserve, protect, and defend the constitution of the United States."

The President was saluted by three cheers of the people, and then retired.

In 1797, John Adams, who was then elected President, gave notice, soon after his election, to both Houses of Congress, that he would attend in the Chamber of the House of Representatives to take his oath of office, according to the requirements of the constitution. Accordingly, agreeably to the notice, on Saturday, at 12 o'clock, the President took his seat in the chair of the Speaker—the Vice President, the late President and the Secretary of the Senate on the right; the Speaker and Clerk of the House on his left; the Chief Justice and the Associate Judges at a table in the centre; the foreign ministers, ambassadors, Heads of Departments, Gen. Wilkinson, Commander-in-Chief, and a large auditory from the city. The

President proceeded to address the audience; and, after concluding, he descended from his seat to receive the oath of office from the Chief Justice, who pronounced it with great solemnity, which was repeated by the President in an audible and solemn manner. Having taken the oath, he resumsd his seat—after sitting a moment, rose, bowed to the audience, and retired.

In 1801 Thomas Jefferson was elected President of the United States. On Wednesday, March 2d, he addressed the following letter to the Speaker, to be laid before the House:

WASHINGTON, *March* 2, 1801.

SIR: I beg leave, through you, to inform the Hon. House of Representatives of the United States, that I shall take the oath which the constitution prescribes to the President of the United States before he enters on the execution of his office, on Wednesday, the 4th instant, at 12 o'clock, in the Senate Chamber.

I have the honor to be, &c.,

THOMAS JEFFERSON.

Accordingly, at 12 o'clock, on the 4th of March, Mr. Jefferson appeared in the Senate Chamber, accompanied by numerous friends and official personages, when he delivered an address, and at 12 o'clock took the oath. The assemblage of people was immense; and immediately after the inauguration several discharges of artillery took place. There were about a thousand persons in the Senate Chamber, besides the members of the legislature, and about one hundrod and fifty ladies. The address of the President was referred to a committee of the Senate, who, on Monday, reported the form of a reply. Aaron Burr the next morning took his seat in the Senate as President of that body, and Vice President of the United States. This was the first inaugural that took place in the city of Washington.

In 1805 President Jefferson was re-elected to office, and George Clinton, sen., elected Vice President, in place of Mr. Burr, who, on Friday, March 2d, took leave of the Senate in a handsome speech of some length. On Monday, March 4th, the President and Vice President were sworn in. The concourse of spectators was immense. Four of the Judges of the Supreme Court attended—Chief Justice Marshall, Cushing, Patterson, and Washington. The Vice President was barely sworn in when the company dispersed.

The civil, military and navy officers, were there in great numbers, and among them the gallant Preble was distinguished with great pleasure.

In 1809, Mr. Madison succeeded Thomas Jefferson as President of the United States. On the 4th March, his Excellency appeared in the hall of the House of Representatives, to take the oath of office, before an immense concourse of spectators, and delivered his inaugural address. In a bill brought before the House on February 28, it appears that the executive mansion upon this occasion was newly and splendidly furnished. On the 4th of March, 1813, Madison was re-elected President for the next four years. The oath of office was administered by Chief Justice Marshall, in the presence of many members of Congress, judges of the Supreme Court, foreign ministers, and a great concourse of ladies. The President was escorted to the Capitol by the cavalry of the District, and was received by companies from Georgetown and Alexandria and the military of Washington. The scene was brilliant, at the same time it was solemn and truly repub ican. Previous to taking the oath, the President delivered an elegant and appropriate address. In the evening there was a ball at Davis' Hotel, probably at that time the leading fashionable resort, at which were present the President, the foreign ministers and most of the distinguished ladies and gentlemen of the city. Mr. Clay, at the adjournment of this Congress, received the thanks of the House for the able manner in which he had discharged the duty of Speaker.

In 1817, James Monroe was elected to the head of the Government, and on Thursday, March 4, was sworn into office with the following ceremonies: The ceremony and the spectacle were simple, but grand, animating and impulsive. At half past 10 a. m. the President, and with him the Vice President, left his residence, attended by a large number of citizens on horseback, and reached the Congress Hall a little before 12. At the same time the Ex-President and the Judges of the Supreme Court arrived.

All having entered the Senate Chamber, the Vice President took the chair, and the oath of office was administered to him. This ceremony having ended, the Vice President, Judges, Senate and marshals of the day, attended the President to the elevated portico, erected for the occasion, when, in the presence of the assembled multitude, he delivered his opening address. Having concluded, the oath was administered to him, by the Chief Justice of the United States. The oath was announced by a single gun, followed by a salute of artillery on the ground and at the Navy-yard. The President on his arrival was received with military honors by the military companies of the District, and also upon h s return. It was estimated about 10,000 people were on the ground. The President and lady received at their dwelling the visits of their friends and of the Heads of Departments. The evening concluded with a ball at Davis's, which was attended by the President and family.

In 1821, President Monroe was re-elected for the next four years. The 4th f March coming on Sunday, the President attended on Monday, the 5th, to take the oath of office, which was administered by Chief Justice Marshall, and notwithstanding the day proved very inclement, a great deal of snow having fallen the previous night, an immense crowd thronged the doors of the Capitol. The ceremony took place in the hall of the House of Represent ti es. On the entrance of the President, the music of the marine band enlivened the scene. The President was placed on the platform in front of the Speaker's chair. The Chief Justice stood by his side during the delivery of his speech. The Judges of the Supreme Court, President of the Senate, Speaker of the House, the Heads of Departments, and many distinguished military and naval officers were near him. The seats in the interior were principally occupied by ladies, and around, above and below, were countless numbers of the people, who were admitted without discrimination, after the ladies and privileged persons were seated.

In 1825, John Quincy Adams succeeded to the Presidency, and was inaugurated as usual, on Friday, the 4th March. At an early hour the approaches to the Capitol were throng d, and about nine o'clock the crowd began to accumulate, and although ladies were allowed admittance, entrance was effected with much difficulty, and not without severe struggles upon the part of their attendants.

Towards 12 o'clock the military received the President, his predecessor, and several officers of the Government. The cavalry led the way and the procession moved towards the Capitol, attended by thousands of citizens. The President was attended by the marshal, on horseback. At the Capitol he was received by the marine corps, stationed in front of the Capitol, whose excellent band of music saluted on their entrance into the building.

The galleries, though filled to overflowing, were remarkable for the stillness and decorum which prevailed. At twenty minutes past 12 the marshals made their appearance, with the officers of both Houses of Congress, who entered with the President elect. He was followed by the Ex-President and family, Judges of the Supreme Court, in their robes of office, and members of the Senate, preceded by the Vice President.

Mr. Adams, in a plain suit of black, ascended the steps to the Speaker's Chair and took his seat. The Chief Justice was in front of the clerk's table, having before him another table on the floor of the hall. On the opposite side sat the remaining judges with their faces to the chair. Mr. Adams then read his address, which occupied about forty minutes, when, as soon as it was finished, a general plaudit commenced in the galleries.

The President then placed himself on the right hand side of the table, and received from the Chief Justice a volume of the Laws of the United States, from which he read the oath of office. General Jackson was present on the occasion, and was among the earliest who took the hand of the President. Shortly after 1 o'clock the procession commenced leaving the hall. The President was then escorted back as he came, and on his arrival at his residence received the compliments of a great many of his friends. This inauguration approached very near in form to that of the second inauguration of Madison.

In 1829, Andrew Jackson was elected to succeed Mr. Adams, who was in office four years. On Wednesday, March 4th, at 11 o'clock, John C. Calhoun was sworn into office as Vice President, and took the chair of the Senate. At half past 11 o'clock the President elect appeared in the Senate Chamber, attended by the marshal of the District and the committee of arrangements, and took his seat immediately in front of the Secretary's desk. The Judges of the Supreme Court soon after entered and were seated on the right of the President's chair. The foreign ministers with their suites in their official costume were on the left A large number of ladies were present, and occupied seats in the rear of the senators. The western gallery was reserved for members of the House of Representatives. At 12 o'clock the Senate adjourned to the eastern portico of the Capitol, where, in the presence of an immense concourse of spectators, filling the portico, the steps, and the enclosure, the President delivered his inaugural address; and having concluded, the oath was administered to him by Chief Justice Marshall. Salutes were fired by artillery stationed near the Capitol, which were repeated by the forts, and at the Navy-Yard. When the President retired the procession was re-formed, and he was conducted to the Presidential mansion. This was altogether a civic procession; the old hero having positively declined an escort or anything like a military programme. On his arrival at his residence he received the congratulations of thousands upon his accession to the Presidency. The number of persons present was estimated at about ten or twelve thousand.

In 1833 President Jackson was again re-elected for the next four years, and Martin Van Buren Vice President. On Tuesday the President and Vice President, at the hour of 12, repaired to the Hall of the House of Representatives, and in the presence of a number of senators, representatives, foreign ministers, public officers of the United States, and a great concourse of ladies and citizens, each took the oath of office, which was administered to them by the Chief Justice of the United States. The President delivered an address. The Vice President made no speech to the assembled public upon this occasion.

In 1837 Martin Van Buren succeeded Gen. Jackson as President of the United States, and Richard M. Johnson, Vice President. The Senate met on Saturday, the 4th of March, at 10 o'clock, and was called to order by Mr. King. The Vice President elect was conducted to the Secretary's table by Senator Grundy, and the oath to support the constitution of the United States having been taken, he took his seat as President of the Senate, when he rose and addressed the Senate in a short speech. At 12 o'clock the late Chief Magistrate, with his successor by his side, took his seat in the beautiful phaeton built of the wood of the frigate Constitution, and presented to him by the citizens of New York city, and preceded by a splendid escort of cavalry and infantry, with a fine band of music, proceeded to the Capitol, through Pennsylvania avenue. A lovely day of brightest sunshine gladdened every heart. The avenue, more than a mile in extent, was thronged with citizens from every quarter of the Union, dressed in holiday suits, and cheering with eager salutations. An immense crowd filled the square on the east front of the Capitol. The procession proceeded to the Senate Chamber, when it was formed anew, and proceeded, with the two Presidents, members of the Senate, Cabinet, and the foreign ministers in their splendid robes, to the rostrum erected on the ascent to the eastern portico. Mr. Van Buren then delivered his inaugural address in clear and impressive tones; and at the close the oath of office was administered by Chief Justice Taney. Nothing disturbed the profound interest which those within the reach of the speaker's voice gave to the address, while the organ of our civil institutions spoke in the gentlest tones, and was listened to with rapt attention. The thunder of our cannon, which spoke the prowess of our country abroad, rolled over the Capitol and died away in silence upon the distant air. Mr. Webster and Mr. Clay were both present at the inauguration, whose spirits are eclipsed in the day that has passed from light unto darkness. The President immediately after the ceremony was escorted to the Presidential mansion, when he received the congratulations of the numerous citizens and foreigners, whose sense of democracy gave them a kind impulse to American liberty, civil and religious.

In 1841 Gen. Harrison succeeded Mr. Van Buren as President. For several days previous to Friday, the 4th March, the metropolis of the nation had been gradually filling with visitors from the most distant States of the Union. At sunrise, on the

4th, a salute of twenty-six guns was fired from the mall by a party of the artillery. Soon after the entire body of our citizens and numerous visitors thronged Pennsylvania avenue and the principal streets. The throng continued to increase until eight o'clock, when the various delegations and military companies assembled at their posts. Soon after 10 the procession moved toward the quarters of the President elect. Having there received him, the procession moved down Pennsylvania avenue to the south gate of the eastern yard of the Capitol. The cheers of the citizens who lined the Avenue, and the appearance of Gen. Harrison, who returned the greetings of the ladies, was exhilirating. The military portion of the procession was remarkably fine, consisting of five companies. After the officers and soldiers who fought under Gen. Harrison, came the President elect, mounted on a white charger, accompanied by a suite of personal friends. On his right were the marshal and his aids. The approaches to the Capitol were such as to gratify the eye of a painter. In the Senate Chamber, though reserved for the privileged persons, there was a crowd at an early hour. The Senate having been called to order by the Secretary, the oath of office was administered to Mr. King, who was reelected President *pro tem.* of that body. The diplomatic corps entered the hall, and assumed the seats in front and left of the Chair—a most brilliant appearance they made, covered with the different insignia of their orders. On the opposite side appeared the Judges of the Supreme Court. The late Vice President and Vice President elect were in attendance; when Mr. Tyler, having been presented to the presiding officer, took the oath, and ascending the chair which was vacated by Mr. King, delivered an address to the Senate of moderate length. At 20 minutes past 12, Gen. Harrison made his appearance, and took the seat prepared for him at the secretary's table. In a few minutes the procession was formed to the platform prepared for the ceremony of inauguration, erected on the east front of the Capitol. The new President forthwith proceeded to read his address to the nation. Previous to delivering the closing sentences, the oath was tendered to him by the Chief Justice, in tones loud, distinct, and solemn; after which the President pronounced the remaining part of his address. The cannon then announced to the country that it had a new Chief Magistrate. The procession then re-formed, and the President was escorted to his residence, where thousands paid their personal respects to the Chief Magistrate of the Union. The close of the day was marked by salutes of artillery, and the evening by balls and places of amusement open, at several of which, in the course of the evening, the President attended, and was received with the warmest marks of respect and attachment.

In consequence of the decease of President Harrison, on the 4th of April, 1841, John Tyler, Vice President, assumed the Presidential chair. At 12 o'clock on the morning of April 6, 1841, the Heads of the Departments called at his residence, when the President took and subscribed to the following oath of office:

I do solemnly swear that I will faithfully execute the office of President of the United States, and will, to the best of my ability, preserve, protect, and defend the constitution of the United States. JOHN TYLER.

April 6, 1841.

DISTRICT OF COLUMBIA,
City and County of Washington, } *ss.*

I, William Cranch, Chief Judge of the Circuit Court of the District of Columbia, certify that the above named John Tyler personally appeared before me this day, and although he deems himself qualified to perform the duties and exercise the powers and office of President, on the death of W. H. Harrison, late President of the United States, and without any other oath than that which he has taken as Vice President, yet, as doubts may arise, and for greater caution, took and subscribed the foregoing oath before me. W. CRANCH.

April 6, 1841.

1845, succeeding President Tyler, James K. Polk was elected President of the United States, and George M. Dallas, Vice President. On Tuesday, the 4th March, the weather was very unfavorable, which marred the brilliancy of the display. At sunrise a discharge of artillery announced the important day. Between 11 and 12 o'clock the President elect leit his residence, and the procession took up the line of march, making a very handsome display—there being eleven companies from the District and neighboring cities. The Empire Club, from the city of New York, followed the military. The whole under the direction of marshal McCalla. Next the military and naval officers and reverend clergy.

The President elect rode in an open carriage, escorted by Gen. Hunter, marshal of the District; the carriage was escorted by the Fairfax cavalry. After the carriage came various corporate bodies and distinguished civilians; the professors and students of Georgetown College closed the procession. When at the Capitol a most interesting scene took place. The avenues to the building had been closely guarded till the hour appointed in the plan of proceedings, and when that hour arrived the rush was fearful. The gentlemen's gallery in the Senate Chamber was crowded in a moment; the ladies occupied the gallery opposite, but had to leave their escort behind, as their was no admittance for gentlemen. When the senators had taken their seats in a semicircle on the right of the chair of the President of the Senate, the oath of office was administered to Mr. Dallas, who immediately took his seat, after which he delivered a brief address. While speaking, the diplomatic corps entered and took seats on the left, opposite the judges. At length the actual and elect Presidents arrived, when a procession was formed to the eastern portico. Here a stage had been erected, and Mr. Polk read his address in a firm tone, and with the air of a man impressed with its importance. The oath of office was then administered to him by the Chief Justice, and the new President was saluted by loud cheers. The procession was re-formed, and the President escoited to the executive mansion, where he received the congratulations of a large number of his fellow-citizens.

In 1849, Zachary Taylor succeeded Mr. Polk as President, and Millard Fillmore was elected Vice President; the 4th March falling upon Sunday, the ceremony of inauguration took place on Monday, the 5th. At break of day the strains of martial music resounded through the city, the star spangled banner waved to the breeze in hundreds of places throughout the city, the bells rang a merry peal, and long before the usual breakfast hour hundreds were on foot wending their way to the Capitol.

At nine o'clock, a band of gentlemen who were appointed aids by the marshal, proceeded in a body, mounted, to Willard's hotel, for the purpose of paying their respects to Gen. Taylor. The general was dressed in a plain suit of black, and appeared, leaning upon the arm of the Mayor of the city, and returned the salutation of the gentlemen. At half past eleven the procession took up its line of march; consisting of twelve military companies. The carriage in which was the President elect, was drawn by four handsome grey horses; accompanying him was the Speaker of the late House of Representatives, and the Mayor of Washington. Upon arriving at the Irving House, the procession halted, and Ex-president Polk was handed into the carriage, and was seated on the right of Gen. Taylor, who shook his predecessor cordially by the hand. Both sides of Pennsylvania avenue were thronged with a countless multitude, from Willard's to the Capitol.

The scene within the Capitol was highly impressive. It would be difficult, in any other country than this to include within the same space, more of distinction, whether we attach to the term elevation of place, or that true elevation which is the prerogative of men born great by the gifts of God. The ladies as usual crowded the galleries to the exclusion of the sterner sex, and some few were admitted to the senatorial seats. The chamber was soon filled with senators and members, when the ceremonies were commenced by a prayer delivered by the Rev. Mr. Slicer; the Vice-president elect entered in company with Mr. Dallas, when Mr. Atchison administered to him the oath of office, when he delivered with calmness and dignity a brief address. At 12 o'clock the two Presidents arrived, and took seats side by side, which had been prepared for them. After a brief pause, the procession was formed passing through the rotunda to the eastern portico of the capitol, where at least 20,000 persons met the eye, representing every State and territory of the Union. The address was delivered in a remarkably distinct tone, and as soon as the applause had subsided, the oath, with due solemnity was administered to him by Chief

Justice Taney. The ceremonies were terminated by salvos of artillery, when the President and suite retraced their steps, and, escorted as before by the military and marshals, arrived at the residence of the successive Presidents of the United States. The President entered the mansion, and then received the salutes and congratulations of some thousands of persons. The hopes of the people were disappointed in the administration of Gen. Taylor, by his untimely death, which took place on Tuesday, July 9, 1850, by which calamity Mr. Fillmore succeeded to the office of President of the United States. Accordingly, on Thursday, July 11, at 12 o'clock, the Senate entered the Hall of the House of Representatives, the Speaker and members standing. Soon after, Mr. Fillmore, attended by a member of each House, entered the Hall and took a seat at the table of the Clerk of the House. After a brief pause, he rose and pronounced the oath of fidelity to the constitution of the United States, and the act of installation was complete—a ceremony so brief and simple—and thus Millard Fillmore became President of the United States.

GENERAL INFORMATION

FOR

INVENTORS, PATENTEES, AND THOSE INTERESTED IN PATENTED INVENTIONS.

Inventors are a most useful and valuable class of citizens, whose labors generally benefit the public more than themselves. The fee required upon an application for a patent is thirty dollars, and the inventor is required to furnish a model or specimen of his invention, with duplicate drawings, and a description such as would enable a person skilled in the art to which the invention appertains, to make and use it. The usual charge for making drawings, and preparing the description and other papers, is thirty dollars, which includes any explanations required at the Patent Office during the progress of the case. If the invention requires several figures, showing different views of the machine or thing for which a patent is desired, and a long description, the expense of preparing the papers is proportionally increased; but in most cases the expense of procuring a patent is sixty dollars, exclusive of the model, which may be a cheap one, but should be neatly made, and not more than one foot square; and, if made of soft wood, it should be stained and varnished. If the patent is granted, it is sent to the applicant free of postage. If the application is rejected, the applicant is referred to such inventions as in the opinion of the Examiner prevent the granting of letters patent; and the applicant may then relinquish his claim to the mode, withdraw his application, and receive back twenty of the thirty dollars paid into the office, and suffer a loss of forty dollars, exclusive of the time and money expended in perfecting his invention and procuring a model; or, if he is dissatisfied with the rejection of his application, he can appeal from the Commissioner's decision to the Chief Justice of the Circuit Court, in the District of Columbia, or file a bill in equity in that court; in either, it will cost from $50 to $100. Only about two-fifths of the applications for patents are granted —1,409 applications having been rejected in 1849, 1,038 in 1850, and 1,403 in 1851.

Now, allowing the expense of each application to have been sixty dollars, (many of them were doubtless much more,) and deducting the twenty dollars returned on the application being withdrawn, and the amount of money spent by inventors in the last three years, exclusive of the cost of models and other incidental expenses, is the enormous sum of one hundred and fifty-four thousand dollars, which is lost to a class of people that can ill afford to lose it, and of which much the greater part might have been saved if they had pursued a course which will now be suggested.

Let each inventor, after completing his invention, make a rough drawing or sketch of it, with pencil or ink, write a description of its use and operation, and enclosing five dollars, send it to some competent agent for procuring patents in the city of Washington, D. C.—(apply to me, and I will recommend a suitable person) —one who has some practical knowledge of machinery and manufactures will be most likely to understand it, who will examine it, and compare it with the inventions already in the Patent Office; and if he finds that there is little or no probability of a patent being obtained, if applied for, he will advise the inventor accordingly. In this way thirty-five dollars, at least, of the forty above mentioned, might in general be saved, which, for the 3,850 inventors whose applications were rejected in the three years above mentioned, would amount to one hundred and thirty-four thousand seven hundred and fifty dollars ($134,750.)

If, on the other hand, the invention is found to be patentable, there is still no loss by this course, for the agent will count the $5 paid for a preliminary examination as a part of the $30 charged for preparing the papers and drawings. Many inventors consult some one living near them, who visits the Patent Office, perhaps two or three times a year, or has visited it a few times in his life, as to the probability of their obtaining a patent; but when it is known that from fifteen to twenty patents are issued weekly, it will be at once seen that the opinion of one not actually visiting the office to compare the invention in question with those already deposited, cannot be of much value. Even if a stranger should come to the Patent Office for the purpose of making an examination, he could hardly expect to do it effectually among so many thousands of models, drawings, and descriptions, without the assistance of some one familiar with the contents of the office, and in the practice of making such examinations; for one patented and several rejected models have frequently been found constructed upon precisely the same principles as the one sent for examination.

Again, some inventors make an invention and send to the Commissioner of Patents for directions how to proceed in procuring a patent, and as the officers employed in the Patent Office are prohibited from giving any opinion in regard to the patentability of any invention until the application for a patent in due form, and a fee of $30 paid, the Commissioner sends them a circular; and although it contains information and instructions, many inventors complain that they have been misled by such circulars, and they prepare their own drawings and descriptions, or employ some one for that purpose in their own neighborhood to do so, without knowing whether the same thing is already in the Patent Office or not; and the person they employ has perhaps very little (if any) knowledge of the patent laws, or experience in preparing papers to procure patents; and it has been observed that such applications are almost certain to be rejected, for inventions have multiplied to such an extent, that it is hardly possible for any person to make a specification and claim that will not be rejected, or require amendment, if he does not know what inventions already exist in the Patent Office; and attorneys who have had long experience in making drawings and specifications, often find it very difficult to get patents, after making a thorough examination of the models, drawings, and records in the Patent Office. Hence it will be perceived that there is very little chance for those to procure patents who do not previously make a proper examination of the inventions in the Patent Office, and ascertain wherein the new invention differs from those which have preceded it, so as to know what is new and what is old—what to claim and what to omit.

And further, when an inventor's agent resides in Washington, he may make verbal explanations during the examination of the invention, and point out the improvements and represent the advantages it has over the previous inventions for the same purpose; and if the application is rejected, he receives immediate notice, and can examine the models, drawings and specifications of the inventions referred to at once, and answer the objections of the examiners, make the requisite explanations, and any necessary alterations in the specification and claim, and have the case attended to at once, while it is fresh before the examiner. But when the agent of the inventor is not in Washington, the case is far otherwise, and the inventor loses the advantage of explanations that might be made during the progress of the examination. Besides, it is some time before he gets the letter of rejection, and then he has not the models, drawings, and specifications of the inventions referred to at hand to compare with the invention of his client; but he may send and get copies of the drawings, by paying the expense of making the same, and of the specifications by paying ten cents for every hundred words; but the obtaining of these copies is attended with delay, and when he gets them he has not the advantage of the models, nor of explaining them personally to the examiner. He may write out the explanations, and state the difference between his client's invention and those referred to in the rejection, and send it to the Patent office; in the mean time, the examiner has turned his attention to other applications, and so much time has elapsed that he has almost or quite forgotten the case, and having examined and decided it once, he may feel reluctant about examining it again: so that the inventor suffers by the delay, and loses the advantage of the verbal explanations and examinations which might have been made by his agent in person, while the invention was fresh before the mind of the examiner. Besides, numerous inventors could be referred to, who have employed agents at a distance from Washington, and who having had their applications rejected, have paid their agent for coming to Washington, or employed an agent here, or have come themselves and employed an agent after they got here, to amend or prepare new papers before they obtained their patent; when, if they had employed a competent agent in the vicinity of the Patent Office, they would not have been subject to the delay, and might have saved the additional expense above mentioned. And further, the papers in numerous applications have been examined, which were rejected because they were not properly prepared, and which would, without doubt, have been successful in obtaining patents, had a competent agent, possessing some practical knowledge of machinery and manufactures, been employed to present the case in person before the Patent Office.

A Commencement of a New Era in the Arts.

JACKSON STATUE.

It is but just that posterity should know whatever merit is due to those who have done anything in giving to America and to the world the magnificent bronze equestrian statue of General Jackson, now in Lafayette Square. Especially should the name, the character, and a knowledge of the difficulties of the artist, be handed down to future ages. I have collected the facts from the artist himself—Mr. Clark Mills.

The trials of genius appear to be the crucible of artists, where the pure metal is separated from the base ore. Whoever contemplates the equestrian statue of Mr. Mills', will have his pleasure augmented by knowing that its designer early studied in the great temple of Nature.

In 1844 a committee was formed of gentlemen of this city, who collected the sum of twelve thousand dollars. To their exertions we owe the credit of having this remarkable statue amongst us. But at the time, no one deeming it possible that any artist could make a bronze equestrian statue of General Jackson for the small sum collected, it was seriously debated whether or not a pedestrian statue should be erected, and the work given to Mr. Powers.

In the year 1848, while the Jackson statue committee were looking for an artist, Mr. Mills chanced to be passing through Washington city. He then proposed to make the equestrian statue. Some of the committee, doubting his capacity, were disposed to have a pedestrian statue by Powers. But when Mr. Mills produced his model, and offered to give security for the due performance of the work, the contract was made with him for the twelve thousand dollars.

The accounts that we have of Mr. Mills was, that his first efforts in art were directed to making plaster busts, in Charleston, South Carolina. He succeeded in giving such admirable likenesses, that he soon was much employed, and resolved to make a bust of Mr. Calhoun in martle; when finished, it was the admiration and astonishment of all. The city of Charleston, as an appreciation of the work, presented him with a splendid gold medal, and placed the bust in the City Hall.

When he offered to make the Jackson statue, he knew the amount offered would not pay him, much less remunerate him for his days and nights of sleepless toil. But, working for a future, he risked the loss of friends who had kindly cheered him in his humbler efforts, but would not encourage him in this undertaking, which was more grand and unique in its design than any of the efforts of the masters who had preceded him. But his model being approved, and he accepting of the moderate sum allowed for the work, ten gentlemen were his bondmen for the due performance of the work, all men of property in the city of Charleston, S. C. I give their names, as it is highly honorable to them, for this act of confidence and kindness. Their names are—James Rose, James Gadsden, H. Gourdin, F. H. Elmore, C. B. Northrop, Charles D. Carr, Edward Frost, N. M. Porter, J. Schnierle, and George Kinlock. The contract required the statue to be a third larger than life. It is a little more than that. Government furnished the metal, which was old cannon, and some of which was captured by General Jackson.

Mr. Mills is thirty-two years of age—a man in whose personal appearance there is nothing remarkable to strike an ordinary observer—has a searching light gray eye, good regular Caucasian features, and gray hair, turned gray during the period of his labor and anxiety over the great work he has accomplished.

On a vacant lot of government ground near the President's House, at the corner of Fifteenth street and Pennsylvania avenue, he erected a small frame building, for a workshop and a residence. He bought a horse in Virginia, known in the Turf Register as Olympus. This he trained to present the attitude he wanted. This horse is well known in Washington now as the "model horse."

He studied the character of Jackson, and the best likenesses that could be found, so as to give a faithful representation of him. He took from the military dress of Gen. Jackson, deposited in the National Museum, the model by which he clothed the hero. The very sword he wore, and every minutiæ of the saddle, holsters, bridle, and even the old fashioned Dutch buckles, are copied faithfully from the originals. He was not quite two years in modelling the group in plaster. The public admired it for its beauty, but the academy artists declared that it was a departure from the rules, and it would never be more than a myth of the artist; all the celebrated statues of the old world—Peter the Great, George III., and the Duke of Wellington—were all different. People could not realize the fact that the first equestrian statue in America (executed by an untaught American artist) could be superior in this respect to all the art of the Old World. Mills, however, following the dictates of his own genius and nature, had discovered that a natural horse, to get in such a position, must throw the centre of gravity through the rider to his hind feet. He staked his reputation on that principle, and has, contrary to the predictions of the learned and scientific, triumphed.

The next thing was a foundry. His means were limited, but the resources of his genius were inexhaustible. With limited means, and in a small miserable shanty, he built a foundry *upon a new principle*, without a chimney, smoke-stack, or draught of any kind—an invention of his own—and cast his colossal statue. What is not the human mind equal to when conscious of its power and pressed by difficulties! Of this foundry, as well as of balancing the statue, scientific men had said it was contrary to experience and to all the known rules of science.

With three-eighths of a cord of wood he melted sixteen hundred pounds of metal, and cast four bells. It was impossible, however, to foresee everything. His idea of doing the work was correct, but his experience was insufficient. The sides of the horse were to be cast whole. These were large pieces, to be cast by such means as he had at his command. He failed several times, by unforeseen accidents, in producing perfect casts. Every one of his attempts cost him $400, and he made six successive trials. Not discouraged, he continued to re-cast, until, in the month of October, 1852, he finished the casting all complete.

Those who have read the account of the casting of the famous Amazone by the German artist Kiss—(exhibited at the World's Fair, London; and, in particular, the celebrated Benevenuto Cellini's account of the casting of his Perseus, now in the grand square at Florence)—will be surprised that Mr. Mills has succeeded so well, and performed his work in so short a time. From the first successful casting in the month of October to the eighth of January following, the day on which the statue was inaugurated—that is, in less than three months—Mr. Mills put the statue together, and placed it on its pedestal. There was $5,000 appropriated by Congress for the pedestal; and had he not been limited as to time, he would have made a more imposing structure. It is, however, a plain, handsome, white marble base. The cap-stone alone weighs about eighteen tons. The entire height of the pedestal and mound is about fourteen feet; and the whole group, with the pedestal, about thirty feet.

During the progress of the work, and especially while he was making unsuccessful castings, Mr. Mills had to encounter the scepticism of the world. Who can appreciate his difficulties and mental suffering? "I have been ready," he says, "to throw myself in the Potomac." None but a man of unconquerable will and perseverance could have overcome such obstacles. He had spent all his means—the twelve thousand dollars of his contract—and had not finished casting the statue. The world said he would never do it. Where could he raise money under such circumstances? There was one man, a member of the committee, who sympathised with him, who believed in him. John W. Maury, the present mayor of Washington, advanced him money, from time to time, as he needed—in all over four thousand dollars. Eternal honor to the man! Let his fellow-citizens and future ages know that he generously aided, at the critical moment, the poor, struggling artist to finish his beautiful creation.

The entire cost of the statue has been about nineteen thousand dollars, or seven thousand dollars over the contract. This is the actual expenditure, without reckoning Mr. Mills' five years' labor, or the value of his work as a work of art.

On the 8th of January, 1853—the anniversary of the battle of New Orleans—the statue was inaugurated. The day was bright and beautiful, suitable to the occasion. In the presence of the President of the United States, the commander-in-chief, both Houses of Congress, many of the personal friends and companions-in-arms of the old Hero, and twenty thousand people, the artist had the satisfaction of seeing the end of his labor and the idol of his soul received with applauding admiration. The Hon. Stephen A. Douglass was the orator chosen to deliver the inaugural address. That address, and the whole proceedings, have been published. What a proud day for Mills! After the oration, he was introduced to the assembled thousands; he raised his hand to the statue for the curtain which covered it to fall, as his speech in response to the enthusiastic plaudits. It was the moment of his life; then again, he saw that Genius which had inspired him to action, holding the laurel crown over his head. He had "followed Nature" as it directed him, and had acquired fame. Well does he deserve it. We believe—and it is also the judgment of men of taste, of travelers, of artists, and of the public who have seen it—that Mills' bronze equestrian statue of General Jackson, in Lafayette Square, is the first work of art of the kind in the world.

It is a pleasure to state that the people, through Congress, has appreciated his genius, and will reward his labors, in employing him to erect a statue to Washington; which resolution was passed in 1783, according to the account in my book, of the design to beautify the Capitol grounds and make it a second Versailles. They have passed an act appropriating $50,000 for the work, and designating him as the artist to carry the design into execution.

It has been proposed that this statue should be placed upon the Mall near where the Monument now stands, as this was the ground that was originally proposed for the statue in 1783, and that this place should be preserved, in all future time, for such statues as might be ordered by Congress or erected by the contributions of individuals—thus beautifying the city, and making it a school for the arts.

OFFICIAL DIRECTORY.

An Alphabetical List of all persons, with their office and salary specified, who hold immediate or intermediate appointments from the General Government, their permanent or present place of business being within the District of Columbia.

Abbot, G. S., clerk Consular Bureau, State Department $1,700
Abbot, Charles, clerk Third Auditor's, Treasury Department 1,200
Abbott, G. J., Diplomatic Bureau, State Department 1,700
Abbott, T. J., clerk Quartermaster General's, War Department 1,000
Abbott, George D., clerk Second Comptroller's, Treasury Department 1,400
Adams, T. N., clerk Pension Office .... $3 33 per diem.
Adams, J. H., jr., clerk Pension Office .... $3 33 per diem.
Adams, C. B., clerk P. O. Department 1,200
Adams, Corn. B., clerk Auditor for P. O. Dep't, Treas. Dep't 1,000
Addison, S. R., assistant surgeon Bureau Medicine, Navy Dep't 1,400
Addison, Thomas B., clerk Auditor for P. O. Dep't, Treasury Department. 1,200
Addison, W., clerk Auditor for P. O. Dep't, Treasury Department 1,000
Addison, James L., clerk War Department 1,400
Addison, J., clerk Pension Office .... $3 33 per diem.
Adler, Morris, clerk Interior Department 1,150
Agg, John, clerk P. O. Department 1,400
Allyn, L. B., clerk Bureau Provisions and Clothing, Navy Dep't 1,100
Allyn, Lucius B., clerk Navy Department 1,100
Ames, C., messenger State Department 700
Amiss, A. D., clerk Census Bureau 1,000
Anderson, William, clerk First Comptroller's, Treasury Department 1,400
Anderson, Thomas F., clerk First Comptroller's, Treasury Department 1,150
Anderson, Leonard J., clerk Auditor P. O. Dep't, Treasury Department 1,200
Anderson, A. H., messenger Pension Office 400
Anderson, J. L., clerk Pension Office .... $3 33 per diem.
Archer, E. W., clerk Auditor for P. O. Dep't, Treas. Dep't 1,000
Armstrong, George B., clerk P. O. Department 1,000
Ashby, J. R., clerk Census Bureau 1,000
Atkinson, E. G., clerk Paymaster General's, War Department 700
Atlee, Samuel Y., clerk Register's, Treasury Department 1,500
Bailey, Wm. L., clerk Quartermaster General's, War Department 1,000
Bailey, Wm., clerk Second Comptroller's, Treas. Department 1,200
Baker, Charles, messenger War Department 500
Baird, T. H., jr., clerk Census Bureau 1,000
Baldwin, H., jr., clerk Census Bureau 1,000
Baldwin, Benjamin H., clerk Interior Department 1,100
Baldwin, Henry, examiner Patent Office, Interior Department 2,500
Ball, Gideon J., chief clerk Auditor Treasury for P. O. Dep't 2,000
Ball, S. M., clerk Pension Office .... $3 33 per diem.
Balmain, Andrew, clerk War Department 1,000
Balmain, Henry W., clerk Second Auditor's, Treasury Department 1,000
Bankin, James M., clerk P. O. Department 1,400
Barbarin, Francis N., chief clerk Eng. Dep't, War Dep't 1,200
Barclay, John D., chief clerk Commissioner Customs, Treas. Dep't 1,700
Barker, James N., Commissioner of Customs, Treasury Department 3,000
Barnes, Abr'm, clerk Interior Department 1,200

Barnhill, J. L., clerk Interior Department.. $1,300
Barrell, O. K., Diplomatic Bureau, State Department........................ 1,500
Barrell, O. K., clerk Census Bureau.. 1,000
Barry, George, clerk Register's, Treasury Department........................ 1,000
Bartell, George, clerk State Department.. 1,400
Bartlett, Thomas, jr., clerk Auditor for P. O. Dep't, Treas. Dep't........... 1,000
Bates, E. H., assistant messenger P. O. Department........................... 450
Bates, Robert W., clerk Third Auditor's, Treasury Department............. 1,000
Beall, George W., clerk Interior Department...................................... 1,100
Beard, Lewis, clerk Second Auditor's, Treasury Department............... 1,400
Bell, Edward, clerk Pension Office............................$3 33 per diem.
Bell, Wm., clerk P. O. Department.. 1,200
Bender, George, chief clerk Ordnance Bureau, Interior Dep't.............. 1,200
Benson, S. E., clerk Second Auditor's, Treasury Department.............. 1,000
Berret, John J., recording clerk Navy Department............................. 1,000
Berret, J. H., Census Bureau..$3 per diem
Berrien, H., clerk Fourth Auditor's, Treasury Department................. 1,150
Berryman, Leroy H., clerk Indian Bureau, Interior Department............ 1,200
Berryman, Wm. B., clerk Register's, Treasury Department.................. 1,000
Bess, L., clerk Pension Office..$3 33 per diem.
Bielaski, A., clerk Interior Department.. 1,200
Billings, J. J. L., clerk Census Bureau... 1,000
Birge, H. W., Census Bureau... 1,000
Birge, Cyrus, clerk Second Comptroller's, Treas. Dep't....................... 1,150
Birnie, C., clerk Pension Office...$3 33 per diem.
Biscoe, George W., clerk Second Auditor's, Treasury Department......... 1,000
Bittinger, Henry, messenger Indian Bureau, Interior Dep't.................. 500
Blake, John B., clerk Register's, Treasury Department...................... 1,400
Blake, J. H., clerk Interior Department.. 1,300
Blanchard, C. D., clerk Paymaster General's, War Department............ 700
Boak, W L., clerk Pension Office...$3 33 per diem.
Boardman, G. W., clerk Interior Department..................................... 1,100
Bogan, Benjamin L., clerk Third Auditor's, Treasury Department......... 1,200
Boone, John F., clerk Auditor Treasury for P. O. Department.............. 1,400
Bootes, Samuel M., Treasury Department... 1,200
Borden, E R., clerk Pension Office.......................................$3 33 per diem.
Boswell, R. H , messenger Treasury Department................................ 700
Bowers, C. B., clerk Auditor for P. O. Dep't, Treas. Dep't.................... 1,200
Bowers, A. L., Census Bureau... 1,000
Bowie, Robert, clerk Interior Department.. 1,300
Boynton, S. C., clerk Fifth Auditor's, Treasury Department................. 1,150
Bradley, J. T., clerk Paymaster General's, War Department................. 700
Bradley, G. H., clerk Paymaster General's, War Department................ 700
Brady, Peter, clerk Second Auditor's, Treasury Department................ 1,400
Breed, Daniel, assistant examiner Patent Office, Interior Department...... 1,500
Brenner, A , Census Bureau... 850
Brewer, E., clerk Pension Office..$3 33 per diem.
Brewer, Moreau, clerk Auditor for P. O. Dep't, Treas. Dep't................. 1,000
Broadhead, John M., clerk Second Comptroller's, Treas. Dep't............. 1,400
Broadus, Wm. A., clerk Pension Office...................................$3 33 per diem.
Bromwell, J. R., Census Bureau.. 1,000
Bronaugh, S. W., clerk First Auditor's, Treasury Department.............. 1,150
Bronaugh, jr., J. W., clerk Auditor for P. O. Department, Treas. Dep't.... 1,200
Bronaugh, John W., clerk Bureau of Construction, Navy Department...... 1,000
Bronough, Wm. J., clerk Auditor Treasury for P. O. Department........... 1,200
Brooke, W. T., clerk Interior Department.. 1,200
Brooke, Wm. N., Census Bureau.. 850
Brown, L. J., clerk Pension Office..$3 33 per diem.
Brown, Joseph F., clerk War Department... 1,000
Brown, Thomas, clerk Third Auditor's, Treasury Department............... 1,000

Brown, Eleazar, clerk Second Auditor's, Treasury Department ... $1,400
Brown, James W., clerk Second Auditor's, Treasury Department ... 1,200
Brown, John H., clerk Second Auditor's, Treasury Department ... 1,000
Brown, A. H., clerk Auditor for P. O. Dep't, Treas. Dep't ... 1,000
Browne, D. Jay, Census Bureau ... 1,000
Browne, J. A., clerk Auditor for P. O. Dep't, Treas. Dep't ... 1,200
Bryan, J., clerk Pension Office ... $3 33 per diem.
Bull, M., clerk Pension Office ... $3 33 per diem.
Burch, J. H., clerk Pension Office ... $3 33 per diem.
Burch, R. W., clerk War Department ... 800
Burche, J. C., Census Bureau ... 1,000
Burr, De Vere, clerk Third Auditor's, Treasury Department ... 1,150
Burr, H. A., topographer P. O. Department ... 1,600
Busey, Wm. G., messenger Pension Office ... 500
Butterfield, F., clerk Auditor for P. O. Dep't, Treas. Dep't ... 1,000
Butz, J. S., messenger Auditor for P. O. Dep't, Treas. Dep't ... 750
Cabell, D. S. G., clerk Interior Department ... 1,100
Cabell, E. A., principal clerk of Public Lands, Interior Department ... 1,800
Cahill, B., Census Bureau ... 1,000
Caldwell, J. F., clerk Auditor for P. O. Depart't, Treasury Department ... 1,400
Calvert, Charles, clerk War Department ... 1,400
Campbell, A., clerk War Department ... 1,600
Campbell, M., clerk Second Comptroller's, Treasury Department ... 1,200
Canfield, C. J., Census Bureau ... 1,000
Cantine, J. J. C., clerk Third Auditor's, Treasury Department ... 1,150
Carper, Jas. S., clerk Third Auditor's, Treasury Department ... 1,000
Carr, J. G., Census Bureau ... 1,000
Carter, Joseph, clerk Auditor for P. O. Dep't, Treasury Department ... 1,200
Casson, J. L., clerk Paymaster General's, War Department ... 700
Cathcart, Thos. J., clerk Second Comptroller's, Treasury Department ... 1,000
Causin, N. P., Census Bureau ... 1,000
Chamberlayne, B., clerk Pension Office ... $3 33 per diem.
Chapman, E., clerk Bureau of Construction, Navy Department ... 1,000
Chapman, Edward, clerk Navy Department ... 1,000
Chapman, Alfred, clerk Indian Bureau, Interior Department ... 1,600
Charles, J. P., clerk Pension Office ... $3 33 per diem.
Chase, J. P., clerk Pension Office ... $3 33 per diem.
Chew, R. S., clerk State Department ... 2,000
Childs, E. L., clerk P. O. Department ... 1,600
Chilton, R. S., clerk State Department ... 1,000
Chipman, George, clerk State Department ... 1,400
Clark, Edward M., clerk Second Auditor's, Treasury Department ... 1,000
Clark, Marsh B., messenger Bureau of Medicine, Navy Department ... 700
Clarke, R. W., clerk Pension Office ... 800
Clarke, George A. D., clerk Interior Department ... 1,400
Clarke, John M., clerk Third Auditor's, Treasury Department ... 1,000
Clayton, Philip, Second Auditor, Treasury Department ... 3,000
Cleary, Nicholas, clerk Interior Department ... 1,300
Cleary, Wm., clerk Interior Department ... 1,200
Cleary, Timothy, Census Bureau ... $3 per diem
Clements, J. T., clerk P. O. Department ... 1,000
Clements, Bennett, clerk Third Auditor's, Treasury Department ... 1,200
Clyde, W., clerk Interior Department ... 1,200
Cobb, Jas. D., clerk Third Auditor's, Treasury Department ... 1,000
Coburn, W. A., Census Bureau ... 1,000
Cochran, Robt., clerk First Comptroller's, Treasury Department ... 1,400
Cole, S., clerk Pension Office ... 1,400
Cole, S. L., Census Bureau ... 1,000
Colegate, Jas., clerk First Auditor's, Treasury Department ... 1,400
Colledge, Wm. H., clerk Auditor for P. O. Dep't, Treasury Department ... 1,200

Collins, D. W., clerk Pension Office.. $1,000
Collins, Jas. H., messenger (Surgeon General's) War Department.......... 500
Collins, W. B., clerk First Auditor's, Treasury Department.................. 1,000
Collins, J. H., Census Bureau.. 1,000
Colson, C. W., Census Bureau.. 850
Colston, P., clerk Pension Office ....$3 33 per diem.
Colt, Chester A., clerk P. O. Department.................................. 1,200
Connolly, T. C., Census Bureau.. 1,000
Cooke, J. M., clerk Quartermaster General's, War Department.............. 1,000
Coolidge, Saml., clerk Auditor for P. O. Depart't, Treasury Department... 1,200
Coolidge, P. H., clerk Paymaster General's, War Department............... 700
Coolige, J. H., Census Bureau... 1,000
Coombs, J. W., Census Bureau.. 1,000
Cooper, W., Census Bureau... 1,000
Cooper, A., clerk Pension Office ....$3 33 per diem.
Cosby, F., clerk Second Auditor's, Treasury Department.................... 1,200
Cosby, R. T., Census Bureau... 1,000
Coulson, G. J. A., Census Bureau.. 1,000
Cowan, Wm. J., clerk Register's, Treasury Department...................... 1,400
Cowan, Wm., clerk Interior Department..................................... 1,100
Cowing, G., clerk Second Auditor's, Treasury Department.................. 1,009
Cox, Thos. C., clerk Paymaster General's, War Department.................. 700
Cox, George G., clerk Auditor for P. O. Dep't, Treasury Department...... 1,200
Coyle, A., Census Burean 850
Craighil, J. A., clerk Third Auditor's, Treasury Department............... 1,000
Crider, Michael, Census Bureau....................................$3 per diem
Crittenden, Timothy R., clerk Indian Bureau, Interior Department......... 1,400
Cronise, J. S., Census Bureau... 1,000
Crosson, H. J., clerk Third Auditor's, Treasury Department................ 1,000
Crupper, A. B.. clerk Pension Office............................$3 33 per diem.
Crupper, J. Q. A., clerk Interior Department.............................. 1,200
Cunningham, A. F., clerk Third Auditor's, Treasury Department........... 1,150
Cunningham, E. M., clerk Bureau of Construction, Navy Department...... 1,200
Cutter, George W., clerk Treasury Department.............................. 1,400
Cutts, J. M., chief clerk Second Comptroller's, Treasury Department..... 1,700
Cutts, Stephen S., Census Bureau.. 1,000
Dabney, John, clerk Interior Department................................... 1,100
Dade, John B., clerk Interior Department.................................. 1,100
Dagger, J. F., clerk First Auditor's, Treasury Department................. 1,000
Daggy, Peter, clerk Interior Department................................... 1,400
Daives, R., clerk Fourth Auditor's, Treasury Department................... 1,000
Dale, George, clerk Auditor for P. O. Dep't, Treasury Department 1,000
Daniel, Thos. C., clerk Third Auditor's, Treasury Department.............. 1,400
Darby, Wm., clerk Interior Department..................................... 1,100
Darden, Wm. S., clerk P. O. Department.................................... 1,200
Darrell, Wm. S., clerk Auditor for P. O. Dep't, Treasury Department..... 1,400
Datcher, T., messenger War Department..................................... 400
Davidge, F. H., clerk P. O. Department.................................... 1,400
Davis, Charles A., clerk Interior Department.............................. 1,300
Davis, C. E., clerk Interior Department................................... 1,100
Davis, Levi, clerk War Department... 1,000
Davis, Eli, watchman P. O. Department..................................... 500
Davis, Jesse L., clerk Auditor for P. O. Dep t, Treasury Department 1,000
Daws. Josephus, clerk Auditor for P. O. Dep't, Treasury Department...... 1,000
Dayton, A. O., Fourth Auditor, Treasury Department........................ 3,000
Debrill, Edward, clerk Register's, Treasury Department.................... 1,000
Decker, J., jr., Census Bureau.. 1,000
Deeble, J. W,, clerk P. O. Department 1,200
De Hass, Willis, clerk Interior Department................................ 1,200
Deitz, W. H., Census Bureau.. **850**

DeKrafft, J. W., clerk Interior Department.. $1,400
Delaroche, G. F., draughtsman Bur. of N. Yards and Docks, Navy Dep't. 1,000
Dement, Richard, clerk Auditor for P. O. Dep't, Treasury Department.... 1,200
Deming, Chester, clerk First Auditor's, Treasury Department 1,000
Denheim, O. B., messenger War Department.. 500
Dennison, W. W., Census Bureau.. 1,000
Derrick, Alexander H., Diplomatic Bureau, State Department............... 1,600
Devlin, John, clerk Fifth Auditor's, Treasury Department..................... 1,150
Dickinson, C. H., messenger Pension Office 500
Dickinson, J. P., clerk Pension Office...........................$3 33 per diem.
Dinies, A. J., clerk Interior Department.. 1,100
Donaho, T. S., Census Bureau.. 1,000
Douglass, John, clerk Auditor for P. O. Dep't, Treasury Department 1,300
Dove, Richard G., clerk Third Auditor's, Treasury Department............. 1,000
Dowling, John, clerk Indian Bureau, Interior Department..................... 1,600
Downes, S., assistant messenger Fourth Auditor's, Treasury Department.. 500
Doyle, Francis, clerk First Auditor's, Treasury Department.................. 1,000
Draine, Charles, messenger Indian Bureau, Interior Department........... 700
Dubois, E. J., Census Bureau.. 850
Duncan, Stephen, clerk Pension Office.........................$3 33 per diem.
Duncan, Stephen, clerk Third Auditor's, Treasury Department.............. 1,000
Duncanson, J. A. M., clerk Auditor for P. O. Dep't, Treas. Department... 1,400
Dundas, Wm. H., Second Assistant Postmaster General....................... 2,500
Dunkinson, Wm. H., clerk Third Auditor's, Treasury Department.......... 1,000
Dunn, J. W., clerk Paymaster General's, War Department.................... 700
Dunn, J. R., Census Bureau.. 1,000
Dunn, J. R., Census Bureau..$2 per diem
Dusenberry, C., Census Bureau.. 850
Dyer, Giles, clerk Auditor for P. O. Dep't, Treasury Department.. 1,000
Edwards, Evans, clerk Treasury Department.. 1,000
Edwards, Saml. M., clerk Auditor for P. O. Dep't, Treasury Department. 1,400
Edwards, A. L., clerk First Comptroller's, Treasury Department............ 1,000
Ellicott, E., Census Bureau.. 1,000
Elliot, Wm. C., messenger Navy Department.. 700
Elliot, Alexander, clerk Second Auditor's, Treasury Department........... 1,200
Elliot, Wm. G., clerk Auditor for the P. O. Dep't, Treasury Department.. 1,600
Elliott, W. A., messenger Bureau of Construction, Navy Department...... 700
Elwell, Wm. S., clerk Third Auditor's, Treasury Department................ 1,150
Erwin, S. Bulow, clerk Navy Department 1,500
Erwin, S. B., clerk Bur. of Provisions and Clothing, Navy Department... 1,400
Estell, Isaac, clerk Register's, Treasury Department........................... 1,000
Etheridge, John, chief clerk Navy Department.................................... 2,000
Evans, Wm, A., clerk Second Comptroller's, Treasury Department......... 1,200
Evans, W., clerk Auditor for P. O. Dep't, Treasury Department............ 1,000
Evans, John W. C., clerk Treasury Department.................................... 1,200
Eveleth, Eben, clerk Third Auditor's, Treasury Department.................. 1,400
Eveleth, James, clerk War Department... 1,250
Evans, Benjamin, clerk Interior Department.. 1,300
Everett, Thos. T., assistant Examiner Patent Office 1,500
Ewell, F. M., clerk Pension Office..............................$3 33 per diem.
Fales, N. W., clerk Interior Department.. 800
Fales, George W., messenger Treasury Department 600
Farrelly, John W., Auditor of the Treas. for P. O. Dep't, Treas. Dep't.... 3,000
Fendall, T. D., clerk Auditor for P. O. Dep't, Treasury Department........ 1,000
Feran, Thomas, clerk Treasury Department.. 1,400
Ferguson, John, clerk First Comptroller's, Treasury Department........... 1,000
Ferguson, William M., Census Bureau... 1,000
Fillebrown, Thomas, chief clerk Bureau of Provisions, Navy Department. 1,700
Finckel, S. D., clerk Quartermaster General's, War Department............ 1,000
Finney, A. C., clerk Auditor for P. O. Dep't, Treasury Department......... 1,200

Fitch, Timothy, clerk P. O. Department	$1,000
Fitnam, T., jr., clerk Pension Office.....$3 33 per diem.	
Fitzhugh, Saml., clerk Auditor for P. O. Dep't, Treasury Department	1,400
Flenner, Wm., clerk Interior Department	1,100
Fletcher, C., clerk Pension Office.....$3 33 per diem.	
Fletcher, Arthur W., clerk Interior Department	1,200
Ford, John N., clerk Interior Department	1,100
Ford, William, assistant messenger Interior Department	120
Ford, S. Calvert, clerk Second Auditor's, Treasury Department	1,200
Forrest, Charles W., clerk Second Auditor's, Treasury Department	1,400
Fortney, E. W., clerk Auditor for P. O. Dep't, Treasury Department	1,200
Foster, Joseph C., clerk P. O. Department	1,200
Foster, Thos., messenger Treasury Department	700
Foulkes, J., Census Bureau	1,000
Fowler, Robert B., clerk War Department	1,000
Frailey, Charles S., clerk Interior Department	1,500
French, E. F., clerk Second Comptroller's, Treasury Department	1,000
French, G. E., Census Bureau	850
Fuller, F. W., clerk Register's, Treasury Department	800
Fuller, E. H., Census Bureau	1,000
Fuller, H. L., Census Bureau	1,000
Fulton, J. B. H., Census Bureau	1,000
Furtner, R., watchman P. O. Department	500
Gallaher, John S., Third Auditor, Treasury Department	3,000
Gallaher, M., clerk Third Auditor's, Treasury Department	1,000
Gale, L. D., examiner Patent Office, Interior Department	2,500
Gardner, Franklin, clerk Auditor for P. O. Dep't, Treas. Dep't	1,200
Garner, James W., messenger Treasury Department	700
Garner, G. W., watchman Post Office Department	500
Garnett, A. S., Census Bureau	850
Gaston, J. A., Census Bureau	1,000
Gatton, A. H., messenger Bureau of Ordnance, Navy Department	700
Geddes, C. W., second assistant engineer, Navy Department	800
Geddes, R., clerk Pension Office.....$3 33 per diem.	
Getty, G. T., clerk Pension Office.....$3 33 per diem.	
Gibbon, John W., clerk Second Comptroller's, Treasury Dep't	1,200
Gillchrist, G. L., clerk First Auditor's, Treasury Department	1,150
Gillespie, W. L, Census Bureau	1,000
Gilman, E., assistant draughtsman Interior Department	1,200
Goddard, Solomon, messenger Treasury Department	500
Goodloe, D. R., clerk Bureau of Construction, Navy Dep't	800
Goodloe, D. R., draught man Navy Department	800
Goolrick, J. C., clerk Quartermaster General's, War Dep't	1,000
Gordon, Wm., clerk Pension Office	1,000
Gordon, Wm. A., chief clerk Quartermaster General's, War Dep't	1,600
Gordon, John, messenger Post Office Department	750
Gordon, C. V., clerk State Department	900
Gordon, J. T., Census Bureau	1,000
Goszler, James, clerk Quartermaster General's, War Dep't	1,200
Gough, Stephen, clerk Bureau of Navy Yards, Navy Department	1,000
Grame, R., clerk Third Auditor's, Treasury Department	1,000
Gratiot, C., Census Bureau	1,000
Gray, Thomas, clerk Auditor for P. O. Dep't, Treas. Dep't	1,400
Grayson, E. B., clerk Indian Bureau, Interior Department	1,400
Green, George F., Census Bureau.....$3 per diem	
Greer, R. A., Census Bureau	1,000
Grist, ——, clerk Navy Department	1,000
Gunton, Thomas, clerk Third Auditor's, Treasury Department	1,400
Gurley, R. R., clerk Interior Department	1,100
Guy, R. M., Census Bureau	1,000

Hackie, J. S., clerk State Department........ $1,500
Haines, D. W., clerk Register's, Treasury Department........ 1,200
Hall, Wm. F., clerk P. O. Department........ 1,400
Hall, G. W., clerk Third Auditor's, Treasury Department........ 1,000
Hall, Alexander, clerk First Auditor's, Treasury Department........ 1,150
Hall, B., messenger Third Auditor's, Treasury Department........ 350
Halter, N., clerk P. O. Department........ 1,400
Hamilton, John, assistant messenger Second Auditor's, Treas. Dep't........ 500
Hamilton, James H., clerk P. O. Department........ 1,200
Hamilton, M. G., Census Bureau........ 1,000
Hammersley, L. R., Census Bureau........ 1,000
Hampton, James W., clerk Third Auditor's, Treasury Department........ 1,200
Handy, C. W., Treasury Department........ 900
Hanson, Richard M., clerk War Department........ 1,000
Hanson, T. H., jr., clerk Pension Office........$3 33 per diem.
Hanson, I. K., clerk Second Comptroller's, Treasury Department........ 800
Hanson, Grafton D., clerk Auditor for P. O. Dep't, Treas. Dep't........ 1,200
Hanson, James M., clerk Auditor P. O. Dep't, Treas. Dep't........ 1,200
Hardin, Wm., clerk Third Auditor's, Treasury Department........ 1,000
Hardin, L. B., Register Navy Department........ 1,400
Hardy, Henry, clerk Indian Bureau, Interior Department........ 1,200
Harkness, Samuel, clerk Auditor for P. O. Dep't, Treas. Dep't........ 1,200
Harleston, G. B., clerk P. O. Department........ 1,200
Harmon, A. D., clerk Auditor for P. O. Dep t, Treas. Dep't........ 1,000
Harper, Kenton, clerk Interior Department........ 1,400
Harris, W. A., clerk Interior Department........ 1,200
Harris, Thomas, chief Bureau of Medicine, Navy Department........ 3,000
Harte, Edward, Census Bureau........ 1,000
Hartwell, Joseph R., clerk Third Auditor's, Treas. Dep't........$4 per diem.
Harvey, Henry L., warrant clerk Navy Department........ 1,200
Haskins, G. W., clerk P. O. Department........ 1,200
Haskins, R., jr., Census Bureau........ 1,000
Haviland, J. C., clerk Register's, Treasury Department........ 800
Hawke, R. A., assistant messenger Treasury Department........ 450
Hawks, John, clerk Third Auditor's, Treasury Dep't........$4 per diem.
Head, George M., clerk Fourth Auditor's, Treasury Department........ 1,400
Heath. J. E., Commissioner of Pensions........ 3,000
Heath, R. M., clerk Pension Office........ 1,200
Heaton, J. G., Census Bureau........ 1,000
Hedgeman, John G., Treasury Department........ 1,000
Hedrick, Robert G., clerk P. O. Department........ 1,400
Helfer, H. H., recording clerk Navy Department........ 1,000
Henry, Patrick M , clerk War Department........ 1,000
Henry R., clerk Pension Office........$3 33 per piem.
Henry J. M., assistant examiner Patent Office, Interior Department........ 1,500
Herbert, Alfred, clerk Interior Department........ 1,000
Hibbs, C., messenger Pension Office........ 700
Higgins, D., clerk Fourth Auditor's, Treasury Department........ 1,150
Hill, Silas H., clerk Third Auditor's, Treasury Department........ 1,400
Hines, Philip, messenger Treasury Department........ 700
Hines, A., assistant messenger Interior Department........ 500
Hitchcox, M. M., Census Bureau........ 1,000
Hobletzell, H., jr., clerk Pension Office........$3 33 per diem.
Hodges, Silas H., Commissioner Patent Office, Interior Department........ 3,000
Hoffman, R. H., Census Bureau........ 1,000
Hogan, J. D., Census Bureau........ 850
Hogan, W., Census Bureau........ 1,000
Hogan, jr., Wm., clerk Third Auditor's, Treasury Department........ 1,000
Hogg, John W., clerk Regisfer's, Treasury Department........ 1,000
Holcombe, L. C., Census Bureau........ 1,000

Holland, J. E., messenger Fourth Auditor's, Treasury Department.........	700
Hollingshead, John S., Census Bureau..	1,000
Hollister, A. D., clerk P. O. Department..	1,200
Holtzman, George H., clerk Indian Bureau, Interior Department...........	1,000
Hood, J. H., clerk Pension Office ....$3 33 per diem.	
Hood, John, clerk Interior Department...	1,300
Hooe, B., clerk Pension Office..	1,200
Hopkins, R. F., clerk P. O. Department...	1,200
Horn, A., clerk P. O. Department..	1,000
Houston, John H., clerk Fifth Auditor's, Treasury Department..............	1,400
Houston, Samuel A., clerk Auditor for P. O. Dep't, Treas. Dep't...........	1,400
Howard, Wm. E., clerk Pension Office........................$3 33 per diem.	
Howard, Joseph, clerk Pension Office..	1,600
Howell, Wm. R., clerk Register's, Treasury Department.......................	1,000
Hull, Wm. H., clerk Pension Office...........................$3 33 per diem.	
Hume, Charles, clerk Second Auditor's, Treasury Department...............	1,200
Hume, Francis, clerk Auditor for P. O. Dep't, Treas. Dep't.................	1,000
Humphreys, G. W., clerk Pension Office......................$3 33 per diem.	
Hungerford, H., clerk Pension Office ....$3 33 per diem.	
Hunter, Wm., chief clerk State Department..	2,000
Hunter, Wm., clerk Fourth Auditor's, Treasury Department.................	1,400
Hunter, John, clerk P. O. Department..	1,400
Huntt, Charles, messenger Bureau of Navy Yards, Navy Dep't..............	700
Hutter, F. C., clerk Paymaster General's, War Department..................	700
Hyde, Samuel G., clerk Interior Department.......................................	1,200
Ingle, Joseph, clerk First Auditor's, Treasury Dep't...........$4 per diem.	
Ingraham, Benjamin S., clerk Interior Department..............................	1,200
Irving, William, Census Bureau..	1,000
Irwin, J. W., clerk Interior Department..	1,300
Isherwood, B. F., Chief Engineer, Navy Department...........................	1,500
Jackson, S. A., Census Bureau..	850
Jacobs, Solomon D., First Assistant Postmaster General......................	2,500
Janney, Samuel H., clerk Third Auditor's, Treasury Department...........	1,150
Janvier, Benjamin A., clerk Third Auditor's, Treasury Department.........	1,000
Jaudon, P., clerk State Department..	800
Jenison, Hartwell, clerk Register's, Treasury Department....................	1,100
Jewell, James G., Census Bureau	1,000
Jewett, J., clerk Pension Office..................................$3 33 per diem	
Johnson, P. C., chief clerk Pension Office...	1,700
Johnson, Richmond, clerk War Department	1,150
Johnson, H. L., clerk P. O. Department..	1,200
Johnson, Philip C., chief clerk Bureau of Construction, Navy Dep't........	1,400
Johnson, George, clerk First Comptroller's, Treasury Department..........	1,000
Johnson, Martin, clerk Auditor for P. O. Dep't, Treas. Dep't................	1,200
Johnson, B. C., clerk Bureau of Construction and Equipment, N. Dep't....	1,400
Johnson, Thomas C., clerk Second Comptroller's, Treasury Department...	1,200
Johnson, L. D., Census Bureau..	1,000
Johnst n, R. W. M., assistant examiner Patent Office, Interior Dep't......	1,500
Jones, Tubman, clerk P. O. Department..	1,000
Jones, Aifred H., clerk P. O. Department..	1,000
Jones, Levin, clerk Third Auditor's, Treasury Department.....................	1,400
Judkins, W. N. B., Census Bureau..	850
Kauffman, E. M., Census Bureau...	1,000
Kayser, J. A., Census Bureau..	1,000
Kean, J. D., Pension Office..	1,000
Keller, J. P., Interior Department..	1,000
Kel y, Moses, Interior Department...	1,300
Kelly, R., Census Bureau ....$3 per diem	
Kennaugh, W. E., Census Bureau...	1,000
Kennedy, W. A., P. O. Department..	1,000

Kennedy, Joseph C. G., Superintendent of Census, Census Bureau......... $3,000
Kennedy, John C., clerk Auditor for P. O. Dep't, Treas. Dep't.............. 1,600
Kent, De Witt, Interior Department... 1,300
Kepler, Samuel, clerk Auditor for P. O. Dep't, Treas. Dep't................. 1,000
Kerr, George C., Third Auditor's, Treasury Department........................ 1,000
Kerr, James D., War Department... 1,000
Kerr, J. L. M., Census Bureau.. 1,000
Kershaw, Henry J., Second Auditor's, Treasury Department.................. 1,200
Kershner, Joseph, Third Auditor's, Treasury Department..................... 1,150
King, W. W., Interior Department... 1,300
King, N. G., principal clerk P. O. Department.................................. 1,600
King, Horatio, principal clerk P. O. Department................................ 1,600
King, T. J., Quartermaster General's, War Department........................ 1,000
King, Charles K., Bureau of Ordnance, Navy Department...................... 1,000
King, William, Bureau of Medicine, Navy Department........................... 1,400
Kinsey, Samuel, Interior Department... 1,400
Knight, T. D., P. O. Department... 1,000
Lacy, R. A., P. O. Department.. 1,400
Lammond, Peter, Register's, Treasury Department.............................. 800
Lane, T. H., Fourth Auditor's, Treasury Department........................... 1,150
Lane, J. H., examiner U. S. Patent Office, Interior Department.............. 2,500
Langdon, Wm. C., assistant examiner Patent Office, Interior Dep't......... 1,500
Langtry, H., First Comptroller's, Treasury Department......................... 1,150
Lannam, Charles, Consular Bureau, State Department.......................... 1,400
Larned, C. J., clerk Auditor for P. O. Dep't, Treas. Dep't.................... 1,000
Lasselle, H., Interior Department... 1,300
Latham, J. D., Interior Department... 1,100
Latham, Woodville, clerk Auditor for P. O. Dep't, Treas. Dep't.............. 1,400
Laub, J. Y., First Comptroller's, Treasury Department......................... 1,400
Lauck, H. C., Pension Office....................................$3 33 per diem.
Laurie, James, Register's, Treasury Department................................. 1,000
Laurie, C., P. O. Department... 1,200
Law, John G., War Department... 1,200
Lawrenson, James, P. O. Department... 1,200
Lea, Luke, Commissioner Indian Affairs, Interior Department................ 3,000
Leal, E. Maxwell, P. O. Department.. 1,400
Lee, Charles H., War Department... 1,000
Lee, Wm. B., clerk War Department.. 1,000
Leech, D. D. T., P. O. Department.. 1,400
Lenthall, John, Chief Naval Constructor, Navy Department.................... 3,000
Lewis, John S., First Auditor's, Treasury Department......................... 1,000
Lewis, J. F., P. O. Department... 1,200
Lewis, T. P., Pension Office.....................................$3 33 per diem.
Lightner, Hopkins, Treasury Department.. 1,200
Lippitt, E. R., Pension Office.....................................$3 33 per diem.
Lipscomb, Wm. C., jr., Bureau of Ordnance, Navy Department.............. 1,000
Lipscomb, Wm. C., clerk Auditor for P. O. Dep't, Treas. Dep't.............. 1,400
Littell, J. D. B., Census Bureau... 1,000
Little, Amos B., second receiving and assignment clerk, Pat. Off., Int. D'pt. 1,200
Long, B. B., Pension Office.......................................$3 33 per diem.
Loundes, Francis, Register's, Treasury Department............................ 1,150
Loving, L. L., Fourth Auditor's, Treasury Department......................... 1,150
Loving, H. C., Census Bureau.. 850
Lowber, John, Interior Department.................................$4 per diem.
Lowry, W. H., Interior Department.. 1,400
Lowry, James H., War Department.. 1,150
Lucas, Ignatius, messenger Navy Department..................................... 700
Lucas, J., messenger Bur. of Provisions and Clothing, Navy Department. 700
Lumsden, W. O., clerk Auditor for P. O. Dep't, Treas. Dep't................. 1,000
Mackall, R. L., chief clerk Fourth Auditor's, Treasury Department....... 1,700

Mackall, Benj. F., Treasury Department.......... $1,200
Macou, J. H., Pension Office..........$3 33 per diem.
Macy C., Census Bureau.......... 1,000
Madora, F.. clerk Pension Office..........$3 33 per diem.
Magill, Samuel, P. O. Department.......... 1,200
Magill, Wm. B., Third Auditor's, Treasury Department.......... 1,150
Magill, C. A., Census Bureau.......... 1,000
Magill, John W., Census Bureau.......... 850
Mahon, David W., First Auditor's, Treasury Department.......... 1,150
Mahon, Alexander, First Auditor's, Treasury Department.......... 1,150
Malcolm, Wm. B.. clerk Pension Office..........$3 33 per diem.
Mandell, George, Treasury Department.......... 1,000
Mangum, W. P.. jr., Census Bureau.......... 1,000
Mark, J. B., Census Bureau.......... 1,000
Markland, M , Quartermaster General's, War Department.......... 1,000
Markle, N. B., clerk Auditor for P. O. Dep't, Treasury Department.......... 1,200
Markle, L., clerk Pension Office..........$3 33 per diem.
Markoe, Francis, chief clerk Diplomatic Bureau, State Department.......... 2,000
Marr, A. N., P. O. Department.......... 1,200
Marr, James H., P. O. Department.......... 1,400
Marron, John, Third Assistant Postmaster General.......... 2,500
Marsh, E., clerk Pension Office..........$3 33 per diem.
Marsh, O. W., clerk Pension Offi e..........$3 33 per diem.
Marshall, W. W. L., clerk Auditor for P. O. Dep't, Treasury Department 1,000
Marshall, J. G., laborer Pension Office.......... 400
Martin, Thomas, Treasury Department.......... 1,000
Mason, Henry, first assistant engineer Navy Department.......... 1,000
Matthews, W. R., Third Auditor's, Treasury Department.......... 1,000
Matthews, Richard T., Third Auditor's, Treasury Department.......... 1,150
Matthews, R. H., Census Bureau..........$3 per diem.
Mayo, A. W., clerk Pension Office..........$3 33 per diem.
McAllister, J. R., clerk Auditor for P. O. Dep't, Treasury Department.... 1,000
McCann, Edward, Third Auditor's, Treasury Department.......... 1,000
McCeney, George, Fourth Auditor's, Treasury Department.......... 1,000
McCleary, James, Register's, Treasury Department.......... 1,400
McClery, E. J., P. O. Department.......... 1,000
McCorkle, J. P., Bureau of Ordnance, Navy Department.......... 1,200
McCorkle, James R., Treasury Department.......... 1,150
McCormick, Hugh, disbursing clerk Patent Office, Interior Depart't.......... 1,200
McCormick, Alexander, Interior Department.......... 1,200
McCrury, W. W., Pension Office..........$3 33 per diem.
McCutchew, John, messenger Treasury Department.......... 700
McDermott, Wm., Interior Department.......... 1,000
McDonnell, E. M., P. O. Department.......... 1,000
McDuell, John, Census Bureau.......... 1,000
McElderry, John P., Bureau Navy Yards, Navy Department.......... 800
McElvaine, J. T., Census Bureau.......... 1,000
McGehee, Lewis, Third Auditor's, Treasury Department.......... 1,000
McGill, R. T., Fourth Auditor's, Treasury Department.......... 1,150
McGill, Henry M., Census Bureau.......... 1,000
McGrorty, W., Paymaster General's, War Department.......... 700
McIlvaine, Joseph, Register's, Treasury Department.......... 800
McIntire, Arthur L., draughtsman Patent Office, Interior Department.......... 1,200
McKean, S. M., Sup't southeast Executive Building, Treas. Department.. 500
McKee, J. S., State Department.......... 1,400
McKenney, John, clerk Auditor for P. O. Dep't, Treasury Department.... 1,400
McKnight, F. M., Census Bureau..........$3 per diem.
McLaughlin, James A., clerk Auditor for P. O. Dep't, Treasury Dep't.... 1,000
McLean, Anthony, Treasury Department.......... 1,200
McLeod, Matthew, Third Auditor's, Treasury Department.......... 1,000

McNeill, Archibald, Third Auditor's, Treasury Department........ $1,000
McNerhany, J., Census Bureau........ 1,000
McPherson, J. D., War Department........ 1,600
McRae, Richard, Pension Office........ $3 33 per diem.
McRea, A. H., clerk Auditor for P. O. Dep't, Treasury Department........ 1,200
McRoberts, T. B., Census Bureau........ 1,000
McSherry, James, Third Auditor's, Treasury Department........ 1,000
Mechlin, Wm., chief clerk Second Auditor's, Treasury Department........ 1,800
Meech, L. W., Census Bureau........ 1,000
Meiere, J., Census Bureau........ 1,000
Meire, J. E., clerk Pension Office........ $3 33 per diem.
Mercer, George W., Second Auditor's, Treasury Department........ 1,200
Messerve, John M., Census Bureau........ $3 per diem.
Mickum, Samuel, messenger Navy Department........ 700
Middleton, L. S., clerk Auditor for P. O. Dep't, Treasury Department........ 1,200
Middleton, Robert W., Second Auditor's, Treasury Department........ 1,200
Miles, T. H., Pension Office........ $3 33 per diem.
Miller, Mitchel H., chief clerk First Auditor's, Treasury Department........ 1,700
Miller, J. Frank, First Auditor's, Treasury Dep't........ $4 per diem
Miller, T. J., Pension Office........ $3 33 per diem.
Miller, W. J., P. O. Department........ 1,200
Miller, Wm., Treasury Department........ 1,400
Miller, Hezekiah, Indian Bureau, Interior Department........ 1,400
Miller, James J., Indian Bureau, Interior Department........ 1,400
Miller, E. P., Census Bureau........ 1,000
Mitchell, Geo. W., clerk Auditor for P. O. Dep't, Treasury Department........ 1,000
Mitchell, H., Pension Office........ $3 33 per diem.
Mitchell, George, Census Bureau........ 850
Mix, Charles E., chief clerk Indian Bureau, Interior Department........ 2,000
Monroe, Charles, clerk Auditor for P. O. Dep't, Treasury Dep't........ 1,000
Monroe, T., Census Bureau........ 1,000
Moody, T. L., Second Auditor's, Treasury Department........ 1,400
Moore, J. S., Quartermaster General's, War Department........ 1,000
Moore, F. H., Third Auditor's, Treasury Department........ 1,000
Moore, John M., principal clerk of Surveys, Interior Department........ 1,800
Moore, James, messenger Treasury Department........ 700
Moore, P. M., principal cor. clerk Navy Department........ 1,500
Moore, John J., Census Bureau........ 1,000
Moran, Wm. E., messenger Interior Department........ 700
Moran, W. P., additional clerk Navy Department........ 1,200
Morehead, S. W., clerk Auditor for P. O. Dep't, Treasury Department........ 1,400
Morgan, M., Treasury Department........ 1,200
Morris, Charles, chief of Bureau of Ordnance, Navy Department........ 3,500
Morris, Robert, P. O. Department........ 1,400
Morris, G. W., Census Bureau........ $3 per diem.
Morrison, Wm. W., assistant cor. clerk Navy Department........ 1,200
Morton, L. M., clerk Paymaster General's, War Department........ 700
Moss, H. H., clerk Pension Office........ $3 33 per diem.
Mullikin, N., messenger Pension Office........ 500
Muse, L., assistant messenger Navy Department........ 400
Mustin, Thomas, chief clerk Fifth Auditor's, Treasury Dep't........ 1,700
Nevins, John C., Census Bureau........ 1,000
Nevins, John S., Register's, Treasury Department........ 1,000
Newcombe, J. W., War Department........ 1,000
Niles, Benjamin F., Third Auditor's, Treasury Department........ 1,000
Niles, Wm. Ogden, Pension Office........ 1,400
Niles, Samuel V., Interior Department........ 1,100
Nimmocks, T. B., Paymaster General's, War Department........ 700
Norment, Samuel, Third Auditor's, Treasury Department........ 1,150
North, J. Bartram, Treasury Department........ 1,400

Nourse, Michael, chief clerk Register's, Treasury Department	$1,700
Nourse, John R., Register's, Treasury Department	1,400
Noyes, J. H., Pension Office.........$3 33 per diem.	
Nutt, Wm. D., Treasury Department	1,200
O'Brien, J., P. O. Department	1,000
O'Dell, T. T., Pension Office.........$3 33 per diem.	
Offutt, St. George H., clerk Auditor for P. O. Dep't, Treas. Department	1,000
Oliphant, John, Register's, Treasury Department	1,600
Oliver, J. B., clerk Fourth Auditor's, Treasury Department	1,000
O'Neale, H. G., clerk Fourth Auditor's, Treasury Department	1,000
Ourand, E., messenger Treasury Department	700
Owens, B. F., Pension Office.........$3 33 per diem.	
Page, Wm. A., Interior Department	1,200
Paine, O. S., Pension Office.........$3 33 per diem.	
Parker, J. E., P. O. Department	1,200
Parker, George S., Census Bureau	600
Parks, John W., third assistant engineer, Navy Department	800
Parris, S. B., clerk Second Comptroller's, Treasury Department	800
Patterson, Edgar, Register's, Treasury Department	1,000
Peake, Wm., laborer Treasury Department	480
Peale, T. R., assistant examiner Patent Office, Interior Department	1,500
Pearce, Allan, Interior Department	1,100
Pearce, Gideon, Third Auditor's, Treasury Department	1,150
Perkins, E. G., Census Bureau	1,000
Pettit, Charles W., Third Auditor's, Treasury Department	1,000
Phelps, E. J., Second Comptroller, Treasury Department	3,000
Phelps, George, messenger War Department	500
Phelps, R. H., Census Bureau	800
Pigott, J., Third Auditor's, Treasury Department	1,000
Pillow, M. L., clerk Paymaster General's, War Department	700
Plater, Wm., Bureau of Medicine, Navy Department	1,200
Platt, J. H., Register's, Treasury Department	1,200
Pleasanton, Stephen, Fifth Auditor, Treasury Department	3,000
Pleasants, Joseph B., Third Auditor's, Treas. Dep't.........$4 per diem.	
Polk, Wm. L., War Department	700
Polk, P. P., Diplomatic Bureau, State Department	1,400
Polk, Josiah F., Second Auditor's, Treasury Department	1,400
Pope, Charles T., clerk Auditor for P. O. Dep't, Treasury Department	1,400
Portier, P. M., Third Auditor's, Treasury Department	1,000
Porter, F. J., Interior Department	1,100
Porter, Daniel P., Third Auditor's, Treasury Department	800
Potts, Samuel, J., Indian Bureau, Interior Department	1,400
Potts, John, chief clerk War Department	2,000
Powell, Robert S., clerk Auditor for P. O. Dep't, Treasury Department	1,200
Powell, Richard, draughtsman Navy Department	800
Powell, W. C., Interior Department	1,200
Powell, Grafton, messenger Interior Department	700
Powers, D., Census Bureau	1,000
Pratt, H. D., State Department	800
Prentice, R., clerk Auditor for P. O. Dep't, Treasury Department	1,200
Preuss, T. K., Third Auditor's, Treasury Department	1,000
Preuss, Henry C., War Department	800
Proctor, J. J., Census Bureau	1,000
Purrington, T., clerk Second Comptroller's, Treasury Department	1,150
Quincy, S. H., assistant messenger Interior Department	500
Quisenberry, Jackson T., Second Auditor's, Treasury Department	1,000
Rady, Morris P., laborer Interior Department	500
Ragan, E. L., Paymaster General's, War Department	700
Rainey, Samuel, Interior Department	1,000

Rainey, J. H., Second Comptroller's, Treasury Department.................... $1,150
Ramsey, J. M., First Comptroller's, Treasury Department.................... 1,400
Randall, Henry K., Third Auditor's, Treasury Department.................... 1,400
Randall, S. S., War Department.................... 1,000
Randall, N. A., Interior Department.................... 1,300
Randolph, Wm. B., Treasurer's, Treasury Department.................... 1,700
Ratcliffe, W. B., Census Bureau.................... 850
Rawlins, E., P. O. Department.................... 1,200
Read, J. G., Paymaster General's, War Department.................... 700
Read, L. F., Paymaster General's, War Department.................... 700
Read, Joseph S., P. O. Department.................... 1,200
Rearden, M., assistant messenger Interior Department.................... 500
Reeve, Samuel, Second Auditor's, Treasury Department.................... 1,000
Reilly, Benjamin T., Interior Department.................... 1,300
Reily, John H., Bureau of Construction, Navy Department.................... 1,200
Reynolds, Joseph, clerk Auditor for P. O. Dep't, Treas. Dep't.................... 1,400
Rhees, William J., Census Bureau.................... 1,000
Rhees, H. H., Census Bureau.................... 1,000
Rice, N., clerk War Department.................... 1,400
Richards, William, Interior Departmenr.................... 1,300
Richardson, Wm. A., Third Auditor's, Treasury Department.................... 1,000
Ricketts, R., Fifth Auditor's, Treasury Department.................... 1,150
Ricketts, Richard, Interior Department.................... 1,100
Riddick, R. H., First Auditor's, Treasury Deparment.................... 1,150
Ridgely, Wm. G., chief clerk Bureau of Navy Yards, Navy Dep't.................... 1,600
Rind, Samuel S., Third Auditor's, Treasury Department.................... 1,600
Rind, Wm. A., Third Auditor's, Treasury Department.................... 1,000
Ringgold, F., First Auditor's, Treasury Department.................... 1,150
Rittenhouse, Benjamin F., Register's, Treasury Department.................... 1,400
Ritter, Frederick W., Register's, Treasury Department.................... 1,000
Robertson, James W., Third Auditor's, Treasury Department.................... 800
Robinson, Wm., miscellaneous clerk, Navy Department.................... 1,000
Robinson, H. E., Pension Office....................$3 33 per diem.
Roche, James R., Indian Bureau, Interior Department.................... 1,200
Rockwell, D., Interior Department....................$4 per diem.
Rogers, B. F., First Comptroller's, Treasury Department.................... 1,150
Rose, T. H., superintendent General P. O. Building.................... 250
Rowzee, G., assistant messenger Interior Department.................... 500
Russell, C. P., P. O. Department.................... 1,200
Russell, A. W., Census Bureau.................... 1,000
Rust, S., Census Bureau.................... 1,000
Saffell, Wm. T. R., Third Auditor's, Treasury Department.................... 1,000
Sands, T. E., Pension Office....................$3 33 per diem.
Sanger, W. P. S., Civil Engineer, Navy Dep't.................... 2,000
Sargent, N., Register, Treasury Department.................... 3,000
Sasscer, Wm. B., clerk Auditor for P. O. Dep't, Treasury Department..... 1,200
Saunders, T. J., Treas. Department.................... 1,150
Saunders, David, P. O. Department.................... 1,400
Saunders, J. D., Census Bureau.................... 1,000
Schaeffer, George C., examiner Patent Office, Interior Department.................... 2,500
Schermerhorn, M., Quartermaster General's, War Department.................... 1,000
Schreiner, Henry J., Navy Department.................... 1,300
Schreiner, Charles W., Third Auditor's, Treasury Dep't.......$4 per diem.
Schreiner, ——, Bureau of Provisions and Clothing, Navy Dep't.................... 1,300
Schwarzmann, G. A., P. O. Department.................... 1,200
Scott, E. M., Third Auditor's, Treasury Department.................... 1,000
Scott, James, Census Bureau.................... 850
Scrivener, John, messenger Interior Department.................... 700
Seaman, E. C., chief clerk First Comptroller's, Treasury Dep't.................... 1,700

Selden, James, Navy Department	$1,000
Semmes, D. R., Census Bureau	1,000
Sessford, John, Second Comptroller's, Treasury Department	1,000
Sewell, Thomas, State Department	1,400
Seybolt, F. S., clerk Auditor for P. O. Dep't, Treasury Department	1,000
Sharretts, John F., clerk Auditor Treasury for P. O. Department	1,600
Shedd, W. P., P. O. Department	1,000
Sheels, R. M., P. O. Department	1,200
Shields, James W., messenger Interior Department	700
Shields, John P., clerk Auditor for P. O. Dep't, Treasury Department	1,200
Shirley, W. H., Interior Department	1,200
Shirley, Charles B., Third Auditor's, Treasury Department	1,000
Shrader, F. M., P. O. Department	1,000
Shriver, A. F., Second Auditor's, Treasury Department	1,400
Shubrick, Com. W. B., chief of Bureau of Construction, Navy Dep't	3,500
Shugert, S. T., Patent Office, Interior Department	14,00
Shulze, Francis S., Third Auditor's, Treasury Department	1,000
Simmons, C., Census Bureau	1,000
Simpson, Presly, clerk Auditor for P. O. Dep't, Treasury Department	1,200
Sims, John M., Second Auditor's, Treasury Department	1,400
Sinclair, Wm., chief of Bureau of Provisions and Clothing, N. Dep't	3,500
Sinclair, Wm., chief of Bureau of Provisions and Clothing, Navy Dep't	3,500
Skinner, F. G., Interior Department	$4 per diem.
Skinner, A. P., Paymaster General's, War Department	700
Slade, W. O., Pension Office	$3 33 per diem.
Slemmer, Charles, Interior Department	1,000
Sloane, John, Treasurer, Treasury Department	3,000
Smith, Joseph, chief of Bureau of Navy Yards, Navy Dep't	3,500
Smith, Andrew K., Interior Department	1,300
Smith, E. Goodrich, Interior Department	1,200
Smith, Caleb P., Interior Department	1,200
Smith, T. C., clerk Auditor for P. O. Dep't, Treasury Department	1,200
Smith, Henry, Pension Office	$3 33 per diem.
Smith, T. L., First Auditor, Treasury Department	3,000
Smith, William B., First Auditor's, Treasury Department	1,150
Smith, J. H., Register's, Treasury Department	1,400
Smith, James M., Third Auditor's, Treasury Department	1,200
Smith, J. T., Paymaster General's, War Department	700
Smith, J. A., Paymaster General's, War Department	700
Smith, F. S., examiner Patent Office, Interior Department	2,500
Smith, John, P. O. Department	1,200
Smith, C., P. O. Department	1,200
Smith, J. B., assistant messenger Interior Department	500
Smith, J. H., Paymaster General's, War Department	700
Smoot, Luther R., Indian Bureau, Interior Department	1,200
Solomon, S. N., Third Auditor's, Treasury Department	1,000
Sommerville, R. A., Pension Office	$3 33 per diem.
Sommerville, B. F., Paymaster General's, War Department	700
Southall, Albert G., sup't timber agency, Navy Dep't	1,500
Speer, A., Fifth Auditor's, Treasury Department	1,150
Spotswood, R. T., Census Bureau	1,000
Spurrier, C., Census Bureau	1,000
Stanley, J. G., Interior Department	1,100
Stansbury, Charles F., Patent Office, Interior Department	1,200
Stanton, H. T., Census Bureau	1,000
Steele, T. R., Pension Office	$3 33 per diem.
Steele, A., Interior Department	1,100
Steele, John H., Indian Bureau, Interior Department	1,600
Steiger, W. T., draughtsman Interior Department	1,500
Stellwagen, Charles K., draughtman Bureau of Ordnance, Navy Dep't	1,000

Stevens, Joseph T., P. O. Department.. $1,400
Stevens, W. W., Census Bureau.. 1,000
Stewart, J. E., Pension Office..$3 33 per diem.
Stewart, Charles B., Engineer-in-Chief, Navy Dep't.. 3,000
Stewart, Charles, Census Bureau.. 850
Stinson, Daniel, Paymaster General's, War Department.. 700
Street, Wm. W., clerk Auditor for P. O. Dep't, Treasury Department...... 1,000
Stroman, Henry C., Treas. Department.. 1,000
Strong, J., W., Interior Department.. 1,400
Stuart, Charles B., Engineer-in-Chief, Navy Department.. 3,000
Stuart, A. A., Pension Office..$3 33 per diem.
Sullivan, Wm. H., clerk Auditor for P. O. Dep't, Treasury Department... 1,200
Sullivan, J. B., Second Auditor's, Treasury Department.. 1,150
Suter, Henderson, clerk Auditor Treasury for P. O. Department.. 1,200
Swearingen, C. E., Pension Office.. 1,200
Sweeney, J. R., Pension Office..$3 33 per diem.
Sylvester, George, messenger Second Auditor's, Treasury Dep't.. 700
Tapscott, A. B., Pension Office..$3 33 per diem.
Tasistro, L. F., translator State Dep't.. 1,600
Tastet, Nicholas, clerk Auditor for P. O. Dep't, Treas. Dep't.. 1,400
Taylor, Walter H. S., ass't chief clerk Third Auditor's, Treas. Dep't....... 1,400
Taylor, Lewis L., First Comptroller's, Treas. Dep't.. 1,400
Taylor, J. T., Pension Office..$3 33 per diem.
Taylor, T. J., Pension Office..$3 33 per diem.
Terrett, W., Paymaster General's, War Dep't.. 700
Terry, E. S., Recorder Land Office, Interior Department.. 2,000
Tessowsky, John, Register's, Treas. Dep't.. 1,150
Thomas, E. M., laborer Pension Office.. 400
Thompson, George W., Interior Department.. 1,300
Thompson, S. W., Interior Department.. 1,100
Thompson, James, chief clerk Third Auditor's, Treas. Dep't.. 1,700
Thompson, Wm., Third Auditor's, Treas. Dep't.. 1,000
Thrall, Wm, B., clerk Auditor for P. O. Dep't, Treas. Dep't.. 1,600
Thruston, T. B., Census Bureau.. 850
Tidball, E. M., Bureau of Ordnance, Navy Department.. 1,0C0
Todd, John, clerk Auditor for P. O. Dep't, Treas. Dep't.. 1,000
Todd, William L., Census Bureau.. 1,000
Todhunter, J. E., P. O. Dep't.. 1,400
Topping, J. H., Census Bureau..$3 per diem.
Torbert, James M., First Auditor's, Treas. Dep't.. 1,400
Townshend, David, Paymaster General's, War Dep't.. 700
Triplett, T., Pension Office..$3 33 per diem.
Trott, Thomas P., chief clerk P. O. Dep't.. 2,000
Trott, John P., P. O. Dep't.. 1,000
Tschiffely, T. A., Interior Department.. 1,300
Tuffts, Servetus, clerk Auditor for P. O. Dep't, Treas. Dep't.. 1,000
Turner, M. A., clerk Auditor for P. O. Dep't, Treas. Dep't.. 1,000
Tustin, S., Pension Office..$3 33 per diem.
Tweedy, R. D., Census Bureau.. 1,000
Tyler, J., Pension Office..$3 33 per diem.
Tyson, Wm., Third Auditor's, Treas. Dep't.. 1,150
Upshur, A. B., recording clerk Navy Department.. 1,000
Upton, C. H., Census Bureau.. 1,000
Van De Venter, E., P. O. Department.. 1,200
Van Zandt, N. B., First Comptroller's, Treas. Department.. 1,400
Vass, D., P. O. Department.. 1,200
Vinson, Charles, Third Auditor's, Treas. Department.. 1,400
Wadsworth, Adrian R., Treasury Department.. 1,150
Waggaman, J. H., Interior Department.. 1,200
Wakeman, N. T., Census Bureau.. 1,000

Walbridge, C., Interior Department........ $1,100
Walker, James C., P. O. Department........ 1,400
Walker, John, War Department........ 1,000
Waller, W. L., Fourth Auditor's, Treasury Department........ 1,000
Walsh, R. M., State Department........ 1,400
Ward, L., Bureau of Construction, Navy Department........ 1,000
Warder, W., Census Bureau........ $3 per diem.
Washington, Perrin, clerk Auditor for P. O. Department, Treas. Dep't..... 1,400
Washington, G. W., Pension Office........ $3 33 per diem.
Washington, R. C., P. O. Department........ 1,400
Washington, L. Q., Treasury Department........ 1,000
Watkins, T., Census Bureau........ 1,000
Watkins, George S., assistant corresponding clerk Navy Department....... 1,200
Watson, George W., Third Auditor's, Treasury Department........ 1,000
Watson, James, W., assistant messenger P. O. Department........ 450
Watson, William, Census Bureau........ 1,000
Watters, John, messenger War Department........ 500
Waugh, Wm. B., Indian Bureau, Interior Department........ 1,400
Weaver, Charles E., State Department........ 1,000
Weems, J. E., jr., Pension Office........ $3 33 per diem.
Weems, J. E., Pension Office........ $3 33 per diem.
Weightman, R. C., chief clerk Patent Office, Interior Department.......... 1,700
Weightman, H. R., Pension Office........ $3 33 per diem.
Welsh, Charles W., additional corresponding clerk, Navy Department...... 1,200
West, Wm. H., Treasury Department........ 1,400
West, John, clerk Auditor for P. O. Dep't, Treasury Department........ 1,000
Wheat, J. H., P. O. Department........ 1,400
Wheeler, John P., clerk Auditor for P. O. Dep't, Treasury Department... 1,200
White, Ashton, S. H., Interior Department........ 1,400
White, L. J., Census Bureau........ $3 per diem.
Whiting, Samuel S., Third Auditor's, Treasury Department........ 1,000
Whiting, George C., chief clerk Interior Department........ 2,000
Whitney, L. F., Pension Office........ $3 33 per diem.
Whittlesey, E. M., clerk First Comptroller's, Treasury Department........ 1,150
Whittlesey, E., First Comptroller, Treasury Department........ 3,500
Whittlesey, Comfort S., P. O. Department........ 1,400
Widdicombe, W. H., messenger War Department........ 650
Williams, Philip, Interior Department........ 1,200
Williams, Samuel F., Bureau of Navy Yards, Navy Department........ 1,000
Williams, J. S., Bureau of Provisions and Clothing, Navy Department..... 1,100
Williams, Wm. B., Pension Office........ 1,200
Williams, J. S., Pension Office........ $3 33 per diem.
Williams, John S., Navy Department........ 1,100
Williamson, G. P., Treasury Department........ 1,200
Willis, F. A., Register's, Treasury Department........ 1,000
Wills, S., Pension Office........ $3 33 per diem.
Wilson, P. F., Interior Department........ 1,200
Wilson, Joseph S., Sup't on Chickasaw business, Interior Department..... 250
Wilson, James C., War Department........ 1,150
Wilson, John, Commissioner General Land Office........ 3,000
Wilson, Wm. R., Pension Office........ $3 33 per diem.
Wilson, J. D., Pension Office........ 1,400
Wilson, Joseph S., principal clerk Private Land Claims, Interior Dep't..... 1,800
Wilson, John C., clerk Second Comptroller's, Treasury Department........ 1,200
Wilson, J. O., clerk Auditor for P. O. Dep't, Treasury Department........ 1,000
Wilson, J. R., clerk Auditor for P. O. Department, Treas. Department.... 1,000
Winston, Isaac, Indian Bureau, Interior Department........ 1,000
Winter, Thomas D., Third Auditor's, Treasury Department........ 1,000
Wise, James M., Register's, Treasury Department........ 1,000
Woodrow, Robert, Interior Department........ 1,400

Woods, J. K., Pension Office ....$3 33 per diem.
Worthington, George F., Third Auditor's, Treasury Department............ $1,000
Wright, Robert, Census Bureau.. 1,000
Yerby, W. W., Interior Department.. 1,200
Young, Coleby, Interior Department.. 1,300
Young, J. F., Interior Department... 1,100
Young, Wm. P., P. O. Department 1,200
Young, John M., Bureau of Navy Yards, Navy Department................. 1,000
Yulee, Elias, Third Auditor's, Treasury Department........................ 1,150
Zantzinger, Wm, C., disbursing agent and sup't N. E. Exec. Building..... 2,000
Zevely, A. M., P. O. Department.. 1,400

Messengers in Census Bureau.

B. Frazier...$1 25 per diem.
John Shorter.. 1 50 per diem.
William Syphax.. 1 25 per diem.
William Cook...$30 per month.

Watchmen in Census Bureau.

William Price... 500
S. Kearney 500

OFFICERS OF THE CORPORATION OF WASHINGTON.

John W. Maury, *Mayor.*
William J. McCormick, *Register.*
William E. Howard, *Tax Clerk.*
Thomas Hutchinson, *Bookkeeper.*
Robert J. Roche, *Collector.*
John H. Bartlett, *Assistant Collector.*
Hugh F. Pritchard, *Assistant Collector.*
Henry W. Ball, *Surveyor.*
Wm. W. De Maine, *Assistant Surveyor.*
James M. Carlisle, *Attorney.*
Jacob Kleiber, *Messenger.*

MEMBERS OF THE BOARD OF ALDERMEN AND BOARD OF COMMON COUNCIL.

FIRST WARD.—*Aldermen*—Wm. B. Magruder and Thomas P. Morgan.
Common Council—Samuel E. Douglass, H. N. Easby, James Kelly.

SECOND WARD.—*Aldermen*—John Wilson and William F. Bayly.
Common Council—Nicholas Callan, J. Russel Barr, Joel W. Downer.

THIRD WARD.—*Aldermen*—John T. Towers and Joseph Borrows.
Common Council—Joseph Bryan, Edward F. Queen, Joseph Davis.

FOURTH WARD.—*Aldermen*—Silas H. Hill and Alexander McD. Davis.
Common Council—John P. Pepper, George Burns, David Hay.

FIFTH WARD.—*Aldermen*—Benjamin B. French and John L. Wirt.
Common Council—Samuel Hanson, jr., John W. Meade, John J. Mulloy.

SIXTH WARD.—*Aldermen*—Thomas Thornley and James A. Gordon,
Common Council—William Morgan, A. W. Miller, James Cull.

SEVENTH WARD.—*Aldermen*—George Page and Ephraim Wheeler.
Common Council—Samuel Pumphrey, Wm. R. Riley, John Van Riswick,

B. B. French, President of the Board of Aldermen.
Nicholas Callan, President of the Board of Common Council.
Erasmus J. Middleton, Secretary of the Board of Aldermen.
Richard Barry, Secretary of the Board of Common Council.
Jacob Kleiber, Porter to the two Boards.

BOARD OF CONTROL WASHINGTON CANAL.

John W. Maury, President.
Thomas P. Morgan,
Joel W. Downer,
Joseph Bryan,
Silas H. Hill,
John W. Meade,
Aaron W. Miller,
Ephraim Wheeler.

TRUSTEES OF THE PUBLIC SCHOOLS.

First District.—Robert Farnham, George J. Abbott, J. F. Haliday.
Second District.—Thomas Donoho, Valentine Harbaugh, Peter F. Bacon.
Third District.—Francis S. Walsh, Charles P. Russell, George R. Ruff.
Fourth District.—Wm. B. Randolph, Samuel Byington, Peter M. Pearson.

Chas. A. Davis, Secretary to the Board of Trustees.

BOARD OF HEALTH.

Dr. Richmond Johnson and Charles Calvert, for First Ward.
Dr. Thomas Miller and John H. Reily, for Second Ward.
Dr. James C. Hall and Wm. R. Young, for Third Ward.
Dr. A. Holmead and G. C. Grammer, for Fourth Ward.
Dr. S. C. Busey and John P. Ingle, for Fifth Ward.
Dr. Samuel A. H. McKim and John E. Bates, for Sixth Ward.
Dr. James E. Morgan and Wm. B. Randolph, for Seventh Ward.

COMMISSIONERS OF ASYLUM.

Charles A. Davis, Theodore Wheeler, George H. Fulmer.

George M. Dove, Physician to Asylum.
Benjamin E. Gittings, Intendent of the Asylum.
Henry Martin, Inspector of Tobacco.
Wm. M. McCauley, Sealer of Weights and Measures.
Jacob Kleiber, Inspector of Flour and Salted Provisions.
James A. Tait, Commissioner Western Section and General Superintendent Canal.
Joseph Cross, Commissioner Eastern Section of the Canal.
Caleb Buckingham, Inspector of Fire Apparatus.

ASSESSORS.

Thomas F. Harkness,
George Plant,
Valentine Harbaugh,
Washington Lewis,
Jeremiah Hepburn,
Daniel E. Kealy,
David Hepburn.

POLICE MAGISTRATES.

Samuel Drury, for the First District.
J. D. Clark, for the Second District.
Saml. Grubb, for the Third District.
B. K. Morsell, for the Fourth District.
Wm. Thompson, for the Fifth District.
James Crandell, for the Sixth District.
Craven Ashford, for the Seventh District.

Horatio N. Steele, Chief of Police.

POLICE OFFICERS.

John H. Craig and Joseph Hilton, for First District.
Wm. H. Barnaclo and Wm. A. Boss, for Second District.
E. G. Handy and J. F. Wollard, for Third District.
R. R. Burr, Wm. Martin, and John Davis, for the Fourth District.
Wm. A. Mulloy, John H. Wise, and J. M. Baker, for Fifth District.
John A. Willett and Josiah Adams, for Sixth District.
Isaac Stoddard and W. B. Mitchell, for Seventh District.

COMMISSIONERS OF IMPROVEMENT.

George W. Harkness, for the First and Second Wards.
Francis B. Lord, for the Third and Fourth Wards.
Thompson Van Reswick, for the Fifth and Sixth Wards.
Henry D. Gunnell, for the Seventh Ward.

COMMISSIONERS OF MARKETS.

Centre Market.—William Orme, John H. Goddard, S. P. Franklin.
East Market.—George H. Fulmer and Lemuel Barnes.
West Market.—Benedict Ransom and Thomas Oxley.
North Market.—Edward F. Queen and Benjamin L. Bogan.

CLERKS OF MARKETS.

F. B. Poston, for the West Market.
John Waters, for the Centre Market.
H. B. Robertson, Assistant Clerk for the Centre Market.
Wm. B. Wilson, Clerk of the Northern Market.
Peter Little, Clerk Eastern Market.

INSPECTORS AND MEASURERS OF LUMBER.

William Burroughs, Wm. G. Deale, John W. Ferguson, Benjamin Bean, Jesse Plowman, John G. Robinson.

WOOD AND COAL MEASURERS.

Robert M. Harrison, Henry Haliday, Richard Winstall, John P. Hilton, John P. Ferguson.

GAUGERS AND INSPECTORS.

Elexius Simms, for the First and Second Wards.
Florian Hitz, for the Third and Fourth Wards.

MEASURERS OF GRAIN, BRAN, SHORTS, &c.

James Gaither, for the First District.
William P. Ferguson, for the Second District.

COMMISSIONERS OF BURIAL GROUNDS.

William Wilson, John C. Harkness, John Wilson, for the Western.
Francis Y. Naylor, John P. Ingle, for East Burial Ground.
Guy Graham, Sexton West Burial Ground.
Thomas J. Bartlett, Sexton East Burial Ground.

SUPERINTENDENTS OE CHIMNEY SWEEPS.

John Lewis, for First Ward.
Ben. L. Bowen, for Second Ward.
Wm. J. Harris, for Third Ward.
Wm. A. Robinson, for Fourth Ward.
Jas. Burgess, for Fifth and Sixth Wards.
Henry C. Bowen, for Seventh Ward.

SCAVENGERS.

William Barr, for the First Ward.
Roger Adamson, for the First District, Second Ward.
James Hollidge, for the Second District, Second Ward.
William Johnson, for the First District, Third Ward.
Thomas Hoodle, for the Second District, Third Ward.
Samuel Curson, for the First District, Fourth Ward.
James Lavender, for the Second District, Fourth Ward.
Hanson Brown, for the Fifth Ward.
William Shepherd, for the Sixth Ward.
John Downs, for the Seventh Ward.

CITY OF WASHINGTON.

Exhibit of the number of Dwellings, &c., erected within the year 1852.

	BRICK DWELLINGS.							WOOD DWELLINGS.						Total No. of Dwellings.	Shops, &c.	Public.	Running feet of brick pavement laid.	Estimated population December 31, 1852.
	On line of streets.				Back from line.			Line of streets.			Back from line.							
Stories	4	3	2	1	3	2	1	3	2	1	3	2	1					
Total Dec. 31, 1848	–	850	1340	26	–	290	3	63	2659	217	6	583	113	6150	390	89	176,196	
Erected in 1849	12	32	24	1	5	–	–	4	84	9	–	13	–	184	9	17	6,322	
Do. 1850	10	57	23	–	6	18	–	9	149	1	–	16	3	292	25	24	6,768	
Do. 1851	1	94	41	–	2	4	–	24	241	3	–	42	1	453	28	44	17,657	
	23	1033	1428	27	13	312	3	100	3133	230	6	654	117	7079	452	174	206,945	
1852. 1st Ward	2	11	7	–	–	–	–	1	41	2	–	2	–	66	3	1	3,185	7,303
2d "	11	56	7	–	–	–	–	11	25	–	–	2	2	114	5	–	2,707	9,673
3d "	4	24	8	–	–	4	–	2	41	1	–	9	–	93	2	–	3,102	6,792
4th "	7	35	15	2	–	3	–	5	71	1	–	17	–	156	4	1	1,659	10,323
5th "	–	6	4	–	1	–	–	2	25	3	–	5	–	46	2	–	2,879	4,287
6th "	1	4	–	–	–	1	–	–	24	1	–	3	–	34	–	–	–	4,292
7th "	–	10	12	–	–	6	–	6	83	–	–	6	–	123	3	1	2,702	6,669
Total built in 1852	25	146	53	2	1	14	–	27	310	8	–	44	2	632	19	3	16,234	49,339

The deepening and walling of the Canal from 15th street to the Anacostia has been completed, and several cesspools made along its margin for the reception of the sediment from drains. The excavations west of 15th street, by dredging, are stiil unfinished, and vessels which can get to 17th street cannot get from thence to the deep water at 15th street, thus continuing the necessity of unloading at 17th street, or of scowing up to the business portion of the city. The work on the Canal should have been begun from the two extremes in sections, and, on the completion of each section, the vessels been admitted bringing in wood, coal, lumber, &c., and thus affording an immediate revenue from wharfage. The Canal itself ought to have been kept free for vessels to pass up through draws in the bridges at 14th, 12th, and 10th streets, to the Centre Market. Had this been done, a lively and active business would have been created, and the revenue from rentals more than trebled, to the great relief of the General and Ward funds; but, instead of this, a narrow, contracted policy has been pursued, to the great injury of the centre portion of the city, by depriving the inhabitants of the free use of the natural highway, and confining the business to boats alone.

The importance of rebuilding the Potomac Bridge is again urged; for no better site can be selected for the interest of the city and adjoining country in Virginia, re-uniting, as it would, the turnpikes leading to it from Alexandria and the Little River turnpike. At its present site, the bridge can be rebuilt at a much less cost than any other, and the evils from freshets prevented by making the openings wide enough to pass all drift wood without hindrance; this alone would prevent the backing of water on the wharves of Georgetown and the central portion of the city, and would leave ample water in the channel of 575 feet on the city side, and 942 feet on the Virginia side, leaving the centre causeway of 1,600 feet permanent, as well as those connecting the two shores. The bridge might be increased somewhat in height and breadth, so as to afford convenience for a railroad over it into the city at 14th street, and continued around the squares facing the river and the Monument Square, to 15th street, on the Canal; and on the south side of the Canal, eastward, to some convenient point near Maryland avenue and 3d street.

The extension of the North Market has produced a beneficial effect, and increased attendance. The extension of the Centre Market on 7th and 9th streets to B street is much wanted; the increased income from which would, no doubt, pay double interest on the outlay, and over which might be rooms for many public purposes.

In the First Ward, K street has been graded from 20th street to Pennsylvania avenue; earth removed from H street; a new brick church for colored people has been erected; D street, from 17th to 19th, partly graded; and the new foundry, erected by Messrs. Cathcart & Schneider, enlarged.

In the Second Ward but little has been done on streets, except casually; several alleys have been graded and paved; and in the Third Ward the same.

In the Fourth Ward some streets have been improved by grading, and a very neat and substantial building erected on the corner of 5th and I streets for a Presbyterian church.

In the Fifth Ward the principal improvement of streets has been on those leading to the new Railroad Depot, changing the appearance of the whole neighborhood.

In the Sixth Ward there has not been much done, either by grading or improving streets; the grading and paving the footways on both sides of 11th street, south of Virginia avenue, would add much to the value and convenience of that neighborhood.

In the Seventh Ward the principal improvements are the new grading of 11th street, and re-laying the footway from D to Water street.

Steamboats are engaged in running hourly to and from Alexandria, daily to Aquia creek, weekly to Baltimore and Norfolk, and occasional trips are made to Mount Vernon. The new steam ferry-boat plying from the south end of 7th street to Alexandria is a great convenience to travelers. Various and important manufacturing establishments are in full operation in the city, giving employment to a large number of workmen, concentrating capital, and furnishing a home market for country and other produce. All around the neighborhood of the city are important improvements, on farms, &c. A plank road has been laid from the termination of 7th street, on the turnpike, to the District line, with a prospect of a further extension. The Army Asylum, on a beautiful elevation near Rock Creek Church, on the farm lately owned by Mr. Riggs, is begun. The beautiful place of Mr. Blagden, south of the Anacostia, it is understood, has been selected for the Lunatic Hospital. A site for a new Cemetery, a mile north of the city, has been purchased—late the farm of Mr. Boyle—on a commanding height, and a commencement made, in preparing and laying out the grounds, to an extent sufficient to do away with the necessity of new grave-yards within the city limits.

The Columbian College, so beautifully located on the heights adjoining the north part of the city, is understood to be in a more flourishing condition than it has hitherto been; but it is to be regretted that so little has been done to improve and embellish the grounds, so as to make them as attractive to the eye as those of Mr. Stone, adjoining; and which might be done at a small cost and a little energy.

The Chesapeake and Ohio Canal is doing a good business, producing a lively trade in Georgetown, and the town is steadily growing to importance. Adjoining to it the new Cemetery on Rock Creek, laid out on a most romantic site, with great taste and judgment, by Mr. De La Roche, is worth visiting.

Alexandria has been much improved this year by the erection of a large number of buildlngs in every part of the town, having water, by pipes, and gaslight introduced. The establishment of Smith & Perkins is very extensive, and superior locomotives, &c., are made at it, thereby keeping capital at home. (See card.)

The commencement of the wings of the Capitol, now up to the level of the first floor, and of most solid workmanship, has given a stimulus to private improvements, affording employment to a large body of workmen, besides creating new establishments for the preparation of the necessary materials, and which, no doubt, will be carried up with vigor as soon as the season opens.

GEORGETOWN COLLEGE, D. C.

In the year 1785, the Rev. John Carroll, D. D., who was the first Archbishop of Baltimore, in conjunction with five gentlemen of property and influence, formed a design of establishing an "Academy at Georgetown, Potomac river, Maryland." Their arrangements being completed, in 1789 the old South East College building was erected, and in 1792 the sessions commenced. In 1798 we find it the "College of Georgetown, Potomac river, State of Maryland."

In 1815, facilities for a more enlarged course of classical and scientific instruction having been increased, the College was raised, by an act of Congress, to the rank of a university, and was empowered to grant and confer degrees in the arts and sciences, &c.

In May 1851, the Medical Department was organized, the lectures of their Faculty being delivered in Washington City.

A Preparatory Department is organized in connection with the College, and is under the immediate supervision of its officers, but is governed by different regulations.

The College buildings, are beautifully situated on the northern bank of the Potomac river, and commands a full view of Washington City, and the adjoining counties of Virginia and Maryland. The scenery on the Potomac is picturesque and highly interesting. The bridge, the aqueduct, (carried over the Potomac on lofty stone piers,) the domes of the Capitol and National Observatory, and the Norman towers and turrets of the Smithsonian Institution, are seen looming in the distance.

The university possesses a select and well-arranged library of 23,000 volumes, and is provided with an extensive philosophical apparatus, and a large first class astronomical observatory, supplied with a transit instrument, meridian circle, an equatorial, &c.

The College is indebted to the liberality and munificence of the late Rev. Thomas Meredith Jenkins, S. J., B. A., one of the Professors, and of the very Rev. Charles Henry Stonestreet, S. J., B. A., and to Robert Jenkins, Esq., of Baltimore, an alumnus of the Institution, for its endowment.

There are literary Debating Societies, and a Reading Room Association in the College, for the improvement of the students.

The first volume of Annals by the Rev. Professor Curley, S. J., the Director, is published.

ODD-FELLOWS.

Central Lodge, No. 1, meets every Friday night, at the Hall on 7th street w.

Washington Lodge, No. 6, meets every Tuesday night, at Hall on 7th st. w.

Eastern Lodge, No. 7, meets every Friday night at Masonic Hall, cor. E and 10th.

Harmony Lodge, No. 9, meets every Monday night at the Hall, cor. 7th e and G s, Navy Yard.

Columbia Lodge, No. 10, meets every Thursday night at the Hall on 7th st. w.

Union Lodge, No. 11, meets every Wednesday night at the Hall, cor. 7th e and G s, Navy Yard.

Friendship Lodge, No. 12, meets every Thursday night at the Hall on 19th st., between Pennsylvania avenue and I st. n, First Ward.

Covenant Lodge, No. 13, meets every Monday night at the Hall on Congress street, Georgetown.

Beacon Lodge, No. 15, meets every Monday night at the Hall on 7th st. w.

Metropolis Lodge, No. 16, meets every Friday night at the Hall on 7th st. w.

Excelsior Lodge, No. 17, meets every Tuesday night at the Hall on 7th st. w.

Mechanics' Lodge, No. 18, meets every Wednesday night at the Hall on Bridge street, Georgetown.

Oriental Lodge, No. 19, meets every Thursday night at the Hall on 7th st. w.

Ridgley Encampment, No. 5, meets second and fourth Wednesdays of every month, at the Hall on 19th street, between Pennsylvania avenue and I street n.

Mount Nebo Encampment, No. 6, meets first and third Wednesdays of every month, at the Hall on 7th st. w.

Grand Encampment of the District of Columbia meets fourth Tuesday January and July, at the Hall on 7th street w.

Columbian Encampment, No. 1, meets first and fourth Wednesdays of every month, at the Hall on 7th street w.

Mount Pisgah Encampment, No. 3, meets first and third Tuesdays of every month, at the Hall on Bridge street, Georgetown.

Maganeu Encampment, No. 4, meets first and third Wednesdays of every month, at the Hall on 7th street w.

Grand Lodge of the District of Columbia meets annually on the second Monday in November, and quarterly on the second Monday of January, April, July, and October.

FREE MASONS.

Grand Lodge meets at Masonic Hall, corner of E and 10th streets, or at Island Hall, at the will of the M. W. Grand Master, on the first Tuesday in May, first Tuesday in November, and on St. John's day, 27th December.

Federal Lodge, No. 7, meets at Masonic Hall, corner of E and 10th streets, on first and third Tuesdays of every month.

Washington Naval Lodge, No. 4, meets at their Hall at the Navy Yard, first Saturday of every month.

Potomac Lodge, No. 5, meets at their Hall in Georgetown, fourth Monday in each month.

Lebanon Lodge, No. 7, meets at Masonic Hall, corner of E and 10th streets, first and third Fridays of each month.

New Jerusalem Lodge, No. 9, meets at Masonic Hall, corner of E and 10th sts., second and fourth Thursdays of each month.

Hiram Lodge, No. 10, meets at Hall on 19th st., on —— Friday of each month.

St. John's Lodge, No. 11, meets at Masonic Hall, corner of E and 10th streets, second and fourth Fridays of each month.

National Lodge, No. 12, meets at Masonic Hall, corner of E and 10th streets, second Saturday of each month.

Washington Centennial Lodge, No. 14, meets at Island Hall, first Thursday in each month.

RED MEN.

Anacostia Tribe, No. 3, meets every Tuesday night, at Masonic Hall, Navy Yard.

Tuscarora Tribe, No. 5, meets every Thursday night, at Odd-Fellows' Hall, corner 7th street e and G street s, Navy Yard.

Osage Tribe, No. 6, meets every Monday night, at Odd-Fellows' Hall, Island.

Grand Council of the District of Columbia meets quarterly, on the second Tuesday of January, April, July, and October, at one of the Halls alternately.

WASHINGTON NATIONAL MONUMENT SOCIETY.

OFFICERS.

Millard Fillmore, *ex officio President.*
Arch. Henderson, *First Vice President.*
John W. Maury, Mayor of Washington, *Second Vice President.*
Tho. Carbery, *Third Vice President.*
J. B. H. Smith, *Treasurer.*
Geo. Watterston, *Secretary.*

MANAGERS.

Winfield Scott,
N. Towson,
Peter Force,
W. W. Corcoran,
W. A. Bradley,
P. R. Fendall,
Walter Jones,
Tho. Blagden,
W. W. Seaton,
M. F. Maury,
T. Hartley Crawford,
Benj. Ogle Tayloe,
Elisha Whittlesey.

WASHINGTON AND ALEXANDRIA BOATS.

The steamer George Washington leaves the wharf, foot of 12th street, at the following hours, viz:

Leaves Alexandria at 7½, 9, 11, 1½, 3, 4½.
Leaves Washington at 8, 10, 12, 2¼, 3¾, 5.
Coaches leave the Capitol at 7½, 9, 11, 1½, 3, 4½.—Fare 12½ cents.

SAMUEL GEDNEY, *Captain.*

The steamer Union leaves the wharf foot of 7th street, at the following hours:

Leaves Alexandria at 8, 10, 12, 2½, 3¾.
Leaves Washington at 9, 11, 1, 3, 4½.
Fare 12½ cents.

JAMES GUY, *Captain.*

MOUNT VERNON.

The steamers George Washington or Thomas Collyer leaves the wharf every Tuesday, Thursday, and Saturday, at 10½ o'clock, a. m., for Mount Vernon and Fort Washington. A line of omnibuses which connects with the boat leaves the Capitol at a quarter to 10 o'clock each day.

TEMPERANCE DIRECTORY FOR THE DISTRICT OF COLUMBIA.

Sons of Temperance.

Grand Division of the District meets second week in October, January, April, and July.

Timothy Division No. 1, meets every Wednesday night at Temperance Hall, (West Room.)

Crystal Fount Division No. 3, meets every Monday night at Temperance Hall, (West Room.)

Potomac Division No. 5, meets every Tuesday night at Georgetown.

Equal Division No. 6, meets every Monday night at Temperance Hall, (East Room.)

Howard Division No. 10, meets every Friday night at Odd Fellows' Hall, Navy Yard.

Northern Liberties Division No. 12, meets every Tuesday night at Temperance Hall, (West Room.)

Mount Vernon Division No. 13, meets every Tuesday night at Island Hall.

Metropolitan Division No. 14, meets every Friday night at Temperance Hall, (East Room.)

George Washington Division No. 15, meets every Monday night at Masonic Hall, Navy Yard.

Independent Order of Rechabites.

Mizpah Encampment meets every 2d and 4th Wednesday at the Hall, corner 7th and D streets,

Mount Vernon Tent No. 208, meets every Thursday night at the Hall, corner 7th and D streets.

George Washington Tent No 265, meets every Monday night at the Hall, corner 7th and D streets.

Potomac Tent No, 290, meets every Tuesday night at Odd Fellows' Hall, 19th street, above Pa. avenue.

Heber Tent No. 298, meets every Thursday night at Odd Fellows' Hall, Georget'n.

Eagle Tent No. 299, meets every Tuesday night at Odd Fellows' Hall, Navy Yard.

Arlington Tent No. 322, meets every Friday night at the Hall, cor. 7th and D sts.

Independent Brothers of Temperance, meets every Friday night at Temperance Hall, (West Room.)

Cadets of Temperance.

George Washington Section No. 1, meets every Thursday night at Temperance Hall, (West Room.)

Junior Order of Rechabites.

Mount Vernon Tent No. 2, meets every Thursday night at Georgetown.

Eagle Tent No. 5, meets every Wednesday night at Navy Yard.

Freemen's Vigilant and Total Abstinence Society, meets every Sunday night at Temperance Hall, E street. Its meetings are open to the public, and addresses are delivered every week.

Columbia Temperance Beneficial Society, meets monthly at Anacostia Hall, Navy Yard.

Temperance Hall, Washington City, E street, between 9th and 10th streets.

Rechabite Hall, Washington City, northeast corner of D and 7th streets.

NORTHERN LIBERTY BUILDING ASSOCIATION, meets at Temperance Hall, first Tuesday of every month.

COURTS IN THE DISTRICT OF COLUMBIA.

Circuit Court meets fourth Monday in March and third Monday in October.

William Cranch, Chief Judge,* - - -	$2,700
James S. Morsell, Assistant Judge, - - -	2,500
James Dunlop, Assistant Judge, - - -	2,500
P. R. Fendall, District Attorney, - - -	fees.
Richard Wallach, Marshal, - - - -	fees.
John A. Smith, Clerk, - - - - -	fees.

Criminal Court meets first Monday in March, third Monday in June, and first Monday in December.

T. Hartley Crawford, Judge, - - - -	$2,000
P. R. Fendall, District Attorney, - - -	fees.
Richard Wallach, Marshal, - - - -	fees.
E. H. Middleton, Clerk, - - - -	fees.

Orphans' Court of Washington County—

W. F. Pursell, Judge, - - - -	$1,500
Edward N. Roach, Register of Wills, - - -	fees.

CIRCULAR.

The Washington City Young Men's Christian Association is a *union* of the young men of all the Evangelical Churches of the city, for the moral, mental, and religious improvement of themselves, and all who shall come within their influence.

Rooms have been taken in *Fowler's Buildings, on Seventh, near E street,* where a *Library* and *Reading Room* is established, and where young men who are strangers in the city will be at all times welcome. A course of *popular lectures* will also be furnished, during the lecture season, by gentlemen of eminence for their scientific, moral, and religious attainments.

Strangers visiting the city are respectfully invited to the rooms of the Association, and referred for information to the *officers*, or any of the undermentioned gentlemen of the *Standing Committee.* This committee consists of *two delegates* from each Evangelical Church in the city, and it is made their *special duty* to "meet the young stranger as he enters our city, take him by the hand, direct him to a boarding place, where he may find a quiet home, pervaded with Christian influences, introduce him to the Church and Sabbath School, bring him to the rooms of the Association, and in every way throw around him good influences, so that he may feel that he is not a stranger, but that noble and christian spirits care for his soul."

The Association respectfully solicits the active co-operation of all young men, and the prayers and contributions (in money, books, papers, or periodicals) of all who would do good to those who, though *young men* now, must soon take the places of their seniors in the church, the family, the State, the community.

OFFICERS.

The following officers were unanimously elected, December, 1852:

President.—Z. Richards, Fourteenth street and New York avenue.

Vice Presidents.—Dr. Jas. S. McKie, State Department; Dr. Richd. H. Coolidge, Navy Department; W. B. Waugh, Indian office; W. Q. Force, cor. 10th and D sts.

Corresponding Secretary.—William Chauncy Langdon, U. S. Patent Office.

Recording Secretary.—Wm. J. Rhees, Census Office.

Treasurer.—Mitchel H. Miller, First Auditor's Office.

Librarian.—A. L. Edwards, First Comptroller's Office.

* Allowed $100 additional from the patent fund.

STANDING COMMITTEE.

Baptist Church.

Church	Committee
First Church, Tenth street,	J. W. Clarke, 7th street, near N. Y. avenue. S. W. Grubb, M street, between 6th and 7th streets.
Second Church, Navy Yard,	Jas. A. Dunnington, B st., between 6th and 7th streets. William Mills, Navy Yard.
Third Church, E st.,	Dr. Samuel C. Smoot, Pa. av., btw. 19th and 20th sts. T. C. McIntyre, corner I and 7th streets.
Fourth Church,	G. W. Dutton, Pa. av., between 4½ and 6th streets. George R. D. Teasdale, 7th street, above E.

Episcopal.

Church	Committee
St. John's Church, H street,	Dr. Richard H. Coolidge, Keller's, President Square. L. B. Hardin, 14th and H streets.
Trinity Church, Third st.,	T. M. Hanson, Potomac Bank. H. J. Kershaw, 13th, between G and H.
Church of the Epiphany, C street,	Ferdinand F. Myer, 12th st., betw H and N. Y avenue. Prof. J. H. C. Coffin, 19th and I streets.
Church of the Ascension, H street,	Chas. W. Schreiner, Third Auditor's Office. Charles F. Perrie, 8th street, near F.
Grace Ch , Island,	C. F. Stansbury, Patent Office. William S. Roberts, B st., near Smithsonian Institution.
Christ Church, Navy Yard,	John W. McKim, opposite City Hall. Dr. S. A. H. McKim, 8th street east, Capitol Hill.

Lutheran.

Church	Committee
St. Paul's, Church, Eleventh st.,	Andrew Noerr, corner E and 11th streets. U. H. Ridenaur, 8th st., betw. D and Pa. avenue.

Methodist.

Church	Committee
McKendry Chapel, New York av.,	L. Durbin Walter, 7th street, between G and H. B. F. Jacobs, 9th and L streets.
Foundry, Ch., Fourteenth street,	R. L. Smallwood, 9th street and Pa avenue. Wm. Bond, 9th, between D and E streets.
Wesley Chapel, F st.,	Joel C. Green, 7th, near Pa. avenue. Wm. Wright, Pa. av., near 6th street.
Union Chapel, Nineteenth street,	J. B. Hines, 20th street, near Pa. avenue. J. L. Hawkins.
Ryland Chapel, Island,	Wm. G. Brock, 10th and G, Island. F. L. Harvey, 10th, near Smithsonian Institution.
Methodist Episcopal, Ch. South, 8th st.,	Alexander G. Brown, Pa. av., between 6th and 7th streets. Samuel H. Latimer, 7th, between Pa. av. and D streets.
Methodist Protestant Church, 9th st.,	W. H. Bangs, 11th, between E and F streets. George H. B. White, 6th, between H and I streets.
Meth. Prot. Church, Navy Yard,	Wm. P. Ferguson, Navy Yard. John McFarland, Navy Yard.
Ebenezer Church, Navy Yard,	Rev. S. A. Marks, Navy Yard. Wm. H. Pritchett, Navy Yard.

Presbyterian.

Church	Committee
First Church, 4½ st.,	John C. Whitwell, Pa. av., btw. 7th and 8th sts. Jay Spurrier, Census office.

Second Church, New York avenue,	Z. D. Gilman, Pa. av., btw. 6th and 7th sts. Prof. William Flyc, K street, near 8th street.
F street Church, (Old School.)	Dr. J. S. Mackie, H, between 7th and 8th streets. Joseph H. Nourse, F, between 12th and 13th streets.
Fourth Ch., Ninth street,	John T. Cochrane, Pa. av., btw 9th and 10th streets. David Bassett, 9th street, between N. Y. av. and L street.

BANK OF THE METROPOLIS.

President—John W. Maury.

Directors—Thomas Carbery, George W. Graham, Charles Hill, Lewis Johnson, George Parker, James Thompson.

Cashier—Richard Smith.

Discount day—Monday.

Residences.

John W. Maury, south side C street west, near Third street.
Thomas Carbery, west side 14th street west, near Canal.
George W. Graham, 15th street west, corner of H north, and in Maryland.
Charles Hill, 14th street west, cor. of Mass. Avenue, and in Maryland.
Lewis Johnson, north side G street north, between 10th nnd 11th streets.
George Parker, south side C street north, corner of 4½ street.
James Thompson, south side L street north, between 26th and 27th streets.

BANK OF WASHINGTON.

President—Wm. Gunton.
Cashier—James Adams.
Paying Teller—Chas. A. James.
Receiving Teller—Wm. E. Howard.
Book Keeper—S. B. Boarman.
Disc. and Note Clk.—G. W. Venable.
Messenger—John Willey.

Trustees.

William Gunton, Jacob Gideon, B. F. Middleton, Stans. Murray, John F. Callan. Archibald Henderson.

PATRIOTIC BANK OF WASHINGTON.

President—Gottlieb C. Grammer.

Directors—Thomas Blagden, William J. McDonald, Eleazar Lindsley, Josiah F. Caldwell, John Purdy, David Saunders, Fitzhugh Coyle.

Cashier—Chancey Bestor.

Discount day—Thursday.

Residences.

Gottlieb C. Grammer, corner 4½ and C streets.
Thomas Blagden, New Jersey avenue, near canal bridge.
Eleazar Lindsley, near the plank road and Park Hotel.
William J. McDonald, C street north, Capitol Hill.
Josiah F. Caldwell, Maryland avenue, between 12th and 13th streets west.
John Purdy, Pennsylvania avenue, between 1st and 2d streets west.
David Saunders, at Mrs. Lamb's, opposite Willard's Hotel.
Fitzhugh Coyle, Missouri avenue, between 4½ and 6th streets.
Chancey Bestor, at Mrs. Taylor's, Penna. avenue, between 4½ and 6th sts.

EXCHANGE BANK OF SELDEN, WITHERS & CO.,

Seventh street, near D street.

PROPRIETORS.

William Selden, late Treas'r U. S., s. side New York av., btw. 13th and 14th sts.
John Withers, Alexandria.
Robert W. Latham, corner of 8th and G streets.
L. P. Bayne, Alexandria.
G. W. C. Whiting, Franklin Row.

OFFICERS.

William Selden, President.
W. C. Bestor, Cashier, south side D street, near 3d st.
David Walker, Bookkeeper, west side Missouri avenue, between 3d and 4½ sts.
Charles E. Thomas, Assistant, west side 12th st., between I and K sts.
Joseph L. Peabody, Collection Clerk.
Wm. H. Selden, Discount Clerk.
Thomas J. Latham, Paying Teller.
H. C. Smith, Assistant.
Joseph M. Adams, Receiving Teller.
John H. Smith, Messenger.
Samuel V. Leech, Messenger.
John Sanderson, Porter.

COLUMBIA BANK.

President—R. P. Stowe.

BANK OF THE REPUBLIC.

President—J. K. Bailey.

FARMERS AND MERCHANTS' BANK OF STATHAM, SMITHSON AND CO.

President—Charles W. Statham; residence, Lynchburg, Virginia.
Cashier—William S. Smithson; residence, Washington, D. C.

BANK OF COMMERCE, GEORGETOWN.

President—C. E. Rittenhouse, *Cashier*—H. B. Sweeney.
Discount Clerk and Notary Public—Francis Harper. *Note Clerk*—A. Wetherill.

COMMERCIAL BANK, GEORGETOWN.

President—J. P. Wiggins. *Cashier*—L. Bostwick.

MECHANICS' BANK, GEORGETOWN.

President—G. Myers. *Cashier*—F. Couch.

FARMERS AND MECHANICS' BANK, GEORGETOWN.

President—Robert Read. *Cashier*—W. Laird, jr.
Book Keeper—J. L. Bangs. *Discount Clerk*—A. H. Porter.

TABLE OF MORTALITY OF THE CITY OF WASHINGTON FOR THE YEAR 1852.

CORRECTED BY DR. RICHARDS.

The following interesting table of mortality of this city, for the year just closed, is worthy the attention of the general reader, and will doubtless command an attentive examination. It has been compiled with care and accuracy, from the official report of the Board of Health.

	January.	February.	March.	April.	May.	June.	July.	August.	September.	October.	November.	December.	Total.
Apoplexy	3	2	2	3	1	3			2	1	1		19
Bronchitis		2											2
Brain congestion, of	2	2		5	1		5	2		4	1	2	24
Brain, dropsy of		1	5		2	4	2	1		1	2		18
Brain, fever	2		2	1	3	2							10
Brain, inflammation of			1		1	1	1	2					6
Brain, softening of				1									1
Cancer			1		3		1	1	1		3		10
Casualty		2		3	4	1	1			2			13
Childbirth	1				1					1	1	1	6
Cholera-infantum	2					11	38	28	3				82
Cholera morbus								1	2				3
Congestion of lungs	2		1	1				1					5
Congestion of bowels					1								1
Consumption	12	14	13	8	9	10	6	10	10	8	13	15	133
Congestive chill	1					1	2	2					6
Convulsions	9	5	7	5	2	10	5	6		4	5	4	62
Croup	1	1	4	1	1	1				1	1	6	17
Cyanosis				1									1
Carbuncle					1								1
Cachexia						1			1				2
Dropsy	4	3	2	4	2	3	1	2		3		2	26
Diarrhœa	1					6	7	2		2	1	1	20
Dyspepsia		1				1	1						3
Drowned							1	3	2		1		7
Dysentery		1				4	15	16		1		1	38
Exposure	1			2							2		5
Epilepsy	1			1	1	1				1			5
Erysipelas	4	2		1				1		1			9
Exhaustion				1									1
Fever, bilious					1		3	2	2		4		12
Fever, catarrh	1	2	3					1				2	9
Fever, typhus							1	1			1	2	5
Fever, gastric											1	1	2
Fever, puerperal	3							1				4	8
Fever, scarlet	4	4	3	5	5	1		4	5	6	9	9	55
Fever, typhoid	1		4		1	1	1			1			9
Gravel						1							1
Gunshot wound					1					1			2
Gangrene								1					1
Gout							1						1
Hysterics													

Table of Mortality of the City of Washington.

TABLE OF MORTALITY—Continued.

	January.	February.	March.	April.	May.	June.	July.	August.	September.	October.	November.	December.	Total.
Hemorrhage	1	3	2	1	1		1				1	1	11
Enlarged Heart					2								2
Hernia							1			1			2
Hooping cough	1	1		1			4		2	1	2		12
Hepatitis							1			1		1	3
Hydrothorax							2				1		3
Inflammation of the bowels	2			3		1		1			1		8
Inflammation of the kidneys											1		1
Inflammation of the lungs			2	1		1				1			5
Inflammation of the bladder	1				1								2
Inflammation of the throat			1										1
Intemperance	3	1	1		1	4	2		3		3		18
Inthrosusception					1	1	1						3
Inanition	1	1	1				1					1	5
Jaundice			1	1							1		3
Mania-a-potu				1	1								2
Metroperitonitis				1									1
Measles		2	7	8	3	4	1						25
Murdered	1		1		1	1		2					6
Marasmus			1	2	2	4	4			3			16
Nervous disease		1											1
Old age	5	1	5	2		1	3	2	2	5	1		27
Ovarian disease			1								1		2
Obstruction of the rectum			1										1
Paralysis		5	4	1	3	1	2	1	3		2		22
Pleurisy				1	1							1	3
Pneumonia	7	10	4	6	2	2	1	1	6	1	3	5	48
Poisoned						1		1				1	3
Peritonitis	1	1	3		1	5	1				1	1	14
Premature births	8	1	5	2	5	5	2	2	6	11	1	4	52
Quinsy					1								1
Rheumatism					2	1							8
Scrofula								1			1	3	5
Putrid throat											1		1
Small-pox	1	1	1	1							1	1	6
Suicide			1										1
Spine affection								2					2
Tetanus		2				2							4
Teething						1	5	4	4				14
Ulcered bowels		1		1									2
Worms											1	1	2
Visitation of God	6	3	7	1	4	5	7	4	15		2	3	57
	102	79	102	83	78	107	136	111	75	66	72	76	1087

Of the above, 410 were white males, 377 white females, 148 colored males, 141 colored females; 7 white, sex not reported; 4 colored, sex not reported. Under one year, 323; 1 to 5, 215; 5 to 10, 44; 10 to 15, 20; 15 to 20, 22; 20 to 30, 90; 30 to 40, 78; 40 to 50, 75; 50 to 60, 70; 60 to 80, 103. Over 80, 33; 100, 1; 102, 1; 115, 1.

By a reference to the weekly reports of interments, I find that the colored population died in greater numbers during the winter months—a fact also noticed in the reports of Baltimore city, published in the *Sun*; a fact proving that they cannot endure cold as well as heat. These statistics show favorably the healthiness of the city as compared with the bills of mortality of other cities, there being three persons over the age of 100, and one reaching the extraordinary age of 115.

GAS WORKS.

President—Silas H. Hill.
Secretary—James F. Brown.
Superintendent—James Keene.
Directors—Silas H. Hill, John W. Maury, Charles B. Dungan, Charles H. Rogers, Beach Vanderpool.

OFFICERS OF THE AMERICAN COLONIZATION SOCIETY.

President—John H. B. Latrobe, Esq.
Secretary and Treasurer—Rev. W. McLain.
Recording Secretary—J. W. Lugenbeel, M. D.
Executive Committee—Harvey Lindsly, M. D., Hon. Elisha Whittlesey, Joseph H. Bradley, Esq., A. O. Dayton, Esq., Rev. J. S. Bacon, D. D., William Gunton, Esq. W. W. Seaton, Esq.

PREFACE.

THE following work is offered to the public in the confident hope that it will be found both interesting and useful; whether as a Guide-Book for the Traveller, a Directory for the Business-man, or a Manual of Facts and Charts for those who seek information concerning the large and increasing cities of our extensive Republic, scattered along the Atlantic slope, through its central valleys, and on the Pacific shore.

The plan of this work is *unique;* the design entirely practical; *nothing* of the kind has before been published.

The reading matter gives a large amount of historical and descriptive information, which will be profitable for study and convenient for reference.

The tables of Railroad Distances have been prepared with great care, and present a mass of valuable statistics, and highly serviceable to the traveller.

The Maps constitute an "*Atlas of Cities*," and form, perhaps, the most interesting and useful, as they do the most costly part of the work. They have been prepared with accuracy and at great expense, and the purposes they are intended to answer are various and important. The *business-man* will be able to see at a glance, the particular street and location where he has done, or wishes to do, his business; while the *tourist* and pleasure-seeker will have a prompt and truthful guide to those great marts of commerce. Persons at a distance will instantly trace the office or residence of their *city friends; and should a conflagration, or other calamity occur*, or important changes take place, they would locate them at once, and accurately, by reference to these maps.

It is commended to the popular favor, as it was prepared for the popular use.

CONTENTS.

MAPS AND ILLUSTRATIONS.

100

AMERICAN CITIES.

BANGOR, Me.

A CITY, and the seat of justice of Penobscot county, situated on the west side of Penobscot river, at the head of tide water, 58 miles from the Atlantic, 68 northeast from Augusta, 230 northeast of Boston. Vast quantities of lumber are annually floated down the river to this place, whence it is shipped to the West Indies and various parts of the Union. This city is built on elevated ground, affording a fine view of the surrounding country, and is tastefully laid out and adorned with trees. The public, as well as the private buildings, are, many of them, neat and elegant. The harbor is inaccessible for four months in the winter, but will admit, at other times, vessels of 300 or 400 tons, the tide alone rising to the height of 17 feet. Lines of steamboats connect the city with Portland, and a railroad extends 12 miles up the river to Oldtown. The Bangor Theological Seminary was incorporated in 1834, and is in prosperous condition.

Population in 1790, 169; in 1800, 277; in 1810, 850; in 1820, 1,221; in 1830, 2,867; in 1840, 8,627; in 1850, 14,538.

BATH, Me.

THIS is a flourishing town, situated in Lincoln county, on the west bank of Kennebec river, at the head of winter navigation, 12 miles from the ocean, 37 miles south of Augusta, 153 northeast of Boston. It occupies a gentle slope about a mile and a half along the river, and extends back about three quarters of a mile. The harbor is safe and commodious, admitting vessels drawing 16 feet of water. A large amount of capital is employed in manufactures and ship-building. The village is connected with Portland, Portsmouth, and Boston, by both railroad and steamboat lines.

Population, in 1810, 2,491; in 1820, 3,056; in 1830, 3,773; in 1840, 5,148; in 1850, 8,108.

RAILROADS.

From Portland to Haverhill via Exeter.

	MILES.	
To Scarborough ...	7	
Saco..............	5	12
Biddeford	2	14
Kennebunkport....	4	18
Kennebunk........	4	22
Wells	5	27
North Berwick....	6	33
Berwick Junc.....	4	37
South Berwick....	1	38
Salmon Falls......	1	39
Rollinsford	1	40
Dover	3	43
Madbury	4	47
Durham	3	50
Newmarket	5	55
Newmarket Junc..	2	57
Exeter	5	62
East Kingston.....	5	67
Newtown	4	71
Plaistow..........	3	74
Haverhill..........	5	79

From Portland to Portsmouth.

To South Berwick as above.........		38
Elliot..............	7	45
Kittery	5	50
Portsmouth........	1	51

From Portland to Gorham.

To Woodford......	2	
Morrell's	1	3
Saccarappa	4	7
Gorham	3	10

From Portland to Montreal and Quebec.

To Falmouth.......	4	
Chamberlain.......	5	9
Yarmouth	2	11
Yarmouth	1	12
North Yarmouth...	3	15
Webber's..........	4	19
North Gloucester..	3	22
Cobb's Bridge	2	24
Danville Junc......	3	27
Hotel Road........	2	29
Empire Road......	3	32
Mechanics' Falls...	4	36
Exford	4	40
South Paris........	7	47
North Paris........	8	55

AUGUSTA, Me.

The capital of the state, is situated on both sides of Kennebec river, at the head of sloop navigation, 42 miles from the ocean, 163, northeast of Boston, and 595 miles from Washington. In 1831, the seat of government was removed from Portland to this place. The statehouse is situated a little south of the town, on the west side of the river, and is constructed of granite, after the plan of the Massachusetts statehouse, in Boston. Length of the central part, 84 feet; depth 56 feet, with a wing on each side 34 by 54 feet. It is entered by a Doric portico of eight granite columns 21 feet high. The central part of the building is surmounted by a handsome cupola and dome, and the whole is embosomed in a spacious park of ornamental trees. An elegant and costly stone-bridge of two arches, each of 180 feet span, connects the two parts of the village. Among other public structures, are the United States Arsenal, which is on the east side of the river, the State Lunatic Asylum, and the Augusta High School. The growth of the place has been rapid, since it became the capital of the state.

Population in 1810, 1,805; in 1820, 2,475; in 1830, 3,800; in 1840, 5,314; in 1850, 8,255.

PORTLAND, Me.

This flourishing city, and seat of justice of Cumberland county, is pleasantly situated on a peninsula, at the southwest extremity of Casco bay, facing the Atlantic, from which it presents a beautiful view. It is 50 miles southwest of Augusta, 110 northeast of Boston, and 545 miles from Washington. The harbor is one of the best in the United States, being capacious and protected by the islands at its entrance, from the severity of the northeast storms, which prevail on this coast. A lighthouse, 72 feet high, built in 1790, still in good preservation, stands on Portland Head. On an eminence, in the northeast part of the city, is an observatory, 70 feet high, which affords a fine view of the neighboring harbor and islands, and the surrounding country, extending to the White mountains in New Hampshire. Railroads extend from this city to the valley of the Androscoggin, Augusta, Portsmouth, Boston, &c., and steamboats and packets ply to Boston and other ports, during the season of navigation. Cumberland and Oxford canal communicates with Sebago and Long ponds in the interior of the county. Portland has an extensive inland and coasting-trade, and exports large quantities of lumber, ice, and provisions, to the West Indies and elsewhere. The city is regularly laid out with wide streets, some of which are lined with beautiful shade trees and handsome dwellings. The hospitality and intelligence of the citizens, and the sea-breezes by which the city is fanned, render it a pleasant resort in the warm season.

The population in 1790, was 2,240; in 1800, 3,677; in 1810, 7,169; in 1820, 8,581; in 1830, 12,601; in 1840, 15,218; in 1850, 26,819.

Bryant's Pond	7	62
Lock's Mills	3	65
Bethel	5	70
West Bethel	4	74
Gilead	6	80
Sherburn	6	86
Gorham	5	91
unfinished.		

From Portland to Waterville.

To Danville Junc. as above		27
Auburn	5	32
Lewistown	1	33
Greene	8	41
Leeds	3	44
Monmouth	3	47
Winthrop	6	53
Readville	6	59
Belgrade	8	67
North Belgrade	3	70
West Waterville	5	75
Waterville	7	82

Portland to Augusta.

To Westbrook	2	
Falmouth	4	6
Cumberland	3	9
Yarmouth Junc.	4	13
Freeport	6	19
Oak Hill	4	23
Brunswick	4	27
Topsham	1	28
Bowdoinham	7	35
Harwood rd	4	39
Richmond	3	42
South Gardiner	6	48
Gardiner	5	53
Hallowell	5	58
Augusta	2	60

From Bedford to Mechanics' Falls.

To E. Hebron	4	
West Minot	5	9
Mechanics' Falls	4	13

From Portland to Boston.

To Haverhill, as above		79
Bradford	1	80
North Andover	4	84
Lawrence	2	86
Andover	3	89
Ballardsvale	2	91
Wilmington	6	97
Reading	3	100
South Reading	2	102
Greenwich	1	103
Stoneham	1	104
Melrose	1	105
Wyoming	1	106
Malden	1	107
Somerville	2	109
Charlestown	1	110
Boston	1	111

From Bangor to Oldtown.

To Steammill	4	
Half Way	2	6
Upper Stillwater	3	9
Oldtown	3	12

STAGE-ROADS.

From Bath to Calais	218
From Portland to Fryeburg	48
From Augusta to Quebec	238
From Bangor to Castine	35
From Bangor to Narridgewock	53
From Augusta to Shelburn, N. H.	77

MANCHESTER, N. H.

A REMARKABLY growing city, or manufacturing town, in Hillsborough county, situated on the east bank of Merrimac river, which affords extensive water-power for propelling the machinery. The great chain of railroads leading from Boston and Lowell through Concord, toward Montreal and Vermont, pass through this city, and Amoskeag Falls canal here facilitates navigation between Boston and Concord. Before the year 1810, this place constituted a part of the town of Derryfield.

The population in 1810, was 615; in 1820, 761; in 1830, 877; in 1840, 3,235: in 1850, 18,933.

CONCORD, N. H.

THE capital of the state of New Hampshire, and seat of justice of Merrimac county, is situated on both sides of Merrimac river, 65 miles northwest of Boston, and 475 from Washington. Four handsome bridges connect the principal part of the town with the east side of the river, and the Contoocook, flowing through its northwest corner, at its confluence with the Merrimac, forms Dustan island, so named after Mrs. Dustan, famed in heroic Indian history. Its central position, the well cultivated and productive surrounding region, and the communication by railroad with Boston and the interior country, contribute to Concord a steady growth and prosperity. The statehouse, built of white granite, taken from the neighboring quarries, is a fine structure in the centre of the town, 126 feet long, 49 feet wide, with projections of four feet on each front, surmounted by a fine cupola. Here also is the stateprison, constructed of the same kind of material. The Portsmouth and Concord, and the Boston, Concord, and Montreal railroads are nearly finished.

The population in 1775, was 1,052; in 1790, 1,747; in 1800, 2,052; 1810, 2,393; in 1820, 2,838; in 1830, 3,727; in 1840, 4,897; in 1850, 8,584.

PORTSMOUTH, N. H.

THE largest and only seaport in New Hampshire, occupies a peninsula on the south side of Piscataqua river, three miles from the Atlantic. It has one of the finest harbors in the world, being completely land-locked, defended by several forts, and having from 45 to 53 feet of water at low-tide. The town is built on ground gradually sloping toward the river, presenting a beautiful aspect from the ocean. It is well built, and possesses much wealth, many of the houses being spacious and elegant. Its public buildings are an ornament to the city, consisting of the court-house, churches, banking houses, markets, and Athenæum. A United States navy-yard is situated on Continental, or Navy island, on the east side of the river, opposite the town. Ship-building and cotton-manufactures, employ a large amount of capital. The Eastern railroad connects the place with Boston and Portland. Another railroad extends toward Concord as far as Raymond.

The population in 1810, was 6,934; in 1820, 7,327; in 1830, 8,082; in 1840, 7,887; in 1850, 9,739.

RAILROADS.

From Portsmouth to Boston.

To Greenland	5	
North Hampton	3	8
Hampton	2	10
Hampton Falls	2	12
Seabrook	2	14
Salisbury	4	18
Newburyport	2	20
Rowley	5	25
Ipswich	4	29
Wenham	5	34
Beverly	4	38
Salem	2	40
Lynn	5	45
North Chelsea	5	50
Boston	4	54

From Concord to Burlington.

To West Concord	3	
Fisherville	4	7
Boscawen	3	10
North Boscawen	5	15
Franklin	4	19
East Andover	6	25
Andover	3	28
Potter Place	2	30
West Andover	3	33
Danbury	6	39
Grafton	5	44
Canaan	8	52
West Canaan	4	56
Enfield	3	59
East Lebanon	2	61
Lebanon	4	65
West Lebanon	4	69
Burlington (see Vermont)	102	171

From Concord to Nashua.

To Robinson's Fe'y	5	
Hooksett	4	9
Martin's Ferry	4	13
Manchester	5	18
Goff's Falls	4	22
Reed's Ferry	4	26
Thornton's Ferry	3	29
Nashua	6	35

From Concord to Boston.

To Nashua, as above		35
Little's	5	40
Tyngsborough	4	44
Chelmsford	3	47
Middlesex	2	49
Lowell	2	51
Boston (see Massachusetts)	26	77

From Nashua to Worcester	45
From Wilton to Boston	56
Concord to Andover	28
Concord to Warren	71
Contocookville to Hillsboro' Bridge	14
Concord to Bradford	25
Manchester to Lawrence	26
Keene to Bellows' F'ls	22
Keene to Boston	92
Fitchburg to Brattlebo'	69
Brattleboro' to Greenfield	24
Portsmouth to Newburyport (as above)	20

BURLINGTON, Vt.

This is a thriving town, the seat of justice of Chittenden county, and the chief port of entry of Vermont. It is pleasantly situated on a beautiful bay of Champlain, and commands the principal trade of the country and of the lake. To this point flow a large portion of the products of the Green Mountain state, and thence they are conveyed by railroad, steamboats, or other vessels, to Troy, Albany, New York, St. Johns, and other places. Rising from the water by a gentle acclivity, and laid out in regular streets, adorned with pleasant gardens and dwellings, Burlington is as conspicuous for its pleasant and healthful location, as for its commercial advantages. The dome of the University of Vermont, which stands on an eminence 250 feet above the lake, commands a most varied, extensive, and delightful prospect. A light-house on Juniper island, marks the entrance of the harbor, and a breakwater, erected by the general government, protects it from the west winds of the lake. This village communicates by railroad with Montpelier, Boston, and the intermediate places.

Population in 1810, 1,690; in 1820, —,—; in 1830, 3,525; in 1840, 4,271; in 1850, 5,211.

MONTPELIER, Vt.

The capital of Vermont, and seat of justice of Washington county, is pleasantly situated amid rugged hills, 160 miles northwest of Boston, and 524 miles from Washington. It is the thoroughfare and centre of an extensive trade from Boston and other points. The dwellings are neat and handsome, and the architecture of the state capitol is admired for its purity and beauty. The edifice is built of dark granite, in the form of a cross, and is of the Doric order. The centre is 72 feet wide and 100 feet deep; the two wings are each 39 feet wide and 50 feet deep; the top of the dome is 36 feet above the ridge and 100 feet from the ground.

Montpelier is connected by railway with Burlington and Boston and the intermediate places.

The population in 1810, was 1,877; in 1820, —,—; in 1830, 1,792; in 1840, 3,725; in 1850, 4,112.

BENNINGTON, Vt.

An important town, and semi-capital of Bennington county, is situated 130 miles west-northwest of Boston, Mass., and about 37 miles northeast of Albany, N Y., and was named from Bennington Wentworth, who, in 1749, was the royal governor of New Hampshire. It is drained by branches of Hoosick river, which afford good water-power. Marble, iron ore, and yellow ochre, are found here. The principal village is on elevated ground, and makes a good appearance. A little to the east is a considerable manufacturing village. In 1777, General Stark, with 800 Americans, defeated a superior British force, on the west border of this town.

RAILROADS.

From Windsor to Montpelier.

To Hartland	4	
North Hartland	4	8
White R. Junc.	6	14
Woodstock	3	17
West Hartford	4	21
Sharon	6	27
South Royalton	5	32
Royalton	2	34
Bethel	5	39
Randolph	7	46
Braintree	5	51
Roxbury	9	60
Northfield	7	67
Montpelier	10	77

Montpelier to Rousse's Point.

To Middlesex	6	
Waterbury	5	11
Bolton	6	17
Jones'	4	21
Richmond	3	24
Williston	5	29
Essex Junc.	4	33
Winooski	4	37
Burlington	3	40
Colchester	3	43
Milton	4	47
Georgia	4	51
St. Albans	9	60
Swanton	10	70
Missisco	6	76
Alburgh	2	78
West Alburgh	5	83
Rousse's Point	2	85

Rutland to Bennington.

To Clarendon	6	
Wallingford	3	9
South Wallingford	4	13
Danby	5	18
North Dorset	4	22
East Dorset	4	26
Manchester	6	32
Sunderland	5	37
Arlington	3	40
Shaftsbury	7	47
N. Bennington	5	52

From Rutland to Troy.

Rutland Centre	2	
West Rutland	2	4
Castleton	7	11
Poultney	7	18
Granville	6	24
Granville Centre	2	26
Pawlet	3	29
Rupert	7	36
West Rupert	2	38
Salem	6	44
Shashan	7	51
Cambridge	6	57
Wait's Corners	3	60
Eagle Bridge	2	62
Troy (see N. Y.)	23	85

Bellows' Falls to Burlington	120
Bellows' Falls to Rutland	53
Bellows' Falls to Middlebury	85
Bellows' Falls to Vergennes	98
Bellows' Falls to Windsor	25
Bellows' Falls to Brattleboro'	24
Windsor to St. Albans	138
White River Junc. to St. Johnsbury	61

BOSTON, Mass.

This flourishing city, the capital of Massachusetts and metropolis of New England, occupies a peninsula and other adjacent points, at the head of Massachusetts bay. The original town was confined to the peninsula, but this, although enlarged by artificial means, has long since proved too narrow for the growing city, which, passing the barriers thrown around it by nature, now embraces, independently of the populous towns and villages that are its offspring, the triple division of "Old Boston," "South Boston," and "East Boston." The "Neck" was formerly the only avenue from the town to the main land, but it is now united by bridges, and other avenues, to Charlestown, Cambridge, South Boston, and other surrounding points. From the west side of the city, Western avenue is continued to Brookline, on the opposite side of Charles river bay, by a costly dam one mile and a half in length, and one hundred feet broad. Proceeding from the middle of this, on which are several tide mills, a second dam divides the bay into two spacious basins. Several of the Boston railroads also enter the city, by bridges built expressly for that purpose.

The harbor extends from Nantasket to the city, and spreads from Chelsea and Nahant to Hingham, containing about seventy-five square miles. It is bespangled with upward of fifty islands, or rocks, and receives the waters from the Mystic, Charles, Neponset, and Manatticut rivers, with several other smaller streams. One of the most remarkable features connected with the harbor, is the costly and splendid wharves. These marks of commercial enterprise and prosperity are about 100 in number, and of various dimensions. Long wharf is 1,800 feet long, and 200 feet wide: Central wharf, 1,397 feet long, and 150 feet wide; India wharf, 980 feet long, and from 246 to 280 feet wide; and Commercial wharf is 1,100 feet long, and 160 feet wide. These, like most of the others, are lined with extensive and magnificent warehouses, constructed of the most substantial materials.

Another valuable acquisition is Boston Common, a pleasant park of about fifty acres, situated at the southwesterly slope of Beacon hill. It is pleasantly diversified with knolls, avenues, fountains, a small lake, or pond, and trees, some of the latter of which are interesting relics of colonial and revolutionary times. The Common is surrounded by an iron fence, over one mile in extent. Between the common and Charles river bay, lies the Botanic garden, a beautiful and tasteful enclosure. On the north side of the Common, and at the summit of the hill, stands the statehouse, an elegant structure, 173 feet in length, 61 feet in depth, and 120 feet in height. The top of the dome is 230 feet above tide-water. The view from the top of the statehouse is very extensive and variegated; perhaps nothing in the country is superior to it. To the east appears the bay and harbor of Boston, interspersed with beautiful islands; and in the distance beyond, the wide extended ocean. To the north the eye is met by Charlestown, with its interesting and memorable heights, of Bunker hill, crowned with the monument, 220 feet in height, and the navy-yard of the United States; the towns of Chelsea, Malden, and Medford, and other villages, and the natural forests

RAILROADS.

From Boston to Portland via Haverhill.

To Charlestown....	1	
Summerville.......	1	2
Malden	3	5
Wyoming	1	6
Melrose	1	7
Stoneham..........	1	8
Greenwood.........	1	9
South Reading	1	10
Reading	2	12
Wilmington	3	15
Ballardsvale	6	21
Andover	2	23
Lawrence	3	26
North Andover....	2	28
Bradford	4	32
Haverhill	1	33
Boston (see N. H.).	78	111

From Boston to Portland, via Portsmouth.

To North Chelsea..	4	
Lynn	5	9
Salem	5	14
Beverly	2	16
Wenham	4	20
Ipswich	5	25
Rowley.............	4	29
Newburyport	5	34
Salisbury	2	36
Seabrook	4	40
Hampton Falls.....	2	42
Hampton	2	44
North Hampton....	2	46
Greenland	3	49
Portsmouth.........	5	54
Portland (see N. H.)	51	105

Boston to Lowell.

To East Cambridge	1	
Summerville........	2	3
West Medford.....	2	5
Winchester.........	3	8
Woburn	2	10
Wilmington	5	15
Billerica & Tewks.	4	19
Billerica Mills......	2	21
Lowell	5	26

Boston to Nashua.

To Lowell, as above		26
Middlesex.........	2	28
Chelmsford	2	30
Tyngsboro'	3	33
Little's	4	37
Nashua.............	4	41

Boston to Fitchburgh.

To Summerville & Porter's	3	
West Cambridge..	3	6
Waltham	4	10
Stony Brook.......	2	12
Weston.............	1	13
Lincoln............	4	17
Concord	3	20
South Acton.......	5	25
West Acton........	2	27
Littleton............	4	31
Groton	4	35
Shirley	5	40
Lunenburgh	2	42
Leominster.........	4	46
Fitchburgh	4	50

Boston to Albany.

To Brighton.......	5	
Newtown Corner..	2	7
West Newtown....	2	9
Grantville	4	13
West Needham....	2	15
Natick	2	17
Framingham.......	4	21
Ashland	3	24
Southborough	4	28
Westborough......	4	32
Grafton	6	38
Worcester..........	7	45

mingling in the distant horizon. To the west, is a fine view of the Charles river and bay, the ancient town of Cambridge, rendered venerable for the university, now about two hundred years old; of the flourishing villages of Cambridgeport and East Cambridge, in the latter of which is a large glass manufacturing establishment; of the highly cultivated towns of Brighton, Brookline, and Newton; and to the south is Roxbury, which seems to be only a continuation of Boston, and which is rapidly increasing: Dorchester, a rich, agricultural town, with Milton and Quincy beyond; and farther south, the Blue hills, at the distance of eight miles, which seem to bound the prospect.

Faneuil hall, which is justly styled the "cradle of American liberty," was originally built in 1740, for a town-hall and market-house. It has been enlarged and beautified on several occasions, and will always be a place of historical interest to the lovers of liberty. Adjoining it on the east is Faneuil-Hall market, one of the most splendid and commodious edifices of the kind in the country. It is constructed of Quincy granite, or sienite, 540 feet in length, 50 feet wide, and two stories high. The court-house, merchants' exchange, postoffice, customhouse, Massachusetts general hospital, the Old South meetinghouse, Park street, Brattle street, and Trinity churches, the Tremont house, Revere house, the Athæneum, the jail, Society of Natural History, the Houses of Industry, Correction, and Reformation, are among other objects of interest. The water-works may be regarded as one of the most important of the recent improvements. By a series of pipes and reservoirs, water is conveyed to all parts of the city proper, and East and South Boston, from Long Pond, or Lake Cochituate, a distance of nearly 20 miles. It will supply 10,000,000 gallons of water daily, and cost about $5,000,000.

Railroads diverge from this city in various directions, connecting it with Plymouth, Cape Cod, New Bedford, Fall River, Providence, Stonington, New York (via Worcester, Springfield, Hartford, and New Haven); with Albany, via Worcester and Springfield; with Vermont, via Fitchburgh; also, with Lake Winnipisiogee and the White mountains, in New Hampshire, via Nashua, Concord, and Meredith Bridge; also, via Haverhill, Exeter, and Dover; with Lawrence, via Lowell and Manchester; with Augusta, Me., via Salem, Newburyport, Portsmouth, Portland, and Bath.

Boston is pre-eminently distinguished for its efforts in behalf of education. Its public schools are unrivalled in excellence, and it numbers among its citizens some of the most munificent patrons of learning, literature, and science; which, with its many eminent literary and philosophical societies, has led to its being honored with the title of the "Athens of America."

Mount Auburn, a beautiful cemetery, belonging to Boston, is picturesquely situated in Cambridge, about five miles out of the city. Within this interesting "city of the dead" rest the remains of many of the illustrious sons of New England.

The population of Boston in 1700, was 7,000; in 1722, 10,567; in 1765, 15,520; in 1790, 18,033; in 1800, 24,937; in 1810, 33,250; in 1820, 43,298; in 1830, 61,392; in 1840, 93,383; in 1850, 138,788.

RAILROADS.

Clappville	9	54
Charlton	3	57
Spencer	5	62
East Brookfield	2	64
South Brookfield	3	67
West Brookfield	2	69
Warren	4	73
Palmer	10	83
Indian Orchard	9	92
Springfield	6	98
West Springfield	2	100
Westfield	8	108
Russel	8	116
Chester Village	3	119
Chester Factory	7	126
Becket	9	135
Washington	3	138
Kinsdale	5	143
Dalton	3	146
Pittsfield	5	151
Shaker Village	3	154
Richmond	5	159
State Line	3	162
Canaan	5	167
East Chatham	5	172
Chatham 4-Corners	5	177
Chatham Centre	4	181
Kinderhook	3	184
Schoodack	8	192
Greenbush	8	200
Albany	1	201

Boston to Providence.

To Roxbury	2	
Jamaica Plains	1	3
Readville	5	8
Canton	6	14
Sharon	3	17
Foxboro'	4	21
Mansfield	3	24
Tobey's	2	26
Attleboro'	5	31
Dodgeville	1	32
Pawtucket	7	39
Providence	4	43

Boston to Stonington and New York.

To Providence (as above)		43
Junction	4	47
Warwick	7	54
Greenwich	3	57
Wickford	6	63
Kingston	7	70
Carolina	6	76
Richmond	3	79
Charlestown	4	83
Westerly	5	88
Stonington	5	93
Thence to N. York by steamboat	128	221

Boston to New York, via Fall River.

To Crescent Ave	2	
Harrison Square	2	4
Neponset	1	5
Quincy	3	8
South Braintree	3	11
Randolph	4	15
East Stoughton	2	17
North Bridgewater	3	20
Campello	3	23
Keith's Furnace	1	24
E & W Bridgewater	1	25
Bridgewater	2	27
Titicut	4	31
Middleboro'	4	35
Haskins	2	37
Myrick's	5	42
Assonet	3	45
Miller's	5	50
Fall River	4	54
Thence by steamboat to Newport	18	72
New York	163	235

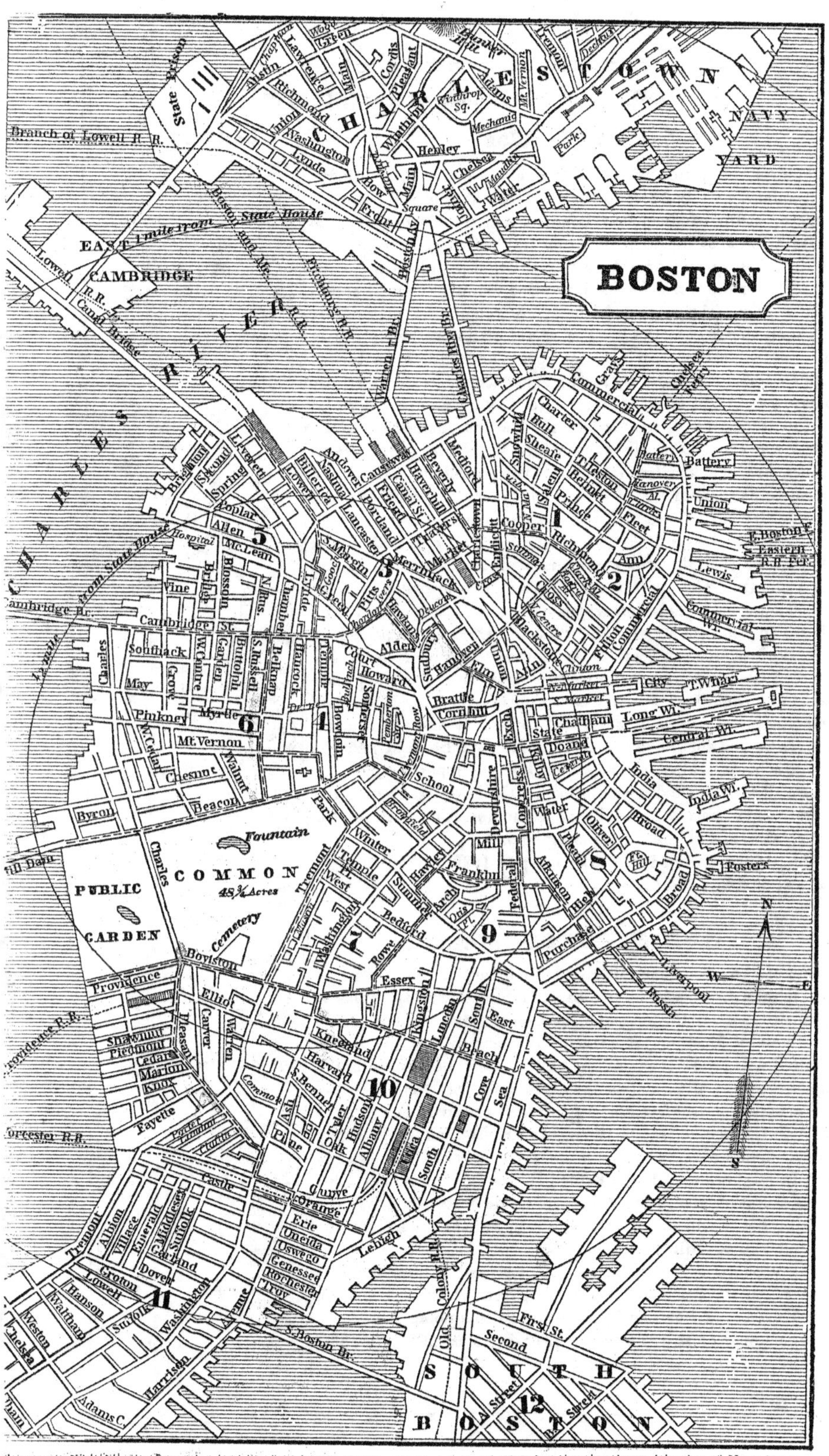
BOSTON
CHARLESTOWN
NAVY YARD
CHARLES RIVER
EAST CAMBRIDGE
1 mile from State House
COMMON
48¾ Acres
Fountain
PUBLIC GARDEN
Cemetery
SOUTH BOSTON
Boston and Me. R.R.
Providence R.R.
Worcester R.R.
Old Colony R.R.
Lowell R.R.
Branch of Lowell R.R.
Canal Bridge
Charles Riv. Br.
Warren Br.
Cambridge Br.
S. Boston Br.
Chelsea Ferry
E. Boston F.
Eastern R.R. Fer.
Mill Dam

LOWELL, Mass.

The seat of justice, with Cambridge and Concord, of Middlesex county, and the second city in the state in population, is situated at the confluence of Concord and Merrimac rivers, 25 miles northwest of Boston. From an insignificant village, in 1822, it has sprung up into a wealthy and populous city, celebrated over the world for its unrivalled manufactories of cotton and woollen fabrics, by which it has gained the title of the "Manchester of America." The secret of its prosperity lies in the vast water-power, which enterprise and skill have turned into available channels. By a canal which connects the Merrimac below Pawtucket falls, with Concord river, water is conveyed to the town and distributed to the various factories. About thirty are engaged in the manufacture of cotton; a number of others produce woollen fabrics of various kinds, as carpets, broadcloths, cassimeres, calicoes, machinery for railroads, &c. About $20,000,000 are invested in these operations.

Lowell is pleasantly situated, and is laid out with broad streets, and the inhabitants are distinguished for industry and good morals. The operatives in the factories, are far above the ignorance and degradation which belong to those similarly employed in other countries. The "Lowell Offering," a periodical composed of communications from the young women of the "mills," is an instance of the truth of this remark. The principal public buildings are the court-house, city-hall, Mechanics' hall (the latter of which is devoted to literary and scientific intelligence, and furnished with a museum and library), and the public schools, which receive a very liberal support.

Lowell is connected with Boston by the Middlesex canal, and by railroad; there is also railroad communication with all the principal towns of the surrounding country.

The population in 1822, 100 or less; in 1830, 6,474; in 1840, 20,796; in 1850, 28,841.

SPRINGFIELD, Mass.

One of the most flourishing and important inland towns of Massachusetts, the seat of justice of Hampden county, is pleasantly situated on the east side of Connecticut river, 91 miles southwest of Boston. It principally occupies a single street, parallel with the river, and contains many handsome buildings. Pleasant alluvial meadows gradually rise from the river into a region of less fertility. A bridge here spans the river to West Springfield. Manufactures of various kinds are largely produced, and give to the place its prosperity. The most important establishment is the United States arsenal, which, built on an elevation above the village, presents within and without an imposing spectacle. Small arms are made at the factory one mile distant, on Mill river.

The Western railroad between Albany and Boston, and the chain of railways through Connecticut river valley to Hartford, New Haven, and New York, concentre at this point.

The population in 1810, was 2,767; in 1820, 3,914; in 1830, 6,784; in 1840, 10,985; in 1850, 21,602.

RAILROADS.

Boston to New York, via Norwich and New London.

To Worcester (see Boston to Albany)		45
Auburn	5	50
Oxford	7	57
North Village	4	61
Webster	1	62
Wilsonsville	3	65
Fisherville	1	66
Thompson	3	69
Pomfret	3	72
Dayville	5	77
Danielson Village	3	80
Central Village	6	86
Plainfield	3	89
Jewett City	3	92
Greeneville	9	101
Norwich	1	102
Allyn's Point	7	109
New London by st.	7	116
New York by steam boat	125	241

Boston to New York, via Springfield and Hartford.

To Springfield (see Boston to Albany		98
Longmeadow	4	102
Thompsonville	4	106
Enfield Bridge	2	108
Warehouse Point	1	109
Windsor Locks	2	111
Windsor	6	117
Hartford	7	124
N. Haven (see Ct.)	36	160
New York (see Ct.)	76	236

Boston to Blackstone.

To Dedham		10
West Dedham	3	13
South Dedham	1	14
Durfee's	1	15
Plympton	3	18
Walpole	1	19
North Wrentham	4	23
City Mills	2	25
Franklin	2	27
Wadsworth	3	30
Mill River	3	33
Blackstone	3	36

Boston to Dover, (see Boston to Portland). 63

Boston to Portsmouth, (see Bos. to Portland) 51

Worcester to Nashua.

To West Boylston	9	
Oakdale	1	10
Sterling	2	12
Clinton	4	16
New Boston	2	18
Lancaster	1	19
Still River	4	23
Harvard	2	25
Groton Junction	3	28
Groton Centre	3	31
Pepperville	5	36
Hollis	3	39
Nashua	6	45

Springfield to Keene.

To Cabotville	3	
Willimansett	3	6
Holyoke	2	8
Smith's Ferry	4	12
Northampton	5	17
Hatfield	4	21
Whately	5	26
South Deerfield	2	28
Deerfield	4	32
Greenfield	4	36
Bernard's Town	6	42
South Vernon	8	50
Hinsdale	4	54
West Winchester	4	58
Winchester	2	60
Westport	5	65
Swanzey	3	68
Keene	5	73

SALEM, Mass.

THIS is a pleasant, and one of the oldest towns in the state. Like Boston, it occupies a peninsula, from which it is distant 14 miles northeast. This tongue of land is nearly surrounded by water, and comprises the oldest and most irregular part of the town. Two bridges over each inlet of the sea, connect this with the more modern parts. The position of the city is low, and its harbor shallow; but here, as elsewhere, obstacles seem to have stimulated, rather than prevented, effort. Next to Plymouth and Weymouth, Salem is the oldest town in Massachusetts, and from an early period, it has been distinguished for the extent of its maritime operations. Its ships and sailors were active in the Revolution, and since that period, it has been celebrated for its East India trade. At present, though other towns more favorably situated, have outstripped it in commerce and population, its vessels are as numerous as ever, and visit every quarter of the globe. Several millions of dollars in capital, are invested in the manufacture of machinery, useful and precious metals, &c. In the centre of the city is a park, or "common," of about nine acres. The streets are not very regular, but some of the houses are handsome. The most noted public buildings are the Athenæum, East-Indian museum, city-hall, courthouse, hospital, customhouse, jail, and about twenty churches of various denominations.

The population in 1790, was 7,921; in 1800, 9,457; in 1810, 12,613; in 1820, 12,721; in 1830, 13,886; in 1840, 15,082; in 1850, 18,846.

WORCESTER, Mass.

This beautiful and flourishing town, lies in the heart of a well-cultivated region, 42 miles west of Boston, in a pleasant valley, surrounded by gentle hills, laid out with regularity and taste, its streets animated by industry, and beautified by nature with shady trees and pleasant gardens. It is, in fact, a New England village. Here, as veins at the heart, concentre railroads from Boston, Providence, Norwich, Springfield, Hartford, and New Haven, New York, the valley of the Hudson, New Hampshire and Vermont, which discharge their burdens, and bear away as swiftly the productions of Worcester and the fruitful region which surrounds it. The Blackstone Canal, 45 miles long, forms another channel of communication with Providence. The state lunatic asylum, and the hall of the American Antiquarian Society, are the most prominent and interesting public buildings.

The population in 1810, was 2,577; in 1820, 2,962; in 1830, 4,172; in 1840, 7,497; in 1850, 15,864.

NEW BEDFORD, Mass.

THE seat of justice, with Taunton, of Bristol county, is 58 miles south of Boston. The Acushnet, an inlet of Buzzard's bay, running up on the east of the town, affords a good harbor for vessels. The town is built on a bold elevation, contains

RAILROADS.

Boston to New Bedford.

To Mansfield (see Boston and Providence)		24
Norton	4	28
Crane's	3	31
Taunton	4	35
Myrick's	6	41
New Bedford	14	55

From Salem to Lawrence.

To South Danvers	2	
Davenport	3	5
North Danvers	1	6
Middleton	3	9
Boxford Station	5	14
North Andover	5	19
Sutton's Mills	1	20
Lawrence	1	21

From Salem to Lowell.

To Carltonville	1	
South Danvers	1	2
Proctor's Corner	2	4
West Danvers	2	6
Middleton	2	8
North Reading	2	10
Wilmington	4	14
Wilmington Junc'n	1	15
Burtt's Mills	1	16
Tewksbury Junc.	2	18
Tewksbury	1	19
Bleacher	4	23
Lowell	1	24

From Lowell to Lawrence.

To Tewksbury	6	
Shed's Crossing	2	8
Lawrence	5	13

From Fitchburg to Greenfield.

To West Fitchburgh	2	
Westminster	3	5
Ashburnham	6	11
Gardner	4	15
Dadmunville	4	19
Baldwinville	2	21
Royalston	6	27
Athol	6	33
Orange	4	37
Wendell	3	40
Erving	2	42
Grout's Corner	6	48
Montague	4	52
Greenfield	4	56

From Fitchburg to Brattleboro'.

Erving (as above)		42
Montague	7	49
Northfield Farms	2	51
Northfield	6	57
South Vernon	2	59
Vernon	5	64
Brattleboro'	5	69

From Boston to Sandwich, Cape Cod route.

To Middleboro' (see Fall River route).		35
Rock Station	5	40
South Middleboro'	3	43
West Wareham	3	46
South Wareham	2	48
Wareham	2	50
Agawam	2	52
Cohasset Narrows	3	55
Monument	1	56
North Sandwich	3	59
West Sandwich	1	60
Sandwich	3	63
Provincetown (by stage)	73	136

many fine buildings, and appears with advantage from the harbor. A bridge across the Acushnet leads to Fairhaven, on the opposite side. Perhaps no other place in the country is engaged so exclusively and extensively in the whaling business as this. About $5,000,000 of capital and two hundred vessels are employed.

The New Bedford and Taunton railroad joins the Boston and Providence railroad at Mansfield, and communicates with this place.

The population in 1810, was 5,651; in 1820, 3,947; in 1830, 7,592; in 1840, 12,087; in 1850, 16,464.

CAMBRIDGE, Mass.

Is situated three quarters of a mile west of Boston. In the old part of the city, stands Harvard University, the most ancient and wealthy collegiate institution in America. This includes a theological, medical, and law school, and has a library of about 100,000 volumes, the largest in the Union. Merchants and others doing business in Boston, reside in this city, and some of the dwellings are costly and splendid. At Cambridge, were the entrenchments of the American army when besieging Boston under Washington. Glass and other manufactures are extensively produced. From its proximity to Boston, the railroads and other lines of travel are common to both places.

One mile west of the college is Mount Auburn Cemetery consecrated by nature and by art to the holy purpose to which it is devoted.

The population in 1810, was 2,323; in 1820 ——; in 1830, 6,071; in 1840, 8,409; in 1850, 14,624.

NEWBURYPORT, Mass.

This is a pleasant and thriving town, in Essex county. It is situated on the south bank of Merrimac river, three miles from its entrance into the ocean, and 30 miles north of Boston. It embraces about one mile square, with regular streets, those parallel with the river rising one above the other, after the manner of terraces. That nearest the water is occupied by stores and warehouses, and the higher ones by neat and commodious dwellings, which command a beautiful prospect of the harbor and ocean. A road and bridge lead to Plumb island, at the mouth of the river, which is a pleasant summer resort. A suspension bridge and a railroad bridge, extend across the Merrimac to Salisbury. The harbor is ample, and is protected by a breakwater, but is obstructed by a sand-bar at its entrance. Newburyport has been and is still extensively engaged in commerce and fisheries; and although of late its maritime trade has diminished, its population and general prosperity has increased. The town contains a customhouse of rough granite with a Grecian Doric portico, churches, a courthouse, jail, market, and other public buildings. The Eastern railroad from Boston and Salem, enters the place, and unites it to the Portsmouth, Portland, and Saco railroads.

The population in 1810, was 7,634; in 1820, 6,852; in 1830 6,375; in 1840, 7,161; in 1850, 9.534.

RAILROADS.

From Pittsfield to North Adams.

To Packard's	3	
East Lanesboro'	3	6
Cheshire	3	9
Cheshire Harbor	2	11
Maple Grove	2	13
South Adams	1	14
North Adams	6	20

From Worcester to Providence.

To Grand Junction	1	
Millbury	5	6
Sutton	2	8
Grafton	1	9
Farnum's	1	10
Northbridge	2	12
Whitins	5	17
Uxbridge	1	18
Millville	5	23
Blackstone and Waterford	2	25
Woonsocket	2	27
Hamlet	1	28
Manville	2	30
Albion	2	32
Ashton	1	33
Lonsdale	3	36
Boston Switch	1	37
Pawtucket	2	39
Providence	4	43

From Worcester to Fitchburgh.

To Sterling Junct'n	12	
Sterling Village	2	14
Pratt's	2	16
Leominster	5	21
South Fitchburgh	3	24
Fitchburgh	2	26

From Beverly to Gloucester 12

From Salem to Marblehead 4

From Newbury to Georgetown 7

From Manchester to Lawrence.

To Londonderry	6	
Derry	5	11
Windham	3	14
Salem	5	19
Methuen	5	24
Lawrence	2	26

From Lowell to Groton.

To Chelmsford	4	
Factory Village	1	5
Westford	2	7
Forge Village	4	11
Groton	6	17

Fm Boston to Watertown.

To Fresh Pond	5	
Mount Auburn	1	6
Watertown	2	8

From Groton to Mason Village.

West Groton	4	
Townsend Harbor	4	8
Townsend Centre	2	10
West Townsend	2	12
Wilton	8	20
Mason Village	3	23

From Boston to Taunton.

To Mansfield (see Bos. & Prov. RR)		24
Norton's	4	28
Crane's	3	31
Taunton	4	35

FALL-RIVER, Mass.

This pleasant town is one of those enterprising and flourishing places in which the "Bay State" abounds. It lies on the outlet of Watuppa pond, a considerable body of water, which passes through Fall river into the Taunton, affording a good and constant water-power. Along this stream are numerous mills, and factories of cotton, wool, machinery, &c., which produce articles to a large amount. Having a good harbor at the entrance of Taunton river into Bristol bay, its commerce is considerable. Ships of a large class, engaged in both the whale-fishery and foreign trade, anchor at its wharves. Besides manufactories, the town contains churches, banks, hotels, and schools of a superior order.

There is a line of splendid steamboats running daily between this place and New York, and the Fall-River railroad connects it with Boston.

The population in 1840, was 9,000; in 1850, in 13,209.

RAILROADS.

From Pittsfield to Sheffield.

To Lenox	8	
Lee	3	11
Stockbridge	6	17
Van Deusenville	6	23
Great Barrington	2	25
Sheffield	6	31

STAGE-ROUTES.

From New Bedford to Sandwich.

To Fairhaven	1	
Mattaposet	4	5
Sippican	4	9
Wareham	5	14
East Wareham	3	17
North Sandwich	5	22
West Sandwich	2	24
Sandwich	7	31

Fm Taunton to Duxbury.

To Scotland	9	
Bridgewater	6	15
Halifax	4	19
North Plympton	3	22
Kingston	4	26
Duxbury	4	30

PROVIDENCE, R. I.

The capital, with Newport, of the state of Rhode Island, is the second city in population of New England, is situated at the head of Narraganset bay, on either side of Providence river, 42 miles southwest of Boston, and 173 miles northeast of New York. The older part of the city lies on the east side of the river, and though many of the streets partake of that irregularity which seems peculiar to the olden times, they contain many splendid stores, warehouses, dwellings, and public buildings. Ascending by an abrupt acclivity from the river, the streets and houses become more regular, many of the residences being of a superior style of elegance and structure, and affording delightful views of the harbor and the surrounding country. Crowning the elevation, are the buildings of Brown University, a flourishing institution. Crossing the river by one of the bridges, the west part of the city is laid out with more regularity upon ground less uneven. Here is the "Arcade," the largest and most important edifice in the city, built of granite, and adorned with a Grecian-Doric portico and columns. It is 225 feet long, 80 feet deep, and 72 feet high.

The name of the city, which it received from the Rev. Roger Williams, its founder, may serve to indicate its prosperity. Its location upon a spacious and convenient harbor, sufficient for a great number of the largest vessels, the manufacturing facilities of the surrounding districts, their facility of access to the city, and the enterprising spirit which has improved and adapted these advantages, are the sources of its increasing wealth and population. The Blackstone canal, beginning at Worcester, and winding through the productive regions and manufacturing towns of Massachusetts, brings large stores to its market. On

RAILROADS.

From Providence to Boston.

To Pawtucket	4	
Dodgeville	7	11
Attleboro'	1	12
Tobey's	5	17
Mansfield	2	19
Foxboro'	3	22
Sharon	4	26
Canton	3	29
Readville	6	35
Jamaica Plain	5	40
Roxbury	1	41
Boston	2	43

Fm Providence to Stonington and New York.

To Junction	4	
Warwick	7	11
Greenwich	3	14
Wickford	6	20
Kingston	7	27
Carolina	6	33
Richmond Switch	3	36
Charlestown	4	40
Westerly	5	45
Stonington	5	50
N. York, by steamboat	128	178

From Providence to Worcester.

To Pawtucket	4	
Lonsdale	3	7
Ashton	2	9
Albion	2	11
Manville	1	12
Hamlet	3	15
Woonsocket	1	16
Waterford & Blackstone	2	18
Millville	2	20
Uxbridge	5	25
Whitins	1	26
Northbridge	5	31
Farnum's	2	33
Grafton	1	34
Sutton	1	35
Millbury	2	37
Grand Junction	5	42
Worcester	1	43

Pawtucket river, and the other streams of Providence county, are extensive factories of cotton, wool, machinery, calico printing, and dyeing; and within the city are also various similar establishments. These are chiefly kept in operation by capitalists of Providence, and employ more than $3,000,000 of capital. This city communicates by railroad with Boston, Worcester, and Stonington, and, in a great measure, has dispensed with the steamboat lines which traversed Long Island sound and the Atlantic to New York, Boston, and other places.

The population in 1810, was 10,071; in 1820, 11,767; in 1830, 16,833; in 1840, 23,171; in 1850, 41,513.

NEWPORT, R. I.

The capital, with Providence, of the state, is finely situated on the southwest side of the isle of Rhode Island, at the main entrance to Narraganset bay, 30 miles south of Providence. It occupies a gentle eminence fronting the harbor, from which it presents a fine appearance. Its pleasant scenery, embracing many spacious views of the ocean and its rocky shores, its healthful climate, abundance and variety of fish in its waters, and its interesting historic associations and relics of early times, render Newport one of the most attractive places of summer resort in the country. Not far from the town stands a curious monument of antiquity—the Old Tower. Its age and origin are unknown, and have been the subject of much learned but fruitless disquisition.

Newport harbor is one of the most accessible, safe, and capacious in America. Long before the Revolution, it gave to the town a rapid growth and prosperity, which, at one time, seemed likely to outstrip that of New York. Here, at different periods, anchored the British fleets, and occupied the town as well as the surrounding country. Here, also, the French fleets entered, under Count D'Estaing and Admiral de Ternay. From these naval operations, Newport suffered greatly, but soon recovered its former vigor, and continued to be one of the chief commercial ports in the Union, until the manufacturing success of Providence diverted the tide of enterprise into other channels. Manufactures and commerce are still extensively prosecuted.

The population in 1810, was 7,907; in 1820, 7,319; in 1830, 8,010; in 1840, 8,333; in 1850, 9,563.

SMITHFIELD, R. I.

This is one of the principal manufacturing towns in the state, being situated on Blackstone river, 10 miles north of Providence. Its resources consist in a favorable position in a region naturally productive, and affording lime and several useful stones, and in the extensive water-power, which keep numerous manufactories in active operation. A number of these are congregated at Woonsocket falls, on the Blackstone, where there is a pleasant village of the same name.

The population in 1810, was 3,828; in 1820, ——; in 1830, 6,857; in 1840, 9,534; in 1850, 11,386.

RAILROADS.

From Providence to Hartford.

unfinished.

To Willimantic, by stage		47
Andover	6	53
Bolton	3	56
Vernon	6	62
Manchester	4	66
Scotland	2	68
East Hartford	8	76
Hartford	2	78

STAGE-ROUTES

From Providence to Killingly.

To North Scituate		10
West Scituate	3	13
Foster	5	18
East Killingly	5	23
Killingly	2	25

From Providence to New London.

To Centreville		10
Coventry	2	12
West Greenwich	5	17
Hopkinton	14	31
North Stonington	7	38
Mystick	6	44
Croton	7	51
New London	1	52

From Providence to Plainfield, Conn.

To South Scituate		11
Mount Vernon	8	19
Sterling	6	25
Plainfield	4	29

From Providence to New Bedford.

To South Seekonk	5	
Swansey	6	11
Fall River	4	15
Westport	7	22
New Bedford	7	29

BY STEAMBOAT.

From Stonington to New York.

Off New London		14
Saybrook Light and mouth of Connecticut river	11	25
Faulkner's Island	15	40
N Haven lighthouse	15	55
Stratford Point	12	67
Bridgeport	3	70
Black Rock	3	73
Norwalk Island	12	85
Greenwich Point	12	97
New Rochelle	11	108
Throgg's Neck	8	116
Hell-Gate	8	124
Blackwell's Island	3	127
New York	4	131

HARTFORD, Conn.

The capital, with New Haven, of the state of Connecticut, is situated on Connecticut river, at the head of sloop navigation, 45 miles from its entrance into Long Island sound, 100 miles southwest of Boston, and 123 northeast of New York. The city is built on the west bank of the river, which rises suddenly into an elevation, and stretches away into an undulating and diversified country. Seated in the centre of the state, and in its richest region, and communicating with the whole valley of the Connecticut from Vermont to the sound, it enjoys an extensive and valuable trade in all the manufactures and productions peculiar to New England. The plan of the city is not very regular, but many of its buildings are elegant and beautiful for situation. On a public-square, stands the state-house, a fine structure of the Doric order, 116 feet long, 75 wide, and 54 high. Trinity College, an Episcopal institution, has a fine location near the city. The city-hall in the Doric, and the Athæneum of the Gothic architecture, are conspicuous edifices. But the buildings most honorable to Hartford, are the American Asylum for the education of the Deaf and Dumb, and the Retreat of the Insane. Both of these institutions are widely known, and include persons from all parts of the country. The former is situated on Tower hill, about a mile west of the city, and receives a revenue from grants made by the general government, and from other sources. The buildings of the Insane Asylum are located toward the southwest of the city, upon an eminence, in the midst of picturesque and delightful scenery, well-suited to minister to the injured mind that peace and quietude which nature can best impart.

A beautiful freestone bridge spans Mill river, which winds through the city into the Connecticut, by a single arch of 100 feet, and a substantial and costly bridge connects the town with East Hartford. Perhaps the object of most universal interest in the vicinity of Hartford, is the Charter Oak, which still flourishes as in its pristine verdure, though age has robbed it of some of its limbs. It stands on a beautiful elevation south of the city.

The New Haven and Hartford, the Hartford and Springfield, and the Connecticut River railroads, traverse the best part of Massachusetts and Connecticut; and sloops and steamboats ply upon the river and Long Island sound.

The population in 1810, was 3,955; in 1820, 4,726: in 1830, 7,074; in 1840, 12,793; in 1850, 17,966.

NEW HAVEN, Conn.

The capital, with Hartford, of the state, is situated on a bay of Long Island sound, which is here about twenty miles broad. It is 76 miles northeast of New York, and 300 from Washington. The city is built on a plain, or gentle slope, at the foot of two bold spurs from the Green Mountain range, which here terminate in two abrupt cliffs, called "East Rock" and "West Rock," rising like sentinels on either side. From the top of these, the eye beholds a wide and enchanting prospect. Below the feet,

RAILROADS.

From Hartford to New Haven.

To Newington	8	
Berlin and Junction of Middletown RR	3	11
Meriden	7	18
Wallingford	6	24
North Haven	6	30
New Haven	6	36

From New Haven to New York.

To Milford		10
Naugatuck Junc	2	12
Stratford	2	14
Bridgeport	4	18
Fairfield	4	22
Southport	2	24
Westport	5	29
Norwalk	3	32
Darien	3	35
Stamford	5	40
Greenwich	5	45
Port Chester	2	47
Rye	2	49
Mumaroneck	4	53
New Rochelle	3	56
Williams' Bridge	7	63
Fordham	2	65
Morrisania	1	66
Mott Haven	1	67
Harlem	1	68
New York	8	76

Fm Hartford to New York.

To New Haven, as above		36
N. York, as above	76	112

From Hartford to Springfield.

To Windsor	7	
Windsor Locks	6	13
Warehouse Point	2	15
Enfield Bridge	2	17
Thompsonville	1	18
Long Meadow	4	22
Springfield	4	26

From Hartford to Boston.

To Springfield, as above		26
Boston (see Boston and Albany route)	98	124

Fm Norwich to Worcester.

To Greenville	1	
Jewett City	8	9
Plainfield	7	16
Central Village	3	19
Danielsonville	6	25
Dayville	3	28
Pomfret	5	33
Thompson	2	35
Masonville	2	37
Fisherville	1	38
Wilsonville	2	40
Webster	3	43
North Village	1	44
Oxford	4	48
Auburn	6	54
Grand Junction	4	58
Worcester	1	59

Fm New London to Palmer and Springfield.

To Montville	6	
Mohegan	3	9
Norwich Landing	4	13
Norwich	1	14
Yantic	2	16
Franklin	4	20
Lebanon	2	22
South Windham	4	26
Willimantic Junct. of Hartford and Providence R.R.	4	30

New Haven lies in quiet beauty, with its white mansions and steeples embowered amid clusters of rich foliage. Far around stretch hills, slopes, and valleys, rich with the colors of nature and cultivation; away to the south and east, like an ocean, spreads the sound, sprinkled here and there by a mote-like sail, and dimly bounded by the cloud-like shores of Long Island. New Haven is one of the most beautiful of cities. Its streets are broad and regular; tasteful, chaste, and splendid buildings are surrounded by pleasant gardens, parks, and trees. Many of these are elms, stately and venerable, planted by the fathers of the town, and cherished with commendable pride and care by their descendants. This profusion of foliage and freedom from contracted and uncleanly streets, combine for New Haven the advantages of the city and the country. The "Green" is a pleasant spot of ground, shaded by rows of lofty elms; in the centre, stand the three oldest churches in the city. Toward the west is the statehouse, a large and imposing structure; still further to the west, are the buildings of Yale College, one of the oldest, most flourishing, and respectable institutions of America. Hillhouse avenue, bordered by sides of undulating green, from which spring rows of stately trees, runs between splendid mansions and gardens, that rival Italian villas in loveliness. Northwest of the city, is the cemetery, beautifully laid out, and adorned with an imposing entrance in Egyptian architecture.

The harbor is spacious, but so shallow that large vessels are obliged to anchor at Long wharf, which, from time to time, has been extended to a length of 3,943 feet. New Haven prosecutes an extensive coasting-trade with New York and the towns along the sound. Several ships from foreign shores also make this city their port. The New York and New Haven railroad has largely increased the communication between the two cities, and the New Haven and Hartford railroad joins the lines at Springfield, which traverse the valley of Connecticut river, and other parts of Massachusetts.

The population in 1810, was 5,772; in 1820 7,147; in 1830, 10,180; in 1840, 14,890; in 1850, 22,539.

NEW LONDON, Conn.

A FLOURISHING city, the principal port of entry in Connecticut, occupies a gentle elevation facing the southeast, on the west bank of the Thames river, three miles from its entrance into Long Island sound, 53 east of New Haven, and 353 from Washington. The ground on which it stands is rocky and rough, and seems to have discouraged the builders from attempting to construct it with regularity. The houses erected within a few years, however, are superior to the rest, and the appearance of the town is much improved.

New London harbor is deep and convenient, although its entrance is narrow, and might be easily blockaded, if it were not defended by two fortifications. Fort Griswold, in Groton, opposite the city, and Fort Trumbull, one mile below, shared severely the struggles of the Revolution, and the former, especially, was

RAILROADS.

South Coventry....	4	34
Eagleville	2	36
Mansfield..........	2	38
South Willington..	4	42
Tolland and Willington	3	45
Stafford............	5	50
Monson............	12	62
Palmer	4	66
Indian Orchard....	9	75
Springfield	6	81
From New Haven to Tariffville.		
To Hamden Plain..	4	
Centreville	2	6
Ives'...............	1	7
Mount Carmel.....	1	8
Bradley's	2	10
Brooks'............	2	12
Cheshire...........	3	15
Hitchcock	4	19
Southington Corner	2	21
Southington	1	22
Plainville..........	5	27
Farmington........	3	30
Avon	7	37
Weatogue	3	40
Simsbury	2	42
Tariffville..........	3	45
From Bridgeport to Pittsfield and Albany.		
To Stipney.........	10	
Bottsford	5	15
Newtown..........	4	19
Hawleyville	4	23
Brookfield	6	29
New Milford.......	6	35
Gaylord's..........	7	42
Kent...............	6	48
Cornwall Bridge..	9	57
West Cornwall....	4	61
Falls Village.......	6	67
Canaan	6	73
Sheffield	6	79
Barrington.........	6	85
Van Dusenville....	2	87
Alger's	3	90
Glendale	2	92
Stockbridge	1	93
South Lee..........	2	95
Lee	4	99
Lenox	1	100
Pittsfield	1	101
Albany (see Massachusetts route)...	49	150
From Winsted to N. York.		
To Burrville.......	5	
Wolcottville	5	10
Litchfield	3	13
Camp's Mills	2	15
Plymouth	5	20
Waterbury	7	27
Waterville.........	3	30
Naugatuck.........	5	35
Seymour...........	7	42
Ansonia	4	46
Dirly	2	48
Junction	9	57
Stratford..........	1	58
Bridgeport	4	62
New York (see N. Haven and New York route)......	58	120
From Bridgeport to Winsted, see above		62
From Hartford to Providence.		
To East Hartford..	2	
Manchester	7	9
Vernon	3	12
Bolton.............	4	16
Andover	6	22
Willimantic........	9	31

unfinished.

the scene of bloody barbarities under Benedict Arnold, who, in 1781, entered the harbor, took Fort Griswold, and burned the town. An obelisk of granite, 125 feet high, preserves the memory of the patriots who here suffered and died.

The business of the city is chiefly whale-fishing and commerce; its tonnage is larger than that of any other town in the state.

The Worcester and Norwich railroad unites with the Thames at Allyn's Point, a few miles above.

The population in 1810, was 3,238; in 1820, 3,330; in 1830, 4,356; in 1840, 5,519; in 1850, 9,006

BRIDGEPORT, Conn.

This pleasant, prosperous, and growing city, is situated on a cove of Long Island sound, which here runs up three miles inland, and affords a good, though not deep harbor. It is 17 miles west of New Haven, and 62 northeast of New York The city is built on a plain, which, as it retreats from the water, rises into an elevation that affords a fine prospect of the surrounding country, and thence spreads away into undulations and hills. It is well laid out with handsome houses. In the last few years especially, a large number of substantial brick stores and dwellings, have added much to the appearance and wealth of the place.

The Housatonick railroad, traversing the valley of Housatonick river, meets the West Stockbridge railroad in Massachusetts, which is the connecting link between Albany and Boston.

Several vessels sail from this port, and it would probably carry on a more extensive foreign commerce, if the harbor were not obstructed by a sand-bar, 13 feet below high-water mark. A bridge, 1,236 feet long, extends across the harbor, admitting vessels through a draw.

The population in 1810, was 5,72; in 1820, ——; in 1830, 2,803; in 1840, 4,570; in 1850, 7,558.

NORWICH, Conn.

This city is situated at the head of navigation of Thames river, at the junction of the Shetucket and Yantic rivers, 14 miles from Long island sound. The main part of the city is situated on a steep acclivity, the houses being built in tiers rising one above another, present a beautiful appearance when approached from the south. Here are extensive manufactures of cotton and woollen goods, paper, hardware, pottery, &c. This location was the scene of severe conflicts between the Mohegan and Narraganset Indians. It was the stronghold of the latter, and here the burial-place of their kings is still to be seen. Near the city there are several picturesque falls, or cataracts, and from a high rock which overhangs these water-falls, the Mohegan Indians, plunged and perished, rather than fall into the hands of the Narragansets, who were pursuing them.

The population in 1840, 7,239; in 1850, 10,261.

RAILROADS.

From Stonington to Providence.

To Westerly	5	
Charlestown	5	10
Richmond Switch	4	14
Carolina	3	17
Kingston	6	23
Wickford	7	30
Greenwich	6	36
Warwick	4	40
Junction	6	46
Providence	4	50

From New Haven to New London.

Fair Haven	2	
East Haven	2½	4½
Bromford	3½	8
Stony Creek	3	11
Guilford	4½	15½
East River	2	17½
Madison	2½	20
Clinton	3½	23½
Westbrook	4½	28
Saybrook	3½	31½
Lynn	2	33½
South Lynn	4½	38
East Lynn	4½	42½
Waterford	4	46½
New London	3½	50

STAGE-ROUTES.

From Hartford to Wilbraham.

To East Windsor	7	
Scantic Village	7	14
Broadbrook	3	17
Somers	8	25
North Somers	2	27
Wilbraham	7	34

From Hartford to Canaan

To West Hartford	4	
Avon	7	11
Canton	3	14
New Hartford	6	20
Winsted	6	26
Norfolk	9	35
Canaan	6	41

From Hartford to West Granville.

To Bloomfield	6	
Weatogue	5	11
North Canton	6	17
Barkhamsted	5	22
West Hartland	5	27
West Granville	5	32

Fm Hartford to Westfield.

To Bloomfield	6	
Tariffville	5	11
Granby	4	15
Southwick	7	22
Westfield	5	27

From New London to Stonington.

To Groton	1	
Pequot	3	4
Mystic	4	8
Portersville	3	11
Mystic Bridge	2	13
Stonington	5	18

From Plainfield to Providence.

To Sterling	4	
Rice City	5	9
Mount Vernon	2	11
South Scituate	6	17
Providence	12	29

NEW YORK, N. Y

THE great commercial metropolis of the United States, and in population, commerce, and wealth, one of the first cities of the globe, is situated in latitude 40° 42′ 40″ north, and in longitude 74° 1′ 8″ west from Greenwich, and 3° 0′ 22″ east from Washington, 216 miles southwest of Boston, and 86 miles northeast of Philadelphia.

The city is located on Manhattan island, between Hudson and East rivers, which unite at its southern extremity, forming one of the most admirable harbors for beauty and convenience in the world. The island is 13½ miles long, bounded on the north by Harlem river, formerly Spuytendevil creek, and embraces an area of about 20 square miles. On the south part of this, the compact part of the city is built, extending northward about four miles from river to river, and spreading by a rate of progress which will soon cover the whole island. Its admirable position for foreign commerce, with its noble bay, and its remarkable facilities of internal communication with every portion of the Union, have been the unfailing sources of its extraordinary growth and prosperity. Here the noble Hudson, after a course of more than 200 miles, through a rich and populous region, sweeps majestically along, bearing on its bosom the vast commerce of the Erie canal and the West, expands into the upper bay, and passes through the "Narrows" into the ocean. Here, too, on the opposite side, courses the strong tide of East river, which, winding between Long island and the main land, forms the rocky pass of "Hell-Gate," and several islands. This stream, which averages about three fourths of a mile in width, and thirty feet in depth, affords a passage for vessels of a large class into Long island sound and the Atlantic; while those engaged in foreign commerce, as well as in the southern coasting-trade, usually enter and leave the harbor through the Narrows, between Staten and Long islands. The best anchorage for these is at the wharves along the East river, which is more secure from ice than the Hudson. British packets, coasting vessels, and canal-boats generally, lie along the former river; some at Brooklyn, and the Atlantic dock, on the opposite bank; while the Hudson is thickly lined with steamboats and ships from England, France, Spain, Portugal, Holland, Sweden, and other foreign countries. On this river, also, at the foot of Canal street, is the wharf of the Collins' line of steamers, between Liverpool and New York. The Cunard steamers land at Jersey city, on the opposite side of the river. Other splendid lines run between the city and Southampton, Bremen, and Havre, in Europe, Charleston, Savannah, New Orleans, Havana, Chagres, Nicaragua, and Panama. Steamboats of different grades, from the magnificent floating palaces of the Hudson, to the lesser propeller and steam-ferry boats, are constantly leaving or approaching the city, and animate its waters with the most varied prospect of life and activity. For pleasant, salubrious position, and beauty of surrounding country, New York is as conspicuous as it is for commercial advantages. Entering the outer bay, from the Atlantic, the traveller sees on the left of the broad expanse of water, the blue hills of New Jersey, formerly known as the highlands of

RAILROADS.

From New York to New Haven.

To Harlem	7	
Mott Haven	1	8
Morrisania	1	9
Fordham	2	11
Williams' Bridge	2	13
New Rochelle	7	20
Mamaroneck	3	23
Rye	4	27
Port Chester	2	29
Greenwich	2	31
Stamford	5	36
Darien	5	41
Norwalk	3	44
Westport	3	47
Southport	5	52
Fairfield	2	54
Bridgeport	4	58
Stratford	4	62
Naugatuck Junc.	2	64
Millford	2	66
New Haven	10	76

From New York to Boston.

To New Haven, as above		76
Springfield (see Ct.)	62	138
Boston (see Mass.)	98	236

From New York to Philadelphia, via Newark and New Brunswick.

To Jersey City	1	
Newark	8	9
Elizabethtown	6	15
Rahway	5	20
Uniontown	3	23
Campbell's	4	27
New Brunswick	4	31
Dean's Pond	8	39
Kingston	4	43
Aqueduct Town	2	45
Princeton	2	47
Clarksville	4	51
Trenton	6	57
Morrisville	1	58
Bristol	10	68
Cornwallis	6	74
Tacony	5	79
Philadelphia	8	87

From New York to Philadelphia, via Perth Amboy.

To Perth Amboy (by steamboat)		25
South Amboy	2	27
Spottswood	11	38
West's	4	42
Cranberry street	3	45
Hightstown	4	49
Centreville	4	53
Newtown	3	56
Sand Hill	2	58
Bordentown	5	63
South Bordentown	1	64
Kincora	3	67
Hammelstown	1	68
Burlington	3	71
Beverly	6	77
Rancocas	1	78
Palmyra	5	83
Fish House	2	85
Camden	4	89
Philadelphia (by Ferry)	1	90

From New York to Newark (see above.) 9

From New York to New Brunswick (se above) 31

From New York to Paterson.

To Jersey City	1	
Bergen	2	3
Aquackanonk	9	12
Paterson	5	17

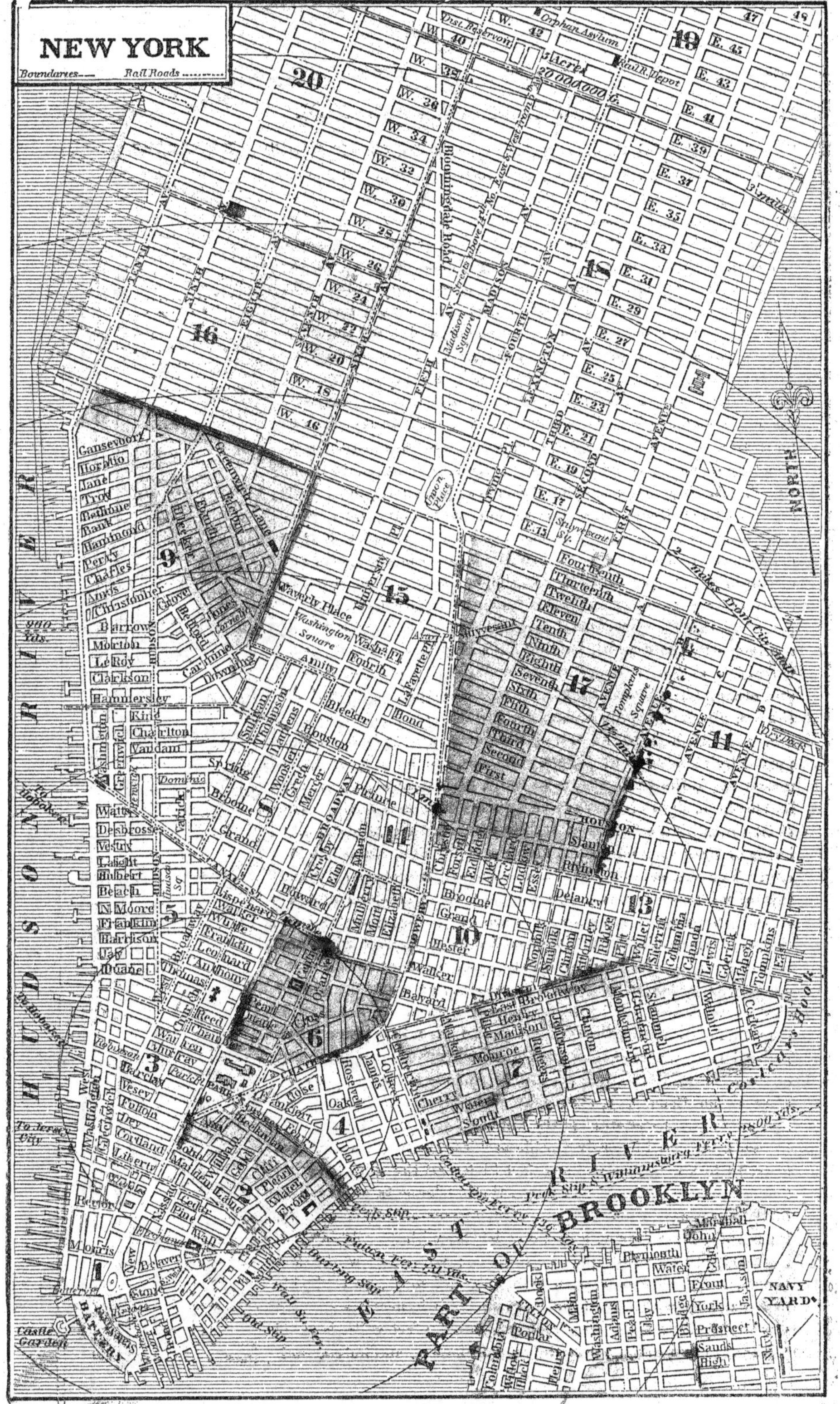
NEW YORK
Boundaries
Rail Roads
HUDSON RIVER
EAST RIVER
PART OF BROOKLYN
NAVY YARD
NORTH
Washington Square
Madison Square
Union Place
Tompkins Square
Stuyvesant Sq.
Waverly Place
BROADWAY
BOWERY
Bloomingdale Road
BATTERY
Castle Garden
Corlears Hook
To Jersey City
To Hoboken
Orphan Asylum
Dist. Reservoir

Navesink. Toward the north, the romantic heights of Staten island rise to view, and on the east, the shores of Long island. Following the Narrows, between the two islands, which are defended by strong fortifications, the upper or inner part of the bay opens an enchanting scene. Staten island recedes, and the shores of New Jersey reappear. Long island continues on the right, and after passing Governor's island, with its fortifications, the great city displays its forest of masts and spires, its domes and its houses, relieved by the green foliage of the "Battery," set, like an emerald, in some darker stone. The ground rises from the Battery, and from both rivers, by a gradual ascent, of which Broadway is the ridge, or summit. This surface, with the outline of the city, which rapidly widens from its southern point to a breadth of two miles, at Corlear's Hook, on the East river, gives an imposing effect, unequalled by almost any in the world. At the lower and ancient part of the city, the streets are somewhat irregular, but not unpleasant, being lined with rows of warehouses and stores of the most splendid and solid construction. Many of these are brick, some of freestone, and others of white marble. This is the business part of the city, and embraces comparatively few residences. Wall street is the principal theatre of financial and mercantile operations, and is a broad, straight avenue, leading from East river to Broadway. On either side of this are numerous splendid banking-houses, and other public buildings, among which is the Merchants' Exchange, of blue granite, or sienite, 200 feet long, 171 feet wide, and 124 feet high to the top of the dome, with a portico supported by massive solid pillars. Within, the most remarkable apartment is the exchange, a rotunda, 80 feet in diameter, and 80 feet high, lighted from above by the dome, and resting upon eight Corinthian columns of Italian marble. The whole building is of fire-proof materials, and is a splendid ornament to the city. The customhouse, on the same street, is a beautiful structure of white marble, in Doric architecture, surrounded by rows of Corinthian columns, with a portico extending across the entire front on Wall street. It is 200 feet long, 90 feet wide, and 80 feet high, and contains numerous apartments for the different offices, the principal of which is of circular form, 80 feet in diameter, surrounded by columns, and lighted by a beautiful dome. This structure occupies the site of where once stood Federal Hall, where Washington was inaugurated first president of the United States, April 30, 1789. At the head of Wall street, fronting on Broadway, stands Trinity church, the most costly and magnificent structure of the kind in America. It is of light-brown freestone, in purely Gothic architecture, and is 192 feet deep, 84 feet wide, the walls 60 feet high, and the spire reaching 284 feet above the ground. From the battlements, at the base of the spire, appears a magnificent panorama of New York bay, its islands, New Jersey, and Long island, with Brooklyn, Williamsburgh, and other populous towns; while below the feet the giant city spreads east, west, north, and south, on each side of Broadway, which for three miles bisects it in nearly a straight direction. This splendid street, which is 80 feet wide, is lined with large and magnificent stores, warehouses, and hotels, built

RAILROADS.

From New York to Dunkirk, via Piermont.

To Piermont Dock (by steamboat.)..		24
Blauvettville	5	29
Clarkstown	4	33
Spring Valley	2	35
Monsey's	2	37
15 Mile Turnout	2	39
Sufferns	3	42
Ramapo	2	44
Sloatsburgh	1	45
Shultz's Turn-Out	3	48
Monro Works	4	52
Wilkes'	2	54
Turner's	3	57
Monroe	2	59
Oxford	3	62
East Junction	1	63
West Junction	1	64
Chester	1	65
Goshen	5	70
North Hampton	4	74
Middletown	3	77
Howell	4	81
Otisville	4	85
Shin Hollow	7	92
Delaware	6	98
Ross' Turn	10	108
Middaugh's	4	112
Barryville	5	117
Lackawaxen	4	121
Mast Hope	5	126
Narrowsburgh	6	132
Nobodystown	5	137
Cochecton	4	141
Callicoon	5	146
Hankin's	7	153
Equinunk	10	163
Stockport	6	169
Hancock	5	174
Dickinson's T.	6	180
Hale's Eddy	2	182
Deposite	5	187
Summit	7	194
Susquehannah	8	202
Great Bend	8	210
Kirkwood	6	216
Windsor Road	4	220
Binghamton	5	225
Union	8	233
Campville	7	240
Owego	7	247
Tioga	5	252
Smithboro'	4	256
Barton	3	259
Waverley	7	266
Chemung	4	270
Wellsburgh	6	276
Elmira	7	283
Junction	4	287
Big Flats	6	293
Noyes' Turn	2	295
Corning	6	301
Painted Post	1	302
Addison	10	312
Rathboneville	5	317
Cameron	7	324
Canisteo	13	337
Hornellsville	5	342
Almond	4	346
Alfred	4	350
Andover	8	358
Shoemaker's	5	363
Gennesee	4	367
Scio	4	371
Phillipsville	4	375
Belvidere	4	379
Friendship	3	382
Cuba	8	390
Hindsdale	7	397
Olean	7	404
Allegany	4	408
Tunungwant	8	416
Great Valley	5	421
Bucktooth	4	425
Little Valley	6	431
Catarangus	7	438
Dayton	9	447
Cooper's Corner	4	451
Forestville	10	461
Dunkirk	8	469

BIRD'S-EYE VIEW OF NEW YORK,

SHOWING THE CITIES OF NEW YORK, BROOKLYN, AND WILLIAMSBURGH, WITH THE HARBOR AND RIVERS

THE CITY-HALL.

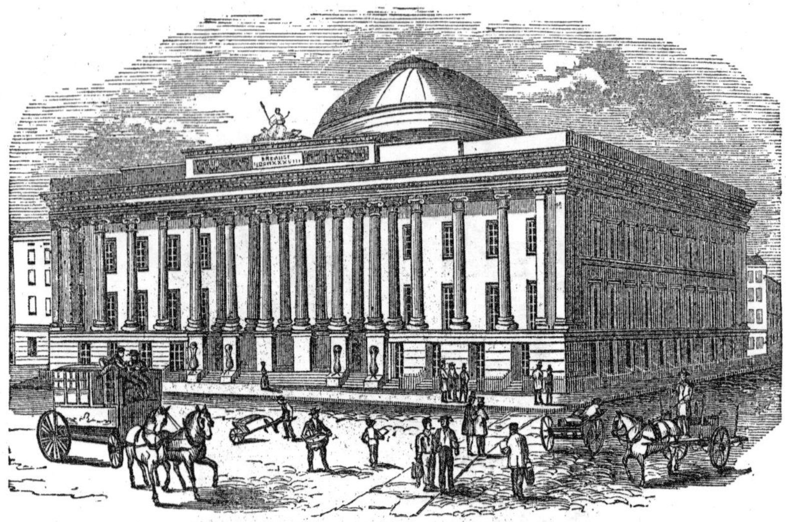

MERCHANTS' EXCHANCE, WALL STREET.

of white marble, freestone, and other durable materials. Below Trinity church, besides a number of fine hotels, there is the United States bonded warehouse. Proceeding northward, successively appear the Astor house, occupying an entire square, built of blue granite, the city-hall, the Irving house, opposite to which is Stuart's dry-goods palace, a massive structure of white marble, the Society library, hospital, American institute, Academy of Design, Metropolitan hotel, and Grace church, of pure white marble, elaborately sculptured. At Tenth street, Broadway makes a small angle, and, after passing Union park, and Madison square, proceeds nearly northward to the upper end of the island. Among the public buildings in the lower part of the city is the city-hall, in the "Park," a pleasant triangular enclosure, of ten acres. This edifice is of white marble, except the back, which is of brown freestone. Its architecture is a combination of the Ionic, Corinthian, and Composite orders. It is 216 feet long, 105 feet deep, and 65 feet high. Upon the roof is a cupola, with a clock, illuminated at night, and an enormous bell, the powerful tones of which send the alarm of fire over an area of many miles. Within are well-furnished apartments for different offices of the city government; and in the second story the governor's room, which is decorated with portraits of the presidents, governors of the state, mayors of the city, and many American heroes and statesmen. In front of this edifice a splendid fountain rises, from the middle of a circular basin, surrounded by flowers and shrubs. The park also contains the new city-hall, the hall of records, and several other public buildings, for the accommodation of the courts, and city business. The halls of justice, often called, from its architecture, the "Egyptian Tombs," is a massive and large building, on Centre street, of light-colored granite, 253 feet long, and 200 feet wide. It contains the city prison, and other departments of justice. Colum-

RAILROADS.

Fm New York to Dunkirk, via Paterson & Sufferns.

To Jersey City (by Ferry)	1	
Bergen	2	3
Seacocus	2	5
Hackensack	2	7
Boiling Spring	3	10
Passaic Bridge	2	12
Huyler's	1	13
Paterson	4	17
Rock Road	4	21
Hokokus	3	24
Allendale	2	26
Ramsey's	2	28
Sufferns	5	33
To Dunkirk (see above)	427	460

New York to Binghamton (see N. Y. to Dunkirk) 225

N. York to Hornellsville (see N. Y. to Dunkirk) 342

N. York to Corning (see N. Y. to Dunkirk)................ 301

Fm New York to Albany, by Hudson River R.R.

Manhattanville	8	
152d street	1	9
Spuytendevil Creek	3	12
Yonkers	5	17
Hastings'	4	21
Dobb's Ferry	1	22
Dearman	3	25
Tarrytown	2	27
Sing-Sing	5	32
Croton	4	36
Haverstraw	2	38
Verplank's	3	41
Peekskill	2	43
Fort Montgomery	3	46
Garrison's	5	51
Cold Spring	3	54
Fishkill	6	60
Low Point	4	64

MAP OF HUDSON RIVER and Hudson River Railroad.

The Hudson river proper rises by two branches, in the mountainous regions of Hamilton and Essex counties, New York. The Eastern branch is composed of two streams, which unite in Warren county. Fifteen miles below this, the Sacandagua unites with the Hudson at Jessup's falls; eighteen miles below this, it passes Hadley's falls; and twenty miles further is Glen's falls. The only considerable tributary below this, is the Mohawk, ten miles above Albany. Its whole course, from its source to its entrance into New York bay, is 320 miles. The tide flows as far as Albany. The city of New York owes much of its prosperity to this river, connected as it is with the Erie and Champlain canals. The Hudson River railroad, which connects Albany with New York, together with the river travel, are greater thoroughfares than any other highway on this continent.

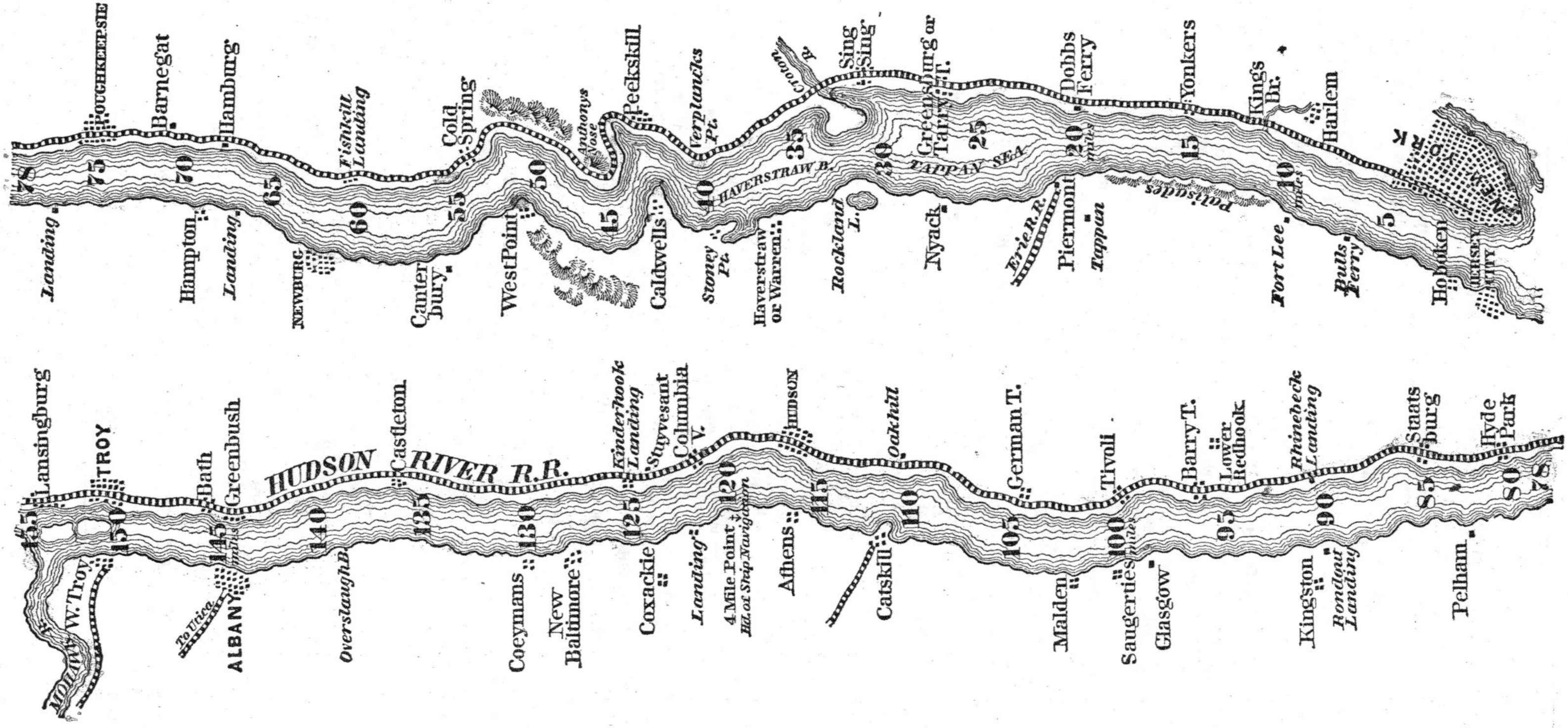

bia college is pleasantly situated westward of the park, fronting a beautiful green, the west side of which once overlooked the Hudson, but it is now at a distance of about a fourth of a mile. This institution was founded under George II., in 1754, and has educated some of the most distinguished men of the country. The New York Postoffice occupies the old Middle Dutch church on Nassau, Cedar, and Liberty streets. Other prominent buildings worthy of note are Clinton hall, occupied by the Mercantile library; Odd-Fellows hall, an imposing structure of freestone; the New York university, an elegant white marble Gothic structure; the university medical college, on Fourteenth street; the New York college of physicians and surgeons, on Crosby street; the New York medical college; the general theological seminary of the protestant episcopal church; the Union theological seminary; the free academy; the Astor library; the institution for the blind; the deaf and dumb asylum; the New York orphan asylum, upon an attractive slope overlooking the Hudson; the colored orphan asylum; the asylum for friendless boys; the sailors' home; the colored home, and many other noble, charitable institutions, which form a most enviable ornament of pride and honor for the metropolis of America.

New York is well furnished with educational and literary privileges, and manifests its high interest in mental culture, by the number and excellence of its libraries, schools, colleges, lectures, and journals, the latter of which are, in general, superior to those of any other city in the Union, for intrinsic merits, despatch, and for every requisite of newspaper literature.

The public grounds of New York are numerous, but scarcely commensurate with its greatness and wealth. The "Battery," at the south extremity, is an airy and delightful resort in summer, carpeted with greensward, shaded with large trees, and fanned by the breezes of the bay. At the southwest side, built up from the water, is Castle-Garden, once a fortification, but now used for public gatherings, and for the magnificent annual fairs of the American Institute. Its vast amphitheatre will contain 10,000 persons. Not far from the battery, at the foot of Broadway, is the "Bowling-Green," a small elliptical enclosure, containing a fountain and lofty trees. Here, before the Revolution, stood a gilded leaden statue of George III., which was converted by the patriots into bullets, to be fired at the troops of the king, whom it represented. The park has been already noticed. Union square is a pleasant oval ground, adorned with flowers, grass, trees, and a fountain. Washington square, formerly a potter's field, lies westward of Broadway, and affords a pleasant promenade. Tompkin's, Stuyvesant, and Madison squares, are the other public grounds. none of which are sufficiently ample for the wants of the city. St. John's, and Grammercy, are beautiful private parks.

It remains to notice a work which, in grandeur of design, and magnificent execution, is truly worthy of the commercial metropolis of America: the Croton water-works, the most extensive and costly structure of the kind in the country, and probably in the world, if we except those at Marseilles, in France. A dam across Croton river, 40 miles north of the city-

RAILROADS.

New Hamburgh	2	66
Milton Ferry	3	69
Poughkeepsie	6	75
Hyde Park	6	81
Rhinebeck	10	91
Barrytown	5	96
Tivoli	4	100
East Camp	5	105
Oak Hill	5	110
Hudson	6	116
Stockport	4	120
Coxsackie	3	123
Stuyvesant	3	126
Schodack	7	133
Castleton	3	136
East Albany	8	144
Albany (by Ferry)	1	145

See Hudson River Railroad.

New York to Yonkers 17

N. York to Tarrytown 27

N. York to Sing-Sing. 32

New York to Fishkill. 60

New York to Poughkeepsie 75

New York to Hudson. 116

New York to Albany, via White Plains, by Harlem Railroad.

To Harlem	7	
Morrisania	3	10
Fordham	2	12
Williams' Bridge	2	14
Turkahoe	6	20
Scarsdale	2	22
White Plains	4	26
Kensico	3	29
Pleasantville	5	34
New Castle	6	40
Bedford	2	42
Mechanicsville	3	45
Croton Falls	6	51
Brewster's	4	55
Paterson	8	63
Paulings	4	67
South Dover	6	73
Dover Plains	7	80
Wassaic	5	85
Amenia	3	88
Millerton	8	96
Boston Corners	7	103
Copake	5	108
Hillsdale	4	112
Bush Bash	3	115
Martindale	3	118
Philmount	4	122
Ghent	6	128
Chatham 4-Corners	2	130
Chatham Centre	4	134
Kinderhook	3	137
Schodack	8	145
Greenbush	7	152
Albany (by Ferry)	1	153

See Harlem Railroad.

New York to White Plains............. 26

New York to Croton Falls............... 51

New York to Amenia. 88

New York to Chatham 4-Corners.......... 130

New York to Albany, via Housatonic R.R. to Bridgeport, (see New York and New Haven route)...... 193

New York to Pittsfield (see Bridgeport to Albany, in Conn)... 159

hall, creates an exhaustless and beautiful lake, of about 400 acres in area, five miles in circumference, and capable of containing 550,000,000 gallons of water. The aqueduct extends from this point to Harlem river, without interruption, conveying the water through a conduit of masonwork, which has a descent of about one foot to a mile, is six feet three inches wide at the bottom, seven feet eight inches at the top, and eight feet five inches high. It passes Harlem river upon the "High Bridge," which has been pronounced equal to the most magnificent structures, of a similar kind, in ancient Rome. Fourteen piers of solid masonry support arches, upon which rests the bridge, 1,450 feet long, and 114 feet above tide-water. After crossing the river, the aqueduct conveys the water to the receiving reservoir, 836 feet wide, 1,825 feet long, and containing 150,000,000 gallons. The water is separated by a partition of masonry, forming two divisions, which may be alternately full and empty, or both full at the same time. The whole area of the surface of the water is equal to 35 acres. From this basin the water is conveyed through iron pipes to the distributing reservoir, two miles southward, whence it is distributed through iron pipes under ground, enters the houses, and cleanses the streets, administering comfort, beauty, and health, to the city and its denizens. The area of the latter reservoir is equal to four acres; its capacity is 20,000,000 gallons. The water-works can supply 60,000,000 gallons daily; the average quantity is 30,000,000. The cost of the aqueduct and reservoirs was over $12,000,000.

The manufactures of New York, like its commerce, are more extensive than those of any other American city. Ship-building and machinery, are among the branches most largely carried on. Here are built the magnificent ocean steamers, packets, and steamboats, that are the glory of New York.

The principal streets are traversed in various directions by omnibus lines, connecting the important points. Ferries communicate with Hoboken, Jersey city, Staten island, Brooklyn, Williamsburgh, and Astoria.

The railroads diverging from New York are, the Harlem; the Hudson River, to Albany; the New York and New Haven; the Camden and Amboy; the Philadelphia; the New Jersey Central; the Morris and Essex; the Paterson and Ramapo; the Erie; and the Long Island. Not all of these enter the city; many communicate by steamboats from different distances.

The population in 1653, was 1,120; in 1661, 1,743; in 1675, 2,580; in 1696, 4,455; in 1730, 8,256; in 1756, 10,530; in 1774, 22,861; in 1786, 23,688; in 1790; 33,131; in 1800, 60,489; in 1810, 96,373; in 1820, 123,706; in 1825, 166,136; in 1830, 202,589; in 1835, 270,089; in 1840, 312,710; in 1845, 371,280; and in 1850, 515,547.

Population by Wards in 1850.—First Ward, 19,755; Second, 6,616; Third, 10,350; Fourth, 23,256; Fifth, 22,691; Sixth, 24,699; Seventh, 32,697; Eighth, 34,413; Ninth, 40,675; Tenth, 23,316; Eleventh, 43,772; Twelfth, 10,453; Thirteenth, 28,244; Fourteenth, 25,206; Fifteenth, 22,564; Sixteenth; 52,887; Seventeenth, 43,780; Eighteenth, 31,557; Nineteenth, 18,463.

RAILROADS.

From New York to Dover, N. J. (see N. Jersey) 44

From New York to Easton, Pa. (see N.J) 78

From N. York to Morristown (see N. Y. to Dover.).......... 34

From Albany to Buffalo.

To Centre House..	8	
Schenectady	9	17
Hoffman's	10	27
Amsterdam	6	33
Tribe's Hill........	6	39
Fonda	5	44
Yost's	5	49
Palatine Bridge....	6	55
Fort Plain	3	58
St. Johnsville......	6	64
Little Falls.........	10	74
Herkimer..........	7	81
Frankfort..........	5	86
Utica	9	95
Whitesboro'	4	99
Oriskany	3	102
Rome...............	7	109
Green's Corners...	5	114
Verona Centre.....	4	118
Oneida	4	122
Wampsville	3	125
Canastota..........	2	127
Canaseraga.........	4	131
Chittenango	2	133
Kirkville	4	137
Manlius	3	140
Syracuse	3	143
Geer's..............	2	145
Camillus...........	5	150
Marcellus..........	7	157
Half Way..........	5	162
Skaneateles........	2	164
Sennett	6	170
Auburn.............	4	174
Shunpike	11	185
Cayuga Bridge....	6	191
Seneca Falls.......	3	194
Waterloo	7	201
Geneva.............	7	208
East Vienna.......	6	214
Clifton Springs....	2	216
Shortsville.........	4	220
Canandaigua	3	223
Paddleford	3	226
Victor	6	232
Fisher's	5	237
Pittsford...........	5	242
Rochester	10	252
Chili...............	5	257
Churchville	9	266
Bergen	3	269
Byron	8	277
Batavia............	8	285
Alexander	8	293
Attica.............	3	296
Darien	5	301
Darien Centre.....	1	302
Alden	6	308
Town Line........	5	313
Lancaster.........	5	318
Clark's Branch....	4	322
Buffalo	6	328

From New York to Buffalo, via Hornellsville & Attica.

To Hornellsville (see N. York and Dunkirk route)..		342
Burns	8	350
Whitney's Valley..	4	354
Nunda.............	12	366
Portage............	6	372
Carlisle...........	8	380
Warsaw	10	390
Gaines'	7	397
Attica	7	404
Buffalo (see Buffalo & Albany route.).	65	469

BROOKLYN, N. Y.

THE second city in population in the state, is situated at the west end of Long island, on the easterly side of East river, opposite the city of New York. Its surface was originally rough and broken, but has since been graded sufficiently low to be passed with ease. From the top of the "Heights," the city spreads over a gentle, or undulating slope, for several miles, toward Gowanus bay on the south and Williamsburgh on the northeast. It is destined, like each in the constellation of cities which cluster around New York, to attain inconceivable greatness. Its ample limits, and fine situation close to the business part of the great commercial emporium, with which it is connected by six steam-ferries — two of them, the Fulton and the South ferry, probably unsurpassed for elegance and despatch by any in the world — render it a favorite residence of merchants and others who do business in New York, and to these causes it is indebted for its rapid growth in population and wealth. Most of the streets are broad and pleasant, lined with handsome shade-trees, and substantial and often princely dwellings, which are lighted in the night with gas. The new avenues toward the east part of the city, are arranged with great regularity and taste, with open, airy gardens attached to the dwellings.

The city-hall, in a central situation, at the union of several of the principal streets, is a fine edifice of white marble. The United States Naval hospital, on a gentle swell near Wallabout bay, seen with its white marble walls through groups of trees, makes an agreeable picture. On this bay, at the north side of the city, appear also the large buildings of the navy-yard, which includes an area of 45 acres, enclosed by a substantial brick-wall. Here, too, is the Brooklyn dry-dock, a structure of almost unequalled vastness. The foundation is 406 feet long, and 120 feet wide. The main chamber is 286 feet long, and 30 feet wide at the bottom; at the top 307 feet long, and 98 feet wide. The iron folding-gates weigh 150 tons. Pumps discharge 40,000 gallons of water per minute. Ships-of-war of the largest class, here enter and are repaired. Sixteen years were occupied in the construction of this dock. The churches, which, in proportion to the population of the place, are equalled in number and beauty by no other city, except, perhaps, by those of New York, are of all orders of architecture, from the chaste and simple Grecian, to the pure Gothic, with lofty walls, richly-sculptured columns, and tinted windows. The literary advantages of Brooklyn are also numerous and valuable. Libraries, lectures, scientific, and literary societies, and schools of various grades, are flourishing and well-supported.

The harbor of Brooklyn is deep, spacious, and sufficient for any number of vessels. Along the southwest front, opposite Governor's island, extends the Atlantic dock, a deep and spacious basin, of 42 acres, which is surrounded by piers and bulkheads, containing a large number of substantial warehouses, built of stone. More than thirty of these are leased by the general government, for depositing bonded-goods. Other warehouses and factories of various kinds line the wharves along East river, from the Atlantic dock to Wallabout bay.

RAILROADS.

From Albany to Schenectady (see Albany to Buffalo.)......... 17

From Albany to Utica (see Albany to Buffalo.)............... 95

Fm Albany to Auburn (see Albany to Buffalo)............... 174

From Albany to Rochester (see Albany to Buffalo.)......... 252

From Albany to Boston.

To Greenbush (by Ferry.)...........	1	
Schodac............	7	8
Kinderhook.......	8	16
Chatham Centre...	4	20
Chatham 4-Corners	3	23
East Chatham......	5	28
Canaan............	10	38
State Line..........	..	38
Richmond..........	3	41
Shaker Village.....	5	46
Pittsfield..	3	49
Dalton.............	5	54
Hinsdale..........	3	57
Washington.......	5	62
Becket............	3	65
Middlefield........	4	69
Chester Factory...	5	74
Chester Village....	7	81
Russell............	3	84
Westfield..........	8	92
West Springfield..	8	100
Springfield........	2	102
Boston (see Mass).	98	200

From Albany to Pittsfield (see above.)... 49

From Albany to Troy 6

From Albany to Saratoga Springs.

To Troy...........	6	
Waterford..........	4	10
Mechanicsville.....	7	17
Ballston...........	13	30
Saratoga Springs..	8	38

From Albany to Castleton, Vermont.

To Whitehall (see next page).......		80
State Line..........	6	86
Fairhaven..........	2	88
Hydeville..........	2	90
Castleton..........	3	93

From Albany to Rutland, Vermont.

To Troy............	6	
Lansingburg.......	3	9
Schaghticoke......	9	18
Pittstown..........	2	20
Johnsonville.......	2	22
Buskirk's Bridge..	5	27
Eagle Bridge......	2	29
Wait's Corner.....	2	31
Cambridge...... ..	3	34
Shushan...........	6	40
Salem.............	13	53
West Rupert.......	2	55
Rupert.............	7	62
Pawlet............	3	65
Granville Corner..	2	67
Granville..........	5	72
Poultney..........	2	74
Castleton..........	7	81
West Rutland.....	5	86
Rutland Centre....	2	8[illegible]
Rutland...........	2	9[illegible]

A few miles south of the city, beyond Gowanus bay, lies the beautiful and enchanting Greenwood cemetery, which, for combination of romantic nature with splendid art, is probably surpassed by no necropolis in the world.

The Long Island railroad terminates in Brooklyn, at the South ferry

The population in 1800, was 3,298; in 1810, 4,402; in 1820, 7,175; in 1830, 12,042; in 1840, 36,233; in 1850, 96,850.

WILLIAMSBURGH, N. Y.

This thriving city lies on the East river, opposite New York, and adjoins Brooklyn on the south. It is built on a slope, gently rising from the water for about a third of a mile, and then descending toward the east a distance of about a mile more. From the pleasant heights of North Brooklyn, at the south of this city, appears an interesting panorama of the towns which thickly cluster around this part of Long Island. Brooklyn, resting on somewhat elevated ground, and bending around a wide circuit, is every day blending more closely with Williamsburgh. Far toward the east and north, spreads the latter city, and north of this the pleasant villas of Greenpoint, Ravenswood, and Astoria; while East river separates these from the great forest of masts and spires on the opposite shores. From the river, Williamsburgh presents a fine effect — its tall steeples, and a number of imposing manufactories along its water-front, add much to the picturesqueness of the place. Its streets are regular, generally well-paved, lighted with gas, and ornamented with trees. Here a large number of persons who do business in New York reside, crossing daily by the four steam-ferries, the boats of which ply constantly between the two cities; other citizens are extensively engaged in ship-building, and in the manufacture of blocks, cordage, marble, glue, glass, chemicals, oil, castings, buttons, and lamps.

The progress of Williamsburgh is one of the phenomena of the age. Thirty years ago, a few insignificant buildings stood on the ground now covered by its northern part. After slowly increasing for about twenty years, it received a new impetus, and rose, in ten years, from a village of 5,000 souls, to the sixth city of the Empire state. It is destined to a still higher rank. Williamsburgh was formerly a part of the town of Bushwick, and was incorporated as a village in 1827; with extended powers in 1835, and as a city in 1851.

The population of Bushwick, in 1820, was 930; of Williamsburgh, in 1830, 1,620; in 1840, 5,680; in 1850, 30,786.

ALBANY, N. Y.

The capital of the state, is situated on the west side of Hudson river, 145 miles north of New York, and 164 miles west of Boston. Rising by a bold ascent from the water, and crowned with the glittering domes of the capitol and city-hall, it presents an interesting appearance from the river, and creates anticipations which are rarely realized on entering its streets; many of these retain their early irregularity and narrowness, but the

RAILROADS.

From Albany to Whitehall.

To Troy	6	
Waterford	4	10
Mechanicsville	7	17
Ballston	13	30
Saratoga	11	41
Gansevoort's	11	52
Moreau	5	57
Fort Edward	1	58
Dunham's Bridge	3	61
Smith's Basin	5	66
Fort Ann	3	69
Comstock's L.	4	73
Whitehall	7	80

From Albany to New York, via Hudson River RR to Albany 145

Albany to Hudson (see N. York to Albany) 29

Albany to Poughkeepsie (see N. York to Albany) 70

Albany to Sing Sing (see New York to Albany) 113

From Owego to Cayuga.

To South Candor	5	
Candor	5	10
Wilseyville	4	14
Pugsley's	5	19
Ithaca	14	33
Ovid Landing	20	53
Andover	6	59
Union Spring	5	64
Cayuga	6	70

From Corning to Blosburg.

To Cook's Furnace	8	
Lawrenceville	7	15
Tioga	5	20
Mansfield	10	30
Covington	5	35
Blosburg	5	40

From Buffalo to Niagara Falls.

To Rock	3	
Black Rock Dam	1	4
Tonawanda	7	11
Cayuga Creek	6	17
Niagara Falls	5	22

From Niagara Falls to Lewistown.

To Junction	7	
Lewistown	3	10

Fm Ogdensburg to Rouse's Point.

To Lisbon	9	
Madrid	8	17
Potsdam	8	25
Knapp's	3	28
Stockholm	8	36
Lawrence	5	41
Moira	6	47
Brush's Mills	3	50
Bangor	5	55
Malone	6	61
Burke	8	69
Chateaugay	4	73
Summit	8	81
Gravel Pit	2	83
Brandy Brook	5	88
Ellenberg	1	89
Chazy	6	95
Sand Pit	2	97
Centreville	6	103
Mooer's	3	106
Champlain	8	114
Rouse's Point	4	118

more modern avenues and buildings are generally spacious and elegant. The capitol, at the head of State street, a broad avenue, ascending steeply from the river, stands on the east side of a beautiful public square. In the north part of this square, which is divided by a street running from east to west, stands the city-hall and the statehouse, both of white-marble, the former adorned with a beautiful gilded dome. The other public buildings are: churches, over thirty in number, the Albany academy, and the Female academy

Few inland cities combine so many natural advantages for trade, improved by such extensive and costly public-works, as Albany. It is the terminus of the Erie canal, and the great chain of railroads which connects the central counties of New York, the great lakes, and their vast shores. The Green mountain state sends its productions to Albany through Lake Champlain and the Champlain canal. Some of the products brought through these channels, pass through Massachusetts to Boston by railroad; more are whirled in a few hours to New York, by the gigantic Hudson River railroad, which now sweeps majestically through the solid mountains and rocky headlands which skirt that mighty stream. Steamboats, schooners, and sloops, also convey large cargoes to and from the towns along the route.

The population in 1790, was 3,498; in 1800, 5,349; in 1810, 9,356; in 1820, 12,630; in 1830, 24,238; in 1840, 33,721; in 1850, 50,771.

BUFFALO, N. Y.

The most important inland city, in point of commercial position, in the state of New York, is situated at the confluence of Buffalo creek with the east end of Lake Erie, and at the western terminus of the Erie canal, by which route, it is 363 miles distant from Albany. It occupies a slope, chiefly on the north side of the creek, which is here deep enough for vessels drawing eight feet of water. The streets are generally regular, the buildings substantial, and many of them imposing. The longest and broadest is Main street, the Broadway of Buffalo, on each side of which, for more than two miles, extend lines of stores and other buildings. From the top of the elevation above the city, appears a wide panorama of the lake, Black Rock basin, Niagara river, the Erie canal, and the surrounding country.

Buffalo is the offspring of the Erie canal, and ever since the completion of that stupendous work, has continued to increase in population, wealth, and importance. It is the gate through which the vast commerce of the great lakes and the western states passes on its way to New York and the east. A great chain of railroads binds Buffalo to New York, Boston, Albany, and the richest portion of the Empire state along the course of the Erie canal; and another, traversing the valleys of the Susquehannah and Delaware, links it with New Jersey, New York city, and Philadelphia. By either of these routes, the passenger may reach Buffalo from New York, a distance of about 500 miles, in less than 20 hours. The Lake-shore railroad, connects it with the vast network of railroads in the western states.

RAILROADS.

From Ogdensburg to Montreal.

To Rouse's Point (see page 31)		118
Lacolle	..	...
Stott's	..	...
St. John's		140
Laprairie	15	155
Montreal	9	164

Fm Hudson to West Stockbridge.

To Claverack	4	
Mellenville	5	9
Ghent	6	15
Chatham 4-Corners	8	23
Edward's	6	29
Mass. State Line	2	31
West Stockbridge	3	34

Fm Whitehall to Castleton.

To State Line	6	
Fairhaven	2	8
Hydeville	2	10
Castleton	3	13

From Schenectady to Saratoga.

To Ballston	15	
Saratoga	7	22

Fm Brooklyn to Greenport.

To Bedford	2	
East New York	3	5
Cypress Hills	2	7
Union Course	1	8
Woodville	1	9
Jamaica	2	11
Brushville	3	14
Hyde Park	3	17
Branch	3	20
Carll Place	2	22
Westbury	1	23
Hicksville	3	26
Farmingdale	5	31
Deer Park	6	37
Thompson	4	41
Suffolk	2	43
Lakeland	6	49
Waverly	4	53
Medford	2	55
Yaphank	5	60
Wampmissic	4	64
Manor	2	66
Riverhead	8	74
Jamesport	5	79
Mattituck	4	83
Catchogue	3	86
Hermitage	3	89
Southhold	2	91
Greenport	4	95

From Brooklyn to Jamaica (see Brookiyn to Greenport) 11

From Rochester to Niagara Falls.

To Spencerport	10	
Adams' Basin	2	12
Brockport	5	17
Halley	5	22
Murray	3	25
Albion	5	30
Medina	10	40
Middleport	5	45
Mabee's	4	49
Orangeport	2	51
Lockport	5	56
Pekin	10	66
S. Bridge	8	74
Niagara Falls	2	76

From Syracuse to Oswego.

Baldwinville	12	
Lamson's	5	17
Fulton	7	24
Oswego	11	35

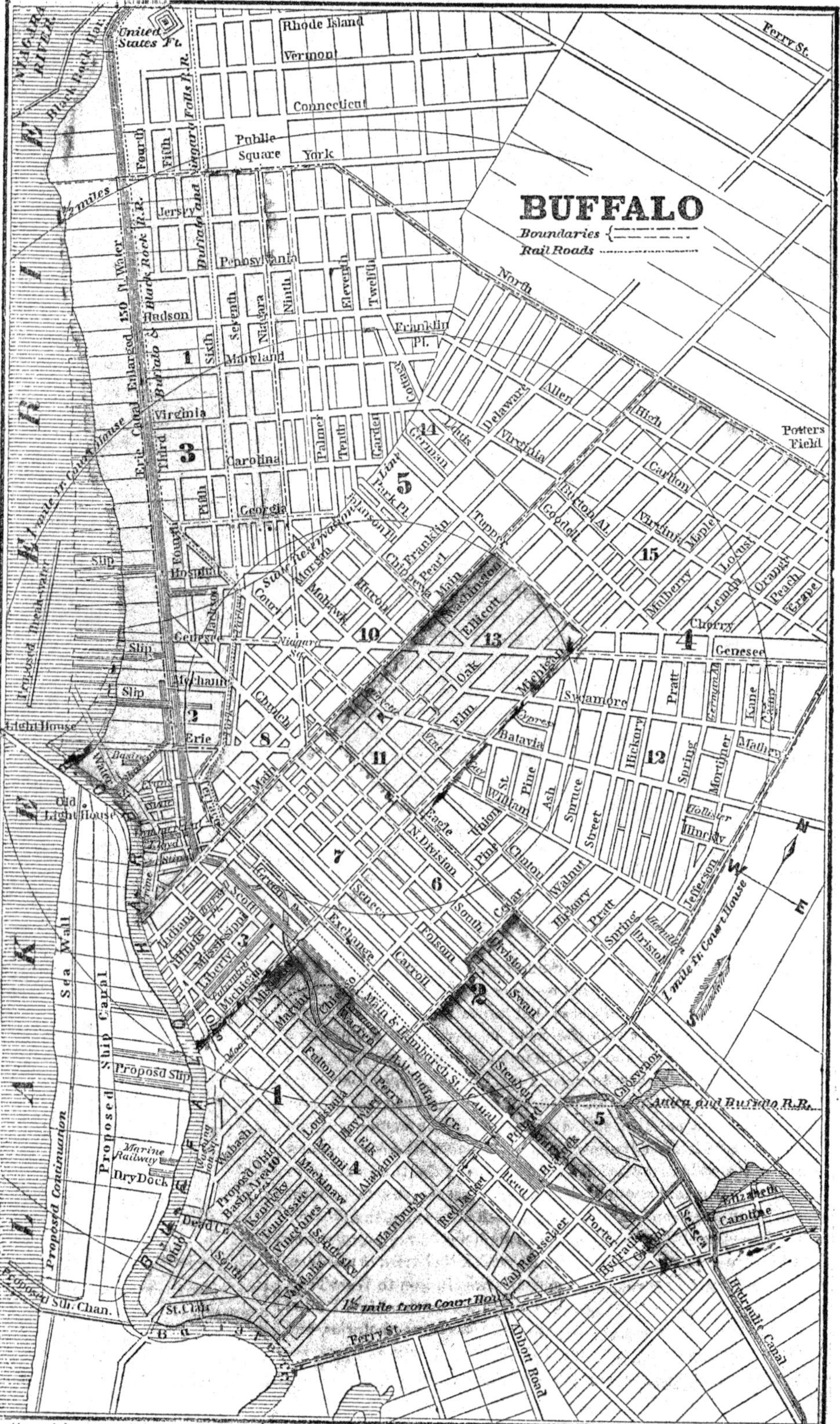
BUFFALO
Boundaries
Rail Roads

The harbor of Buffalo was formerly impeded by sands which the winds and storms of Lake Erie deposited at its entrance. By the construction of a mole and pier, 1,500 feet long, this obstruction is removed, and vessels drawing eight feet of water, now enter the creek. Here, in the winter-season, a large number of vessels, steamboats, ships, schooners, and canal-boats, are congregated and protected from ice and storms. Several hundred schooners, and a number of steamboats, navigate Lake Erie from Buffalo to the different ports on its shores. A large amount of capital is invested in manufactures.

The population in 1810, was 1,508; in 1820, 2,095; in 1830, 8,653: in 1840, 18,213; in 1850, 40,266.

ROCHESTER, N. Y

Is the most important city, next to Buffalo, of Western New York, and is situated on both sides of Genesee river 7 miles from its entrance into Lake Ontario, 73 miles northeasterly from Buffalo, and 220 miles northwest of Albany. Three bridges, and the magnificent aqueduct of the Erie canal, span the river from the west to the east part of the city. The public buildings are generally substantial and imposing; but the most interesting structures are the flour-mills along the rapids and falls of Genesee river, which here descend 270 feet. Here the vast stores of wheat produced in Genesee valley and the surrounding country, as well as the western states, are ground and prepared for market. To its vast water-power and the Erie canal, Rochester owes its prosperity and surprising growth. Thirty years ago, the site of the city was a marshy, unhealthy wilderness; now, it is populous with men, and active with industry.

The population in 1820, was 1,502; in 1830, 9,269; in 1840, 20,191; in 1850, 36,561.

TROY, N. Y.

This enterprising and pleasant city, the seat of justice of Rensselaer county, is situated on the east side of Hudson river, 6 miles north of Albany, and 151 miles north of New York. Formerly, this point was the head of sloop-navigation, but a dam across the river above, 1,100 feet long, and 9 feet high, with a lock, enables sloops to ascend to Lansingburgh, four miles higher up. The city is built on level ground, at the foot of steep hills, the two chief of which have the classic names, "Mount Ida" and "Mount Olympus." From both of these eminences, spreads a wide prospect of the Hudson and the towns along its valley. It is laid out with broad and pleasant streets, and the houses are neat and substantial. South of the city, the Poestenkill comes tumbling and foaming through a wild ravine, affording a fine water-power for several mills, which lie buried in the deep, dark gorge. A railroad bridge spans the Hudson to West Troy, a flourishing village, in Albany county, where there is a United States arsenal, an extensive bell-foundry, cotton factories, and other establishments. Among the public builings of Troy, besides its churches, the Troy Female institute, and the Troy acad-

RAILROADS.

From Buffalo to Cleveland

To Rodgers's Road	10	
18-Mile Creek	5	15
Evans' Centre	7	22
Lagrange	7	29
Silver Creek	2	31
Dunkirk	10	41
Centreville	10	51
Westfield	6	57
Quincy	8	65
Pa. State Line	4	69

To Erie and Cleveland (see Penn. and Ohio routes) 123

From Rome to Watertown and Cape Vincent.

To Taberg	11	
M'Connellsville	2	13
Camden	5	18
West Camden	5	23
Williamstown	5	28
Kasoag	3	31
Albion	6	37
Richland	5	42
Sandy Creek	5	47
Mannsville	5	52
Pierrepont	2	54
Adams	5	59
Adams Centre	3	62
Watertown	10	72
Brownville	4	76
Limerick	4	80
Chaumont	6	86
Cape Vincent	11	97

From Newburgh to Chester, on the Erie Railroad.

To Craigsville	10	
Washingtonville	10	20
Salisbury	5	25
Vail's Gate	10	35
Newburgh	10	45

From Elmira to Canandaigua.

To Junction	4	
Horse Heads	1	5
Millport	7	12
Havana	6	18
Jefferson	3	21
Rock Stream	6	27
Big Stream	2	29
Starkey	3	32
Hemrod's	4	36
Milo Centre	3	39
Penn Yan	4	43
Benton	3	46
Bellona	3	49
Hall's Corners	3	52
Gorham	2	54
Hopewell	4	58
Canandaigua	8	66

BY STEAMBOAT.

From New York to Albany and Troy.

To Bull's Ferry	6	
Manhattanville	2	8
Fort Lee	2	10
Yonkers	7	17
Hastings	3	20
Dobb's Ferry	2	22
Piermont	2	24
Tarrytown	3	27
Sing Sing	6	33
Verplank's Point	7	40
Caldwell's Landing	4	44
West Point	8	52
Cold Spring	2	54
Cornwall	3	57
Newburgh	4	61
New Hamburgh	6	67
Milton	3	70
Poughkeepsie	4	74
Hyde Park	6	80
Pelham	4	84

emy, deserve notice from the reputation which they enjoy. Water is conveyed to the city from a basin in Lansingburgh, elevated 72 feet above the level of the streets, through which it is distributed by iron-pipes buried under ground. One million and a half gallons are thus supplied for daily consumption, or to extinguish fires.

Troy is united to Lake Champlain by railroad, via Saratoga and Whitehall, to Greenbush; opposite Albany, and to Schenectady, on the great central line, by one of two branch railroads; the other proceeding from Schenectady to Albany. There has been considerable rivalry in enterprise between Albany and Troy, which has probably injured neither city. The Erie canal passes through West Troy, and steamboats and numerous vessels, communicate with New York and the other towns on the river.

The population in 1810, was 3,885; in 1820, 5,264; in 1830, 11,401; in 1840, 19,334; in 1850, 28,785.

SYRACUSE, N. Y.

This flourishing and rapidly increasing city, like Buffalo and Rochester, is one of the wonderful fruits of the Erie canal. It lies 133 miles west of Albany, on the great central railroad route to Buffalo. Few inland towns have a more advantageous position; in the midst of a region rich in exhaustless salt springs, it communicates with Lake Ontario by the Oswego canal, and the Oswego and Syracuse railroad, which here join respectively the Erie canal and the great central railroad of New York. The buildings of Syracuse are chiefly of brick; it also contains an elegant hotel and several churches. A branch canal connects the place with Salina, about a mile distant, and between the two places, are extensive manufactories, yielding a vast quantity of salt, and a large annual revenue to the state.

The population in 1830, was 2,565; in 1840, 6,502; in 1850, 22,235.

POUGHKEEPSIE, N. Y.

This is one of the largest and pleasantest towns on the Hudson, at the head of ship-navigation. It lies on the east side of the river, in Dutchess county, 75 miles north of New York 71 miles south of Albany, and 301 miles from Washington. Wappinger's creek bounds the town on the east, the Hudson on the west. From the latter river, the village is concealed, being delightfully seated on an elevated plain, one mile eastward. At the landing, there are a number of wharves, where steamboats and other vessels stop on their way between Albany and New York. Ascending by the road, the steep bank, the village bursts upon the sight, presenting an interesting spectacle of industry and prosperity. It has the appearance of a city, with its compact buildings, regular streets, stores, churches, banks, and manufactories. Upon a neighboring elevation stands the Poughkeepsie collegiate school, a fine building in Grecian architecture; besides this there are an academy and other schools. Formerly whaling vessels were owned in Poughkeepsie, and returned

BY STEAMBOAT.

Rhinebeck	6	90
Redhook, Lower Landing	7	97
Redhook, Upper Landing	3	100
Saugerties	1	101
Bristol	1	102
Catskill	9	111
Hudson	5	116
Coxsackie	8	124
Kinderhook Land'g	3	127
New Baltimore	4	131
Coryman's	2	133
Castleton	4	137
Overslaugh	5	142
Albany	3	145
Troy	6	151

Nrom New York to Stonington and Providence.

To Blackwell's Isl'd	4	
Ravenswood	2	6
Hell-Gate (Astoria)	1	7
Throgg's Point	9	16
Sands' Point	7	23
Mamaroneck	5	28
Greenwich Point	7	35
Long Neck Point	5	40
Norwalk Harbor	4	44
Farm's Point	7	51
Bridgeport Harbor	5	56
Stratford Point	4	60
New Haven Light	10	70
Goose Island	14	84
Hamonasset Point	7	91
Saybrook Light, and mouth of Conn. R.	11	102
Off New London	12	114
Stonington	14	128
Providence, by railroad (see p. 17)	50	178

From Buffalo to Chicago.

To Hamburgh	11	
Cattaraugus	10	21
Dunkirk	17	38
Portland	17	55
Erie, Pa	33	88
Fairview	11	99
Conneaut Harbor	20	119
Ashtabula	13	132
Grand River	30	162
Cleveland	32	194
Black River	26	220
Vermilion River	9	229
Huron	14	243
Sandusky	14	257
Port Clinton	15	272
Toledo	32	304
Erie	12	316
Monroe	14	330
Gibraltar	25	355
Detroit	24	379
Fort Gratiot	80	459
Mouth of Saginaw Bay	75	534
Thunder Bay Isl'd	75	609
Presqu' Island Lighthouse	35	644
Mackinaw	83	727
Fox Island Point	30	757
Manitou Islands	70	827
Manitowoc	97	924
Sheboyagan	30	954
Milwaukie	50	1004
Racine	23	1027
Kenosha	10	1037
Waukegan	12	1049
Chicago	50	1099

From Oswego to Lewiston.

To Little Sodus Bay	12	
Sodus Bay	10	22
Poultneyville	15	37
Port Genesee	35	72
Oak Orchard Creek	38	110
18-Mile Creek	25	135
Fort Niagara	10	145
Youngstown	1	146
Lewistown	6	152

hither from their voyages. An expensive aqueduct supplies the village with water from neighboring springs. The Hudson River railroad passes through the place.

The population, in 1810, was 4,670; in 1820, 5,726; in 1830, 7,222; in 1840, 10,006; in 1850, 11,080.

UTICA, N. Y.

Is another of the numerous and vigorous progeny of the Erie canal. It is situated south of Mohawk river, 92 miles northwest of Albany, and 233 miles east of Buffalo. The city is built on a pleasant slope, facing the river, its streets are generally broad and regular, and its aspect exhibits the signs of prosperity, business, activity, and successful industry. The Erie canal, and the great central chain of railroads, pass through Utica, and the former is here joined by the Chenango canal, which extends to Binghamton, on the Erie railroad, and furnishing an outlet for the agricultural products of the surrounding country. Manufactures of various kinds are extensively carried on.

The population in 1820, was 2,972; in 1830, 8,323; in 1840, 12,782; in 1850, 17,240.

NEWARK, N. J.

The principal city of New Jersey, is situated on the west side of Passaic river, 3 miles from its entrance into Newark bay, 9 miles west of New York, and 215 miles from Washington. It has a pleasant location on level ground, somewhat elevated above the river. The streets are broad and straight, lighted with gas, and supplied through iron-pipes with pure water from a neighboring spring. Two spacious public parks, shaded by lofty trees, add much to the beauty of the place. The houses are generally of wood, or brick, the former white and neat, the latter substantial and elegant. Toward the west, the elevated ground affords a commanding site for residences; and the court-house, which is a large structure of brown freestone, in the Egyptian style of architecture. The materials for this, were wrought from the neighboring quarries, which furnish large quantities of material for buildings in New York and elsewhere. The New Jersey railroad, connecting New York with Newark, Trenton, and Philadelphia, here enters a splendid depot, which is one of the most prominent buildings in the city. The Morris and Essex railroad, also terminates here. Newark has also a number of churches, of which some are elegant and beautiful; also several banks, literary institutions, and libraries.

In proportion to its population, few cities are more extensively engaged in manufactures. Whalebone, oil, carriages, varnish, leather, shoes, candles, soap, harness, machinery, castings, zinc, paint, and jewelry, are among the articles most largely produced.

Steamboats ply several times a-day to New York; and the Morris canal, traversing the fruitful county from which it is named, has contributed much to the trade and prosperity of the place.

The population in 1810, was 5,000 (in whole township, 8,008); in 1820, 6,507; in 1830, 10,953; in 1840, 17,290; in 1850, 38,885.

BY STEAMBOAT.

From Oswego to Ogdensburg, on L. Ontario and River St. Lawrence.

To Sackett's Harbor	43	
Kingston, C. W.	48	91
French Creek, N. Y.	28	119
Alexandria, N. Y.	14	133
Brockville, C. W.	25	158
Morristown, N. Y.	2	160
Ogdensburg, N. Y.	15	175

From New York to New Haven.

To N. Haven Light (see page 35)	70	
New Haven	3	73

CANALS.

Fm Albany to Buffalo. 364

Fm Albany to Whitehall 73

From Utica to Binghamton 99

From Syracuse to Oswego 38

Fm Rochester to Olean 104

RAILROADS.

From New York to Philadelphia.

To Jersey City (by Ferry)	1	
Newark	8	9
Elizabethtown	6	15
Rahway	5	20
Uniontown	3	23
Campbell's	4	27
New Brunswick	4	31
Dean's Pond	8	39
Kingston	4	43
Aqueduct T.	2	45
Princeton	2	47
Clarksville	4	51
Trenton	6	57
Morrisville	1	58
Bristol	10	68
Cornwallis	6	74
Tacony	5	79
Philadelphia (by steamboat)	8	87

From Jersey City to Newark (as above).. 8

From Jersey City to New Brunswick (as above) 30

From Jersey City to Trenton (as above).. 57

From N. York to Perth Amboy (by steamb't) 25

Fm Perth Amboy to Philadelphia.

To South Amboy	2	
Spotswood	11	13
West's	4	17
Cranberry st.	3	20
Hightstown	4	24
Centreville	4	28
Newtown	3	31
Sand Hill	2	33

PATERSON, N. J.

This flourishing and rapidly increasing city, is situated on both sides of the Passaic river, 17 miles northwest of New York. It owes its existence and prosperity to the great water-power furnished by the Passaic. A large number of cotton factories, as well as other establishments for making machinery, firearms, and paper, are here in successful operation. The genius of Alexander Hamilton, first perceived these natural advantages, and devised the means for their application. Difficulties at first prevented the success of his plans, but time has proved their practicability and sagacity. The beauty of Passaic falls, which are near this place, is not less admirable than their utility. Hither many resort in the summer, to enjoy the picturesque scenery and healthful air.

Paterson contains several churches and institutions for improvement in knowledge. The Morris canal passes near the south part of the city; the Paterson railroad connects it with Jersey City and New York, and the Ramapo and Paterson railroad communicates with the Erie railroad at Ramapo.

The population in 1810, was 292; in 1820, 1,578; in 1830. 7,731; in 1840, 7,596; in 1850, 21,341.

JERSEY CITY, N. J.

This flourishing city is situated upon a peninsula, on the west bank of the Hudson, opposite the lower extremity of New York. In the days of the Revolution, it was known as Paulus Hook, and was the scene of several events interwoven in American history. Upon the neck of the peninsula, a little in advance of Bergen hill, was quite a strong fortification, which was occupied as a British outpost during a long period of the war. It was surprised, and its force made prisoners, in July, 1779, by Major Henry Lee, and a part of his legion.

Here the Paterson railway, connected with the Erie; the Morris and Essex railway; the Central railway, reaching toward Easton, on the Delaware; the New Jersey railway, extending to Trenton, and connecting with routes to Philadelphia; all have a terminus. Here, also, the Morris canal terminates, after pursuing a circuitous route of 100 miles from the Delaware river. Here the Cunard British Steam Navigation company have an extensive wharf, from which their magnificent ocean-steamers sail for Europe at regular intervals. Manufactories of various kinds are giving to Jersey City the most active prosperity, and its population, like that of all the towns near New York, is rapidly increasing. Several ferries communicate with New York.

Population in 1830, about 1,500; in 1840, 3,072; in 1850, 16,856.

TRENTON, N. J.

Is situated on the east side of Delaware river, at the head of sloop-navigation, 30 miles northeast of Philadelphia, 60 miles miles southwest of New York, and 166 miles from Washington. The city is pleasantly located on ground somewhat uneven, the streets regular, and many of the buildings are elegant and substantial. The statehouse, built of stone, and covered with stucco, in imitation of granite, is finely situated, and commands a delightful prospect of the Delaware and surrounding country. Above the city, the river descends by rapids, or falls, and at the foot of this descent it is spanned by a fine bridge, 1,100 feet long, with five arches, supported by stone piers. One side of this

RAILROADS.

Bordentown	5	38
Bordentown S.	1	39
Kincora	3	42
Hammel's T.	1	43
Burlington	3	46
Beverly	6	52
Rancocas	1	53
Palmyra	5	58
Fish-House	2	60
Camden	4	64
Philadelphia (by Ferry)	1	65

From Perth Amboy to Burlington (as above) 46

Fm P. Amboy to Bordentown (as above). 39

From Jersey City, opposite New York, to Easton.

To Newark	8	
Elizabethtown P't.	6	14
Elizabethtown	2	16
Cranesville	5	21
Westfield	2	23
Scotch Plains	3	26
Plainfield	2	28
New Market	3	31
Bound Brook	4	35
Dunn's Landing	5	40
Somerville	1	41
North Branch	4	45
Whitehouse	5	50
Clinton	8	53
Clarkville		
New Hampton		
Asbury		
Jaytown		
Bloomsburg		
Springtown		
Greene's Mills		
Easton		78

From Jersey City to Somerville (as above) 41

From Jersey City to Dover.

To Newark	8	
Orange	4	12
South Orange	2	14
Millville	4	18
Summit	3	21
Chatham	3	24
Madison	3	27
Morristown	4	31
Morris Plains	2	33
Denville	5	38
Rockaway	1	39
Dover	4	43

Fm Jersey City to Morristown (as above).. 31

From Jersey City to Paterson.

To Bergen	2	
Seacocus	2	4
Hackensack	2	6
Boiling Spring	3	9
Passaic Bridge	2	11
Huyler's	1	12
Paterson	4	16

Fm Jersey City to Sufferns. Junction of Erie R. R.

To Paterson (as above)		16
Rock Road	4	20
Hokokus	3	23
Allendale	2	25
Ramsey's	2	27
Sufferns	5	32

Fm Burlington to Mt. Holly 6

Fm Jersey City to Allendale (see above).. 25

bridge is appropriated to the railroad from New York to Philadelphia. At Trenton, the Delaware and Raritan canal meets a feeder, which enters the river 23 miles above the city. The falls afford an extensive water-power for manufacturing purposes, which has been increased by means of a dam across the river, and a raceway along its bank. Trenton is united to New Brunswick and New York by the New Jersey railroad, and by the Philadelphia and Trenton railroad, with the metropolis of Pennsylvania.

The population in 1810, was 3,003; in 1820, 3,942: in 1830, 3,925 (township); in 1840, 4,035; in 1850, 6,766.

PHILADELPHIA, Pa.

The first city of Pennsylvania, in population, wealth, and manufactures, and the second in the United States, is situated on a peninsula, formed by the confluence of Delaware and Schuylkill rivers. The city was laid out with beautiful regularity, in 1683, by its illustrious founder, William Penn, who gave it its name, signifying "brotherly love." Many of the noble trees which grew on the site, are now commemorated by the names of the streets running east and west, as Chesnut, Walnut, Pine, &c., while those crossing them are designated by numerals.

The ground on which Philadelphia is built is even, rising gently from each river, along which it extends for several miles. On the Delaware, the scenery is monotonous, but the water being deeper than that of the other river, the commerce and business of the city tends to this side; while the Schuylkill affords pleasing landscapes and agreeable places of residence. Many of the smaller vessels, sloops, and boats, here congregate, laden with coal, and other products of the valley of the Schuylkill; this part of the city is now rapidly increasing in wealth and business. No feature of Philadelphia is more striking than the regularity and neatness of its streets. The latter peculiarity is chiefly owing to the convenient grade, which allows the water to descend and find its way through sewers and other channels, into the Delaware. The houses, also, are more remarkable for neatness and solidity, than for splendor and show; they are mostly of brick, adorned with steps and basements of white marble, which the neighboring quarries furnish in abundance, and of fine quality. Of this material, a number of the public buildings are constructed, among which are the United States Marine hospital, the Pennsylvania bank, the Girard bank, the building formerly occupied by the United States bank, and the Girard college, which deserves more than a passing mention. A bequest of $2,000,000, with grounds beautifully situated on an elevation near the city, was made in 1831, by Stephen Girard, an eccentric, though wealthy citizen of Philadelphia, for the purpose of founding a college for orphans. With part of these funds, has been erected one of the most magnificent structures in the United States. The college consists of five buildings, the main edifice in the centre is devoted to the education of pupils and students of various ages and acquirements; the other four, two on each side, are residences for the instructors and students. The whole is of richly-wrought white marble. The central structure is 218 feet long, and 160 feet wide, surrounded by 34 Corinthian columns, 55 feet high, and six feet in diameter. The interior is in a corresponding style of splendor. The four other buildings are each 125 feet long, and 52 feet wide.

Another building in Philadelphia, of less magnificence, probably excites greater interest. This is the old statehouse, or Independence hall, where the Declaration of American Independ-

RAILROADS.

From Trenton to N. York.

To Clarksville	6	
Princeton	4	10
Aqueduct T.	2	12
Kingston	2	14
Dean's Pond	4	18
New Brunswick	8	26
Campbell's	4	30
Uniontown	4	34
Rahway	3	37
Elizabethtown	5	42
Newark	6	48
Jersey City	8	56
New York	1	57

RAILROADS.

From Philadelphia to New York, via Trenton.

To Tacony	8	
Cornwallis	5	13
Bristol	6	19
Morrisville	10	29
Trenton	1	30
Clarksville	6	36
Princeton	4	40
Aqueduct T.	2	42
Kingston	2	44
Dean's Pond	4	48
New Brunswick	8	56
Campbell's	4	60
Uniontown	4	64
Rahway	3	67
Elizabethtown	5	72
Newark	6	78
Jersey City	8	86
N. York (by Ferry)	1	87

From Philadelphia to Trenton (see above) 30

From Philadelphia to New Brunswick (see above) 56

From Philadelphia to Princeton (see above) 40

From Philadelphia to New York, via Burlington.

To Camden (by Ferry)	1	
Fish-House	4	5
Palmyra	2	7
Rancocas	5	12
Beverly	1	13
Burlington	6	19
Hammelstown	3	22
Kincora	1	23
Bordentown S.	3	26
Bordentown	1	27
Sand Hill	5	32
Newtown	2	34
Centreville	3	37
Hightstown	4	41
Canterbury st.	4	45
West's	3	48
Spotswood	4	52
South Amboy	11	63
Perth Amboy	2	65
New York (by st.)	25	90

From Philadelphia to Bordentown (see above) 27

From Philadelphia to Burlington (see above) 19

From Philadelphia to South Amboy (see above) 83

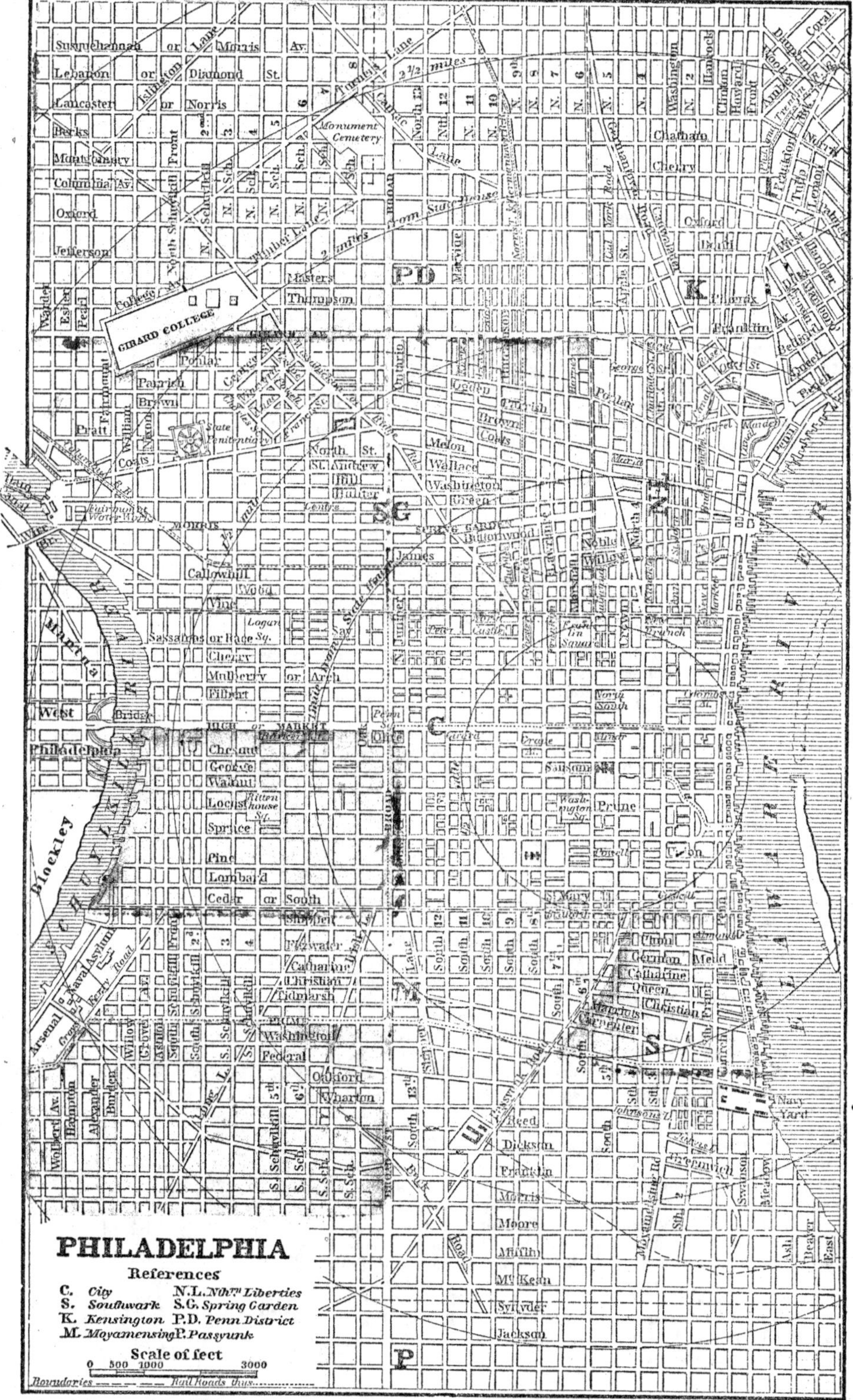
PHILADELPHIA
References
C. City
N.L. Nth.n Liberties
S. Southwark
S.G. Spring Garden
K. Kensington
P.D. Penn District
M. Moyamensing
P. Passyunk
Scale of feet
0 500 1000 3000
Boundaries
Rail Roads thus
GIRARD COLLEGE
Monument Cemetery
State Penitentiary
Fairmount Water Works
West Philadelphia
Blockley
Naval Asylum
Arsenal
Navy Yard
Logan Sq.
Franklin Square
Washington Sq.
Rittenhouse Sq.
2 miles from State House
1 mile from State House
2 1/2 miles
BROAD
HIGH or MARKET
Sassafras or Race
Mulberry or Arch
Cedar or South
Susquehanna or Morris Av.
Lebanon or Diamond St.
Lancaster or Norris

ence was decreed and signed by the first continental congress. The bell which announced to the anxious people the adoption of this great instrument, is carefully preserved in the cupola; it bears the prophetic inscription: "Proclaim Liberty throughout this land unto all the inhabitants thereof." These words were imprinted on the bell long before the use which was afterward made of it could have been known. In this building are a statue of Washington, in wood, and many other relics of the Revolution.

Philadelphia contains a large number of important public buildings and institutions. Among them are the Pennsylvania hospital, which owes its origin to Doctors Franklin and Bond; the Insane asylum, outside of the city; the Almshouse, fronting Schuylkill river on its west side; institutions for the deaf and for the blind, and several other charitable establishments. Besides these, there are the American Philosophical society, founded in 1743, by the exertions of Dr. Franklin, and possessing a large and valuable library and cabinet; the Philadelphia library, also established under the auspices of Franklin; the Franklin institute; the Academy of Natural Sciences; the Pennsylvania Academy of Fine Arts; and numerous other flourishing institutions for improvement in knowledge and art.

Another great structure is the United States mint, built of white marble, with two porticoes, resting on Ionic columns, one fronting Chestnut, the other Olive street. Here a vast amount of bullion, from California and other parts of the Union, is coined.

The markets of Philadelphia are among the most convenient, well-supplied, and well-conducted, in the country. To these come vast quantities of provisions from the surrounding region, with the rich and varied fruits of New Jersey and Delaware.

By the water-works on the Schuylkill, at Fairmount, a large body of water is raised into elevated reservoirs, whence it is distributed over the city by iron-pipes. A beautiful suspension bridge spans the Schuylkill at Fairmount, and several railroad bridges also lead to the city.

There are in Philadelphia a number of public parks, laid out with taste and beauty, shaded by trees, and adorned with walks, fountains, and other appropriate ornaments. In the rear of Independence-hall, is Independence square, a favorite and agreeable public report. Other public grounds are Franklin, Washington, Logan, and Rittenhouse squares.

Outside of the city are Pratt's gardens, on the Schuylkill, near the water-works, and below, Barton's gardens, both of which are interesting spots. These, with the beautiful villas, and soft but rich scenery of the river, render Philadelphia as agreeable a place of residence as any large city in the country.

Properly forming a part of the city, but having distinct municipal incorporations, are the five districts, Southwark, Moyamensing, Northern Liberties, Kensington, and Spring Garden. These, with several adjacent villages, though for convenience of government and for local causes, separated from the city, in nature, connection, and interest, and for all practical purposes, may be identified with it, except perhaps in the crookedness of their streets, which form one distinctive feature from the city itself.

The manufactures of Philadelphia are varied and important, embracing nearly all the articles produced by American industry.

The railroads diverging from Philadelphia, are the Philadelphia, Wilmington, and Baltimore; the Philadelphia, Harrisburgh, and Pittsburgh; the Philadelphia, Reading, and Pottsville; the Philadelphia, Germantown, and Norristown; the Camden and Amboy; the Columbia and Philadelphia; the Philadelphia and Westchester; the Philadelphia and Trenton branch; the Philadelphia and Germantown branch; and the New York and Philadelphia steamer line.

RAILROADS.

From Philadelphia to Baltimore, via Havre de Grace.

To Gray's	3	
Lazaretto	?	11
Chester	4	15
Marcus Hook	3	18
Naaman's	2	20
Wilmington	8	28
Newport	4	32
Staunton	2	34
Newark	6	40
Elkton	6	46
Northeast	6	52
Broad Creek	3	55
Charleston	2	57
Perryville	4	61
Havre-de-Grace	1	62
Hall's ⋈ Roads	5	67
Perryman's	4	71
Magnolia	8	79
Chase's	4	83
Stemmer's Run	7	90
Baltimore	8	98

From Philadelphia to Havre-de-Grace (see above) 62

Fm Philadelphia to Balti. via New-Castle & Frenchtown Railroad.

By Steamboat on the Delaware river to Fort Mifflin	9	
Lazaretto	5	14
Chester	4	18
Marcus Hook	4	22
New-Castle	13	35
By Frenchtown R. R.		
Fm New-Castle to Frenchtown	17	52
By Steamboat.		
Mouth of Elk River	13	65
Pool's Island		
Chesapeake Bay	22	87
North Point	15	102
Fort M'Henry	10	112
Baltimore	4	116

From Philadelphia to New-Castle (see above) 35

From Philadelphia to Pittsburgh.

To Hestonville	4	
Athensville	5	9
Whitehall	2	11
Morgan's Corner	3	14
Eagle	3	17
Paoli	4	21
Steamboat	5	26
Oakland	4	30
Downingtown	3	33
Gallaghersville	2	35
Coatesville	6	41
Parkesburg	4	45
Penningtonville	3	48
Gap	4	52
Kinzer's	3	55
Lemon Place	3	58
Bird-in-Hand	5	63
Lancaster	7	70
Dillerville	1	71
Mount Joy	11	82
Elizabethtown	6	88
Middletown	9	97
High Spire	4	101
Harrisburgh	6	107
Rockville	6	113
Cove	5	118
Duncannon	4	122
Aqueduct	3	125
Baileysburg	5	130
Newport	4	134
Millerstown	6	140
Tuscarora	7	147
Mexico	4	151
Perryville	2	153
Mifflin	3	156

The canals, communicating directly, or through rivers, with Philadelphia, are the Schuylkill Navigation, which extends to Port Carbon; the Pennsylvania; the Morris, which enters the Delaware at Easton; and the Delaware and Raritan, between Bordentown and New Brunswick on the Raritan river, which is navigable for steamboats from New York.

The population in 1685 was 2,500; in 1790, 42,520; in 1800, 70,287; in 1810, 96,664; in 1820, 108,116; in 1830, 167,188; in 1840, 258,037; in 1850, 409,353.

HARRISBURGH, Pa.

THE capital of the state, is situated on the east bank of Susquehannah river, 97 miles northwest of Philadelphia, and 110 miles from Washington. It is a borough, built on rising ground, which subsides toward Paxton creek into a plain. From the elevation upon which the statehouse stands, appears a wide and varied prospect of hills, fertile vales, and winding streams. Across the Susquehannah and the island which here divides it, extends the Harrisburgh bridge, nearly a mile in length, and not far below, the bridge of the Cumberland Valley railroad. These channels of communication, the Pennsylvania lines of railroad and canal, besides opening a way to the remote parts of the state, convey to Harrisburgh the products of the neighboring fertile region, of which it is a profitable market. The Susquehannah, with its large volume of water, is not navigable, except for timber rafts, which can only descend with its swift current.

The capitol is an imposing structure, consisting of a main building and two wings, each adorned with a portico and Ionic pillars. The central edifice is 180 feet wide, 80 feet deep, and 108 feet from the ground to the top of the dome. The whole is surrounded by an open space, adorned with trees, walks, and an iron-railing. The other prominent buildings, are a Masonic-hall, two banks, a prison, and a number of churches.

By the Mount Airy water-works, water is elevated from the Susquehannah into a reservoir, on a hill above the borough, and thence is distributed through iron-pipes.

Manufactures, to a considerable extent, are produced in Harrisburgh, and the town is gradually increasing in population and wealth.

The population in 1810, was 2,287; in 1820, 2,990: in 1830, 4,311; in 1840, 6,020; in 1850, 8,173.

PITTSBURGH, Pa.

THIS flourishing city, the second in population and business in Pennsylvania, has justly been styled the "Birmingham of America." It is situated at the head of Ohio river, which is here formed by the confluence of the Alleghany and Monongahela rivers. It is 297 miles westerly from Philadelphia, and 226 miles from Washington.

The city is built on a broad level point of land, between the two rivers, and is enclosed by hills, which are filled with bituminous coal. This constitutes the fuel for the vast number of factories, the tall chimneys of which bristle the town, belching black clouds of smoke, that darken the air and stain the houses a dusky hue. In point of beauty, therefore, Pittsburgh has little that is attractive; yet there is something interesting in the concentration of industry and enterprise which this dark city exhibits. Here, before the settlement of the town, in 1760, stood Fort du Quesne, for a long time one of the most important posts in the hands of the French, who abandoned it in 1758, when it was named by the British Fort Pitt. The dwellings are mostly

RAILROADS.

Lewistown	12	168
Anderson's	7	175
M'Veytown	5	180
N. Hamilton	10	190
Mount Union	3	193
Mapleton	3	196
Mill Creek	3	199
Huntingdon	5	204
Petersburg	7	211
Spruce Creek	6	217
Tyrone	7	224
Fostoria	6	230
Altona	8	238
Hollidaysburg	6	244
Plane No. 9	4	248
Plane No. 8	2	250
Summit of the Mountains	4	254
Plane No. 4	3	257
Plane No. 2	3	260
Jefferson	4	264
Half-Way-House	4	268
Viaduct	3	271
Tunnel	3	274
Connaugh	2	276
Johnstown	2	278
Nineveh	10	288
New Florence	5	293
Lockport	5	298
Bolivar	2	300
Blairsville Junction	5	305
Hill Side	4	309
Derry	5	314
Latrobe	6	320
Turnpike	2	322
Tuttle Creek	26	348
Wilkinsburg	5	353
Liberty	5	358
Pittsburgh	5	363

From Philadelphia to Lancaster (see above) 70

From Philadelphia to Harrisburgh (see route from Phila. to Pittsburgh) 107

From Philadelphia to Hollidaysburg (see Phila. & Pittsburgh route) 244

Fm Philadelphia to Pottsville.

To Schuylkill Viaduct	3	
Manyunk	7	10
Conshohocken	3	13
Norristown	4	17
Port Kennedy	4	21
Valley Forge	2	23
Phœnixville	4	27
Rogers' Ford	5	32
Limerick	2	34
Pottstown	6	40
Douglassville	4	44
Birdsboro'	5	49
Reading	9	58
Atthouse	8	66
Mohrsville	2	68
Hamburg	7	75
Port Clinton	3	78
Auburn	5	83
Orwigsburg	3	86
Schuylkill Haven	3	89
Mount Carbon	3	92
Pottsville	1	93

From Philadelphia to Norristown (see above) 17

From Philadelphia to Reading (see above) 58

Fm Pottsville to Turnout.

To Sch'lkill Haven	4	
Minersville	8	12
Turnout	4	16

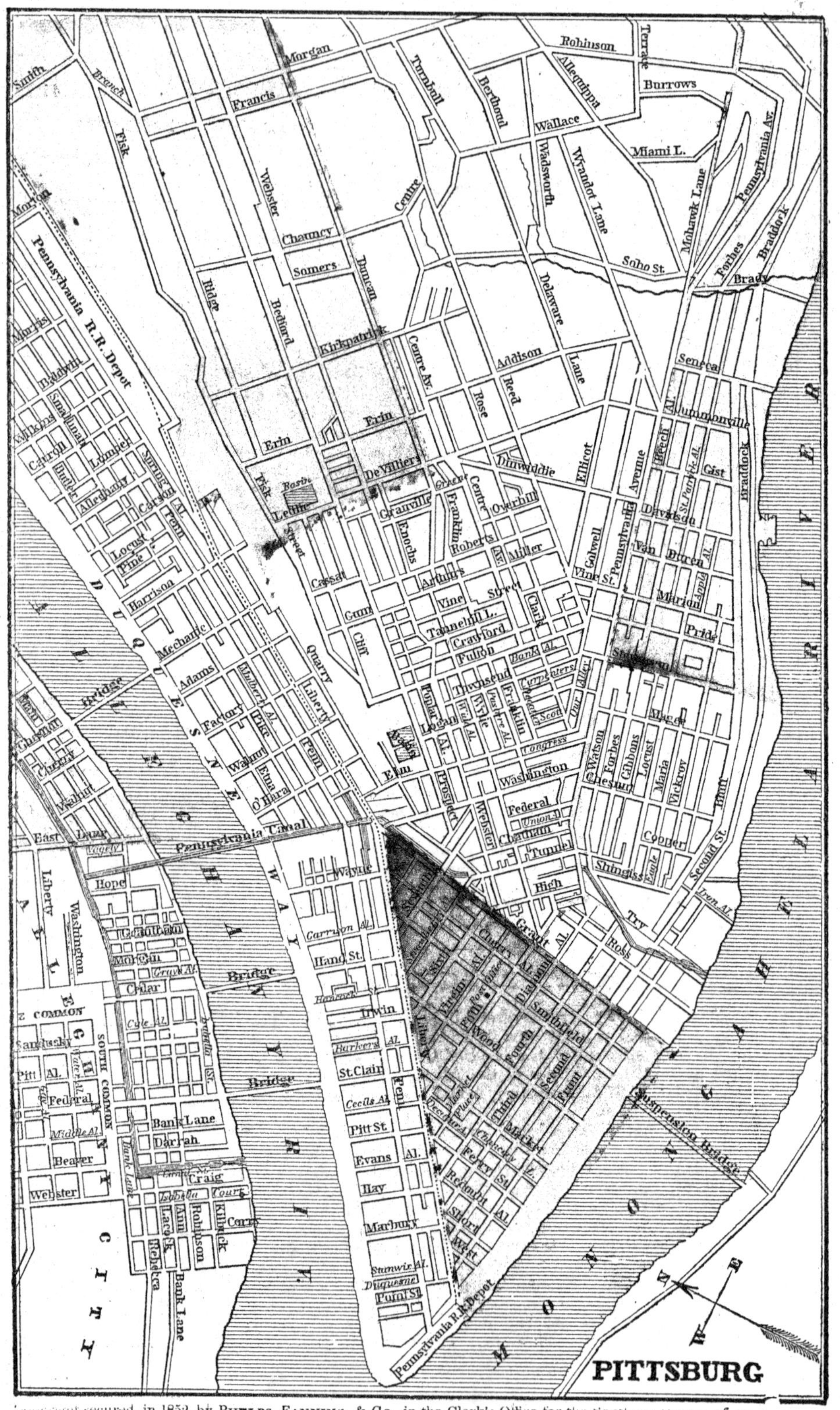
PITTSBURG
Robinson
Terrace
Burrows
Allequippa
Morgan
Francis
Turnbull
Berthoud
Wallace
Miami L.
Pennsylvania Av.
Mohawk Lane
Braddock
Forbes
Brady
Smith
Branch
Fisk
Webster
Centre
Wadsworth
Wyandot Lane
Soho St.
Chauncy
Somers
Ridge
Bedford
Duncan
Kirkpatrick
Delaware
Lane
Addison
Centre Av.
Rose
Reed
Erin
Seneca
Summonville
Ellicot
Avenue
Beech Al.
Gist
Dinwiddie
DeVilliers
Basin
Granville
Franklin
Overhill
Davison
Van Buren
Pennsylvania R.R. Depot
Morris
Carroll
Lumper
Allegheny
Carson
Locust
Pine
Harrison
Mechanic
Adams
Factory
Walnut
Pike
Etna
O'Hara
Penn
Liberty
Quarry
Cassat
Gum
Cliff
Enochs
Roberts
Miller
Vine St.
Vine Street
Arthurs
Tannehill L.
Crawford
Fulton
Bank Al.
Townsend
Logan
Poplar
Marion
Pride
Colwell
Pennsylvania
Watson
Forbes
Gibbons
Locust
Maria
Vickroy
Magee
Chesnut
Congress
Washington
Federal
Union
Chatham
Tunnel
High
Elm
Prospect
Webster
Cooper
Shingiss
Second St.
Bluff
Iron Al.
Try
Ross
Grant Al.
Cherry Al.
Diamond
Smithfield
Wood
Fourth
Second
Front
Third
Market
Ferry St.
Chancery
Redoubt Al.
Short
West
Liberty
Pennsylvania Canal
Pennsylvania R.R. Depot
Wayne
Garrison Al.
Hand St.
Irwin
Hancock St.
Barkers Al.
St. Clair
Cecils Al.
Pitt St.
Evans Al.
Hay
Marbury
Duquesne
Point St.
DUQUESNE WAY
ALLEGHENY RIVER
MONONGAHELA RIVER
Monongahela Bridge
Bridge
East Lane
Hope
Washington
Liberty
Morgan
Cedar
COMMON
SOUTH COMMON
Sandusky
Pitt Al.
Federal
Middle Al.
Bank Lane
Darrah
Beaver
Webster
Craig
Isabella Court
Killbuck
Robinson
Anna
Lacock
Rebecca
Bank Lane
ALLEGHENY CITY
N
E
S
W

of brick, many of them elegant and substantial, though dingy with smoke. The flourishing towns and villages which surround this city, afford pleasant sites for residence. Of these places, which are virtual suburbs of Pittsburgh, Alleghany city, on the opposite bank of the Alleghany, is the most important. The river is here spanned by a fine bridge, 1,122 feet long, resting upon five stone piers; two bridges cross it at other points, and the Pennsylvania canal has a splendid aqueduct, 1,200 feet long, over the same stream. On the Monongahela are Birmingham and other settlements, which are connected by a bridge 1,500 feet long, and several ferries.

From its position, Pittsburgh is a great commercial as well as manufacturing emporium. It holds to Pennsylvania the same relation as Buffalo does to New York, being the gate of commerce between the east and the west. Hither come a large number of steamboats, during the season of navigation, from New Orleans and the valley of the Mississippi and Ohio rivers. The Pennsylvania canal, after traversing the whole state, and crossing the Alleghany on its great aqueduct, passes by a tunnel under a hill near the city, and enters the Monongahela. Pittsburgh is connected with Lake Erie by the Ohio and Pennsylvania and the Cleveland and Pittsburgh railroads, and with Philadelphia by the Grand Trunk railroad.

The city contains an elegant courthouse, 165 feet long, 100 feet wide, and 148 feet from the ground to the top of the dome, which affords a delightful view of the populous neighborhood and rich and picturesque surrounding region; also a prison, the Western University of Pennsylvania, finely seated on an adjacent elevation, and numerous churches, banks, hotels, and other prominent buildings. The Alleghany river affords a plentiful supply of water, which is distributed over the city by expensive and convenient water-works; and the bituminous coal of the adjoining hills yields gas for illuminating the town.

The manufactures embrace almost every article of domestic necessity and convenience. Machinery, cutlery, glass, cotton, cloth, pottery, paints, and drugs, are a few of the vast and innumerable variety produced.

The population in 1800, was 1,565; in 1810, 4,768; in 1820, 7,248; in 1830, 12,542; in 1840, 21,115; in 1850, 50,519.

READING, Pa.

Is a flourishing and pleasant town on the east side of Schuylkill river, 57 miles northwest of Philadelphia, and 52 miles east of Harrisburgh, and has a delightful situation amid picturesque vales, hills, and streams. In the regularity of its streets, the neatness of its houses, and the industry and good order of its inhabitants, it still retains the character stamped upon it by its founders, Thomas and Richard Penn, the sons of William Penn.

Reading is a town of considerable trade and manufactures, for which it has great natural and improved advantages. Tulpehocken creek and the Schuylkill furnish excellent water-power, by which numerous manufactories are kept in successful operation. Hats are the fabrics most extensively made.

Reading contains an imposing courthouse, several elegant churches, and market-houses, banks, an academy, and other public buildings. A neighboring spring supplies the town with an abundant supply of pure water, which is distributed by means of a reservoir and iron-pipes. Here the Schuylkill Navigation canal meets the Union canal, which terminates at Middletown, on the Susquehannah, and the Philadelphia and Reading railroad communicates with this town.

The population in 1810, was 3,463; in 1820, 4,332; in 1830, 5 850; in 1840, 8,410; in 1850, 15,821.

RAILROADS.

From Philadelphia to Westchester.

To County Line....	5	
Whitehall..........	5	10
Morgan's Corner...	3	13
Eagle Hotel.......	3	16
Paoli	3	19
Junction...........	2	21
Westchester	9	30

From Harrisburgh to Baltimore.

To Bridgeport		
Goldsboro'		
York		25
Fork's Codd's......	4	29
Tunnell............	3	32
Gladfetter's........	3	35
Smyser's	1	36
Heathcote's........	5	41
Seitzland	1	42
Strasburgh.........	1	43
Summit............	1	44
Freeland's.........	3	47
Bee-Tree	3	50
Parkton............	4	54
Whitehall..........	2	56
Monkton...........	4	60
Love's.............	2	62
Phœnix............	2	64
Ashland	2	66
Texas	3	69
Timonium	2	71
Rider's Line.......	1	72
Relay-House	3	75
Washington Fac...	1	76
Melvale	2	78
Woodbury..........	1	79
Baltimore	3	82

From Erie to Cleveland.

Ohio State Line....		25
Ashtabula..........	15	40
Madison	15	55
Painesville	11	66
Willoughby	10	76
Cleveland	19	95

From Blosburg to Corning.

To Covington......	5	
Mansfield..........	5	10
Tioga..............	10	20
Lawrenceville	5	25
Cook's Turnout....	7	32
Corning	8	40

From Great Bend to Scranton, on the Erie R. R.

To New Milford...	6	
Montrose	7	13
Tunkhannock	14	27
Factoryville	8	35
Abington	5	40
Clark's Summit....	3	43
Scranton...........	7	50

From Erie to Dunkirk and Buffalo.

To Harbor Creek..	.9	
N. Y. State Line....	10	19
Quincy	5	24
Westfield	8	32
Centreville	6	33
Dunkirk	10	43
Silver Creek.......	10	58
Lagrange..........	2	60
Evans' Centre.....	7	67
18-Mile Creek......	7	74
Rodgers' Road....	5	79
Buffalo	10	89

From Easton to New York (see N. York to Easton).......... 69

LANCASTER, Pa.

This pleasant, healthy, and increasing city, is situated 36 miles southeast of Harrisburgh, and 62 miles west of Philadelphia. In 1812, the state government was transferred from this place to Harrisburgh. In the midst of the beautiful and fertile valley of Conestoga creek, it constitutes the centre of an extensive trade with the surrounding region, and a thoroughfare between Philadelphia and the west. This is one of those towns which are interesting for both age and prosperity. Some of its buildings are antiquated; others are modern; but generally all are neat and pleasant. By a series of dams and locks, forming the Conestoga canal, the navigation of the creek has been improved to the Susquehannah, a distance of 18 miles.

The manufacturing establishments are various and flourishing.

The Columbia and Philadelphia railroad, communicates with Lancaster, and leads toward Harrisburgh; and here, the Westchester branch diverges toward York.

The population in 1810, was 5,405; in 1820, 6,633; in 1830, 7,704; in 1840, 8,417; in 1850, 12,369.

DOVER, Del.

The capital of the state, and seat of justice of Kent county, is a borough, on Jones' Creek, 10 miles from its entrance into Delaware bay, 50 miles south of Wilmington, and 120 miles from Washington. It is built on four principal streets, which, intersecting, form a square in the centre of the town. Here is an elegant statehouse, and several churches, banks, and other public buildings, are in the vicinity. The buildings are neat, and generally of brick. It contains a monument erected to the memory of Col. John Haslett, who fell at the battle of Princeton, in 1777.

The population, in 1810, was about 900; in 1820, 600; in 1830, 1,300; in 1840, 3,790; in 1850, ——.

WILMINGTON, Del.

The principal city and port of entry in the state, is situated between Christiana creek and Brandywine river, two miles from the entrance of the latter into the Delaware, 28 miles southwest of Philadelphia, and 70 miles northeast of Baltimore. The ground on which it is built rises from the river to an elevation of 112 feet, and offers a pleasant prospect of the neighboring scenery. The streets are broad and rectangular, and the houses, generally of brick, are many of them costly and beautiful. Wilmington has the usual number of public buildings, but the most interesting are the flour-mills, to which it owes its celebrity. These are situated near the falls of the Brandywine, not far from the town, and afford an extensive water-power. To this point, vessels ascend drawing eight feet of water, those of 14 feet draught navigating both streams to the city. The Christiana admits vessels of eight feet draught, 8 miles further up. A large number of ships anchor at Wilmington, receiving and exporting the produce of the mills and manufactories in its vicinity; others are employed in the whale-fishery. Each of the streams are crossed by bridges, and the Philadelphia, Wilmington, and Baltimore railroad communicates with this city.

Five miles from Wilmington are the Brandywine Chalybeate springs, the salubrious waters of which contribute much to the health and recreation of the visiters.

The population in 1810, was 4,416; in 1820, 5,268; in 1830, 6,628; in 1840, 8,367; in 1850, 13,979.

RAILROADS.

Fm Easton to Somerville (see N. Jersey Route from Jersey City to Easton)..... 40

From Summit Hill to Mauch Chunk...... 9

Fm Harrisburgh to Chambersburg.

To Bridgeport.....		
Mechanicsburg		
Carlisle............		
Newville		
Shippinsburg		
Chambersburg		

From Chambersburg to Hagerstown.

To Greencastle....	11	
Hagerstown	11	22

From Philadelphia to Germantown........ 6

RAILROADS.

Fm New Castle to Frenchtown.

To Red Lion......	6	
Glasgow	5	11
Frenchtown	5	16
To Baltimore (by steamboat).......	64	80

From Wilmington to Philadelphia.

To Naaman's Creek	8	
Marcus Hook......	2	10
Chester............	3	13
Lazaretto	5	18
Gray's Ferry.......	7	25
Philadelphia	4	29

From Wilmington to Baltimore.

To Newport.......	4	
Staunton...........	2	6
Newark	6	12
Elkton.............	6	18
Northeast..........	6	24
Broad Creek......	3	27
Perryville	6	33
Havre-de-Grace ...	1	34
Hall's ✕ Roads....	6	40
Perryman's........	4	44
Magnolia	8	52
Chace's............	4	56
Stemmer's Run....	6	62
Baltimore	9	71

STAGE-ROUTES.

Fm Wilmington to Dover and Georgetown.

To New-Castle....	5	
St. George's.......	12	17
Smyrna............	18	35
Dover	12	47
Camden	3	50
Canterbury	6	56
Frederica..........	5	61
Milford	7	68
Milton.............	11	79
Georgetown	8	87

Fm Georgetown to Princess Ann, Md.

To Concord	11	
Laurell	6	17
Salisbury	17	34
Forktown	5	39
Princess Ann......	11	50

ANNAPOLIS, Md.

The capital of the state, is situated on the southwest bank of Severn river, three miles from its entrance into Chesapeake bay, 20 miles southeast of Baltimore, and 40 miles from Washington. Though located favorably enough for commerce, on a good harbor, the tide of trade and prosperity is drawn too strongly toward Baltimore to allow it to flourish as vigorously as it otherwise might. The site and plan of the city are pleasant and agreeable. The statehouse is venerable and interesting from its Revolutionary associations. Here, in 1783, Washington resigned his commission to the continental congress, one month after the departure of the enemy from the American shores. The walls of the senate-chamber are honored with the portraits of Carroll, Chase, Paca, and Stone, signers of the Declaration of Independence, and of other distinguished contemporaries. In the hall of the house of delegates, is a picture of the surrender of Cornwallis at Yorktown. Aside from these attractions, the capitol is beautiful for its situation and architecture, as well as for the magnificent prospect viewed from its dome. Besides several churches, banks, &c., Annapolis contains St. John's college.

The population in 1810, was about 2,000; in 1820, 2,260; in 1830, 2,623; in 1840, 2,792; in 1850, 4,198.

BALTIMORE, Md.

The principal city of the state, and the third city of the United States in population, is situated on the north side of Patapsco river, 14 miles from its entrance into Chesapeake bay, 100 miles southwest of Philadelphia, and 40 miles from Washington. It is built on uneven ground, bending around the innermost of three harbors, which successively diminish in space and depth. The outer one is 22 feet deep, one mile and a quarter long, from its entrance into the second, which is 15 feet deep, half a mile wide, and one mile long. Vessels of about 600 tons enter this harbor, while the third, which enters the city, is deep enough for vessels of 200 tons. The outer entrance is defended by fortifications, which repulsed a British fleet of sixteen ships in 1814.

The appearance of the city, when viewed from the water, is imposing. The most conspicuous and fashionable part is built on a bold, but not steep elevation; and the steeples, monuments, and domes, with which it is crowned, greatly relieve and beautify the scene. Within the town, the streets and buildings exhibit various degrees of beauty and regularity, when viewed from different points. In the construction of the houses, convenience and solidity appear to have been studied, rather than magnificence; but the abodes of wealthy citizens exhibit the same elegance here as in other great cities of the Union. Many of the public structures are also splendid and costly. Baltimore has been named the "Monumental city," chiefly from the two great monuments it contains. Washington monument is a Doric column, of white marble, 180 feet high, resting on a base of the same material, 20 feet high, and surmounted by a statue of the man it commemorates. Ascending by a winding staircase, within the column, the visiter beholds a wide prospect of the city, and its varied environs. Battle monument, also of white marble, is 52 feet high, and was erected in memory of the patriots who fell in defence of this city against the British, in 1814. Many of the churches are remarkable for architectural beauty. The courthouse, state penitentiary, customhouse, St. Mary's college, and the halls of numerous literary and scientific institutions, are among the other important public buildings. The exchange is 225 feet wide, 141 feet deep, and 115 feet to the top of the

RAILROADS

From Baltimore to Washington, D. C.

To Mount Clare....	2	
Relay House......	7	9
Eldridge Landing..	1	10
Jessup's Cut E. E.	5	15
Patuxent Switch...	2	17
Annapolis Junction	1	18
Savage R. R.......	1	19
Laurell Factory....	3	22
Bettsville..........	5	27
Paint Branch......	4	31
Bladensburg.......	2	33
Washington	7	40

From Baltimore to Philadelphia, via Havre-de-Grace.

To Stemmer's Run.	9	
Chace's...........	6	15
Magnolia	3	18
Perryman's........	9	27
Hall's ✕ Roads....	3	30
Havre-de-Grace ...	5	35
Perryville	2	37
Broad Creek......	6	43
Northeast..........	3	46
Elkton.............	5	51
Newark	6	57
Staunton....... ...	7	64
Newport	2	66
Wilmington	4	70
Philadelphia, (see Wilmington and Philadel. Route in Delaware).......	29	99

From Baltimore to Philadelphia, via New-Castle and Frenchtown R. R.

By Steamboat.		
To Fort McHenry.	4	
North Point........	10	14
Chesapeake Bay...	15	29
Pool's Island......	—	—
Mouth of Elk River	22	51
Frenchtown	13	64
By Railroad.		
To New-Castle....	17	81
By Steamboat on the Delaware River.		
To Marcus Hook..	13	94
Chester	4	98
Lazaretto..........	4	102
Fort Mifflin........	5	107
Philadelphia.......	9	116

From Baltimore to Cumberland & Wheeling, Va.

To Mount Clare....	2	
Relay-House.......	7	9
Avalon	1	10
Ilchester...........	3	13
Ellicott's Mills....	2	15
Elysville	6	21
Woodstock	4	25
Marryotsville	4	29
Sykesville	3	32
Hood's Mill........	3	35
Woodbine	3	38
Mount Airy........	6	44
Monrovia	6	50
Ijamsville	4	54
Mocanopy	5	59
Buckeyestone	4	63
Davis'	2	65
Point of Rocks....	5	70
Catoctin Switch...	2	72
Berlin	4	76
Knoxville	3	79
Weverton	1	80
Harper's Ferry....	2	82
Duffield's	6	88
Kearneyville	10	98
Martinsburg	3	101
Tabb's	3	104
North Mountain....	4	108
Sleepy Creek......	9	117
Hancock...........	7	124
St. John's River...	6	130

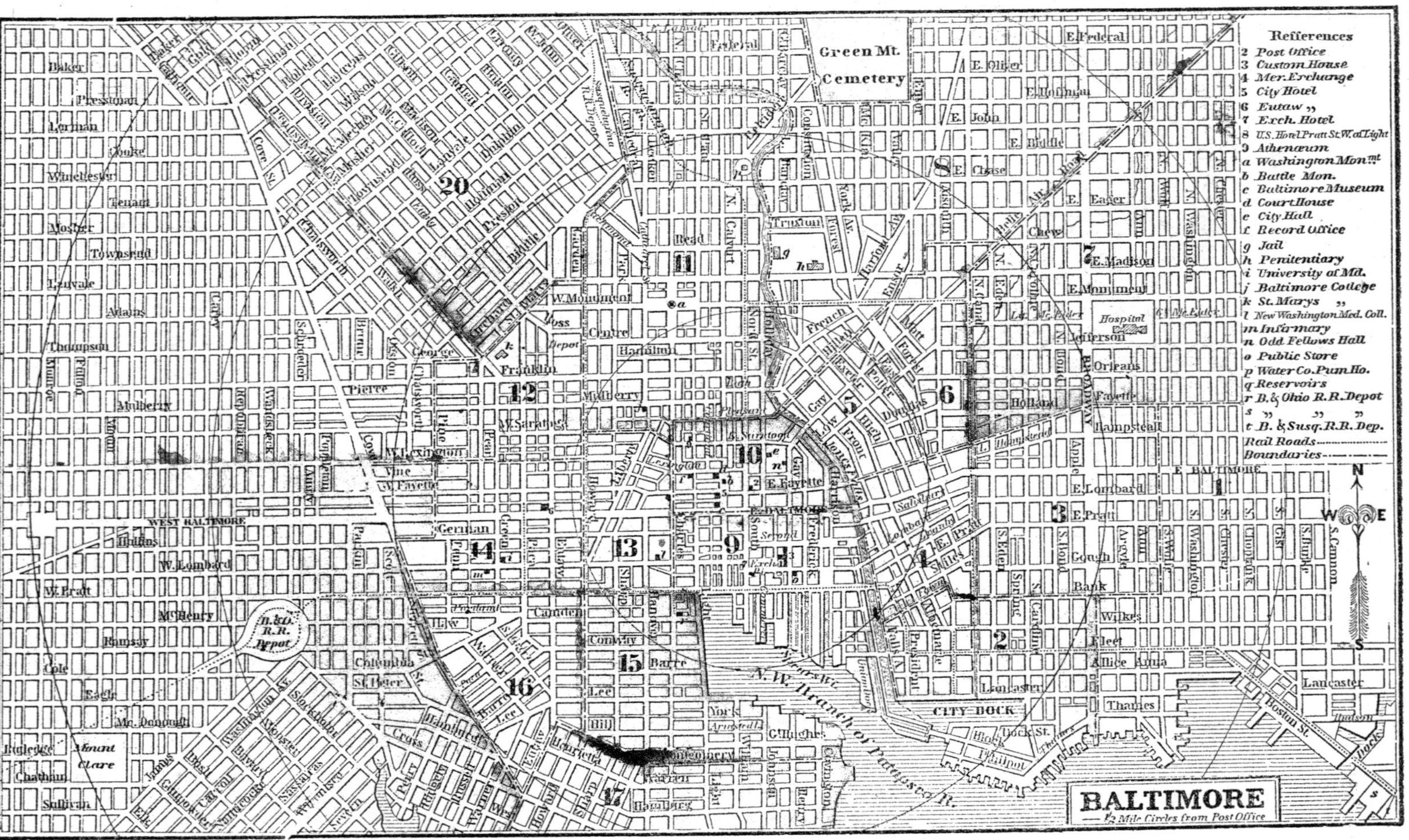
BALTIMORE
½ Mile Circles from Post Office
Refferences
2 Post Office
3 Custom House
4 Mer. Exchange
5 City Hotel
6 Eutaw ,,
7 Exch. Hotel
8 U.S. Hotel Pratt St. W. of Light
9 Athenæum
a Washington Mon.mt
b Battle Mon.
c Baltimore Museum
d Court House
e City Hall
f Record Office
g Jail
h Penitentiary
i University of Md.
j Baltimore College
k St. Marys ,,
l New Washington Med. Coll.
m Infirmary
n Odd Fellows Hall
o Public Store
p Water Co. Pum Ho.
q Reservoirs
r B. & Ohio R.R. Depot
s ,, ,, ,,
t B. & Susq. R.R. Dep.
Rail Roads
Boundaries
N
S
E
W
Green Mt. Cemetery
CITY DOCK
N.W. Branch of Patapsco R.
WEST BALTIMORE
E. BALTIMORE
BROADWAY
Mount Clare
B. & O. R.R. Depot
Susquehanna R.R. Depot

dome. Colonnades of the Ionic order, made of Italian marble, extend across its east and west fronts.

Water is supplied in abundance from fountains in the city, and from Jones's fall, in the vicinity, by an aqueduct and pipes.

In manufactures, as in commerce, Baltimore ranks with the great cities of America. Jones's fall (a small creek dividing the city, and spanned by several beautiful bridges) and the Patapsco, afford numerous excellent seats for mills and manufactories of various kinds.

The population in 1775, was 5,936; in 1790, 13,503; in 1800, 26,614; in 1810, 46,555; in 1820, 62,738; in 1830, 80 625; in 1840, 134,379; in 1850 169 012.

WASHINGTON, D. C.

The capital of the United States, is pleasantly situated on the east bank of the Potomac river, in latitude 38° 53′ 34″ north, and longitude 77° 1′ 30″ west from Greenwich. It is 295 miles from the ocean, following the course of the river, 225 miles southwest of New York, and 1,203 miles northeast of New Orleans. The city is built on a point of land formed by the confluence of the Potomac and the Anacosta rivers, which afford a good harbor for vessels of the largest class. Commerce, however, flows naturally toward Baltimore, leaving to Washington, perhaps, a less rapid growth, but more quiet. A more beautiful site for a city could hardly be obtained. It was selected by Washington as the fittest locality for the seat of the national government, and the city was laid out under his direction. It is said his attention was called to the advantages of this location as long previous as when he had been a youthful surveyor of the country around. Pleasant slopes, decked with elegant mansions, surrounded by hills and varied scenery, and the general aspect and airiness of the town, conduce to render Washington an agreeable place of residence. The city is planned on a grand scale; and if ever built up as originally designed, would be one of the finest cities in the world. By this plan, seven spacious avenues were laid out, to diverge from the Capitol as a centre, and five avenues form rays from the President's House, the latter building and the Capitol being each situated on beautiful eminences, about one mile and a half apart, and connected by Pennsylvania avenue, now the principal street in the city. The avenues are named after different states, and are crossed diagonally by streets running east and west, named after the letters of the alphabet, and others running north and south, which are named after numbers. The avenues and streets leading to public places, are from 120 to 160 feet wide, and the other streets are from 70 to 110 feet wide. Only a comparatively small part of its extensive site is yet covered by buildings, which, in connection with its spacious avenues, has given it the designation of the "city of magnificent distances." A bridge a mile long spans the Potomac, another the Anacosta (sometimes termed the eastern branch of the Potomac), and two others over Rock creek, connect Washington with Georgetown. On the Anacosta is a navy-yard, occupying an area of 27 acres.

The Capitol is justly regarded as one of the finest national buildings in the world. It stands on a gentle eminence, in the midst of a beautiful space of 23 acres, highly ornamented with trees, shrubbery, &c. The dome, which is 120 feet high from the ground, is the first object which strikes the eye from a distance. The edifice is of white freestone, and, as originally built, consisted of a central part and two wings. The width of the whole

RAILROADS.

Great Cacapon....	3	133
D. G. Tunnel	9	142
No. 12 W. Station..	9	151
Pawpaw	3	154
Little Cacapon....	4	158
South Branch......	5	163
Gr. Sp. Run........	2	165
Patterson's	6	171
Cumberland	8	179
Brady's Mill.......	7	186
Rawlin's Station...	6	192
New Creek........	10	202
Piedmont..........	5	207
Frankville	8	215
Allamont	9	224
Oakland	9	.33
Cr. Summit.........	10	243
Rowlesburg	11	254
Tunnelton	7	261
Simpson's	6	267
Thornton	7	274
Fetterman	8	282
By Stage to Wheeling	32	314

From Baltimore to Winchester, via Harper's Ferry.

To Harper's Ferry (see Baltimore & Cumberl'd Route)	82	
Halltown	7	89
Charlestown.......	3	92
Cameron's Depot..	4	96
Wade's Depot.....	5	101
Stephenson's Depot	4	105
Winchester........	5	110

From Baltimore to York and Harrisburgh, Pa.

To Woodbury.....	3	
Melvale............	1	4
Relay-House	3	7
Rider's Lane......	3	10
Timonium	1	11
Texas	2	13
Cockeysville.......	1	14
Ashland	2	16
Westerman's	2	18
Love's.............	2	20
Monkton.	2	22
Whitehall	4	26
Parkton	2	28
Bee Tree..........	4	32
Freeland's.........	3	35
Summit............	3	38
Strasburg..........	1	39
Seitzland	1	40
Heathcote's........	1	41
Smyser's	5	46
Gladfelter's........	1	47
Tunnel	3	50
Forks Codo's......	3	53
York	4	57
Goldsboro'	—	—
Bridgeport	—	—
Harrisburgh.......	—	82

From Baltimore to Pittsburgh.

To Cumberland (see Route from Baltimore to Cumberland)		179
By Stage.		
To Frostburg......	12	191
Little Crossings...	12	203
Addison, Pa.......	13	216
Somerfield	6	222
Uniontown	20	242
Brownsville	12	254
By Steamboat on the Monongahela R.		
To Pittsburgh.....	56	310

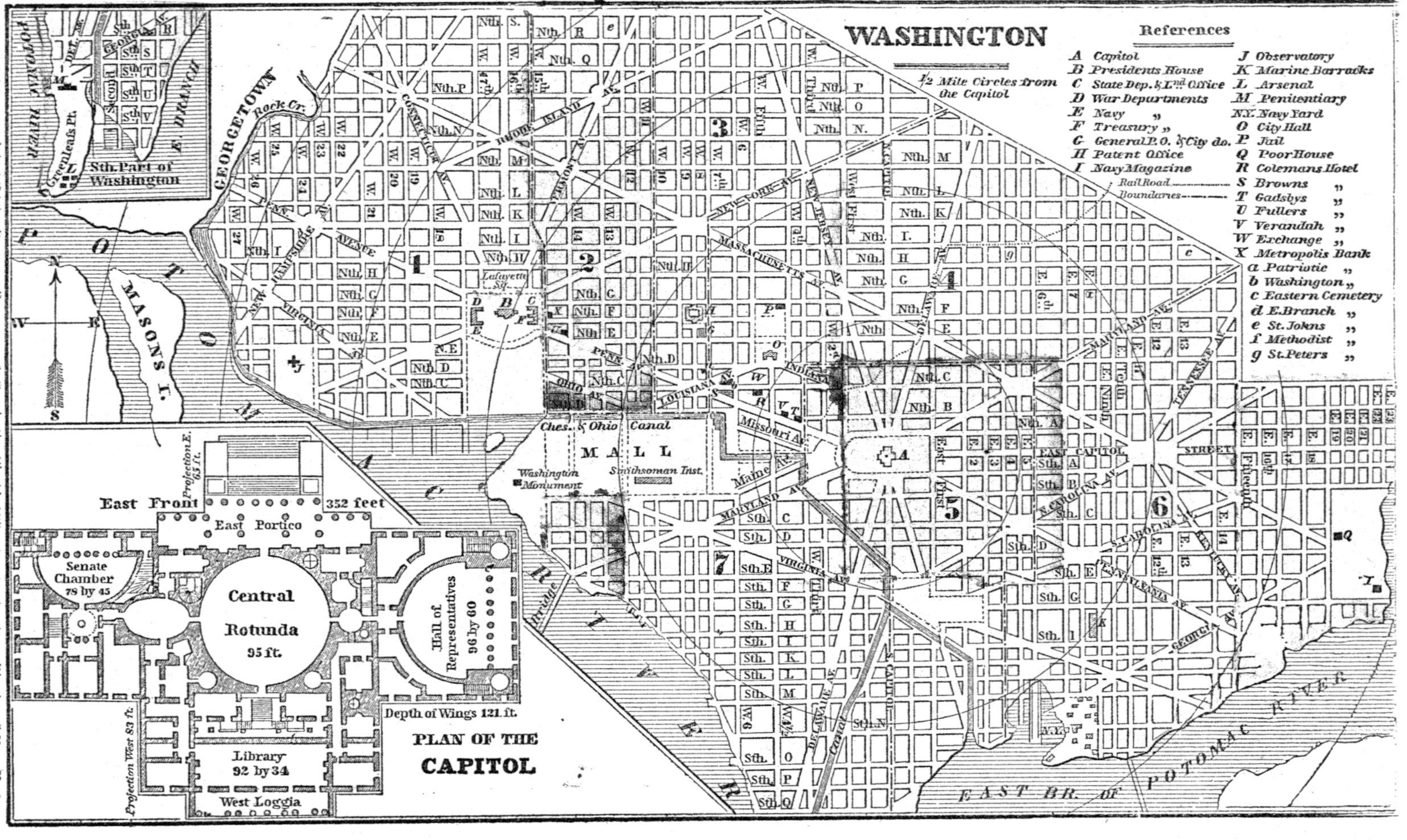
WASHINGTON
½ Mile Circles from the Capitol
References
A Capitol
B Presidents House
C State Dep. & Lnd Office
D War Departments
E Navy "
F Treasury "
G General P.O. & City do.
H Patent Office
I Navy Magazine
J Observatory
K Marine Barracks
L Arsenal
M Penitentiary
N.Y. Navy Yard
O City Hall
P Jail
Q Poor House
R Colemans Hotel
S Browns "
T Gadsbys "
U Fullers "
V Verandah "
W Exchange "
X Metropolis Bank
a Patriotic "
b Washington "
c Eastern Cemetery
d E. Branch "
e St. Johns "
f Methodist "
g St. Peters "
Rail Road
Boundaries
GEORGETOWN
Rock Cr.
MASONS I.
POTOMAC RIVER
EAST BR. OF POTOMAC RIVER
MALL
Ches. & Ohio Canal
Smithsonian Inst.
Washington Monument
Lafayette Sq.
Sth. Part of Washington
Greenleafs Pt.
E. BRANCH
PLAN OF THE CAPITOL
East Front
352 feet
Projection E. 65 ft.
East Portico
Senate Chamber 78 by 45
Central Rotunda 95 ft.
Hall of Representatives 96 by 60
Depth of Wings 121 ft.
Library 92 by 34
West Loggia
Projection West 83 ft.

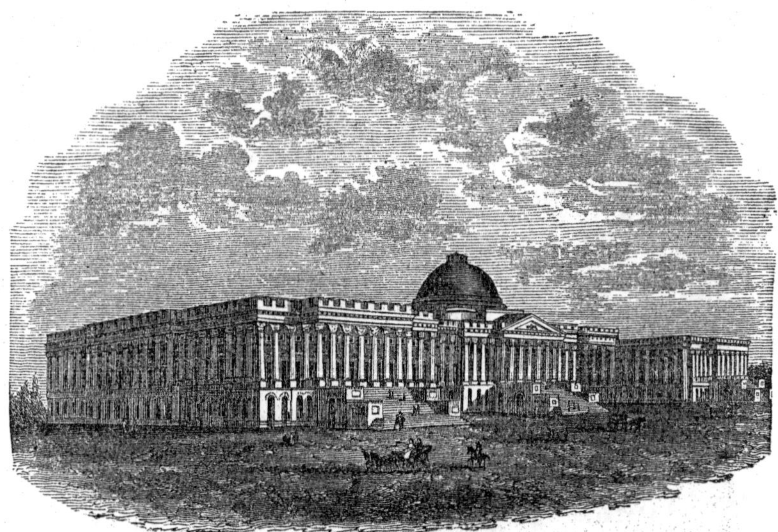

CAPITOL OF THE UNITED STATES.

building was 352 feet, and depth of the wings 121, all occupying an area of one and a half acres. But, in the addition of new states to the Union, with the consequent numerical increase of congressional representation, the Capitol, on its original plan, has become too limited, and an enlargement was commenced in 1851, and is being rapidly pressed to completion. The above engraving is designed to represent this edifice as it will appear when the additions shall have been completed. These additions will consist of two wings at the ends of the building, with which they will be connected by corridors, or piazzas, 44 feet long, and 50 feet wide. The wings will each be 143 feet by 238, exclusive of porticoes and steps; and the entire length of the building, when completed, will be 751 feet, and the area it covers 153,112 square feet, or over 3½ acres. Beneath the dome is the rotunda, a spacious apartment, 75 feet high, and 95 feet in diameter. On its walls the magnificent national paintings of Trumbull, Chapman, Wier, and Vanderlyn, are hung. The room is also adorned with basso-relievo groups, representing prominent events in American history. The senate-chamber is in the north wing, and the hall of the house of representatives in that on the south. Under the senate-chamber is the room where the supreme court sits. These apartments are all richly furnished, and ornamented with statuary and paintings.

The President's House is a noble and spacious edifice, also of white freestone. It is 170 feet long, and 86 feet wide, with Ionic pilasters, comprehending two lofty stories, with a stone balustrade. The north front is ornamented with a portico, sustained by four Ionic columns, with three projecting columns, affording a shelter for carriages to drive under. The garden, or southern front, is embellished by a circular colonnade of six Ionic columns. The interior of the President's House possesses one superb reception-room, commonly known as the "East-room," and two oval drawing-rooms, one in each story, of very beautiful proportions. The house stands in an enclosed area of some twenty acres, and commands, from its balcony, one of the loveliest prospects in the country.

Near the President's House are the buildings occupied by the

RAILROADS.

From Baltimore to Annapolis.

To Mount Clare....	2	
Relay-House	7	9
Elkridge Landing..	1	10
Annapolis Junction	8	18
Millersville........	10	28
Annapolis	10	38

DIS. COLUMBIA.

RAILROADS.

From Washington to Richmond, Va.

By Steamboat on the Potomac River.		
To Alexandria.....	8	
Fort Washington..	6	14
Mount Vernon.....	2	16
Glymont...........	6	22
Sandy Point.......	18	40
Aqua Creek L	12	52
By Railroad.		
To Brooks'........	6	58
Fredericsburg	12	70
Guinney's	12	82
Milford	10	92
Chesterfield........	7	99
Junction...........	2	101
Taylorsville	3	104
Hungary	12	116
Richmond	8	124

From Washington to Fredericksburg (see above) 70

From Washington to Wilmington, N. C.

To Richmond (see above)...........		124
Wilmington (see Richmond & Wilmington Route).	248	372

UNITED STATES SENATE CHAMBER.

UNITED STATES REPRESENTATIVE CHAMBER.

state, treasury, war, and navy departments. The United States Treasury is 300 feet long, with a wing in the rear of 100 feet. Along the front is a colonnade, composed of 23 columns, of massive proportions. The General Postoffice is a splendid marble building, with two wings, and adorned with large fluted marble columns. The Patent-Office is a spacious and noble looking building. The models of such inventions as receive a patent-right, are here placed on exhibition, and form an interesting development of the genius of our country.

The erection of the Washington monument is steadily progressing, and has already reached a considerable altitude. The most prominent and imposing object of this colossal structure, will be the obelisk shaft rising through the centre to the height of 600 feet, 70 feet square at the base, and 40 at the top. The several states of the Union, and many associations, have each prepared a stone, bearing an appropriate inscription, to be placed in the monument.

The Smithsonian Institute, founded by the munificent bequest of an English gentleman, after whom it is named, to the American government for the advancement of knowledge among men, is one of the purest specimens of architecture in the world.

The manufactures of Washington are by no means contemptible; and its trade the surrounding country, is facilitated by the Chesapeake and Ohio canal, which extends to Cumberland, Maryland, on the Potomac river.

The Washington Branch railroad connects the city with Baltimore; and the Washington and Wilmington line, through Virginia and North Carolina, diverges from this point.

The population in 1800 was 3,210; in 1810, 8,208; in 1820, 13,247; in 1830, 18,827; in 1840, 23,364; in 1850, 40,001.

RICHMOND, Va.

The capital of the state, is situated on the north side of James river, 150 miles from its entrance into Chesapeake bay, and 120 miles south of Washington. In trade, manufactures, and population, it is the principal city of the state. Directly above it, the river has a descent of about 80 feet in six miles, forming a natural barrier to navigation, which has been overcome by a canal around the falls, and extending 176 miles farther up the river. Through these channels, Richmond has become the entrepot of a fertile region, and receives large quantities of flour, tobacco, and coal. Vessels of 10 feet draught pass the bar, six miles below the city, and those of 14 feet navigate the river below this point. The location of the city is pleasant and healthful, and is situated on two hills, though not densely built, and in the valley between them runs Shockoe creek, a rapid stream. Many beautiful mansions are scattered on these elevations, and on the level top of the westerly one, stands the statehouse, a chaste and beautiful building, in the centre of an open square. Near this is the city-hall, a large and elegant edifice of Grecian architecture. In 1811, a theatre was burned on the site where an Episcopal church now stands, and a large number of respectable citizens, including the governor of the state, perished. To commemorate this sad event, the Monumental church was erected on the spot where it took place. Near the city is a penitentiary, extending with its grounds over an area of several acres.

The manufactures of Richmond are varied and valuable, the neighboring streams affording fine water-power, which has been extensively supplied. Here are cotton factories, flouring mills,

RAILROADS.

From Washington to Baltimore.

To Bladensburg...	7	
Paint Branch......	2	9
Beltsville..........	4	13
Laurel Factory....	5	18
Savage Railroad...	3	21
Annapolis Junc....	1	22
Patuxent Station...	1	23
Jessup's Cut E. E.	2	25
Elkridge Landing.	5	30
Relay-House......	1	31
Mount Clare.......	7	38
Baltimore..........	2	40

STAGE-ROUTES.

Fm Washington to Staunton, Va.

To Mouth of Aquia Creek by Steamboat on the Potomac River (see Washington to Richmond)	52	
By Railroad.		
To Fredericksburg	18	70
By Stage.		
Chancellorsville ..	10	80
Wilderness.........	6	86
Locust Grove......	5	91
Orange C. House..	18	109
Gordonsville	12	121
Everettsville	14	135
Charlottesville.....	6	141
Yancy's Mills......	16	157
Brookville.........	5	162
Waynesboro'......	7	169
Staunton...........	11	180

RAILROADS.

From Richmond to Lynchburg.

To Robois.........	10	
Coalfield...........	3	13
Tomahawk	4	17
Powhattan..........	5	22
Mattoax	5	27
Scott's Shop........	6	33
Amelia C. House...	3	36
Weyanoke..........	7	43
Jenning's..........	7	50
Hatokah	4	54
By Stage.		
Farmville..........	15	69
Walker's Church..	15	84
Sprout Spring......	15	99
Concord	5	104
Lynchburg	15	119

From Richmond to Charlottesville.

To Atley's.........	9	
Peake's............	6	15
Hanover C. House.	3	18
Junction...........	9	27
Noel's	5	32
Hewlett's..........	4	36
Beaver Dam........	4	40
Bumpass's..........	6	46
Frederick's Hall...	5	51
Tolersville.........	6	57
Louisa C. H......	6	63
Trevillian's........	5	68
Gordonsville	9	77
Lindsay's..........	5	82
Cobham	2	84
Kiswick	7	91
Shadwell	3	94
Charlottesville.....	4	98

nail, and iron works, and numerous other prosperous establishments.

Besides the canal before noticed, the city is connected with Norfolk, New York, and other points, by steamboats and sailing-packets. Two bridges extend over James river to Manchester, a flourishing suburb of Richmond, upon one of which the Washington and Wilmington railroad enters the city, whence it traverses Virginia and North Carolina. The Virginia Central railroad begins at Richmond, and penetrates the interior of the state.

The water-works, by which Richmond is supplied, raise the water, by hydraulic power, into three reservoirs, each containing a million of gallons, and from these lead off to all parts of the city.

The spot on which this large and fine city stands was first visited by white men in 1609, when "Master West" penetrated to the falls in search of provisions for the young colony at Jamestown, but found nothing edible except acorns. Richmond was founded in 1742, and made the capital of the state in 1780, since which it has been steadily increasing.

The population in 1800, was 5,537; in 1810, 9,735; in 1820, 12,046; in 1830, 16,060; in 1840, 20,153; in 1850, 27,483.

PETERSBURG, Va.

Is a prosperous borough and port of entry, on the south bank of Appomattox river, 12 miles from its entrance into the James, 23 miles south of Richmond, and 140 miles from Washington. The houses, which are principally of brick, have risen on the ruins of about 400 less elegant ones that were destroyed by fire, in 1815. Like Richmond, it is situated at the foot of falls in the river, which afford valuable water-power; while the barrier that they present to navigation has been surmounted by a canal, passing around the falls, and admitting boats to navigate the river 80 miles above. Vessels of 100 tons anchor at Petersburg; those of larger burden come to the City Point, at the confluence of the Appomattox with the James. A railroad connects the two points; and the Washington and Wilmington railroad line communicates with the place.

The population in 1810, was 5,668; in 1820, ——; in 1830, 8,322; in 1840, 11,136; in 1850, 14,603.

NORFOLK, Va.

The principal port of entry of the state, is situated on Elizabeth river, opposite Portsmouth, 32 miles from its entrance through Hampton Roads into the ocean, 106 miles southeast of Richmond, and 230 miles from Washington. This town is more remarkable for its deep and spacious harbor, than for its appearance. The ground is low and marshy, the Great Dismal swamp covering a large portion of Norfolk county. The streets are generally irregular, and the houses not splendid, though some of the principal avenues are wide, straight, and neat. Hampton roads are the basin formed by James and Elizabeth rivers before passing into the Atlantic. The entrance to these from the ocean, is defended by strong fortifications. At Gosport, near Portsmouth, on the west side of Elizabeth river, is a navy-yard, with a dry-dock built of hewn granite.

The Seaboard and Roanoke railroad connects Portsmouth with Weldon, on the route of the Washington and Wilmington line.

The commerce of Norfolk exceeds that of any other place in Virginia, and several hundred thousand dollars are invested in manufactures.

The population in 1810, was 9,193; in 1820, 8,478; in 1830, 9,816; in 1840, 10,920; in 1850, 14,320.

RAILROADS.

From Richmond to Petersburg, Weldon, and Wilmington, N. C.

To Water-Station..	11	
Clover Hill Junc..	2	13
Pt. Walthal Junc..	3	16
Petersburg	6	22
Stony Creek.......	21	43
Jarratt's	10	53
Belfield.............	10	63
Junction	3	66
Pleasant Hill......	8	74
Weldon	12	86
Halifax	8	94
Enfield	11	105
Battles	10	115
Rocky Mount......	8	123
Joiner's	9	132
Tosnot..............	8	140
Barden's	6	146
Nahunta	7	153
Goldsboro'	10	163
Dudley	10	173
Faisons	12	185
Warsaw	8	193
Strickland	8	201
Teachey's	9	210
Washington	8	218
Burgaw	7	225
Rocky Point.......	9	234
Northeast...........	4	238
Wilmington	10	248

From Richmond to Petersburgh (as above). 22

From Richmond to Washington.

To Hungary.......	8	
Taylorsville	12	20
Junction............	3	23
Chesterfield........	2	25
Milford	7	32
Guinney's	10	42
Fredericksburg	12	54
Brook's..............	12	66
Aqua Creek.........	6	72
By Steamboat on the Potomac River.		
Sandy Point........	12	84
Glymont.............	18	102
Fort Washington..	6	108
Alexandria	8	116
Washington	8	124

Fm Richmond to Fredericksburg (as above) 54

Fm Richmond to Weldon, N. C. (see route from Washington to Wilmington) 86

From Harper's Ferry to Winchester.

To Halltown.......	7	
Charlestown.......	3	10
Cameron's Depot..	4	14
Summit Point......	4	18
Wade's Depot.....	5	23
Stephenson's Depot	4	27
Winchester.........	5	32

Fm Gaston to Raleigh, N. C.

To Littleton.......	9	
Macon...............	11	20
Warrenton	4	24
Ridgeway	5	29
Henderson..........	13	42
Franklin	18	60
Forestville..........	11	71
Huntsville	7	78
Raleigh.............	9	87

From Hicksford to Gaston.

To Ryland's.......	10	
Summit.............	8	18
Gaston	3	21

WILMINGTON, N. C.

Has a commercial, but somewhat unhealthy situation, on Cape Fear river, 35 miles from the sea, 148 miles southeastly from Raleigh, and 365 miles from Washington. A large shoal at the mouth of the harbor, in a great measure destroys the effect of its other natural advantages. Two islands divide the river into three channels opposite the town. They afford the finest rice fields in the state. The great body of the exports and imports of North Carolina pass through this port, and it is the terminus of the Washington and Wilmington chain of railroads.

The population in 1810, was about 2,000; in 1820, ——; in 1830, 2,700; in 1840, 4,744; in 1850, 11,218.

RALEIGH, N. C.

One of the pleasantest and most tasteful towns in North Carolina, is the capital of the state. It is about six miles west of Neuse river, which is not generally navigable for ordinary vessels above Smithfield, 27 miles southeast of this place. Four broad avenues divide the town into as many squares, which are each again subdivided into four squares by streets of less width. At the junction of the main avenues, in the midst of an open park of 10 acres, stands the statehouse, a chaste and elegant structure of granite, 166 feet long, and 90 feet wide, surrounded by massy columns and crowned by a beautiful dome. In 1831, the statehouse upon the same site was destroyed by fire, with a marble statue of Washington by Canova. The Gaston and Raleigh railroad extends to the former place, 85 miles distant, where the Greenville and Roanoke connects it with Petersburg.

In 1810, the population was about 1,000; in 1820, 2,674; in 1830, 1,700; in 1840, 2,224; in 1850, 3,091.

RAILROADS.

From Gaston to Raleigh.

To Littleton	9	
Macon	11	20
Warrenton	4	24
Ridgeway	5	29
Henderson	13	42
Franklin	18	60
Forestville	11	71
Huntsville	7	78
Raleigh	9	87

From Gaston to Warrenton (as above).. 24

F'm Weldon to Wilmington

To Halifax	8	
Enfield	11	19
Battles	10	29
Rocky Mount	8	37
Joiners	9	46
Tosnot	8	54
Barden's	6	60
Nahunta	7	67
Goldsboro'	10	77
Dudley	10	87
Faisons	12	99
Warsaw	8	107
Strickland	8	115
Teachey's	9	124
Washington	8	132
Burgaw	7	139
Rocky Mount	9	148
North East	4	152
Wilmington	10	162

The contemplated Railroads from Wilmington to Columbia, S. C., and from Salisbury to Columbia, S. C., and from Raleigh to Hillsboro', are not surveyed.

CHARLESTON, S. C.

Occupies a point of land formed by the confluence of Ashley and Cooper rivers, which together enter the ocean by a spacious and deep harbor, extending seven miles below the city. It is 120 miles southeast of Columbia, the state capital, and 540 miles from Washington. Four channels of different depths afford an entrance into the harbor through a sand-bar which obstructs it. The deepest of these admits ships with 16 feet draught. The harbor is defended by Fort Moultrie, on Sullivan island, lying at its mouth, and by Forts Pinckney and Johnson.

The city stands on ground somewhat elevated above tide-water, and may be said to resemble New York on a smaller scale. It is constructed with regularity and taste, and many rich and varied trees of southern climes lend their charms. Besides the city proper, there are populous suburbs, which afford fine sites for residences, and are identified with its growth and interests. Charleston may be considered as the metropolis of the southern Atlantic states, as New Orleans is of those on the Mexican gulf and the Mississippi. Into this basin, flow many of the products of North Carolina and Georgia. Its foreign commerce is extensive and valuable, as is also its coasting-trade, and packets, as well as splendid steamships, ply to New York and other maritime cities. The Santee canal connects Santee with Cooper river, thus opening a communication from Columbia, the state capital, to Charleston.

The public buildings and institutions of the city, indicate the

RAILROADS.

F'm Charleston to Augusta.

To 7-Mile Pump	7	
Sineath's	6	13
Ladson's	4	17
Summerve	5	22
Lawrence's	6	28
Ridgeville	3	31
Ross'	6	37
41-Mile Turnout	4	41
George's	6	47
Reeve's	5	52
Branchville	10	62
Midway	10	72
Graham's	9	81
Blackville	9	90
Williston	9	99
Windsor	8	107
Johnson's	8	115
Aiken	5	120
Graniteville	6	126
Marsh's	2	128
Hamburg	8	136
Augusta, S. C	1	137

Charleston to Columbia.

To Branchville (see above)		62
Rowes	9	71
Orangeburg	8	79
Jamison's	7	86
Lewisville	6	92
Fort Mott	7	99
Camden Junc	6	105
Gadsden	5	110
Hopkins'	8	118
Woodlands	6	124
Columbia	5	129

wealth, intelligence, and liberality of the people. There are a number of banks, churches, and hotels, some of them splendid and costly. Other prominent buildings are the customhouse, guard-house, exchange, city-hall, state citadel, almshouse, orphan asylum, jail, and the College of Charleston. The literary and scientific institutions and libraries, are generally respectable and flourishing. No city is more justly noted for hospitality and refinement, and its climate is more salubrious than that of most southern cities, affording a delightful and safe summer resort for planters from the low country and the West Indies, and a pleasant winter resort for people from the north.

The South Carolina railroad extends to Augusta, on the Savannah, 137 miles, where it communicates with the Georgia railroad. At Branchtown, 62 miles from Charleston, the Columbia branch diverges to Camden and Columbia.

The population in 1790, was 16,359; in 1800, 18,712; in 1810, 24,711; in 1820, 24,480; in 1830, 30,289; in 1840, 29,261; in 1850, 42,985.

COLUMBIA, S. C.

A PLEASANT village, situated on the east side of Congaree river, below the confluence of its constituents, the Broad and the Saluda, is the capital of South Carolina, 120 miles northwest of Charleston, and 506 miles from Washington. The bank of the river gradually ascends to an elevation of about 200 feet, from which the town overlooks an extensive and interesting prospect. The streets are remarkable for breadth and regularity, and the houses for their neat and tasteful appearance. Here is located the College of South Carolina, a flourishing institution, which is liberally supported by the state. A substantial and well-built bridge extends on eight stone piers across the Congaree, and the Saluda canal, making a circuit of six and a quarter miles around the falls, passes through the town. The river affords steamboat communication with the ocean and with Charleston. The Columbia Branch railroad meets the South Carolina railroad from Charleston, at Branchville.

Water from springs 1 mile from the town, is forced by steam to an elevated point, whence it is conveyed to all sections of the village.

The population in 1830, was 3,400; in 1840, 4,340; in 1850, 6,060.

SAVANNAH, Ga.

ON the south side of the river from which it is named, 17 miles from the sea, and 158 miles southeast of Milledgeville, the state capital, is the principal city of Georgia, and one of the most favorably located ports in the southern states. It is 90 miles southwest of Charleston, and 662 miles from Washington. Near the river, the bank is about 40 feet high. Along the foot of this bluff, are stores and warehouses; while the streets of the city extend over the level at the top of this eminence. They are rendered remarkably pleasant by lines of trees along their sides and through their middle, shading the traveller from the southern sun, affording delightful walks at all times of the day. In 1820, a conflagration destroyed a great portion of the city, but it has been rebuilt with increased solidity and beauty. Formerly, the rice swamps in the vicinity, and other circumstances, contributed to render Savannah as unhealthy as it is

RAILROADS.

From Columbia to Greenville.

To Frost's Mills	7	
Littleton	8	15
Alston	10	25
Pomaria	7	32
Prosperity	8	40
Newbury C. House	7	47
Helena	1	48
Silver Street	6	54
Saluda Turnout	7	61
Chappel's Bridge	4	65
Ninety-Six	10	75
Greenwood	10	85
Cokesbury	9	94
By Stage.		
Greenville	46	140

From Camden to Charleston.

To Boykin's	9	
Claremont	10	19
Middleton	7	26
Junction	11	37
To Charleston (see above)	105	142

BY STEAMBOAT.

From Charleston to Savannah.

To Sullivan's Isl'd	4	
Lighthouse	7	11
Stono Entrance	3	14
North Edisto	12	26
St. Helena Sound	15	41
P. Royal Entrance	28	69
Mouth of Savannah River	20	89
Savannah	12	101

Charleston to Wilmington

To Bull's Bay	18	
Cape Romain	10	28
Santee River	8	36
Georgetown Entr.	40	76
8-Mile Inlet	20	96
Little River Inlet	24	120
Cape Fear	25	145
Wilmington	42	187

From Columbia to Ebenezer 78

RAILROADS.

From Savannah to Macon.

To Station No. 1	9	
Eden	11	20
Reform	10	30
Station No. 4	6	36
Armenia	10	46
Halcyondal	4	50
Ogucbee	12	62
Scarboro'	8	70
Millen	9	79
Cushingville	4	83
Birdsville	7	90
Midville	4	94
Holcomb	6	100
Spear's Turn	12	112
Davisboro'	10	122
Tennille	14	136
Oconee	11	147
Emmett	5	152
Gordon	18	170
Griswoldville	13	183
Macon	8	191

now salubrious. This change is owing to the improvements in the culture of rice, and in the condition of the city. The exchange, courthouse, hospital, arsenal, guard-house, jail, and numerous churches and banks, display the characteristic enterprise and liberality of the citizens; while airy, verdant, and shady parks, are interspersed more frequently in this than in most other American cities. Among other splendid trees, the "Pride of China" (azederach) holds a conspicuous rank.

Savannah has an excellent harbor, with a safe and easy entrance from the ocean. Several islands are formed by the embouchures of the river, affording both protection and ornament. Upon Tybee island, a lighthouse marks the entrance to the port, while two forts protect the city from outward assault. Vessels of 13 feet draught anchor at the wharves of the city, those of larger size at a point several miles below. Above Savannah, the river is navigable for steamboats of 150 tons to Augusta, 150 miles. By this and other channels, most of the cotton, tobacco, sugar, lumber, and other staples of Georgia, are conveyed to Savannah, where they find a market, or are exported. This city, from its favorable commercial situation, on a coast not well supplied with good harbors, is the receptacle of productions from an extensive region. Late improvements in railroads and other channels of communication, have added largely to its growth and prosperity. A canal connects Ogeechee river with the Savannah. Steamboats navigate the principal rivers of the state, and sail to Charleston and other cities on the coast, and regular steam and sailing-packets communicate with New York.

The Central railroad extends 191 miles to Macon, whence the Macon and Western railroad proceeds 101 miles, in a northwesterly direction, to Atlanta. Through this place, passes the Georgia and Western and Atlantic railroad, from Augusta to Chattanooga, on Tennessee river, in Hamilton county, Tennessee.

The population in 1810, was 5,595; in 1820, 7,523; in 1830, 9,748; in 1840, 11,214; in 1850, 27,841.

MILLEDGEVILLE, Ga.

HAS a pleasant and central situation, at the head of steamboat navigation on Oconee river, 300 miles from the sea, and 648 miles from Washington. The city is built on elevated and somewhat uneven ground, in the midst of a rich and populous cotton-producing region. It is the capital of Georgia, and is laid out with broad streets and pleasant squares. The statehouse is a fine edifice of Gothic architecture, surmounted by a cupola, and containing in its halls portraits of General Oglethorpe and other eminent men of early times. Among the other prominent buildings, are banks, a market-house, governor's house, state arsenal, and churches. A bridge extends to the west bank of the river.

The population in 1810, was [illegible]256; in 1820, ——; in 1830, 1,599; in 1840, 2,095; in 1850, ——.

AUGUSTA, Ga.

Is situated on the west side of the Savannah river, 98 miles east-northeast of Milledgeville, and 125 from Savannah. The streets cross each other at right angles, and are lined with beautiful shade-trees, giving the city a fine appearance. The public, and many of the private buildings, are costly and elegant. It is connected with Charleston, Savannah, and the interior of the states of Georgia, Alabama and Tennessee, by railroads, and is a city of much commercial enterprise.

Population in 1830, was 4,634; in 1840, 6,436; in 1850, ——.

RAILROADS.

Fm Savannah to Atlanta

To Macon (see page 55)		191
Howard's	6	197
Crawford's	7	204
Smarr's	6	210
Forsyth's	5	215
Collier's	6	221
Goggin's	5	226
Barnesville	5	231
Milner's	7	238
Griffin	11	249
Fayette	7	256
Jonesboro'	14	270
Rough and Rendy	11	281
East Point Junc	5	286
Atlanta	6	292

From Savannah to Chattanooga.

To Atlanta (see above)		292
Balton	8	300
Marietta	3	303
Moon's	10	313
Acworth	5	318
Altoona	5	323
Etowah	10	333
Cartersville	—	333
Cass	5	338
Kingston	5	343
Adairsville	10	353
Calhoun	10	363
Resaca	5	368
Tilton	7	375
Dalton	8	383
Tunnel Hill	8	391
Ringgold	8	399
Opelika	4	403
Chickamany	9	412
Chatanooga	11	423

From Augusta to Atlanta and Chatanooga, Tenn.

To Bell Air	11	
Berzelia	10	21
Dearing	8	29
Thompson	9	38
Camac	9	47
Cuming	10	57
Crawfordville	8	65
Union Point	11	76
Greensboro'	8	84
Madison	20	104
Social Circle	16	120
Covington	10	130
Conyer's	11	141
Lithonia	6	147
S. Mountain	9	156
Decatur	9	165
Atlanta	6	171
To Chatanooga (see see above)	140	311

From Augusta to Nashville.

To Chatanooga (as above)		311
To Nashville (see Tennessee)	151	462

From Atlanta to Montgomery, Ala.

To East Point	6	
Fairburn	12	18
Palmetto	7	25
Newman	15	40
Hagansville	19	59
Lagrange	13	72
West Point	15	87
Cusetta	10	97
Rough and Ready	5	102
Opelika	4	106
Auburn	7	113
Lockapoka	7	120
Natasulga	6	126
Chehaw	7	133
Franklin	5	138
Fort Decten	5	143
M'Gar's	10	153
Tippecanoe	9	162
Montgomery	11	173

TALLAHASSEE, Fla.

The capital of the state, is about 292 miles from Augustine, and 896 miles from Washington. It is situated in the midst of a fertile and undulating region, upon elevated ground, from which several pure springs issue and unite in a good mill-stream. This city, like the state, is of recent growth. Thirty years ago, its site was a luxuriant but unpeopled wilderness. It is now an increasing town, laid out with streets and public-squares, with respectable buildings. It has a statehouse, churches, jail, market-house, bank, and other conspicuous edifices. Twenty miles south of Tallahassee is St. Marks, on the Gulf of Mexico, where ships discharge their cargoes bound for the capital, to which a railroad conveys them.

The population varies in winter and in summer. In the former season, many resort to this place from colder regions to enjoy the mild and salubrious climate.

In 1826, there were about 800 inhabitants; in 1830, 1,500; in 1840, from 1,616 to 2,500; in 1850 ——.

PENSACOLA, Fla.

On the bay of the same name, in Escambria county, Florida, about 10 miles from the Gulf of Mexico, 242 milest west of Tallahassee, and 1,042 miles from Washington, is the principal port of entry and city in Florida. The site is a low sandy plain, extending into the harbor, making it too shallow near the town for large vessels, which are obliged to anchor at a distance. The entrance to the port is deeper than any other on the north coast of the gulf. Five miles above the mouth, is one of the United States navy-yards. The city is a parallelogram, with regular streets and public squares. It was among the earliest settlements in Florida, having been founded in 1699, by a Spanish officer.

The population in 1830, was about 2,000; in 1840, about 2,000; in 1850, ——.

RAILROADS.

From Tallahassee to Port Leon.......... 22

BY STEAMBOAT.

From Apalachicola to Columbus, Ga.

To Fort Gadsden..	30	
Iola..............	31	61
Chatahoochee......	70	131
Woodville, Ala....	53	184
Columbia..........	20	204
Fort Gaines, Ga...	40	244
Eufaula, Ala......	28	272
Roanoke...........	22	294
Fort Mitchell, Ala..	55	349
Columbus, Ga......	15	364

From Pensacola to St. Marks.

To Fort Barancas..	7	
St. Rosa's Inlet.....	48	55
St. Andrew's Inlet..	60	115
Cape St. Joseph...	15	130
Cape St. Blas......	35	165
Fox Island.........	45	210
Dog Island.........	10	220
South West Cape..	18	238
St. Mark's.........	22	260

From St. Augustine to Savannah.

To St. John's Inlet.	40	
Talbot Inlet........	9	49
Nassau Inlet.......	6	55
Cumberland Sound.	20	75
St. Andrew's Sound	24	99
St. Simond's Sound	10	109
Altamahaw Sound.	17	126
Sapelo Island......	5	131
Sapelo Sound......	15	146
St. Catherine's S...	15	161
Osabaw Sound.....	15	176
Warsaw Sound....	10	186
Savannah Light....	10	196
Savannah..........	15	211

MOBILE, Ala.

Thirty miles north of the Gulf of Mexico, on Mobile bay, 160 miles east of New Orleans, and 1,013 miles from Washington, is the principal city and only port of entry of Alabama. It occupies an elevated plain, overlooking the pleasant bay, and is fanned by its breezes. Fires have several times injured the city, but it has been rebuilt with improved appearance and solidity. From its position in the state, it is the receptacle of the commerce of Alabama. Vast quantities of cotton are annually exported. The harbor is difficult of access, being obstructed by marshy islands and shoals, but within, deep and spacious enough for large vessels. These, by a circuit around an island, in front of the city, anchor at its wharves. The entrance to the bay is defended by a fortification and marked by a lighthouse. Good water, from a neighboring source, is distributed over the city by iron-pipes. Railroads are in process of construction to connect the city with the Ohio river, and also with the Atlantic states through Georgia. It has daily communication, by steamboat, to Proctorsville, and thence, by railroad with New Orleans. There are a customhouse courthouse, hospitals, banks, and churches.

In 1813, the period when Mobile passed from the hands of Spain into possession of the United States, it contained about 100 buildings. In 1830, the population was 3,194; in 1840, 12,672; in 1850, 20,513.

RAILROADS.

From Montgomery to Atlanta, Ga.

To Tippecanoe....	11	
M'Gar's	9	20
Shorter's...........	5	25
Fort Decatur.......	5	30
Franklin	5	35
Chehaw	5	40
Notasulga	7	47
Lockapoka	6	53
Auburn	7	60
Opelika............	7	67
Rough and Ready..	4	71
Cusetta	5	76
West Point.........	10	86
Lagrange..........	15	101
Hogansville	13	114
Newman	19	133
Palmetto...........	15	148
Fairburn...........	7	155
East Point.........	12	167
Atlanta	6	173

Fm Tuscumbia to Decatur and Huntsville.

To Leighton.......	11	
Cortland...........	14	25
Hillsboro'	9	34
Decatur............	10	44
By Stage.		
Mooresville	12	56
Huntsville.........	20	76

MONTGOMERY, Ala.

Now the capital of the state, having succeeded Tuscaloosa, as the seat of government in 1847, has a central situation in Montgomery county, of which it is also the seat of justice, 220 miles northeast of Mobile, and —— miles from Washington. It is the centre of an extensive trade in cotton, which is brought from the surrounding country to this point, the head of steamboat navigation on Alabama river. It contains the usual number of public buildings.

The Montgomery and West Point and the Lagrange railroads, unite the city to Atlanta, on the route of the Georgia railroad, and to the intermediate points.

The population in 1840, was 2,179; in 1850 ——.

RAILROADS.

From Mobile to Citronville.

To Mauvila	13	
Citronville	20	33

BY STEAMBOAT.

From Mobile to Wetumpka.

To Fort Minns	73	
Little River	18	91
Clairborne	42	133
Bell's Landing	25	153
Dale Town	58	216
Portland	45	261
Selma	40	301
Vernon	75	376
Washington	22	398
Montgomery	13	411
Wetumpka	50	461

NATCHEZ, Miss.

The principal city of Mississippi, is situated on the east bank of Mississippi river, 292 miles from New Orleans, and 1,110 miles from Washington. Along the river, at the foot of the bluff, which rises 200 feet from the water, there are stores, warehouses, and other buildings, but the more respectable part of the city occupies the top of the elevation, which affords fine sites for residence, and from its heights a beautiful view of the river and its banks. Broad streets divide pleasant mansions; which indicate the wealth and taste of their owners. Rich and varied trees lend their charms to the other attractions of the city. Natchez is the mart of the interior of Mississippi, receiving the vast quantities of cotton and other staples, which are conveyed by numerous steamboats to New Orleans and other towns on the river. There is a railroad, 30 miles long, from Natchez to Malcolm.

The population in 1810, was 1,511; in 1820, 2,184; in 1830, 2,789; in 1840, 4,800; in 1850, 5,239.

JACKSON, Miss.

The capital of the state, is situated at the head of boat navigation, on the west bank of Pearl river. It is built on a beautiful level ground, half a mile square. It contains a magnificent statehouse, governor's house, a penitentiary, and other elegant public buildings. It is connected with Jackson by a railroad 45 miles long. It lies 1,015 miles southwest of Washington.

The population in 1840 was, 2,126; in 1850 ——.

COLUMBUS, Miss.

At the head of steamboat navigation, on the east bank of Tombigbee river, is an important and growing city, 141 miles northeast of Jackson, and 885 miles from Washington. Like the other flourishing towns of Mississippi, it is an extensive market for cotton, which finds its way from this point down the Tombigbee to Mobile, and thence to various domestic and foreign ports. The city is well laid out, on an elevation, about 120 feet above the level of the Tombigbee. An elegant bridge spans this stream, and some of the public buildings are beautiful and imposing.

The population in 1840, was 4,000; in 1850, 9,312.

RAILROADS.

Fm Vicksburg to Brandon.

To Mount Alban	6	
Bovina	4	10
Big Black	2	12
Edward's	6	18
Bolton's	9	27
Clinton	9	36
Jackson	10	46
Brandon	14	60

Fm Vicksburg to Clinton (see above)		36

Fm Vicksburg to Raymond.

To Bolton's (as above)	27	
Raymond	6	33

From Woodville to Bayou Sara & St. Franciisville.

To Laurell Hill	14	
Bayou Sara and St. Francisville	12	26

STAGE-ROUTES.

Fm Jackson to St. Francisville, via Natchez.

To Newtown	10	
Line Store	11	21
Gallatin	20	41
Malcolm	32	73
Hamburg	10	83
Washington	12	95
Natchez	7	102
Cold Spring	23	125
Woodville	15	140
By Railroad.		
Laurell Hill	14	154
St. Francisville	12	166

From Jackson to Memphis, Tenn., via Holly Springs.

To Canton	25	
Benton	26	51
Lexington	18	69
Black-Hawk	15	84
Carrollton	15	99
Grenada	21	120
Ockachickam	14	134
Oxford	33	167
Wyatt	15	182
Waterford	10	192
Holly Springs	10	202
North Mt. Pleasant	15	217
Germantown	25	242
Memphis	15	257

NEW ORLEANS, La.

Sometimes called the "Crescent City," from its form, bending parallel with the Mississippi, is situated on the north bank of that river, 100 miles from its entrance into the gulf of Mexico, 1,185 miles below the mouth of the Missouri, and 1,172 miles from Washington. Its position and appearance are both singularly different from those of other American cities. The ground, as it recedes from the river, descends by a gentle inclination, causing the houses, when viewed from a point not much above the level of high water, to seem to rise immediately from it. A "levee," or dike, forms a margin between the city and the river, and protects the former from inundation by the latter. It is built of wood, 200 feet wide, and extends for four miles, presenting a most animated scene of commercial prosperity. Within, not only the houses, but the inhabitants, are of many descriptions. Except New York, no city includes Americans from so many different states, while the number of blacks, with the French and Spanish Creoles, and the foreigners, is still greater. These representatives of many nations are drawn to New Orleans by its geographical and commercial relation to the West Indies, South America, Mexico, and the southern parts of North America. The Creole citizens are descendants of the French, Spanish, and Germans, who originally founded and peopled the city, and constitute a large portion of the population. The position of New Orleans, with regard to the interior of the United States, is still more important. Situated near the mouth of the great river of the American continent, the Mississippi, with its immense confluents, the Ohio and the Missouri, almost the whole trade of those streams, and of their thousand tributaries, flows toward this point, as to a vast receiving and distributing reservoir. Hence the exports of New Orleans are exceeded by those of no other American city, New York excepted. The great staples of the southern and western states, sugar, cotton, wheat, flour, and corn, are the articles chiefly shipped from this port. The harbor is excellent, deep, and spacious. Ships, and vessels of every description, from the flatboat of the Mississippi to the magnificent ocean-steamer, here congregate, or enliven the scene, as they move from point to point. From the city to the bar, near the gulf, 100 miles below, the river has an average

CITY OF NEW ORLEANS.

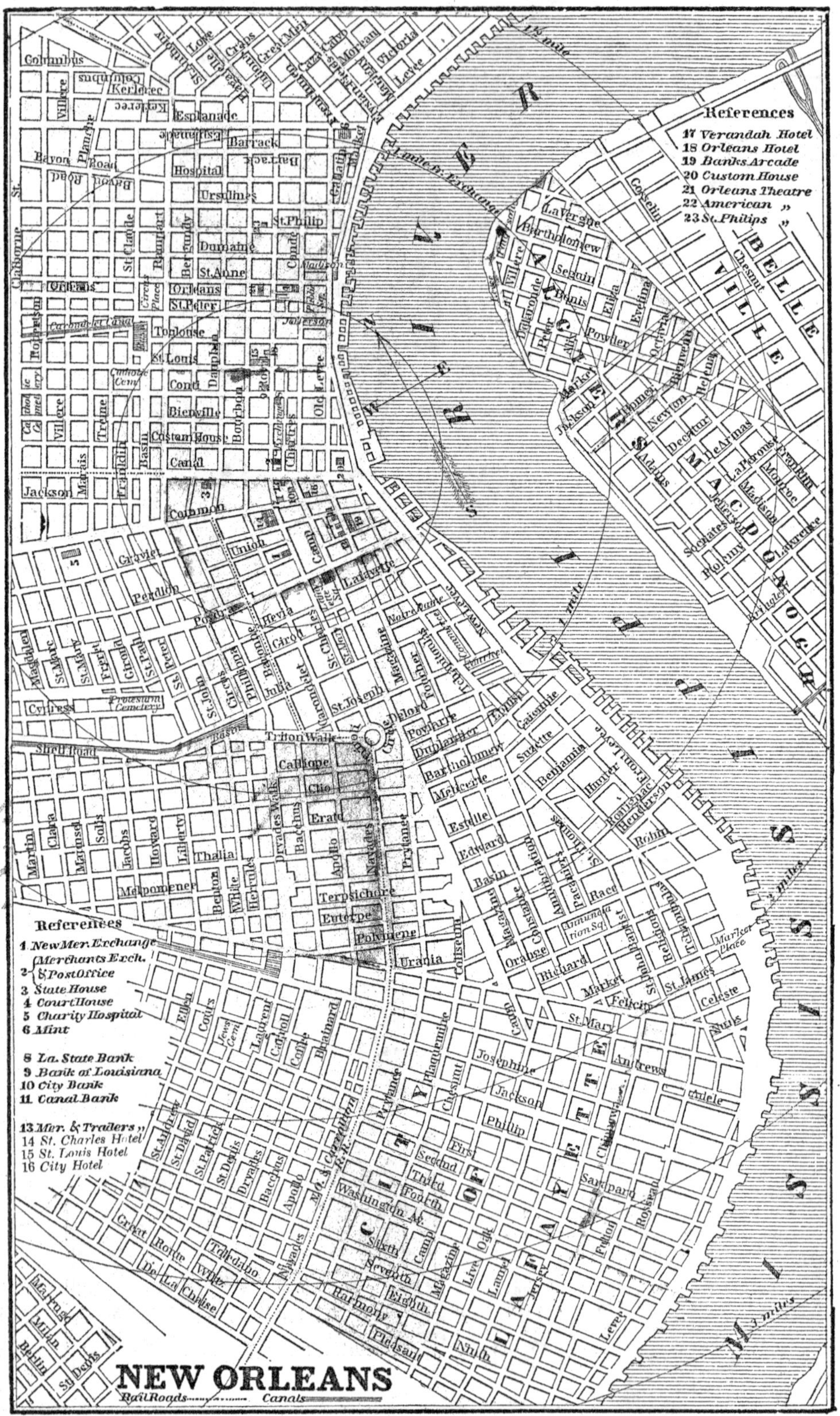

NEW ORLEANS
Rail Roads
Canals
References
1 New Mer. Exchange
2 Merchants Exch. & Post Office
3 State House
4 Court House
5 Charity Hospital
6 Mint
8 La. State Bank
9 Bank of Louisiana
10 City Bank
11 Canal Bank
13 Mer. & Traders „
14 St. Charles Hotel
15 St. Louis Hotel
16 City Hotel
References
17 Verandah Hotel
18 Orleans Hotel
19 Banks Arcade
20 Custom House
21 Orleans Theatre
22 American „
23 St. Philips „

depth of 100 feet, affording anchorage for several miles along the wharves. The bed of the river, and its banks toward the mouth, are gradually rising. In 1722 there were 25 feet of water on the bar. In 1767 there were but 20, and now there are but 9 feet. The present mouth of the river is three miles beyond the mouth of 1724.

The city is gradually extending toward Lake Ponchartrain on the north, which communicates with the Mississippi by a canal, the Bayou St. John, and a railroad six miles long, and with the Gulf of Mexico, by Lake Borgne and intermediate passages. The Mexican Gulf railroad communicates with Proctorsville, 27 miles distant. From the nature of the commercial advantages which New Orleans possesses, it is apparent that its prosperity is almost unlimited, and is the necessary result of the settlement of the vast region of the valley of the Mississippi. It is now the sixth city in population, and the third in commerce, in the Union, and perhaps would already have held a higher rank, but from the check it receives from the prevalence of yellow fever, and other maladies, consequent upon its situation. There were formerly three municipalities and the city of Lafayette, with district councils for the management of internal affairs, in the geographical limits of the city; these were consolidated in 1852 under one municipal government. This city was also the capital of Louisiana until 1849, when the seat of government was removed to Baton Rouge. It contains churches of various ages and styles of architecture; hospitals, charitable institutions, theatres, banks, warehouses, hotels, and the United States branch mint, a large building, 108 feet deep, 282 feet long, and three stories high; also the University of Louisiana, and many excellent schools. The city is supplied with water, elevated by steam from the Mississippi into a reservoir, and thence distributed through iron-pipes.

The population in 1763, was 3,190; in 1785, 4,980; in 1810, 17,242; in 1820,27,176; in 1830, 46,310; in 1840, 102,193; in 1850, 116,348. It was first settled in 1722.

BATON ROUGE, La.

The capital of Louisiana, occupies a pleasant slope on the east bank of the Mississippi river, 117 miles northwest of New Orleans and 1,237 miles from Washington. Upon the elevation east of the city, stand the United States barracks; it also contains Baton Rouge college, and other prominent public buildings. This place is not otherwise particularly remarkable, except in being the seat of the state government, having succeeded New Orleans in that relation in December, 1849. Opposite is the village of West Baton Rouge. The town is pleasantly located with good facilities for business, being nearly equally distant from Natchez and from New Orleans, from which places, and other points on the Mississippi, come steamboats to its wharves.

The population in 1830, was about 1,000; in 1840, 2,269; in 1850, 4,200.

AUSTIN, Texas,

The capital of the state, is situated on the northeasterly side of Colorado river, 200 miles northwest of Galveston. The site is salubrious, being removed from the unhealthy atmosphere of the seaboard. The city is laid out on an extensive scale, with regular streets and avenues, which, when lined with the contemplated rows of buildings, will present an imposing spectacle.

RAILROADS.

From New Orleans to Proctorsville.

To Congress St....		
U. S. Barrack......		
Versailles..........		
Ducro's Landing...		12
Terre Aux Bœuf...		
Bœuf C. House....		
Santiagos..........		
Tautauts...........		
Proctorsville.......		27

From St. Francisville to Woodville, Miss.

To Laurel Hill....	12	
Woodville.........	14	26

From Port Hudson to Clinton............. 24

From New Orleans to Carrollton.......... 6

From New Orleans to Lake Ponchartrain. 6

STAGE-ROUTES.

Fm New Orleans to Baton Rouge.

To Springfield	32	
Van Buren.........	8	40
Baton Rouge......	32	72

From Baton Rouge to Opelousas.

To West Baton Rouge...........	2	
Atchafalaya River.	38	40
Opelousas	22	62

From New Orleans to Natchitoches.

To Baton Rouge (see above)......	72	
To Opelousas (as above)...........	62	134
Bayou Chicot......	28	162
Cheneyville	18	130
Alexandria	25	205
Red River.........	50	255
Natchitoches.......	20	275

From New Orleans to Covington, via Madisonville....... 45

BY STEAMBOAT.

From New Orleans to Baton Rouge....... 138

From New Orleans to Natchitoches....... 396

For distances on the Western Rivers see last of the book.

STAGE-ROUTES.

Fm Austin to Rio Grande.

To Bastrop........	30	
R. San Marcos......	44	74
R. Gaudalupe......	22	86
San Antonio	48	134
R. San Miguel......	42	176
Rio Frio............	28	204
R. Neuces	60	264
Rio Grande.........	55	319

At present, the buildings are not remarkable for elegance or number. In 1845, a convention met at this place, and organized a state government and constitution, which were ratified by the popular vote in the same year. In 1846, the first state legislature met at Austin, where it has since held biennial sessions.

The population in 1840, was about 400; in 1850, 4,846.

GALVESTON, Texas.

This city is situated at the northeast part of Galveston island, which lies off the mouth of a large bay of the same name. Between the town and Pelican island, on the northwest, the entrance to the bay is deep and spacious, affording a good harbor and anchorage. Steamboats and other vessels arrive at Galveston from different points on the Gulf of Mexico; and it is the chief commercial place in the state. There are a number of stores, dwellings, and other buildings, the white walls of which appear finely from the water, but occasion disappointment when more closely viewed.

The population in 1840, was from 5,000 to 7,000; in 1850, 6,000.

LITTLE ROCK, Ark.

As its name imports, is situated on a rock, or bluff, on the south side of Arkansas river, at the head of steamboat navigation, except during high water, when Fort Gibson, 1,100 miles further up, may be reached. It is the capital of Arkansas, and is 300 miles by the river from the Mississippi, and 1,065 miles from Washington. The town is well laid out, and has the usual number of churches and other public buildings, among which may be mentioned the statehouse, courthouse, and penitentiary.

The population in 1840, was 3,000; in 1850 4,138.

NASHVILLE, Tenn.

On the south bank of Cumberland river, at the head of steamboat navigation, 120 miles from its entrance into the Mississippi, and 648 miles from Washington, is the capital of the state. Built upon an uneven surface, amid the picturesque scenery of a fertile and populous region, few southern cities combine a pleasant situation, with more attractive hospitality and refinement, or display, in proportion to their population, a greater number of elegant public structures. Of these, a new statehouse is the most magnificent. The courthouse is a spacious and convenient edifice; the churches are beautiful and costly; and the schools are excellent. Nashville university is a prosperous institution, with commodious buildings, well supplied with apparatus and other means of instruction.

Vessels of 400 tons, chiefly steamboats, navigate Cumberland river to Nashville, during the greater part of the year. When the water is low, the stream admits only those of 30 or 40 tons burden. These carry on an extensive trade with New Orleans and intermediate places.

Water is elevated from the river into a reservoir, and thence distributed over the city.

The population in 1830, was 5,566; in 1840, 6,929; in 1850, 17,502.

STAGE-ROUTES.

Fm Washington to Austin.

To Independence..	10	
Industry	30	40
Rutersville	20	60
Lagrange	6	66
Bastrop	44	110
Austin	30	140

From Austin to Galveston.

To Bastrop	30	
Lagrange	44	74
Rutersville	6	80
San Felipe	40	120
Houston	55	175
Galveston	75	250

BY STEAMBOAT.

From Galveston to New Orleans.

To Sabine Island.	55	
Atchafalaya	145	200
Southwest Pass	140	340
Southeast Pass	25	365
Fort St. Philip	20	385
Fort St. Leon	58	443
New Orleans	20	463

STAGE-ROUTES.

From Little Rock to Fort Smith.

To Lewisburg	48	
Dwight	33	81
Pittsburg	14	95
Ozark	39	134
Van Buren	39	173
Fort Smith	5	178

From Little Rock to Hick's Ferry....... 180

For Steamboat Routes, see last of book.

RAILROADS.

From Nashville to Chattanooga.

To Antioch	10	
Smyrna	11	21
Murfreesboro'	11	32
Christiana	9	41
Fosterville	4	45
Bell Buckle	5	50
Wartrace	5	55
Normandy	8	63
Tallahoma	7	70
Allisonia	7	77
Dichera	7	84
Cowan	5	89
Tantallon	7	96
Anderson	9	105
Stevenson	10	115
Shell Mound	15	130
Station	10	140
Chattanooga	11	151

Fm Nashville to Murfreesboro' (as above) 32

From Nashville to Savannah, Ga.

To Chattanooga (as above)	151	
To Savannah (see Georgia Routes)	432	583

FRANKFORT, Ky.

One of the most pleasant towns of Kentucky, is the capital of the state. It is situated on a circular bend, on the north side of Kentucky river, 60 miles from its entrance into the Ohio, and 452 miles from Washington. The river here winds through deep limestone banks, which afford a level site for the town, and for South Frankfort, on the opposite side, with which it is connected by a bridge. Behind the town, the plain rises several hundred feet into a table-land, from which appears a magnificent prospect of the river and a wide extent of country. Frankfort is a well-built village, with neat and solid dwellings, of brick or white marble. Of this material, which the limestone region along the river furnishes in great plenty and excellence, the statehouse is constructed, a splendid building, with a portico supported by Ionic pillars at the front, and a lighted cupola upon the roof. There are also a penitentiary, courthouse, churches, banks, &c. The citizens of Frankfort display the accustomed intelligent hospitality which is characteristic of Kentuckians. The manufactures of the town are considerable, and steamboats ascending to this point with high water, carry on a trade with the valleys of the Mississippi and Ohio rivers.

The Lexington and Ohio railroad, between Lexington and Louisville, 92 miles long, communicates with Frankfort.

The population in 1810, was 1,099; in 1820, 1,679; in 1830, 1,680; in 1840, 1,917; in 1850, 4,372.

LOUISVILLE, Ky.

At the head of steamboat navigation on the Ohio, except during three months in the year, when the river is high, is the principal city of Kentucky, and a commercial metropolis of the western states. Here the Ohio descends by rapids over a limestone ledge, forming a barrier to navigation, which is now surmounted by a canal from below the city to a point above the falls. From the water, the ground rises gently and with undulations, affording a fine site, and a magnificent and varied prospect of the river and its islands, foaming rapids, pleasant villages, and fertile shores. The city is intersected by broad and pleasant streets, parallel with the river, crossed at right angles by other streets and alleys. Beargrass creek, passing through the upper part of the town, falls into the Ohio, above the rapids, and is spanned by bridges. The public buildings are numerous, and commensurate with the importance and prosperity of Louisville, including banks, churches, hospitals, jails, a city-hall, and court-house, medical institute, and other benevolent, scientific, and educational establishments.

The Medical institute at Louisville, is a very important institution, founded in 1837, with six professors, and about two hundred and fifty students. The Kentucky Historical society, has a considerable library with numerous manuscripts.

This city may be regarded as one of the great magazines for provisions in the west. It is the market of a vast agricultural region, extending through Kentucky, Ohio, Indiana, and Illinois, and trades extensively with the whole valleys of the Mississippi and the Ohio. Manufactures of numerous kinds are also prosecuted with great enterprise and success. It is supplied by an aqueduct with pure and abundant water, and is brilliantly illuminated with gas.

Louisville is the terminus of the Lexington and Ohio railroad, and the port of a large number of steamboats from New Orleans, St. Louis, and other places in the great valley of the west.

The population, in 1778, was 30; in 1800, 600; in 1810, 1,357; in 1820, 4,012; in 1830, 10,352; in 1840, 21,210; in 1850, 43,217.

RAILROADS.

From Memphis to Somerville.

To Nashobo	12	
Germantown	2	14
Colliersville	10	24
Moscow	16	40
Somerville	15	55

STAGE-ROUTES.

From Nashville to Huntsville, Ala.

To Cold Spring	12	
Franklin	6	18
Spring Hill	12	30
Columbia	14	44
Cave Spring	12	56
Lynnville	7	63
Pulaski	14	77
Elkton	17	94
Huntsville	30	124

From Nashville to Frankfort, Ky.

To Pleasant Hill	6	
Hendersonville	9	15
Gallatin	10	25
Scottsville	30	55
Lewis	14	69
Glasgow	12	71
Blue Spring Grove	12	83
Monroe	10	93
Greensburg	13	106
Campbellsville	11	117
Lebanon	20	137
Perryville	18	155
Harrodsburg	10	165
Salvisa	11	176
Lawrenceburg	10	186
Frankfort	12	198

Fm Nashville to Memphis 241

Fm Nashville to Middleburg 177

Fm Memphis to Somerville 46

KENTUCKY.

RAILROADS.

From Lexington to Frankfort.

To Midway	14	
Frankfort	15	29

From Lexington to Louisville.

To Frankfort	29	
Milaning	6	35
Consolution	6	41
Bagdad	1	42
Christianburg	2	44
Pleasureville	5	49
Bellevue	3	52
Eminence	2	54
Smithfield	5	59
Walnut Grove	2	61
Lagrange	6	67
Williamson	12	79
Louisville	15	94

Projected Railroads.

Lexington to Covington.
Lexington to Maysville.

LEXINGTON, Ky.

This city is situated on a branch of the Elkhorn river, 70 miles from Louisville, and 515 from Washington. It is the oldest town in the state, and was formerly the capital. It has many handsome, paved streets, Main street being 75 feet wide, and 1½ miles in length. The noble shade-trees that border the streets, give it a pleasing appearance. A large public square adorns the centre of the place, which is surrounded by stately private mansions. The public buildings are, a splendid court-house, Masonic hall, jail, state lunatic asylum, and the halls of the Transylvania university, together with several churches and academies, and the hospitality and intelligence of its citizens, render it a desirable southern residence.

The population in 1820, was 5,283; in 1830, 6,408· in 1840, 6,984; in 1850 ——.

STAGE-ROUTES.

Fm Lexington to Madison Indiana.

To Laputa	10	
Pleasureville	10	20
New Castle	7	27
Campbellsburg	6	33
Bedford	11	44
Milton	11	55
Madison (by Ferry)	1	56

From Lexington to Cincinnati, Ohio.

To Delphton	7	
Georgetown	6	13
Fishville	10	23
Williamstown	22	45
Crittenden	12	57
Walton	9	66
Florence	8	74
Covington	10	84
Cincinnati (Ferry)	1	85

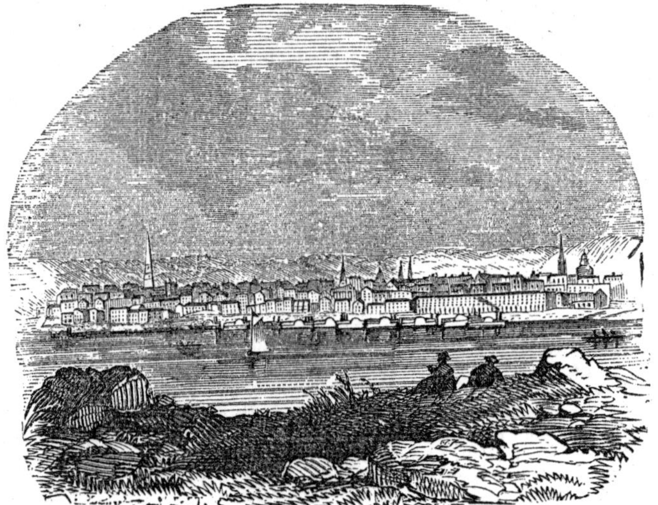

VIEW OF CINCINNATI, OHIO.

CINCINNATI, Ohio,

The "Queen City of the West," in population, commerce, and general enterprise, is situated on the north bank of Ohio river, 494 miles from its entrance into the Mississippi, 1,447 miles from New Orleans, and 492 miles from Washington. It occupies two terraces, or even surfaces, the higher rising by a regular grade, about 60 feet above the lower. Great uniformity characterizes the streets, and the city is more splendid than it appears from the water. The surrounding country is a pleasant, fertile valley, bounded by undulating slopes and hills, which command delightful views of the city, the river, and its banks. Near Cincinnati, are several thriving villages and towns, which are connected with it in prosperity and interests. Like most rapidly increasing American cities, Cincinnati exhibits great diversity in the appearance of its buildings. Some are of wood and cheap material; others are solid, durable, and splendid. Extensive warehouses, stores, and dwellings, adorn the compact central portions; toward the outskirts, the buildings are more scattered and less comely.

The public buildings are numerous and generally elegant, consisting of from seventy to eighty churches; market-houses;

RAILROADS.

From Cincinnati to Columbus, via Xenia.

To Engine House	3	
Plainville	6	9
Milford	5	14
Miamiville	3	17
Loveland	6	23
Foster's	4	27
Deerfield	5	32
Morrow	4	36
Fort Ancient	5	41
Oregon	4	45
Corwin	6	51
Claysville	4	55
Spring Valley	3	58
Xenia	7	65
Cedarville	8	73
Selma	6	79
S. Charleston	5	84
London	11	95
West Jefferson	10	105
Rome	7	112
Columbus	8	120

From Cincinnati to Xenia (see above).. 65

From Cincinnati to Deerfield (see above) 32

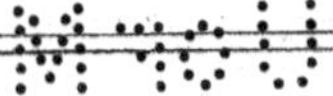

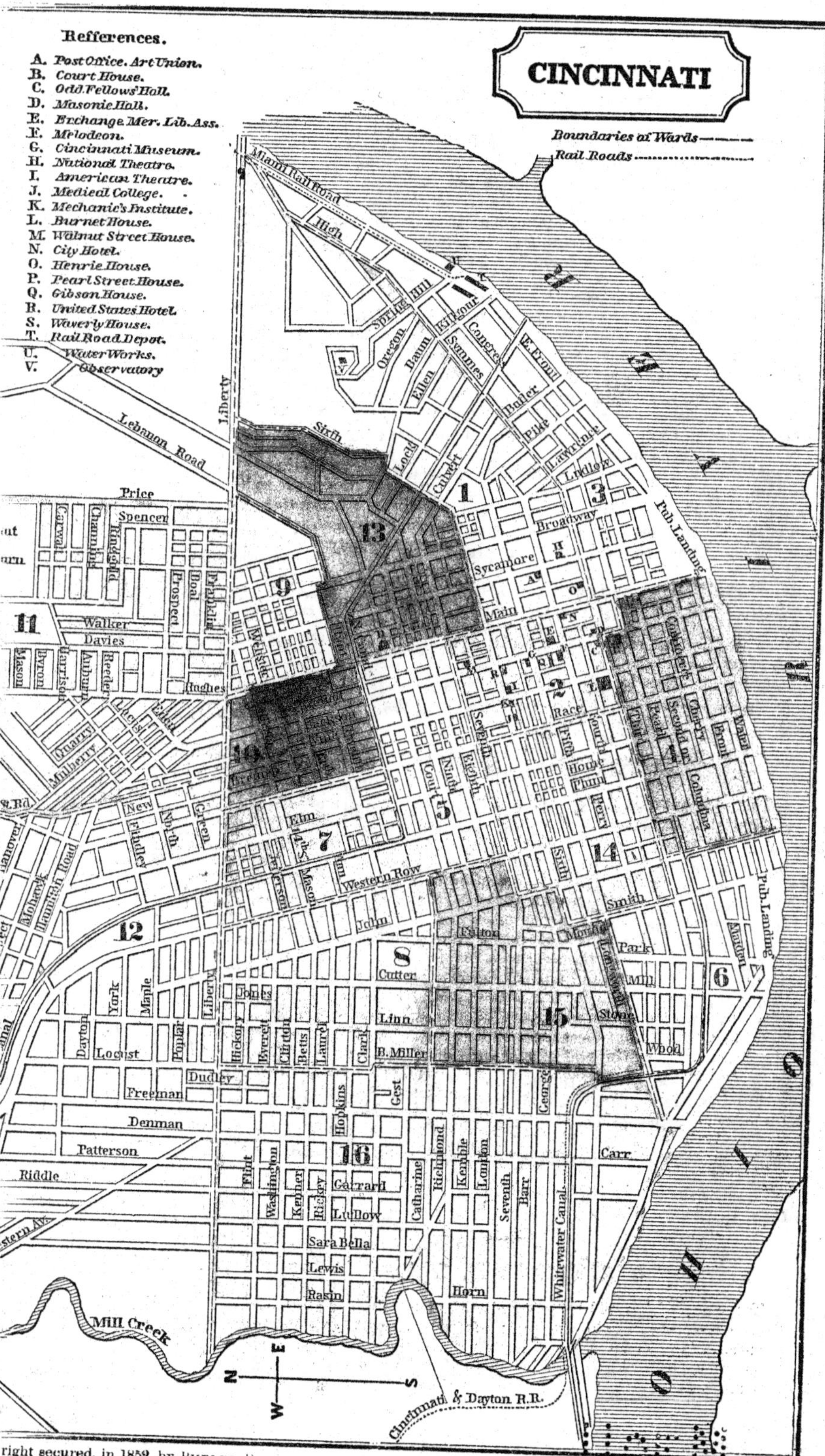
CINCINNATI
Refferences.
A. Post Office. Art Union.
B. Court House.
C. Odd Fellows' Hall.
D. Masonic Hall.
E. Exchange Mer. Lib. Ass.
F. Melodeon.
G. Cincinnati Museum.
H. National Theatre.
I. American Theatre.
J. Medical College.
K. Mechanic's Institute.
L. Burnet House.
M. Walnut Street House.
N. City Hotel.
O. Henrie House.
P. Pearl Street House.
Q. Gibson House.
R. United States Hotel.
S. Waverly House.
T. Rail Road Depot.
U. Water Works.
V. Observatory
Boundaries of Wards
Rail Roads
Miami Rail Road
Lebanon Road
Mill Creek
Cincinnati & Dayton R.R.
Whitewater Canal
Pub. Landing
OHIO

a courthouse, 120 feet high to the top of the dome; several banks, asylums, and hospitals; large and splendid hotels; public schools; libraries; the Observatory; scientific and literary institutions. Cincinnati, St. Xavier, and Woodward colleges, and Lane seminary, are located in the city, and exhibit the high regard for education which is cherished in the west.

The manufactures of Cincinnati include a great variety of articles of necessity, comfort, and luxury. Nature has supplied no remarkable water privileges; yet enterprise has constructed extensive appliances for the prosecution of manufactures. Several canals, approaching the city from different points, by means of locks and dams, perform the functions of rivers in respect to industry and trade. Cincinnati is the market and emporium of a wide extent of country, exchanging its manufactures for vast numbers of hogs and other agricultural products. This extensive trade is facilitated by the numerous natural and artificial channels of communication from various points. From its position on the Ohio, it commands the commerce of its valley with that of the Mississippi, while Licking river enters the Ohio opposite the city, after meandering 230 miles in Kentucky. Whitewater and Miami rivers, with their navigation improved by extensive canals, largely contribute to the trade and prosperity of the place.

The water-works of Cincinnati consist of a steam engine and reservoirs on the Ohio, which contain 1,600,000 gallons.

From Cleveland and Sandusky city, 60 miles apart, on Lake Erie, two lines of railroad traverse the state, meet at Xenia, and terminate at Cincinnati.

The population in 1800, was 750; in 1810, 2,540; in 1820, 9,644; in 1830; 24,831; in 1840, 46,338; in 1850, 115,436.

COLUMBUS, Ohio.

This pleasant city, the growth of but thirty years, is the capital of the state. It occupies a gentle slope on the east side of Scioto river, 110 miles northeast of Cincinnati, and 363 miles from Washington. A large public square, of 10 acres, in the centre of the city, is formed by the intersection of rectangular streets, and contains the statehouse, an imposing edifice of brick, with a cupola 106 feet above the ground, which displays an interesting view of a wide surface of country. Fronting this square, are also the federal courthouse, and a building for state purposes. The penitentiary is a solid and extensive structure of limestone. There are also asylums for the insane, and for the blind, deaf, and dumb; banks, churches, and numerous other prominent buildings. Columbus owes much of its prosperity to the circumstance of its being the seat of state government; but manufactures and trade are increasing with the facilities of communication. The Columbus Branch canal extends 10 miles, to the Ohio and Erie canal, which traverses the state from Portsmouth, on the Ohio, to Cleveland, on Lake Erie, a distance of 307 miles. The Cincinnati, Cleveland, and Columbus railroad, communicates with this place.

The population in 1820, was 1,400; in 1830, 2,435; in 1840, 6,048; in 1850, 18,183.

CLEVELAND, Ohio.

This enterprising and beautiful city, the emporium of northern Ohio, and with Buffalo, the mart of the great lakes, is finely situated on the south shore of Lake Erie, at the mouth of Cuyahoga river. It is the seat of justice of Cuyahoga county, and is 200 miles east of Columbus, and 359 miles from Washington.

RAILROADS.

From Cincinnati to Cleveland.

To Columbus (as above)		120
Worthington	9	129
Orange	7	136
Berlin	4	140
Delaware	3	143
Eden	4	147
Ashley	4	151
Cardington	7	158
Gilead	5	163
Iberia	7	170
Galion	6	176
Vernon	4	180
Shelby	8	188
Salem	7	195
Greenwich	6	201
New London	7	208
Rochester	6	214
Wellington	5	219
Lagrange	7	226
Grafton	4	230
Columbia	7	237
Olmsted	3	240
Berea	3	243
Rockport	5	248
Cleveland	7	255

Fm Cleveland to Columbus (see above). 135

Fm Cleveland to Cincinnati (see above). 255

From Sandusky to Cincinnati, via Bellefontaine, Springfield, and Dayton.

To Margaretta		
Bellville		15
Lodi	—	—
Republic	—	30
Tiffin	8	38
Oregon	—	—
Carey	—	54
Patterson	14	68
Kenton	10	78
Bell Centre	—	90
Richland	—	—
Huntsville	—	—
Bellefontaine	—	102
West Liberty	8	110
Urbanna	10	120
Tremont	—	—
Springfield	—	134
Enon	7	141
Osborn	7	148
Dayton	10	158
Carrolton	5	163
Miamisburg	6	169
Carlisle	4	173
Post Town	5	178
Middletown	3	181
Trenton	4	185
Busenback's	3	188
Hamilton	5	193
Jones'	5	198
Glendale	5	203
Lockland	4	207
Carthage	1	208
Ludlow	2	210
Spring Grove	1	211
Cummingsville	2	213
Cincinnati	5	218

Fm Sandusky to Dayton (as above)..... 158

From Columbus to Zanesville.

To Black Lick	11	
Pataskala	6	17
Summit	5	22
Union	4	26
Newark	7	33
Clay Lick	5	38
Rockdale	2	40
Black Hand	3	43
Claypool Mill	3	46
Pleasant Valley	3	49
Dillon's Falls	7	56
Zanesville	3	59

The shore of Lake Erie here is a bold bluff, about 80 feet high, upon the level top of which the largest and best part of the city is built. Here the streets are straight and spacious, the buildings neat and pleasant, and an open park, shaded with trees, occupies the centre. Fronting this square, are the courthouse, a church, and other prominent buildings. Hitherto, the rapid growth of Cleveland, has caused it to want that aspect of permanence which is the result of slower increase; but solid stores, hotels, and dwellings, are now rising in every quarter, making it as substantial as it is flourishing. Toward Cuyahoga river, the ground descends steeply, affording a convenient locality for stores, warehouses, and places of business. Here, the plan of the town is less regular and not so attractive. The mouth of the river constitutes the harbor, which is deep, spacious, and accessible. Two piers of solid masonry project 1,200 feet into the lake, and mark the entrance. At the end of one of these piers, stands a lighthouse; another occupies the brow of the hill on the lake. Vessels of the largest class enter the harbor, and proceed some distance up the river, but the Ohio and Erie canal, along the stream and through its bed, is the principal channel of inland navigation. This great canal connects Portsmouth, 307 miles distant, on the Ohio river, with Cleveland, and traverses the rich interior of the state. It meets the Ohio and Pennsylvania canal at Akron, in Summit county, and thus communicates with Pittsburgh and the east. By these channels, and the facilities of intercouse with New York, Canada, and Michigan, which lakes Erie, Ontario, and Huron afford, Cleveland maintains a commerce as varied as it is extensive. Here congregate steamboats and other vessels, from every point on the vast shores of the great lakes, exchanging many foreign articles for the grain and other agricultural products of Ohio. Here, also, terminate the Cleveland and Pittsburgh, and the Cincinnati, Columbus, and Cleveland railroads. The Lake-shore railroad connects it with the Erie at Dunkirk, the Central at Buffalo, and the Southern Michigan at Toledo.

The manufacturing facilities of this city are not equal to its commercial advantages. The only water-power is afforded by the Cuyahoga river and the Ohio canal, which serve to keep several establishments in operation. Such articles as are necessary to supply the demand for domestic manufacture, existing in every flourishing city, are produced by the aid of steam and other mechanical powers.

The population in 1802, was about 200; in 1810, 547; in 1820, 606; in 1830, 1,076; in 1840, 6,071; in 1850, 17,034.

SANDUSKY CITY, Ohio,

An interesting, pleasant, and thriving village, and one of the principal ports of entry on Lake Erie, is finely located on the inner shore of Sandusky bay, 60 miles west of Cleveland, 110 miles north of Columbus, and 414 miles from Washington. Few western towns combine so pleasant a situation with so many sources of prosperity. On a beautiful site, overlooking the whole bay, its entrance, and lake beyond, the harbor, dotted with sails and steamboats, moving in different directions, the town and its environs form a pleasing picture of industry and comfort. A rich quarry of fine limestone, furnishes a foundation for the village and material for its buildings. Of these, a number are conspicuous for beauty and elegance.

Besides the numerous steamboats and other vessels which visit Sandusky city from different points on the lake, it is the terminus of railroads from Cincinnati, Columbus, and intermediate towns.

The population in 1830, was 597; in 1840, 2,000; in 1850, 5,088.

RAILROADS.

From Sandusky to Newark.

To Ladd's	8	
Monroeville	8	16
Pontiac	4	20
Havanna	4	24
Centreville	4	28
New Haven	6	34
Plymouth	2	36
Shelby	9	45
Spring Mill	6	51
Mansfield	5	56
Lexington	9	65
Bellville	5	70
Independence	6	76
Ankenneytown	5	81
Fredericktown	5	86
Mount Vernon	6	92
Hunt's	6	98
Utica	7	105
St. Louisville	4	109
Newtown	3	112
Newark	5	117

From Cleveland to Wellsville, on the Ohio River.

To Newbury	8	
Bedford	6	14
Macedonia	6	20
Hudson	6	26
Earlville	6	32
Ravenna	6	38
Rootstown	10	48
Atwater	2	50
Lima	3	53
Alliance	5	58
Winchester	5	63
Moultrie	3	66
Bayard	3	69
Rochester	1	70
Hanover	5	75
Brush Run	6	81
Salineville	5	86
Steubenville Road	5	91
Hammond's	4	95
Yellow Creek	2	97
Wellsville	2	99

From Cleveland to Pittsburgh, Pa.

To Alliance (see Route from Cleveland to Wellsville)		58
Stanley	8	66
Salem	5	71
Franklin	4	75
Columbiana	6	81
Bull Creek	5	86
Palestine	5	91
Enon	5	96
Darlington	6	102
N. Brighton	10	112
Rochester	3	115
Freedom	2	117
Baden	3	120
Economy	3	123
Shousetown	3	126
Sewickley	2	128
Haysville	2	130
Courtney's	4	134
Pittsburgh	6	140

Fm Cleveland to Erie, Pa.

To Willoughly	19	
Painesville	10	29
Madison	11	40
Ashtabula	15	55
N. Y. State Line	15	70
Erie	25	95

From Dayton to Greenville.

To Higgin's Station	6	
Brookville	7	13
Dodson	2	15
Baltimore	3	18
Gordon	3	21
Arcunum	5	26
Jay's	4	30
Greenville	5	35

ZANESVILLE, Ohio.

Finely situated on the east side of Muskingum river, opposite the mouth of the Licking, and one of the most enterprising and flourishing towns in the interior of the state. It is 54 miles east of Columbus, and 359 miles from Washington. The river is navigable to the falls near the town; and a canal, passing round this obstruction, enables boats to ascend to Coshocton, about 25 miles above, and furnishes a great water-power. A number of dams and locks in the vicinity, serve to keep in operation the various manufactories of woollen, cotton, and other fabrics, which contribute to Zanesville its prosperity and importance, as well as to afford means of communication with the Ohio canal and surrounding points. On the west bank of the Muskingum, are Putnam and West Zanesville, two flourishing villages, intimately connected with the town, not only by two bridges, but also by reciprocal interests and operations.

The population in 1830, was 3,216; in 1840, 4,766 or including the adjacent places, 7,000; in 1850, 10,355.

RAILROADS.

Cincinnati to Hillsboro'.

To Plainville	9	
Milford	5	14
Miamisville	3	17
Loveland	6	23
Spence's Station	6	29
Goshen & Wilmington	3	32
Blanchester	7	39
Westboro'	4	43
Lynchburg	7	50
Hoagland's	6	56
Hillsboro'	4	60

Fm Toledo to Chigago, Ill., via Adrian.

To Sylvania	11	
Knight's	9	20
Blissfield	2	22
Palmyra	6	28
Adrian	5	33
Chicago (see Route from Monroe to Chicago, in Michigan)	211	244

CITY OF DETROIT, MICHIGAN.

DETROIT, Mich.

This commercial and rapidly increasing city, occupies a pleasant and commanding situation, on the west bank of Detroit river, 18 miles from Lake Erie, and 7 miles from Lake St. Clair. Between the two great lakes, Huron and Erie, upon both of which, its vessels carry on an extensive trade, through Lakes Superior and Michigan, and with Canada, Pennsylvania, and New York. It is an important metropolis of the western states, and is destined to a still higher rank than it now holds. The city is agreeably laid out with broad streets, some of which converge at the "Circus," a spacious public ground. Among the other parks, is the "Campus Martius," near the centre of the city. Parallel with the river, at the foot of the eminence upon which the town is built, is a street lined with warehouses and stores. Above this, another street runs in the same direction, and still further to the west, is the principal business street, which is closely built with stores, dwellings, and public buildings. Here, until 1847 when the seat of government was removed to

RAILROADS.

From Detroit to Chicago, Illinois.

To Dearborn	10	
Wayne	7	17
Ypsilanti	12	29
Ann Arbor	8	37
Dexter	10	47
Chelsea	9	56
Grass Lake	9	65
Jackson	11	76
Parma	9	85
Albion	11	96
Marshall	12	108
Battle Creek	12	120
Galensburg	15	135
Kalamazoo	8	143
Pawpaw	17	160
Decatur	8	168
Dowagiac	11	179
Niles	12	191
Buchanan	6	197
New Buffalo	21	218
Michigan City	10	228
Gibson's	32	260
Chicago	21	281

Lansing, stood the statehouse, from the high dome of which appears an enchanting prospect of the river, Lake St. Clair, and their picturesque and romantic shores. Other buildings are the city-hall, bank of Michigan, churches, markets, schools, and various scientific and literary institutions. Several hundred steamboats and other vessels, from various places on the lakes, visit Detroit during the season of navigation, which lasts about two thirds of the year.

The Michigan Central railroad extends 281 miles to Chicago, on Lake Michigan; and the Detroit and Pontiac railroad is 25 miles long.

The population in 1810, was 770; in 1820, 1,422; in 1830, 2,222; in 1840, 9,102; in 1850, 21,057.

LANSING, Mich.

This town, situated on the east side of Grand river, in Ingham county, near the centre of Michigan, succeeded Detroit as the capital of the state, in December, 1847. It is 95 miles northwest of Detroit, and 80 miles east of Lake Michigan. The state and public buildings are projected, and finishing on a scale creditable to this great state.

INDIANAPOLIS, Ia.

In the centre of the state, of which it is the capital, and on the east side of White river, is situated in the midst of a rich and rapidly populating country, 108 miles northwest of Cincinnati, and 573 miles from Washington. Thirty years ago, a dense forest occupied the site of this city. In 1821, it became the seat of the state government, and has since continued to increase in population and prosperity. It is laid out with ingenuity and beauty. A circular street surrounds an open space, with the governor's mansion in the middle. From this diverge several streets, intersecting, diagonally, the others, which are rectangular. Besides a number of churches, mills, and factories, the city contains a splendid statehouse, 180 feet long, 85 wide, and 45 feet high, adorned by Ionic porticoes and columns, and surmounted by a dome. The courthouse is also a conspicuous edifice. White river is here spanned by an elegant bridge. The whole is an interesting specimen of industry, enterprise, and thrift, and bids fair to become one of the principal cities in the west. When high, the river is navigable to this point for steamboats. Indianapolis is connected by railroad with Madison, on the Ohio, 86 miles distant, and railways also extend toward Peru, as well as toward Bellefontaine, in Logan county, Ohio.

The population in 1830, was about 1,200; in 1840, 2,692; in 1850, 8,034.

NEW ALBANY, Ia.

The largest city in the state, is pleasantly located on the north bank of the Ohio, 4 miles below Louisville, and 2 miles below the falls, 121 miles southerly from Indianapolis, and 600 miles from Washington. Like most other favorably-situated western towns, it has more than doubled in population within ten years, and exhibits all the signs of enterprise and prosperity. Here, steamboats and other vesssels are extensively built, and carry on a brisk trade with the valleys of the Ohio and Mississippi.

The population in 1830, was about 1,900; in 1840, 4,226; in 1850, 9,785.

RAILROADS.

Fm Monroe to Chicago, Ill.

To Ida	13	
Petersburg	7	20
Deerfield	4	24
Adrian	12	36
Clayton	11	47
Hudson	6	53
Pittsford	6	59
Osceo	5	64
Hillsdale	5	69
Jonesville	5	74
Quincy	11	85
Cold Water	7	92
Bronson	11	103
Burr Oak	7	110
Sturgis'	5	115
White Pigeon	12	127
Bristol, Ind	10	137
Elkhart	9	146
Mishawakie	11	157
South Bend	4	161
Terre Coupee	11	172
Laporte	16	188
Michigan City	18	206
Bailey Town	13	219
Miller's	5	224
Ainsworth	13	237
Chicago	10	247

RAILROADS.

From Indianapolis to Madison, on the Ohio river, 90 miles below Cincinnati.

To Greenwood	10	
Franklin	10	20
Adams'	5	25
Edinburg	5	30
Taylorsville	5	35
Columbus	6	41
Clifty Switch	7	48
Elizabethtown	7	55
Rock River Station	3	58
Scipio	6	64
Queensville	2	66
Vernon	4	70
Champion's Mill	2	72
Dupont	2	74
North Madison	10	84
Madison	2	86

From Evansville to Terre Haute.

To Mechanicsville.	4	
Sandersville	6	10
Princeton	18	28

Fm Madison to Shelbyvillle.

To Edinburg (see above)	30	
Conover	2	32
Clark's Depot	6	33
Shelbyville	8	46

From New Albany to Juliet.

To Bennettsville	10	
N. Providence	9	19
Pekin	5	24
Hurristown	6	30
Salem	5	35
Buena-Vista	10	45
Orleans	10	55
Juliet	10	65

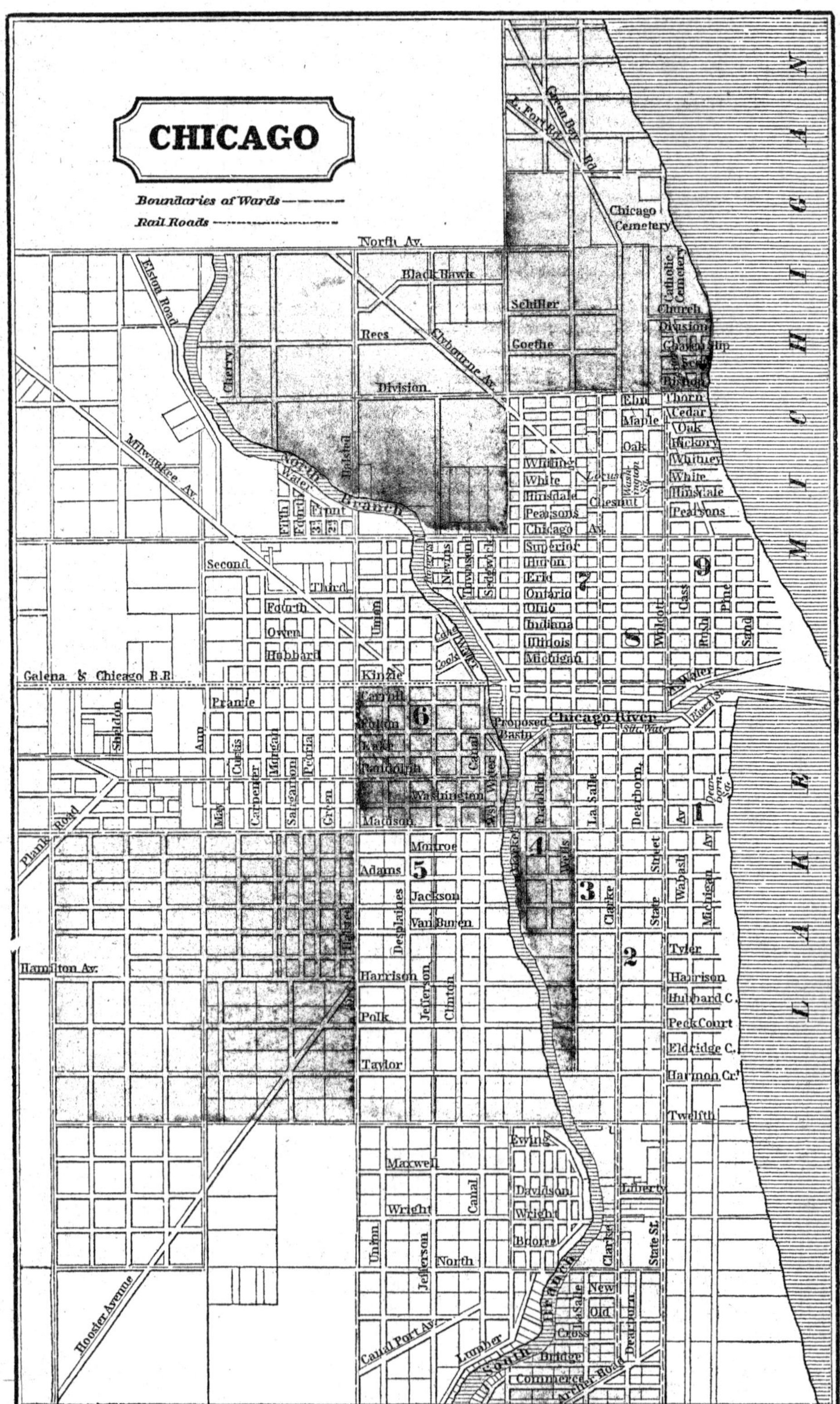

CHICAGO
Boundaries of Wards
Rail Roads
North Av.
Black Hawk
Elston Road
Rees
Clybourne Av.
Division
Cherry
Schiller
Goethe
Green Bay Rd.
Chicago Cemetery
Catholic Cemetery
Church
Division
Milwaukee Av.
North Branch
Halsted
Second
Third
Fourth
Owen
Hubbard
Union
Kinzie
Galena & Chicago R.R.
Prairie
Carroll
Fulton
Lake
Randolph
Washington
Madison
Sheldon
Ann
Curtis
May
Carpenter
Morgan
Sangamon
Peoria
Green
Canal
Water
Proposed Basin
Chicago River
Elm
Maple
Oak
Thorn
Cedar
Oak
Hickory
Whitney
White
Hinsdale
Pearsons
Whiting
White
Hinsdale
Pearsons
Chicago Av.
Superior
Huron
Erie
Ontario
Ohio
Indiana
Illinois
Michigan
Wolcott
Cass
Rush
Pine
Sand
N. Water
Franklin
Wells
La Salle
Dearborn
State Street
Wabash Av
Michigan Av
Monroe
Adams
Jackson
Van Buren
Clarke
Plank Road
Hamilton Av.
Desplaines
Harrison
Jefferson
Clinton
Polk
Taylor
Tyler
Harrison
Hubbard C.
Peck Court
Eldridge C.
Harmon Ct.
Twelfth
Ewing
Maxwell
Davidson
Wright
Canal
Brown
Union
Jefferson
North
Liberty
State St.
Clark St.
New
Old
Cross
Bridge
Commerce
Archer Road
Dearborn
La Salle
Hoosier Avenue
Canal Port Av.
Lumber
South Branch
1
2
3
4
5
6
7
8
9
LAKE MICHIGAN

CITY OF CHICAGO, ILLINOIS.

CHICAGO, Ill.

THE commercial emporium of Lake Michigan, and of the adjacent states, is remarkable for its rapid increase in population, wealth, and enterprise. It occupies both sides of the river, from which it takes its name, and is built on the border of a prairie, elevated a little above the level of the lake. Few towns have a more advantageous position. The river, formed by the confluence of two branches, in the upper part of the city, is deep and spacious enough for a vast number of steamboats and vessels of various kinds, which here assemble from different points on the lakes, the St. Lawrence, the Erie, and Welland canals, and thickly line the wharves for some distance up the streams, which form the harbor. The shore of the lake, naturally shallow, has been extended into deep water, by means of two piers, which, projecting from both sides of the harbor, protect it from the accumulation of sand. The streets of Chicago are generally broad and pleasant, lined with trees, and leading to the open prairie, or affording fine views of the lake. The buildings have the appearance of unusual comfort and convenience, while many of the public edifices are surpassed by those of few cities in the Union. Large warehouses and stores, five or six stories high, splendid hotels, churches, fine public-schools, and dwellings, frequently magnificent, are some of the structures which strike the eye and excite admiration. Twenty years ago, the lands of the adjacent prairie were the property of the Pottawatomie Indians. In 1833, the tribe removed, by treaty, to lands in Missouri, and gave up their prairie to the settlers of Chicago; since then, it has continued to increase, and of late with unexampled rapidity. The Illinois and Michigan canal, by connecting the navigation of the lake with that of the great river of the state, has caused the current of trade, which formerly flowed toward Mississippi river, to turn toward the "garden city," making it the market of the rich productions of Illinois, and of vast quantities of goods from New York and other eastern cities. The branches of commerce in which Chicago is most extensively engaged, are

RAILROADS.

Fm Indianapolis to Terrehaute.

To Bridgeport	9	
Plainfield	5	14
Cartersburg	3	17
North Bellville	2	19
Clayville	2	21
Morristown	4	25
Crittenden	2	27
Coatsville	2	29
Fillmore	4	33
Green Castle	6	39
Hendrick's	5	44
Reel's Mill	4	48
Croy's Creek	4	52
Brazil	5	57
Highland	4	61
Cloverland	2	63
Wood's Mills	2	65
Terrehaute	8	73

Fm Shelbyville to Knightstown.

To Marion	—	—
Hanover	—	—
Morristown	—	—
Carthage	—	—
Knightstown	—	27

From Indianapolis to Bellefontaine, Ohio.

To Delzell's Mill	5	
Laneville	4	9
Oakland	5	14
M'Card's Mill	2	16
Fortville	4	20
Alfort	3	23
Pendleton	5	28
Anderson	8	36
Chesterfield	6	42
Yorktown	6	48
Muncie	6	54
Selma	6	60
Farmland	6	66
Winchester	8	74
Union	9	83

lumber, grain, and cattle. It exceeds all other western cities in the quantity of lumber exported; vast forests of pine and other trees, covering the northern part of Wisconsin, while immense numbers of cattle, from the interior, are here slaughtered and transported eastward, frequently to New York. The canal, which has contributed so largely to the growth of Chicago, is worthy of extended notice. Commencing about 3 miles above the mouth of the river, it traverses the valley of that stream, and of the Des Plaines, and terminates at Peru, the head of steamboat navigation on the Illinois. The whole length is 106 miles, width 60 feet, depth 6 feet. A navigable feeder, four miles long, communicates with Fox river, and the canal descends 20 feet by two locks toward the Illinois. It was begun in 1836, and finished in 1849.

The Galena and Chicago Union railroad, commences at Chicago, and extends to Galena, the head of steamboat navigation on the Mississippi, and the depot of a region rich in lead. The Central road will unite it with Mississippi river near the mouth of the Ohio, while the Southern and Central Michigan roads connect it with the eastern states.

The population in 1840, was 4,479; in 1850, 28,269, in 1852, 38,733.

SPRINGFIED, Ill.

Delightfully located near the central part of Illinois, four miles south of Sangamon river, became the capital of the state, in 1840. It is surrounded by a rich and populous region, picturesquely varied with prairies, forests, vales, and gentle elevations. The village is one of the most pleasant and beautiful in the west, situated on the border of extensive prairie, laid out with broad and shaded streets, interspersed with spacious lawns and squares, and indicating, in its neat and comfortable dwellings, prosperity and vigorous health. It contains a number of fine public-schools, academies, churches, a jail, market-house, court-house, and the statehouse, a costly and elegant structure.

The Sangamon and Morgan railroad extends to Naples on Illinois river, 54 miles distant.

The population in 1840 was 2,579; in 1850, ——.

GALENA, Ill.

This thriving city is situated on both sides of Fevre, or Bean river, six miles above its entrance into the Mississippi, and the largest boats ascend to this point at all stages of the water. The city is mostly built on the west side of the river, yet it is rapidly extending on the opposite side, with which it is connected by three substantial bridges. This is the centre of the great lead region, which occupies the northwestern portion of Illinois, and the southwestern corner of Wisconsin, together with a strip of a few miles in width on the opposite side of the Mississippi in Iowa, equal to a surface of nearly three thousand square miles. In riding over the country from Galena to the Wisconsin river, the most remarkable feature presented is the numerous "diggings." Its trade with the surrounding country is extensive, embracing a circuit of 30 to 100 miles. The town presents a very metallic appearance, inasmuch as its wharves, for quite a distance, are lined with piles of pig-lead. It is estimated by those whose knowledge and experience render them competent to judge, that if the mines already opened were well worked, they are capable of producing 150,000,000 pounds annually for ages to come.

The population in 1850, was 8,510.

RAILROADS.

From Shelbyville to Rushville 20

From Lafayette to Indianapolis.

To Baker's Corner.	14	
Midway	3	17
Clarksville........	5	22
Thornton	5	27
Lebanon..........	10	37
Indianapolis		62

From Indianapolis to Noblesville 22

ILLINOIS.

RAILROADS.

Fm Springfield to Naples.

To Schuyler.......	9	
Prairie Farm.......	4	13
Berlin	3	16
Island Grove......	3	19
Franklin..........	6	25
Jacksonville.......	8	33
Jones' Switch.....	6	39
Morgan City.......	6	45
Van Grundy's.....	5	50
Naples............	4	54

From Chicago to Galena.

To Desplaines.....	10	
Cottage Hill.......	6	16
Babcock's	4	20
Danby	—	—
Wheaton	—	25
Aurora Junction...	5	30
Wayne	3	33
Climon	5	38
Elgin..............	4	42
Gilbert's...........	8	50
Huntley's..........	5	55
Union	7	62
Marengo	4	66
Garden Prairie....	6	72
Belvidere..........	6	78
Cherry Valley.....	7	85
Rockford	7	92
By Stage.		
Vanceburg	16	108
Freeport...........	20	128
Wadham's Grove..	17	145
Galena	25	170

From Chicago to Monroe, Mich.

To Ainsworth......	11	
Miller's............	13	24
Bailey Town......	13	37
Michigan City.....	13	50
Laporte	10	60
Terre Coupee......	14	74
South Bend........	12	86
Mishawakie	4	90
Elkhart	11	101
Bristol.............	9	110
White Pigeon	10	120
Sturgis	12	132
Burr Oak..........	6	138
Bronson	7	145
Cold Water.........	11	156
Quincy	6	162
Jonesville	11	173
Hillsdale	6	179
Osceo	4	183
Pittsford...........	5	188
Hudson............	7	195
Clayton............	5	200
Adrian	12	212
Deerfield	12	224
Petersburg	4	228
Ida	7	235
Monroe............	13	248

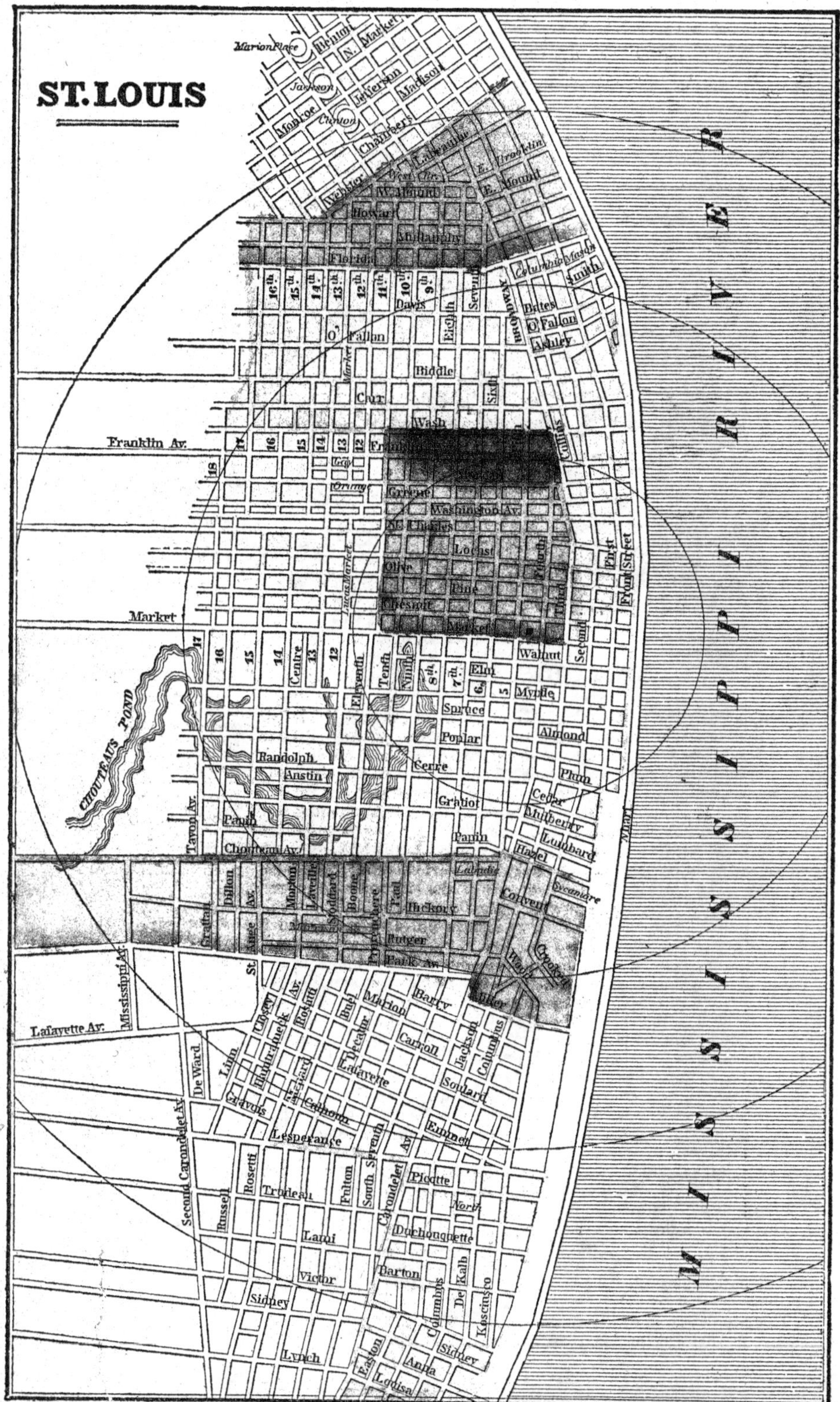
ST. LOUIS
MISSISSIPPI RIVER
CHOUTEAU'S POND
Marion Place
Jackson
Clinton
Monroe
Jefferson
Madison
N. Market
Chambers
Webster
Lafayette
Franklin
E. Mound
W. Mound
Howard
Florida
Davis
O'Fallon
Biddle
Carr
Wash
Franklin Av.
Greene
Washington Av.
St. Charles
Locust
Olive
Pine
Chesnut
Market
Walnut
Elm
Myrtle
Spruce
Almond
Poplar
Randolph
Austin
Cerre
Plum
Gratiot
Cedar
Mulberry
Lombard
Hazel
Convent
Rutger
Park Av.
Barry
Miller
Marion
Carroll
Lafayette
Soulard
Emmet
Calhoun
Lesperance
Picotte
Trudeau
North
Duchouquette
Lami
Barton
Victor
Sidney
Lynch
Anna
Louisa
Chouteau Av.
Tayon Av.
Mississippi Av.
Lafayette Av.
Second Carondelet Av.
De Ward
Russell
Rosetti
Fulton
South Seventh
Carondelet Av.
Columbus
De Kalb
Kosciusco
Jackson
Decatur
Buel
Rosatti
Linn
Gravois
Grattan
Dillon
St. Ange Av.
Morton
Laveille
Stoddard
Boone
Tenth
Ninth
Eleventh
Centre
Hickory
Second
First
Front Street
Third
Fourth
Collins
Sixth
Seventh
Eighth
Broadway
Bates
Ashley
Smith
Columbia
Mason

CITY OF ST. LOUIS.

ST. LOUIS, Mo.,

Is situated on the west bank of Mississippi river, 20 miles below the junction of the Missouri, 180 miles above the Ohio, 1,150 miles from New Orleans, and 856 miles from Washington. It is built upon two elevations, the lower 20 feet above the river, and the higher 60 feet. The terrace, as it may be styled, next the water, affords room for several business streets, some of which are lined with rows of spacious and imposing warehouses. Above, are many fine sites for residence and for public buildings, churches, asylums, schools, banks, and various other prominent edifices. The thickly-peopled part of the city extends several miles along the river, and about a mile westward. The whole area is much larger, including 36 square miles or more, and is filling up with unexampled rapidity.

The commercial position and advantages are remarkable, as its growing prosperity conclusively testifies. Few towns on the Mississippi have so favorable a position with respect to that river, while it is the entrepot of a vast trade from the valleys of Ohio and Missouri rivers. It is thus identified in progress with an extensive section of the West, to which it holds an important relation. The surrounding land is fertile, populous, and well-cultivated, and of course contributes largely to the maintenance and trade of the city. The harbor is sufficient for steamboats of the largest class, many hundred of which stop at this point every year.

The manufactures of St. Louis are also extensive and varied, embracing articles of different descriptions, to the amount of many hundred thousand dollars.

The city is lighted with gas, and supplied with water from the river, elevated into reservoirs by steam-engines, and thence distributed by iron-pipes. It is the seat of St. Louis university, and contains other scientific and literary institutions of different grades.

The population in 1810, was 1,600; in 1820, 4,598; in 1830, 5,852; in 1840 16,469; in 1850, 82,744.

STAGE-ROUTES.

From Jefferson City to Independence, via Boonville.

To Marion	17	
Moniteau	6	23
Clark's Fork	15	38
Boonville	12	50
Lamine	10	60
Arrow Rock	13	73
Bryan	8	81
Marshall	8	89
Grand Pass	17	106
Mount Hope	12	118
Dover	8	126
Lexington	12	138
Wellington	14	152
Fort Osage	15	167
Independence	12	179

From Jefferson City to Boonville....... 50

From Jefferson City to Lexington....... 138

From Jefferson City to Santa Fe, New Mexico.

To Independence (as above)		179
Round Grove	37	216
Narrows	33	249
Bridge Creek	8	257
Council Grove	44	301
Diamond Spring	17	318
Cottonwood Creek	15	333
Little Arkansas R.	42	375
Arkansas River	20	395
Arkansas Creek, up the Arkansas R.	25	420
Corn Creek	46	466
Ford of Arkansas	56	522
Willow Bar	110	632
Cold Spring	25	657
Round Mound	[illegible]	712
Point of Rocks	[illegible]	740
Rio Colorado	22	762
Rio Mora	[illegible]3	815
San Miguel	45	860
Pecros Village	25	885
Santa Fe	25	910

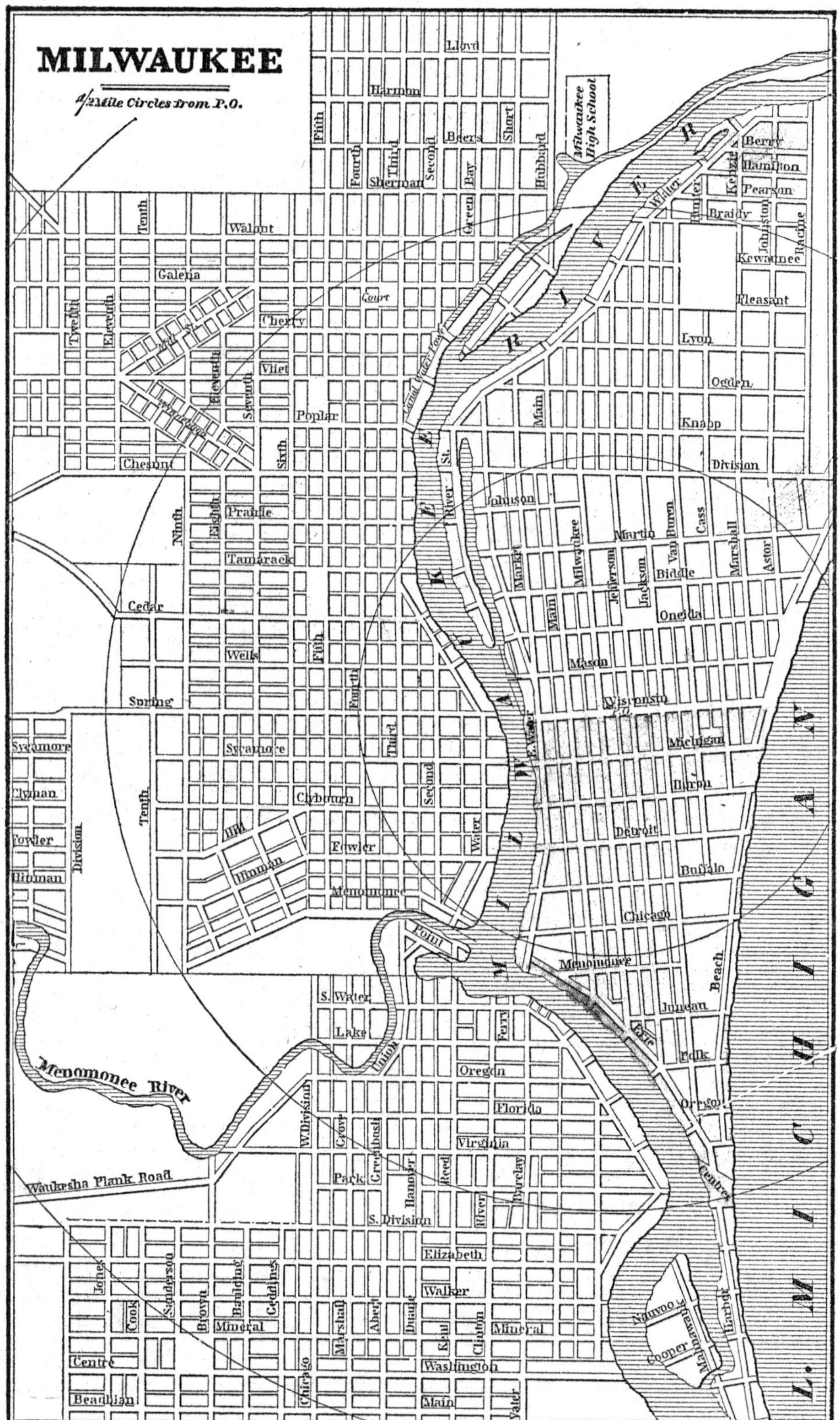
MILWAUKEE
1/2 Mile Circles from P.O.
Milwaukee High School
Menomonee River
Waukesha Plank Road
L. MICHIGAN

JEFFERSON CITY, Mo.

THE capital of the state, is situated near the central part of the state, on the south bank of the Missouri, nine miles from the mouth of Osage river, 134 miles west of St. Louis, and 936 miles from Washington. Its site is elevated, and it contains the statehouse, governor's mansion, penitentiary, and other public buildings, and is gradually and substantially rising in wealth and intelligence.

The population in 1830, was 1,200; in 1840, 1,174; in 1850, 3,721.

BURLINGTON, Iowa,

FORMERLY the capital, and the largest town in the state, and the seat of justice of Des Moines county, occupies a pleasant slope on the west bank of the Mississippi, 75 miles southeast of Iowa city, 248 miles north of St. Louis, 1,429 miles north of New Orleans, and 871 miles from Washington. Pleasant hills and woody slopes rise behind the city, and enhance the effect of its other advantages. It is the centre of an active, extended, and increasing commerce, with the rich interior of the state, together with that of Illinois, and the valley of the Mississippi. Possessing a combination of so many favorable circumstances, it has already received a vigorous impulse, and will undoubtedly advance with accelerated growth. Its broad and delightful streets, either along the water, or on higher ground, are admirably suited for business, as well as for residence, and the number of public buildings, elegant stores, and dwellings, is already large, and receives almost daily accessions. A steam-ferry connects the town with the opposite side of the river.

The population in 1840, was 1,300; in 1850, 5 102.

IOWA CITY, Iowa.

THIS delightful and thriving town is situated on the east bank of Iowa river, about 50 miles from its entrance into the Mississippi, and 75 miles northwest of Burlington. It is the capital of Iowa, and, for romantic and agreeable scenery, as well as in some measure for commercial advantages, it is eminently worthy to be the seat of government of so flourishing a state. It is built on successive elevations, rising, like terraces, one above the other. The ground, near the river, is level and open. Above and beyond, upon two heights, run broad and beautiful avenues, and, at right angles to this, is "Iowa avenue," a magnificent street, at the head of which stands the statehouse, a splendid edifice of richly-variegated stone, called "bird's eye marble." It is in the Grecian-Doric architecture, 60 feet wide, and 100 feet long, surmounted by a beautiful dome. There are churches, schools, stores, and all the accompaniments of civilization and prosperity in the west. The river is navigable to Iowa city for steamboats and vessels of ordinary draught, and navigation will doubtless be speedily improved by canals and other channels of intercommunication.

The population in 1840, was 800; in 1850, 2,308.

MILWAUKIE, Wis.

THE chief city of Wisconsin, and, next to Chicago, the largest on Lake Michigan, is finely located for commerce, on both sides of Milwaukie river, at its entrance into the lake, 90 miles north of Chicago, 90 miles east of Madison, and 805 miles from Washington. It is the market of a large part of the productions of the state. Steamboats and other vessels, navigating Lake Michigan, touch here, on their way to and from Detroit and points on Lake Erie, and the St. Lawrence, Erie, and Welland canals. The surrounding region is rich, and rapidly increasing in an industrious and enterprising population, of whiich Milwaukie is the nucleus and the centre of trade. This city is remarkable for the peculiarly bright straw-color and excellent quality of its bricks, for which the rich clay-beds along the lake afford abundant material. Besides the large quantities of these which are exported, they are used for the majority of the buildings, some of which, in large and uniform rows of dwellings or stores, present a beautiful and splendid effect. Here are churches, a jail, courthouse, and other prominent edifices.

The Milwaukie and Mississippi railroad is completed to Palmyra, 43 miles westward.

The population in 1840, was 1,700; in 1850, 20,026.

MADISON, Wis.

The capital of the state, occupies a delightful position on a strip of land between "Third" and "Fourth" lakes, two of a chain of four beautiful sheets of water, not far apart, and connected by streams. It is 90 miles west of Milwaukie, and 847 miles from Washington. From the former lake, the shore rises abruptly 50 feet, and, gradually, 20 feet higher. Upon this elevation

STAGE-ROUTES.

From Jefferson City to St. Louis.

To Lisle	10	
Linn	8	18
Union	52	70
Port William	9	79
Manchester	24	103
St. Louis	20	123

STAGE-ROUTES.

Burlington to Iowa City.

To Dodgeville	18	
Florence	7	25
Wapello	7	32
Harrison	4	36
Grandview	7	43
Bloomington	12	55
Overman's Ferry	10	65
West Liberty	12	77
Iowa City	12	89

From Davenport to Dubuque.

To De Witt	20	
Andrew	28	48
Dubuque	27	75

From Burlington to Waterloo, Mo.

To Augusta	10	
Fort Madison	12	22
Montrose	12	34
St. Francisville	13	47
Waterloo	6	53

From Iowa City to Knoxville.

To Mills	23	
Sigourney	27	50
Rose Hill	15	65
Oskaloosa	7	72
Knoxville	28	100

Fm Iowa City to Dubuque.

To Cedar River	18	
Tipton	11	29
Walnut Fork	15	44
Edinburg	12	56
Dubuque	44	100

RAILROADS.

Fm Milwaukie to Palmyra.

To Wauwatosa	5	
Elm Grove	5	10
Power's Mill	4	14
Forest House	3	17
Waukesha	3	20
Genesee	8	28
North Prairie	3	31
Palestine	2	33
Eagle Prairie	3	36
Palmyra	7	43

To be continued to Madison.

STAGE-ROUTES.

From Milwaukie to Janesville.

To Greenfield	8	
New Berlin	4	12
Vernon	6	18
Mukwonago	6	24
East Troy	10	34
Troy	3	37
Richmond	14	51
Janesville	18	69

stands the statehouse, a prominent structure of stone, in the centre of a large park, which overlooks an enchanting panorama of lakes, lawns, groves, hills, vales, and winding streams. Toward Fourth lake, the ground again descends with different degrees of steepness, the whole distance from one shore to the other being about three fourths of a mile. The University of Wisconsin is delightfully situated upon an eminence, 125 feet above the lakes. The beauty and healthfulness of location, central position, business, and political advantages of Madison, are elements of permanent prosperity, if not of rapid progress, and it bids fair to become one of the largest towns in the state.

The population in 1840, was 376; in 1850, 1,871.

SAN FRANCISCO, Cal.

THE "Empire City" of the Pacific, is situated just within the entrance of San Francisco bay, and, for growing importance, commercial advantages, and the enterprise of its citizens, deserves the rank of one of the great cities of the Union. The bay is safe and commodious, being capable of holding the combined navies of the world. Although this city has been repeatedly destroyed by fire, it has each time risen, phœnix-like, from its own ashes, with new beauty and with greater splendor than before. It contains a large number of elegant brick fire-proof stores and banking-houses, and the streets are paved with heavy timbers and planks, which will soon give place to more durable materials. There are several daily lines of steamers to Sacramento, Marysville, Stockton, San Joaquin city, and other points on the rivers, and in the northern and southern mines; while ocean-steamers ply from San Francisco to Panama and San Juan del Sur, the port of Nicaragua. Vessels from the Atlantic coast, and all parts of the world, constantly arrive or depart.

The population, in 1852, was estimated at 30,000.

SACRAMENTO CITY, Cal.

IN Sacramento county, 125 miles from San Francisco, on the east bank of Sacramento river, is the second city in point of location and importance in California. It is the principal depot for the greater part of the northern mining district. This city is destined to be of great importance, as it is the highest point to which steamers and other vessels can ascend at low water. A good and substantial levee has been constructed around the city, to protect it from the overflow of the river, during the annual and occasional freshets. The city is rapidly increasing, and must become a large commercial town, from the fact of its being a central point in the northern section of the state.

The population in 1850, was 8,000.

ST. PAUL'S, Minnesota.

THIS new town is remarkable for being the capital of Minnesota. It occupies a plateau, at the head of the bold bank of the Mississippi, on its north side, eight miles below the Falls of St. Anthony, the head of navigation. The central position of the town is level, terminating on the bluff, 80 feet high, which recedes from the river at the upper and lower end of the village, forming two landings. Though yet in embryo, it bids fair to become an important point on the westward stream of civilization. In 1850, its population was 1,135.

OREGON CITY, Oregon.

THIS is the principal settlement in the territory, and from its favorable position in the fertile valley of Willamette, or Muttonah river, 30 miles from its entrance into the Columbia, will probably become the business and political metropolis of the territory. It is in latitude 45° 20′ north, and longitude 45° 45′ west of Washington, at the head of navigation, below the falls of the Willamette, which furnish a most valuable water-power. From Fort Vancouver, on the Columbia, it is 20 miles south; from Astoria, 100 miles southeast; and 2,171 miles northwest of Independence, on Missouri river, which is 1,072 miles west of Washington. Most of the settlers are Americans, and the swift tide of migration toward California, has contributed considerably to its growth. There are a number of stores, dwellings, mills, schools, &c., which are receiving accessions. The population, in 1848, was from 200 to 300; in 1850, 702.

SANTA FE, New Mexico.

THIS commercial town, the capital of New Mexico, is situated east of the Rio del Norte, about 600 miles from the Gulf of Mexico. It has long been an important rendezvous of traders from the United States and Mexico. Between 1834 and 1841, the annual value of the trade passing through this place, was from $2,000,000 to $3,000,000. The hostilities between the United States and Mexico checked this prosperity, but the annexation of New Mexico, and the rapid settlement of California, are sources of permanent advantage, of which the influence has been already felt. The annoyances from hostile Indians, to which traders have always been more or less exposed, are the principal obstacles to its rapid increase.

The population in 1840, was about 6,000; in 1850, 7,713.

STAGE-ROUTES.

From Madison to Galena, Illinois.

To Cross Plains	12	
Blue Mound	13	25
Ridgeway	10	35
Messersburg	5	40
Dodgeville	3	43
Mineral Point	8	51
Belmont	14	65
Plattville	4	69
Hazel Green	16	85
Galena	9	94

Fm Galena, Ill., to Prairie Du Chien.

To Fairplay	11	
Dickeysville	8	19
Potosi	4	23
Beetown	14	37
Patch Grove	13	50
Brooklyn	7	57
Prairie Du Chien	10	67

CALIFORNIA.

BY STEAMBOAT.

From San Francisco to Sacramento City.

To Benicia	40	
New York	25	65
Sutterville	58	123
Sacramento City	2	125

Fm San Francisco to Butler City.

To Sacramento (as above)		125
Springfield	17	142
Fremont	2	144
Buteville	75	219
Colusi	3	222
Tehama	6	228
Butler City	5	233

From San Francisco to Stockton.

To Benicia	40	
New York	25	65
Mouth of the Mokelumne	24	89
Mokelumne	3	92
Middle Channel	8	100
Lone Tree	24	124
Stockton	8	132

From San Francisco to Sonora.

To New York	65	
Middle Channel	41	106
Doak's Ferry	3	109
San Joaquin City	23	132
Belcher's Ferry	7	139
Tuolumne River	4	143
Grayson	7	150
Tuolumne City	5	155
Islip's	6	161
Knight's	12	173
Sonora	65	238

From San Francisco to Panama.

To Monterey	104	
Cape St. Lucas	1225	1329
Mazatlan	200	1529
Acapulco	620	2140
Panama	2280	4420

From San Francisco to Astoria, Oregon.

To Humboldt Bay	225	
Cape Blanco	190	445
Astoria	240	655

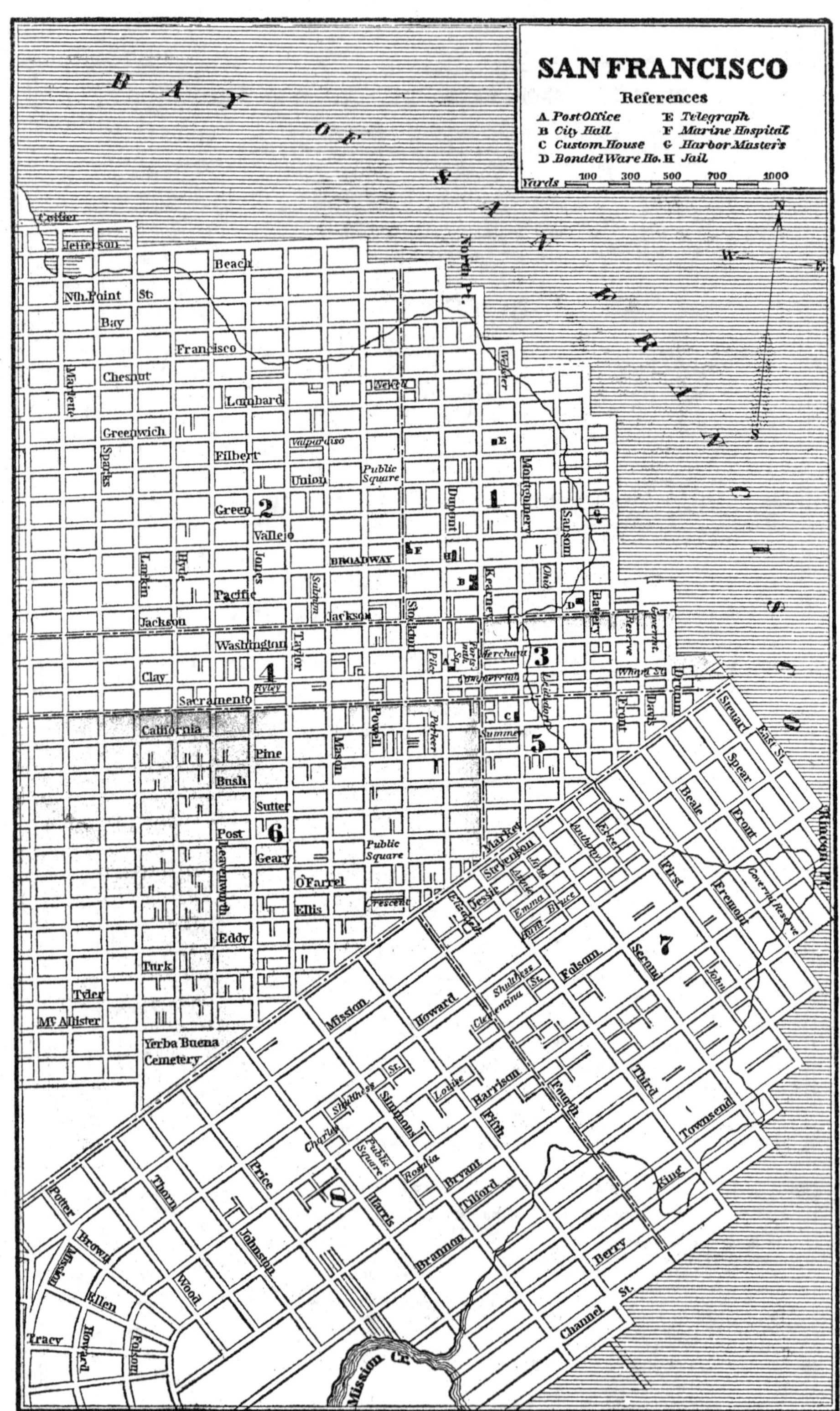
SAN FRANCISCO
References
A. Post Office
B. City Hall
C. Custom House
D. Bonded Ware Ho.
E. Telegraph
F. Marine Hospital
G. Harbor Master's
H. Jail
Yards 100 300 500 700 1000
BAY OF SAN FRANCISCO
N
W
E
S
Jefferson
Beach
Nth. Point St.
Bay
Francisco
Chesnut
Lombard
Greenwich
Filbert
Union
Green
Vallejo
Broadway
Pacific
Jackson
Washington
Clay
Sacramento
California
Pine
Bush
Sutter
Post
Geary
O'Farrel
Ellis
Eddy
Turk
Tyler
Mc. Allister
Yerba Buena Cemetery
Sparks
Larkin
Hyde
Jones
Leavenworth
Taylor
Mason
Powell
Stockton
Dupont
Kearney
Montgomery
Sansom
Battery
Front
Davis
Drumm
Public Square
North P.
Market
Stevenson
Jessie
Mission
Howard
Folsom
Harrison
Bryant
Brannon
Townsend
King
Berry
Channel St.
Steuart
Spear
Beale
Fremont
First
Second
Third
Fourth
Fifth
Simmons
Harris
Price
Thorn
Johnston
Wood
Potter
Brown
Ellen
Tracy
Tilford
Mission Cr.
Rincon Pt.
1
2
3
4
5
6
7
8

PLACES & DISTANCES ON THE WESTERN RIVERS.

MISSISSIPPI RIVER,

From the Falls of St. Anthony to the Gulf of Mexico, with the distance from place to place. Those on the east side of the river, have a star (*) after the State.*

NAMES OF PLACES.	States.	Miles.	Miles.
To Horse Shoe C.	Mi.	4	
Ft Snelling, Mendota and Mouth of St. Peter's R.	Mi.	4	8
Carver's Cave	Mi.*	2	10
St. Paul's	Mi.*	3	13
Point Douglass & Mouth of Saint Croix River	Mi.	27	40
Head of L. Pepin	Mi.	22	62
Maiden's Rock	Mi.	12	74
Foot of Lake Pepin & Mouth of Chippewa R.	Mi.	15	89
Nelson's	Wn*	—	—
Holme's Landing	Wn*	40	129
Mouth of Black R.	Wn*	35	164
Prairie La Crosse	Wn*	11	175
Iowa State Line	Io.	35	210
Lansing	Io.	18	228
Lynxville	Wn*	8	236
Prairie du Chien	Wn*	16	252
Fort Crawford	Wn*	1	253
Wisconsin River	Wn*	2	255
Clayton City	Io.	9	264
Mendota	Wn*	10	274
Cassville	Wn*	8	282
Buena Vista	Io.	6	288
Osceola	Wn*	15	303
Dubuque	Io.	10	313
Fever R. (*Galena* is six miles from its mouth)	Ill.*	20	333
Bellevue	Io.	8	341
Portsmouth	Ill.*	11	352
Savannah	Ill.*	5	357
Charleston	Io.	2	359
Sabula	Io.	3	362
Bluffville	Ill.*	7	369
Fulton / Lyons	Ill.* / Io.	5	374
Albany	Ill.*	8	382
Camanche	Io.	1	383
Seclaire	Io.	18	401
Hampton	Ill.*	12	413
Davenport & Rock Island	Io. / Ill.*	12	425
Andalusia	Ill.*	11	436
Fairport	Io.	8	444
Muscatine City	Ill.*	8	452
New Boston / Mouth of Iowa R	Ill.* / Io.	23	475
Kiethsburg	Ill.*	5	480
Huron	Io.	6	486
Benton	Ill.*	3	489
Oquawka	Ill.*	6	495
Burlington	Io.	18	513
Dallas	Ill.*	5	518
Fort Madison	Io.	10	528
Nauvoo	Ill.*	7	535
Montrose	Io.	1	536
Montabello	Ill.*	2	538
Keokuk	Io.	8	546
Warsaw & Desmoine River	Io.	1	547
Alexandria	Mo.	4	551
Hazleton	Mo.	6	557
Tully	Mo.	11	568
Lagrange	Mo.	5	573
Quincy	Ill.*	12	585
Boonville	Ill.*	18	603
Hannibal	Mo.	6	609
Louisiana	Mo.	25	634
Clarksville	Mo.	12	646
Hamburg	Ill.*	14	660
Gilead	Ill.*	12	672
Milan	Ill.*	27	699
Illinois River	Ill.*	5	704
Grafton	Ill.*	2	706
Randolph	Ill.*	9	715
Alton	Ill.*	9	724
Missouri River	Mo.	3	727
Chippeway	Ill.*	4	731
Madison	Ill.*	2	733
St. Louis	Mo.	12	745
Jefferson Barracks	Mo.	10	755
Oakville	Mo.	5	760
Sulphur Spring	Mo.	7	767
Harrisonville	Ill.*	10	777
Herculaneum	Mo.	2	779
Selma	Mo.	4	783
St. Genevieve	Mo.	28	811
Chester	Ill.*	16	827
Wittenberg	Mo.	20	847
Bainbridge	Mo.	25	872
Cape Girardeau	Mo.	14	886
Commerce	Mo.	12	898
Cairo (M. Ohio R.)	Ill.*	30	928
Columbus	K .*	17	945
Hickman	Ky.*	16	961
Obionville	Te.*	28	989
New Madrid	Mo.	14	1003
Little Prairie	Mo.	32	1035
Obion River	Te.*	30	1065
Ashport	Te.*	8	1073
Fulton	Te.*	11	1084
Randolph	Te.*	10	1094
Greenock	Ark.	32	1126
Memphis	Te.*	36	1162
Commerce	Mis*	25	1187
Peyton	Mis*	35	1222
Sterling	Ark.	10	1232
Helena	Ark.	12	1244
Delta	Mis*	8	1252
Victoria	Mis*	72	1324
Montgomery	Ark.	1	1325
Bolivia	Mis*	15	1340
Napoleon (Mouth of Arkansas R.	Ark.	8	1348
Columbia	Ark.	50	1398
Villemont	Ark.	5	1403
Princeton	Mis*	40	1443
Providence	La.	30	1473
Yazoo River	Mis*	62	1535
Vicksburg	Mis*	14	1549
Warrenton	Mis*	8	1557
Palmyra	Mis*	18	1575
Carthage	La.	1	1576
Point Pleasant	La.	14	1590
Grand Gulf	Mis*	14	1604
Bruinsburg	Mis*	12	1616
St. Joseph	La.	8	1624
Rodney	Mis*	4	1628
Vidalia	La.	30	1658
Natchez	Mis*	1	1659
Homochitto River	Mis*	40	1699
Fort Adams	Mis*	11	1710
Upper Mouth of Red River	La.	12	1722
St. Francisville	La.*	58	1780
Point Coupee	La.	1	1781
Port Hudson	La.*	12	1793
Baton Rouge	La.*	28	1821
Manshac & Iberville River	La.*	16	1837
Plaquemine	La.	9	1846
New Hampton	La.*	22	1868
Donaldsonville	La.*	13	1881
Jefferson College	La.*	21	1902
Red Church	La.*	40	1942
Carrolton	La.*	20	1962
Lafayette	La.*	4	1966
New Orleans	La.*	2	1968
Fort St. Leon	La.	20	1988
Woodville	La.*	14	2002
Fort St. Philip	La.*	44	2046
Fort Jackson	La.*	6	2052
Gulf of Mexico	La.	40	2092

OHIO RIVER,

From Pittsburgh to Cairo and New Orleans. Those having a star (*) attached are on the southerly side of the river.

NAMES OF PLACES.	States.	Miles.	Miles.
Middletown	Pa.*	10	
Economy	Pa.	10	20
Beaver	Pa.	8	28
Georgetown	Pa.*	10	33
Liverpool	O.	5	43
Wellsville	O.	5	48
Elliottsville	O.	12	60
Wintersville	O.	12	72
Steubenville	O.	3	75
Wellsburg	Va.*	8	83
Warrenton	Va.*	8	91
Wheeling	Va.*	10	101
Bridgeport	O.	—	—
Bellaire	O.	5	106
Elizabethtown	Va.*	6	112
Archville	Va.*	4	116
New Martinsville	Va.*	23	139
Sistersville	Va.*	12	151
Newport	O.	24	175
Marietta (Mouth of Muskingum river)	O.	18	193
Belpre	O.	12	205
Parkersburg	Va.*	1	206
Blannerhassett's Is	O.	2	208
Centre	O.	5	213
Hockhocking	O.	4	217
Belleville	Va.*	13	230
Letartville	O.	28	258
Nyesville	O.	7	265
Pomeroy	O.	1	266
Cheshire	O.	10	276
Point Pleasant (Mouth of the Gt. Kanawha).	Va.*	10	286
Gallipolis	O.	4	290
Great Bottom	Va.*	18	308
Guyandotte	Va.*	19	327
Burlington	O.	6	333
Catletsburg	Va.*	4	337
Coal Grove	O.	10	347
Hanging Rock	O.	10	357
Greenupsburg	Ky.*	5	362
Little Sciota River	O.	15	377
Portsmouth & Mouth of Scioto River	O.	6	383
Alexandria	O.	2	385
Bradford	O.	3	388
Rockville	O.	10	398
Vanceburg	Ky.*	5	403
Rome	O.	6	409
Concord	Ky.*	6	415

* The Falls of St. Anthony are 800 miles below the source of the Mississippi.

NAMES OF PLACES.	States.	Miles.	Miles.
Manchester	O.	6	421
Aberdeen	O.	13	434
Maysville	Ky.*	—	—
Ripley	O.	11	445
Lavanna	O.	2	447
Higginsport	O.	5	452
Augusta	Ky.*	3	455
Chilo	O.	7	462
Neville	O.	4	466
Moscow	O.	4	470
Point Pleasant	O.	4	474
Flag Spring	Ky.*	1	475
Carthage	Ky.*	3	478
New Richmond	O.	1	479
Little Miami River	O.	10	489
Columbia	O.	2	491
Newport	Ky.*	3	494
Cincinnati	O.	1	495
Covington	Ky.*	1	496
Warsaw	Ky.*	8	504
North Bend	O.	8	512
Great Miami River	O.	5	517
Lawrenceburg	Ia.*	1	518
Aurora	Ia.*	5	523
Rising Sun	Ia.*	10	533
Patriot	Ia.	14	547
Warsaw	Ky.*	12	559
Ghent	Ia.	4	563
Vevay	Ia.	10	573
Port William & Mouth of Kentucky River	Ky.*	11	584
Madison	Ia.	12	596
New London	Ia.	10	606
Bethlehem	Ia.	4	610
Westport	Ky.*	16	626
Utica	Ia.	18	644
Jeffersonville	Ia.	9	653
Louisville	Ky.*	1	654
Shippingsport	Ky.*	2	656
New Albany	Ia.	1	657
Portland	Ky.*	—	—
Baird's Town	Ia.	12	669
Westpoint	Ky.*	8	677
Bradensburg	Ky.*	18	695
Muckport	Ia.	4	699
Northampton	Ia.	8	707
Amsterdam	Ia.	4	711
Leavenworth	Ia.	7	718
Fredonia	Ia.	4	722
Alton	Ia.	10	732
Concordia	Ky.*	12	744
Stevensport	Ky.*	10	754
Rome	Ia.	1	755
Cloversport	Ky.*	12	767
Hawleyville	Ky.*	8	775
Troy	Ia.	12	787
Rockport	Ia.	20	807
Owensboro'	Ky.*	10	817
Enterprise	Ia.	5	822
Newburg	Ia.	12	834
Green River	Ky.*	7	841
Evansville	Ia.	9	850
Hendersonville	Ky.*	10	860
Mount Vernon	Ia.	26	886
Carthage	Ky.*	13	899
Uniontown	Ky.*	2	901
Wabash River	Ky.*	6	907
Raleigh	Ky.*	6	913
Shawneetown	Ill.	4	917
Cave-in-Rock	Ill.	22	939
Elizabethtown	Ill.	8	947
Golconda	Ill.	14	961
Smithland, Mouth of Cumberland River	Ky.*	16	977
Paducah, Mouth of Tennessee River	Ky.*	16	993
Metropolis	Ill.	8	1001
Napoleon	Ill.	10	1011
Caledonia	Ill.	15	1026
Trinity	Ill.	8	1034
Cairo, Ill., and Mouth of Ohio River	Ill.	5	1039

From Cincinnati to Cairo.. 543
Fm Cincinnati to Louisville 158
From Louisville to Cairo.. 383

MISSOURI RIVER.

From St. Louis to Independence and Council Bluffs.

NAMES OF PLACES.	Miles.	Miles.
Mouth of Missouri River		18
Jamestown	8	26
St. Charles	16	42
Missouritan	20	62
Marthasville	20	82
Newport	8	90
Griswold City	9	99
Hermann	14	113
Portland	20	133
Hibernia	28	161
Jefferson City	2	163
Marion	16	179
Moniteau	6	185
Nashville	3	188
Rockport	14	202
Booneville	11	213
Franklin	—	—
Glasgow	14	227
Chariton	3	230
Brunswick	18	248
Grand River	1	249
De Witt	3	252
Miami	15	267
Lexington	48	315
Wellington	10	325
Camden	30	355
Napoleon	14	369
Fort Osage*	10	379
Randolph	35	414
Kanzas River	16	430
Parksville	16	446
Platte River	2	448
Fort Leavenworth	25	473
Weston	10	483
St. Joseph	63	546
Nodaway River	18	564
Lower Nemaha River	20	584
Upper Nemaha River	44	628
Platte River	75	703
Bellevue Trading-house	18	721
Boyer's River	33	754
Council Bluffs	12	766

* To Independence 12 miles.

ILLINOIS RIVER.

From Peru, head of steamboat navigation, to St. Louis.

Names of Places	Miles.	Miles.
To Hennipin	17	
West Hennipin	2	19
Webster	9	28
Lacon	7	35
Chillicothe	12	47
Rome	2	49
Detroit	12	61
Peoria	5	66
Wesley City	4	70
Pekin	5	75
Duncan	14	89
Liverpool	11	100
Havanna	8	108
Schuyler City	26	134
Beardstown	6	140
Lagrange	8	148
Meredosia	9	157
Naples	8	165
Portland	6	171
Florence	3	174
Montezuma	4	178
New Bedford & Bridgeport	6	184
Newport	10	194
Guilford	20	214
Mouth of Illinois River.	17	231
On the Mississippi River.		
Grafton	2	233
Randolph	9	242
Alton	9	251
Missouri River	3	254
Chippeway	4	258
St. Louis	14	272

WABASH RIVER.

From Lafayette to its entrance into the Ohio, 10 miles above Shawneetown.

NAMES OF PLACES.	Miles.	Miles.
To Cincinnatus	4	
Lagrange	9	13
Independence	3	16
Williamsport	12	28
Portland	5	33
Baltimore	9	42
Covington	3	45
Perryville	9	54
Gilderoy	13	67
Newport Ferry	12	79
Montezuma	7	86
Clinton	12	98
Gallatin	3	101
Terre-Haute	13	114
Smyrna	8	122
Darwin	17	139
York	10	149
Merom	17	166
Russellville	22	188
Vincennes	14	202
St. Francisville	12	214
Mount Carmel	24	238
Coffee Island Rapids	12	250
Graysville	18	268
New Harmony	15	283
Tecumseh	26	309
Junction with Ohio R.	23	332

RED RIVER.

From New Orleans to Shreveport, on the Red River.

Names of Places	Miles.	Miles.
To Mouth of Red River (see Mississippi R..		370
Black River	33	403
Alexandria	65	468
Natchitoches	85	553
Shreveport	80	633

ARKANSAS RIVER,

From New Orleans to Fort Gibson, on Arkansas River.

Names of Places	Miles.	Miles.
To Napoleon, Mouth of Arkansas River, (see Mississippi R).		644
Wellington	20	664
Arkansas	32	696
Gascony	80	776
Pine Bluff	25	801
Little Rock	95	896
Cadron	48	944
Marion	1	945
Lewisburg	11	956
Point Remove	7	963
Norristown	35	998
Dardanelle	1	999
Scotia	35	1034
Morrison's Bluff	22	1056
Lagan's	2	1058
Ozark	23	1081
Van Buren	55	1136
Fort Smith	6	1142
Fort Coffee, Ind. Ter.	16	1158
Canadian River	36	1194
Fort Gibson	46	1240

From Buffalo to Chicago.

(By Steamboat.)

Names of Places	Miles.	Miles.
To Dunkirk	44	
Erie	51	95
Ashtabula	45	140
Cleveland	62	202
Sandusky	60	262
Detroit	85	347
Mackinaw	372	719
Manitou Islands	95	814
Milwaukee	155	969
Racine	27	996
Southport	13	1009
Chicago	56	1065

ADVERTISEMENTS

APPENDED TO

THE WASHINGTON AND GEORGETOWN

DIRECTORY.

For the Index, see end of the book.

ADVERTISEMENT.

NOTICE TO PURCHASERS.

It is an axiom in trade that a person who cannot afford to advertise cannot sell so cheap, nor have they the variety of other tradesmen, who put their articles before the public for competition. In the following pages you will find the cards and notices of every kind of business to supply every want you may desire; therefore, if you are in want of any article, turn over my Directory until you find the place you want, and go directly there, as you may be assured that you will be waited upon with more politeness, promptness, and withal cheaper than those who do not let you know where they are, or that they have anything to sell.

ADVERTISEMENTS.

GREEN & SCOTT,

AUCTION AND COMMISSION MERCHANTS,

AND

HOUSE FURNISHING ESTABLISHMENT,

WASHINGTON HALL,

CORNER OF SIXTH STREET AND PENNSYLVANIA AVENUE.

JOHN W. McKIM,

ATTORNEY AND COUNSELLOR AT LAW,

Office on Indiana avenue, opposite the East Wing of the City Hall,

WASHINGTON, D. C.

Practices in the several Courts of the District. Attends to Collections, Conveyancing, and to the prosecution of Claims before Congress and the various Departments of Government.

J. T. NEELY,

Attorney at Law and General Agent,

CORNER OF 4½ STREET AND PENNA. AVENUE,

WASHINGTON, D. C.

WILLIAM H. PHILIP,

ATTORNEY AND COUNSELLOR AT LAW,

LANE & TUCKER'S BUILDING,

Pennsylvania avenue, between Four-and-a-half and Sixth streets,

WASHINGTON, D. C.

NICHOLAS CALLAN,

NOTARY PUBLIC,

Conveyancer, and Commissioner of Deeds

FOR THE STATES OF

NEW YORK, PENNSYLV'A, MARYLAND, OHIO, IOWA, INDIANA, & LOUISIANA.

South side F street north, between 14th and 15th streets west.

JAMES C. McGUIRE,

AUCTION, COMMISSION,

AND

HOUSE-FURNISHING

CORNER OF 10th STREET AND PENNA. ANENUE,

HAS ALWAYS ON HAND AN EXTENSIVE ASSORTMENT OF

FURNITURE,

AND

House Furnishing Goods.

HE WILL ATTEND TO THE

PURCHASE OR SALE OF REAL ESTATE,

either at Auction or at Private Sale, and will cash all deferred payments, on sales of Real or Personal property, at the lowest rates.

THE WASHINGTON CITY
SAVINGS BANK,

CORNER OF TENTH STREET AND PENNA. AVENUE.

The undersigned have established in this city an institution to be designated and styled

THE WASHINGTON CITY SAVINGS BANK,

for the purpose of receiving such sums of money as are the profits of industry and economy, or legacies or donations to widows, children, and others, who may need its aid, and investing the same in public stocks or other safe securities, as may from time to time be deemed expedient, and thereby afford to such persons the twofold advantage of security and profit. Guardians may deposit for the benefit of their wards, and parents for their children, and, if desired at the time of deposite, subject the same to the control of such guardian or parent.

Depositors shall have the right to withdraw their deposites at any time, by giving one week's notice in writing of their intention, and this notice may be dispensed with at the discretion of the undersigned, or a majority of them.

Interest at the rate of four per cent. per annum will be allowed on deposites for any calendar month they may be continued, computing from the first day of the month succeeding the deposite; but, to avoid tedious calculations on small sums, none will be estimated on a fractional part of a month or of a dollar; nor will any interest be allowed on a sum less than one dollar standing to the credit of the depositor; no interest will be allowed where an account has not been continued with the bank three calendar months; all accruing interest shall be paid on the first days of May and November in each year, unless the principal shall have been withdrawn between those periods.

The Undersigned have, by good and sufficient bond, bound themselves and their assigns, and their respective property; and will at all times hold the books and affairs of the said bank open to the inspection of depositors.

The Washington City Savings Bank is situated at the corner of Tenth street and Pennsylvania avenue, where some of the undersigned will be in attendance through the day. Those persons who may not be able to call during ordinary hours of business will be attended to upon application to either of the undersigned at his place of residence.

April 20, 1847.

LEWIS JOHNSON,
STANISLAUS MURRAY,
EDWARD SIMMS,
JOHN PURDY.

LEWIS JOHNSON, *Treasurer.*

The above institution, being permanently established in its present location, a central and convenient situation for business, and resting on a basis that the proprietors flatter themselves entitle it to universal confidence, is now prepared for a moderate and prudent extension of its usefulness to the community, so far at least as to receive deposites of cash and collections on current account, without departing in any degree from its original object of fostering the cause of the "Saving Bank" principle, the true motive of its first inception, and exercising the general functions of banking business, except the issue of notes for circulation as currency, to which its *conductors are decidedly opposed*, unless authorized by law, *and especially all such issues under five dollars*. The operations of the Washington City Savings Bank gives activity and useful employment to a large amount of capital deposited on interest, which would otherwise lie dormant, and supplies business men with extensive facilities on satisfactory terms.

LEWIS JOHNSON, *Treasurer.*

MRS. GARRET ANDERSON,

BOOKSELLER AND STATIONER,

AND DEALER IN

FOREIGN AND AMERICAN MUSIC, PIANO FORTES, GUITARS, BASS VIOLS, and VIOLINS, and a general assortment of Musical merchandise, Staple and Fancy Stationery, Fancy Articles, Perfumery, &c.

PENNSYLVANIA AVENUE, BETWEEN ELEVENTH AND TWELFTH STREETS.

MRS. H. N. GILBERT'S

BOARDING-HOUSE,

Penna. avenue, first square west of the Capitol Yard,

WASHINGTON, D. C.

H. N. GILBERT has an Agency to sell FARMS in Virginia, Maryland, and the District of Columbia.

CHARLES H. BURGESS,

WASHINGTON CITY,

Will attend to POSTING and DISTRIBUTING Theatre, Concert, and Exhibition Bills, of every description; Sale Bills for Auctions; Circulars, Invitations, and Business Cards, promptly distributed.

☞ All orders left at Mr. Henry Polkinhorn's Printing Office, cor of 11th st. and Pennsylvania avenue; and at Hunter's Book Store, Pennsylvania avenue, will be faithfully attended to.

JOSEPH DAWSON,

WASHINGTON BREWERY,

MALTSTER & HOP MERCHANT,

BREWER AND BOTTLER OF

ALES, PORTER, SCOTCH ALE,

LONDON BROWN STOUT, CIDER, &c.

A stock of the above articles always on hand, ready for immediate use.

THE IRON HALL

DRY GOODS STORE

HAS ALWAYS ON HAND A CHOICE SELECTION OF ALL KINDS OF

DRY GOODS,

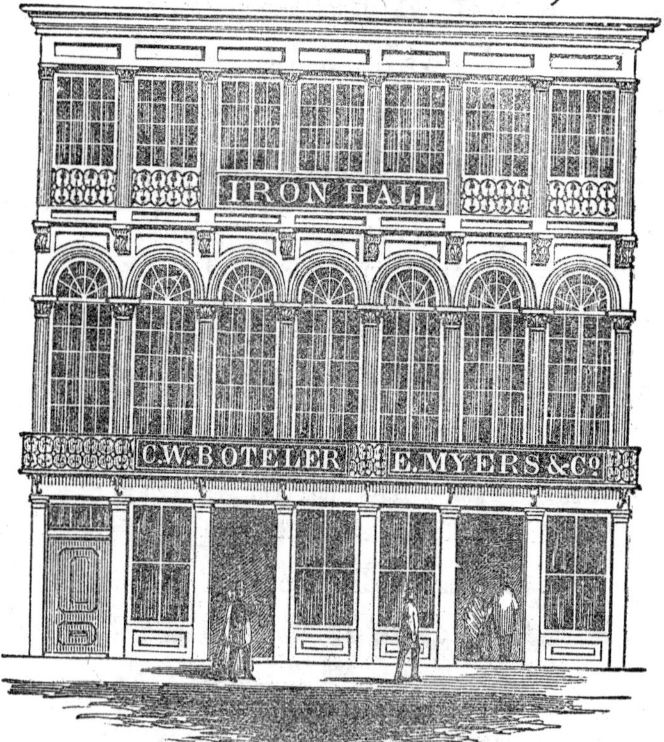

SILKS AND DRESS GOODS, SHAWLS AND MANTILLAS,

GLOVES AND HOSIERY,

LACES AND EMBROIDERIES.

As our motto is "SMALL PROFITS AND QUICK SALES," purchasers will find it greatly to their advantage to examine our stock and prices before purchasing. We are sure to please in both.

E. MYERS & CO.,
Iron Building, Pennsylvania avenue,
Between Ninth and Tenth streets, Washington city.

IRON HALL

House Furnishing Store.

The Subscriber keeps for sale the largest stock of HOUSEKEEPING ARTICLES that can be found in any one Establishment south of New York, and he pledges himself to sell them at prices that cannot fail to please.

C. W. BOTELER, *Iron Hall.*

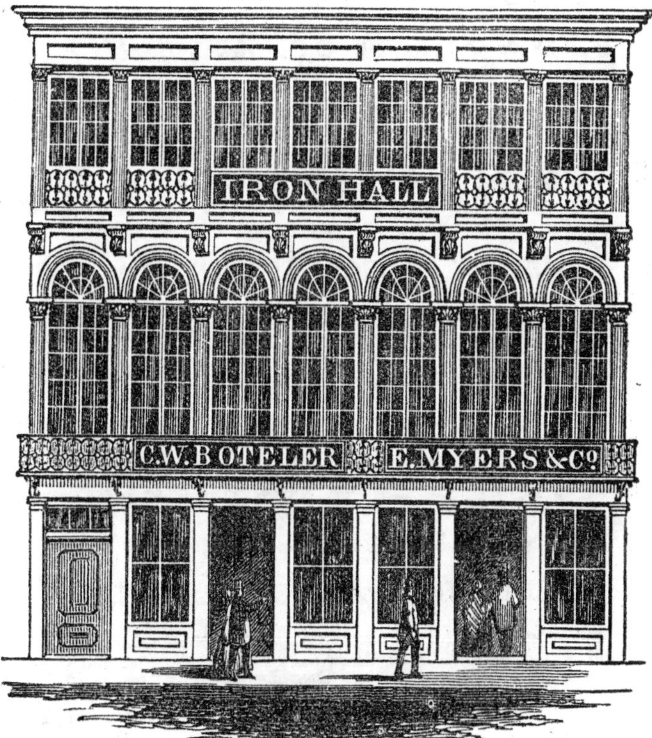

AUCTION NOTICE.

The Subscriber begs leave to announce that he has again renewed his auction license, and tenders his services to sell Real and Personal Property of every description. He will bestow particular attention to the arrangement and disposal of Household Furniture; and should a family desire to avoid a sale at their residence, he will have the goods carefully removed to the large Hall over his store, where every effort will be used to render satisfactory all sales intrusted to his care.

C. W. BOTELER, Iron Hall.

C. H. VENABLE,

DAGUERREAN ARTIST,

Corner Seventh street and Penna. avenue, over Stott's Drug Store.

Pictures taken in cloudy as well as clear weather. Likenesses of the sick, aged, or deceased taken at their residences. Paintings, Statuary, and Daguerreotypes copied. A clear day should be selected for Children or Family Groups. The public are respectfully invited to call and examine specimens.

KIDWELL & LAURENCE,

DEALERS IN

DRUGS, CHEMICALS,

Perfumery, Fancy Articles, &c.,

CORNER PENNSYLVANIA AVENUE AND 14TH STREET,

WASHINGTON, D. C.

Z. D. GILMAN,

CHEMIST AND DRUGGIST,

WHOLESALE AND RETAIL DEALER IN

DRUGS & MEDICINES, PAINTS, OILS, AND GLASS,

And inventor and sole proprietor of GILMAN'S INSTANTANEOUS LIQUID HAIR DYE. Agent for all the *Patent* or *Proprietory Medicines* of the day, *Letter and Cap Paper, Superior Inks, Pure Wines and Brandies for medicinal purposes, Fancy articles, &c.*

Pennsylvania avenue, between Sixth and Seventh streets, Washington, D. C.

J. S. MAXWELL. J. W. COLLEY. J. W. SEARS.

MAXWELL, SEARS, & COLLEY,

DEALERS IN

FANCY AND STAPLE DRY GOODS

PENNA. AVENUE, BETWEEN 9th AND 10th STS.

WASHINGTON, D. C.

F. E. HASSLER,

GENERAL AGENT FOR CLAIMS,

TRANSLATOR OF FRENCH AND SPANISH,

OFFICE FOUR-AND-A-HALF STREET, NEAR PENNA. AVENUE,

BOARDS AT FITZGERALD'S, PENNA. AVENUE.

HUGH CAMERON,

GENERAL AGENT,

TODD'S BUILDING, PENN. AVENUE,

WASHINGTON CITY, D. C.

PEKIN TEA COMPANY'S AGENCY,

EIGHTEENTH ST., BETWEEN H AND I STS.

PEOPLE'S MUTUAL HEALTH ASSURANCE COMPANY,

Incorporated by the Legislature of Massachusetts. Capitol stock $50,000.

EMIGRANT INTELLIGENCE OFFICE,

for finding situations for foreigners, of whatever class, nation, or creed.

J. THOMPSON GREHAM. Agent,

Office Eighteenth street, between H and I streets.

C. R. BYRNE,

DEALER IN ALL KINDS OF

FAMILY GROCERIES, WINES, LIQUORS, CIGARS, &C.,

SOUTHEAST CORNER OF TENTH ST. AND PENNA. AVENUE,

Washington, D. C.

SAMUEL BACON & CO.,

WHOLESALE AND RETAIL DEALERS IN

WINES, LIQUORS, & GROCERIES,

CORNER SEVENTH STREET AND PENNA. AVENUE,

WASHINGTON, D. C.

GROCER,

POULUS THYSON,

DEALER IN

HARDWARE, PAINTS AND OILS,

GROCERIES, FEED, AND FLOUR,

SEVENTH STREET, BETWEEN H AND I STREETS.

J. W. BADEN,

IMPORTER AND DEALER IN

HARDWARE, CUTLERY,

GUNS, PISTOLS, ETC.,

WASHINGTON, D. C.

FASHIONABLE HAT ESTABLISHMENT.

FRANCIS MATTINGLY

Informs his Friends and the Public, he has opened, in his New Store on Seventh street, east side, between D and E streets,

A LARGE ASSORTMENT OF HATS AND CAPS OF THE LATEST FASHION,

Also Ladies' Dress and Fancy Furs.

The quality of his Hats are superior to any in the market, and sold on terms so as to be satisfactory to his Customers.

TODD & CO.,

HATTERS,

AND DEALERS IN CAPS AND FURS,

MARBLE BUILDING, PENNSYLVANIA AVENUE,

EVANS, JR.,

HAT, CAP, FUR, AND BONNET MANUFACTORY,

PENNA. AVENUE, BETWEEN TWELFTH AND THIRTEENTH STREETS,

Washington, D. C.

WASHINGTON GAS-LIGHT COMPANY.

S. H. HILL, President.

J. F. BROWN, Secretary.

OFFICE OPPOSITE CENTRE MARKET,

Corner of Eighth street, (over Riley's Store.)

The Works are situated on Maine avenue, east of Four-and-a-half street.

All applications respecting the Gas and individuals' accounts should be made at the office, (where payments of dues are required,) to

JAMES KEENE,
Superintendent.

MAGUIRE'S

FASHIONABLE HAT AND CAP ESTABLISHMENT,

Penna. avenue, bet. 3d and 4½ sts., adjoining Odeon Hall,
WASHINGTON.

CAPS AND SOFT HATS IN GREAT VARIETY.

NATIONAL HOTEL,

Corner of Penna. avenue and Sixth street,
WASHINGTON, D. C.

M. A. DEXTER.

WILLARD'S CITY HOTEL,

WASHINGTON, D. C.

H. A. WILLARD.

SITUATED ON PENNA. AVENUE, CORNER FOURTEENTH STREET,
Near the President's House and Executive Offices.

T. P. BROWN. M. BROWN.

BROWNS' HOTEL,

MARBLE BUILDINGS,

WASHINGTON CITY.

FRANKENBERGER & WITTENAUER,
SUCCESSORS TO F. SCHAD,

EUROPEAN HOUSE,

CORNER OF SEVENTH AND G STREETS,
Washington, D. C.

CHAS. FRANKENBERGER. ALEX. WITTENAUER.

C. WARRINER. H. SEMKEN.

C. WARRINER & CO.,

Wholesale and Retail Dealers in

WATCHES, JEWELRY, SILVER WARE, AND FANCY GOODS,

Penna. avenue, between 9th and 10th streets,

WASHINGTON D. C.

JOHN KELLY'S

FAREMRS' HOTEL,

CORNER OF EIGHTH AND D STREETS,

WASHINGTON, D. C.

☞BOARD BY THE DAY OR WEEK.☜

KEYWORTH'S

JEWELRY AND FANCY STORE,

PENNA. AVENUE, BETWEEN NINTH AND TENTH STREETS,

WASHINGTON, D. C.

Watches and Jewelry carefully repaired.

S. MASI,

DEALER IN

FINE WATCHES, JEWELRY, AND FANCY GOODS,

PENNA. AVENUE, WASHINGTON CITY.

Watches and Jewelry repaired.

STEPHEN EDDY,

DEALER IN FINE

WATCHES, JEWELRY, & SILVER WARE.

Sole agent for the sala of Paine's celebrated Perifocal Spectacles.

No. 100 Penna. avenue, north side, between 4½ and 6th sts., Washington City, D. C.

☞Fine watches carefully repaired.

W. W. HOLLINGSWORTH, *Watch Maker.*

CLAGETT & DODSON'S

HOUSE FURNISHING

WAREROOMS.

The citizens of Washington are respectfully invited to the GENERAL HOUSE-FURNISHING DRY GOODSWARE ROOMS of CLAGETT & DODSON, one door east of the corner of Pennsylvania avenue and Ninth street, that you may have an early opportunity of seeing their stock of goods in the above line, all of which are of the very latest importations and styles, and will be sold on the very best terms which can be afforded in any city or house in the Union. Should you be pleased to make any purchases with us, we warrant them as described, and will pack and transport them to your address in the most perfect manner.

In our stock may be found CARPETINGS of the following descriptions, to wit: Belgian, French, English, and American Tapestry Velvet and Brussels, and plain Brussels, Imperial Three-ply, Scotch, English, and American Double Ingrain, Floor Oil Cloth, in Gothic, Brussels, Tapestry, and Mosaic pave patterns, from $1 50 per square yard to 37½ cents, for rooms and halls, which will be cut as per diagram; Brussels, Tapestry, Twilled, and Plain Venitian Carpeting, for passages and steps; also Step Rods to suit the widths, in silver-plate and brass, at prices from $12 to $1 50 per dozen.

In CURTAIN MATERIALS, we have India Satan Damask, Satin Lains, Brochatels, Damask Lains, and worsted Damask and Moreens, in all or any contrast or plain colors which may be desired; with Drapery Cords and Tassels, Side Loops, Gimps; exquisitely embroidered and plain Muslin Under Curtains, Cornices, Side Pins or Brackets, in Lilly and Historic designs, of all qualities and prices.

FOWLER & SHILES'

LUMBER YARD,

CORNER OF 14TH STREET AND MARYLAND AVENUE, AND CORNER OF 3D STREET AND MARYLAND AVENUE,

WASHINGTON, D. C.

JOHN B. WARD,

LUMBER DEALER,

Has always on hand a good supply of BUILDING LUMBER, which will be sold on as good terms as can be obtained in the District.

YARD ON TWELFTH ST., NEAR THE CANAL.

LUMBER,

LIME, AND COAL.

The Subscriber has always on hand a large supply of

SEASONED LUMBER

OF ALL DESCRIPTIONS;

Also, the best

WOOD BURNT LIME;

Also,

COAL

Of all kinds and sizes ;

CALCINED PLASTER AND CEMENT,

Of the best make ;

In full, everything to be found in a No. 1 yard,

Which will be sold cheap for cash on short credits.

Yard on First Street, opposite the Capitol, Washington, D. C.

JOHN PURDY.

Paper-Hanging Establishment—Plumbing.

THE COLUMBIAN,

CORNER OF EIGHTH AND E STREETS, WASHINGTON CITY, D. C.

F. WINGENROTH.

This House is located opposite the Post Office Department, and in the immediate vicinity of the Patent Office. A Refectory is attached, from which every delicacy, in its season, will at all hours be served up by experienced cooks. The BAR is at all times filled with the best Liquors.

To strangers visiting Washington, The Columbian offers superior attractions, both as to locality and accommodations.

W. H. HARROVER,

COPPER, TIN, AND SHEET IRON WARE MANUFACTURER,

Has always on hand and makes to order, Tin Ware, Stoves, Parlor Grates, Cooking Ranges; Hot Air Furnaces, portable and stationary, for Public or Private Buildings; Copper Boilers, Pump Cylinders, Lead Pipe, &c.

Also, Roofing and Spouting, Lead Cisterns; Bath Tubs, with hot water circulation, Bath Fixtures, Water Closets, Basins and Sinks; Metallic Pumps, put up by experienced hands and warranted. Also Agent for Reip's Patent Wall Bake-oven; every housekeeper should not be without one.

SEVENTH STREET, OPPOSITE PATRIOTIC BANK, WASHINGTON CITY, D. C.

W. H. GOODS.

Saddle, Harness, and Trunk Manufacturer,

CORNER OF SEVENTH AND I STREETS, OPPOSITE DORSEY'S HOTEL,

WASHINGTON, D. C.

W. H. G. keeps constantly on hand, Saddles, Harness, Trunks, Whips and Collars, with every other article in their line of business, all of which will be sold on the most reasonable terms.

N. B.—Old Saddles and Harness taken in exchange for new. Also, repaired at the shortest notice.

THOMAS CREASER,

LADIES' FRENCH BOOT AND SHOE MAKER,

Keeps on hand, of his own make, and makes to order, Ladies', Misses', and Children's black and white satin Gaiter Boots and Slippers. French, English and American black and white Kid, colored Morocco, and patent leather Boots and Shoes, made to order.

F street, between Eighth and Ninth, opposite the Patent Office.

CARD.

Ladies', Misses', and Children's FRENCH SHOES offered for sale in the basement story of the new building with the high marble steps, 15th street, just above Corcoran & Riggs's. A very superior assortment of Ladies', Misses', and Children's French Gaiter Walking Shoes, White and Black Satin Gaiters and Slippers, &c., made to order, of the best materials, and in the latest Parisian styles.

The Ladies of Washington, Georgetown, and Alexandria, and vicinity, are respectfully invited to call and judge for themselves.

H. WEIRMAN, of Phildelphia.

ENCOURAGE YOUR OWN MECHANICS AND MANUFACTURERS.

SHIRTS! SHIRTS! SHIRTS!

Members of Congress, Citizens, and Strangers are invited to call at

WM. H. FAULKNER'S

Fashionable Shirt Manufactory and leave their measures.

His Shirts are warranted to fit in all cases, the style and pattern of which has received the unqualified commendation of gentlemen in all parts of the United States.

All Shirts made at his establishment are as good and as cheap as they can be purchased in New York. Thankful for the favors already received, he respectfully solicits a continuance of the same.

Also on hand, a splendid assortment of Silk and Merino Undershirts and Drawers.

Also, Gloves, Cravats, Socks, and every other article suitable for a gentleman's wardrobe, at prices which cannot fail to suit.

WM. H. FAULKNER, *Sign of the Shirt,*
South side Penn. avenue, between 3d and 4½ streets,
Opposite the United States Hotel.

HARRIS & GRIFFIN'S

BOOT AND SHOE STORE,

Pennsylvania avenue, between 9th and 10th streets,

WASHINGTON, D. C.

A. HOOVER & SON,

DEALERS IN

BOOTS AND SHOES OF ALL DESCIPTIONS,

South side Penna. avenue, between 6th and 7th sts.

FRANCIS Y. NAYLOR,

COPPER, TIN, SHEET IRON, AND STOVE MANUFACTURER.

ROOFING, GUTTERING, SPOUTING, ETC.,

South side of Pennsylvania avenue, near Third street,

Washington City, D. C.

D. E. GROUX,

TEACHER OF

MODERN LANGUAGES,

ESPECIALLY

FRENCH, SPANISH, AND GERMAN.

TRANSLATIONS MADE WITH CORRECTNESS AND PUNCTUALITY IN

FRENCH, SPANISH, GERMAN, SWEDISH, DANISH, RUSSIAN, ETC.

PROFESSOR OF NUMISMATICS,

For the classification and explanation of Medals and Coins.

MUSEUM,

For selling, buying, and exchanging Coin and Medals, Minerals, Fossils, Shells, Pictures, Engravings, Old Books, Antiquities, Ancient Furniture, old China and Porcelain, Bohemian Glass. Small shells, for shell work, for sale in great variety.

OPEN ONLY FROM THREE TO FIVE O'CLOCK.

COLLECTIONS OF COMPOSITION,

Or Imitation Medals of American History and eminent men, likewise of other nations.

RELIGIOUS MEDALS,

For the use of Colleges and Schools, in large and small quantities, and at reasonable prices.

Penna. avenue, opposite Browns' Hotel,

WASHINGTON CITY.

FURNISHED ROOMS TO RENT.

GOOD OPPORTUNITY TO LEARN LANGUAGES, IN THE BEST LOCATION IN THE CITY.

INDEX TO ADVERTISERS.

www.ingramcontent.com/pod-product-compliance
Lightning Source LLC
LaVergne TN
LVHW010130110826
845151LV00002B/313
* 9 7 8 1 4 2 5 5 4 0 5 1 7 *